Contents

D1367018

Credits

Online Supplements 649

NOTE FROM THE AUTHORS

● LECTURE VIDEOS: A SEA CHANGE IN INSTRUCTIONAL METHODOLOGY

We are excited to announce the availability of instructional videos that explain the content associated with every learning objective introduced throughout the text. ***These videos have been developed by a member of the author team and are available when assigned through McGraw-Hill Connect Accounting.*** They have the touch and feel of a live lecture as opposed to a canned PowerPoint presentation. The benefits are enormous. Videos allow students to pause for contemplation and note-taking. They permit students to repeat difficult concepts or fast-forward through content they have mastered. In other words, videos enable self-paced learning. No longer is the lecture too fast for some and too slow for others. Now the lecture satisfies the needs of each individual student.

Many accounting educators have taught in professional exam prep courses that make extensive use of video lectures. Now you can bring that prep course learning approach into your everyday classroom. You can use the videos we provide to transform the traditional classroom from a passive listening exercise into an active learning experience. Here are some examples of how you can use instructional videos to improve the classroom environment.

Flip Courses

Instructional videos enable instructors to flip the traditional teaching model. Specifically, instead of providing a lecture in class and then assigning homework, ***flip courses*** deliver the lecture at home and use the classroom as a place for students to work problems and ask questions. The teacher's function moves from lecturer to coach and tutor. Without a requirement to deliver a lecture, the instructor is free to tutor students in small groups or individually. Instruction becomes more focused and individualized. Indeed, when coupled with *Connect*® technology, instructors can obtain real-time feedback that allows them to identify and approach specific students who are having difficulty without disturbing those students who are able to digest the material independently.

Competency-Based Learning Courses

Video instruction enables the implementation of a competency-based grading system. Since learning is self-paced, grades can be assigned on the basis of how deep students go into the content as opposed to an averaging approach. For example, content could be divided into modules. Grades could be assigned based on the number of modules completed successfully. Weaker students could repeat lower-level modules, while stronger students move on to more advanced topics. When you are no longer forced to move students through your class in a lock-step fashion, the potential for improving the learning environment is virtually limitless.

There are many different competency-based models that can be applied to introductory accounting. At this point, our objective is to introduce the general possibilities for improving learning. If you are interested in developing a specific competency-based approach for your classroom, you can speak directly with a member of the author team who has used videos in a variety of settings (contact information is provided on the following page). Standardized lesson plans that can be adapted for use in your individual classroom are available upon request.

Mass Section Courses

Many schools deliver live lectures to mass section classes. Students then break into small groups that are led by teaching assistants or adjunct faculty. While this approach is cost effective, it frequently results in dissatisfaction. Students often find it difficult to see and hear in large lecture halls. Also, the lecture must be set at an average pace which by its nature is too fast for many students and too slow for others. Prerecorded video lectures resolve these issues. They enable students to study the lecture before class. They can then bring questions about the lecture to the breakout sessions. Since videos eliminate the need for mass lectures, there is more time for students to meet in small groups where they are able to receive more individualized attention.

Distance Learning Courses

One of the fastest-growing markets in higher education today is Internet-based courses. Many students struggle with these courses. Generally, they would prefer to learn from a lecture but due to timing or location are unable to attend class. Prerecorded video lectures solve this problem by allowing students to access lectures on demand. Until now, the only way to provide video coverage was for the instructor to make personal recordings. Anyone who has tried this knows it is a time-consuming activity. We offer a standardized turn-key course that is composed of prerecorded instructional videos, self-assessment quizzes, and instructor-generated evaluative exams. The instructor simply selects the learning objectives to be covered. There is no simpler way to develop a distance learning course.

Supplement Your Traditional Lecture-Based Course

You do not have to change the way you teach your class to reap many of the benefits available from video instruction. Students who have to miss class or who have trouble comprehending certain concepts can benefit from watching video lectures. Also, many students who attend class will be able to build confidence by watching videos that reinforce the concepts presented in class. Since the videos are tied directly to the learning objectives, you can develop a specific plan for students who are struggling with specific topics. Alternatively, you may offer video instruction to enable advanced students to cover additional topics.

These are only a few opportunities made possible by video lectures. If you would like to discuss these or other possible applications, please contact Chris Edmonds at **cedmonds@gmail.com**.

INSTRUCTOR SUPPLEMENTS

Assurance of Learning Ready

Many educational institutions today are focused on the notion of assurance of learning, an important element of some accreditation standards. *Survey of Accounting*, 4e, is designed specifically to support your assurance of learning initiatives with a simple, yet powerful, solution. Each test bank question for *Survey of Accounting*, 4e, maps to a specific chapter learning outcome/objective listed in the text. You can use our test bank software, EZ Test, and *Connect*® to easily query for learning outcomes/objectives that directly relate to the learning objectives for your course. You can then use the reporting features of EZ Test and *Connect*® to aggregate student results in similar fashion, making the collection and presentation of assurance of learning data simple and easy.

AACSB Statement

The McGraw-Hill Companies, Inc., is a proud corporate member of AACSB International. Recognizing the importance and value of AACSB accreditation, we have sought to recognize the curricula guidelines detailed in AACSB standards for business accreditation by connecting selected questions in Edmonds 4e with the general knowledge and skill guidelines found in the AACSB standards. The statements contained in Edmonds 4e are provided only as a guide for the users of this text. The AACSB leaves content coverage and assessment clearly within the realm and control of individual schools, the mission of the school, and the faculty. The AACSB does also charge schools with the obligation of doing assessment against their own content and learning goals. While Edmonds 4e and its teaching package make no claim of any specific AACSB qualification or evaluation, we have labeled selected questions according to the six general knowledge and skills areas. The labels or tags within Edmonds 4e are as indicated. There are, of course, many more within the test bank, the text, and the teaching package which might be used as a "standard" for your course. However, the labeled questions are suggested for your consideration.

McGraw-Hill *Connect*® *Accounting*

 McGraw-Hill *Connect*® *Accounting* offers a number of powerful tools and features to make managing your classroom easier. *Connect*® *Accounting* with Edmonds 4e offers enhanced features and technology to help both you and your students make the most of your time inside and outside the classroom. See page xvi for more details.

Online Learning Center
(www.mhhe.com/edmondssurvey4e)

The password-protected instructor side of the book's Online Learning Center (OLC) houses all the instructor resources you need to administer your course, including:

• Solutions Manual
• Test Bank
• Instructor PowerPoint® slides
• Instructor's Manual
• Text exhibits
• Sample syllabus

If you choose to use *Connect*® *Accounting* with Edmonds 4e, you will have access to these same resources via the Instructor Library.

Instructor's Manual

This comprehensive manual includes step-by-step, explicit instructions on how the text can be used to implement teaching methods. The guide includes lesson plans and demonstration problems with student work papers, as well as solutions. Available on the password-protected Instructor side of the Online Learning Center and the *Connect*® Instructor Library.

STUDENT SUPPLEMENTS

Solutions Manual

Prepared by the authors, the solutions manual contains complete solutions to all the text's end-of-chapter review questions, exercises, problems, and cases. Available on the password-protected Instructor side of the Online Learning Center and the *Connect®* Instructor Library.

PowerPoint Presentations

This resource includes a complete set of Instructor PowerPoints, following the chapter-by-chapter content.

Available on the password-protected Instructor side of the Online Learning Center and the *Connect®* Instructor Library.

Test Bank

This test bank contains multiple-choice questions, essay questions, and short problems. Each test item is coded for level of difficulty, learning objective, AACSB, AICPA, and Bloom's.

EZ Test Online

McGraw-Hill's EZ Test is a flexible electronic testing program. The program allows instructors to create tests from book-specific items. It accommodates a wide range of question types.

McGraw-Hill *Connect®* Accounting and *Connect®* Plus Accounting

McGraw-Hill *Connect®* Accounting helps prepare you for your future by enabling faster learning, more efficient studying, and higher retention of knowledge. See page xvi for more details.

CourseSmart

CourseSmart is a new way to find and buy eTextbooks. At Course-Smart you can save up to 60 percent off the cost of a print textbook, reduce your impact on the environment, and gain access to powerful web tools for learning. CourseSmart has the largest selection of eTextbooks available anywhere, offering thousands of the most commonly adopted textbooks from a wide variety of higher education publishers. CourseSmart eTextbooks are available in one standard online reader with full text search, notes and highlighting, and e-mail tools for sharing notes between classmates.

Online Learning Center and *Connect®* Student Library
www.mhhe.com/edmondssurvey4e

The Online Learning Center (OLC) and *Connect®* Student Library follow *Survey of Accounting* chapter by chapter, offering all kinds of supplementary help for you as you read. The following resources are available to help you study more efficiently:

- Online quizzes
- Student PowerPoint presentations
- Check figures
- Review problems

Student PowerPoint Presentations

Presentation slides are located on the text's Online Learning Center and the *Connect®* Library.

McGraw-Hill's *Connect®* Accounting

See page xvi for details.

CHAPTER 1

An Introduction to Accounting

LEARNING OBJECTIVES

After you have mastered the material in this chapter, you will be able to:

SECTION 1: COLLECTING AND ORGANIZING INFORMATION

LO 1-1   Explain the role of accounting in society.

LO 1-2   Construct an accounting equation and show how business events affect the equation.

LO 1-3   Interpret information shown in an accounting equation.

LO 1-4   Classify business events as asset source, use, or exchange transactions.

SECTION 2: REPORTING INFORMATION

LO 1-5   Use general ledger account information to prepare four financial statements.

LO 1-6   Explain the closing process.

LO 1-7   Record business events using a horizontal financial statements model.

 Video lectures and accompanying self-assessment quizzes are available for all learning objectives through McGraw-Hill Connect® Accounting.

The Curious Accountant

Who owns Google? Who owns the American Heart Association (AHA)? Many people and organizations other than owners are interested in the operations of Google and the AHA. These parties are called *stakeholders*. Among others, they include lenders, employees, suppliers, customers, benefactors, research institutions, local governments, heart patients, lawyers, bankers, financial analysts, and government agencies such as the Internal Revenue Service and the Securities and Exchange Commission. Organizations communicate information to stakeholders through *financial reports*.

How do you think the financial reports of Google differ from those of the AHA? (Answer on page 11.)

SECTION 1:

COLLECTING AND ORGANIZING INFORMATION

Why should you study accounting? You should study accounting because it can help you succeed in business. Businesses use accounting to keep score. Imagine trying to play football without knowing how many points a touchdown is worth. Like sports, business is competitive. If you do not know how to keep score, you are not likely to succeed.

Accounting is an information system that reports on the economic activities and financial condition of a business or other organization. Do not underestimate the importance of accounting information. If you had information that enabled you to predict business success, you could become a very wealthy Wall Street investor. Communicating economic information is so important that accounting is frequently called the *language of business.*

4   Chapter 1

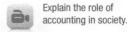

ROLE OF ACCOUNTING IN SOCIETY

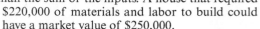

How should society allocate its resources? Should we spend more to harvest food or cure disease? Should we build computers or cars? Should we invest money in IBM or General Motors? Accounting provides information that helps answer such questions.

Using Free Markets to Set Resource Priorities

Suppose you want to start a business. You may have heard "you have to have money to make money." In fact, you will need more than just money to start and operate a business. You will likely need such resources as equipment, land, materials, and employees. If you do not have these resources, how can you get them? In the United States, you compete for resources in open markets.

A **market** is a group of people or entities organized to exchange items of value. The market for business resources involves three distinct participants: consumers, conversion agents, and resource owners. *Consumers* use resources. Resources are frequently not in a form consumers want. For example, nature provides trees but consumers want furniture. *Conversion agents* (businesses) transform resources such as trees into desirable products such as furniture. *Resource owners* control the distribution of resources to conversion agents. Thus resource owners provide resources (inputs) to conversion agents who provide goods and services (outputs) to consumers.

For example, a home builder (conversion agent) transforms labor and materials (inputs) into houses (output) that consumers use. The transformation adds value to the inputs, creating outputs worth more than the sum of the inputs. A house that required

$220,000 of materials and labor to build could have a market value of $250,000.

Common terms for the added value created in the transformation process include **profit, income,** or **earnings.** Accountants measure the added value as the difference between the cost of a product or service and the selling price of that product or service. The profit on the house described above is $30,000, the difference between its $220,000 cost and $250,000 market value.

Conversion agents who successfully and efficiently (at low cost) satisfy consumer preferences are rewarded with high earnings. These earnings are shared with resource owners, so conversion agents who exhibit high earnings potential are more likely to compete successfully for resources.

Return to the original question. How can you get the resources you need to start a business? You must go to open markets and convince resource owners that you can produce profits. Exhibit 1.1 illustrates the market trilogy involved in resource allocation.

The specific resources businesses commonly use to satisfy consumer demand are financial resources, physical resources, and labor resources.

Financial Resources

Businesses (conversion agents) need **financial resources** (money) to get started and to operate. *Investors* and *creditors* provide financial resources.

- **Investors** provide financial resources in exchange for ownership interests in businesses. Owners expect businesses to return to them a share of the business including a portion of earned income.

- **Creditors** lend financial resources to businesses. Instead of a share of the business, creditors expect the businesses to repay borrowed resources plus a specified fee called **interest.**

EXHIBIT 1.1

Market Trilogy in Resource Allocation

Investors and creditors prefer to provide financial resources to businesses with high earnings potential because such companies are better able to share profits and make interest payments. Profitable businesses are also less likely to experience bankruptcy.

Physical Resources

In their most primitive form, **physical resources** are natural resources. Physical resources often move through numerous stages of transformation. For example, standing timber may be successively transformed into harvested logs, raw lumber, and finished furniture. Owners of physical resources seek to sell those resources to businesses with high earnings potential because profitable businesses are able to pay higher prices and make repeat purchases.

Labor Resources

Labor resources include both intellectual and physical labor. Like other resource providers, workers prefer businesses that have high income potential because these businesses are able to pay higher wages and offer continued employment.

Accounting Provides Information

How do providers of financial, physical, and labor resources identify conversion agents (businesses) with high profit potential? Investors, creditors, and workers rely heavily on accounting information to evaluate which businesses are worthy of receiving resources. In addition, other people and organizations have an interest in accounting information about businesses. The many **users** of accounting information are commonly called **stakeholders.** Stakeholders include resource providers, financial analysts, brokers, attorneys, government regulators, and news reporters.

The link between conversion agents (businesses) and those stakeholders who provide resources is direct: businesses pay resource providers. Resource providers use accounting information to identify companies with high earnings potential because those companies are more likely to return higher profits, make interest payments, repay debt, pay higher prices, and provide stable, high paying employment.

The link between conversion agents and other stakeholders is indirect. Financial analysts, brokers, and attorneys may use accounting information when advising their clients. Government agencies may use accounting information to assess companies' compliance with income tax laws and other regulations. Reporters may use accounting information in news reports.

Types of Accounting Information

Stakeholders such as investors, creditors, lawyers, and financial analysts exist outside of and separate from the businesses in which they are interested. The accounting information these *external users* need is provided by **financial accounting.** In contrast, the accounting information needed by *internal users,* stakeholders such as managers and employees who work within a business, is provided by **managerial accounting.**

The information needs of external and internal users frequently overlap. For example, external and internal users are both interested in the amount of income a business earns. Managerial accounting information, however, is usually more detailed than financial accounting reports. Investors are concerned about the overall profitability of Wendy's versus Burger King; a Wendy's regional manager is interested in the profits of individual Wendy's restaurants. In fact, a regional manager is also interested in nonfinancial measures, such as the number of employees needed to operate a restaurant, the times at which customer demand is high versus low, and measures of cleanliness and customer satisfaction.

Nonbusiness Resource Usage

The U.S. economy is not *purely* market based. Factors other than profitability often influence resource allocation priorities. For example, governments allocate resources to national defense, to redistribute wealth, or to protect the environment. Foundations, religious groups, the Peace Corps, and other benevolent organizations prioritize resource usage based on humanitarian concerns.

Like profit-oriented businesses, civic or humanitarian organizations add value through resource transformation. For example, a soup kitchen adds value to uncooked meats and vegetables by converting them into prepared meals. The individuals who consume the meals, however, are unable to pay for the kitchen's operating costs, much less for the added value. The soup kitchen's motivation is to meet humanitarian needs, not to earn profits. Organizations that are not motivated by profit are called **not-for-profit entities** (also called *nonprofit* or *nonbusiness organizations*).

Stakeholders interested in nonprofit organizations also need accounting information. Accounting systems measure the cost of the goods and services not-for-profit organizations provide, the efficiency and effectiveness of the organizations' operations, and the ability of the organizations to continue to provide goods and services. This information serves a host of stakeholders, including taxpayers, contributors, lenders, suppliers, employees, managers, financial analysts, attorneys, and beneficiaries.

The focus of accounting, therefore, is to provide information that is useful to a variety of business and nonbusiness user groups for decision-making. The different types of accounting information and the stakeholders that commonly use the information are summarized in Exhibit 1.2.

Careers in Accounting

An accounting career can take you to the top of the business world. *Bloomberg Businessweek* studied the backgrounds of the chief executive officers (CEOs) of the 1,000 largest public corporations. More CEOs had backgrounds in finance and accounting than any other field. Exhibit 1.3 provides additional detail regarding the career paths followed by these executives.

EXHIBIT 1.2

Accounting as Information Provider

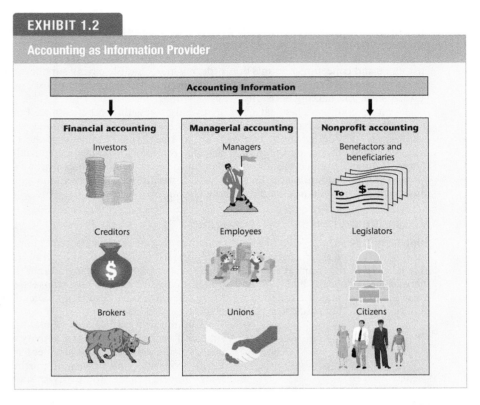

What do accountants do? Accountants identify, record, analyze, and communicate information about the economic events that affect organizations. They may work in either public accounting or private accounting.

Public Accounting

You are probably familiar with the acronym CPA. CPA stands for certified *public* accountant. Public accountants provide services to various clients. They are usually paid a fee that varies depending on the service provided. Services typically offered by public accountants include (1) audit services, (2) tax services, and (3) consulting services.

- *Audit services* involve examining a company's accounting records in order to issue an opinion about whether the company's financial statements conform to generally accepted accounting principles. The auditor's opinion adds credibility to the statements, which are prepared by the company's management.

- *Tax services* include both determining the amount of tax due and tax planning to help companies minimize tax expense.

- *Consulting services* cover a wide range of activities that includes everything from installing sophisticated computerized accounting systems to providing personal financial advice.

All public accountants are not certified. Each state government establishes certification requirements applicable in that state. Although the requirements vary from state to state, CPA candidates normally must have a college education, pass a demanding technical examination, and obtain work experience relevant to practicing public accounting.

EXHIBIT 1.3

Career Paths of Chief Executive Officers

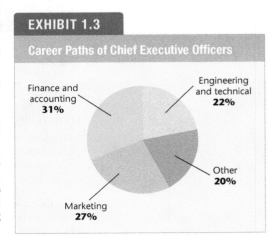

Finance and accounting **31%**

Engineering and technical **22%**

Other **20%**

Marketing **27%**

Private Accounting

Accountants employed in the private sector usually work for a specific company or nonprofit organization. Private sector accountants perform a wide variety of functions for their employers. Their duties include classifying and recording transactions, billing customers and collecting amounts due, ordering merchandise, paying suppliers, preparing and analyzing financial statements, developing budgets, measuring costs, assessing performance, and making decisions.

Private accountants may earn any of several professional certifications. For example, the Institute of Management Accountants issues the *Certified Management Accounting (CMA)* designation. The Institute of Internal Auditors issues the *Certified Internal Auditor (CIA)* designation. These designations are widely recognized indicators of technical competence and integrity on the part of individuals who hold them. All professional accounting certifications call for meeting education requirements, passing a technical examination, and obtaining relevant work experience.

Measurement Rules

Suppose a store sells an MP3 player in December to a customer who agrees to pay for it in January. Should the business *recognize* (report) the sale as a December transaction or as a January transaction? It really does not matter as long as the storeowner discloses the rule the decision is based on and applies it consistently to other transactions. Because businesses may use different reporting rules, however, clear communication also requires full and fair disclosure of the accounting rules chosen.

Communicating business results would be simpler if each type of business activity were reported using only one measurement method. World economies and financial reporting practices, however, have not evolved uniformly. Even in highly sophisticated countries such as the United States, companies exhibit significant diversity in reporting methods. Providers of financial reports assume that users are educated about accounting practices.

The **Financial Accounting Standards Board (FASB)**[1] is a privately funded organization with the primary authority for establishing accounting standards in the United States. The measurement rules established by the FASB are called **generally accepted accounting principles (GAAP)**. Financial reports issued to the public must follow GAAP. This textbook introduces these principles so you will be able to understand business activity reported by companies in the USA.

Companies are not required to follow GAAP when preparing *management accounting* reports. Although there is considerable overlap between financial and managerial accounting, managers are free to construct internal reports in whatever fashion best suits the effective operation of their companies.

Reporting Entities

Think of accountants as you would of news reporters. A news reporter gathers and discloses information about some person, place, or thing. Likewise, an accountant gathers and discloses financial information about specific people or businesses. The

---

[1]The FASB consists of seven full-time members appointed by the supporting organization, the Financial Accounting Foundation (FAF). The FAF membership is intended to represent the broad spectrum of individuals and institutions that have an interest in accounting and financial reporting. FAF members include representatives of the accounting profession, industry, financial institutions, the government, and the investing public.

FOCUS ON INTERNATIONAL ISSUES

IS THERE GLOBAL GAAP?

As explained in this chapter, accounting is a measurement and communication discipline based on rules referred to as *generally accepted accounting principles (GAAP).* The rules described in this text are based on GAAP used in the United States, but what rules do the rest of the world use? Is there a global GAAP, or does each country establish its own unique GAAP?

Until recently, each country developed its own unique GAAP. Global companies were required to prepare multiple sets of financial statements to satisfy each country's GAAP. The use of multiple accounting standards across the globe made comparing company performance difficult and expensive. To address the need for a common set of financial standards, the International Accounting Standards Committee was formed in 1973. The committee was reorganized as the **International Accounting Standards Board (IASB)** in 2001. The IASB issues **International Financial Reporting Standards (IFRS),** which are rapidly gaining support worldwide. In 2005,

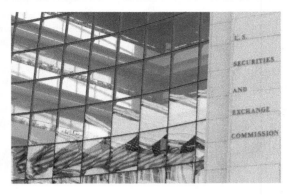

companies in the countries who were members of the European Union were required to use the IFRS as established by the IASB, which is headquartered in London. Today, over 100 countries require or permit companies to prepare their financial statements using IFRS.

As of 2013 most of the major economic countries had switched from their local GAAP to IFRS. One notable exception is the United States, but even here, the Securities and Exchange Commission announced in 2008 that it was seriously considering adopting rules that would allow our companies to use either GAAP or IFRS. Although not finalized when this book was being prepared, many accountants in the United States believe this will occur. Additionally, there is an active process in place to reduce the differences between IFRS and U.S. GAAP.

There are many similarities between the IASB and the FASB. Both the FASB and the IASB are required to include members with a variety of backgrounds, including auditors, users of financial information, academics, and so forth. Also, both groups primarily require that their members work full-time for their respective boards; they cannot serve on the board while being compensated by another organization. (The IASB does allow up to three of its members to be part-time.) Members of each board serve five-year terms, and can be reappointed once. The funds to support both boards, and the large organizations that support them are obtained from a variety of sources, including selling publications and private contributions. To help maintain independence of the board's members, fundraising is performed by separate sets of trustees.

There are significant differences between the IASB and the FASB, and one of these relates to size and geographic diversity. The FASB has only seven members, all from the United States. The IASB has sixteen members, and these must include at least four from Asia, four from Europe, four from North America, one from Africa, and one from South America.

Not only is the structure of the standards-setting boards different but the standards and principles they establish may also differ significantly. In this chapter, you will learn that GAAP employs the *historical cost concept.* This means that the assets of most U.S. companies are shown on the balance sheet at the amount for which they were purchased. For example, land that has a market value of millions of dollars may be shown on US Steel's financial statements with a value of only a few hundred thousand dollars. This occurs because GAAP requires US Steel to show the land at its cost rather than its market value. In contrast, IFRS permits companies to show market values on their financial statements. This means that the exact same assets may show radically different values if the statements are prepared under IFRS rather than GAAP.

Throughout this text, where appropriate, we will note the differences between U.S. GAAP and IFRS. However, by the time you graduate, it is likely that among the major industrialized nations, there will be a global GAAP.

---

people or businesses accountants report on are called **reporting entities.** When studying accounting you should think of yourself as the accountant. Your first step is to identify the person or business on which you are reporting. This is not always as easy as it may seem. To illustrate, consider the following scenario.

Jason Winston recently started a business. During the first few days of operation, Mr. Winston transferred cash from his personal account into a business account for a company he named Winston Enterprises. Mr. Winston's brother, George, invested cash in Winston Enterprises for which he received an ownership interest in the company. Winston Enterprises borrowed cash from First Federal Bank. Winston Enterprises paid cash to purchase a building from Commercial Properties, Inc. Winston Enterprises earned cash revenues from its customers and paid its employees cash for salaries expense.

How many reporting entities are described in this scenario? Assuming all of the customers are counted as a single entity and all of the employees are counted as a single entity, there are a total of seven entities named in the scenario. These entities include: (1) Jason Winston, (2) Winston Enterprises, (3) George Winston, (4) First Federal Bank, (5) Commercial Properties, Inc., (6) the customers, and (7) the employees. A separate set of accounting records would be maintained for each entity.

Your ability to learn accounting will be greatly influenced by how you approach the entity concept. Based on your everyday experiences you likely think from the perspective of a customer. In contrast, this text is written from the perspective of a business entity. These opposing perspectives dramatically affect how you view business events. For example, as a customer you consider a sales discount a great bargain. The view is different from the perspective of the business granting the discount. A sales discount means an item did not sell at the expected price. To move the item, the business had to accept less money than it originally planned to receive. From this perspective, a sales discount is not a good thing. To understand accounting, train yourself to interpret transactions from the perspective of a business rather than a consumer. Each time you encounter an accounting event ask yourself, how does this affect the business?

 CHECK YOURSELF 1.1

In a recent business transaction, land was exchanged for cash. Did the amount of cash increase or decrease?

Answer The answer depends on the reporting entity to which the question pertains. One entity sold land. The other entity bought land. For the entity that sold land, cash increased. For the entity that bought land, cash decreased.

ELEMENTS OF FINANCIAL STATEMENTS

 LO 1-2

Construct an accounting equation and show how business events affect the equation.

The individuals and organizations that need information about a business are called *stakeholders.* Stakeholders include owners, lenders, government agencies, employees, news reporters, and others. Businesses communicate information to stakeholders through four financial statements:[2] (1) an income statement, (2) a statement of changes in equity, (3) a balance sheet, and (4) a statement of cash flows.

The information reported in **financial statements** is organized into ten categories known as **elements.** Eight financial statement elements are discussed in this chapter: assets, liabilities, equity, contributed capital, revenue, expenses, distributions, and net income. The other two elements, gains and losses, are discussed in a later chapter. In practice, the business world uses various titles to identify several of the financial statement elements. For example, business people use net income, net *earnings,* and net *profit* interchangeably to describe the same element. Contributed capital may be called *common stock* and equity may be called *stockholders' equity, owner's capital,* and *partners' equity.* Furthermore, the transfer of assets from a business to its owners may be called *distributions, withdrawals,* or *dividends.* Think of accounting as a language. Different terms can describe the same business event. Detailed definitions of the elements and their placement on financial statements will be discussed in the following sections of the chapter.

---

[2]In practice these statements have alternate names. For example, the income statement may be called *results of operations* or *statement of earnings.* The balance sheet is sometimes called the *statement of financial position.* The statement of changes in equity might be called *statement of capital* or *statement of stockholders' equity.* Since the Financial Accounting Standards Board (FASB) called for the title *statement of cash flows,* companies do not use alternate names for that statement.

Answers to The Curious Accountant

Anyone who owns stock in Google owns a part of the company. Google has many owners. In contrast, nobody actually owns the American Heart Association (AHA). The AHA has a board of directors that is responsible for overseeing its operations, but the board is not its owner.

Ultimately, the purpose of a business entity is to increase the wealth of its owners. To this end, it "spends money to make money." The expense that Google incurs for developing software is a cost incurred in the hope that it will generate revenues when it sells advertising. The financial statements of a business show, among other things, whether and how the company made a profit during the current year. For example, Google's income statements show how much expense was incurred from "research and development" operations versus from "sales and marketing."

The AHA is a not-for-profit entity. It operates to provide services to society at large, not to make a profit. It cannot increase the wealth of its owners, because it has no owners. When the AHA spends money to conduct CPR classes, it does not spend this money in the expectation that it will generate revenues. The revenues of the AHA come from contributors who wish to support efforts related to fighting heart disease. Because the AHA does not spend money to make money, it has no reason to prepare an *income statement* like that of Google. The AHA's statement of activities shows how much revenue was received from "contributions" versus from "special events."

Not-for-profit entities do prepare financial statements that are similar in appearance to those of commercial enterprises. The financial statements of not-for-profit entities are called the *statement of financial position,* the *statement of activities,* and the *cash flow statement.*

Using Accounts to Gather Information

Detailed information about the elements is maintained in records commonly called **accounts.** For example, information regarding the element *assets* may be organized in separate accounts for cash, equipment, buildings, land, and so forth. The types and number of accounts used by a business depends on the information needs of its stakeholders. Some businesses provide very detailed information; others report highly summarized information. The more detail desired, the greater number of accounts needed. Think of accounts like the notebooks students keep for their classes. Some students keep detailed notes about every class they take in a separate notebook. Other students keep only the key points for all of their classes in a single notebook. Similarly, some businesses use more accounts than other businesses.

Diversity also exists regarding the names used for various accounts. For example, employee pay may be called salaries, wages, commissions, and so forth. Do not become frustrated with the diversity of terms used in accounting. Remember, accounting is a language. The same word can have different meanings. Similarly, different words can be used to describe the same phenomenon. The more you study and use accounting, the more familiar it will become to you.

Accounting Equation

You have probably heard the adage "you have to have money to make money." Indeed, you usually need a lot more than just money. For example, Carmike Cinemas, Inc., uses buildings, seating, screens, projection equipment, vending machines, cash registers, and so on in order to make money from ticket sales. The resources a business uses to make money are called **assets.** So, where do businesses get assets? There are three distinct sources.

First, a business can borrow assets from creditors. Usually a business acquires cash from creditors and then uses the cash to purchase the assets it needs to conduct its operations. When a business receives cash from creditors it accepts an obligation to return the cash to the creditors at some future date. In accounting terms, the obligations a business has to its creditors are called **liabilities.**

The second source of assets is investors. When a business acquires assets from investors it commits to keep the assets safe and to use the assets in a manner that benefits the investors. The business also grants the investor an ownership interest in the business thereby allowing the investor (owner) to share in the profits generated by the business. The specific commitments made to the investors are described in certificates called **common stock.** In accounting terms investors are called **stockholders.** Further, the business's commitment to the stockholders is called **stockholders' equity.**

The third source of assets is operations. Businesses use assets in order to produce higher amounts of other assets. For example, Best Buy may sell a TV that cost the company $500 for $600. The $100 difference between the sales price and the cost of the TV results in an increase in Best Buy's total assets. This explains how operations can be a source of assets. Of course operations may also result in a decrease in assets. If Best Buy has to discount the sales price of the TV to $450 in order to sell it, the company's total assets decrease by $50.

Net increases in assets generated from operations are commonly called *earnings* or *income.* Net decreases in assets caused by operations are called *losses.* As a result of their ownership status, the stockholders reap the benefits and suffer the sacrifices that a business experiences from its operations. A business may distribute all or part of the assets generated through operations to the shareholders. The distribution of assets generated through earnings is called a *dividend.*

Notice that paying dividends is an option not a legal requirement. Instead of paying dividends, a business may retain the assets it generates through operations. If a business retains the assets, it commits to use those assets for the benefit of the stockholders. This increase in the business's commitments to its stockholders is normally called **retained earnings.** Also, note that earnings that have been retained in the past can be used to pay dividends in the future. However, a company that does not have current or prior retained earnings cannot pay dividends.

As a result of providing assets to a business the creditors and investors are entitled to make potential **claims**[3] on the assets owned by the business. The relationship between a business's assets and the claims on its assets is frequently expressed in an equality called the **accounting equation.** Based on the relationships described above the accounting equation can be developed as follows:

$$\text{Assets} = \text{Claims}$$

$$\text{Assets} = \text{Liabilities} + \text{Stockholders' equity}$$

$$\text{Assets} = \text{Liabilities} + \text{Common stock} + \text{Retained earnings}$$

☑ CHECK YOURSELF 1.2

Gupta Company has $250,000 of assets, $60,000 of liabilities, and $90,000 of common stock. What percentage of the assets was provided by retained earnings?

Answer First, using algebra, determine the dollar amount of retained earnings:

Assets = Liabilities + Common stock + Retained earnings
Retained earnings = Assets − Liabilities − Common stock
Retained earnings = $250,000 − $60,000 − $90,000
Retained earnings = $100,000

---

[3]A claim is a legal action to obtain money, property, or the enforcement of a right against another party.

Second, determine the percentage:

Percentage of assets provided by retained earnings = Retained earnings/Total assets

Percentage of assets provided by retained earnings = $100,000/$250,000 = 40%

RECORDING BUSINESS EVENTS UNDER THE ACCOUNTING EQUATION

An **accounting event** is an economic occurrence that changes an enterprise's assets, liabilities, or stockholders' equity. A **transaction** is a particular kind of event that involves transferring something of value between two entities. Examples of transactions include acquiring assets from owners, borrowing money from creditors, and purchasing or selling goods and services. The following section of the text explains how several different types of accounting events affect a company's accounting equation.

Asset Source Transactions

As previously mentioned, businesses obtain assets (resources) from three sources. They acquire assets from owners (stockholders); they borrow assets from creditors; and they earn assets through profitable operations. Asset source transactions increase total assets and total claims. A more detailed discussion of the effects of asset source transactions is provided below:

EVENT 1 Rustic Camp Sites (RCS) was formed on January 1, 2014, when it acquired $120,000 cash from issuing common stock.

When RCS issued stock, it received cash and gave each investor (owner) a stock certificate as a receipt. Since this transaction provided $120,000 of assets (cash) to the business, it is an **asset source transaction.** It increases the business's assets (cash) and its stockholders' equity (common stock).

	Assets			=	Liab.	+	Stockholders' Equity		
	Cash	+	Land	=	N. Pay.	+	Com. Stk.	+	Ret. Earn.
Acquired cash through stock issue	120,000	+	NA	=	NA	+	120,000	+	NA

Notice the elements have been divided into accounts. For example, the element *assets* is divided into a Cash account and a Land account. Do not be concerned if some of these account titles are unfamiliar. They will be explained as new transactions are presented. Recall that the number of accounts a company uses depends on the nature of its business and the level of detail management needs to operate the business. For example, Sears would have an account called Cost of Goods Sold although GEICO Insurance would not. Why? Because Sears sells goods (merchandise) but GEICO does not.

Also, notice that a stock issue transaction affects the accounting equation in two places, both under an asset (cash) and also under the source of that asset (common stock). All transactions affect the accounting equation in at least two places. It is from this practice that the **double-entry bookkeeping** system derives its name.

EVENT 2 RCS acquired an additional $400,000 of cash by borrowing from a creditor.

This transaction is also an asset source transaction. It increases assets (cash) and liabilities (notes payable). The account title Notes Payable is used because the borrower

(RCS) is required to issue a promissory note to the creditor (a bank). A promissory note describes, among other things, the amount of interest RCS will pay and for how long it will borrow the money.[4] The effect of the borrowing transaction on the accounting equation is indicated below.

	Assets			=	Liab.	+	Stockholders' Equity		
	Cash	+	Land	=	N. Pay.	+	Com. Stk.	+	Ret. Earn.
Beginning balances	120,000	+	NA	=	NA	+	120,000	+	NA
Acquired cash by issuing note	400,000	+	NA	=	400,000	+	NA	+	NA
Ending balances	520,000	+	NA	=	400,000	+	120,000	+	NA

The beginning balances above came from the ending balances produced by the prior transaction. This practice is followed throughout the illustration.

Asset Exchange Transactions

Businesses frequently trade one asset for another asset. In such cases, the amount of one asset decreases and the amount of the other asset increases. Total assets are unaffected by asset exchange transactions. Event 3 is an asset exchange transaction.

EVENT 3 RCS paid $500,000 cash to purchase land.

This asset exchange transaction reduces the asset account Cash and increases the asset account Land. The amount of total assets is not affected. An **asset exchange transaction** simply reflects changes in the composition of assets. In this case, the company traded cash for land. The amount of cash decreased by $500,000 and the amount of land increased by the same amount.

	Assets			=	Liab.	+	Stockholders' Equity		
	Cash	+	Land	=	N. Pay.	+	Com. Stk.	+	Ret. Earn.
Beginning balances	520,000	+	NA	=	400,000	+	120,000	+	NA
Paid cash to buy land	(500,000)	+	500,000	=	NA	+	NA	+	NA
Ending balances	20,000	+	500,000	=	400,000	+	120,000	+	NA

Another Asset Source Transaction

EVENT 4 RCS obtained $85,000 cash by leasing camp sites to customers.

Revenue represents an economic benefit a company obtains by providing customers with goods and services. In this example the economic benefit is an increase in the asset cash. Revenue transactions can therefore be viewed as *asset source transactions*. The asset increase is balanced by an increase in the retained earnings section of stockholders' equity because producing revenue increases the amount of earnings that can be retained in the business.

[4]For simplicity, the computation of interest is ignored in this chapter. Interest computation is discussed in the appendix to Chapter 2 and in subsequent chapters.

	Assets			=	Liab.	+	Stockholders' Equity				
	Cash	+	Land	=	N. Pay.	+	Com. Stk.	+	Ret. Earn.	Acct. Title
Beginning balances	20,000	+	500,000	=	400,000	+	120,000	+	NA	
Acquired cash by earning revenue	85,000	+	NA	=	NA	+	NA	+	85,000	Revenue
Ending balances	105,000	+	500,000	=	400,000	+	120,000	+	85,000	

Note carefully that the $85,000 ending balance in the retained earnings column is *not* in the Retained Earnings account. It is in the Revenue account. It will be transferred to the Retained Earnings account at the end of the accounting period. Transferring the Revenue account balance to the Retained Earnings account is part of a process called *closing the accounts.*

Asset Use Transactions

Businesses use assets for a variety of purposes. For example, assets may be used to pay off liabilities or they may be transferred to owners. Assets may also be used in the process of generating earnings. All **asset use transactions** decrease the total amount of assets and the total amount of claims on assets (liabilities or stockholders' equity).

EVENT 5   RCS paid $50,000 cash for operating expenses such as salaries, rent, and interest. (RCS could establish a separate account for each type of expense. However, the management team does not currently desire this level of detail. Remember, the number of accounts a business uses depends on the level of information managers need to make decisions.)

In the normal course of generating revenue, a business consumes various assets and services. The assets and services consumed to generate revenue are called **expenses.** Revenue results from providing goods and services to customers. In exchange, the business acquires assets from its customers. Since the owners bear the ultimate risk and reap the rewards of operating the business, revenues increase stockholders' equity (retained earnings), and expenses decrease retained earnings. In this case, the asset account, Cash, decreased. This decrease is balanced by a decrease in the retained earnings section of stockholders' equity because expenses decrease the amount of earnings retained in the business.

	Assets			=	Liab.	+	Stockholders' Equity				
	Cash	+	Land	=	N. Pay.	+	Com. Stk.	+	Ret. Earn.	Acct. Title
Beginning balances	105,000	+	500,000	=	400,000	+	120,000	+	85,000	
Used cash to pay expenses	(50,000)	+	NA	=	NA	+	NA	+	(50,000)	Expense
Ending balances	55,000	+	500,000	=	400,000	+	120,000	+	35,000	

Like revenues, expenses are not recorded directly into the Retained Earnings account. The $50,000 of expense is recorded in the Expense account. It will be transferred to the Retained Earnings account at the end of the accounting period as part of the closing process. The $35,000 ending balance in the retained earnings column shows what would be in the Retained Earnings account after the balances in the Revenue and Expense accounts have been closed. The current balance in the Retained Earnings account is zero.

EVENT 6   RCS paid $4,000 in cash dividends to its owners.

To this point the enterprise's total assets and equity have increased by $35,000 ($85,000 of revenue − $50,000 of expense) as a result of its earnings activities. RCS can keep the additional assets in the business or transfer them to the owners. If a business transfers some or all of its earned assets to owners, the transfer is frequently called a **dividend.** Since assets distributed to stockholders are not used for the purpose of generating revenue, *dividends are not expenses.* Furthermore, dividends are a transfer of *earnings,* not a return of the assets acquired from the issue of common stock.

	Assets			=	Liab.	+	Stockholders' Equity				
	Cash	+	Land	=	N. Pay.	+	Com. Stk.	+	Ret. Earn.	Acct. Title
Beginning balances	55,000	+	500,000	=	400,000	+	120,000	+	35,000	
Used cash to pay dividends	(4,000)	+	NA	=	NA	+	NA	+	(4,000)	Dividends
Ending balances	51,000	+	500,000	=	400,000	+	120,000	+	31,000	

Like revenues and expenses, dividends are not recorded directly into the Retained Earnings account. The $4,000 dividend is recorded in the Dividends account. It will be transferred to retained earnings at the end of the accounting period as part of the closing process. The $31,000 ending balance in the retained earnings column shows what would be in the Retained Earnings account after the balances in the Revenue, Expense, and Dividend accounts have been closed. The current balance in the Retained Earnings account is zero.

EVENT 7   The land that RCS paid $500,000 to purchase had an appraised market value of $525,000 on December 31, 2014.

Although the appraised value of the land is higher than the original cost, RCS will not increase the amount recorded in its accounting records above the land's $500,000 historical cost. In general, accountants do not recognize changes in market value. The **historical cost concept** requires that most assets be reported at the amount paid for them (their historical cost) regardless of increases in market value.

Surely investors would rather know what an asset is worth instead of how much it originally cost. So why do accountants maintain records and report financial information based on historical cost? Accountants rely heavily on verification. Information is considered to be more useful if it can be independently verified. For example, two people looking at the legal documents associated with RCS's land purchase will both conclude that RCS paid $500,000 for the land. That historical cost is a verifiable fact. The appraised value, in contrast, is an opinion. Even two persons who are experienced appraisers are not likely to come up with the same amount for the land's market value. Accountants do not report market values in financial statements because such values are not reliable.

There are exceptions to the application of the historical cost rule. When market value can be clearly established, GAAP not only permits but requires its use. For example, securities that are traded on the New York Stock Exchange must be shown at market value rather than historical cost. We will discuss other notable exceptions to the historical cost principle later in the text. However, as a general rule you should assume that assets shown in a company's financial statements are valued at historical cost.

Summary of Transactions

The complete collection of a company's accounts is called the **general ledger.** A summary of the accounting events and the general ledger account information for RCS's 2014 accounting period is shown in Exhibit 1.4. The Revenue, Expense, and Dividend account data appear in the retained earnings column. These account titles are shown immediately to the right of the dollar amounts listed in the retained earnings column.

EXHIBIT 1.4

Accounting Events

1.	RCS issued common stock, acquiring $120,000 cash from its owners.
2.	RCS borrowed $400,000 cash.
3.	RCS paid $500,000 cash to purchase land.
4.	RCS received $85,000 cash from earning revenue.
5.	RCS paid $50,000 cash for expenses.
6.	RCS paid dividends of $4,000 cash to the owners.
7.	The land that RCS paid $500,000 to purchase had an appraised market value of $525,000 on December 31, 2014.

General Ledger Accounts Organized under the Accounting Equation

Event No.	Assets			=	Liabilities	+	Stockholders' Equity			Other Account Titles
	Cash	+	Land	=	Notes Payable	+	Common Stock	+	Retained Earnings	
Beg. bal.	0		0		0		0		0	
1.	120,000						120,000			
2.	400,000				400,000					
3.	(500,000)		500,000							
4.	85,000								85,000	Revenue
5.	(50,000)								(50,000)	Expense
6.	(4,000)								(4,000)	Dividend
7.	NA		NA		NA		NA		NA	
	51,000	+	500,000	=	400,000	+	120,000	+	31,000	

INTERPRETING INFORMATION SHOWN IN THE ACCOUNTING EQUATION

In the United States, the amounts shown in an accounting equation are normally expressed in dollars. However, the dollar amounts shown on the right side of the equation are not related to the amount of actual cash a company has on hand.

LO 1-3

 Interpret information shown in an accounting equation.

The Left versus the Right Side of the Accounting Equation

To illustrate the relationship between the left and right sides of the accounting equation, assume Educate Inc. acquires $600 cash from creditors, $300 cash from investors, and $100 cash from operations. This information can be organized under an accounting equation as follows:

Assets	= Liabilities	+ Common stock	+ Retained earnings
$1,000 Cash =	$600	+ $300	+ $100

Now assume that Educate Inc. uses its cash to purchase land. Immediately after this purchase, the company's accounting equation is a follows:

Assets	= Liabilities	+ Common stock	+ Retained earnings
$1,000 Land =	$600	+ $300	+ $100

At this point the company has zero cash. This highlights the fact that the amounts in liabilities, common stock, and retained earnings do not represent cash. Instead they represent the original sources of the company's assets. Indeed, the right side of the accounting equation could be expressed as percentages instead of dollars. Specifically, the equation could be written as:

$$\text{Assets} = \text{Liabilities} + \text{Common stock} + \text{Retained earnings}$$
$$\$1{,}000 \text{ Land} = 60\% + 30\% + 10\%$$

This equation suggests 60 percent of Educate's assets came from creditors, 30 percent came from owner's, and 10 percent from its earnings. However, this does not explain what has happened to the company's assets since they were acquired. Specifically, the right side of the equation does not show that the company acquired cash and then used the cash to purchase land. The right side identifies the sources of assets, not their composition.

Two Views of the Right Side of the Accounting Equation

Another important point to recognize is that there are two views of the right side of the accounting equation. In the above case the right side is viewed as sources of assets. Clearly, when a company borrows money from a bank the business receives an asset, cash. Therefore, we say creditors are a source of assets. However, borrowing money creates an obligation for the business to return the amount borrowed to creditors. Thus, we can view the liabilities of a company as its obligations to return assets to its creditors. In summary, liabilities can be viewed as sources of assets or, alternatively, as obligations of the business.

Similarly, a business may acquire assets from its owners by issuing stock or it may earn assets through its operations. Therefore, common stock and retained earnings can be viewed as sources of assets. However, the business has a **stewardship** function, which means that it has a duty to protect and use the assets for the benefit of the owners. As a result, common stock and retained earnings can be viewed as sources of assets or, alternatively, as commitments to the investors. In summary, the right side of the accounting equation can be viewed either as sources of assets or as obligations and commitments of the business.

Cash and Retained Earnings

While the amount of retained earnings does not represent the amount of cash a company has on hand, it does limit the amount of cash that can be used to pay dividends. To illustrate, we assume that Educate Inc. earns an additional $150 of cash. This event would cause assets and retained earnings to increase, thereby resulting in the following accounting equation:

$$\text{Assets} = \text{Liabilities} + \text{Common stock} + \text{Retained earnings}$$
$$\$150 \text{ Cash} + \$1{,}000 \text{ Land} = \$600 + \$300 + \$250$$

Given that the company has $250 in retained earnings, can the company pay a $200 cash dividend? The answer is no. Remember, there is no cash in retained earnings. The only cash the company has is listed on the left side of the equation. In this case, the maximum cash dividend that can be paid is $150 because that is all the cash the company has. Suppose Educate decides it no longer needs the land and sells it for $1,000 cash. After this event, the accounting equation appears as follows:

$$\text{Assets} = \text{Liabilities} + \text{Common stock} + \text{Retained earnings}$$
$$\$1{,}150 \text{ Cash} = \$600 + \$300 + \$250$$

Given that Educate now has $1,150 in cash, can the company pay a $400 dividend? The answer is no. Based on the information in the accounting equation,

Educate has only increased its assets by $250 as a result of its operations. Since dividends are a distribution of assets that were generated through earnings, the maximum dividend Educate can distribute at this time is $250. In summary, the payment of dividends is limited by both the amount of cash and the amount of retained earnings. In other words, to pay a cash dividend a company must have both cash and retained earnings.

Distributions in Business Liquidations

If a business ceases to operate, its remaining assets are sold and the sale proceeds are returned to the creditors and investors through a process called business **liquidation.** Creditors have priority in business liquidations. This means the business uses its assets first to settle the obligations to the creditors. Any assets remaining after the creditors have been paid are then distributed to the investors.

To illustrate, suppose Cruz Company acquired $100 cash from investors and $200 cash from creditors. Also assume Cruz had a net operating loss of $75. After these events, Cruz's accounting equation is as follows:

Assets	= Liabilities + Common stock + Retained earnings
$225 Cash =	$200 + $100 + $(75)

If Cruz is forced to liquidate at this point the creditors would receive $200 and the owners (investors) would receive only $25.

Return to the original scenario where Cruz acquires $100 cash from investors and $200 cash from creditors. Now suppose instead of experiencing a $75 loss Cruz experiences a $120 loss. In this scenario, Cruz's accounting equation would be:

Assets	= Liabilities + Common stock + Retained earnings
$180 Cash =	$200 + $100 + $(120)

If Cruz is forced to liquidate at this point the investors would receive zero and the creditors would receive only $180 even though the business owes them $200. Simply stated, Cruz cannot distribute assets that it does not have. This case shows that creditors as well as investors are at risk to lose some or all of the resources they provide to businesses.

It is interesting to note that even profitable companies can be forced to liquidate. For example, return to the illustration where Cruz Company acquires $100 cash from investors and $200 cash from creditors. Now assume that Cruz earns a net income of $75 cash instead of experiencing a net loss. Also assume Cruz pays $350 to purchase land. After these events, Cruz would have the following accounting equation.

Assets	= Liabilities + Common stock + Retained earnings
$25 Cash + $350 Land =	$200 + $100 + $75

At this point, if the liabilities come due and the creditors demand payment, Cruz could be forced into bankruptcy because it has only $25 cash to settle a $200 debt. A company must properly manage its assets as well as its liabilities and stockholders' equity in order to remain a **going concern.** The going concern doctrine assumes that a business is able to continue its operations into the foreseeable future. Many procedures and practices used by accountants are based on a going concern assumption. If a company's going concern status becomes uncertain, accountants are required to notify creditors and investors.

In practice, the relationships between a business and its creditors and investors are determined by complex legal documents that may conflict with the general conditions described above. We will discuss some of these details in later chapters. However, it is important to clearly establish the basic guidelines before we begin discussing the refinements.

20   Chapter 1

RECAP: TYPES OF TRANSACTIONS

Classify business events as asset source, use, or exchange transactions.

The transactions described above have each been classified into one of three categories: (1) asset source transactions; (2) asset exchange transactions; and (3) asset use transactions. A fourth category, claims exchange transactions, is introduced in a later chapter. In summary:

▪ **Asset source transactions** increase the total amount of assets and increase the total amount of claims. In its first year of operation, RCS acquired assets from three sources: first, from owners (Event 1); next, by borrowing (Event 2); and finally, through earnings activities (Event 4).

▪ **Asset exchange transactions** decrease one asset and increase another asset. The total amount of assets is unchanged by asset exchange transactions. RCS experienced one asset exchange transaction; it used cash to purchase land (Event 3).

▪ **Asset use transactions** decrease the total amount of assets and the total amount of claims. RCS used assets to pay expenses (Event 5) and to pay dividends (Event 6).

As you proceed through this text, practice classifying transactions into one of the four categories. Businesses engage in thousands of transactions every day. It is far more effective to learn how to classify the transactions into meaningful categories than to attempt to memorize the effects of thousands of transactions.

The Curious Accountant

The RCS case includes only seven business events, one of which is not recognized in the ledger accounts. These events are assumed to have taken place over the course of a year. In contrast, real-world companies engage in thousands, even millions, of transactions in a single day. For example, think of the number of sales events Walmart processes in a day or how many tickets Delta Airlines sells. Presenting this many events in accounting equation format would produce such a volume of data that users would be overwhelmed with details. To facilitate communication, accountants summarize and organize the transaction data into reports called financial statements. This section discusses the information contained in financial statements and explains how they are prepared. While the RCS illustration contains only a few transactions, the financial statements prepared for this company contain the same basic content as those of much larger companies.

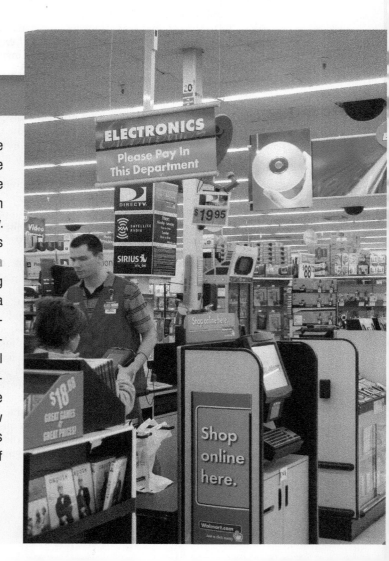

SECTION 2:

REPORTING INFORMATION

As indicated earlier, accounting information is normally presented to external users in four general-purpose financial statements. The information in the ledger accounts is used to prepare these financial statements. The data in the ledger accounts in Exhibit 1.4 are color coded to help you understand the source of information in the financial statements. The numbers in *green* are used in the *statement of cash flows*. The numbers in *red* are used to prepare the *balance sheet*. Finally, the numbers in *blue* are used to prepare the *income statement*. The numbers reported in the statement of changes in stockholders' equity have not been color coded because they appear in more than one statement. The next section explains how the information in the accounts is presented in financial statements.

PREPARING FINANCIAL STATEMENTS

The financial statements for RCS are shown in Exhibit 1.5. The information used to prepare these statements was drawn from the ledger accounts shown in Exhibit 1.4. Information in one statement may relate to information in another statement. For example, the amount of net income reported on the income statement also appears on the statement of changes in stockholders' equity. Accountants use the term **articulation** to describe the interrelationships among the various elements of the financial statements. The key articulated relationships in RCS's financial statements are highlighted with arrows (Exhibit 1.5). A description of each statement follows.

LO 1-5

 Use general ledger account information to prepare four financial statements.

Income Statement and the Matching Concept

A business must make sacrifices in order to obtain benefits. For example, RCS must sacrifice cash to pay for employee salaries, rent, and interest. In turn, RCS receives a benefit when it collects cash from its customers. As this example implies, sacrifices are defined as decreases in assets; and benefits are increases in assets. In accounting terms sacrifices are called expenses; and benefits are called revenues. *Therefore, expenses are decreases in assets; and revenues are increases in assets.*[5]

The **income statement** matches the expenses with the revenues that occur during a period when operating a business. If revenues exceed expenses, the difference is called **net income.** If expenses are greater than revenues, the difference is called **net loss.** The practice of pairing revenues with expenses on the income statement is called the **matching concept.**

The income statement in Exhibit 1.5 indicates that RCS has earned more assets than it has used. The statement shows that RCS has increased its assets by $35,000 (net

---

[5]The definitions for revenue and expense are expanded in subsequent chapters as additional relationships among the elements of financial statements are introduced.

EXHIBIT 1.5   Financial Statements

RUSTIC CAMP SITES
Income Statement
For the Year Ended December 31, 2014

Rental revenue (*asset increases*)	$ 85,000
Operating expenses (*asset decreases*)	(50,000)
Net income	$ 35,000

RUSTIC CAMP SITES
Statement of Changes in Stockholders' Equity
For the Year Ended December 31, 2014

Beginning common stock	$ 0	
Plus: common stock issued	120,000	
Ending common stock		$120,000
Beginning retained earnings	0	
Plus: Net income	35,000	
Less: Dividends	(4,000)	
Ending retained earnings		31,000
Total stockholders' equity		$151,000

RUSTIC CAMP SITES
Balance Sheet
As of December 31, 2014

Assets		
Cash	$ 51,000	
Land	500,000	
Total assets		$551,000
Liabilities		
Notes payable		$400,000
Stockholders' equity		
Common stock	$120,000	
Retained earnings	31,000	
Total stockholders' equity		151,000
Total liabilities and stockholders' equity		$551,000

RUSTIC CAMP SITES
Statement of Cash Flows
For the Year Ended December 31, 2014

Cash flows from operating activities:		
Cash receipts from revenue	$ 85,000	
Cash payments for expenses	(50,000)	
Net cash flow from operating activities		$ 35,000
Cash flows from investing activities:		
Cash payments to purchase land		(500,000)
Cash flows from financing activities:		
Cash receipts from borrowing funds	400,000	
Cash receipts from issuing common stock	120,000	
Cash payments for dividends	(4,000)	
Net cash flow from financing activities		516,000
Net increase in cash		51,000
Plus: beginning cash balance		0
Ending cash balance		$ 51,000

income) as a result of operating its business. Observe the phrase *For the Year Ended December 31, 2014,* in the heading of the income statement. Income is measured for a span of time called the **accounting period.** While accounting periods of one year are normal for external financial reporting, income can be measured weekly, monthly, quarterly, semiannually, or over any other desired time period. Notice that the cash RCS paid to its stockholders (dividends) is not reported as expense. The decrease in assets for dividend payments is not incurred for the purpose of generating revenue. Instead, dividends are transfers of wealth to the owners of the business. Dividend payments are not reported on the income statement.

 CHECK YOURSELF 1.3

Mahoney, Inc., was started when it issued common stock to its owners for $300,000. During its first year of operation Mahoney received $523,000 cash for services provided to customers. Mahoney paid employees $233,000 cash. Advertising costs paid in cash amounted to $102,000. Other cash operating expenses amounted to $124,000. Finally, Mahoney paid a $25,000 cash dividend to its stockholders. What amount of net income would Mahoney's report on its earnings statement?

Answer   The amount of net income is $64,000 ($523,000 Revenue − $233,000 Salary Expense − $102,000 Advertising Expense − $124,000 Other Operating Expenses). The cash received from issuing stock is not revenue because it was not acquired from earnings activities. In other words, Mahoney did not work (perform services) for this money; it was contributed by owners of the business. The dividends are not expenses because the decrease in cash was not incurred for the purpose of generating revenue. Instead, the dividends represent a transfer of wealth to the owners.

Statement of Changes in Stockholders' Equity

The **statement of changes in stockholders' equity** explains the effects of transactions on stockholders' equity during the accounting period. It starts with the beginning balance in the common stock account. In the case of RCS, the beginning balance in the common stock account is zero because the company did not exist before the 2014 accounting period. The $120,000 of stock issued during the accounting period is added to the beginning balance to determine the ending balance in the common stock account.

In addition to reporting the changes in common stock, the statement describes the changes in retained earnings for the accounting period. RCS had no beginning balance in retained earnings. During the period, the company earned $35,000 and paid $4,000 in dividends to the stockholders, producing an ending retained earnings balance of $31,000 ($0 + $35,000 − $4,000). Since equity consists of common stock and retained earnings, the ending total equity balance is $151,000 ($120,000 + $31,000). This statement is also dated with the phrase *For the Year Ended December 31, 2014,* because it describes what happened to stockholders' equity during 2014.

Balance Sheet

The **balance sheet** draws its name from the accounting equation. Total assets balance with (equal) liabilities and stockholders' equity. The balance sheet for RCS is shown in Exhibit 1.5. In this case, total assets equals total liabilities plus stockholders' equity ($551,000 = $551,000).

Note the order of the assets in the balance sheet. Cash appears first, followed by land. Assets are displayed in the balance sheet based on their level of **liquidity.** This means that assets are listed in the order of how rapidly they can be converted into cash. Finally, note that the balance sheet is dated with the phrase *As of December 31, 2014,* indicating that it describes the company's financial condition on the last day of the accounting period.

CHECK YOURSELF 1.4

To gain a clear understanding of the balance sheet, try to create one that describes your personal financial condition. First list your assets, then your liabilities. Determine the amount of your equity by subtracting your liabilities from your assets.

Answer   Answers for this exercise will vary depending on the particular assets and liabilities each student identifies. Common student assets include automobiles, computers, stereos, TVs, phones, MP3 players, clothes, and textbooks. Common student liabilities include car loans, mortgages, student loans, and credit card debt. The difference between the assets and the liabilities is the equity.

Statement of Cash Flows

The **statement of cash flows** explains how a company obtained and used *cash* during the accounting period. Receipts of cash are called *cash inflows,* and payments are *cash outflows.* The statement classifies cash receipts (inflows) and payments (outflows) into three categories: financing activities, investing activities, and operating activities.

Businesses normally start with an idea. Implementing the idea usually requires cash. For example, suppose you decide to start an apartment rental business. First, you would need cash to finance acquiring the apartments. Acquiring cash to start a business is a financing activity. **Financing activities** include obtaining cash (inflow) from owners or paying cash (outflow) to owners (dividends). Financing activities also include borrowing cash (inflow) from creditors and repaying the principal (outflow) to creditors. Because interest on borrowed money is an expense, however, cash paid to creditors for interest is reported in the operating activities section of the statement of cash flows.

After obtaining cash from financing activities, you would invest the money by building or buying apartments. **Investing activities** involve paying cash (outflow) to purchase long-term assets or receiving cash (inflow) from selling long-term assets. Long-term assets are normally used for more than one year. Cash outflows to purchase land or cash inflows from selling a building are examples of investing activities.

After investing in the productive assets (apartments), you would engage in operating activities. **Operating activities** involve receiving cash (inflow) from revenue and paying cash (outflow) for expenses. Note that cash spent to purchase short-term assets such as office supplies is reported in the operating activities section because the office supplies would likely be used (expensed) within a single accounting period.

The primary cash inflows and outflows related to the types of business activity introduced in this chapter are summarized in Exhibit 1.6. The exhibit will be expanded as additional types of events are introduced in subsequent chapters.

The statement of cash flows for Rustic Camp Sites in Exhibit 1.5 shows that the amount of cash increased by $51,000 during the year. The beginning balance in the Cash account was zero; adding the $51,000 increase to the beginning balance results in a $51,000 ending balance. Notice that the $51,000 ending cash balance on the statement of cash flows is the same as the amount of cash reported in the asset section on the December 31 year-end balance sheet. Also, note that the statement of cash flows is dated with the phrase *For the Year Ended December 31, 2014,* because it describes what happened to cash over the span of the year.

EXHIBIT 1.6

Classification Scheme for Statement of Cash Flows

Cash flows from operating activities:
  Cash receipts (inflows) from customers
  Cash payments (outflows) to suppliers

Cash flows from investing activities:
  Cash receipts (inflows) from the sale of long-term assets
  Cash payments (outflows) for the purchase of long-term assets

Cash flows from financing activities:
  Cash receipts (inflows) from borrowing funds
  Cash receipts (inflows) from issuing common stock
  Cash payments (outflows) to repay borrowed funds
  Cash payments (outflows) for dividends

CHECK YOURSELF 1.5

Classify each of the following cash flows as an operating activity, investing activity, or financing activity.

1. Acquired cash from owners.
2. Borrowed cash from creditors.
3. Paid cash to purchase land.
4. Earned cash revenue.
5. Paid cash for salary expenses.
6. Paid cash dividend.
7. Paid cash for interest.

Answer (1) financing activity; (2) financing activity; (3) investing activity; (4) operating activity; (5) operating activity; (6) financing activity; (7) operating activity.

The Closing Process

As previously indicated, transaction data are recorded in the Revenue, Expense, and Dividend accounts during the accounting period. At the end of the accounting period the data in these accounts are transferred to the Retained Earnings account. The process of transferring the balances is called **closing.** Since the Revenue, Expense, and Dividend accounts are closed each period, they are called **temporary accounts.** At the beginning of each new accounting period, the temporary accounts have zero balances. The Retained Earnings account carries forward from one accounting period to the next. Since this account is not closed, it is called a **permanent account.**

LO 1-6

Explain the closing process.

Since RCS started operations on January 1, 2014, the beginning Retained Earnings account balance was zero. In other words, there were no previous earnings available to be retained by the business. During 2014, amounts were recorded in the Revenue, Expense, and Dividend accounts. Since the Retained Earnings account is separate from the Revenue, Expense, and Dividend accounts, the entries in these temporary accounts did not affect the Retained Earnings balance. Specifically, the *before closing* balance in the Retained Earnings account on December 31, 2014, is still zero. In contrast, the Revenue account has a balance of $85,000; the Expense account has a balance of $50,000; and the Dividends account has a balance of $4,000. The closing process transfers the balances in the Revenue, Expense, and Dividend accounts to the Retained Earnings account. Therefore, *after closing* the balance in the Retained Earnings account is $31,000 ($85,000 − $50,000 − $4,000) and the Revenue, Expense, and Dividend accounts have zero balances.

Since the asset, liability, common stock, and retained earnings accounts are permanent accounts, they are not closed at the end of the accounting period. After the closing account process, RCS's general ledger will contain the following account balances as of December 31, 2014.

Cash	+	Land	=	Notes Payable	+	Common Stock	+	Retained Earnings
51,000	+	500,000	=	400,000	+	120,000	+	31,000

Take note that the December 31, 2014, ending account balances become the January 1, 2015, beginning account balances. So, RCS will start the 2015 accounting period with these same account balances. In other words, the current period's after closing ending balances become the next period's beginning balances.

☑ CHECK YOURSELF 1.6

After closing on December 31, 2014, Walston Company had $4,600 of assets, $2,000 of liabilities, and $700 of common stock. During January of 2015, Walston earned $750 of revenue and incurred $300 of expense. Walston closes its books each year on December 31.

1. Determine the balance in the Retained Earnings account as of December 31, 2014.

2. Determine the balance in the Retained Earnings account as of January 1, 2015.

3. Determine the balance in the Retained Earnings account as of January 31, 2015.

Answer

1. Assets = Liabilities + Common Stock + Retained Earnings

   $4,600 = $2,000 + $700 + Retained Earnings

   Retained Earnings = $1,900

2. The balance in the Retained Earnings account on January 1, 2015, is the same as it was on December 31, 2014. This year's ending balance becomes next year's beginning balance. Therefore, the balance in the Retained Earnings account on January 1, 2015, is $1,900.

3. The balance in the Retained Earnings account on January 31, 2015, is still $1,900. The revenue earned and expenses incurred during January are not recorded in the Retained Earnings account. Revenue is recorded in a Revenue account and expenses are recorded in an Expense account during the accounting period. The balances in the Revenue and Expense accounts are transferred to the Retained Earnings account during the closing process at the end of the accounting period (December 31, 2015).

THE HORIZONTAL FINANCIAL STATEMENTS MODEL

LO 1-7

Record business events using a horizontal financial statements model.

Financial statements are the scorecard for business activity. If you want to succeed in business, you must know how your business decisions affect your company's financial statements. This text uses a **horizontal statements model** to help you understand how business events affect financial statements. This model shows a set of financial statements horizontally across a single page of paper. The balance sheet is displayed first, adjacent to the income statement, and then the statement of cash flows. Because the effects of equity transactions can be analyzed by referring to certain balance sheet columns, and because of limited space, the statement of changes in stockholders' equity is not shown in the horizontal statements model.

The model frequently uses abbreviations. For example, activity classifications in the statement of cash flows are identified using OA for operating activities, IA for investing activities, and FA for financing activities. NC designates the net change in cash. The statements model uses "NA" when an account is not affected by an event. The background of the *balance sheet* is red, the *income statement* is blue, and the *statement of cash flows* is green. To demonstrate the usefulness of the horizontal statements model, we use it to display the seven accounting events that RCS experienced during its first year of operation (2014).

1. RCS acquired $120,000 cash from the issuance of common stock.
2. RCS borrowed $400,000 cash.
3. RCS paid $500,000 cash to purchase land.
4. RCS received $85,000 cash from earning revenue.
5. RCS paid $50,000 cash for expenses.
6. RCS paid $4,000 of cash dividends to the owners.
7. The market value of the land owned by RCS was appraised at $525,000 on December 31, 2014.

Event No.	Balance Sheet										Income Statement						Statement of Cash Flows	
	Assets			=	Liab.	+	Stockholders' Equity											
	Cash	+	Land	=	N. Pay.	+	Com. Stk.	+	Ret. Earn.		Rev.	−	Exp.	=	Net Inc.			
Beg. bal.	0	+	0	=	0	+	0	+	0		0	−	0	=	0		NA	
1.	120,000	+	NA	=	NA	+	120,000	+	NA		NA	−	NA	=	NA		120,000	FA
2.	400,000	+	NA	=	400,000	+	NA	+	NA		NA	−	NA	=	NA		400,000	FA
3.	(500,000)	+	500,000	=	NA	+	NA	+	NA		NA	−	NA	=	NA		(500,000)	IA
4.	85,000	+	NA	=	NA	+	NA	+	85,000		85,000	−	NA	=	85,000		85,000	OA
5.	(50,000)	+	NA	=	NA	+	NA	+	(50,000)		NA	−	50,000	=	(50,000)		(50,000)	OA
6.	(4,000)	+	NA	=	NA	+	NA	+	(4,000)		NA	−	NA	=	NA		(4,000)	FA
7.	NA	+	NA	=	NA	+	NA	+	NA		NA	−	NA	=	NA		NA	
Totals	51,000	+	500,000	=	400,000	+	120,000	+	31,000		85,000	−	50,000	=	35,000		51,000	NC

Recognize that statements models are learning tools. Because they are helpful in understanding how accounting events affect financial statements, they are used extensively in this book. However, the models omit many of the details used in published financial statements. For example, the horizontal model shows only a partial set of statements. Also, since the statements are presented in aggregate, the description of dates (i.e., "as of" versus "for the period ended") does not distinguish periodic from cumulative data.

Real-World Financial Reports

As previously indicated, organizations exist in many different forms, including *business* entities and *not-for-profit* entities. Business entities are typically service, merchandising, or manufacturing companies. **Service businesses,** which include doctors, attorneys, accountants, dry cleaners, and housekeepers, provide services to their customers. **Merchandising businesses,** sometimes called *retail* or *wholesale companies,* sell goods to customers that other entities make. **Manufacturing businesses** make the goods that they sell to their customers.

Some business operations include combinations of these three categories. For example, an automotive repair shop might change oil (service function), sell parts such as oil filters (retail function), and rebuild engines (manufacturing function). The nature of the reporting entity affects the form and content of the information reported in an entity's financial statements. For example, governmental entities provide statements of activities while business entities provide income statements. Similarly, income statements of retail companies show an expense item called *cost of goods sold,* but service companies that do not sell goods have no such item in their income statements. You should expect some diversity when reviewing real-world financial statements.

Throughout this book we usually present income statements that end with "Net income." Due to an accounting rule that became effective at the end of 2009, income statements of large, real-world companies often appear to have three lines for net income. The partial income statements for Merck & Company, a large pharmaceutical company, shown in Exhibit 1.7, illustrate this issue. Notice that the third line from the bottom of the statement is called "Net income." However, "Net income attributable to noncontrolling interest" is subtracted from this first net income to arrive at "Net income attributable to Merck & Co., Inc." The illustrations in this text always assume that there is no net income attributable to noncontrolling interests, therefore our examples simply end with the term "Net income."

Some real-world companies with complex operations report information related to *comprehensive income.* Comprehensive income is determined by adding or subtracting certain items to or from net income. A description of the items used to determine

EXHIBIT 1.7	Real-World Financial Reporting		

MERCK & CO., INC. AND SUBSIDIARIES
Consolidated Statement of Income (partial)
Years Ended December 31
($ in millions except per share amounts)

	2012	2011	2010
Sales	$47,267	$48,047	$45,987
Costs, expenses, and other			
Materials and production	16,446	16,871	18,396
Marketing and administrative	12,776	13,733	13,125
Research and development	8,168	8,467	11,111
Restructuring costs	664	1,306	985
Equity income from affiliates	(642)	(610)	(587)
Other (income) expense, net	1,116	946	1,304
	38,528	40,713	44,334
Income before taxes	8,739	7,334	1,653
Taxes on income	2,440	942	671
Net income	6,299	6,392	982
Less: Net income attributable to noncontrolling interests	131	120	121
Net income attributable to Merck & Co., Inc.	$ 6,168	$ 6,272	$ 861

comprehensive income is complex and beyond the scope of this course. Even so, the reader should be aware that, as of 2011, companies that must report comprehensive income may do so in one of two ways. First, comprehensive income items can be added to the bottom of the primary statement of earnings. Alternatively, a separate statement showing the determination of comprehensive income can be presented immediately following the primary statement of earnings. If a company chooses to report comprehensive income in a separate statement, the company's annual report will contain five financial statements. This text limits coverage to the four financial statements that traditionally appear in real-world annual reports. The optional statement of comprehensive income is not covered.

Annual Report for Target Corporation

Organizations normally provide information, including financial statements, to *stakeholders* yearly in a document known as an **annual report.** The annual report for Target Corporation is referred to in some of the end-of-chapter assignments, and it is worth your while to review it as an example of a real-world annual report. This report can be found online at http://investors.target.com. On the webpage that appears, under the "Investors" link, click on "sec filings." Next, under "filter by form type," select "annual filings" and then select the most recent "10-k" form from the list that appears. The pdf format is the easiest to work with. This report includes the company's financial statements (see pages 33–37 of the 2012 annual report). Immediately following the statements are a set of notes that

REALITY BYTES

On April 19, 2010, the stock of BP, Plc. (formally known as British Petroleum) was trading at $59.48 per share. On that same day the stock of Chevron Corp. was trading at $81.32 and the stock of Exxon Mobil Corp. was trading at $68.23. About six weeks later, on June 4, 2010, these companies' stocks had fallen to $37.16, $71.28, and $59.53 per share, respectively. Why did this happen? Did the companies report a large drop in their net earnings during these six weeks? No. What happened was that on April 20, 2010, the Deepwater Horizon oil well, owned by BP, failed and began discharging 60,000 barrels of oil daily into the Gulf of Mexico.

While it is easy to see why this event could cause BP's stock to lose 38 percent of its value, why would this cause Chevron's stock to fall 12 percent and Exxon's stock to fall 13 percent? These two companies did not have any oil spills during this time. One reason that the stock price of most oil companies declined significantly after BP's problems was that investors were concerned the failure would result in tighter regulation of all oil companies. Additionally, there was the concern that the government would ban, or seriously reduce, all future deepwater drilling. More regulations, and certainly a ban on future drilling, could drastically reduce the future earnings potential of all oil companies, not just BP.

As this situation illustrates, investors frequently use information not yet reported in a company's annual report. The annual report focuses on historical data, but investors are more concerned about the future. The historical information contained in the annual report is important because the past is frequently a strong predictor of what will occur in the future. However, current negative news, such as an oil spill, may give investors more information about a company's future than last year's annual report. For example, while the oil spill was bad news for the oil companies, it was, in financial terms, good news for companies that manufacture the oil-booms used to prevent oil from reaching the beaches. Similarly, a new company that has never earned a profit may have such an innovative idea that investors rush to buy its stock, even though they expect it to be a few years before the company has positive earnings. Also, investors and creditors may be motivated by nonfinancial considerations such as social consciousness, humanitarian concerns, or personal preferences. While accounting information is critically important, it is only one dimension of the information pool that investors and creditors use to make decisions.

---

provide additional details about the items described in the statements (see pages 38–64 of the 2012 annual report). The annual report contains the *auditors' report,* which is discussed in Chapter 4. Annual reports also include written commentary describing management's assessment of significant events that affected the company during the reporting period. This commentary is called *management's discussion and analysis* (MD&A).

The U.S. Securities and Exchange Commission (SEC) requires public companies to file an annual report in a document known as a 10-K. The SEC is discussed in more detail later. Even though the annual report is usually flashier (contains more color and pictures) than the 10-K, the 10-K is normally more comprehensive with respect to content. As a result, the 10-K report frequently substitutes for the annual report, but the annual report cannot substitute for the 10-K. In an effort to reduce costs, many companies now use the 10-K report as their annual report.

Special Terms in Real-World Reports

The financial statements of real-world companies include numerous items relating to advanced topics that are not covered in introductory accounting textbooks, especially the first chapter of an introductory accounting textbook. Do not, however, be discouraged from browsing through real-world annual reports. You will significantly enhance your learning if you look at many annual reports and attempt to identify as many items as you can. As your accounting knowledge grows, you will likely experience increased interest in real-world financial reports and the businesses they describe.

We encourage you to look for annual reports in the library or ask your employer for a copy of your company's report. The Internet is another excellent source for obtaining annual reports. Most companies provide links to their annual reports on their home pages. Look for links labeled "about the company" or "investor relations" or other phrases that logically lead to the company's financial reports. The best way to learn accounting is to use it. Accounting is the language of business. Learning the language will serve you well in almost any area of business that you pursue.

A Look Back

This chapter introduced the role of accounting in society and business: to provide information helpful to operating and evaluating the performance of organizations. Accounting is a measurement discipline. To communicate effectively, users of accounting must agree on the rules of measurement. *Generally accepted accounting principles (GAAP)* constitute the rules used by the accounting profession in the United States to govern financial reporting. GAAP is a work in progress that continues to evolve.

This chapter has discussed eight elements of financial statements: *assets, liabilities, equity, common stock (contributed capital), revenue, expenses, dividends (distributions),* and *net income.* The elements represent broad classifications reported on financial statements. Four basic financial statements appear in the reports of public companies: the *balance sheet,* the *income statement,* the *statement of changes in stockholders' equity,* and the *statement of cash flows.* The chapter discussed the form and content of each statement as well as the interrelationships among the statements.

This chapter introduced a *horizontal financial statements model* as a tool to help you understand how business events affect a set of financial statements. This model is used throughout the text. You should carefully study this model before proceeding to Chapter 2.

 A Look Forward

To keep matters as simple as possible and to focus on the interrelationships among financial statements, this chapter considered only cash events. Obviously, many real-world events do not involve an immediate exchange of cash. For example, customers use telephone service throughout the month without paying for it until the next month. Such phone usage represents an expense in one month with a cash exchange in the following month. Events such as this are called *accruals.* Understanding the effects that accrual events have on the financial statements is included in Chapter 2.

 Video lectures and accompanying self-assessment quizzes are available for all learning objectives through McGraw-Hill *Connect*® *Accounting.*

SELF-STUDY REVIEW PROBLEM

During 2015 Rustic Camp Sites experienced the following transactions.

1. RCS acquired $32,000 cash by issuing common stock.
2. RCS received $116,000 cash for providing services to customers (leasing camp sites).
3. RCS paid $13,000 cash for salaries expense.
4. RCS paid a $9,000 cash dividend to the owners.
5. RCS sold land that had cost $100,000 for $100,000 cash.
6. RCS paid $47,000 cash for other operating expenses.

Required

a. Record the transaction data in a horizontal financial statements model like the following one. In the Cash Flow column, classify the cash flows as operating activities (OA), investing activities (IA), or financing activities (FA). The beginning balances have been recorded as an example. They are the ending balances shown on RCS's December 31, 2014, financial statements illustrated in the chapter. Note that the revenue and expense accounts have a zero beginning balance. Amounts in these accounts apply only to a single accounting period.

Revenue and expense account balances are not carried forward from one accounting period to the next.

Event No.	Balance Sheet											Income Statement						Statement of Cash Flows
	Assets			=	Liab.	+	Stockholders' Equity											
	Cash	+	Land	=	N. Pay.	+	Com. Stk.	+	Ret. Earn.			Rev.	−	Exp.	=	Net Inc.		
Beg. bal.	51,000	+	500,000	=	400,000	+	120,000	+	31,000			NA	−	NA	=	NA		NA

b. Explain why there are no beginning balances in the Income Statement columns.
c. What amount of net income will RCS report on the 2015 income statement?
d. What amount of total assets will RCS report on the December 31, 2015, balance sheet?
e. What amount of retained earnings will RCS report on the December 31, 2015, balance sheet?
f. What amount of net cash flow from operating activities will RCS report on the 2015 statement of cash flows?

Solution

a.

Event No.	Balance Sheet											Income Statement						Statement of Cash Flows	
	Assets			=	Liab.	+	Stockholders' Equity												
	Cash	+	Land	=	N. Pay.	+	Com. Stk.	+	Ret. Earn.			Rev.	−	Exp.	=	Net Inc.			
Beg. bal.	51,000	+	500,000	=	400,000	+	120,000	+	31,000			NA	−	NA	=	NA		NA	
1.	32,000	+	NA	=	NA	+	32,000	+	NA			NA	−	NA	=	NA		32,000	FA
2.	116,000	+	NA	=	NA	+	NA	+	116,000			116,000	−	NA	=	116,000		116,000	OA
3.	(13,000)	+	NA	=	NA	+	NA	+	(13,000)			NA	−	13,000	=	(13,000)		(13,000)	OA
4.	(9,000)	+	NA	=	NA	+	NA	+	(9,000)			NA	−	NA	=	NA		(9,000)	FA
5.	100,000	+	(100,000)	=	NA	+	NA	+	NA			NA	−	NA	=	NA		100,000	IA
6.	(47,000)	+	NA	=	NA	+	NA	+	(47,000)			NA	−	47,000	=	(47,000)		(47,000)	OA
Totals	230,000	+	400,000	=	400,000	+	152,000	+	78,000			116,000	−	60,000	=	56,000		179,000	NC*

*The letters NC on the last line of the column designate the net change in cash.

b. The revenue and expense accounts are temporary accounts used to capture data for a single accounting period. They are closed (amounts removed from the accounts) to retained earnings at the end of the accounting period and therefore always have zero balances at the beginning of the accounting cycle.

c. RCS will report net income of $56,000 on the 2015 income statement. Compute this amount by subtracting the expenses from the revenue ($116,000 Revenue − $13,000 Salaries expense − $47,000 Other operating expense).

d. RCS will report total assets of $630,000 on the December 31, 2015, balance sheet. Compute total assets by adding the cash amount to the land amount ($230,000 Cash + $400,000 Land).

e. RCS will report retained earnings of $78,000 on the December 31, 2015, balance sheet. Compute this amount using the following formula: Beginning retained earnings + Net income − Dividends = Ending retained earnings. In this case, $31,000 + $56,000 − $9,000 = $78,000.

f. Net cash flow from operating activities is the difference between the amount of cash collected from revenue and the amount of cash spent for expenses. In this case, $116,000 cash inflow from revenue − $13,000 cash outflow for salaries expense − $47,000 cash outflow for other operating expenses = $56,000 net cash inflow from operating activities.

KEY TERMS

Accounting 3	Elements 10	International Accounting	Not-for-profit entities 6
Accounting equation 12	Expenses 15	Standards Board	Operating activities 24
Accounting event 13	Financial accounting 6	(IASB) 9	Permanent accounts 25
Accounting period 23	Financial Accounting	International Financial	Physical resources 5
Accounts 11	Standards Board	Reporting Standards	Profit 4
Annual report 28	(FASB) 8	(IFRS) 9	Reporting entities 9
Articulation 21	Financial resources 4	Investing activities 24	Retained earnings 12
Asset exchange transaction 14	Financial statements 10	Investors 4	Revenue 14
Asset source transaction 13	Financing activities 24	Labor resources 5	Service businesses 27
Asset use transaction 15	General ledger 16	Liabilities 12	Stakeholders 5
Assets 11	Generally accepted accounting	Liquidation 19	Statement of cash flows 24
Balance sheet 23	principles (GAAP) 8	Liquidity 23	Statement of changes in
Claims 12	Going concern 19	Managerial accounting 6	stockholders' equity 23
Closing 25	Historical cost concept 16	Manufacturing businesses 27	Stewardship 18
Common stock 12	Horizontal statements	Market 4	Stockholders 12
Creditors 4	model 26	Matching concept 21	Stockholders' equity 12
Dividend 16	Income 4	Merchandising businesses 27	Temporary accounts 25
Double-entry bookkeeping 13	Income statement 21	Net income 21	Transaction 13
Earnings 4	Interest 4	Net loss 21	Users 5

QUESTIONS

1. Explain the term *stakeholder*. Distinguish between stakeholders with a direct versus an indirect interest in the companies that issue financial reports.

2. Why is accounting called the *language of business*?

3. What is the primary mechanism used to allocate resources in the United States?

4. In a business context, what does the term *market* mean?

5. What market trilogy components are involved in the process of transforming resources into finished products?

6. Give an example of a financial resource, a physical resource, and a labor resource.

7. What type of income or profit does an investor expect to receive in exchange for providing financial resources to a business? What type of income does a creditor expect from providing financial resources to an organization or business?

8. How do financial and managerial accounting differ?

9. Describe a not-for-profit or nonprofit enterprise. What is the motivation for this type of entity?

10. What are the U.S. rules of accounting information measurement called?

11. Explain how a career in public accounting differs from a career in private accounting.

12. Distinguish between elements of financial statements and accounts.

13. What role do assets play in business profitability?

14. To whom do the assets of a business belong?

15. Describe the differences between creditors and investors.

16. Name the accounting term used to describe a business's obligations to creditors.

17. What is the accounting equation? Describe each of its three components.

18. Who ultimately bears the risk and collects the rewards associated with operating a business?

19. What does a *double-entry bookkeeping system* mean?

20. How does acquiring capital from owners affect the accounting equation?

21. What is the difference between assets that are acquired by issuing common stock and those that are acquired using retained earnings?

22. How does earning revenue affect the accounting equation?

23. What are the three primary sources of assets?

24. What is the source of retained earnings?

25. How does distributing assets (paying dividends) to owners affect the accounting equation?

26. What are the similarities and differences between dividends and expenses?

27. What four general-purpose financial statements do business enterprises use?

28. Which of the general-purpose financial statements provides information about the enterprise at a specific designated date?

29. What causes a net loss?

30. What three categories of cash receipts and cash payments do businesses report on the statement of cash flows? Explain the types of cash flows reported in each category.

31. How are asset accounts usually arranged in the balance sheet?

32. Discuss the term *articulation* as it relates to financial statements.

33. How do temporary accounts differ from permanent accounts? Name three temporary accounts. Is retained earnings a temporary or a permanent account?

34. What is the historical cost concept and how does it relate to verifiability?

35. Identify the three types of accounting transactions discussed in this chapter. Provide an example of each type of transaction, and explain how it affects the accounting equation.

36. What type of information does a business typically include in its annual report?

37. What is U.S. GAAP? What is IFRS?

 ## MULTIPLE-CHOICE QUESTIONS

Multiple-choice questions are provided on the text website at www.mhhe.com/edmondssurvey4e.

SECTION 1 EXERCISES

 All applicable Exercises are available with McGraw-Hill's *Connect® Accounting.*

Exercise 1-1   *The role of accounting in society*

LO 1-1

Resource owners provide three types of resources to conversion agents that transform the resources into products or services that satisfy consumer demands.

Required

Identify the three types of resources. Write a brief memo explaining how resource owners select the particular conversion agents to which they will provide resources. Your memo should include answers to the following questions: If you work as a private accountant, what role would you play in the allocation of resources? Which professional certification would be most appropriate to your career?

Exercise 1-2   *Careers in accounting*

LO 1-1

Accounting is commonly divided into two sectors. One sector is called public accounting. The other sector is called private accounting.

Required

a. Identify three areas of service provided by public accountants.

b. Describe the common duties performed by private accountants.

Exercise 1-3   *Identifying the reporting entities*

LO 1-1

Ray Steen recently started a business. During the first few days of operation, Mr. Steen transferred $100,000 from his personal account into a business account for a company he named Steen Enterprises. Steen Enterprises borrowed $60,000 from First Bank. Mr. Steen's father-in-law, Stan Rhoades, invested $75,000 into the business for which he received a 25 percent ownership interest. Steen Enterprises purchased a building from Zoro Realty Company. The building cost $150,000 cash. Steen Enterprises earned $56,000 in revenue from the company's customers and paid its employees $31,000 for salaries expense.

Required

Identify the entities that were mentioned in the scenario and explain what happened to the cash accounts of each entity that you identify.

Exercise 1-4   *Missing information in the accounting equation*

LO 1-2

Required

Calculate the missing amounts in the following table.

Company	Assets	=	Liabilities	+	Stockholders' Equity — Common Stock	+	Stockholders' Equity — Retained Earnings
A	$?		$30,000		$ 50,000		$62,000
B	50,000		?		10,000		25,000
C	85,000		20,000		?		40,000
D	215,000		60,000		100,000		?

34   Chapter 1

Exercise 1-5   *Effect of events on the accounting equation*

Hansen Enterprises experienced the following events during 2014:

1. Acquired cash from the issue of common stock.
2. Provided services to clients for cash.
3. Paid utilities expenses with cash.
4. Paid cash to reduce the principal on a bank note.
5. Sold land for cash at an amount equal to its cost.
6. Paid a cash dividend to the stockholders.

Required

Explain how each of the events would affect the accounting equation by writing the letter I for increase, the letter D for decrease, and NA for does not affect under each of the components of the accounting equation. The first event is shown as an example.

				Stockholders' Equity	
Event Number	Assets	= Liabilities	+	Common Stock	+ Retained Earnings
1	I	NA		I	NA

LO 1-2

Exercise 1-6   *Effect of transactions on general ledger accounts*

At the beginning of 2014, Foster Corp.'s accounting records had the following general ledger accounts and balances.

FOSTER CORP. Accounting Equation							
Event	Assets		=	Liabilities	+	Stockholders' Equity	Acct. Titles for RE
	Cash	Land		Notes Payable		Common Stock	Retained Earnings	
Balance 1/1/2014	30,000	16,000		10,000		20,000	16,000	

Foster Corp. completed the following transactions during 2014:

1. Purchased land for $20,000 cash.
2. Acquired $10,000 cash from the issue of common stock.
3. Received $90,000 cash for providing services to customers.
4. Paid cash operating expenses of $65,000.
5. Borrowed $20,000 cash from the bank.
6. Paid a $5,000 cash dividend to the stockholders.
7. Determined that the market value of the land purchased in event 1 is $30,000.

Required

a. Record the transactions in the appropriate general ledger accounts. Record the amounts of revenue, expense, and dividends in the Retained Earnings column. Provide the appropriate titles for these accounts in the last column of the table.
b. As of December 31, 2014, determine the total amount of assets, liabilities, and stockholder's equity and present this information in the form of an accounting equation.
c. What is the amount of total assets, liabilities, and stockholders' equity as of January 1, 2015?

Exercise 1-7 *Missing information and recording events*

LO 1-2

As of December 31, 2014, Post Company had total cash of $156,000, notes payable of $85,600, and common stock of $52,400. During 2015, Post earned $36,000 of cash revenue, paid $20,000 for cash expenses, and paid a $3,000 cash dividend to the stockholders.

Required

a. Determine the amount of retained earnings as of December 31, 2014.
b. Create an accounting equation and record the beginning account balances under the appropriate elements.
c. Record the revenue, expense, and dividend events under the appropriate elements of the accounting equation created in Requirement *b*.
d. Prove the equality of the accounting equation as of December 31, 2015.
e. Identify the beginning and ending balances in the Cash and Common Stock accounts. Explain why the beginning and ending balances in the Cash account are different, but the beginning and ending balances in the Common Stock account remain the same.

Exercise 1-8 *Account titles and the accounting equation*

LO 1-2

The following account titles were drawn from the general ledger of Gutter Control, Incorporated (GCI): Cash, Notes Payable, Land, Accounts Payable, Office Furniture, Salaries Expense, Common Stock, Service Revenue, Interest Expense, Utilities Payable, Utilities Expense, Trucks, Supplies, Operating Expenses, Rent Revenue, Dividends, Computers, Building, Supplies Expense, Gasoline Expense, Retained Earnings, Dividends.

Required

a. Create an accounting equation using the elements assets, liabilities, and stockholders' equity. List each account title under the element of the accounting equation to which it belongs.
b. Will all businesses have the same number of accounts? Explain your answer.

Exercise 1-9 *Components of the accounting equation*

LO 1-3

Lang Enterprises was started when it acquired $4,000 cash from creditors and $6,000 from owners. The company immediately purchased land that cost $9,000.

Required

a. Record the events under an accounting equation.
b. After all events have been recorded, Lang's obligations to creditors represent what percent of total assets?
c. After all events have been recorded, Lang's stockholder's equity represents what percent of total assets?
d. Assume the debt is due. Given that Lang has $6,000 in stockholders' equity, can the company repay the creditors at this point? Why or why not?

Exercise 1-10 *Components of the accounting equation*

LO 1-3

The financial condition of GreyCo Inc. is expressed in the following accounting equation:

Assets	= Liabilities + Common stock + Retained earnings
$800 Cash + $9,200 Land =	$7,000 + $2,000 + $1,000

Required

a. Are dividends paid to creditors or investors? Explain why.
b. How much cash is in the Retained Earnings account?
c. Determine the maximum dividend GreyCo can pay.
d. If the obligation to creditors is due, can GreyCo repay the loan? Why or why not?
e. Suppose the land sinks into the sea as a result of an earthquake and a resulting tsunami. The business is then liquidated. How much cash will creditors receive? How much cash will investors receive? (Assume there are no legal fees or other costs of liquidation.)

LO 1-3

Exercise 1-11 *Differences between interest and dividends*

The following account balances were drawn from the financial records of Crystal Company (CC) as of January 1, 2014. Assets, $14,000; Liabilities, $4,000; Common Stock, $7,000; and Retained Earnings, $3,000. CC has agreed to pay the creditors $400 of interest per year. Further, CC agrees that for the 2014 fiscal year any annual earnings remaining after the interest charges will be paid out as dividends to the owners.

Required

a. Assuming CC earns a before interest expense recognition profit of $900 during 2014, determine the amount of interest and dividends paid.

b. Assuming CC earns a before interest expense recognition profit of $500 during 2014, determine the amount of interest and dividends paid.

c. Assuming CC earns a before interest expense recognition profit of $100 during 2014, determine the amount of interest and dividends paid.

LO 1-3

Exercise 1-12 *Distribution in a business liquidation*

Assume that Clinton Company acquires $1,200 cash from creditors and $1,700 cash from investors.

Required

a. Explain the primary differences between investors and creditors.

b. If Clinton has net income of $800 and then liquidates, what amount of cash will the creditors receive? What amount of cash will the investors receive?

c. If Clinton has a net loss of $800 cash and then liquidates, what amount of cash will the creditors receive? What amount of cash will the investors receive?

d. If Clinton has a net loss of $1,900 cash and then liquidates, what amount of cash will the creditors receive? What amount of cash will the investors receive?

LO 1-4

Exercise 1-13 *Classifying events as asset source, use, or exchange*

Dale's Business Services experienced the following events during its first year of operations:

1. Acquired $20,000 cash from the issue of common stock.
2. Borrowed $12,000 cash from First Bank.
3. Paid $5,000 cash to purchase land.
4. Received $25,000 cash for providing boarding services.
5. Acquired an additional $5,000 cash from the issue of common stock.
6. Purchased additional land for $4,000 cash.
7. Paid $10,000 cash for salary expense.
8. Signed a contract to provide additional services in the future.
9. Paid $1,200 cash for rent expense.
10. Paid a $1,000 cash dividend to the stockholders.
11. Determined the market value of the land to be $18,000 at the end of the accounting period.

Required

Classify each event as an asset source, use, or exchange transaction or as not applicable (NA).

SECTION 2 EXERCISES

LO 1-5

Exercise 1-14 *Missing information for determining net income*

The December 31, 2013, balance sheet for Thomas Company showed total stockholders' equity of $156,000. Total stockholders' equity increased by $65,000 between December 31, 2013, and December 31, 2014. During 2014 Thomas Company acquired $20,000 cash from the issue of common stock. Thomas Company paid a $5,000 cash dividend to the stockholders during 2014.

Required

Determine the amount of net income or loss Thomas reported on its 2014 income statement. (*Hint:* Remember that stock issues, net income, and dividends all change total stockholders' equity.)

Exercise 1-15   *Preparing an income statement and a balance sheet*

LO 1-5

Topez Company was started on January 1, 2014. During 2014, the company experienced the following three accounting events: (1) earned cash revenues of $14,500, (2) paid cash expenses of $9,200, and (3) paid a $500 cash dividend to its stockholders. These were the only events that affected the company during 2014.

Required

a. Create an accounting equation and record the effects of each accounting event under the appropriate general ledger account headings.
b. Prepare an income statement, statement of changes in stockholder's equity, and a balance sheet dated December 31, 2014, for Topez Company.
c. Explain why the income statement uses different terminology to date the income statement than is used to date the balance sheet.

Exercise 1-16   *Historical cost versus market value*

LO 1-5

Mountain View, Inc., purchased land in January 2009 at a cost of $250,000. The estimated market value of the land is $425,000 as of December 31, 2014.

Required

a. Name the December 31, 2014, financial statement(s) on which the land will be shown.
b. At what dollar amount will the land be shown in the financial statement(s)?
c. Name the key concept that will be used in determining the dollar amount that will be reported for land that is shown in the financial statement(s).

Exercise 1-17   *Statement of cash flows*

LO 1-5

On January 1, 2014, Palmetto, a fast-food company, had a balance in its Cash account of $32,000. During the 2014 accounting period, the company had (1) net cash inflow from operating activities of $15,600, (2) net cash outflow for investing activities of $23,000, and (3) net cash outflow from financing activities of $4,500.

Required

a. Prepare a statement of cash flows.
b. Provide a reasonable explanation as to what may have caused the net cash inflow from operating activities.
c. Provide a reasonable explanation as to what may have caused the net cash outflow from investing activities.
d. Provide a reasonable explanation as to what may have caused the net cash outflow from financing activities.

Exercise 1-18   *Prepare a statement of cash flows*

LO 1-5

American General Company experienced the following accounting events during 2014:

1. Paid $4,000 cash for salary expense.
2. Borrowed $8,000 cash from State Bank.
3. Received $30,000 cash from the issue of common stock.
4. Purchased land for $8,000 cash.
5. Performed services for $14,000 cash.
6. Paid $4,200 cash for utilities expense.
7. Sold land for $7,000 cash.
8. Paid a cash dividend of $1,000 to the stockholders.
9. Hired an accountant to keep the books.
10. Paid $3,000 cash on the loan from State Bank.

Required

a. Indicate how each of the events would be classified on the statement of cash flows as operating activities (OA), investing activities (IA), financing activities (FA), or not applicable (NA).

b. Prepare a statement of cash flows for 2014. Assume American General had a beginning cash balance of $9,000 on January 1, 2014.

LO 1-3, 1-5

Exercise 1-19   *Preparing financial statements*

Carolina Company experienced the following events during 2014.

1. Acquired $50,000 cash from the issue of common stock.
2. Paid $15,000 cash to purchase land.
3. Borrowed $25,000 cash.
4. Provided services for $60,000 cash.
5. Paid $12,000 cash for rent expense.
6. Paid $22,000 cash for other operating expenses.
7. Paid a $5,000 cash dividend to the stockholders.
8. Determined that the market value of the land purchased in Event 2 is now $16,500.

Required

a. The January 1, 2014, general ledger account balances are shown in the following accounting equation. Record the eight events in the appropriate general ledger accounts. Record the amounts of revenue, expense, and dividends in the Retained Earnings column. Provide the appropriate titles for these accounts in the last column of the table. The first event is shown as an example.

CAROLINA COMPANY Accounting Equation							
Event	**Assets**		**=**	**Liabilities**	**+**	**Stockholders' Equity**		**Acct. Titles for RE**
	Cash	**Land**		**Notes Payable**		**Common Stock**	**Retained Earnings**	
Balance 1/1/2014	15,000	10,000		0		20,000	5,000	
1.	50,000					50,000		

b. Prepare an income statement, statement of changes in equity, year-end balance sheet, and statement of cash flows for the 2014 accounting period.

c. Determine the percentage of assets that were provided by retained earnings. How much cash is in the retained earnings account?

LO 1-4, 1-5

Exercise 1-20   *Relating accounting events to entities*

Pandora Company paid $40,000 cash to purchase land from Donnelley Company. Donnelley originally paid $40,000 for the land.

Required

a. Was this event an asset source, use, or exchange transaction for Pandora Company?

b. Was this event an asset source, use, or exchange transaction for Donnelley Company?

c. Was the cash flow an operating, investing, or financing activity on Pandora Company's 2014 statement of cash flows?

d. Was the cash flow an operating, investing, or financing activity on Donnelley Company's 2014 statement of cash flows?

Exercise 1-21   *Preparing financial statements—retained earnings emphasis*   LO 1-3, 1-4, 1-5

On January 1, 2014, the following information was drawn from the accounting records of Wilson Company: cash of $200; land of $1,800; notes payable of $600; and common stock of $1,000.

Required

a. Determine the amount of retained earnings as of January 1, 2014.

b. After looking at the amount of retained earnings, the chief executive officer (CEO) wants to pay a $300 cash dividend to the stockholders. Can the company pay this dividend? Why or why not?

c. As of January 1, 2014, what percent of the assets were acquired from creditors?

d. As of January 1, 2014, what percent of the assets were acquired from investors?

e. As of January 1, 2014, what percent of the assets were acquired from retained earnings?

f. Create an accounting equation using percentages instead of dollar amounts on the right side of the equation.

g. During 2014, Wilson Company earned cash revenue of $500, paid cash expenses of $300, and paid a cash dividend of $50. Prepare an income statement, statement of changes in stockholders' equity, a balance sheet, and a statement of cash flows dated December 31, 2014. (*Hint:* It is helpful to record these events under an accounting equation before preparing the statements.)

h. Comment on the terminology used to date each statement.

i. An appraiser determines that as of December 31, 2014, the market value of the land is $2,000. How will this fact change the financial statements?

j. What is the balance in the Revenue account on January 1, 2015?

Exercise 1-22   *Preparing financial statements—cash flow emphasis*   LO 1-5

As of January 1, 2014, Concepts Inc. had a balance of $4,500 in Cash, $2,500 in Common Stock, and $2,000 in Retained Earnings. These were the only accounts with balances in the ledger on January 1, 2014. Further analysis of the company's cash account indicated that during the 2014 accounting period, the company had (1) net cash inflow from operating activities of $5,100, (2) net cash outflow for investing activities of $13,000, and (3) net cash inflow from financing activities of $7,600. All revenue and expense events were cash events. The following accounts and balances represent the general ledger of Concepts Inc. as of December 31, 2014, before closing.

CONCEPTS INC.
General Ledger

Assets	=	Liabilities	+	Stockholders' Equity		
Cash		**Notes Payable**		**Common Stock**		**Revenue**
Bal. 4,200		Bal. 3,000		Bal. 8,000		Bal. 9,900
Land				**Retained Earnings**		**Expenses**
Bal. 13,000				Bal. 2,000		Bal. 4,800
						Dividends
						Bal. 900

Required

a. Assume that the net cash inflow from financing activities of $7,600 was caused by three events. Based on the information above, identify these events and determine the cash flow associated with each event.

b. What did the company purchase that resulted in the cash outflow from investing activities?

c. Prepare an income statement, statement of changes in stockholders' equity, balance sheet, and statement of cash flows.

LO 1-5, 1-6

Exercise 1-23 *Retained earnings and the closing process*

As of December 31, 2014, Blue Haven Company had total assets of $100,000, total liabilities of $30,000, and common stock of $50,000. The company's 2014 income statement contained revenue of $16,000 and expenses of $11,000. The 2014 statement of changes in stockholder's equity stated that $2,000 of dividends were paid to investors.

Required

a. Determine the before-closing balance in the Retained Earnings account on December 31, 2014.

b. Determine the after-closing balance in the Retained Earnings account on December 31, 2014.

c. Determine the before-closing balances in the Revenue, Expense, and Dividend accounts on December 31, 2014.

d. Determine the after-closing balances in the Revenue, Expense, and Dividend accounts on December 31, 2014.

e. Explain the difference between common stock and retained earnings.

f. On January 1, 2015, Blue Haven Company raised $40,000 by issuing additional common stock. Immediately after the additional capital was raised. Blue Haven reported total equity of $110,000. Are the stockholders of Blue Haven in a better financial position than they were on December 31, 2014?

LO 1-6

Exercise 1-24 *The closing process*

Sammy's Pizza opened on January 1, 2014. Sammy's reported the following for cash revenues and cash expenses for the years 2014 to 2016:

	Cash Revenues	Cash Expenses
2014	$20,000	$11,000
2015	$30,000	$14,000
2016	$40,000	$22,000

Required

a. What would Sammy's Pizza report for net income and retained earnings for the years 2014, 2015, and 2016?

b. Explain the difference between net income and retained earnings.

c. Assume that Sammy's Pizza paid a $5,000 dividend to stockholders in 2015. What would Sammy's Pizza report for net income and retained earnings for 2015 and 2016?

LO 1-6

Exercise 1-25 *Retained earnings and the closing process*

Davis Company was started on January 1, 2014. During the month of January, Davis earned $4,600 of revenue and incurred $3,000 of expenses. During the remainder of 2014, Davis earned $52,000 and incurred $42,000 of expenses. Davis closes its books on December 31 of each year.

Required

a. Determine the balance in the Retained Earnings account as of January 31, 2014.

b. Determine the balance in the Revenue and Expense accounts as of January 31, 2014.

c. Determine the balance in the Retained Earnings account as of December 31, 2014, before closing.

d. Determine the balances in the Revenue and Expense accounts as of December 31, 2014, before closing.

e. Determine the balance in the Retained Earnings account as of January 1, 2015.

f. Determine the balance in the Revenue and Expense accounts as of January 1, 2015.

Exercise 1-26 *Types of transactions and the horizontal statements model* LO 1-4, 1-7

Happy Pet Store experienced the following events during its first year of operations, 2014:

1. Acquired cash by issuing common stock.
2. Borrowed cash from a bank.
3. Signed a contract to provide services in the future.
4. Purchased land with cash.
5. Paid cash for operating expenses.
6. Paid a cash dividend to the stockholders.
7. Determined that the market value of the land is higher than the historical cost.

Required

a. Indicate whether each event is an asset source, use, or exchange transaction.
b. Use a horizontal statements model to show how each event affects the balance sheet, income statement, and statement of cash flows. Indicate whether the event increases (I), decreases (D), or does not affect (NA) each element of the financial statements. Also, in the Cash Flows column, classify the cash flows as operating activities (OA), investing activities (IA), or financing activities (FA). The first transaction is shown as an example.

Event No.	Balance Sheet										Income Statement						Statement of Cash Flows
	Cash	+	Land	=	N. Pay	+	C. Stock.	+	Ret. Ear.		Rev.	−	Exp.	=	Net Inc.		
1.	I	+	NA	=	NA	+	I	+	NA		NA	−	NA	=	NA		I FA

Exercise 1-27 *International Financial Reporting Standards* LO IFRS

Corrugated Boxes Inc. is a U.S.–based company that develops its financial statements under GAAP. The total amount of the company's assets shown on its December 31, 2014, balance sheet was approximately $305 million. The president of Corrugated is considering the possibility of relocating the company to a country that practices accounting under IFRS. The president has hired an international accounting firm to determine what the company's statements would look like if they were prepared under IFRS. One striking difference is that under IFRS the assets shown on the balance sheet would be valued at approximately $345 million.

Required

a. Would Corrugated Boxes' assets really be worth $40 million more if it moves its headquarters?
b. Discuss the underlying conceptual differences between U.S. GAAP and IFRS that cause the difference in the reported asset values.

SECTIONS 1 AND 2 PROBLEMS

 All applicable Problems are available with McGraw-Hill's *Connect® Accounting.*

Problem 1-28 *Accounting's role in not-for-profits* LO 1-1

Karen White is struggling to pass her introductory accounting course. Karen is intelligent but she likes to party. Studying is a low priority for Karen. When one of her friends tells her that she is going to have trouble in business if she doesn't learn accounting, Karen responds that she doesn't plan to go into business. She says that she is arts oriented and plans someday to be a director of a museum. She is in the school of business to develop her social skills, not her quantitative skills. Karen says she won't have to worry about accounting, since museums are not intended to make a profit.

Required

a. Write a brief memo explaining whether you agree or disagree with Karen's position regarding accounting and not-for-profit organizations.
b. Distinguish between financial accounting and managerial accounting.
c. Identify some of the stakeholders of not-for-profit institutions that would expect to receive financial accounting reports.
d. Identify some of the stakeholders of not-for-profit institutions that would expect to receive managerial accounting reports.

LO 1-1

CHECK FIGURE

1. Entities mentioned: Chris Hann and Classic Auto Sales

Problem 1-29   *Accounting entities*

The following business scenarios are independent from one another:

1. Chris Hann purchased an automobile from Classic Auto Sales for $10,000.
2. Sal Pearl loaned $15,000 to the business in which he is a stockholder.
3. First State Bank paid interest to Strong Co. on a certificate of deposit that Strong Co. has invested at First State Bank.
4. Cindy's Restaurant paid the current utility bill of $135 to Midwest Utilities.
5. Sun Corp. borrowed $50,000 from City National Bank and used the funds to purchase land from Carriage Realty.
6. Sue Wang purchased $10,000 of common stock of International Sales Corporation from the corporation.
7. Chris Gordon loaned $6,000 cash to his daughter.
8. Motor Service Co. earned $20,000 in cash revenue.
9. Poy Imports paid $4,000 for salaries to each of its four employees.
10. Borg Inc. paid a cash dividend of $4,000 to its sole shareholder, Mark Borg.

Required

a. For each scenario, create a list of all of the entities that are mentioned in the description.
b. Describe what happens to the cash account of each entity that you identified in Requirement *a*.

LO 1-4

Problem 1-30   *Classifying events as asset source, use, or exchange*

The following unrelated events are typical of those experienced by business entities:

1. Pay cash for operating expenses.
2. Pay an office manager's salary with cash.
3. Receive cash for services that have been performed.
4. Pay cash for utilities expense.
5. Acquire land by accepting a liability (financing the purchase).
6. Pay cash to purchase a new office building.
7. Discuss plans for a new office building with an architect.
8. Repay part of a bank loan.
9. Acquire cash by issuing common stock.
10. Purchase land with cash.
11. Purchase equipment with cash.
12. Pay monthly rent on an office building.
13. Hire a new office manager.
14. Borrow cash from a bank.
15. Pay a cash dividend to stockholders.

Required

Identify each of the events as an asset source, use, or exchange transaction. If an event would not be recorded under generally accepted accounting principles, identify it as not applicable (NA).

Also indicate for each event whether total assets would increase, decrease, or remain unchanged. Organize your answer according to the following table. The first event is shown in the table as an example.

Event No.	Type of Event	Effect on Total Assets
1	Asset use	Decrease

Problem 1-31 *Relating titles and accounts to financial statements*   LO 1-5

Required

Identify the financial statements on which each of the following items (titles, date descriptions, and accounts) appears by placing a check mark in the appropriate column. If an item appears on more than one statement, place a check mark in every applicable column.

Item	Income Statement	Statement of Changes in Stockholders' Equity	Balance Sheet	Statement of Cash Flows
For the period ended (date)				
Net income				
Investing activities				
Net loss				
Ending cash balance				
Salary expense				
Consulting revenue				
Dividends				
Financing activities				
Ending common stock				
Interest expense				
As of (date)				
Land				
Beginning cash balance				
Notes payable				
Beginning common stock				
Service revenue				
Utility expense				
Stock issue				
Operating activities				

Problem 1-32 *Preparing financial statements for two complete accounting cycles*   LO 1-2, 1-3, 1-5, 1-6

Susan's Consulting experienced the following transactions for 2014, its first year of operations, and 2015. *Assume that all transactions involve the receipt or payment of cash.*

44   Chapter 1

Transactions for 2014

1. Acquired $50,000 by issuing common stock.
2. Received $100,000 cash for providing services to customers.
3. Borrowed $15,000 cash from creditors.
4. Paid expenses amounting to $60,000.
5. Purchased land for $40,000 cash.

Transactions for 2015

Beginning account balances for 2015 are:

Cash	$65,000
Land	40,000
Notes payable	15,000
Common stock	50,000
Retained earnings	40,000

1. Acquired an additional $20,000 from the issue of common stock.
2. Received $130,000 for providing services.
3. Paid $10,000 to creditors to reduce loan.
4. Paid expenses amounting to $75,000.
5. Paid a $15,000 dividend to the stockholders.
6. Determined that the market value of the land is $50,000.

Required

a. Write an accounting equation, and record the effects of each accounting event under the appropriate headings for each year. Record the amounts of revenue, expense, and dividends in the Retained Earnings column. Provide appropriate titles for these accounts in the last column of the table.

b. Prepare an income statement, statement of changes in stockholders' equity, year-end balance sheet, and statement of cash flows for each year.

c. Determine the amount of cash that is in the Retained Earnings account at the end of 2014 and 2015.

d. Examine the balance sheets for the two years. How did assets change from 2014 to 2015?

e. Determine the balance in the Retained Earnings account immediately after Event 2 in 2014 and in 2015 are recorded.

LO 1-2, 1-3, 1-5, 1-6

Problem 1-33   *Interrelationships among financial statements*

Crawford Enterprises started the 2014 accounting period with $75,000 of assets (all cash), $15,000 of liabilities, and $25,000 of common stock. During the year, Crawford earned cash revenues of $46,000, paid cash expenses of $26,000, and paid a cash dividend to stockholders of $5,000. Crawford also acquired $15,000 of additional cash from the sale of common stock and paid $10,000 cash to reduce the liability owed to a bank.

Required

a. Prepare an income statement, statement of changes in stockholders' equity, period-end balance sheet, and statement of cash flows for the 2014 accounting period. (*Hint:* Determine the amount of beginning retained earnings before considering the effects of the current period events. It also might help to record all events under an accounting equation before preparing the statements.)

b. Determine the percentage of total assets that were provided by creditors, investors, and earnings.

c. Determine the balance in the Revenue, Expense, and Dividends accounts as of January 1, 2015.

LO 1-2, 1-3, 1-4, 1-5, 1-6, 1-7

Problem 1-34   *Recording events in a horizontal statements model*

Davidson Company was started on January 1, 2014, and experienced the following events during its first year of operation:

1. Acquired $52,000 cash from the issue of common stock.
2. Borrowed $20,000 cash from National Bank.

3. Earned cash revenues of $42,000 for performing services.
4. Paid cash expenses of $23,000.
5. Paid a $6,000 cash dividend to the stockholders.
6. Acquired an additional $10,000 cash from the issue of common stock.
7. Paid $10,000 cash to reduce the principal balance of the bank note.
8. Paid $45,000 cash to purchase land.
9. Determined that the market value of the land is $55,000.

Required

a. Record the preceding transactions in the horizontal statements model. Also, in the Cash Flows column, classify the cash flows as operating activities (OA), investing activities (IA), or financing activities (FA). The first event is shown as an example.

Event No.	Balance Sheet													Income Statement							Statement of Cash Flows
	Cash	+	Land	=	N. Pay	+	C. Stock.	+	Ret. Ear.				Rev.	−	Exp.	=	Net Inc.			
1.	52,000	+	NA	=	NA	+	52,000	+	NA				NA	−	NA	=	NA			52,000 FA

b. Determine the amount of total assets that Davidson would report on the December 31, 2014, balance sheet.
c. Identify the asset source transactions and related amounts for 2014.
d. Determine the net income that Davidson would report on the 2014 income statement. Explain why dividends do not appear on the income statement.
e. Determine the net cash flows from operating activities, financing activities, and investing activities that Davidson would report on the 2014 statement of cash flows.
f. Determine the percentage of assets that were provided by investors, creditors, and earnings.
g. What is the balance in the Retained Earnings account immediately after Event 3 is recorded?

ANALYZE, THINK, COMMUNICATE

ATC 1-1   Business Applications Case   *Understanding real-world annual reports*

Required

Use the Target Corporation's Form 10-K to answer the following questions related to Target's 2012 fiscal year (year ended February 2, 2013). Target's Form 10-K is available on the company's website or through the SEC's EDGAR database. Appendix A provides instructions for using the EDGAR database.

Target Corporation

a. What was Target's net income for 2012 (the year ended February 2, 2013)?
b. Did Target's net income increase or decrease from 2011 to 2012, and by how much?
c. What was Target's accounting equation for 2012?
d. Which of the following had the largest percentage change from 2011 to 2012: net sales; cost of sales; or selling, general, and administrative expenses? Show all computations.

ATC 1-2   Group Assignment   *Missing information*

The following selected financial information is available for HAS, Inc. Amounts are in millions of dollars.

Income Statements	2017	2016	2015	2014
Revenue	$ 860	$1,520	$ (a)	$1,200
Cost and expenses	(a)	(a)	(2,400)	(860)
Income from continuing operations	(b)	450	320	(a)
Unusual items	-0-	175	(b)	(b)
Net income	$ 20	$ (b)	$ 175	$ 300

(continued)

Balance Sheets	2017	2016	2015	2014
Assets				
Cash and marketable securities	$ 350	$1,720	$ (c)	$ 940
Other assets	1,900	(c)	2,500	(c)
Total assets	2,250	$2,900	$ (d)	$3,500
Liabilities	$ (c)	$ (d)	$1,001	$ (d)
Stockholders' equity				
Common stock	880	720	(e)	800
Retained earnings	(d)	(e)	800	(e)
Total stockholders' equity	1,520	1,345	(f)	2,200
Total liabilities and stockholders' equity	$2,250	$ (f)	$3,250	$3,500

Required

a. Divide the class into groups of four or five students each. Organize the groups into four sections. Assign Task 1 to the first section of groups, Task 2 to the second section, Task 3 to the third section, and Task 4 to the fourth section.

Group Tasks

(1) Fill in the missing information for 2014.

(2) Fill in the missing information for 2015.

(3) Fill in the missing information for 2016.

(4) Fill in the missing information for 2017.

b. Each section should select two representatives. One representative is to put the financial statements assigned to that section on the board, underlining the missing amounts. The second representative is to explain to the class how the missing amounts were determined.

c. Each section should list events that could have caused the unusual items category on the income statement.

ATC 1-3 Research Assignment *Finding real-world accounting information*

This chapter introduced the basic four financial statements companies use annually to keep their stakeholders informed of their accomplishments and financial situation. Complete the requirements below using the most recent (20xx) financial statements available on the McDonald's Corporation's website. Obtain the statements on the Internet by following the steps below. (The formatting of the company's website may have changed since these instructions were written.)

1. Go to www.mcdonalds.com.
2. Click on the "Corporate" link at the bottom of the page. (Most companies have a link titled "investors relations" that leads to their financial statements; McDonald's uses "corporate" instead.)
3. Click on the "INVESTORS" link at the top of the page.
4. Click on "*Annual Reports*" and then on "*20xx Financial Report.*"
5. Go to the company's financial statements that begin on page 45 of the annual report.

Required

a. What was the company's net income in each of the last three years?

b. What amount of total assets did the company have at the end of the most recent year?

c. How much retained earnings did the company have at the end of the most recent year?

d. For the most recent year, what was the company's cash flow from operating activities, cash flow from investing activities, and cash flow from financing activities?

ATC 1-4 Writing Assignment *Elements of financial statements defined*

Sam and his sister Blair both attend the state university. As a reward for their successful completion of the past year (Sam had a 3.2 GPA in business, and Blair had a 3.7 GPA in art), their father gave each of them 100 shares of The Walt Disney Company stock. They have just received their first annual report. Blair does not understand what the information means and has asked Sam to explain it to her. Sam is currently taking an accounting course, and she knows he will understand the financial statements.

Required

Assume that you are Sam. Write Blair a memo explaining the following financial statement items to her. In your explanation, describe each of the two financial statements and explain the financial information each contains. Also define each of the elements listed for each financial statement and explain what it means.

Balance Sheet
Assets
Liabilities
Stockholders' equity

Income Statement
Revenue
Expense
Net income

CHAPTER 2

Accounting for Accruals and Deferrals

LEARNING OBJECTIVES

After you have mastered the material in this chapter, you will be able to:

SECTION 1: SHOW HOW ACCRUALS AFFECT FINANCIAL STATEMENTS

LO 2-1   Show how receivables affect financial statements.

LO 2-2   Show how payables affect financial statements.

SECTION 2: SHOW HOW DEFERRALS AFFECT FINANCIAL STATEMENTS

LO 2-3   Show how supplies affect financial statements.

LO 2-4   Show how prepaid items affect financial statements.

LO 2-5   Show how unearned revenues affect financial statements.

LO 2-6   Explain the accounting cycle including adjustments and the closing process.

LO 2-7   Prepare financial statements based on accrual accounting.

LO 2-8   Classify accounting events into one of four categories.

 Video lectures and accompanying self-assessment quizzes are available for all learning objectives through McGraw-Hill Connect® Accounting.

SECTION 1:

ACCOUNTING FOR ACCRUALS

Users of financial statements must distinguish between the terms *recognition* and *realization*. **Recognition** means formally *reporting* an economic item or event in the financial statements. **Realization** refers to collecting money, generally from the sale of products or services. Companies may recognize (report) revenue in the income statement in a different accounting period from the period in which they collect the cash related to the revenue. Furthermore, companies frequently make cash payments for expenses in accounting periods other than the periods in which the expenses are recognized in the income statement.

To illustrate assume Johnson Company provides services to customers in 2014 but collects cash for those services in 2015. In this case, realization occurs in 2015. When should Johnson recognize the services revenue?

Users of *cash basis* accounting recognize (report) revenues and expenses in the period in which cash is collected or paid. Under cash basis accounting Johnson would recognize the revenue in 2015 when it collects the cash. In contrast, users of **accrual accounting** recognize revenues and expenses in the period in which they occur, regardless of when cash is collected or paid. Under accrual accounting Johnson would recognize the revenue in 2014 (the period in which it performed the services) even though it does not collect (realize) the cash until 2015.

Accrual accounting is required by generally accepted accounting principles. Virtually all major companies operating in the United States use it. Its two distinguishing features are called *accruals* and *deferrals*.

- The term **accrual** describes a revenue or an expense event that is recognized *before* cash is exchanged. Johnson's recognition of revenue in 2014 related to cash realized in 2015 is an example of an accrual.

- The term **deferral** describes a revenue or an expense event that is recognized *after* cash has been exchanged. Suppose Johnson pays cash in 2014 to purchase office supplies it uses in 2015. In this case the cash payment occurs in 2014 although supplies expense is recognized in 2015. This example is a deferral.

50   Chapter 2

The Curious Accountant

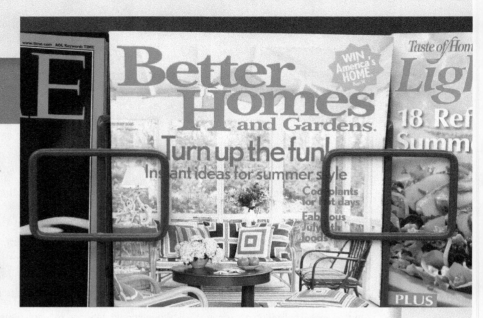

On September 15, 2014, Janet McGeorge purchased a subscription to *Better Homes and Gardens* magazine for her mother's birthday. She paid $12 for a one-year subscription to the Meredith Corporation, the company that publishes *Fitness, American Baby, Better Homes and Gardens, The Ladies Home Journal,* and several other magazines. The company also owns 12 television stations. Janet's mother will receive her first issue of the magazine in October.

How should Meredith Corporation account for the receipt of this cash? How would this event be reported on its December 31, 2014, financial statements? (Answer on page 64.)

ACCRUAL ACCOUNTING

LO 2-1

Show how receivables affect financial statements.

This section of the text describes seven events experienced by Cato Consultants, a training services company that uses accrual accounting.

EVENT 1   Cato Consultants was started on January 1, 2014, when it acquired $5,000 cash by issuing common stock.

The issue of stock for cash is an **asset source transaction.** It increases the company's assets (cash) and its equity (common stock). The transaction does not affect the income statement. The cash inflow is classified as a financing activity (acquisition from owners). These effects are shown in the following financial statements model:

Assets	=	Liab.	+	Stockholders' Equity							
Cash	=			Com. Stk.	+	Ret. Earn.		Rev.	−	Exp.	=	Net Inc.	Cash Flow
5,000	=	NA	+	5,000	+	NA		NA	−	NA	=	NA	5,000 FA

Accounting for Accounts Receivable

EVENT 2   During 2014 Cato Consultants provided $84,000 of consulting services to its clients. The business has completed the work and sent bills to the clients, but not yet collected any cash. This type of transaction is frequently described as providing services *on account.*

Accrual accounting requires companies to recognize revenue in the period in which the work is done regardless of when cash is collected. In this case, revenue is recognized in 2014 even though cash has not been realized (collected). Recall that revenue represents the economic benefit that results in an increase in assets from providing goods and services to customers. The specific asset that increases is called **Accounts Receivable.** The balance in Accounts Receivable represents the amount of cash the company expects to collect in the future. Since the revenue recognition causes assets (accounts receivable) to increase, it is classified as an asset source transaction. Its effect on the financial statements follows:

Assets			=	Liab.	+	Stockholders' Equity				Rev.	−	Exp.	=	Net Inc.	Cash Flow
Cash	+	Accts. Rec.	=			Com. Stk.	+	Ret. Earn.							
NA	+	84,000	=	NA	+	NA	+	84,000		84,000	−	NA	=	84,000	NA

Notice that the event affects the income statement but not the statement of cash flows. The statement of cash flows will be affected in the future when cash is collected.

EVENT 3   Cato collected $60,000 cash from customers in partial settlement of its accounts receivable.

The collection of an account receivable is an **asset exchange transaction.** One asset account (Cash) increases and another asset account (Accounts Receivable) decreases. The amount of total assets is unchanged. The effect of the $60,000 collection of receivables on the financial statements is as follows:

Assets			=	Liab.	+	Stockholders' Equity				Rev.	−	Exp.	=	Net Inc.	Cash Flow
Cash	+	Accts. Rec.	=			Com. Stk.	+	Ret. Earn.							
60,000	+	(60,000)	=	NA	+	NA	+	NA		NA	−	NA	=	NA	60,000 OA

Notice that collecting the cash did not affect the income statement. The revenue was recognized when the work was done (see Event 2). Revenue would be double counted if it were recognized again when the cash is collected. The statement of cash flows reflects a cash inflow from operating activities.

Other Events

EVENT 4   Cato paid the instructor $10,000 for teaching training courses (salary expense).

Cash payment for salary expense is an **asset use transaction.** Both the asset account Cash and the equity account Retained Earnings decrease by $10,000. Recognizing the expense decreases net income on the income statement. Since Cato paid cash for the expense, the statement of cash flows reflects a cash outflow from operating activities. These effects on the financial statements follow:

Assets			=	Liab.	+	Stockholders' Equity				Rev.	−	Exp.	=	Net Inc.	Cash Flow
Cash	+	Accts. Rec.	=			Com. Stk.	+	Ret. Earn.							
(10,000)	+	NA	=	NA	+	NA	+	(10,000)		NA	−	10,000	=	(10,000)	(10,000) OA

EVENT 5 Cato paid $2,000 cash for advertising costs. The advertisements appeared in 2014.

Cash payments for advertising expenses are asset use transactions. Both the asset account Cash and the equity account Retained Earnings decrease by $2,000. Recognizing the expense decreases net income on the income statement. Since the expense was paid with cash, the statement of cash flows reflects a cash outflow from operating activities. These effects on the financial statements follow:

Assets			=	Liab.	+	Stockholders' Equity							
Cash	+	Accts. Rec.	=			Com. Stk.	+	Ret. Earn.	Rev.	–	Exp.	=	Net Inc.	Cash Flow
(2,000)	+	NA	=	NA	+	NA	+	(2,000)	NA	–	2,000	=	(2,000)	(2,000) OA

EVENT 6 Cato signed contracts for $42,000 of consulting services to be performed in 2015.

The $42,000 for consulting services to be performed in 2015 is not recognized in the 2014 financial statements. Revenue is recognized for work actually completed, *not* work expected to be completed. This event does not affect any of the financial statements.

Assets			=	Liab.	+	Stockholders' Equity							
Cash	+	Accts. Rec.	=			Com. Stk.	+	Ret. Earn.	Rev.	–	Exp.	=	Net Inc.	Cash Flow
NA	+	NA	=	NA	+	NA	+	NA	NA	–	NA	=	NA	NA

Accounting for Accrued Salary Expense (Adjusting Entry)

LO 2-2

 Show how payables affect financial statements.

It is impractical to record many business events as they occur. For example, Cato incurs salary expense continually as the instructor teaches courses. Imagine the impossibility of trying to record salary expense second by second! Companies normally record transactions when it is most convenient. The most convenient time to record many expenses is when they are paid. Often, however, a single business transaction pertains to more than one accounting period. To provide accurate financial reports in such cases, companies may need to recognize some expenses before paying cash for them. Expenses that are recognized before cash is paid are called **accrued expenses.** The accounting for Event 7 illustrates the effect of recognizing accrued salary expense.

EVENT 7 At the end of 2014 Cato recorded accrued salary expense of $6,000 (the salary expense is for courses the instructor taught in 2014 that Cato will pay cash for in 2015).

Accrual accounting requires that companies recognize expenses in the period in which they are incurred regardless of when cash is paid. Cato must recognize all salary expense in the period in which the instructor worked (2014) even though Cato will not pay the instructor again until 2015. Cato must also recognize the obligation (liability) it has to pay the instructor. To accurately report all 2014 salary expense and year-end obligations, Cato must record the unpaid salary expense and salary liability before preparing its financial statements. The entry to recognize the accrued salary expense is called an **adjusting entry.** Like all adjusting entries, it is only to update the accounting records; it does not affect cash.

This adjusting entry decreases stockholders' equity (Retained Earnings) and increases a liability account called **Salaries Payable.** The balance in the Salaries Payable account represents the amount of cash the company is obligated to pay the instructor in the future. The effect of the expense recognition on the financial statements follows:

Assets			=	Liab.	+	Stockholders' Equity								
Cash	+	Accts. Rec.	=	Sal. Pay.	+	Com. Stk.	+	Ret. Earn.	Rev.	−	Exp.	=	Net Inc.	Cash Flow
NA	+	NA	=	6,000	+	NA	+	(6,000)	NA	−	6,000	=	(6,000)	NA

This event is a **claims exchange transaction.** The claims of creditors (liabilities) increase and the claims of stockholders (retained earnings) decrease. Total claims remain unchanged. The salary expense is reported on the income statement. The statement of cash flows is not affected.

Be careful not to confuse liabilities with expenses. Although liabilities may increase when a company recognizes expenses, liabilities are not expenses. Liabilities are obligations. They can arise from acquiring assets as well as recognizing expenses. For example, when a business borrows money from a bank, it recognizes an increase in assets (cash) and liabilities (notes payable). The borrowing transaction does not affect expenses.

> ☑ **CHECK YOURSELF 2.1**
>
> During 2014, Anwar Company earned $345,000 of revenue on account and collected $320,000 cash from accounts receivable. Anwar paid cash expenses of $300,000 and cash dividends of $12,000. Determine the amount of net income Anwar should report on the 2014 income statement and the amount of cash flow from operating activities Anwar should report on the 2014 statement of cash flows.
>
> **Answer**   Net income is $45,000 ($345,000 revenue − $300,000 expenses). The cash flow from operating activities is $20,000, the amount of revenue collected in cash from customers (accounts receivable) minus the cash paid for expenses ($320,000 − $300,000). Dividend payments are classified as financing activities and do not affect the determination of either net income or cash flow from operating activities.

Summary of Events and General Ledger

The previous section of this chapter described seven events Cato Consultants experienced during the 2014 accounting period. These events are summarized in Exhibit 2.1. The associated general ledger accounts are also shown in the exhibit. The information in these accounts is used to prepare the financial statements. The revenue and expense items appear in the Retained Earnings column with their account titles immediately to the right of the dollar amounts. The amounts are color coded to help you trace the data to the financial statements. Data in red appear on the balance sheet, data in blue on the income statement, and data in green on the statement of cash flows.

Vertical Statements Model

The financial statements for Cato Consultants' 2014 accounting period are represented in a vertical statements model in Exhibit 2.2. A vertical statements model arranges a set of financial statement information vertically on a single page. Like horizontal statements models, vertical statements models are learning tools. They illustrate interrelationships among financial statements. The models do not, however, portray the full, formal presentation formats companies use in published financial statements. For example, statements models may use summarized formats with abbreviated titles and dates. As you read the following explanations of each financial statement, trace the color-coded financial data from Exhibit 2.1 to Exhibit 2.2.

EXHIBIT 2.1

Transaction Data for 2013 Recorded in General Ledger Accounts

1	Cato Consultants acquired $5,000 cash by issuing common stock.
2	Cato provided $84,000 of consulting services on account.
3	Cato collected $60,000 cash from customers in partial settlement of its accounts receivable.
4	Cato paid $10,000 cash for salary expense.
5	Cato paid $2,000 cash for 2014 advertising costs.
6	Cato signed contracts for $42,000 of consulting services to be performed in 2015.
7	Cato recognized $6,000 of accrued salary expense.

	Assets			=	Liabilities	+	Stockholders' Equity			
Event No.	Cash	+	Accounts Receivable	=	Salaries Payable	+	Common Stock	+	Retained Earnings	Other Account Titles
Beg. bal.	0		0		0		0		0	
1	5,000						5,000			
2			84,000						84,000	Consulting revenue
3	60,000		(60,000)							
4	(10,000)								(10,000)	Salary expense
5	(2,000)								(2,000)	Advertising expense
6										
7					6,000				(6,000)	Salary Expense
End bal.	53,000	+	24,000	=	6,000	+	5,000	+	66,000	

Income Statement

The income statement reflects accrual accounting. Consulting revenue represents the price Cato charged for all the services it performed in 2014, even though Cato had not by the end of the year received cash for some of the services performed. Expenses include all costs incurred to produce revenue, whether paid for by year-end or not. We can now expand the definition of expenses introduced in Chapter 1. Expenses were previously defined as assets consumed in the process of generating revenue. Cato's adjusting entry to recognize accrued salaries expense did not reflect consuming assets. Instead of a decrease in assets, Cato recorded an increase in liabilities (salaries payable). An **expense** can therefore be more precisely defined as *a decrease in assets or an increase in liabilities resulting from operating activities undertaken to generate revenue.*

Statement of Changes in Stockholders' Equity

The statement of changes in stockholders' equity reports the effects on equity of issuing common stock, earning net income, and paying dividends to stockholders. It identifies how an entity's equity increased and decreased during the period as a result of transactions with stockholders and operating the business. In the Cato case, the statement shows that equity increased when the business acquired $5,000 cash by issuing common stock. The statement also reports that equity increased by $66,000 from earning income and that none of the $66,000 of net earnings was distributed to owners (no dividends were paid). Equity at the end of the year is $71,000 ($5,000 + $66,000).

Balance Sheet

The balance sheet discloses an entity's assets, liabilities, and stockholders' equity at a particular point in time. As of December 31, 2014, Cato Consultants had total assets of $77,000 ($53,000 cash + $24,000 accounts receivable). These assets are equal to the

EXHIBIT 2.2	Vertical Statements Model

CATO CONSULTANTS
Financial Statements*
Income Statement
For the Year Ended December 31, 2014

Consulting revenue	$84,000
Salary expense	(16,000)
Advertising expense	(2,000)
Net income	$66,000

Statement of Changes in Stockholders' Equity
For the Year Ended December 31, 2014

Beginning common stock	$ 0	
Plus: Common stock issued	5,000	
Ending common stock		$ 5,000
Beginning retained earnings	0	
Plus: Net income	66,000	
Less: Dividends	0	
Ending retained earnings		66,000
Total stockholders' equity		$71,000

Balance Sheet
As of December 31, 2014

Assets		
Cash	$53,000	
Accounts receivable	24,000	
Total assets		$77,000
Liabilities		
Salaries payable		$ 6,000
Stockholders' equity		
Common stock	$ 5,000	
Retained earnings	66,000	
Total stockholders' equity		71,000
Total liabilities and stockholders' equity		$77,000

Statement of Cash Flows
For the Year Ended December 31, 2014

Cash flows from operating activities		
Cash receipts from customers	$60,000	
Cash payments for salary expense	(10,000)	
Cash payments for advertising expenses	(2,000)	
Net cash flow from operating activities		$48,000
Cash flow from investing activities		0
Cash flows from financing activities		
Cash receipt from issuing common stock	5,000	
Net cash flow from financing activities		5,000
Net change in cash		53,000
Plus: Beginning cash balance		0
Ending cash balance		$53,000

*In real-world annual reports, financial statements are normally presented separately with appropriate descriptions of the date to indicate whether the statement applies to the entire accounting period or a specific point in time.

obligations and commitments Cato has to its creditors and investors. Specifically, Cato has a $6,000 obligation (liability) to creditors, with the remaining $71,000 of assets available to support commitments (stockholders' equity) to stockholders.

Statement of Cash Flows

The statement of cash flows explains the change in cash from the beginning to the end of the accounting period. It can be prepared by analyzing the Cash account. Since Cato Consultants was established in 2014, its beginning cash balance was zero. By the end of the year, the cash balance was $53,000. The statement of cash flows explains this increase. The Cash account increased because Cato collected $60,000 from customers and decreased because Cato paid $12,000 for expenses. As a result, Cato's net cash inflow from operating activities was $48,000. Also, the business acquired $5,000 cash through the financing activity of issuing common stock, for a cumulative cash increase of $53,000 ($48,000 + $5,000) during 2014.

Comparing Cash Flow from Operating Activities with Net Income

The amount of net income measured using accrual accounting differs from the amount of cash flow from operating activities. For Cato Consulting in 2014, the differences are summarized below.

	Accrual Accounting	Cash Flow
Consulting revenue	$84,000	$60,000
Salary expense	(16,000)	(10,000)
Advertising expense	(2,000)	(2,000)
Net income	$66,000	$48,000

Many students begin their first accounting class with the misconception that revenue and expense items are cash equivalents. The Cato illustration demonstrates that a company may recognize a revenue or expense without a corresponding cash collection or payment in the same accounting period.

The Closing Process

Recall that the temporary accounts (revenue, expense, and dividend) are closed prior to the start of the next accounting cycle. The closing process transfers the amount in each of these accounts to the Retained Earnings account, leaving each temporary account with a zero balance.

Exhibit 2.3 shows the general ledger accounts for Cato Consultants after the revenue and expense accounts have been closed to retained earnings. The closing entry labeled C1.1 transfers the balance in the Consulting Revenue account to the Retained Earnings account. Closing entries C1.2 and C1.3 transfer the balances in the expense accounts to retained earnings.

Steps in an Accounting Cycle

An accounting cycle, which is represented graphically in Exhibit 2.4, involves several steps. The four steps identified to this point are (1) recording transactions; (2) adjusting the accounts; (3) preparing financial statements; and (4) closing the temporary accounts. The first step occurs continually throughout the accounting period. Steps 2, 3, and 4 normally occur at the end of the accounting period.

The Matching Concept

Cash basis accounting can distort reported net income because it sometimes fails to match expenses with the revenues they produce. To illustrate, consider the $6,000 of accrued salary expense that Cato Consultants recognized at the end of 2014. The instructor's teaching produced revenue in 2014. If Cato waited until 2015 (when it paid

EXHIBIT 2.3

General Ledger Accounts for Cato Consultants

Assets		=	Liabilities		+	Stockholders' Equity	
Cash			**Salaries Payable**			**Common Stock**	
(1)	5,000		(7)	6,000		(1)	5,000
(3)	60,000		Bal.	6,000			
(4)	(10,000)					**Retained Earnings**	
(5)	(2,000)					Cl.1	84,000
Bal.	53,000					Cl.2	(16,000)
						Cl.3	(2,000)
Accounts Receivable						Bal.	66,000
(2)	84,000						
(3)	(60,000)					**Consulting Revenue**	
Bal.	24,000					(2)	84,000
						Cl.1	(84,000)
						Bal.	0
						Salary Expense	
						(4)	(10,000)
						(7)	(6,000)
						Cl.2	16,000
						Bal.	0
						Advertising Expense	
						(5)	(2,000)
						Cl.3	2,000
						Bal.	0

the instructor) to recognize $6,000 of the total $16,000 salary expense, then $6,000 of the expense would not be matched with the revenue it generated. By using accrual accounting, Cato recognized all the salary expense in the same accounting period in which the consulting revenue was recognized. A primary goal of accrual accounting is to appropriately match expenses with revenues, the **matching concept.**

Appropriately matching expenses with revenues can be difficult even when using accrual accounting. For example, consider Cato's advertising expense. Money spent on advertising may generate revenue in future accounting periods as well as in the current period. A prospective customer could save an advertising brochure for several years before calling Cato for training services. It is difficult to know when and to what extent advertising produces revenue. When the connection between an expense and the corresponding revenue is vague, accountants commonly match the expense with the period in which it is incurred. Cato matched (recognized) the entire $2,000 of advertising cost with the 2013 accounting period even though some of that cost might generate revenue in future accounting periods. Expenses that are matched with the period in which they are incurred are frequently called **period costs.**

Matching is not perfect. Although it would be more accurate to match expenses with revenues than with periods, there is sometimes no obvious direct connection between expenses and revenue.

EXHIBIT 2.4

The Accounting Cycle

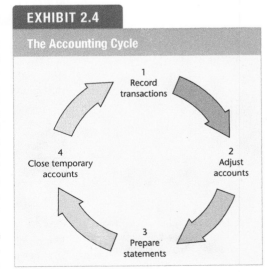

1 Record transactions

2 Adjust accounts

3 Prepare statements

4 Close temporary accounts

Accountants must exercise judgment to select the accounting period in which to recognize revenues and expenses. The concept of conservatism influences such judgment calls.

The Conservatism Principle

When faced with a recognition dilemma, **conservatism** guides accountants to select the alternative that produces the lowest amount of net income. In uncertain circumstances, accountants tend to delay revenue recognition and accelerate expense recognition. The conservatism principle holds that it is better to understate net income than to overstate it. If subsequent developments suggest that net income should have been higher, investors will respond more favorably than if they learn it was really lower. This practice explains why Cato recognized all of the advertising cost as expense in 2014 even though some of that cost may generate revenue in future accounting periods.

SECTION 2:

ACCOUNTING FOR DEFERRALS

As previously discussed cash may be exchanged before revenue or expense is recognized. In this case the business defers recognition. This section introduces three common deferrals.

SECOND ACCOUNTING CYCLE

The effects of Cato Consultants' 2015 events are as follows:

EVENT 1   Cato paid $6,000 to the instructor to settle the salaries payable obligation.

Cash payments to creditors are *asset use transactions.* When Cato pays the instructor, both the asset account Cash and the liability account Salaries Payable decrease. The cash payment does not affect the income statement. The salary expense was recognized in 2014 when the instructor taught the classes. The statement of cash flows reflects a cash outflow from operating activities. The effects of this transaction on the financial statements are shown here.

Assets	=	Liab.	+	Stk. Equity		Rev.	−	Exp.	=	Net Inc.	Cash Flow	
Cash	=	Sal. Pay.				Rev.	−	Exp.	=	Net Inc.	Cash Flow	
(6,000)	=	(6,000)	+	NA		NA	−	NA	=	NA	(6,000)	OA

LO 2-3

Show how supplies affect financial statements.

Accounting for Supplies Purchase

EVENT 2   Cato purchased $800 of supplies on account.

The purchase of supplies on account is an *asset source transaction.* The asset account Supplies and the liability account Accounts Payable increase. The income statement is unaffected. Expense recognition is deferred until the supplies are used. The statement of cash flows is not affected. The effects of this transaction on the financial statements are shown here.

Assets	=	Liab.	+	Stk. Equity		Rev.	−	Exp.	=	Net Inc.	Cash Flow
Supplies	=	Accts. Pay.				Rev.	−	Exp.	=	Net Inc.	Cash Flow
800	=	800	+	NA		NA	−	NA	=	NA	NA

Prepaid Items (Cost versus Expense)

EVENT 3   On March 1, 2015, Cato signed a one-year lease agreement and paid $12,000 cash in advance to rent office space. The one-year lease term began on March 1.

Show how prepaid items affect financial statements.

Accrual accounting draws a distinction between the terms *cost* and *expense*. A **cost** *might be either an asset or an expense*. If a company has already consumed a purchased resource in the process of earning revenue, the cost of the resource is an *expense*. For example, companies normally pay for electricity the month after using it. The cost of electric utilities is therefore usually recorded as an expense. In contrast, if a company purchases a resource it will use in the future to generate revenue, the cost of the resource represents an *asset*. Accountants record such a cost in an asset account and *defer* recognizing an expense until the resource is used to produce revenue. Deferring the expense recognition provides more accurate *matching* of revenues and expenses.

The cost of the office space Cato leased in Event 2 is an asset. It is recorded in the asset account *Prepaid Rent*. Cato expects to benefit from incurring this cost for the next twelve months. Expense recognition is deferred until Cato uses the office space to help generate revenue. Other common deferred expenses include *prepaid insurance* and *prepaid taxes*. As these titles imply, deferred expenses are frequently called **prepaid items**. Exhibit 2.5 illustrates the relationship between costs, assets, and expenses.

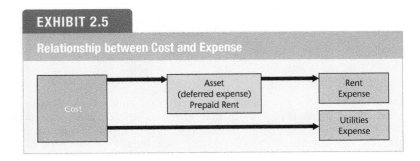

EXHIBIT 2.5

Relationship between Cost and Expense

Purchasing prepaid rent is an asset exchange transaction. The asset account Cash decreases and the asset account Prepaid Rent increases. The amount of total assets is unaffected. The income statement is unaffected. Expense recognition is deferred until the office space is used. The statement of cash flows reflects a cash outflow from operating activities. The effects of this transaction on the financial statements are shown here.

Assets			=	Liab.	+	Stk. Equity		Rev.	−	Exp.	=	Net Inc.	Cash Flow
Cash	+	Prep. Rent	=	Liab.	+	Stk. Equity		Rev.	−	Exp.	=	Net Inc.	Cash Flow
(12,000)	+	12,000	=	NA	+	NA		NA	−	NA	=	NA	(12,000) OA

Show how unearned revenues affect financial statements.

Accounting for Receipt of Unearned Revenue

EVENT 4   Cato received $18,000 cash in advance from Westberry Company for consulting services Cato agreed to perform over a one-year period beginning June 1, 2015.

Cato must defer (delay) recognizing any revenue until it performs (does the work) the consulting services for Westberry. From Cato's point of view, the deferred revenue is a liability because Cato is obligated to perform services in the future. The liability is called **unearned revenue.** The cash receipt is an *asset source transaction.* The asset account Cash and the liability account Unearned Revenue both increase. Collecting the cash has no effect on the income statement. The revenue will be reported on the income statement after Cato performs the services. The statement of cash flows reflects a cash inflow from operating activities. The effects of this transaction on the financial statements are shown here.

Assets	=	Liab.	+	Stk. Equity		Rev.	−	Exp.	=	Net Inc.	Cash Flow
Cash	=	Unearn. Rev.				Rev.	−	Exp.	=	Net Inc.	Cash Flow
18,000	=	18,000	+	NA		NA	−	NA	=	NA	18,000 OA

Other 2015 Events

EVENT 5   Cato provided $96,400 of consulting services on account.

Providing services on account is an *asset source transaction.* The asset account Accounts Receivable and the stockholders' equity account Retained Earnings increase. Revenue and net income increase. The statement of cash flows is not affected. The effects of this transaction on the financial statements are shown here.

Assets	=	Liab.	+	Stk. Equity		Rev.	−	Exp.	=	Net Inc.	Cash Flow
Accts. Rec.	=			Ret. Earn.		Rev.	−	Exp.	=	Net Inc.	Cash Flow
96,400	=	NA	+	96,400		96,400	−	NA	=	96,400	NA

EVENT 6   Cato collected $105,000 cash from customers as partial settlement of accounts receivable.

Collecting money from customers who are paying accounts receivable is an *asset exchange transaction.* One asset account (Cash) increases and another asset account (Accounts Receivable) decreases. The amount of total assets is unchanged. The income statement is not affected. The statement of cash flows reports a cash inflow from operating activities. The effects of this transaction on the financial statements are shown here.

Assets			=	Liab.	+	Stk. Equity		Rev.	−	Exp.	=	Net Inc.	Cash Flow
Cash	+	Accts. Rec.						Rev.	−	Exp.	=	Net Inc.	Cash Flow
105,000	+	(105,000)	=	NA	+	NA		NA	−	NA	=	NA	105,000 OA

EVENT 7   Cato paid $32,000 cash for salary expense.

Cash payments for salary expense are *asset use transactions.* Both the asset account Cash and the equity account Retained Earnings decrease by $32,000. Recognizing the expense decreases net income on the income statement. The statement of cash flows reflects a cash outflow from operating activities. The effects of this transaction on the financial statements are shown here.

Assets	=	Liab.	+	Stk. Equity						
Cash	=			Ret. Earn.	Rev.	−	Exp.	=	Net Inc.	Cash Flow
(32,000)	=	NA	+	(32,000)	NA	−	32,000	=	(32,000)	(32,000) OA

EVENT 8   Cato incurred $21,000 of other operating expenses on account.

Recognizing expenses incurred on account are *claims exchange transactions.* One claims account (Accounts Payable) increases and another claims account (Retained Earnings) decreases. The amount of total claims is not affected. Recognizing the expenses decreases net income. The statement of cash flows is not affected. The effects of this transaction on the financial statements are shown here.

Assets	=	Liab.	+	Stk. Equity						
		Accts. Pay.	+	Ret. Earn.	Rev.	−	Exp.	=	Net Inc.	Cash Flow
NA	=	21,000	+	(21,000)	NA	−	21,000	=	(21,000)	NA

EVENT 9   Cato paid $18,200 in partial settlement of accounts payable.

Paying accounts payable is an *asset use transaction.* The asset account Cash and the liability account Accounts Payable decrease. The statement of cash flows reports a cash outflow for operating activities. The income statement is not affected. The effects of this transaction on the financial statements are shown here.

Assets	=	Liab.	+	Stk. Equity						
Cash	=	Accts. Pay.			Rev.	−	Exp.	=	Net Inc.	Cash Flow
(18,200)	=	(18,200)	+	NA	NA	−	NA	=	NA	(18,200) OA

EVENT 10   Cato paid $79,500 to purchase land it planned to use in the future as a building site for its home office.

Purchasing land with cash is an *asset exchange transaction.* One asset account, Cash, decreases and another asset account, Land, increases. The amount of total assets is unchanged. The income statement is not affected. The statement of cash flows reports a cash outflow for investing activities. The effects of this transaction on the financial statements are shown here.

Assets			=	Liab.	+	Stk. Equity						
Cash	+	Land	=				Rev.	−	Exp.	=	Net Inc.	Cash Flow
(79,500)	+	79,500	=	NA	+	NA	NA	−	NA	=	NA	(79,500) IA

EVENT 11   Cato paid $21,000 in cash dividends to its stockholders.

Cash payments for dividends are *asset use transactions.* Both the asset account Cash and the equity account Retained Earnings decrease. Recall that dividends are wealth transfers from the business to the stockholders, not expenses. They are not incurred in the process of generating revenue. They do not affect the income statement. The statement of cash flows reflects a cash outflow from financing activities. The effects of this transaction on the financial statements are shown here.

Assets	=	Liab.	+	Stk. Equity						
Cash	=			Ret. Earn.	Rev.	−	Exp.	=	Net Inc.	Cash Flow
(21,000)	=	NA	+	(21,000)	NA	−	NA	=	NA	(21,000) FA

EVENT 12   Cato acquired $2,000 cash from issuing additional shares of common stock.

Issuing common stock is an *asset source transaction.* The asset account Cash and the stockholders' equity account Common Stock increase. The income statement is unaffected. The statement of cash flows reports a cash inflow from financing activities. The effects of this transaction on the financial statements are shown here.

Assets	=	Liab.	+	Stk. Equity						
Cash	=			Com. Stk.	Rev.	−	Exp.	=	Net Inc.	Cash Flow
2,000	=	NA	+	2,000	NA	−	NA	=	NA	2,000 FA

Explain the accounting cycle including adjustments and the closing process.

Adjusting Entries

Recall that companies make adjusting entries at the end of an accounting period to update the account balances before preparing the financial statements. Adjusting entries ensure that companies report revenues and expenses in the appropriate accounting period; adjusting entries never affect the Cash account.

Accounting for Supplies (Adjusting Entry)

EVENT 13   After determining through a physical count that it had $150 of unused supplies on hand as of December 31, Cato recognized supplies expense.

Companies would find the cost of recording supplies expense each time a pencil, piece of paper, envelope, or other supply item is used to far outweigh the benefit derived from such tedious recordkeeping. Instead, accountants transfer to expense the total cost of all supplies used during the entire accounting period in a single year-end adjusting entry. The cost of supplies used is determined as follows:

Beginning supplies balance + Supplies purchased = Supplies available for use

Supplies available for use − Ending supplies balance = Supplies used

Companies determine the ending supplies balance by physically counting the supplies on hand at the end of the period. Cato used $650 of supplies during the year (zero beginning balance + $800 supplies purchase = $800 available for use; $800 available for use − $150 ending balance = $650). Recognizing Cato's supplies expense is an *asset use transaction.* The asset account Supplies and the stockholders' equity account Retained Earnings decrease. Recognizing supplies expense reduces net income. The statement of cash flows is not affected. The effects of this transaction on the financial statements are shown here.

Assets	=	Liab.	+	Stk. Equity						
Supplies	=			Ret. Earn.	Rev.	−	Exp.	=	Net Inc.	Cash Flow
(650)	=	NA	+	(650)	NA	−	650	=	(650)	NA

Accounting for Prepaid Rent (Adjusting Entry)

EVENT 14   Cato recognized rent expense for the office space used during the accounting period.

Recall that Cato paid $12,000 on March 1, 2015, to rent office space for one year (see Event 3). The portion of the lease cost that represents using office space from March 1 through December 31 is computed as follows:

$12,000 Cost of annual lease ÷ 12 Months = $1,000 Cost per month

$1,000 Cost per month × 10 Months used = $10,000 Rent expense

Recognizing the rent expense decreases the asset account Prepaid Rent and the stockholders' equity account Retained Earnings. Recognizing rent expense reduces net income. The statement of cash flows is not affected. The cash flow effect was recorded in the March 1 event. These effects on the financial statements follow:

Assets	=	Liab.	+	Stk. Equity						
Prep. Rent	=			Ret. Earn.	Rev.	−	Exp.	=	Net Inc.	Cash Flow
(10,000)	=	NA	+	(10,000)	NA	−	10,000	=	(10,000)	NA

☑ CHECK YOURSELF 2.2

Rujoub Inc. paid $18,000 cash for one year of insurance coverage that began on November 1, 2014. Based on this information alone, determine the cash flow from operating activities that Rujoub would report on the 2014 and 2015 statements of cash flows. Also, determine the amount of insurance expense Rujoub would report on the 2014 income statement and the amount of prepaid insurance (an asset) that Rujoub would report on the December 31, 2014, balance sheet.

Answer   Since Rujoub paid all of the cash in 2014, the 2014 statement of cash flows would report an $18,000 cash outflow from operating activities. The 2015 statement of cash flows would report zero cash flow from operating activities. The expense would be recognized in the periods in which the insurance is used. In this case, insurance expense is recognized at the rate of $1,500 per month ($18,000 ÷ 12 months). Rujoub used two months of insurance coverage in 2014 and therefore would report $3,000 (2 months × $1,500) of insurance expense on the 2014 income statement. Rujoub would report a $15,000 (10 months × $1,500) asset, prepaid insurance, on the December 31, 2014, balance sheet. The $15,000 of prepaid insurance would be recognized as insurance expense in 2015 when the insurance coverage is used.

Accounting for Unearned Revenue (Adjusting Entry)

EVENT 15   Cato recognized the portion of the unearned revenue it earned during the accounting period.

Recall that Cato received an $18,000 cash advance from Westberry Company to provide consulting services from June 1, 2015, to May 31, 2016 (see Event 4). By December 31, Cato had earned 7 months (June 1 through December 31) of the revenue related to this contract. Rather than recording the revenue continuously as it performed the consulting services, Cato can simply recognize the amount earned in a single adjustment to the accounting records at the end of the accounting period. The amount of the adjustment is computed as follows:

$18,000 ÷ 12 months = $1,500 revenue earned per month

$1,500 × 7 months = $10,500 revenue to be recognized in 2015

The adjusting entry moves $10,500 from the Unearned Revenue account to the Consulting Revenue account. This entry is a *claims exchange transaction.* The liability account Unearned Revenue decreases and the equity account Retained Earnings increases. The effects of this transaction on the financial statements are shown here.

Assets	=	Liab.	+	Stk. Equity						
		Unearn. Rev.	+	Ret. Earn.	Rev.	−	Exp.	=	Net Inc.	Cash Flow
NA	=	(10,500)	+	10,500	10,500	−	NA	=	10,500	NA

Recall that revenue was previously defined as an economic benefit a company obtains by providing customers with goods and services. In this case the economic benefit is a decrease in the liability account Unearned Revenue. **Revenue** can therefore be more precisely defined as *an increase in assets or a decrease in liabilities that a company obtains by providing customers with goods or services.*

☑ CHECK YOURSELF 2.3

Sanderson & Associates received a $24,000 cash advance as a retainer to provide legal services to a client. The contract called for Sanderson to render services during a one-year period beginning October 1, 2014. Based on this information alone, determine the cash flow from operating activities Sanderson would report on the 2014 and 2015 statements of cash flows. Also determine the amount of revenue Sanderson would report on the 2014 and 2015 income statements.

Answer   Since Sanderson collected all of the cash in 2014, the 2014 statement of cash flows would report a $24,000 cash inflow from operating activities. The 2015 statement of cash flows would report zero cash flow from operating activities. Revenue is recognized in the period in which it is earned. In this case revenue is earned at the rate of $2,000 per month ($24,000 ÷ 12 months = $2,000 per month). Sanderson rendered services for three months in 2014 and nine months in 2015. Sanderson would report $6,000 (3 months × $2,000) of revenue on the 2014 income statement and $18,000 (9 months × $2,000) of revenue on the 2015 income statement.

Answers to The Curious Accountant

Because the Meredith Corporation receives cash from customers before actually sending any magazines to them, the company has not earned any revenue when it receives the cash. Meredith has a liability called *unearned revenue.* If Meredith closed its books on December 31, then $3 of Janet's subscription would be recognized as revenue in 2014. The remaining $9 would appear on the balance sheet as a liability.

Meredith actually ends its accounting year on June 30 each year. The actual June 30, 2012, balance sheet for the company is presented in Exhibit 2.6. The liability for unearned revenue was $322.3 million ($180.9 + $141.4)—which represented about 26.4 percent of total liabilities!

Will Meredith need cash to pay these subscription liabilities? Not exactly. The liabilities will not be paid directly with cash. Instead, they will be satisfied by providing magazines to the subscribers. However, Meredith will need cash to pay for producing and distributing the magazines supplied to the customers. Even so, the amount of cash required to provide magazines will probably differ significantly from the amount of unearned revenues. In most cases, subscription fees do not cover the cost of producing and distributing magazines. By collecting significant amounts of advertising revenue, publishers can provide magazines to customers at prices well below the cost of publication. The amount of unearned revenue is not likely to coincide with the amount of cash needed to cover the cost of satisfying the company's obligation to produce and distribute magazines. Even though the association between unearned revenues and the cost of providing magazines to customers is not direct, a knowledgeable financial analyst can use the information to make estimates of future cash flows and revenue recognition.

EXHIBIT 2.6	Balance Sheet for Meredith Corporation

MEREDITH CORPORATION AND SUBSIDIARIES
Consolidated Balance Sheets
As of June 30 (amounts in thousands)

	2012	2011
Assets		
Current assets		
Cash and cash equivalents	$ 25,820	$ 27,721
Accounts receivable		
(net of allowances of $13,436 in 2012 and $10,823 in 2011)	215,526	212,365
Inventories	22,559	21,529
Current portion of subscription acquisition costs	75,446	54,581
Current portion of broadcast rights	3,408	3,974
Other current assets	16,677	13,568
Total current assets	359,436	333,738
Property, plant, and equipment		
Land	19,517	19,619
Buildings and improvements	129,688	127,916
Machinery and equipment	290,866	289,045
Leasehold improvements	14,816	14,468
Construction in progress	384	8,209
Total property, plant, and equipment	455,271	459,257
Less accumulated depreciation	(260,967)	(272,819)
Net property, plant, and equipment	194,304	186,438
Subscription acquisition costs	75,368	54,286
Broadcast rights	943	1,292
Other assets	66,858	66,940
Intangible assets, net	586,263	545,101
Goodwill	733,127	525,034
Total assets	$2,016,299	$1,712,829
Liabilities and Shareholders' Equity,		
Current liabilities		
Current portion of long-term debt	$ 105,000	$ 50,000
Current portion of long-term broadcast rights payable	6,752	8,548
Accounts payable	72,911	82,878
Accrued expenses		
Compensation and benefits	52,402	53,593
Distribution expenses	12,029	13,937
Other taxes and expenses	52,640	48,205
Total accrued expenses	117,071	115,735
Current portion of unearned subscription revenues	180,852	151,831
Total current liabilities	482,586	408,992
Long-term debt	275,000	145,000
Long-term broadcast rights payable	3,695	5,431
Unearned subscription revenues	141,408	120,024
Deferred income taxes	204,054	160,709
Other noncurrent liabilities	112,111	97,688
Total liabilities	1,218,854	937,844
Shareholders' equity		
Series preferred stock, par value $1 per share	—	—
Common stock, par value $1 per share	35,791	36,282
Class B stock, par value $1 per share, convertible to common stock	8,716	8,776
Additional paid-in capital	53,275	58,274
Retained earnings	722,778	687,816
Accumulated other comprehensive income (loss)	(23,115)	(16,163)
Total shareholders' equity	797,445	74,985
Total liabilities and shareholders' equity	$2,016,299	$1,712,829

Accounting for Accrued Salary Expense (Adjusting Entry)

EVENT 16   Cato recognized $4,000 of accrued salary expense.

The adjusting entry to recognize the accrued salary expense is a ***claims exchange transaction.*** One claims account, Retained Earnings, decreases and another claims account, Salaries Payable, increases. The expense recognition reduces net income. The statement of cash flows is not affected. The effects of this transaction on the financial statements are shown here.

Assets	=	Liab.	+	Stk. Equity						
		Sal. Pay.	+	Ret. Earn.	Rev.	−	Exp.	=	Net Inc.	Cash Flow
NA	=	4,000	+	(4,000)	NA	−	4,000	=	(4,000)	NA

Summary of Events and General Ledger

The previous section of this chapter described sixteen events Cato Consultants experienced the during the 2015 accounting period. These events are summarized in Exhibit 2.7 on page 67. The associated general ledger accounts are also shown in the exhibit. The account balances at the end of 2014, shown in Exhibit 2.3, become the beginning balances for the 2015 accounting period. The 2015 transaction data are referenced to the accounting events with numbers in parentheses. The information in the ledger accounts is the basis for the financial statements in Exhibit 2.8 on pages 68 and 69. Before reading further, trace each event shown in Exhibit 2.7 to the related accounts that are also shown in that exhibit.

Vertical Statements Model

Prepare financial statements based on accrual accounting.

Financial statement users obtain helpful insights by analyzing company trends over multiple accounting cycles. Exhibit 2.8 presents for Cato Consultants a multicycle **vertical statements model** of 2014 and 2015 accounting data. To conserve space, we have combined all the expenses for each year into single amounts labeled "Operating Expenses," determined as follows:

	2014	2015
Other operating expenses	$ 0	$21,000
Salary expense	16,000	36,000
Rent expense	0	10,000
Advertising expense	2,000	0
Supplies expense	0	650
Total operating expenses	$18,000	$67,650

Similarly, we combined the cash payments for operating expenses on the statement of cash flows as follows:

	2014	2015
Supplies and other operating expenses	$ 0	$18,200*
Salary expense	10,000	38,000
Rent expense	0	12,000
Advertising expense	2,000	0
Total cash payments for operating expenses	$12,000	$68,200

*Amount paid in partial settlement of accounts payable

Recall that the level of detail reported in financial statements depends on user information needs. Most real-world companies combine many account balances together to report highly summarized totals under each financial statement caption. Before

EXHIBIT 2.7

Ledger Accounts with 2015 Transaction Data

1. Cato paid $6,000 to the instructor to settle the salaries payable obligation.
2. Cato purchased $800 of supplies on account.
3. On March 1, Cato paid $12,000 cash to lease office space for one year.
4. Cato received $18,000 cash in advance from Westberry Company for consulting services to be performed for one year beginning June 1.
5. Cato provided $96,400 of consulting services on account.
6. Cato collected $105,000 cash from customers as partial settlement of accounts receivable.
7. Cato paid $32,000 cash for salary expense.
8. Cato incurred $21,000 of other operating expenses on account.
9. Cato paid $18,200 in partial settlement of accounts payable.
10. Cato paid $79,500 to purchase land it planned to use in the future as a building site for its home office.
11. Cato paid $21,000 in cash dividends to its stockholders.
12. Cato acquired $2,000 cash from issuing additional shares of common stock.

The year-end adjustments are:

13. After determining through a physical count that it had $150 of unused supplies on hand as of December 31, Cato recognized supplies expense.
14. Cato recognized rent expense for the office space used during the accounting period.
15. Cato recognized the portion of the unearned revenue it earned during the accounting period.
16. Cato recognized $4,000 of accrued salary expense.

| Assets | | = | Liabilities | + | Stockholders' Equity | |

Cash

Bal.	53,000
(1)	(6,000)
(3)	(12,000)
(4)	18,000
(6)	105,000
(7)	(32,000)
(9)	(18,200)
(10)	(79,500)
(11)	(21,000)
(12)	2,000
Bal.	9,300

Accounts Receivable

Bal.	24,000
(5)	96,400
(6)	(105,000)
Bal.	15,400

Supplies

Bal.	0
(2)	800
(13)	(650)
Bal.	150

Prepaid Rent

Bal.	0
(3)	12,000
(14)	(10,000)
Bal.	2,000

Land

Bal.	0
(10)	79,500
Bal.	79,500

Accounts Payable

Bal.	0
(2)	800
(8)	21,000
(9)	(18,200)
Bal.	3,600

Unearned Revenue

Bal.	0
(4)	18,000
(15)	(10,500)
Bal.	7,500

Salaries Payable

Bal.	6,000
(1)	(6,000)
(16)	4,000
Bal.	4,000

Common Stock

Bal.	5,000
(12)	2,000
Bal.	7,000

Retained Earnings

| Bal. | 66,000 |

Dividends

Bal.	0
(11)	(21,000)
Bal.	(21,000)

Consulting Revenue

Bal.	0
(5)	96,400
(15)	10,500
Bal.	106,900

Other Operating Expenses

Bal.	0
(8)	(21,000)
Bal.	(21,000)

Salary Expense

Bal.	0
(7)	(32,000)
(16)	(4,000)
Bal.	(36,000)

Rent Expense

Bal.	0
(14)	(10,000)
Bal.	(10,000)

Supplies Expense

Bal.	0
(13)	(650)
Bal.	(650)

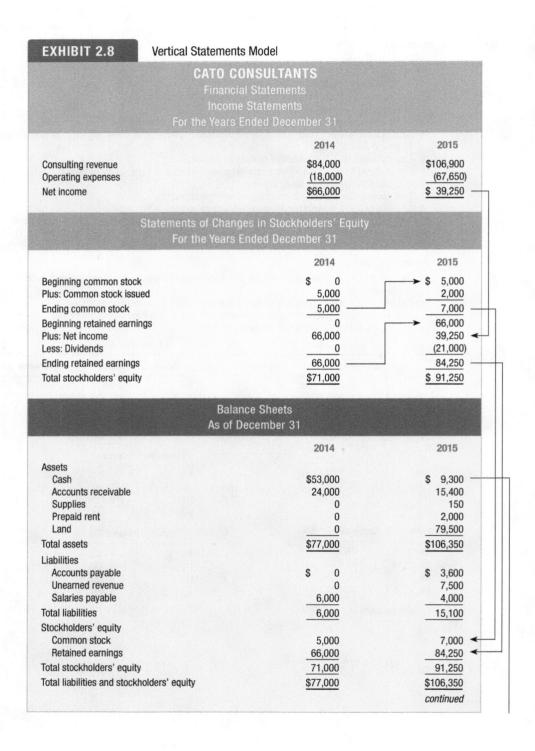

EXHIBIT 2.8   Vertical Statements Model

CATO CONSULTANTS
Financial Statements
Income Statements
For the Years Ended December 31

	2014	2015
Consulting revenue	$84,000	$106,900
Operating expenses	(18,000)	(67,650)
Net income	$66,000	$ 39,250

Statements of Changes in Stockholders' Equity
For the Years Ended December 31

	2014	2015
Beginning common stock	$ 0	$ 5,000
Plus: Common stock issued	5,000	2,000
Ending common stock	5,000	7,000
Beginning retained earnings	0	66,000
Plus: Net income	66,000	39,250
Less: Dividends	0	(21,000)
Ending retained earnings	66,000	84,250
Total stockholders' equity	$71,000	$ 91,250

Balance Sheets
As of December 31

	2014	2015
Assets		
Cash	$53,000	$ 9,300
Accounts receivable	24,000	15,400
Supplies	0	150
Prepaid rent	0	2,000
Land	0	79,500
Total assets	$77,000	$106,350
Liabilities		
Accounts payable	$ 0	$ 3,600
Unearned revenue	0	7,500
Salaries payable	6,000	4,000
Total liabilities	6,000	15,100
Stockholders' equity		
Common stock	5,000	7,000
Retained earnings	66,000	84,250
Total stockholders' equity	71,000	91,250
Total liabilities and stockholders' equity	$77,000	$106,350

continued

EXHIBIT 2.8	*Concluded*		
Statements of Cash Flows For the Years Ended December 31			
		2014	2015
Cash Flows from Operating Activities			
Cash receipts from customers		$60,000	$123,000
Cash payments for operating expenses		(12,000)	(68,200)
Net cash flow from operating activities		48,000	54,800
Cash Flows from Investing Activities			
Cash payment to purchase land		0	(79,500)
Cash Flows from Financing Activities			
Cash receipts from issuing common stock		5,000	2,000
Cash payments for dividends		0	(21,000)
Net cash flow from financing activities		5,000	(19,000)
Net change in cash		53,000	(43,700)
Plus: Beginning cash balance		0	53,000
Ending cash balance		$53,000	$ 9,300

reading further, trace the remaining financial statement items from the ledger accounts in Exhibit 2.7 to where they are reported in Exhibit 2.8.

The vertical statements model in Exhibit 2.8 shows significant interrelationships among the financial statements. For each year, trace the amount of net income from the income statement to the statement of changes in stockholders' equity. Next, trace the ending balances of common stock and retained earnings reported on the statement of changes in stockholders' equity to the stockholders' equity section of the balance sheet. Also, confirm that the amount of cash reported on the balance sheet equals the ending cash balance on the statement of cash flows.

Other relationships connect the two accounting periods. For example, trace the ending retained earnings balance from the 2014 statement of stockholders' equity to the beginning retained earnings balance on the 2015 statement of stockholders' equity. Also, trace the ending cash balance on the 2014 statement of cash flows to the beginning cash balance on the 2015 statement of cash flows. Finally, confirm that the change in cash between the 2014 and 2015 balance sheets ($53,000 − $9,300 = $43,700 decrease) agrees with the net change in cash reported on the 2014 statement of cash flows.

☑ CHECK YOURSELF 2.4

Treadmore Company started the 2014 accounting period with $580 of supplies on hand. During 2014 the company paid cash to purchase $2,200 of supplies. A physical count of supplies indicated that there was $420 of supplies on hand at the end of 2014. Treadmore pays cash for supplies at the time they are purchased. Based on this information alone, determine the amount of supplies expense to be recognized on the income statement and the amount of cash flow to be shown in the operating activities section of the statement of cash flows.

Answer The amount of supplies expense recognized on the income statement is the amount of supplies that were used during the accounting period. This amount is computed below:

$580 Beginning balance + $2,200 Supplies purchases = $2,780 Supplies available for use

$2,780 Supplies available for use − $420 Ending supplies balance = $2,360 supplies used

The cash flow from operating activities is the amount of cash paid for supplies during the accounting period. In this case, Treadmore paid $2,200 cash to purchase supplies. This amount would be shown as a cash outflow.

70   Chapter 2

REALITY BYTES

REVENUE VERSUS CASH FLOW:
THE GAMES PEOPLE PLAY

Most banks have a sign on their door that says "FDIC Insured." The FDIC on the sign refers to the Federal Deposit Insurance Corporation. Insurance provided by the FDIC protects the bank's depositors up to $250,000 per account in the event the bank should fail. To pay for this insurance, the FDIC charges participating banks a fee.

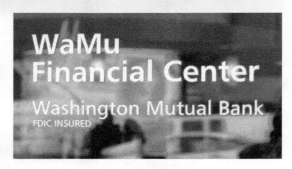

After 164 banks failed during the economic and banking crisis of 2007 and 2008 the FDIC was concerned that its reserves available to pay potential claims were running low. To address this, it required banks to prepay three years of premiums in 2009, rather than pay them in 2009, 2010, and 2011. Although such measures improved the FDIC's cash reserves, it does not mean they earned three year's worth of revenue in 2009, and it did not change the fact that cash payments would still have to be made over the next three years with moneys collected in 2009. And, even though the banks paid three years of premiums in 2009, they spread the expense recognition over 2009, 2010, and 2011.

The FDIC was not the first entity to use such tactics. State and local governments have sometimes delayed payments due near the end of their fiscal year into the next year so as not to show a deficit in the current year.

Near the end of their fiscal year, business entities sometimes try to convince customers to buy more goods and services than they need immediately. The company tells the customer that they can always return the goods next year if they do not need them. The goal is to increase this year's revenues, and profits, and executive bonuses. This tactic, called "trade loading" is at best a violation of GAAP, and in some situations may be illegal.

The problems these tactics create are rather obvious. Cash collected in advance in 2009 by the FDIC means less cash will be collected in 2010 and 2011. Expenses deferred into the next fiscal year by a state government means that next year will have higher expenses to pay than it otherwise would have. These schemes are sometimes referred to as, "kicking the can down the road." Such plans are seldom successful in the long run.

Source of FDIC information: *Birmingham Business Journal,* October 2, 2009.

TRANSACTION CLASSIFICATION

LO 2-8

Classify accounting events into one of four categories.

Chapters 1 and 2 introduced four types of transactions. Although businesses engage in an infinite number of different transactions, all transactions fall into one of four types. By learning to identify transactions by type, you can understand how unfamiliar events affect financial statements. The four types of transactions are

1. *Asset source transactions:* An asset account increases, and a corresponding claims account increases.

2. *Asset use transactions:* An asset account decreases, and a corresponding claims account decreases.

3. *Asset exchange transactions:* One asset account increases, and another asset account decreases.

4. *Claims exchange transactions:* One claims account increases, and another claims account decreases.

<< A Look Back

This chapter introduced the *accrual accounting* concept. Accrual accounting causes the amount of revenues and expenses reported on the income statement to differ significantly from the amount of cash flow from operating activities reported on the statement of cash flows because of timing differences. These differences are readily apparent when relevant events are recorded in a horizontal financial statements model. To review, study the following transactions and the corresponding statements model. Set up a statements model on a piece of paper and try to record the effects of each event before reading the explanation.

Events

1. Provided $600 of services on account.
2. Collected $400 cash from accounts receivable.
3. Accrued $350 of salary expense.
4. Paid $225 cash in partial settlement of salaries payable.

Event No.	Balance Sheet									Income Statement					Statement of Cash Flows	
	Cash	+	Accts. Rec.	=	Sal. Pay.	+	Ret. Earn.		Rev.	−	Exp.	=	Net Inc.			
1	NA	+	600	=	NA	+	600		600	−	NA	=	600		NA	
2	400	+	(400)	=	NA	+	NA		NA	−	NA	=	NA		400	OA
3	NA	+	NA	=	350	+	(350)		NA	−	350	=	(350)		NA	
4	(225)	+	NA	=	(225)	+	NA		NA	−	NA	=	NA		(225)	OA
Totals	175	+	200	=	125	+	250		600	−	350	=	250		175	NC

Notice the $250 of net income differs from the $175 cash flow from operating activities. The entries in the statements model demonstrate the reasons for the difference. Although $600 of revenue is recognized, only $400 of cash was collected. The remaining $200 will be collected in the future and is currently shown on the balance sheet as Accounts Receivable. Also, although $350 of salary expense is recognized, only $225 was paid in cash. The remaining $125 will be paid in the future. This obligation is shown as Salaries Payable on the balance sheet. Study these relationships carefully to develop a clear understanding of how accrual accounting affects financial reporting.

Also, the definitions of revenue and expense have been expanded. The complete definitions of these two elements are as follows:

1. **Revenue:** Revenue is the *economic benefit* derived from operating the business. Its recognition is accompanied by an increase in assets or a decrease in liabilities resulting from providing products or services to customers.

2. **Expense:** An expense is an *economic sacrifice* incurred in the process of generating revenue. Its recognition is accompanied by a decrease in assets or an increase in liabilities resulting from consuming assets and services in an effort to produce revenue.

A Look Forward >>

Chapters 1 and 2 focused on businesses that generate revenue by providing services to their customers. Examples of these types of businesses include consulting, real estate sales, medical services, and legal services. The next chapter introduces accounting practices for businesses that generate revenue by selling goods. Examples of these companies include Wal-Mart, Radio Shack, Office Depot, and Lowes.

Video lectures and accompanying self-assessment quizzes are available for all learning objectives through McGraw-Hill *Connect® Accounting.*

SELF-STUDY REVIEW PROBLEM

Gifford Company experienced the following accounting events during 2014:

1. Started operations on January 1 when it acquired $20,000 cash by issuing common stock.
2. Earned $18,000 of revenue on account.
3. On March 1 collected $36,000 cash as an advance for services to be performed in the future.
4. Paid cash operating expenses of $17,000.
5. Paid a $2,700 cash dividend to stockholders.
6. On December 31, 2014, adjusted the books to recognize the revenue earned by providing services related to the advance described in Event 3. The contract required Gifford to provide services for a one-year period starting March 1.
7. Collected $15,000 cash from accounts receivable.

Gifford Company experienced the following accounting events during 2015:

1. Recognized $38,000 of cash revenue.
2. On April 1 paid $12,000 cash for an insurance policy that provides coverage for one year beginning immediately.
3. Collected $2,000 cash from accounts receivable.
4. Paid cash operating expenses of $21,000.
5. Paid a $5,000 cash dividend to stockholders.
6. On December 31, 2015, adjusted the books to recognize the remaining revenue earned by providing services related to the advance described in Event 3 of 2014.
7. On December 31, 2015, Gifford adjusted the books to recognize the amount of the insurance policy used during 2015.

Required

a. Record the events in a financial statements model like the following one. The first event is recorded as an example.

Event No.	Assets			=	Liab.	+	Stockholders' Equity						
	Cash +	Accts. Rec. +	Prep. Ins.	=	Unearn. Rev.	+	Com. Stk. +	Ret. Earn.		Rev. −	Exp. =	Net Inc.	Cash Flow
1	20,000 +	NA +	NA	=	NA	+	20,000 +	NA		NA −	NA =	NA	20,000 FA

b. What amount of revenue would Gifford report on the 2014 income statement?
c. What amount of cash flow from customers would Gifford report on the 2014 statement of cash flows?
d. What amount of unearned revenue would Gifford report on the 2014 and 2015 year-end balance sheets?
e. What are the 2015 opening balances for the revenue and expense accounts?
f. What amount of total assets would Gifford report on the December 31, 2014 balance sheet?
g. What obligations and commitments would Gifford report on the December 31, 2015 balance sheet?

Solution to Requirement a

The financial statements model follows:

Event No.	Assets			=	Liab.	+	Stockholders' Equity							
	Cash +	Accts. Rec. +	Prep. Ins. =		Unearn. Rev. +		Com. Stk. +	Ret. Earn.	Rev. −	Exp. =	Net Inc.	Cash Flow		
2013														
1	20,000 +	NA +	NA =		NA +		20,000 +	NA	NA −	NA =	NA	20,000	FA	
2	NA +	18,000 +	NA =		NA +		NA +	18,000	18,000 −	NA =	18,000	NA		
3	36,000 +	NA +	NA =		36,000 +		NA +	NA	NA −	NA =	NA	36,000	OA	
4	(17,000) +	NA +	NA =		NA +		NA +	(17,000)	NA −	17,000 =	(17,000)	(17,000)	OA	
5	(2,700) +	NA +	NA =		NA +		NA +	(2,700)	NA −	NA =	NA	(2,700)	FA	
6*	NA +	NA +	NA =		(30,000) +		NA +	30,000	30,000 −	NA =	30,000	NA		
7	15,000 +	(15,000) +	NA =		NA +		NA +	NA	NA −	NA =	NA	15,000	OA	
Bal.	51,300 +	3,000 +	NA =		6,000 +		20,000 +	28,300	48,000 −	17,000 =	31,000	51,300	NC	

	Asset, liability, and equity account balances carry forward								Rev. & exp. accts. are closed					
2014														
Bal.	51,300 +	3,000 +	NA =		6,000 +		20,000 +	28,300	NA −	NA =	NA	NA		
1	38,000 +	NA +	NA =		NA +		NA +	38,000	38,000 −	NA =	38,000	38,000	OA	
2	(12,000) +	NA +	12,000 =		NA +		NA +	NA	NA −	NA =	NA	(12,000)	OA	
3	2,000 +	(2,000) +	NA =		NA +		NA +	NA	NA −	NA =	NA	2,000	OA	
4	(21,000) +	NA +	NA =		NA +		NA +	(21,000)	NA −	21,000 =	(21,000)	(21,000)	OA	
5	(5,000) +	NA +	NA =		NA +		NA +	(5,000)	NA −	NA =	NA	(5,000)	FA	
6*	NA +	NA +	NA =		(6,000) +		NA +	6,000	6,000 −	NA =	6,000	NA		
7†	NA +	NA +	(9,000) =		NA +		NA +	(9,000)	NA −	9,000 =	(9,000)	NA		
Bal.	53,300 +	1,000 +	3,000 =		0 +		20,000 +	37,300	44,000 −	30,000 =	14,000	2,000	NC	

*Revenue is earned at the rate of $3,000 ($36,000 ÷ 12 months) per month. Revenue recognized in 2014 is $30,000 ($3,000 × 10 months). Revenue recognized in 2015 is $6,000 ($3,000 × 2 months).

†Rent expense is incurred at the rate of $1,000 ($12,000 ÷ 12 months) per month. Rent expense recognized in 2015 is $9,000 ($1,000 × 9 months).

Solutions to Requirements b–g

b. Gifford would report $48,000 of revenue in 2014 ($18,000 revenue on account plus $30,000 of the $36,000 of unearned revenue).

c. The cash inflow from customers in 2014 is $51,000 ($36,000 when the unearned revenue was received plus $15,000 collection of accounts receivable).

d. The December 31, 2014, balance sheet will report $6,000 of unearned revenue, which is the amount of the cash advance less the amount of revenue recognized in 2014 ($36,000 − $30,000). The December 31, 2015, unearned revenue balance is zero.

e. Since revenue and expense accounts are closed at the end of each accounting period, the beginning balances in these accounts are always zero.

f. Assets on the December 31, 2014, balance sheet are $54,300 [Gifford's cash at year-end plus the balance in accounts receivable ($51,300 + $3,000)].

g. Since all unearned revenue would be recognized before the financial statements were prepared at the end of 2015, there would be no liabilities on the 2015 balance sheet. In this case, all of the assets are committed to the investors.

KEY TERMS

Accounts receivable 51	Asset source transaction 50	Deferral 49	Recognition 49
Accrual 49	Asset use transaction 51	Expense 54	Revenue 64
Accrual accounting 49	Claims exchange	Matching concept 57	Salaries payable 52
Accrued expenses 52	transaction 53	Period costs 57	Unearned revenue 60
Adjusting entry 52	Conservatism 58	Prepaid items 59	Vertical statements
Asset exchange transaction 51	Cost 59	Realization 49	model 66

74   Chapter 2

QUESTIONS

1. What does accrual accounting attempt to accomplish?

2. Define *recognition*. How is it independent of collecting or paying cash?

3. What does the term *deferral* mean?

4. If cash is collected in advance of performing services, when is the associated revenue recognized?

5. What does the term *asset source transaction* mean?

6. What effect does the issue of common stock have on the accounting equation?

7. How does the recognition of revenue on account (accounts receivable) affect the income statement compared to its effect on the statement of cash flows?

8. Give an example of an asset source transaction. What is the effect of this transaction on the accounting equation?

9. When is revenue recognized under accrual accounting?

10. Give an example of an asset exchange transaction. What is the effect of this transaction on the accounting equation?

11. What is the effect on the right side of the accounting equation when cash is collected in advance of performing services?

12. What does the term *unearned revenue* mean?

13. What effect does expense recognition have on the accounting equation?

14. What does the term *claims exchange transaction* mean?

15. What type of transaction is a cash payment to creditors? How does this type of transaction affect the accounting equation?

16. When are expenses recognized under accrual accounting?

17. Why may net cash flow from operating activities on the cash flow statement be different from the amount of net income reported on the income statement?

18. What is the relationship between the income statement and changes in assets and liabilities?

19. How does net income affect the stockholders' claims on the business's assets?

20. What is the difference between a cost and an expense?

21. When does a cost become an expense? Do all costs become expenses?

22. How and when is the cost of the *supplies used* recognized in an accounting period?

23. What does the term *expense* mean?

24. What does the term *revenue* mean?

25. What is the purpose of the statement of changes in stockholders' equity?

26. What is the main purpose of the balance sheet?

27. Why is the balance sheet dated *as of* a specific date when the income statement, statement of changes in stockholders'

equity, and statement of cash flows are dated with the phrase *for the period ended*?

28. In what order are assets listed on the balance sheet?

29. What does the statement of cash flows explain?

30. What does the term *adjusting entry* mean? Give an example.

31. What types of accounts are closed at the end of the accounting period? Why is it necessary to close these accounts?

32. Give several examples of period costs.

33. Give an example of a cost that can be directly matched with the revenue produced by an accounting firm from preparing a tax return.

34. List and describe the four stages of the accounting cycle discussed in Chapter 2.

MULTIPLE-CHOICE QUESTIONS

Multiple-choice questions are provided on the text website at www.mhhe.com/edmondssurvey4e.

SECTION 1 EXERCISES

≡ connect |ACCOUNTING   **All applicable Exercises are available with McGraw-Hill's *Connect® Accounting.***

Where applicable in all exercises, round computations to the nearest dollar.

LO 2-1   **Exercise 2-1   *Effect of collecting accounts receivable on the accounting equation and financial statements***

Burke Company earned $12,000 of service revenue on account during 2014. The company collected $9,800 cash from accounts receivable during 2014.

Required

Based on this information alone, determine the following for Burke Company. (*Hint:* Record the events in general ledger accounts under an accounting equation before satisfying the requirements.)

a. The balance of the accounts receivable that Burke would report on the December 31, 2014, balance sheet.

b. The amount of net income that Burke would report on the 2014 income statement.

c. The amount of net cash flow from operating activities that would be reported on the 2014 statement of cash flows.
d. The amount of retained earnings that would be reported on the 2014 balance sheet.
e. Why are the answers to Requirements *b* and *c* different?

Exercise 2-2   *Effect of accrued expenses on the accounting equation and financial statements*   LO 2-2

During 2014, Crest Corporation earned $5,000 of cash revenue and accrued $3,000 of salaries expense.

Required

(*Hint:* Record the events in general ledger accounts under an accounting equation before satisfying the requirements.) Based on this information alone:

a. Prepare the December 31, 2014, balance sheet.
b. Determine the amount of net income that Crest would report on the 2014 income statement.
c. Determine the amount of net cash flow from operating activities that Crest would report on the 2014 statement of cash flows.
d. Why are the answers to Requirements *b* and *c* different?

Exercise 2-3   *Effect of accruals on the financial statements*   LO 2-1, 2-2

Coates Inc. experienced the following events in 2014, in its first year of operation:

1. Received $20,000 cash from the issue of common stock.
2. Performed services on account for $38,000.
3. Paid the utility expense of $2,500.
4. Collected $21,000 of the accounts receivable.
5. Recorded $15,000 of accrued salaries at the end of the year.
6. Paid a $2,000 cash dividend to the shareholders.

Required

a. Record the events in general ledger accounts under an accounting equation. In the last column of the table, provide appropriate account titles for the Retained Earnings amounts. The first transaction has been recorded as an example.

COATES INC. General Ledger Accounts							
Event	Assets		=	Liabilities	+	Stockholders' Equity		Acct. Titles for Ret. Earn.
	Cash	Accounts Receivable		Salaries Payable		Common Stock	Retained Earnings	
1.	20,000					20,000		

b. Prepare the income statement, statement of changes in stockholders' equity, balance sheet, and statement of cash flows for the 2014 accounting period.
c. Why is the amount of net income different from the amount of net cash flow from operating activities?

Exercise 2-4   *Effect of accounts receivable and accounts payable transactions on financial statements*   LO 2-1, 2-2

The following events apply to Brown and Birgin, a public accounting firm, for the 2014 accounting period:

1. Performed $96,000 of services for clients on account.
2. Performed $65,000 of services for cash.

3. Incurred $45,000 of other operating expenses on account.
4. Paid $26,000 cash to an employee for salary.
5. Collected $70,000 cash from accounts receivable.
6. Paid $38,000 cash on accounts payable.
7. Paid a $10,000 cash dividend to the stockholders.
8. Accrued salaries were $3,000 at the end of 2014.

Required

a. Show the effects of the events on the financial statements using a horizontal statements model like the following one. In the Cash Flow column, use OA to designate operating activity, IA for investment activity, FA for financing activity, and NC for net change in cash. Use NA to indicate the element is not affected by the event. The first event is recorded as an example.

Event No.	Assets			=	Liabilities			+	Equity							
	Cash	+	Accts. Rec.	=	Accts. Pay.	+	Sal. Pay	+	Ret. Earn.	Rev.	−	Exp.	=	Net Inc.	Cash Flow
1	NA	+	96,000	=	NA	+	NA	+	96,000	96,000	−	NA	=	96,000	NA

b. What is the amount of total assets at the end of 2014?
c. What is the balance of accounts receivable at the end of 2014?
d. What is the balance of accounts payable at the end of 2014?
e. What is the difference between accounts receivable and accounts payable?
f. What is net income for 2014?
g. What is the amount of net cash flow from operating activities for 2014?

LO 2-1, 2-2

Exercise 2-5   *Missing information related to accruals*

Panoramic Inc. had a beginning balance of $2,000 in its Accounts Receivable account. The ending balance of Accounts Receivable was $2,400. During the period, Panoramic recognized $40,000 of revenue on account. Panoramic's Salaries Payable account has a beginning balance of $1,300 and an ending balance of $900. During the period, the company recognized $35,000 of accrued salaries expense.

Required

a. Based on the information provided, determine the amount of net income.
b. Based on the information provided, determine the amount of net cash flow from operating activities.

LO 2-1, 2-2, 2-6

Exercise 2-6   *Effect of accruals on the financial statements*

Valmont Inc. experienced the following events in 2014, its first year of operation:

1. Received $50,000 cash from the issue of common stock.
2. Performed services on account for $67,000.
3. Paid a $5,000 cash dividend to the stockholders.
4. Collected $45,000 of the accounts receivable.
5. Paid $49,000 cash for other operating expenses.
6. Performed services for $10,000 cash.
7. Recognized $2,000 of accrued utilities expense at the end of the year.

Required

a. Identify the events that result in revenue or expense recognition.
b. Based on your response to Requirement *a*, determine the amount of net income reported on the 2014 income statement.
c. Identify the events that affect the statement of cash flows.

d. Based on your response to Requirement *c*, determine the amount of cash flow from operating activities reported on the 2014 statement of cash flows.

e. What is the before- and after-closing balance in the service revenue account? What other accounts would be closed at the end of the accounting cycle?

f. What is the balance of the retained earnings account that appears on the 2014 balance sheet?

Exercise 2-7   *Net income versus changes in cash*   LO 2-1, 2-2

In 2014, Zoe Inc. billed its customers $62,000 for services performed. The company collected $51,000 of the amount billed. Zoe incurred $39,000 of other operating expenses on account. Zoe paid $31,000 of the accounts payable. Zoe acquired $40,000 cash from the issue of common stock. The company invested $21,000 cash in the purchase of land.

Required

(*Hint:* Identify the six events described in the paragraph and record them in general ledger accounts under an accounting equation before attempting to answer the questions.) Use the preceding information to answer the following questions:

a. What amount of revenue will Zoe report on the 2014 income statement?

b. What amount of cash flow from revenue will Zoe report on the statement of cash flows?

c. What is the net income for the period?

d. What is the net cash flow from operating activities for the period?

e. Why is the amount of net income different from the net cash flow from operating activities for the period?

f. What is the amount of net cash flow from investing activities?

g. What is the amount of net cash flow from financing activities?

h. What amounts of total assets, liabilities, and equity will Zoe report on the year-end balance sheet?

SECTION 2 EXERCISES

Exercise 2-8   *Supplies and the financial statements model*   LO 2-2, 2-3

Copy Express Inc. began the 2014 accounting period with $9,000 cash, $5,000 of common stock, and $4,000 of retained earnings. Copy Express was affected by the following accounting events during 2014:

1. Purchased $9,500 of paper and other supplies on account.

2. Earned and collected $32,500 of cash revenue.

3. Paid $7,200 cash on accounts payable.

4. Adjusted the records to reflect the use of supplies. A physical count indicated that $1,700 of supplies was still on hand on December 31, 2014.

Required

a. Show the effects of the events on the financial statements using a horizontal statements model like the following one. In the Cash Flows column, use OA to designate operating activity, IA for investing activity, FA for financing activity, and NC for net change in cash. Use NA to indicate accounts not affected by the event. The beginning balances are entered in the following example:

Event No.	Assets			=	Liab.	+	Stockholders' Equity								
	Cash	+	Supplies	=	Accts. Pay.	+	Com. Stk.	+	Ret. Earn.	Rev.	−	Exp.	=	Net Inc.	Cash Flows
Beg. bal.	9,000	+	0	=	0	+	5,000	+	4,000	0	−	0	=	0	0

b. Explain the difference between the amount of net income and amount of net cash flow from operating activities.

78   Chapter 2

LO 2-3, 2-6

Exercise 2-9   *Supplies on financial statements*

Accounting Professionals Inc. experienced the following events in 2014, its first year of operation:

1. Performed services for $20,000 cash.
2. Purchased $4,000 of supplies on account.
3. A physical count on December 31, 2014, found that there was $1,000 of supplies on hand.

Required

Based on this information alone

a. Record the events under an accounting equation.
b. Prepare an income statement, balance sheet, and statement of cash flows for the 2014 accounting period.
c. What is the balance in the Supplies account as of January 1, 2015?
d. What is the balance in the Supplies Expense account as of January 1, 2015?

LO 2-3, 2-4

Exercise 2-10   *Asset versus expense*

A cost can be either an asset or an expense.

Required

a. Distinguish between a cost that is an asset and a cost that is an expense.
b. List three costs that are assets.
c. List three costs that are expenses.

LO 2-4

Exercise 2-11   *Prepaid items on financial statements*

Therapy Inc. experienced the following events in 2014, its first year of operation:

1. Performed counseling services for $18,000 cash.
2. On February 1, 2014, paid $12,000 cash to rent office space for the coming year.
3. Adjusted the accounts to reflect the amount of rent used during the year.

Required

Based on this information alone

a. Record the events under an accounting equation.
b. Prepare an income statement, balance sheet, and statement of cash flows for the 2014 accounting period.
c. Ignoring all other future events, what is the amount of rent expense that would be recognized in 2015?

LO 2-4, 2-6

Exercise 2-12   *Effect of an error on financial statements*

On June 1, 2014, Cole Corporation paid $8,400 to purchase a 24-month insurance policy. Assume that Cole records the purchase as an asset and that the books are closed on December 31.

Required

a. Show the purchase of the insurance policy and the related adjusting entry to recognize insurance expense in the accounting equation.
b. Assume that Cole Corporation failed to record the adjusting entry to reflect the expiration of insurance. How would the error affect the company's 2014 income statement and balance sheet?

LO 2-5

Exercise 2-13   *Unearned items on financial statements*

Interior Design Consultants (IDC) experienced the following events in 2014, its first year of operation:

1. On October 1, 2014, IDC collected $24,000 for consulting services it agreed to provide during the coming year.
2. Adjusted the accounts to reflect the amount of consulting service revenue recognized in 2014.

Required

Based on this information alone

a. Record the events under an accounting equation.
b. Prepare an income statement, balance sheet, and statement of cash flows for the 2014 accounting period.
c. Ignoring all other future events, what is the amount of service revenue that would be recognized in 2015?

Exercise 2-14   *Unearned revenue defined as a liability*   LO 2-5

Kim Wong received $800 in advance for tutoring fees when she agreed to help Joe Pratt with his introductory accounting course. Upon receiving the cash, Kim mentioned that she would have to record the transaction as a liability on her books. Joe asked, "Why a liability? You don't owe me any money, do you?"

Required

Respond to Joe's question regarding Wong's liability.

Exercise 2-15   *Supplies, unearned revenue, and the financial statements model*   LO 2-3, 2-5

Ross, Attorney at Law, experienced the following transactions in 2014, the first year of operations:

1. Purchased $1,500 of office supplies on account.
2. Accepted $36,000 on February 1, 2014, as a retainer for services to be performed evenly over the next 12 months.
3. Performed legal services for cash of $84,000.
4. Paid cash for salaries expense of $32,000.
5. Paid a cash dividend to the stockholders of $8,000,
6. Paid $1,200 of the amount due on accounts payable.
7. Determined that at the end of the accounting period, $150 of office supplies remained on hand.
8. On December 31, 2014, recognized the revenue that had been earned for services performed in accordance with Transaction 2.

Required

Show the effects of the events on the financial statements using a horizontal statements model like the following one. In the Cash Flow column, use the initials OA to designate operating activity, IA for investing activity, FA for financing activity, and NC for net change in cash. Use NA to indicate accounts not affected by the event. The first event has been recorded as an example.

Event No.	Assets		=	Liabilities			+	Stk. Equity	Rev.	−	Exp.	=	Net Inc.	Cash Flow
	Cash	+ Supplies	=	Accts. Pay.	+	Unearn. Rev.	+	Ret. Earn.						
1	NA	+ 1,500	=	1,500	+	NA	+	NA	NA	−	NA	=	NA	NA

Exercise 2-16   *Unearned revenue and the financial statements model*   LO 2-5

Ed Arnold started a personal financial planning business when he accepted $120,000 cash as advance payment for managing the financial assets of a large estate. Arnold agreed to manage the estate for a one-year period beginning May 1, 2014.

Required

a. Show the effects of the advance payment and revenue recognition on the 2014 financial statements using a horizontal statements model like the following one. In the Cash Flows column, use OA to designate operating activity, IA for investing activity, FA for financing activity, and NC for net change in cash. Use NA if the account is not affected.

Event	Assets	=	Liab.	+	Stockholders' Equity	Rev.	−	Exp.	=	Net Inc.	Cash Flows
	Cash	=	Unearn. Rev.	+	Ret. Earn.						

b. How much revenue would Ed recognize on the 2015 income statement?

c. What is the amount of cash flow from operating activities in 2015?

LO 2-4, 2-5

Exercise 2-17 *Prepaid vs. unearned, the entity concept*

On October 1, 2014, Caldonia Company paid East Alabama Rentals $4,800 for a 12-month lease on warehouse space.

Required

a. Record the deferral and the related December 31, 2014, adjustment for Caldonia Company in the accounting equation.

b. Record the deferral and the related December 31, 2014, adjustment for East Alabama Rentals in the accounting equation.

LO 2-1, 2-2, 2-3, 2-4, 2-5

Exercise 2-18 *Identifying deferral and accrual events*

Required

Identify each of the following events as an accrual, deferral, or neither:

a. Incurred other operating expenses on account.

b. Recorded expense for salaries owed to employees at the end of the accounting period.

c. Paid a cash dividend to the stockholders.

d. Paid cash to purchase supplies to be used over the next several months.

e. Paid cash to purchase land.

f. Provided services on account.

g. Collected accounts receivable.

h. Paid one year's rent in advance.

i. Paid cash for utilities expense.

j. Collected $2,400 in advance for services to be performed over the next 12 months.

k. Recorded interest revenue earned for the period.

LO 2-1, 2-2, 2-3, 2-4, 2-5

Exercise 2-19 *Revenue and expense recognition*

Required

a. Describe a revenue recognition event that results in an increase in assets.

b. Describe a revenue recognition event that results in a decrease in liabilities.

c. Describe an expense recognition event that results in an increase in liabilities.

d. Describe an expense recognition event that results in a decrease in assets.

LO 2-6

Exercise 2-20 *Closing entries*

Rollins Company's accounting records show an after-closing balance of $19,400 in its Retained Earnings account on December 31, 2014. During the 2014 accounting cycle, Rollins earned $15,100 of revenue, incurred $9,200 of expense, and paid $1,500 of dividends. Revenues and expenses were recognized evenly throughout the accounting period.

Required

a. Determine the balance in the Retained Earnings account as of January 1, 2015.

b. Determine the balance in the temporary accounts as of January 1, 2014.

c. Determine the after-closing balance in the Retained Earnings account as of December 31, 2013.

d. Determine the balance in the Retained Earnings account as of June 30, 2014.

LO 2-6

Exercise 2-21 *Adjusting the accounts*

Mikita Inc. experienced the following accounting events during its 2014 accounting period:

1. Paid cash to settle an account payable.

2. Collected a cash advance for services that will be provided during the coming year.

3. Paid a cash dividend to the stockholders.

4. Paid cash for a one-year lease to rent office space.

5. Collected cash from accounts receivable.

6. Recognized cash revenue.

7. Issued common stock.

8. Paid cash to purchase land.

9. Paid cash to purchase supplies.

10. Recognized operating expenses on account.

Required

a. Identify the events that would require a year-end adjusting entry.

b. Are adjusting or closing entries recorded first? Why?

Exercise 2-22   *Closing the accounts*

LO 2-6

The following information was drawn from the accounting records of Swanson Company as of December 31, 2014, before the temporary accounts had been closed. The Cash balance was $6,000, and Notes Payable amounted to $3,000. The company had revenues of $7,000 and expenses of $4,200. The company's Land account had a $4,000 balance. Dividends amounted to $1,000. There was $2,000 of common stock issued.

Required

a. Identify which accounts would be classified as permanent and which accounts would be classified as temporary.

b. Assuming that Swanson's beginning balance (as of January 1, 2014) in the Retained Earnings account was $5,200, determine its balance after the temporary accounts were closed at the end of 2014.

c. What amount of net income would Swanson Company report on its 2014 income statement?

d. Explain why the amount of net income differs from the amount of the ending Retained Earnings balance.

e. What are the balances in the revenue, expense, and dividend accounts on January 1, 2015?

Exercise 2-23   *Closing accounts and the accounting cycle*

LO 2-6

Required

a. Identify which of the following accounts are temporary (will be closed to Retained Earnings at the end of the year) and which are permanent:

   (1) Service Revenue

   (2) Dividends

   (3) Common Stock

   (4) Notes Payable

   (5) Cash

   (6) Rent Expense

   (7) Accounts Receivable

   (8) Utilities Expense

   (9) Prepaid Insurance

   (10) Retained Earnings

b. List and explain the four stages of the accounting cycle. Which stage must be first? Which stage is last?

Exercise 2-24   *Matching concept*

LO 2-7

Companies make sacrifices known as *expenses* to obtain benefits called *revenues*. The accurate measurement of net income requires that expenses be matched with revenues. In some circumstances, matching a particular expense directly with revenue is difficult or impossible. In these circumstances, the expense is matched with the period in which it is incurred.

Required

Distinguish the following items that could be matched directly with revenues from the items that would be classified as period expenses:

a. Sales commissions paid to employees.

b. Advertising expense.

c. Supplies.

d. The cost of land that has been sold.

LO 2-7

Exercise 2-25   *Classifying events on the statement of cash flows*

The following transactions pertain to the operations of Blair Company for 2014:

1. Acquired $30,000 cash from the issue of common stock.

2. Performed services for $12,000 cash.

3. Paid a $7,200 cash advance for a one-year contract to rent equipment.

4. Recognized $15,000 of accrued salary expense.

5. Accepted a $21,000 cash advance for services to be performed in the future.

6. Provided $60,000 of services on account.

7. Incurred $28,000 of other operating expenses on account.

8. Collected $51,000 cash from accounts receivable.

9. Paid a $5,000 cash dividend to the stockholders.

10. Paid $22,000 cash on accounts payable.

Required

a. Classify the cash flows from these transactions as operating activities (OA), investing activities (IA), or financing activities (FA). Use NA for transactions that do not affect the statement of cash flows.

b. Prepare a statement of cash flows. (There is no beginning cash balance.)

LO 2-7

Exercise 2-26   *Relationship of accounts to financial statements*

Required

Identify whether each of the following items would appear on the income statement (IS), statement of changes in stockholders' equity (SE), balance sheet (BS), or statement of cash flows (CF). Some items may appear on more than one statement; if so, identify all applicable statements. If an item would not appear on any financial statement, label it NA.

a. Consulting Revenue

b. Market Value of Land

c. Supplies Expense

d. Salaries Payable

e. Notes Payable

f. Ending Common Stock

g. Beginning Cash Balance

h. Prepaid Rent

i. Net Change in Cash

j. Land

k. Operating Expenses

l. Total Liabilities

m. "As of" Date Notation

n. Salaries Expense

o. Net Income

p. Service Revenue

q. Cash Flow from Operating Activities

r. Operating Income

s. Interest Receivable

t. Interest Revenue

u. Rent Expense

v. Salary Expense

w. Total Stockholders' Equity

x. Unearned Revenue

y. Cash Flow from Investing Activities

z. Insurance Expense

aa. Ending Retained Earnings

bb. Interest Revenue

cc. Supplies

dd. Beginning Retained Earnings

ee. Utilities Payable

ff. Cash Flow from Financing Activities

gg. Accounts Receivable

hh. Prepaid Insurance

ii. Ending Cash Balance

jj. Utilities Expense

kk. Accounts Payable

ll. Beginning Common Stock

mm. Dividends

nn. Total Assets

Exercise 2-27 *Identifying transaction type and effect on the financial statements* LO 2-7, 2-8

Required

Identify whether each of the following transactions is an asset source (AS), asset use (AU), asset exchange (AE), or claims exchange (CE). Also show the effects of the events on the financial statements using the horizontal statements model. Indicate whether the event increases (I), decreases (D), or does not affect (NA) each element of the financial statements. In the Cash Flows column, designate the cash flows as operating activities (OA), investing activities (IA), or financing activities (FA). The first two transactions have been recorded as examples.

Event No.	Type of Event	Assets	=	Liabilities	+	Common Stock	+	Retained Earnings	Rev.	−	Exp.	=	Net Inc.	Cash Flows
						Stockholders' Equity								
a	AE	I/D		NA		NA		NA	NA		NA		NA	D IA
b	AS	I		NA		I		NA	NA		NA		NA	I FA

a. Purchased land for cash.
b. Acquired cash from the issue of common stock.
c. Collected cash from accounts receivable.
d. Paid cash for operating expenses.
e. Recorded accrued salaries.
f. Purchased supplies on account.
g. Performed services on account.
h. Paid cash in advance for rent on office space.
i. Adjusted the books to record supplies used during the period.
j. Performed services for cash.
k. Paid cash for salaries accrued at the end of a prior period.
l. Paid a cash dividend to the stockholders.
m. Adjusted books to reflect the amount of prepaid rent expired during the period.
n. Incurred operating expenses on account.
o. Paid cash on accounts payable.
p. Received cash advance for services to be provided in the future.
q. Recorded accrued interest revenue earned at the end of the accounting period.

Exercise 2-28 *Effect of accounting events on the income statement and statement of cash flows* LO 2-1, 2-2, 2-3, 2-4, 2-5, 2-6, 2-7

Required

Explain how each of the following events or series of events and the related adjusting entry will affect the amount of *net income* and the amount of *cash flow from operating activities* reported on the year-end financial statements. Identify the direction of change (increase, decrease, or NA) and the amount of the change. Organize your answers according to the following table. The first event is recorded as an example. If an event does not have a related adjusting entry, record only the effects of the event.

Event	Net Income		Cash Flows from Operating Activities	
	Direction of Change	Amount of Change	Direction of Change	Amount of Change
a	NA	NA	NA	NA

a. Acquired $60,000 cash from the issue of common stock.
b. Earned $20,000 of revenue on account. Collected $15,000 cash from accounts receivable.
c. Paid $4,800 cash on October 1 to purchase a one-year insurance policy.

84   Chapter 2

d. Collected $12,000 in advance for services to be performed in the future. The contract called for services to start on August 1 and to continue for one year.

e. Accrued salaries amounting to $5,000.

f. Sold land that cost $15,000 for $15,000 cash.

g. Provided services for $9,200 cash.

h. Purchased $2,000 of supplies on account. Paid $1,500 cash on accounts payable. The ending balance in the Supplies account, after adjustment, was $800.

i. Paid cash for other operating expenses of $2,200.

LO 2-8

Exercise 2-29   *Transactions that affect the elements of financial statements*

Required

Give an example of a transaction that will

a. Increase an asset and decrease another asset (asset exchange event).

b. Increase an asset and increase a liability (asset source event).

c. Decrease an asset and decrease a liability (asset use event).

d. Decrease an asset and decrease equity (asset use event).

e. Increase a liability and decrease equity (claims exchange event).

f. Increase an asset and increase equity (asset source event).

g. Decrease a liability and increase equity (claims exchange event).

LO 2-8

Exercise 2-30   *Identifying source, use, and exchange transactions*

Required

Indicate whether each of the following transactions is an asset source (AS), asset use (AU), asset exchange (AE), or claims exchange (CE) transaction:

a. Performed services for clients on account.

b. Paid cash for salary expense.

c. Acquired cash from the issue of common stock.

d. Incurred other operating expenses on account.

e. Performed services for cash.

f. Paid cash on accounts payable.

g. Collected cash from accounts receivable.

h. Paid a cash dividend to the stockholders.

i. Received cash for services to be performed in the future.

j. Purchased land with cash.

LO 2-8

Exercise 2-31   *Identifying asset source, use, and exchange transactions*

Required

a. Name an asset use transaction that will affect the income statement.

b. Name an asset use transaction that will *not* affect the income statement.

c. Name an asset exchange transaction that will *not* affect the statement of cash flows.

d. Name an asset exchange transaction that will affect the statement of cash flows.

e. Name an asset source transaction that will *not* affect the income statement.

SECTIONS 1 AND 2 PROBLEMS

connect |ACCOUNTING   **All applicable Problems are available with McGraw-Hill's *Connect® Accounting.***

LO 2-1, 2-2, 2-3, 2-4, 2-5

CHECK FIGURES
Net Income: $15,200
Ending Cash Balance: $24,600

Problem 2-32   *Recording events in a horizontal statements model*

The following events pertain to James Cleaning Company:

1. Acquired $15,000 cash from the issue of common stock.

2. Provided services for $6,000 cash.

3. Provided $18,000 of services on account.
4. Collected $11,000 cash from the account receivable created in Event 3.
5. Paid $1,400 cash to purchase supplies.
6. Had $100 of supplies on hand at the end of the accounting period.
7. Received $3,600 cash in advance for services to be performed in the future.
8. Performed one-half of the services agreed to in Event 7.
9. Paid $6,500 for salaries expense.
10. Incurred $2,800 of other operating expenses on account.
11. Paid $2,100 cash on the account payable created in Event 10.
12. Paid a $1,000 cash dividend to the stockholders.

Required

Show the effects of the events on the financial statements using a horizontal statements model like the following one. In the Cash Flows column, use the letters OA to designate operating activity, IA for investing activity, FA for financing activity, and NC for net change in cash. Use NA to indicate accounts not affected by the event. The first event is recorded as an example.

Event No.		Assets			=	Liabilities			+	Stockholders' Equity							
	Cash	+	Accts. Rec.	+ Supp.	=	Accts. Pay.	+	Unearn. Rev.	+	Com. Stk.	+	Ret. Earn.	Rev.	− Exp.	=	Net Inc.	Cash Flows
1	15,000	+	NA	+ NA	=	NA	+	NA	+	15,000	+	NA	NA	− NA	=	NA	15,000 FA

Problem 2-33 *Effect of adjusting entries on the accounting equation*

LO 2-1, 2-2, 2-3, 2-4, 2-5, 2-6

Required

Each of the following independent events requires a year-end adjusting entry. Show how each event and its related adjusting entry affect the accounting equation. Assume a December 31 closing date. The first event is recorded as an example.

CHECK FIGURE
b. adjustment amount: $2,200

	Total Assets					Stockholders Equity		
Event/ Adjustment	Cash	+	Other Assets	=	Liabilities	+	Common Stock	+	Retained Earnings
a	−6,000		+6,000		NA		NA		NA
Adj.	NA		−4,500		NA		NA		−4,500

a. Paid $6,000 cash in advance on April 1 for a one-year insurance policy.
b. Purchased $2,400 of supplies on account. At year's end, $200 of supplies remained on hand.
c. Paid $7,200 cash in advance on March 1 for a one-year lease on office space.
d. Received an $18,000 cash advance for a contract to provide services in the future. The contract required a one-year commitment starting September 1.

Problem 2-34 *Closing the accounts*

LO 2-6

The following selected accounts and account balances were taken from the records of Bates Company. Except as otherwise indicated, all balances are as of December 31, 2014, before the closing entries were recorded.

Cash received from common stock issued during 2013	$ 4,500
Cash	10,500
Revenue	18,000
Salary expense	13,000
Cash flow from operating activities	4,500
Notes payable	6,000
Utility expense	1,800
Dividends	1,000
Cash flow from financing activities	5,000
Rent expense	1,600
Land	25,000
Retained earnings, January 1, 2014	19,700
Common stock, December 31, 2014	20,000

Required

a. Prepare the income statement Black would include in its 2014 annual report.

b. Identify the accounts that should be closed to the Retained Earnings account.

c. Determine the Retained Earnings account balance at December 31, 2014. Identify the reasons for the difference between net income and the ending balance in Retained Earnings.

d. What are the balances in the Revenue, Expense, and Dividend accounts on January 1, 2015? Explain.

LO 2-1, 2-2, 2-3, 2-4, 2-5, 2-6

Problem 2-35 *Effect of events on financial statements*

Davis Company had the following balances in its accounting records as of December 31, 2013:

Assets		Liabilities and Equity	
Cash	$ 60,000	Accounts Payable	$ 32,000
Accounts Receivable	45,000	Common Stock	60,000
Land	35,000	Retained Earnings	48,000
Totals	$140,000		$140,000

The following accounting events apply to Davis for 2014:

Jan.   1   Acquired an additional $30,000 cash from the issue of common stock.
April 1   Paid $7,200 cash in advance for a one-year lease for office space.
June   1   Paid a $5,000 cash dividend to the stockholders.
July   1   Purchased additional land that cost $40,000 cash.
Aug.   1   Made a cash payment on accounts payable of $21,000.
Sept. 1   Received $9,600 cash in advance as a retainer for services to be performed monthly during the next eight months.
Sept. 30   Sold land for $20,000 cash that had originally cost $20,000.
Oct.   1   Purchased $1,200 of supplies on account.
Dec. 31   Earned $75,000 of service revenue on account during the year.
      31   Received $62,000 cash collections from accounts receivable.
      31   Incurred $27,000 other operating expenses on account during the year.
      31   Recognized accrued salaries expense of $18,000.
      31   Had $100 of supplies on hand at the end of the period.
      31   The land purchased on July 1 had a market value of $56,000.
      31   Recognized $120 of accrued interest revenue.

Required

Based on the preceding information for Davis Company answer the following questions. All questions pertain to the 2014 financial statements. (*Hint:* Record the events in general ledger accounts under an accounting equation before answering the questions.)

a. What two additional adjusting entries need to be made at the end of the year?

b. What amount would be reported for land on the balance sheet?

c. What amount of net cash flow from operating activities would be reported on the statement of cash flows?

d. What amount of rent expense would be reported in the income statement?

e. What amount of total liabilities would be reported on the balance sheet?

f. What amount of supplies expense would be reported on the income statement?

g. What amount of unearned revenue would be reported on the balance sheet?

h. What amount of net cash flow from investing activities would be reported on the statement of cash flows?

i. What amount of total expenses would be reported on the income statement?

j. What total amount of service revenue would be reported on the income statement?

k. What amount of cash flows from financing activities would be reported on the statement of cash flows?

l. What amount of net income would be reported on the income statement?

m. What amount of retained earnings would be reported on the balance sheet?

Problem 2-36   *Identifying and arranging elements on financial statements*

LO 2-7

The following accounts and balances were drawn from the records of Dawkins Company at December 31, 2014:

CHECK FIGURES
a. Total Assets $91,700
b. Net Income $20,000

Cash	$22,100	Accounts receivable	$21,000
Land	43,000	Cash flow from operating act.	8,600
Insurance expense	2,500	Beginning retained earnings	47,200
Dividends	5,000	Beginning common stock	5,500
Prepaid insurance	3,500	Service revenue	86,000
Accounts payable	15,000	Cash flow from financing act.	9,000
Supplies	2,100	Ending common stock	14,500
Supplies expense	1,000	Cash flow from investing act.	(6,000)
Rent expense	3,500	Other operating expenses	59,000

Required

Use the accounts and balances from Dawkins Company to construct an income statement, statement of changes in stockholders' equity, balance sheet, and statement of cash flows (show only totals for each activity on the statement of cash flows).

Problem 2-37   *Missing information in financial statements*

LO 2-7

Required

Fill in the blanks (indicated by the alphabetic letters in parentheses) in the following financial statements. Assume the company started operations January 1, 2014, and all transactions involve cash.

	For the Years		
	2014	2015	2016
Income Statements			
Revenue	$ 400	$ 500	$ 800
Expense	(250)	(l)	(425)
Net income	$ (a)	$ 100	$ 375
Statement of Changes in Stockholders' Equity			
Beginning common stock	$ 0	$ (m)	$ 9,100
Plus: Common stock issued	(b)	1,100	310
Ending common stock	$8,000	9,100	(s)
Beginning retained earnings	0	25	75
Plus: Net income	(c)	100	375
Less: Dividends	(d)	(50)	(150)
Ending retained earnings	25	(n)	300
Total stockholders' equity	$ (e)	$ 9,175	$ (t)

continued

Balance Sheets					
Assets					
Cash	$	(f)	$	(o)	$ (u)
Land		0		(p)	2,500
Total assets		$11,000		$11,650	$10,550
Liabilities	$	(g)	$	(q)	$ 840
Stockholders' equity					
Common stock		(h)		(r)	9,410
Retained earnings		(i)		75	300
Total stockholders' equity		8,025		9,175	9,710
Total liabilities and stockholders' equity		$11,000		$11,650	$10,550

Statements of Cash Flows					
Cash flows from operating activities					
Cash receipts from customers	$	(j)	$	500	$ (v)
Cash payments for expenses		(k)		(400)	(w)
Net cash flows from operating activities		150		100	375
Cash flows from investing activities					
Cash payments for land		0		(5,000)	0
Cash receipt from sale of land		0		0	2,500
Net cash flows from investing activities		0		(5,000)	2,500
Cash flows from financing activities					
Cash receipts from borrowed funds		2,975		0	0
Cash payments to reduce debt		0		(500)	(x)
Cash receipts from stock issue		8,000		1,100	(y)
Cash payments for dividends		(125)		(50)	(z)
Net cash flows from financing activities		10,850		550	(1,475)
Net change in cash		11,000		(4,350)	1,400
Plus: Beginning cash balance		0		11,000	6,650
Ending cash balance		$11,000		$ 6,650	$ 8,050

LO 2-1, 2-2, 2-3, 2-4, 2-5,
2-6, 2-7, 2-8

Problem 2-38 *Events for two complete accounting cycles*

Alabama Service Company was formed on January 1, 2014.

Events Affecting the 2014 Accounting Period

1. Acquired cash of $60,000 from the issue of common stock.
2. Purchased $1,200 of supplies on account.
3. Purchased land that cost $18,000 cash.
4. Paid $800 cash to settle accounts payable created in Event 2.
5. Recognized revenue on account of $42,000.
6. Paid $21,000 cash for other operating expenses.
7. Collected $38,000 cash from accounts receivable.

Information for 2014 Adjusting Entries

8. Recognized accrued salaries of $3,200 on December 31, 2014.
9. Had $200 of supplies on hand at the end of the accounting period.

Events Affecting the 2015 Accounting Period

1. Acquired an additional $20,000 cash from the issue of common stock.
2. Paid $3,200 cash to settle the salaries payable obligation.

3. Paid $3,600 cash in advance for a lease on office facilities.
4. Sold land that had cost $15,000 for $15,000 cash.
5. Received $4,800 cash in advance for services to be performed in the future.
6. Purchased $1,000 of supplies on account during the year.
7. Provided services on account of $32,000.
8. Collected $33,000 cash from accounts receivable.
9. Paid a cash dividend of $5,000 to the stockholders.
10. Paid other operating expenses of $19,500.

Information for 2015 Adjusting Entries

11. The advance payment for rental of the office facilities (see Event 3) was made on March 1 for a one-year lease term.
12. The cash advance for services to be provided in the future was collected on October 1 (see Event 5). The one-year contract started October 1.
13. Had $300 of supplies on hand at the end of the period.
14. Recognized accrued salaries of $3,900 at the end of the accounting period.
15. Recognized $400 of accrued interest revenue.

Required

a. Identify each event affecting the 2014 and 2015 accounting periods as asset source (AS), asset use (AU), asset exchange (AE), or claims exchange (CE). Record the effects of each event under the appropriate general ledger account headings of the accounting equation.

b. Prepare an income statement, statement of changes in stockholders' equity, balance sheet, and statement of cash flows for 2014 and 2015, using the vertical statements model.

ANALYZE, THINK, COMMUNICATE

ATC 2-1 Business Applications Case *Understanding real-world annual reports*

Required

Use the Target Corporation's Form 10-K to answer the following questions related to Target's 2012 fiscal year (year ended February 2, 2013). Target's Form 10-K is available on the company's website or through the SEC's EDGAR database. Appendix A provides instructions for using the EDGAR database.

a. Which accounts on Target's balance sheet are accrual-type accounts?
b. Which accounts on Target's balance sheet are deferral-type accounts?
c. Compare Target's 2012 *net earnings* (the year ended February 2, 2013) to its 2012 *cash provided by operating activities.* Which is larger?
d. First, compare Target's 2011 net income to its 2012 net income. Next, compare Target's 2011 cash provided by operating activities to its 2012 cash provided by operating activities. Which changed the most from 2011 to 2012, net earnings or cash provided by operating activities?

ATC 2-2 Group Assignment *Financial reporting and market evaluation*

The following financial highlights were drawn from the 2012 annual reports of Exxon Mobil Corporation and Apple Inc.

	Exxon	Apple
Revenue	$482.3 Billion	$156.5 Billion
Net income	$ 44.9 Billion	$ 41.7 Billion
Cash and short-term investments	$ 38.1 Billion	$ 29.1 Billion

90   Chapter 2

Even so, as of February 28, 2013, Wall Street valued Exxon Mobil at $402.9 billion and Apple at $418.6 billion.

Divide the class into groups of four or five students.

Required

Have the members of each group reach a consensus response for each of the following tasks. Each group should elect a spokesperson to represent the group.

Group Tasks

(1) Determine the amount of expenses incurred by each company.
(2) Comment on how the concept of conservatism applies to the information presented in this case.
(3) Speculate as to why investors would be willing to pay more for Apple than Exxon Mobil.

ATC 2-3 Research Assignment *Identifying accruals and deferrals at Netflix*

This chapter defined and discussed accrual and deferral transactions. Complete the requirements below using the most recent financial statements available on the Internet for Netflix, Inc. Obtain the statements by following the steps below. (Be aware that the formatting of the company's website may have changed since these instructions were written.)

1. Go to www.netflix.com.
2. Click on "Investor Relations," which is at the bottom of the page in very small print.
3. Click on the "Annual Reports and Proxies" link at the left side of the page.
4. Click on the "20xx Annual Report." Use the pdf. version of the annual report.
5. Find the company's balance sheet and complete the requirements below. In recent years this has been shown toward the end of the Form 10-K section of the company's annual report, on page 48. The "Index" near the beginning of the report can help you locate the financial statements.

Required

a. Make a list of all the accounts on the balance sheet that you believe are accrual-type accounts.
b. Make a list of all the accounts on the balance sheet that you believe are deferral-type accounts.

ATC 2-4 Writing Assignment *Conservatism and Matching*

Glenn's Cleaning Services Company is experiencing cash flow problems and needs a loan. Glenn has a friend who is willing to lend him the money he needs provided she can be convinced that he will be able to repay the debt. Glenn has assured his friend that his business is viable, but his friend has asked to see the company's financial statements. Glenn's accountant produced the following financial statements.

Income Statement		Balance Sheet	
Service Revenue	$ 38,000	Assets	$85,000
Operating Expenses	(70,000)	Liabilities	$35,000
Net Loss	$(32,000)	Stockholders' Equity	
		Common Stock	82,000
		Retained Earnings	(32,000)
		Total Liabilities and	
		Stockholders' Equity	$85,000

Glenn made the following adjustments to these statements before showing them to his friend. He recorded $82,000 of revenue on account from Barrymore Manufacturing Company for a contract to clean its headquarters office building that was still being negotiated for the next month. Barrymore had scheduled a meeting to sign a contract the following week, so Glenn was sure that he would get the job. Barrymore was a reputable company, and Glenn was confident that he could ultimately collect the $82,000. Also, he subtracted $30,000 of accrued salaries expense and the corresponding liability. He reasoned that since he had not paid the employees, he had not incurred any expense.

Required

a. Reconstruct the income statement and balance sheet as they would appear after Glenn's adjustments.

b. Write a brief memo explaining how Glenn's treatment of the expected revenue from Barrymore violated the conservatism concept.

c. Write a brief memo explaining how Glenn's treatment of the accrued salaries expense violates the matching concept.

Accounting for Merchandising Businesses

LEARNING OBJECTIVES

After you have mastered the material in this chapter, you will be able to:

LO 3-1   Record and report on inventory transactions using the perpetual system.

LO 3-2   Show how transportation costs, cash discounts, returns and allowances, and inventory shrinkage affect financial statements.

LO 3-3   Explain how gains, losses, and other items are shown on a multistep income statement.

LO 3-4   Determine the amount of net sales.

LO 3-5   Use common size financial statements to evaluate managerial performance.

LO 3-6   Identify the primary features of the periodic inventory system. (Appendix)

 Video lectures and accompanying self-assessment quizzes are available for all learning objectives through McGraw-Hill Connect® Accounting.

CHAPTER OPENING

Previous chapters have discussed accounting for service businesses. These businesses obtain revenue by providing some kind of service such as medical or legal advice to their customers. Other examples of service companies include dry cleaning companies, maid service companies, and car washes. This chapter introduces accounting practices for merchandising businesses. **Merchandising businesses** generate revenue by selling goods. They buy the merchandise they sell from companies called suppliers. The goods purchased for resale are called **merchandise inventory.** Merchandising businesses include **retail companies** (companies that sell goods to the final consumer) and **wholesale companies** (companies that sell to other businesses). Sears, JCPenney, Target, and Sam's Club are real-world merchandising businesses.

The Curious Accountant

Richard recently purchased a new Ford automobile from a dealer near his home. When he told his friend Jeff that he was able to purchase the car for $1,000 less than the sticker price, Jeff told Richard he had gotten a lousy deal. "Everybody knows there is a huge markup on cars," Jeff said. "You could have gotten a much lower price if you'd shopped around."

Richard responded, "If there is such a big profit margin on cars, why did so many of the car manufacturers get into financial trouble?" Jeff told him that he was confusing the maker of the car with the dealer. Jeff argued that although the manufacturers may not have high profit margins, the dealers do, and told him again that he had paid too much.

Exhibit 3.1 presents the income statements for AutoNation, Inc., and Ford Motor Company. Based on these statements, do you think either of these guys is correct? For example, if you pay $20,000 for a vehicle from a dealership operated by AutoNation, the largest auto retailer in the United States, how much did the car cost the company? Also, how much did the car cost the Ford Motor Company to manufacture? (Answers on page 110.)

EXHIBIT 3.1	Comparative Income Statements

AUTONATION, INC.
Consolidated Statements of Operations (partial)
For the Years Ended December 31,
(In millions, except per share data)

	2012	2011	2010
Revenue:			
New vehicle	$ 8,906.9	$ 7,498.9	$ 6,669.1
Used vehicle	3,714.7	3,512.8	3,116.1
Parts and service	2,399.2	2,293.1	2,209.1
Finance and insurance, net	571.2	474.5	418.9
Other	76.8	53.0	47.8
Total revenue	15,668.8	13,832.3	12,461.0
Cost of Sales:			
New vehicle	8,327.4	6,951.2	6,217.9
Used vehicle	3,415.4	3,228.0	2,849.4
Parts and service	1,391.3	1,323.0	1,245.9
Other	48.3	26.1	20.3
Total cost of sales	13,182.4	11,528.3	10,333.5
Gross Profit:			
New vehicle	579.5	547.7	451.2
Used vehicle	299.3	284.8	266.7
Parts and service	1,007.9	970.1	963.2
Finance and insurance	571.2	474.5	418.9
Other	28.5	26.9	27.5
Total gross profit	2,486.4	2,304.0	2,127.5
Selling, general, and administrative expenses	1,749.5	1,649.4	1,552.1
Depreciation and amortization	87.3	83.7	76.8
Franchise rights impairment	4.2	—	—
Other expenses (income), net	0.1	(1.1)	2.0
Operating income	645.3	572.0	496.6
Floorplan interest expense	(45.5)	(42.7)	(42.5)
Other interest expense	(86.9)	(66.0)	(56.1)
Loss on debt extinguishment	—	(2.2)	(19.6)
Interest income	0.3	0.7	1.4
Other gains (losses), net	3.6	(0.5)	1.5
Income (loss) from continuing operations before income taxes	516.8	461.3	381.3
Income tax provision	199.5	177.1	146.0
Net income from continuing operations	317.3	284.2	235.3
Loss from discontinued operations, net of income taxes	(0.9)	(2.8)	(8.7)
Net income	$ 316.4	$ 281.4	$ 226.6

FORD MOTOR COMPANY AND SUBSIDIARIES
Consolidated Statement of Operations (Partial)
For the Years Ended December 31, 2012, 2011, and 2010
(in millions, except per share amounts)

	2012	2011	2010
Sales and revenues			
Automotive sales	$126,567	$128,168	$119,280
Financial Services revenues	7,685	8,096	9,674
Total sales and revenues	134,252	136,264	128,954

(continued)

	2012	2011	2010
Costs and expenses			
Automotive cost of sales	112,578	113,345	104,451
Selling, administrative, and other expenses	12,182	11,578	11,909
Interest expense	3,115	3,614	4,345
Financial Services provision for credit and insurance losses	86	(33)	(216)
Total costs and expenses	127,961	128,504	120,489
Automotive interest expense	(713)	(817)	(1,807)
Automotive interest income, expense, and other non-operating income/(expense), net	1,185	825	(362)
Financial Services other income/(loss), net	369	413	315
Equity in net income/(loss) of affiliated companies	588	500	538
Income before income taxes	7,720	8,681	7,149
Provision for/(Benefit from) income taxes	2,056	(11,541)	592
Net income	5,664	20,222	6,557
Less: Income/(Loss) attributable to noncontrolling interests	(1)	9	(4)
Net income/attributable to Ford Motor Company	$ 5,665	$ 20,213	$ 6,561

PRODUCT COSTS VERSUS SELLING AND ADMINISTRATIVE COSTS

Companies report inventory costs on the balance sheet in the asset account Merchandise Inventory. All costs incurred to acquire merchandise and ready it for sale are included in the inventory account. Examples of inventory costs include the price of goods purchased, shipping and handling costs, transit insurance, and storage costs. Since inventory items are referred to as products, inventory costs are frequently called **product costs.**

Costs that are not included in inventory are usually called **selling and administrative costs.** Examples of selling and administrative costs include advertising, administrative salaries, sales commissions, insurance, and interest. Since selling and administrative costs are usually recognized as expenses *in the period* in which they are incurred, they are sometimes called **period costs.** In contrast, product costs are expensed when inventory is sold regardless of when it was purchased. In other words, product costs are matched directly with sales revenue, while selling and administrative costs are matched with the period in which they are incurred.

ALLOCATING INVENTORY COST BETWEEN ASSET AND EXPENSE ACCOUNTS

The cost of inventory that is available for sale during a specific accounting period is determined as follows.

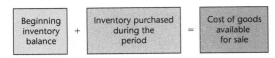

The **cost of goods available for sale** is allocated between the asset account Merchandise Inventory and an expense account called **Cost of Goods Sold.** The cost of inventory items that have not been sold (Merchandise Inventory) is reported as an asset on the balance sheet, and the cost of the items sold (Cost of Goods Sold) is expensed on the income statement. This allocation is depicted graphically as follows.

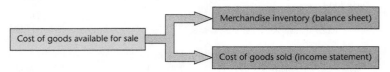

The difference between the sales revenue and the cost of goods sold is called **gross margin** or **gross profit.** The selling and administrative expenses (period costs) are subtracted from gross margin to obtain the net income.

Exhibit 3.1 displays income statements from the annual reports of AutoNation and Ford. For each company, review the most current income statement and determine the amount of gross margin. You should find a gross profit of $2,486.4 for AutoNation and a gross margin of $6,291 ($134,252 − $127,961) for Ford.

PERPETUAL INVENTORY SYSTEM

LO 3-1

Record and report on inventory transactions using the perpetual system.

Most modern companies maintain their inventory records using the **perpetual inventory system,** so-called because the inventory account is adjusted perpetually (continually) throughout the accounting period. Each time merchandise is purchased, the inventory account is increased; each time it is sold, the inventory account is decreased. The following illustration demonstrates the basic features of the perpetual inventory system.

June Gardener loved plants and grew them with such remarkable success that she decided to open a small retail plant store. She started June's Plant Shop (JPS) on January 1, 2014. The following discussion explains and illustrates the effects of the five events the company experienced during its first year of operation.

Effects of 2014 Events on Financial Statements

EVENT 1   JPS acquired $15,000 cash by issuing common stock.

This event is an asset source transaction. It increases both assets (cash) and stockholders' equity (common stock). The income statement is not affected. The statement of cash flows reflects an inflow from financing activities. These effects are shown here.

Assets			=	Liab.	+	Stockholders' Equity							
Cash	+ Inventory	+ Land	=	Accts. Pay.	+	Com. Stk.	+ Ret. Earn.	Rev.	− Exp.	= Net Inc.	Cash Flow
15,000	+ NA	+ NA	=	NA	+	15,000	+ NA	NA	− NA	= NA	15,000 FA

EVENT 2   JPS purchased merchandise inventory for $14,000 cash.

This event is an asset exchange transaction. One asset, cash, decreases and another asset, merchandise inventory, increases; total assets remain unchanged. Because product costs are expensed when inventory is sold, not when it is purchased, the event does not affect the income statement. The cash outflow, however, is reported in the operating activities section of the statement of cash flows. These effects are illustrated below.

Assets			=	Liab.	+	Stockholders' Equity							
Cash	+ Inventory	+ Land	=	Accts. Pay.	+	Com. Stk.	+ Ret. Earn.	Rev.	− Exp.	= Net Inc.	Cash Flow
(14,000)	+ 14,000	+ NA	=	NA	+	NA	+ NA	NA	− NA	= NA	(14,000) OA

EVENT 3A　JPS recognized sales revenue from selling inventory for $12,000 cash.

The revenue recognition is the first part of a two-part transaction. The *sales part* represents a source of assets (cash increases from earning sales revenue). Both assets (cash) and stockholders' equity (retained earnings) increase. Sales revenue on the income statement increases. The $12,000 cash inflow is reported in the operating activities section of the statement of cash flows. These effects are shown in the following financial statements model.

Assets			=	Liab.	+	Stockholders' Equity							
Cash	+ Inventory	+ Land	=	Accts. Pay.	+	Com. Stk.	+ Ret. Earn.	Rev.	− Exp.	= Net Inc.	Cash Flow
12,000	+ NA	+ NA	=	NA	+	NA	+ 12,000	12,000	− NA	= 12,000	12,000 OA

EVENT 3B　JPS recognized $8,000 of cost of goods sold.

The expense recognition is the second part of the two-part transaction. The *expense part* represents a use of assets. Both assets (merchandise inventory) and stockholders' equity (retained earnings) decrease. An expense account, Cost of Goods Sold, is reported on the income statement. This part of the transaction does not affect the statement of cash flows. A cash outflow occurred when the goods were bought, not when they were sold. These effects are shown here.

Assets			=	Liab.	+	Stockholders' Equity							
Cash	+ Inventory	+ Land	=	Accts. Pay.	+	Com. Stk.	+ Ret. Earn.	Rev.	− Exp.	= Net Inc.	Cash Flow
NA	+ (8,000)	+ NA	=	NA	+	NA	+ (8,000)	NA	− 8,000	= (8,000)	NA

EVENT 4　JPS paid $1,000 cash for selling and administrative expenses.

This event is an asset use transaction. The payment decreases both assets (cash) and stockholders' equity (retained earnings). The increase in selling and administrative expenses decreases net income. The $1,000 cash payment is reported in the operating activities section of the statement of cash flows. These effects are illustrated below.

Assets			=	Liab.	+	Stockholders' Equity							
Cash	+ Inventory	+ Land	=	Accts. Pay.	+	Com. Stk.	+ Ret. Earn.	Rev.	− Exp.	= Net Inc.	Cash Flow
(1,000)	+ NA	+ NA	=	NA	+	NA	+ (1,000)	NA	− 1,000	= (1,000)	(1,000) OA

EVENT 5　JPS paid $5,500 cash to purchase land for a place to locate a future store.

Buying the land increases the Land account and decreases the Cash account on the balance sheet. The income statement is not affected. The statement of cash flow shows a cash outflow to purchase land in the investing activities section of the statement of cash flows. These effects are shown below.

Assets			=	Liab.	+	Stockholders' Equity							
Cash	+ Inventory	+ Land	=	Accts. Pay.	+	Com. Stk.	+ Ret. Earn.	Rev.	− Exp.	= Net Inc.	Cash Flow
(5,500)	+ NA	+ 5,500	=	NA	+	NA	+ NA	NA	− NA	= NA	(5,500) IA

98   Chapter 3

Financial Statements for 2014

JPS's financial statements for 2014 are shown in Exhibit 3.2. JPS had no beginning inventory in its first year, so the cost of merchandise inventory available for sale was $14,000 (the amount of inventory purchased during the period). Recall that JPS must allocate the *Cost of Goods (Inventory) Available for Sale* between the *Cost of Goods Sold* ($8,000) and the ending balance ($6,000) in the *Merchandise Inventory* account. The cost of goods sold is reported as an expense on the income statement and the ending balance of merchandise inventory is reported as an asset on the balance sheet. The difference between the sales revenue ($12,000) and the cost of goods sold ($8,000) is labeled *gross margin* ($4,000) on the income statement.

☑ CHECK YOURSELF 3.1

Phambroom Company began 2014 with $35,600 in its Inventory account. During the year, it purchased inventory costing $356,800 and sold inventory that had cost $360,000 for $520,000. Based on this information alone, determine (1) the inventory balance as of December 31, 2014, and (2) the amount of gross margin Phambroom would report on its 2014 income statement.

Answer

1. $35,600 Beginning inventory + $356,800 Purchases = $392,400 Goods available for sale
   $392,400 Goods available for sale − $360,000 Cost of goods sold = $32,400 Ending inventory

2. Sales revenue − Cost of goods sold = Gross margin
   $520,000 − $360,000 = $160,000

Transportation Cost, Purchase Returns and Allowances, and Cash Discounts Related to Inventory Purchases

LO 3-2

 Show how transportation costs, cash discounts, returns and allowances, and inventory shrinkage affect financial statements.

Purchasing inventory often involves: (1) incurring transportation costs, (2) returning inventory or receiving purchase allowances (cost reductions), and (3) taking cash discounts (also cost reductions). During its second accounting cycle, JPS encountered these kinds of events. The final account balances at the end of the 2014 fiscal year become the beginning balances for 2015: Cash, $6,500; Merchandise Inventory, $6,000; Land, 5,500; Common Stock, $15,000; and Retained Earnings, $3,000.

Effects of 2015 Events on Financial Statements

JPS experienced the following events during its 2015 accounting period. The effects of each of these events are explained and illustrated in the following discussion.

EVENT 1　JPS borrowed $4,000 cash by issuing a note payable.

JPS borrowed the money to enable it to purchase a plot of land for a site for a store it planned to build in the near future. Borrowing the money increases the Cash account and the Note Payable account on the balance sheet. The income statement is not affected. The statement of cash flow shows a cash flow from financing activities. These effects are shown below.

		Assets			=	Liabilities		+	Stockholders' Equity						
Cash	+	Accts. Rec.	+ Inventory	+ Land	=	Accts. Pay.	+ Notes Pay.	+	Com. Stk.	+ Ret. Earn.	Rev.	− Exp.	= Net Inc.		Cash Flow
4,000	+	NA	+ NA	+ NA	=	NA	+ 4,000	+	NA	+ NA	NA	− NA	= NA		4,000 FA

EVENT 2　JPS purchased on account merchandise inventory with a list price of $11,000.

The inventory purchase increases both assets (merchandise inventory) and liabilities (accounts payable) on the balance sheet. The income statement is not affected until later, when inventory is sold. Since the inventory was purchased on account, there was no cash outflow. These effects are shown here.

		Assets			=	Liab.		+	Stockholders' Equity						
Cash	+	Accts. Rec.	+ Inventory	+ Land	=	Accts. Pay.	+ Notes Pay.	+	Com. Stk.	+ Ret. Earn.	Rev.	− Exp.	= Net Inc.		Cash Flow
NA	+	NA	+ 11,000	+ NA	=	11,000	+ NA	+	NA	+ NA	NA	− NA	= NA		NA

Accounting for Purchase Returns and Allowances

EVENT 3　JPS returned some of the inventory purchased in Event 2. The list price of the returned merchandise was $1,000.

To promote customer satisfaction, many businesses allow customers to return goods for reasons such as wrong size, wrong color, wrong design, or even simply because the purchaser changed his mind. The effect of a purchase return is the *opposite* of the original purchase. For JPS the **purchase return** decreases both assets (merchandise inventory) and liabilities (accounts payable). There is no effect on either the income statement or the statement of cash flows. These effects are shown below.

		Assets			=	Liab.		+	Stockholders' Equity						
Cash	+	Accts. Rec.	+ Inventory	+ Land	=	Accts. Pay.	+ Notes Pay.	+	Com. Stk.	+ Ret. Earn.	Rev.	− Exp.	= Net Inc.		Cash Flow
NA	+	NA	+ (1,000)	+ NA	=	(1,000)	+ NA	+	NA	+ NA	NA	− NA	= NA		NA

Sometimes dissatisfied buyers will agree to keep goods instead of returning them if the seller offers to reduce the price. Such reductions are called allowances. **Purchase allowances** affect the financial statements the same way purchase returns do.

Purchase Discounts

EVENT 4 JPS received a cash discount on goods purchased in Event 2. The credit terms were 2/10, n/30.

To encourage buyers to pay promptly, sellers sometimes offer **cash discounts.** To illustrate, assume JPS purchased the inventory in Event 2 under terms **2/10, n/30** (two-ten, net thirty). These terms mean the seller will allow a 2 percent cash discount if the purchaser pays cash within 10 days from the date of purchase. The amount not paid within the first 10 days is due at the end of 30 days from date of purchase. Recall that JPS returned $1,000 of the inventory purchased in Event 1 leaving a $10,000 balance ($11,000 list price − $1,000 purchase return). If JPS pays for the inventory within 10 days, the amount of the discount is $200 ($10,000 × .02).

When cash discounts are applied to purchases they are called **purchases discounts.** When they are applied to sales, they are called sales discounts. Sales discounts will be discussed later in the chapter. A *purchase discount* reduces the cost of the inventory and the associated account payable on the balance sheet. A purchase discount does not directly affect the income statement or the statement of cash flow. These effects are shown here.

	Assets				=	Liab.			+	Stockholders' Equity							
Cash	+	Accts. Rec.	+	Inventory	+	Land	=	Accts. Pay.	+	Notes Pay.	+	Com. Stk.	+	Ret. Earn.	Rev. − Exp. = Net Inc.	Cash Flow
NA	+	NA	+	(200)	+	NA	=	(200)	+	NA	+	NA	+	NA	NA − NA = NA	NA

If JPS paid the account payable after 10 days, there would be no purchase discount. In this case the balances in the Inventory and Account Payable accounts would remain at $10,000.

EVENT 5 JPS paid the $9,800 balance due on the account payable.

The remaining balance in the accounts payable is $9,800 ($10,000 list price − $200 purchase discount). Paying cash to settle the liability reduces cash and accounts payable on the balance sheet. The income statement is not affected. The cash outflow is shown in the operating section of the statement of cash flows. These effects are shown below.

	Assets				=	Liab.			+	Stockholders' Equity							
Cash	+	Accts. Rec.	+	Inventory	+	Land	=	Accts. Pay.	+	Notes Pay.	+	Com. Stk.	+	Ret. Earn.	Rev. − Exp. = Net Inc.	Cash Flow
(9,800)	+	NA	+	NA	+	NA	=	(9,800)	+	NA	+	NA	+	NA	NA − NA = NA	(9,800) OA

The Cost of Financing Inventory

Suppose you buy inventory this month and sell it next month. Where do you get the money to pay for the inventory at the time you buy it? One way to finance the purchase is to buy it on account and withhold payment until the last day of the term for the account payable. For example, suppose you buy inventory under terms 2/10, net/30. Under these circumstances you could delay payment for 30 days after the day of purchase. This way you may be able to collect enough money from the inventory you sell

REALITY BYTES

Many real-world companies have found it more effective to impose a penalty for late payment than to use a cash discount to encourage early payment. The invoice from Arley Water Works is an example of the penalty strategy. Notice that the amount due, if paid by the due date, is $18.14. A $1.88 late charge is imposed if the bill is paid after the due date. The $1.88 late charge is in fact interest. If Arley Water Works collects the payment after the due date, the utility will receive cash of $20.02. The collection will increase cash ($20.02), reduce accounts receivable ($18.14), and increase interest revenue ($1.88).

to pay for the inventory you purchased. Refusing the discount allows you the time needed to generate the cash necessary to pay off the liability (account payable). Unfortunately, this is usually a very expensive way to finance the purchase of inventory.

While the amount of a cash discount may appear small, the discount period is short. Consider the terms 2/10, net/30. Since you can pay on the tenth day and still receive the discount, you obtain financing for only 20 days (30-day full credit term − 10-day discount term). In other words, you must forgo a 2 percent discount to obtain a loan with a 20-day term. What is the size of the discount in annual terms? The answer is determined by the following formula.

Annual rate = Discount rate × (365 days ÷ term of the loan)

Annual rate = 2% × (365 ÷ 20)

Annual rate = 36.5%

This means that a 2 percent discount rate for 20 days is equivalent to a 36.5 percent annual rate of interest. So, if you do not have the money to pay the account payable, but can borrow money from a bank at less than 36.5 percent annual interest, you should borrow the money and pay off the account payable within the discount period.

Accounting for Transportation Costs

EVENT 6 The shipping terms for the inventory purchased in Event 2 were FOB shipping point. JPS paid the freight company $300 cash for delivering the merchandise.

The terms **FOB shipping point** and **FOB destination** identify whether the buyer or the seller is responsible for transportation costs. If goods are delivered FOB shipping point, the buyer is responsible for the freight cost. If goods are delivered FOB destination, the seller is responsible. When the buyer is responsible, the freight cost is called **transportation-in.** When the seller is responsible, the cost is called **transportation-out.** The following table summarizes freight cost terms.

Responsible Party	Buyer	Seller
Freight terms	FOB shipping point	FOB destination
Account title	Merchandise inventory	Transportation-out

Event 6 indicates the inventory was delivered FOB shipping point, so JPS (the buyer) is responsible for the $300 freight cost. Since incurring transportation-in costs is necessary to obtain inventory, these costs are added to the inventory account. The freight cost increases one asset account (Merchandise Inventory) and decreases another asset account (Cash). The income statement is not affected by this transaction because transportation-in costs are not expensed when they are incurred. Instead they are expensed as part of *cost of goods sold* when the inventory is sold. However, the cash paid for transportation-in costs is reported as an outflow in the operating activities section of the statement of cash flows. The effects of *transportation-in costs* are shown here.

		Assets			=	Liab.		+	Stockholders' Equity						
Cash	+	Accts. Rec.	+ Inventory	+ Land	=	Accts. Pay.	+ Notes Pay.	+	Com. Stk.	+ Ret. Earn.	Rev.	− Exp.	= Net Inc.	Cash Flow	
(300)	+	NA	+ 300	+ NA	=	NA	+ NA	+	NA	+ NA	NA	− NA	= NA	(300)	OA

EVENT 7A   JPS recognized $24,750 of revenue on the cash sale of merchandise that cost $11,500.

The sale increases assets (cash) and stockholders' equity (retained earnings). The revenue recognition increases net income. The $24,750 cash inflow from the sale is reported in the operating activities section of the statement of cash flows. These effects are shown below.

		Assets			=	Liab.		+	Stockholders' Equity						
Cash	+	Accts. Rec.	+ Inventory	+ Land	=	Accts. Pay.	+ Notes Pay.	+	Com. Stk.	+ Ret. Earn.	Rev.	− Exp.	= Net Inc.	Cash Flow	
24,750	+	NA	+ NA	+ NA	=	NA	+ NA	+	NA	+ 24,750	24,750	− NA	= 24,750	24,750	OA

EVENT 7B   JPS recognized $11,500 of cost of goods sold.

When goods are sold, the product cost—*including a proportionate share of transportation-in and adjustments for purchase returns and allowances*—is transferred from the Merchandise Inventory account to the expense account, Cost of Goods Sold. Recognizing cost of goods sold decreases both assets (merchandise inventory) and stockholders' equity (retained earnings). The expense recognition for cost of goods sold decreases net income. Cash flow is not affected. These effects are shown here.

		Assets			=	Liab.		+	Stockholders' Equity						
Cash	+	Accts. Rec.	+ Inventory	+ Land	=	Accts. Pay.	+ Notes Pay.	+	Com. Stk.	+ Ret. Earn.	Rev.	− Exp.	= Net Inc.	Cash Flow	
NA	+	NA	+ (11,500)	+ NA	=	NA	+ NA	+	NA	+ (11,500)	NA	− 11,500	= (11,500)	NA	

EVENT 8   JPS paid $450 cash for freight costs on inventory delivered to customers.

Assume the merchandise sold in Event 7A was shipped FOB destination. Also assume JPS paid the freight cost in cash. FOB destination means the seller is responsible for the freight cost, which is called transportation-out. Transportation-out is reported on the income statement as an operating expense in the section below gross margin. The cost of freight on goods shipped to customers is incurred *after* the goods are sold. It is not part of the costs to obtain goods or ready them for sale. Recognizing the expense of transportation-out reduces assets (cash) and stockholders' equity (retained earnings). Operating expenses increase and net income decreases. The cash outflow is reported in the operating activities section of the statement of cash flows. These effects are shown below.

Assets				=	Liab.			+	Stockholders' Equity							
Cash +	Accts. Rec. +	Inventory +	Land =		Accts. Pay. +	Notes Pay. +			Com. Stk. +	Ret. Earn.		Rev. −	Exp. =	Net Inc.		Cash Flow
(450) +	NA +	NA +	NA =		NA +	NA +			NA +	(450)		NA −	450 =	(450)		(450) OA

If the terms had been FOB shipping point, the customer would have been responsible for the transportation cost and JPS would not have recorded an expense.

EVENT 9   JPS paid $5,000 cash for selling and administrative expenses.

The effect on the balance sheet is to decrease both assets (cash) and stockholders' equity (retained earnings). Recognizing the selling and administrative expenses decreases net income. The $5,000 cash outflow is reported in the operating activities section of the statement of cash flows. These effects are shown below.

Assets				=	Liab.			+	Stockholders' Equity							
Cash +	Accts. Rec. +	Inventory +	Land =		Accts. Pay. +	Notes Pay. +			Com. Stk. +	Ret. Earn.		Rev. −	Exp. =	Net Inc.		Cash Flow
(5,000) +	NA +	NA +	NA =		NA +	NA +			NA +	(5,000)		NA −	5,000 =	(5,000)		(5,000) OA

EVENT 10   JPS paid $360 cash for interest expense on the note described in Event 1.

The effect on the balance sheet is to decrease both assets (cash) and stockholders' equity (retained earnings). Recognizing the interest expense decreases net income. The $360 cash outflow is reported in the operating activities section of the statement of cash flows. These effects are shown below.

Assets				=	Liab.			+	Stockholders' Equity							
Cash +	Accts. Rec. +	Inventory +	Land =		Accts. Pay. +	Notes Pay. +			Com. Stk. +	Ret. Earn.		Rev. −	Exp. =	Net Inc.		Cash Flow
(360) +	NA +	NA +	NA =		NA +	NA +			NA +	(360)		NA −	360 =	(360)		(360) OA

Adjustment for Lost, Damaged, or Stolen Inventory

EVENT 11 JPS took a physical count of its inventory and found $4,100 of inventory on hand.

Most merchandising companies experience some level of inventory **shrinkage,** a term that reflects decreases in inventory for reasons other than sales to customers. Inventory may be stolen by shoplifters, damaged by customers or employees, or even simply lost or misplaced. Since the *perpetual* inventory system is designed to record purchases and sales of inventory as they occur, the balance in the merchandise inventory account represents the amount of inventory that *should* be on hand at any given time. For example, based on the previous transactions the book balance of the JPS's Inventory account can be computed as follows:

Beginning balance	$ 6,000
Purchases	11,000
Purchase returns	(1,000)
Purchase discounts	(200)
Transportation in	300
Goods available for sale	16,100
Cost of goods sold	(11,500)
Ending balance	$ 4,600

Assume that JPS takes a physical count of its inventory on hand and finds that it has only $4,100 of inventory. By comparing the $4,600 book balance in the Merchandise Inventory account with the $4,100 of actual inventory counted, we determine that the Company has experienced $500 of shrinkage. Under these circumstances JPS must make an adjusting entry to write down the Inventory account so the amount reported on the financial statements agrees with the amount actually on hand at the end of the period. The write-down decreases both assets (inventory) and stockholders' equity (retained earnings). The write-down increases expenses and decreases net income. Cash flow is not affected. The effects on the statements are as follows.

Assets	=	Liab.	+	Equity	Rev.	−	Exp.	=	Net Inc.	Cash Flow
(500)	=	NA	+	(500)	NA	−	500	=	(500)	NA

Theoretically, inventory losses are operating expenses. However, because such losses are normally immaterial in amount, they are usually added to cost of goods sold for external reporting purposes.

REALITY BYTES

"Closed for Inventory Count" is a sign you frequently see on retail stores sometime during the month of January. Even if companies use a perpetual inventory system, the amount of inventory on hand may be unknown because of lost, damaged, or stolen goods. The only way to determine the amount of inventory on hand is to count it. Why count it in January? Christmas shoppers and many after-Christmas sales shoppers are satiated by mid-January, leaving the stores low on both merchandise and customers. Accordingly, stores have less merchandise to count and "lost sales" are minimized during January. Companies that do not depend on seasonal sales (e.g., a plumbing supplies wholesale business) may choose to count inventory at some other time during the year. Counting inventory is not a revenue-generating activity; it is a necessary evil that should be conducted when it least disrupts operations.

RECOGNIZING GAINS AND LOSSES

EVENT 12   JPS sold the land that had cost $5,500 for $6,200 cash.

When JPS sells merchandise inventory for more than it cost, the difference between the sales revenue and the cost of the goods sold is called the *gross margin*. In contrast, when JPS sells land for more than it cost, the difference between the sales price and the cost of the land is called a **gain.** Why is one called *gross margin* and the other a *gain*? The terms are used to alert financial statement users to the fact that the nature of the underlying transactions is different.

JPS's primary business is selling inventory, not land. The term *gain* indicates profit resulting from transactions that are not likely to regularly recur. Similarly, had the land sold for less than cost the difference would have been labeled **loss** rather than expense. This term also indicates the underlying transaction is not from normal, recurring operating activities. Gains and losses are shown separately on the income statement to communicate the expectation that they are nonrecurring.

The presentation of gains and losses in the income statement is discussed in more detail in a later section of the chapter. At this point note that the sale increases cash, decreases land, and increases retained earnings on the balance sheet. The income statement shows a gain on the sale of land and net income increases. The $6,200 cash inflow is shown as an investing activity on the statement of cash flows. These effects are shown below:

LO 3-3

Explain how gains, losses, and other items are shown on a multistep income statement.

Assets				=	Liab.		+	Stockholders' Equity							
Cash	+ Accts. Rec.	+ Inventory	+ Land	=	Accts. Pay.	+ Notes Pay.	+	Com. Stk.	+ Ret. Earn.	Gain	− Exp.	= Net Inc.		Cash Flow	
6,200	+ NA	+ NA	+ (5,500)	=	NA	+ NA	+	NA	+ 700	700	− NA	= 700		6,200	IA

✓ CHECK YOURSELF 3.2

Tsang Company purchased $32,000 of inventory on account with payment terms of 2/10, n/30 and freight terms FOB shipping point. Freight costs were $1,100. Tsang obtained a $2,000 purchase allowance because the inventory was damaged upon arrival. Tsang paid for the inventory within the discount period. Based on this information alone, determine the balance in the inventory account.

Answer

List price of inventory	$32,000
Plus: Transportation-in costs	1,100
Less: Purchase returns and allowances	(2,000)
Less: Purchase discount [($32,000 − $2,000) × .02]	(600)
Balance in inventory account	$30,500

Multistep Income Statement

JPS's 2015 income statement is shown in Exhibit 3.3. Observe the form of this statement carefully. It is more informative than one which simply subtracts expenses from revenues. First, it compares sales revenue with the cost of the goods that were sold to produce that revenue. The difference between the sales revenue and the cost of goods sold is called *gross margin.* Next, the operating expenses are subtracted from the gross margin to determine the *operating income.* **Operating income** is the amount of income that is generated from the normal recurring operations of a business. Items that are not expected to recur on a regular basis are subtracted from the operating income to determine the amount of *net income.*[1]

EXHIBIT 3.3	
JUNE'S PLANT SHOP	
Income Statement	
For the Period Ended December 31, 2015	
Sales revenue	$ 24,750
Cost of goods sold*	(12,000)
Gross margin	12,750
Less: Operating expenses	
Selling and administrative expense	(5,000)
Transportation-out	(450)
Operating income	7,300
Nonoperating items	
Interest expense	(360)
Gain on the sale of land	700
Net income	$ 7,640

*$11,500 inventory sold + $500 shrinkage.

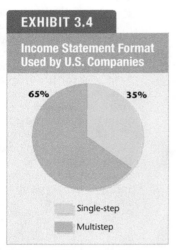

EXHIBIT 3.4

Income Statement Format Used by U.S. Companies

65%   35%

☐ Single-step

☐ Multistep

Data Source: AICPA, *Accounting Trends and Techniques.*

Income statements that show these additional relationships are called **multistep income statements.** Income statements that display a single comparison of all revenues minus all expenses are called **single-step income statements.** To this point in the text we have shown only single-step income statements to promote simplicity. However, the multistep form is used more frequently in practice. Exhibit 3.4 shows the percentage of companies that use the multistep versus the single-step format. Go to Exhibit 3.1 and identify the company that presents its income statement in the multistep format. You should have identified AutoNation as the company using the multistep format. Ford's statement is shown in the single-step format.

Note that interest is reported as a *nonoperating* item on the income statement in Exhibit 3.3. In contrast, it is shown in the *operating* activities section of the statement of cash flows in Exhibit 3.6. When the FASB issued Statement of Financial Accounting Standard (SFAS) 95, it required interest to be reported in the operating activities section of the statement of cash flows. There was no corresponding requirement for the treatment of interest on the income statement. Prior to SFAS 95, interest was considered to be a nonoperating item. Most companies continued to report interest as a nonoperating item on their income statements even though they were required to change how it was reported on the statement of cash flows. As a result, there is frequent inconsistency in the way interest is reported on the two financial statements.

Also note that while the gain on the sale of land is shown on the income statement, it is not included in the operating activities section of the statement of cash flows. Since the gain is a nonoperating item, it is included in the cash inflow from the sale of land shown in the investing activities section. In this case the full cash inflow from the sale of

[1]Revenue and expense items with special characteristics may be classified as discontinued or extraordinary items. These items are shown separately just above net income regardless of whether a company uses a single-step or multistep format. Further discussion of these items is beyond the scope of this text.

EXHIBIT 3.5

JUNE'S PLANT SHOP
Balance Sheet
As of December 31, 2015

Assets		
Cash	$25,540	
Merchandise inventory	4,100	
Total assets		$29,640
Liabilities		
Notes payable		$ 4,000
Stockholders' equity		
Common stock	$15,000	
Retained earnings	10,640	
Total stockholders' equity		25,640
Total liabilities and stockholders' equity		$29,640

EXHIBIT 3.6

JUNE'S PLANT SHOP
Statement of Cash Flows
For the Period Ended December 31, 2015

Operating activities		
Inflow from customers	$ 24,750	
Outflow for inventory*	(10,100)	
Outflow for transportation-out	(450)	
Outflow for selling and administrative expense	(5,000)	
Outflow for interest expense	(360)	
Net cash outflow for operating activities		$ 8,840
Investing activities		
Inflow from sale of land		6,200
Financing activities		
Inflow from issue of note payable		4,000
Net change in cash		19,040
Plus beginning cash balance		6,500
Ending cash balance		$25,540

*Net cost on inventory $9,800 + transportation-in $300 = $10,100

land ($6,200) is shown in the investing activities section of the statement of cash flows in Exhibit 3.6. Finally, note that the ending inventory balance is shown on the balance sheet in Exhibit 3.5.

EVENTS AFFECTING SALES

To this point we assumed JPS did not offer cash discounts to its customers. However, sales, as well as purchases of inventory, can be affected by returns, allowances, and discounts. **Sales discounts** are price reductions offered by sellers to encourage buyers to pay promptly. To illustrate, assume JPS engaged in the following selected events during January 2016.

LO 3-4

 Determine the amount of net sales.

EVENT 1A JPS sold on account merchandise with a list price of $8,500. Payment terms were 1/10, n/30. The merchandise had cost JPS $4,000.

The sale increases both assets (accounts receivable) and shareholders' equity (retained earnings). Recognizing revenue increases net income. The statement of cash flows is not affected. The effects on the financial statements follow.

Assets					=	Liab.	+	Stockholders' Equity				Rev.	−	Exp.	=	Net Inc.	Cash Flow
Cash	+	Accts. Rec.	+	Inventory	=	Note Pay.	+	Com. Stk.	+	Retained Earnings							
NA	+	8,500	+	NA	=	NA	+	NA	+	8,500		8,500	−	NA	=	8,500	NA

EVENT 1B JPS recognized $4,000 of cost of goods sold.

Recognizing the expense decreases assets (merchandise inventory) and stockholders' equity (retained earnings). Cost of goods sold increases and net income decreases. Cash flow is not affected. The effects on the financial statements follow.

Assets					=	Liab.	+	Stockholders' Equity				Rev.	−	Exp.	=	Net Inc.	Cash Flow
Cash	+	Accts. Rec.	+	Inventory	=	Note Pay.	+	Com. Stk.	+	Retained Earnings							
NA	+	NA	+	(4,000)	=	NA	+	NA	+	(4,000)		NA	−	4,000	=	(4,000)	NA

Accounting for Sales Returns and Allowances

EVENT 2A A customer from Event 1A returned inventory with a $1,000 list price. The merchandise had cost JPS $450.

The sales return decreases both assets (accounts receivable) and stockholders' equity (retained earnings) on the balance sheet. Sales and net income decrease. Cash flow is not affected. The effects on the financial statements follow.

Assets					=	Liab.	+	Stockholders' Equity				Rev.	−	Exp.	=	Net Inc.	Cash Flow
Cash	+	Accts. Rec.	+	Inventory	=	Note Pay.	+	Com. Stk.	+	Retained Earnings							
NA	+	(1,000)	+	NA	=	NA	+	NA	+	(1,000)		(1,000)	−	NA	=	(1,000)	NA

EVENT 2B The cost of the goods ($450) is returned to the inventory account.

Since JPS got the inventory back, the sales return increases both assets (merchandise inventory) and stockholders' equity (retained earnings). The expense (cost of goods sold) decreases and net income increases. Cash flow is not affected. The effects on the financial statements follow.

Assets					=	Liab.	+	Stockholders' Equity				Rev.	−	Exp.	=	Net Inc.	Cash Flow
Cash	+	Accts. Rec.	+	Inventory	=	Note Pay.	+	Com. Stk.	+	Retained Earnings							
NA	+	NA	+	450	=	NA	+	NA	+	450		NA	−	(450)	=	450	NA

Accounting for Sales Discounts

EVENT 3 JPS collected the balance of the accounts receivable generated in Event 1A. Recall the goods were sold under terms 1/10, net/30.

ALTERNATIVE 1 The collection occurs before the discount period has expired (within 10 days from the date of the sale).

JPS would give the buyer a 1 percent discount. Given the original sales amount of $8,500 and a sales return of $1,000, the amount of the discount is $75 [($8,500 − $1,000) × .01]. The sales discount reduces the amount of accounts receivable and retained earnings on the balance sheet. It also reduces the amount of revenue and the net income shown on the balance sheet. It does not affect the statement of cash flows. The effects on the financial statements follow.

	Assets			=	Liab.	+	Stockholders' Equity			Rev.	−	Exp.	=	Net Inc.	Cash Flow
Cash	+	Accts. Rec.	+	Inventory =	Note Pay.	+	Com. Stk.	+	Retained Earnings						
NA	+	(75)	+	NA =	NA	+	NA	+	(75)	(75)	−	NA	=	(75)	NA

The balance due on the account receivable is $7,425 ($8,500 original sales − $1,000 sales return − $75 discount). The collection increases the Cash account and decreases the Accounts Receivable account. The income statement is not affected. The cash inflow is shown in the operating activities section of the statement of cash flows. The effects on the financial statements follow.

	Assets			=	Liab.	+	Stockholders' Equity			Rev.	−	Exp.	=	Net Inc.	Cash Flow
Cash	+	Accts. Rec.	+	Inventory =	Accts. Pay.	+	Com. Stk.	+	Retained Earnings						
7,425	+	(7,425)	+	NA =	NA	+	NA	+	NA	NA	−	NA	=	NA	7,425 OA

Net Sales

The gross amount of sales minus **sales returns and allowance** and sales discounts is commonly called **net sales.** Companies are not required by GAAP to show sales returns and allowance and sales discount on their income statement. Indeed, most companies show only the amount of *net sales* on the income statement. In this case the net sales amount to $7,425 ($8,500 original sales − $1,000 sales return − $75 discount).

ALTERNATIVE 2 The collection occurs after the discount period has expired (after 10 days from the date of the sale).

Under these circumstances there is no sales discount. The amount collected is $7,500 ($8,500 original sale − $1,000 sales return). Net sales shown on the income statement would also be $7,500.

COMMON SIZE FINANCIAL STATEMENTS

How good is a $1,000,000 increase in net income? The answer is not clear because there is no indication as to the size of the company. A million dollar increase may be excellent for a small company but would be virtually meaningless for a company the size of Exxon. To enable meaningful comparisons analysts prepare **common size financial statements.** Common size statements display information in percentages as well as absolute dollar amounts.

To illustrate, we expand the income statements for JPS to include percentages. The results are shown in Exhibit 3.7. The percentage data are computed by defining net

LO 3-5

Use common size financial statements to evaluate managerial performance.

110   Chapter 3

Answers to The Curious Accountant

As data from the income statement for AutoNation show, automobile dealers do not have big markups on the cars they sell. The new vehicles the company sold for $8,906.9 million in 2012 cost the company $8,327.4 to purchase, resulting in a gross margin of $579.5, or 6.5 percent. In other words, if you bought an "average" car from AutoNation for $20,000, the company's gross profit on it was only $1,300 ($20,000 × .065), meaning it paid Ford $18,700 ($20,000 − $1,300). Furthermore, the company still had to pay other expenses besides its cost of goods sold. In 2012, only 2.0 percent of each dollar of AutoNation's sales was net profit ($316.4 ÷ $15,668.8) Remember, the amount shown for sales on AutoNation's income statement is based on what customers actually paid for the cars the company sold, not the "sticker price."

Meanwhile, if Ford sold the car to AutoNation for $18,700, it earned a gross margin on the sale of 11.1 percent, or $2,076 [$13,989 ÷ $126,567 = 11.1%; ($126,567 − $112,578 = $13,989)] [$18,700 × .111 = $2.076]. Like AutoNation, Ford still had other expenses to pay for besides the cost of goods sold. In 2012 Ford earned 4.3 percent of net profit on each dollar of sales ($5,665 ÷ $134,252).

Most consumers significantly overestimate the profit margins of the companies from which they buy goods. Retailers, especially, operate with small profit margins, so inventory management is very important to their success.

sales as the base figure, or 100 percent. The other amounts on the statements are then shown as a percentage of net sales. For example, the *cost of goods sold percentage* is the dollar amount of *cost of goods sold* divided by the dollar amount of *net sales*, which produces a percentage of 66.7 percent ($8,000 ÷ $12,000) for 2014 and 48.5 percent ($12,000 ÷ $24,750) for 2015. Other income statement items are computed using the same approach.

| EXHIBIT 3.7 | Common Size Financial Statements |

JUNE'S PLANT SHOP
Income Statement
For the Period Ended

	2014		2015	
Net sales*	$12,000	100.0%	$24,750	100.0%
Cost of goods sold	(8,000)	66.7	(12,000)	48.5
Gross margin	4,000	33.3	12,750	51.5
Less: Operating expenses				
Selling and administrative expense	(1,000)	8.3	(5,000)	20.2
Transportation-out			(450)	1.8
Operating income	3,000	25.0	7,300	29.5
Nonoperating items				
Interest expense			(360)	(1.5)
Gain on the sale of land			700	2.8
Net income	$ 3,000	25.0	$ 7,640	30.9

*Since JPS did not offer sales discounts or have sales returns and allowances during 2014 or 2015, the amount of sales revenue is equal to the amount of net sales. We use the term *net sales* here because it is more commonly used in business practice. Percentages do not add exactly because they have been rounded.

These common size statements provide insight into the company's operating strategy. For example, assume JPS relocated its store in an upscale mall in early 2015. Management realized that the company would have to pay more for operating expenses but believed those expenses could be offset by charging significantly higher prices. The common size income statement confirms that the company's goals were accomplished. Note that the gross margin increased from 33.3 percent of sales to 51.5 percent, confirming that the company was able to increase prices. Also, note that operating expenses increased. Selling and administrative expense increased from 8.3 percent of sales to 20.2 percent. Also, the company experienced a new expense, transportation out, for delivering merchandise to its customers. These increases in expenses confirm the fact that JPS is paying more for rental space and providing additional services to its customers. The common size statements, therefore, support the conclusion that JPS's increase in net income from $3,000 to $7,640 was a result of management's new operating strategy. As a side note, the new operating strategy may also explain why JPS sold its land in late 2015. Considering the success the company experienced at the new location, there was no motive to build a store on the land.

A Look Back

Merchandising companies earn profits by selling inventory at prices that are higher than the cost paid for the goods. Merchandising companies include *retail companies* (companies that sell goods to the final consumer) and *wholesale companies* (companies that sell to other merchandising companies). The products sold by merchandising companies are called *inventory*. The costs to purchase inventory, to receive it, and to ready it for sale are *product costs,* which are first accumulated in an inventory account (balance sheet asset account) and then recognized as cost of goods sold (income statement expense account) in the period in which goods are sold. Purchases and sales of inventory can be recorded continually as goods are bought and sold (perpetual system) or at the end of the accounting period (periodic system, discussed in the chapter appendix).

Accounting for inventory includes the treatment of cash discounts, transportation costs, and returns and allowances. The cost of inventory is the list price less any purchase returns and allowances and purchase discounts, plus transportation-in costs. The cost of freight paid to acquire inventory (*transportation-in*) is considered a product cost. The cost of freight paid to deliver inventory to customers (*transportation-out*) is a selling expense. *Sales returns and allowances* and *sales discounts* are subtracted from sales revenue to determine the amount of *net sales* reported on the income statement. Purchase returns and allowances reduce product cost. Theoretically, the cost of lost, damaged, or stolen inventory is an operating expense. However, because these costs are usually immaterial in amount they are typically included as part of cost of goods sold on the income statement.

Some companies use a *multistep income statement* which reports product costs separately from selling and administrative costs. Cost of goods sold is subtracted from sales revenue to determine *gross margin. S*elling and administrative expenses are subtracted from gross margin to determine income from operations. Other companies report income using a *single-step format* in which the cost of goods sold is listed along with selling and administrative items in a single expense category that is subtracted in total from revenue to determine income from operations.

Managers of merchandising businesses operate in a highly competitive environment. They must manage company operations carefully to remain profitable. *Common size financial statements* (statements presented on a percentage basis) and ratio analysis are useful monitoring tools. Common size financial statements permit ready comparisons among different-size companies. Although a $1 million increase in sales may be good for a small company and bad for a large company, a 10 percent increase can apply to any size company.

112   Chapter 3

 A Look Forward

To this point, the text has explained the basic accounting cycle for service and merchandising businesses. Future chapters more closely address specific accounting issues. For example, in Chapter 5 you will learn how to deal with inventory items that are purchased at differing prices. Other chapters will discuss a variety of specific practices that are widely used by real-world companies.

APPENDIX

 LO 3-6

 Identify the primary features of the periodic inventory system.

Periodic Inventory System

Under certain conditions, it is impractical to record inventory sales transactions as they occur. Consider the operations of a fast-food restaurant. To maintain perpetual inventory records, the restaurant would have to transfer from the Inventory account to the Cost of Goods Sold account the *cost* of each hamburger, order of fries, soft drink, or other food items as they were sold. Obviously, recording the cost of each item at the point of sale would be impractical without using highly sophisticated computer equipment (recording the selling price the customer pays is captured by cash registers; the difficulty lies in capturing inventory cost).

The **periodic inventory system** offers a practical solution for recording inventory transactions in a low-technology, high-volume environment. Inventory costs are recorded in a Purchases account at the time of purchase. Purchase returns and allowances and transportation-in are recorded in separate accounts. No entries for the cost of merchandise purchases or sales are recorded in the Inventory account during the period. The cost of goods sold is determined at the end of the period as shown in Exhibit 3.8.

EXHIBIT 3.8

Schedule of Cost of Goods Sold for 2015	
Beginning inventory	$ 6,000
Purchases	11,000
Purchase returns and allowances	(1,000)
Purchase discounts	(200)
Transportation-in	300
Cost of goods available for sale	16,100
Ending inventory	4,600
Cost of goods sold	$11,500

The perpetual and periodic inventory systems represent alternative procedures for recording the same information. The amounts of cost of goods sold and ending inventory reported in the financial statements will be the same regardless of the method used.

The **schedule of cost of goods sold** presented in Exhibit 3.8 is used for internal reporting purposes. It is normally not shown in published financial statements. The amount of cost of goods sold is reported as a single line item on the income statement. The income statement in Exhibit 3.3 will be the same whether JPS maintains perpetual or periodic inventory records.

Advantages and Disadvantages of the Periodic System versus the Perpetual System

The chief advantage of the periodic method is recording efficiency. Recording inventory transactions occasionally (periodically) requires less effort than recording them continually (perpetually). Historically, practical limitations offered businesses like fast-food restaurants or grocery stores no alternative to using the periodic system. The sheer volume of transactions made recording individual decreases to the Inventory account balance as each item was sold impossible. Imagine the number of transactions a grocery store would have to record every business day to maintain perpetual records.

Although the periodic system provides a recordkeeping advantage over the perpetual system, perpetual inventory records provide significant control advantages over periodic records. With perpetual records, the book balance in the Inventory account should agree with the amount of inventory in stock at any given time. By comparing that book balance with the results of a physical inventory count, management can determine the amount of lost, damaged, destroyed, or stolen inventory. Perpetual records also permit more timely and accurate reorder decisions and profitability assessments.

When a company uses the *periodic* inventory system, lost, damaged, or stolen merchandise is automatically included in cost of goods sold. Because such goods are not included in the year-end physical count, they are treated as sold regardless of the reason for their absence. Since the periodic system does not separate the cost of lost, damaged, or stolen merchandise from the cost of goods sold, the amount of any inventory shrinkage is unknown. This feature is a major disadvantage of the periodic system. Without knowing the amount of inventory losses, management cannot weigh the costs of various security systems against the potential benefits.

Advances in such technology as electronic bar code scanning and increased computing power have eliminated most of the practical constraints that once prevented merchandisers with high-volume, low dollar-value inventories from recording inventory transactions on a continual basis. As a result, use of the perpetual inventory system has expanded rapidly in recent years and continued growth can be expected. This text, therefore, concentrates on the perpetual inventory system.

 Video lectures and accompanying self-assessment quizzes are available for all learning objectives through McGraw-Hill *Connect®* Accounting.

SELF-STUDY REVIEW PROBLEM

Academy Sales Company (ASC) started the 2014 accounting period with the balances given in the financial statements model shown below. During 2014 ASC experienced the following business events.

1. Purchased $16,000 of merchandise inventory on account, terms 2/10, n/30.
2. The goods that were purchased in Event 1 were delivered FOB shipping point. Freight costs of $600 were paid in cash by the responsible party.
3. Returned $500 of goods purchased in Event 1.
4a. Recorded the cash discount on the goods purchased in Event 1.
4b. Paid the balance due on the account payable within the discount period.
5a. Recognized $21,000 of cash revenue from the sale of merchandise.
5b. Recognized $15,000 of cost of goods sold.
6. The merchandise in Event 5a was sold to customers FOB destination. Freight costs of $950 were paid in cash by the responsible party.
7. Paid cash of $4,000 for selling and administrative expenses.
8. Sold the land for $5,600 cash.

Required

a. Record the above transactions in a financial statements model like the one shown below.

Event No.	Cash	+	Inventory	+	Land	=	Accts. Pay.	+	Com. Stk.	+	Ret. Earn.	Rev./ Gain	−	Exp.	=	Net Inc.	Cash Flow
Bal.	25,000	+	3,000	+	5,000	=	–0–	+	18,000	+	15,000	NA	−	NA	=	NA	NA

b. Prepare a schedule of cost of goods sold. (Appendix)
c. Prepare a multistep income statement. Include common size percentages on the income statement.

d. ASC's gross margin percentage in 2013 was 22 percent. Based on the common size data in the income statement, did ASC raise or lower its prices in 2014? (Appendix)

e. Assuming a 10 percent rate of growth, what is the amount of net income expected for 2015?

Solution

a.

Event No.	Cash	+	Inventory	+	Land	=	Accts. Pay.	+	Com. Stk.	+	Ret. Earn.	Rev./ Gain	−	Exp.	=	Net Inc.	Cash Flow
Bal.	25,000	+	3,000	+	5,000	=	–0–	+	18,000	+	15,000	NA	−	NA	=	NA	NA
1		+	16,000			=	16,000	+		+			−		=		
2	(600)	+	600			=		+		+			−		=		(600) OA
3		+	(500)			=	(500)	+		+			−		=		
4a		+	(310)			=	(310)	+		+			−		=		
4b	(15,190)	+				=	(15,190)	+		+			−		=		(15,190) OA
5a	21,000	+				=		+		+	21,000	21,000	−		=	21,000	21,000 OA
5b		+	(15,000)			=		+		+	(15,000)		−	15,000	=	(15,000)	
6	(950)	+				=		+		+	(950)		−	950	=	(950)	(950) OA
7	(4,000)	+				=		+		+	(4,000)		−	4,000	=	(4,000)	(4,000) OA
8	5,600	+			(5,000)	=		+		+	600	600	−		=	600	5,600 IA
Bal.	30,860	+	3,790		–0–	=	–0–	+	18,000	+	16,650	21,600	−	19,950	=	1,650	5,860 NC

b.

ACADEMY SALES COMPANY
Schedule of Cost of Goods Sold
For the Period Ended December 31, 2014

Beginning inventory	$ 3,000
Plus purchases	16,000
Less: Purchase returns and allowances	(500)
Less: Purchases discounts	(310)
Plus: Transportation-in	600
Goods available for sale	18,790
Less: Ending inventory	3,790
Cost of goods sold	$15,000

c.

ACADEMY SALES COMPANY
Income Statement*
For the Period Ended December 31, 2014

Net sales	$21,000	100.0%
Cost of goods sold	(15,000)	71.4
Gross margin	6,000	28.6
Less: Operating expenses		
Selling and administrative expense	(4,000)	19.0
Transportation-out	(950)	4.5
Operating income	1,050	5.0
Nonoperating items		
Gain on the sale of land	600	2.9
Net income	$ 1,650	7.9

*Percentages do not add exactly because they have been rounded.

d. All other things being equal, the higher the gross margin percentage, the higher the sales prices. Since the gross margin percentage increased from 22 percent to 28.6 percent, the data suggest that Academy raised its sales prices.

e. $1,155 [$1,050 + (.10 × $1,050)]. Note that the gain is not expected to recur.

KEY TERMS

Cash discount 100	Gross profit 96	Perpetual inventory system 96	Selling and administrative costs 95
Common size financial statements 109	Loss 105	Product costs 95	Shrinkage 104
	Merchandise inventory 92	Purchase discount 100	
Cost of goods available for sale 95	Merchandising businesses 92	Purchase returns and allowances 99	Single-step income statement 106
Cost of Goods Sold 95	Multistep income statement 106	Retail companies 92	Transportation-in (freight-in) 101
FOB (free on board) destination 101	Net sales 109	Sales discounts 107	Transportation-out (freight-out) 101
FOB (free on board) shipping point 101	Operating income (or loss) 106	Sales returns and allowances 109	2/10, n/30 100
Gain 105	Period costs 95	Schedule of cost of goods sold 112	Wholesale companies 92
Gross margin 96	Periodic inventory system 112		

QUESTIONS

1. Define *merchandise inventory*. What types of costs are included in the Merchandise Inventory account?

2. What is the difference between a product cost and a selling and administrative cost?

3. How is the cost of goods available for sale determined?

4. What portion of cost of goods available for sale is shown on the balance sheet? What portion is shown on the income statement?

5. When are period costs expensed? When are product costs expensed?

6. If PetCo had net sales of $600,000, goods available for sale of $450,000, and cost of goods sold of $375,000, what is its gross margin? What amount of inventory will be shown on its balance sheet?

7. Describe how the perpetual inventory system

works. What are some advantages of using the perpetual inventory system? Is it necessary to take a physical inventory when using the perpetual inventory system?

8. What are the effects of the following types of transactions on the accounting equation? Also identify the financial statements that are affected. (Assume that the perpetual inventory system is used.)
    a. Acquisition of cash from the issue of common stock.
    b. Contribution of inventory by an owner of a company.
    c. Purchase of inventory with cash by a company.
    d. Sale of inventory for cash.

9. Northern Merchandising Company sold inventory that cost $12,000 for $20,000 cash. How does

this event affect the accounting equation? What financial statements and accounts are affected? (Assume that the perpetual inventory system is used.)

10. If goods are shipped FOB shipping point, which party (buyer or seller) is responsible for the shipping costs?

11. Define *transportation-in*. Is it a product or a period cost?

12. Quality Cellular Co. paid $80 for freight on merchandise that it had purchased for resale to customers (transportation-in) and paid $135 for freight on merchandise delivered to customers (transportation-out). The $80 payment is added to what account? The $135 payment is added to what account?

13. Why would a seller grant an allowance to a buyer of his merchandise?

14. Dyer Department Store purchased goods with the terms 2/10, n/30. What do these terms mean?

15. Eastern Discount Stores incurred a $5,000 cash cost. How does the accounting for this cost differ if the cash were paid for inventory versus commissions to sales personnel?

16. What is the purpose of giving a cash discount to charge customers?

17. Define *transportation-out*. Is it a product cost or a period cost for the seller?

18. Ball Co. purchased inventory with a list price of $4,000 with the terms 2/10, n/30. What amount will be added to the Merchandise Inventory account?

19. Explain the difference between purchase returns and sales returns. How do

116   Chapter 3

purchase returns affect the financial statements of both buyer and seller? How do sales returns affect the financial statements of both buyer and seller?

20. Explain the difference between gross margin and a gain.

21. What is the difference between a multistep

income statement and a single-step income statement?

22. What is the advantage of using common size income statements to present financial information for several accounting periods?

23. What is the purpose of preparing a schedule of cost of goods sold?

24. Explain how the periodic inventory system works. What are some advantages of using the periodic inventory system? What are some disadvantages of using the periodic inventory system? Is it necessary to take a physical inventory when using

the periodic inventory system?

25. Why does the periodic inventory system impose a major disadvantage for management in accounting for lost, stolen, or damaged goods?

MULTIPLE-CHOICE QUESTIONS

Multiple-choice questions are provided on the text website at www.mhhe.com/edmondssurvey4e.

EXERCISES

■ **CONNECT**   All applicable Exercises are available with McGraw-Hill's
|ACCOUNTING   ***Connect® Accounting.***

When the instructions for *any* exercise or problem call for the preparation of an income statement, use the *multistep format* unless otherwise indicated.

LO 3-1   **Exercise 3-1   *Determining the cost of financing inventory***

On January 1, 2014, Laura started a small flower merchandising business that she named Laura's Flowers. The company experienced the following events during the first year of operation.

1. Started the business by issuing common stock for $20,000 cash.
2. Paid $14,000 cash to purchase inventory.
3. Sold merchandise that cost $8,000 for $18,000 on account.
4. Collected $15,000 cash from accounts receivable.
5. Paid $3,750 for operating expenses.

Required

a. Organize ledger accounts under an accounting equation and record the events in the accounts.
b. Prepare an income statement, a balance sheet, and a statement of cash flows.
c. Since Laura sold inventory for $18,000, she will be able to recover more than half of the $20,000 she invested in the stock. Do you agree with this statement? Why or why not?

LO 3-1   **Exercise 3-2   *Comparing a merchandising company with a service company***

The following information is available for two different types of businesses for the 2014 accounting period. Lewis CPAs is a service business that provides accounting services to small businesses. Casual Clothing is a merchandising business that sells sports clothing to college students.

Data for Lewis CPAs

1. Borrowed $80,000 from the bank to start the business.
2. Provided $60,000 of services to clients and collected $60,000 cash.
3. Paid salary expense of $40,000.

Data for Casual Clothing

1. Borrowed $80,000 from the bank to start the business.
2. Purchased $50,000 inventory for cash.
3. Inventory costing $32,000 was sold for $60,000 cash.
4. Paid $7,200 cash for operating expenses.

Required

a. Prepare an income statement, a balance sheet, and a statement of cash flows for each of the companies.
b. Which of the two businesses would have product costs? Why?
c. Why does Lewis CPAs not compute gross margin on its income statement?
d. Compare the assets of both companies. What assets do they have in common? What assets are different? Why?

Exercise 3-3   *Effect of inventory transactions on financial statements:*   LO 3-1
                    Perpetual system

Justin Swords started a small merchandising business in 2014. The business experienced the following events during its first year of operation. Assume that Swords uses the perpetual inventory system.

1. Acquired $70,000 cash from the issue of common stock.
2. Purchased inventory for $60,000 cash.
3. Sold inventory costing $48,000 for $82,000 cash.

Required

a. Record the events in a statements model like the one shown below.

Assets			=	Equity			Rev.	−	Exp.	=	Net Inc.	Cash Flow
Cash	+	Inv.	=	Com. Stk.	+	Ret. Earn.						

b. Prepare an income statement for 2014 (use the multistep format).
c. What is the amount of total assets at the end of the period?

Exercise 3-4   *Effect of inventory transactions on the income statement and*   LO 3-1
                    statement of cash flows: Perpetual system

During 2014, King Merchandising Company purchased $30,000 of inventory on account. King sold inventory on account that cost $22,500 for $31,000. Cash payments on accounts payable were $18,000. There was $22,000 cash collected from accounts receivable. King also paid $4,200 cash for operating expenses. Assume that King started the accounting period with $18,000 in both cash and common stock.

Required

a. Identify the events described in the preceding paragraph and record them in a horizontal statements model like the following one:

Assets						=	Liab.	+	Equity				Rev.	−	Exp.	=	Net inc.	Cash Flow
Cash	+	Accts. Rec.	+	Inv.	=	Accts. Pay.	+	Com. Stk.	+	Ret. Earn.								
14,000	+	NA	+	NA	=	NA	+	14,000	+	NA		NA	−	NA	=	NA		NA

    b. What is the balance of accounts receivable at the end of 2014?

    c. What is the balance of accounts payable at the end of 2014?

    d. What are the amounts of gross margin and net income for 2014?

    e. Determine the amount of net cash flow from operating activities.

    f. Explain why net income and retained earnings are the same for King. Normally would these amounts be the same? Why or why not?

LO 3-1

Exercise 3-5 *Recording inventory transactions in a financial statements model*

Hilo Clothing experienced the following events during 2014, its first year of operation:

1. Acquired $25,000 cash from the issue of common stock.
2. Purchased inventory for $12,000 cash.
3. Sold inventory costing $8,000 for $15,000 cash.
4. Paid $1,200 for advertising expense.

Required

Record the events in a statements model like the one shown below.

Assets			=	Equity			Rev.	−	Exp.	=	Net Inc.	Cash Flow
Cash	+	Inv.	=	Com. Stk.	+	Ret. Earn.						

LO 3-2

Exercise 3-6 *Understanding the freight terms FOB shipping point and FOB destination*

Required

Determine which party, buyer or seller, is responsible for freight charges in each of the following situations:

    a. Sold merchandise, freight terms, FOB shipping point.

    b. Sold merchandise, freight terms, FOB destination.

    c. Purchased merchandise, freight terms, FOB shipping point.

    d. Purchased merchandise, freight terms, FOB destination.

LO 3-2

Exercise 3-7 *Effect of purchase returns and allowances and freight costs on the financial statements: Perpetual system*

The beginning account balances for Austin's Auto Shop as of January 1, 2014, follows:

Account Titles	Beginning Balances
Cash	$14,000
Inventory	7,000
Common stock	18,000
Retained earnings	3,000

The following events affected the company during the 2014 accounting period:

1. Purchased merchandise on account that cost $12,000.
2. The goods in Event 1 were purchased FOB shipping point with freight cost of $800 cash.
3. Returned $2,600 of damaged merchandise for credit on account.
4. Agreed to keep other damaged merchandise for which the company received an $1,100 allowance.
5. Sold merchandise that cost $12,000 for $21,500 cash.
6. Delivered merchandise to customers in Event 5 under terms FOB destination with freight costs amounting to $500 cash.
7. Paid $8,000 on the merchandise purchased in Event 1.

Required

a. Organize appropriate ledger accounts under an accounting equation. Record the beginning balances and the transaction data in the accounts.

b. Prepare an income statement and a statement of cash flows for 2014.

c. Explain why a difference does or does not exist between net income and net cash flow from operating activities.

Exercise 3-8 *Accounting for product costs: Perpetual inventory system*   LO 3-2

Which of the following would be *added* to the Inventory account for a merchandising business using the perpetual inventory system?

Required

a. Purchase of a new computer to be used by the business.
b. Purchase of inventory. +1500
c. Allowance received for damaged inventory. 200
d. Transportation-out.
e. Purchase discount. 50
f. Transportation-in. 300

Exercise 3-9 *Effect of product cost and period cost: Horizontal statements model*   LO 3-2

The Sports Store experienced the following events for the 2014 accounting period:

1. Acquired $40,000 cash from the issue of common stock.
2. Purchased $78,000 of inventory on account.
3. Received goods purchased in Event 2 FOB shipping point; freight cost of $900 paid in cash.
4. Sold inventory on account that cost $46,000 for $72,000.
5. Freight cost on the goods sold in Event 4 was $560. The goods were shipped FOB destination. Cash was paid for the freight cost.
6. Customer in Event 4 returned $5,100 worth of goods that had a cost of $2,950.
7. Collected $61,500 cash from accounts receivable.
8. Paid $66,100 cash on accounts payable.
9. Paid $2,600 for advertising expense.
10. Paid $3,100 cash for insurance expense.

Required

a. Which of these events affect period (selling and administrative) costs? Which result in product costs? If neither, label the transaction NA.

b. Record each event in a horizontal statements model like the following one. The first event is recorded as an example.

Assets			=	Liab.	+	Equity			Rev.	−	Exp.	=	Net Inc.	Cash Flow	
Cash	+ Accts. Rec.	+ Inv.	=	Accts. Pay.	+	C. Stk.	+	Ret. Earn.							
40,000	+ NA	+ NA	=	NA	+	40,000	+	NA	NA	−	NA	=	NA	40,000	FA

Exercise 3-10 *Cash discounts and purchase returns*   LO 3-3

On April 6, 2014, Fashion Furnishings purchased $24,800 of merchandise from James's Imports, terms 2/10, n/45. On April 8, Fashion returned $2,400 of the merchandise to James's Imports for credit. Fashion paid cash for the merchandise on April 15, 2014.

120   Chapter 3

Required

a. What is the amount that Fashion must pay James's Imports on April 15?

b. Record the events in a horizontal statements model like the following one.

Assets			=	Liab.	+		Equity		Rev.	–	Exp.	=	Net Inc.	Cash Flow
Cash	+	Inv.	=	Accts. Pay.	+	C. Stock.	+	Ret. Earn.						

c. How much must Fashion pay for the merchandise purchased if the payment is not made until April 20, 2014?

d. Record the payment in event (c) in a horizontal statements model like the one above.

e. Why would Fashion want to pay for the merchandise by April 15?

LO 3-2

Exercise 3-11 *Determining the effect of inventory transactions on the horizontal statements model: Perpetual system*

Mario Company experienced the following events:

1. Purchased merchandise inventory for cash.
2. Sold merchandise inventory on account. Label the revenue recognition 2a and the expense recognition 2b.
3. Returned merchandise purchased on account.
4. Purchased merchandise inventory on account.
5. Paid cash on accounts payable within the discount period.
6. Paid cash for selling and administrative expenses.
7. Sold merchandise inventory for cash. Label the revenue recognition 7a and the expense recognition 7b.
8. Paid cash for transportation-out.
9. Paid cash for transportation-in.
10. Collected cash from accounts receivable not within the discount period.

Required

Identify each event as asset source (AS), asset use (AU), asset exchange (AE), or claims exchange (CE). Also explain how each event affects the financial statements by placing a + for increase, – for decrease, or NA for not affected under each of the components in the following statements model. Assume the company uses the perpetual inventory system. The first event is recorded as an example.

Event No.	Event Type	Assets	=	Liab.	+	Equity	Rev.	–	Exp.	=	Net Inc.	Cash Flow
1	AE	+ –	=	NA	+	NA	NA	–	NA	=	NA	– OA

LO 3-2

Exercise 3-12 *Inventory financing costs*

Nichole Jordan comes to you for advice. She has just purchased a large amount of inventory with the terms 2/10, n/30. The amount of the invoice is $270,000. She is currently short of cash but has decent credit. She can borrow the money needed to settle the account payable at an annual interest rate of 7 percent. Nichole is sure she will have the necessary cash by the due date of the invoice but not by the last day of the discount period.

Required

a. Convert the discount rate into an annual interest rate.

b. Make a recommendation regarding whether Jordan should borrow the money and pay off the account payable within the discount period.

Exercise 3-13   *Effect of shrinkage: Perpetual system*   LO 3-2

Royal Sales experienced the following events during 2014, its first year of operation:

1. Started the business when it acquired $80,000 cash from the issue of common stock.
2. Paid $35,000 cash to purchase inventory.
3. Sold inventory costing $21,000 for $40,500 cash.
4. Physically counted inventory showing $13,500 inventory was on hand at the end of the accounting period.

Required

a. Determine the amount of the difference between book balance and the actual amount of inventory as determined by the physical count.

b. Explain how differences between the book balance and the physical count of inventory could arise. Why is being able to determine whether differences exist useful to management?

Exercise 3-14   *Comparing gross margin and gain on sale of land*   LO 3-3

Phillips Sales Company had the following balances in its accounts on January 1, 2014.

Cash	$35,000
Merchandise Inventory	25,000
Land	60,000
Common Stock	50,000
Retained Earnings	70,000

Phillips experienced the following events during 2014.

1. Sold merchandise inventory that cost $20,000 for $37,500.
2. Sold land that cost $25,000 for $40,000.

Required

a. Determine the amount of gross margin recognized by Phillips.
b. Determine the amount of the gain on the sale of land recognized by Phillips.
c. Comment on how the gross margin versus the gain will be recognized on the income statement.
d. Comment on how the gross margin versus the gain will be recognized on the statement of cash flows.

Exercise 3-15   *Single-step and multistep income statements*   LO 3-3

The following information was taken from the accounts of Healthy Eats, a delicatessen, at December 31, 2014. The accounts are listed in alphabetical order, and each has a normal balance.

Accounts payable	$1,200
Accounts receivable	800
Advertising expense	400
Cash	820
Common stock	400
Cost of goods sold	1,200
Interest expense	140
Merchandise inventory	900
Prepaid rent	80
Retained earnings	1,000
Sales revenue	2,000
Salaries expense	260
Rent expense	220
Loss on sale of land	50

Required

First, prepare an income statement for the year using the single-step approach. Then prepare another income statement using the multistep approach.

LO 3-4

Exercise 3-16   *Effect of sales returns and allowances and freight costs on the financial statements: Perpetual system*

Poole Company began the 2014 accounting period with $36,000 cash, $80,000 inventory, $70,000 common stock, and $46,000 retained earnings. During the 2014 accounting period, Poole experienced the following events:

1. Sold merchandise costing $51,500 for $92,900 on account to Mable's General Store.
2. Delivered the goods to Mable's under terms FOB destination. Freight costs were $500 cash.
3. Received returned goods from Mable's. The goods cost Poole Company $3,200 and were sold to Mable's for $4,700.
4. Granted Mable's a $1,500 allowance for damaged goods that Mable's agreed to keep.
5. Collected partial payment of $71,000 cash from accounts receivable.

Required

a. Record the events in a statements model like the one shown below.

Assets				=	Equity			Rev.	−	Exp.	=	Net Inc.	Cash Flow
Cash	+	Accts. Rec.	+	Inv.	=	Com. Stk.	+	Ret. Earn.					

b. Prepare an income statement, a balance sheet, and a statement of cash flows.
c. Why would Poole grant the $1,500 allowance to Mable's? Who benefits more?

LO 3-4

Exercise 3-17   *Effect of cash discounts on financial statements: Perpetual system*

Clayton Computers was started in 2014. The company experienced the following accounting events during its first year of operation.

1. Started business when it acquired $25,000 cash from the issue of common stock.
2. Purchased merchandise with a list price of $23,000 on account, terms 2/10, n/30.
3. Paid off one-half of the accounts payable balance within the discount period.
4. Sold merchandise on account that had a list price of $24,000. Credit terms were 1/20, n/30. The merchandise had cost Clayton Computers $14,000.
5. Collected cash from the account receivable within the discount period.
6. Paid $1,700 cash for operating expenses.
7. Paid the balance due on accounts payable. The payment was not made within the discount period.

Required

a. Record the events in a horizontal statements model like the following one.

Assets				=	Liab.	+	Equity			Rev.	−	Exp.	=	Net Inc.	Cash Flow
Cash	+	Accts. Rec.	+	Inv.	=	Accts. Pay.	+	Com. Stk.	+	Ret. Earn.					

b. What is the amount of gross margin for the period? What is the net income for the period?
c. Why would Clayton Computers sell merchandise with the terms 1/20, n/30?
d. What do the terms 2/10, n/30 in Event 2 mean to Clayton Computers?

Exercise 3-18   *Using common size statements and ratios to make comparisons*   LO 3-5

At the end of 2014 the following information is available for Fargo and Huston companies:

	Fargo	Huston
Sales	$2,000,000	$2,000,000
Cost of goods sold	1,600,000	1,200,000
Operating expenses	300,000	640,000
Total assets	2,500,000	2,500,000
Stockholders' equity	700,000	1,500,000

Required

a. Prepare common size income statements for each company.
b. One company is a high-end retailer, and the other operates a discount store. Which is the discounter? Support your selection by referring to the common size statements.

Exercise 3-19   *Effect of inventory transactions on the income statement and balance sheet: Periodic system (Appendix)*   LO 3-6

Edd Gant owns Edd's Sporting Goods. At the beginning of the year, Edd's had $16,000 in inventory. During the year, Edd's purchased inventory that cost $65,000. At the end of the year, inventory on hand amounted to $26,300.

Required

Calculate the following:

a. Cost of goods available for sale during the year.
b. Cost of goods sold for the year.
c. Amount of inventory Edd's would report on the year-end balance sheet.

Exercise 3-20   *Determining cost of goods sold: Periodic system (Appendix)*   LO 3-6

Belk Antiques uses the periodic inventory system to account for its inventory transactions. The following account titles and balances were drawn from Belk's records for the year 2014: beginning balance in inventory, $42,000; purchases, $128,000; purchase returns and allowances, $12,000; sales, $520,000; sales returns and allowances, $3,900; freight-in, $1,000; and operating expenses, $130,000. A physical count indicated that $26,000 of merchandise was on hand at the end of the accounting period.

Required

a. Prepare a schedule of cost of goods sold.
b. Prepare a multistep income statement.

PROBLEMS

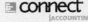 **connect** |ACCOUNTING   **All applicable Problems are available with McGraw-Hill's *Connect® Accounting.***

Problem 3-21   *Identifying product and period costs*   LO 3-2

Required

Indicate whether each of the following costs is a product cost or a period (selling and administrative) cost.

a. Cleaning supplies for the office.
b. Freight on goods purchased for resale.

CHECK FIGURE
a. Period cost

124   Chapter 3

c. Salary of the marketing director.
d. Freight on goods sold to customer with terms FOB destination.
e. Utilities expense incurred for office building.
f. Advertising expense.
g. Insurance on vans used to deliver goods to customers.
h. Salaries of sales supervisors.
i. Monthly maintenance expense for a copier.
j. Goods purchased for resale.

LO 3-2

CHECK FIGURE
Event (b): NA Cost: $0

Problem 3-22   *Identifying freight costs*

Required

For each of the following events, determine the amount of freight paid by Tom's Part House. Also indicate whether the freight cost would be classified as a product or period (selling and administrative) cost.

a. Purchased inventory with freight costs of $500. The goods were shipped FOB shipping point.
b. Sold merchandise to a customer. Freight costs were $800. The goods were shipped FOB shipping point.
c. Purchased merchandise inventory with freight costs of $1,400. The merchandise was shipped FOB destination.
d. Shipped merchandise to customers, freight terms FOB destination. The freight costs were $300.

LO 3-2

CHECK FIGURES
a. Ending Cash: $29,245
b. Net Income: $6,550

Problem 3-23   *Effect of purchase returns and allowances and purchase discounts on the financial statements: Perpetual system*

The following events were completed by Yang's Imports in September 2014.

Sept. 1   Acquired $30,000 cash from the issue of common stock.
       1   Purchased $18,000 of merchandise on account with terms 2/10, n/30.
       5   Paid $400 cash for freight to obtain merchandise purchased on September 1.
       8   Sold merchandise that cost $10,000 to customers for $19,000 on account, with terms 2/10, n/30.
       8   Returned $750 of defective merchandise from the September 1 purchase to the supplier.
      10   Paid cash for the balance due on the merchandise purchased on September 1.
      20   Received cash from customers of September 8 sale in settlement of the account balances, but not within the discount period.
      30   Paid $2,450 cash for selling expenses.

Required

a. Record each event in a statements model like the following one. The first event is recorded as an example.

Assets			=	Liab.	+	Equity			Rev.	−	Exp.	=	Net Inc.	Cash Flow
Cash	+ Accts. Rec.	+ Inv.	=	Accts. Pay.	+	Com. Stk.	+	Ret. Earn.						
30,000	+ NA	+ NA	=	NA	+	30,000	+	NA	NA	−	NA	=	NA	30,000 FA

b. Prepare an income statement for the month ending September 30.
c. Prepare a statement of cash flows for the month ending September 30.
d. Explain why there is a difference between net income and cash flow from operating activities.

Problem 3-24   *Preparing a schedule of cost of goods sold and multistep and single-step income statements: Periodic system (Appendix)*

LO 3-3, 3-6

The following account titles and balances were taken from the adjusted trial balance of Omar Farm Co. for 2014. The company uses the periodic inventory system.

Account Title	Balance
Sales returns and allowances	$ 6,500
Miscellaneous expense	800
Transportation-out	1,400
Sales	139,500
Advertising expense	5,500
Salaries expense	17,000
Transportation-in	3,450
Purchases	84,000
Interest expense	720
Merchandise inventory, January 1	12,400
Rent expense	10,000
Merchandise inventory, December 31	8,100
Purchase returns and allowances	2,500
Loss on sale of land	6,800
Utilities expense	1,420

Required

a. Prepare a schedule to determine the amount of cost of goods sold.
b. Prepare a multistep income statement.
c. Prepare a single-step income statement.

Problem 3-25   *Basic transactions for three accounting cycles: prepetual system*

LO 3-3

Amber's Flower Company was started in 2014 when it acquired $80,000 cash from the issue of common stock. The following data summarize the company's first three years' operating activities. Assume that all transactions were cash transactions.

	2014	2015	2016
Purchases of inventory	$40,000	$55,000	$ 95,000
Sales	75,000	88,000	146,000
Cost of goods sold	38,000	49,000	82,000
Selling and administrative expenses	29,000	35,000	42,000

Required

Prepare an income statement (use multistep format) and balance sheet for each fiscal year. (*Hint:* Record the transaction data for each accounting period in the accounting equation before preparing the statements for that year.)

Problem 3-26   *Comprehensive cycle problem: Perpetual system*

LO 3-2, 3-3, 3-4, 3-5

At the beginning of 2013, the Bradley Company had the following balances in its accounts:

Cash	$ 8,600
Inventory	18,000
Common stock	20,000
Retained earnings	6,600

During 2014, the company experienced the following events:

1. Purchased inventory that cost $4,400 on account from Bivins Company under terms 1/10, n/30. The merchandise was delivered FOB shipping point. Freight costs of $190 were paid in cash.
2. Returned $400 of the inventory that it had purchased because the inventory was damaged in transit. The seller agreed to pay the return freight cost.
3. Paid the amount due on its account payable to Bivins Company within the cash discount period.
4. Sold inventory that had cost $6,000 for $11,000 on account, under terms 2/10, n/45.
5. Received merchandise returned from a customer. The merchandise originally cost $800 and was sold to the customer for $1,450 cash. The customer was paid $1,450 cash for the returned merchandise.
6. Delivered goods FOB destination in Event 4. Freight costs of $120 were paid in cash.
7. Collected the amount due on the account receivable within the discount period.
8. Took a physical count indicating that $15,500 of inventory was on hand at the end of the accounting period.

Required

a. Identify these events as asset source (AS), asset use (AU), asset exchange (AE), or claims exchange (CE).

b. Record each event in a statements model like the following one.

Event	Balance Sheet							Income Statement			Statement of Cash Flows
	Assets	=	Liab.	=	Equity			Rev. − Exp. = Net Inc.			
	Cash + Accts. Rec. + Mdse. Inv.	=	Accts. Pay. +		Ret. Earn.						

c. Prepare a multistep income statement, a statement of changes in stockholders' equity, a balance sheet, and a statement of cash flows.

LO 3-5

Problem 3-27 *Using common size income statements to make comparisons*

The following income statements were drawn from the annual reports of Harper Sales Company.

	2014*	2015*
Net sales	$200,000	$250,000
Cost of goods sold	(140,000)	(170,000)
Gross margin	60,000	80,000
Less: Operating expense		
Selling and administrative expenses	(28,000)	(32,000)
Net income	$ 32,000	$ 48,000

*All dollar amounts are reported in thousands.

The president's message in the company's annual report stated that the company had implemented a strategy to increase market share by spending more on advertising. The president indicated that prices held steady and sales grew as expected. Write a memo indicating whether you agree with the president's statements. How has the strategy affected profitability? Support your answer by measuring growth in sales and selling expenses. Also prepare common size income statements and make appropriate references to the differences between 2014 and 2015.

Problem 3-28   *Comprehensive cycle problem: Periodic system (Appendix)*   LO 3-6

The following trial balance pertains to Cal's Grocery as of January 1, 2014:

CHECK FIGURES
a. Ending Cash: $58,348
b. Cost of Goods Sold: $291,252

Account Title	Beginning Balances
Cash	$ 52,000
Accounts receivable	8,000
Merchandise inventory	100,000
Accounts payable	8,000
Common stock	86,000
Retained earnings	66,000

The following events occurred in 2014. Assume that Cal's uses the periodic inventory method.

1. Purchased land for $40,000 cash.
2. Purchased merchandise on account for $252,000, terms 1/10, n/45.
3. Paid freight of $2,000 cash on merchandise purchased FOB shipping point.
4. Returned $7,200 of defective merchandise purchased in Event 2.
5. Sold merchandise for $172,000 cash.
6. Sold merchandise on account for $240,000, terms 2/10, n/30.
7. Paid cash within the discount period on accounts payable due on merchandise purchased in Event 2.
8. Paid $23,200 cash for selling expenses.
9. Collected $95,000 of the accounts receivable from Event 6 within the discount period.
10. Collected $62,000 of the accounts receivable but not within the discount period.
11. Paid $13,200 of other operating expenses.
12. A physical count indicated that $53,100 of inventory was on hand at the end of the accounting period.

Required

a. Record the above transactions in a horizontal statements model like the following one.

	Balance Sheet									Income Statement				
Event	**Assets**				**=**	**Equity**				**Rev.**	**−**	**Exp.**	**=**	**Net Inc.**	**Statement of Cash Flows**
	Cash +	Accts. Rec. +	Mdse. Inv. +	Land =		Accts. Pay. +	Com. Stock +	Ret. Earn.							

b. Prepare a schedule of cost of goods sold and an income statement.

ANALYZE, THINK, COMMUNICATE

ATC 3-1   Business Application Case   *Understanding real world annual reports*

Use the Target Corporation's Form 10-K to answer the following questions related to Target's 2012 fiscal year (year ended February 2, 2013). Target's Form 10-K is available on the company's website or through the SEC's EDGAR database. Appendix A provides instructions for using the EDGAR database.

Target Corporation

Required

a. What percentage of Target's *total revenues* end up as net earnings?
b. What percentage of Target's *sales* go to pay for the costs of the goods being sold?

c. What costs does Target include in its Cost of Sales account?

d. When does Target recognize revenue from the sale of gift cards?

ATC 3-2   Group Exercise   *Multistep income statement*

The following quarterly information is given for Raybon for the year ended 2014 (amounts shown are in millions).

	First Quarter	Second Quarter	Third Quarter	Fourth Quarter
Net Sales	$736.0	$717.4	$815.2	$620.1
Gross Margin	461.9	440.3	525.3	252.3
Net Income	37.1	24.6	38.6	31.4

Required

a. Divide the class into groups and organize the groups into four sections. Assign each section financial information for one of the quarters.

   (1) Each group should compute the cost of goods sold and operating expenses for the specific quarter assigned to its section and prepare a multistep income statement for the quarter.

   (2) Each group should compute the gross margin percentage and cost of goods sold percentage for its specific quarter.

   (3) Have a representative of each group put that quarter's sales, cost of goods sold percentage, and gross margin percentage on the board.

Class Discussion

b. Have the class discuss the change in each of these items from quarter to quarter and explain why the change might have occurred. Which was the best quarter and why?

ATC 3-3   Research Assignment   *Analyzing Amazon.com's income statement*

Complete the requirements below using the most recent financial statements available [20xx] on Amazon.com's corporate website. Obtain the statements on the Internet by following the steps below. (Be aware that the formatting of the company's website may have changed since these instructions were written.)

■ Go to www.amazon.com.
■ At the bottom of the screen, under "Get to Know Us," click on "Investor Relations."
■ Annual Reports and Proxies.
■ Click on "20xx Annual Report" (the most recent year).

Read the following sections of the annual report:

■ The income statement, which Amazon.com calls the "Consolidated Statement of Operations."
■ In the footnotes section, "Note 1—Description of Business and Accounting Policies," read the subsections titled "*Revenues*" and "*Cost of Sales.*"

Required

a. What percentage of Amazon's sales end up as net income?

b. What percentage of Amazon's sales go to pay for the costs of the goods being sold?

c. What specific criteria are necessary before Amazon will recognize a sale as having been completed and record the related revenue?

d. How does Amazon account for (report on its income statement) the shipping costs it incurs to ship goods to its customers?

ATC 3-4   Written Assignment, Critical Thinking   *Effect of sales returns on financial statements*

Bell Farm and Garden Equipment reported the following information for 2014:

Net Sales of Equipment	$2,450,567
Other Income	6,786
Cost of Goods Sold	1,425,990
Selling, General, and Administrative Expense	325,965
Net Operating Income	$ 705,398

Selected information from the balance sheet as of December 31, 2014, follows.

Cash and Marketable Securities	$113,545
Inventory	248,600
Accounts Receivable	82,462
Property, Plant, and Equipment—Net	335,890
Other Assets	5,410
Total Assets	$785,907

Assume that a major customer returned a large order to Bell on December 31, 2014. The amount of the sale had been $146,800 with a cost of sales of $94,623. The return was recorded in the books on January 1, 2015. The company president does not want to correct the books. He argues that it makes no difference as to whether the return is recorded in 2014 or 2015. Either way, the return has been duly recognized.

Required

a. Assume that you are the CFO for Bell Farm and Garden Equipment Co. Write a memo to the president explaining how omitting the entry on December 31, 2014, could cause the financial statements to be misleading to investors and creditors. Explain how omitting the return from the customer would affect net income and the balance sheet.

b. Why might the president want to record the return on January 1, 2015, instead of December 31, 2014?

CHAPTER 4

Internal Controls, Accounting for Cash, and Ethics

LEARNING OBJECTIVES

After you have mastered the material in this chapter, you will be able to:

LO 4-1   Identify the key elements of a strong system of internal control.

LO 4-2   Prepare a bank reconciliation.

LO 4-3   Discuss the role of ethics in the accounting profession.

LO 4-4   Describe the auditor's role in financial reporting.

 Video lectures and accompanying self-assessment quizzes are available for all learning objectives through McGraw-Hill Connect® Accounting.

CHAPTER OPENING

In the first three chapters, we covered the basics of the accounting system. By now you should understand how basic business events affect financial statements and how the accounting cycle works. Accounting is an elegant system that when implemented correctly provides meaningful information to investors and other stakeholders. However, without effective control, the accounting system can be manipulated in ways that may overstate business performance. This can lead investors to make bad decisions, which can result in huge losses when the true performance is revealed. This chapter discusses the importance of internal control systems. The chapter also discusses accounting for cash, an area where good internal controls are critical. The chapter concludes with a discussion on the importance of ethical conduct in the accounting profession.

The Curious Accountant

On December 11, 2008, Bernard Madoff was arrested on suspicion of having defrauded the clients of his investment company, Bernard L. Madoff Investments (BMI), of $50 billion. Later estimates would put the losses at over $60 billion. Although his clients believed the money they sent to BMI was being invested in the stock market, it was actually just being deposited into bank accounts.

Mr. Madoff was accused of operating the largest Ponzi scheme in history. Clients were sent monthly statements falsely showing that their investments were earning income and growing at a steady rate, even when the overall stock market was falling. When individual investors asked to withdraw their funds, they were simply given money that had been deposited by other investors.

This fraudulent system works as long as more new money is being deposited than is being withdrawn. Unfortunately for BMI, with the severe stock-market decline of 2008 too many clients got nervous and asked to withdraw their money, including the gains they believed they had earned over the years. At this point the Ponzi scheme failed.

How could such a pervasive fraud go undetected for so long? (Answer on page 142.)

132   Chapter 4

KEY FEATURES OF INTERNAL CONTROL SYSTEMS

LO 4-1

 Identify the key elements of a strong system of internal control.

During the early 2000s a number of accounting-related scandals cost investors billions. In 2001, Enron's share price went from $85 to $0.30 after it was revealed that the company had billions of dollars in losses that were not reported on the financial statements. Several months later, WorldCom reported an $11 billion accounting fraud, which included hundreds of millions in personal loans to then CEO, Bernie Ebbers.

The Enron and WorldCom accounting scandals had such devastating effects that they led Congress to pass the Sarbanes-Oxley Act of 2002 (SOX). SOX requires public companies to evaluate their *internal control* and to publish those findings with their SEC filings. **Internal control** is the process designed to ensure reliable financial reporting, effective and efficient operations, and compliance with applicable laws and regulations. Safeguarding assets against theft and unauthorized use, acquisition, or disposal is also part of internal control.

Section 404 of Sarbanes-Oxley requires a statement of management's responsibility for establishing and maintaining adequate internal control over financial reporting by public companies. This section includes an assessment of the controls and the identification of the framework used for the assessment. The framework established by The Committee of Sponsoring Organizations of the Treadway Commission (COSO) in 1992 is the de facto standard by which SOX compliance is judged. COSO's framework titled *Internal Control—An Integrated Framework* recognizes five interrelated components including:

1. *Control Environment.* The integrity and ethical values of the company, including its code of conduct, involvement of the board of directors, and other actions that set the tone of the organization.

2. *Risk Assessment.* Management's process of identifying potential risks that could result in misstated financial statements and developing actions to address those risks.

3. *Control Activities.* These are the activities usually thought of as "the internal controls." They include such things as segregation of duties, account reconciliations, and information processing controls that are designed to safeguard assets and enable an organization to timely prepare reliable financial statements.

4. *Information and Communication.* The internal and external reporting process, and includes an assessment of the technology environment.

5. *Monitoring.* Assessing the quality of a company's internal control over time and taking actions as necessary to ensure it continues to address the risks of the organization.

In 2004 COSO updated the framework to help entities design and implement effective enterprise-wide approaches to risk management. The updated document is titled *Enterprise Risk Management (ERM)—An Integrated Framework.* The ERM framework introduces an enterprise-wide approach to risk management as well as concepts such as risk appetite, risk tolerance, and portfolio view. While SOX applies only to U.S. public companies, the ERM framework has been adopted by both public and private organizations around the world.

The ERM framework does not replace the internal control framework. Instead, it incorporates the internal control framework within it. Accordingly, companies may decide to look to the ERM framework both to satisfy their internal control needs and to move toward a fuller risk management process.

While a detailed discussion of the COSO documents is beyond the scope of this text, the following overview of the more common *control activities* of the internal control framework is insightful.

Separation of Duties

The likelihood of fraud or theft is reduced if collusion is required to accomplish it. Clear **separation of duties** is frequently used as a deterrent to corruption. When duties are separated, the work of one employee can act as a check on the work of another employee. For example, a person selling seats to a movie may be tempted to steal money received from customers who enter the theater. This temptation is reduced if the person staffing the box office is required to issue tickets that a second employee collects as people enter the theater. If ticket stubs collected by the second employee are compared with the cash receipts from ticket sales, any cash shortages would become apparent. Furthermore, friends and relatives of the ticket agent could not easily enter the theater without paying. Theft or unauthorized entry would require collusion between the ticket agent and the usher who collects the tickets. Both individuals would have to be dishonest enough to steal, yet trustworthy enough to convince each other they would keep the embezzlement secret. Whenever possible, the functions of *authorization, recording,* and *custody of assets* should be performed by separate individuals.

Quality of Employees

A business is only as good as the people it employs. Cheap labor is not a bargain if the employees are incompetent. Employees should be properly trained. In fact, they should be trained to perform a variety of tasks. The ability of employees to substitute for one another prevents disruptions when co-workers are absent because of illnesses, vacations, or other commitments. The capacity to rotate jobs also relieves boredom and increases respect for the contributions of other employees. Every business should strive to maximize the productivity of every employee. Ongoing training programs are essential to a strong system of internal control.

Bonded Employees

The best way to ensure employee honesty is to hire individuals with *high levels of personal integrity.* Employers should screen job applicants using interviews, background checks, and recommendations from prior employers or educators. Even so, screening programs may fail to identify character weaknesses. Further, unusual circumstances may cause honest employees to go astray. Therefore, employees in positions of trust should be bonded. A **fidelity bond** provides insurance that protects a company from losses caused by employee dishonesty.

Required Absences

Employees should be required to take regular vacations and their duties should be rotated periodically. Employees may be able to cover up fraudulent activities if they are always present at work. Consider the case of a parking meter collection agent who covered the same route for several years with no vacation. When the agent became sick, a substitute collected more money each day than the regular reader usually reported. Management checked past records and found that the ill meter reader had been understating the cash receipts and pocketing the difference. If management had required vacations or rotated the routes, the embezzlement would have been discovered much earlier.

Procedures Manual

Appropriate accounting procedures should be documented in a **procedures manual.** The manual should be routinely updated. Periodic reviews should be conducted to ensure that employees are following the procedures outlined in the manual.

Authority and Responsibility

Employees are motivated by clear lines of authority and responsibility. They work harder when they have the authority to use their own judgment and they exercise reasonable caution when they are held responsible for their actions. Businesses should prepare an **authority manual** that establishes a definitive *chain of command.* The authority manual should guide both specific and general authorizations. **Specific authorizations** apply to specific positions within the organization. For example, investment decisions are authorized at the division level while hiring decisions are authorized at the departmental level. In contrast, **general authority** applies across different levels of management. For example, employees at all levels may be required to fly coach or to make purchases from specific vendors.

134   Chapter 4

Prenumbered Documents

How would you know if a check were stolen from your check book? If you keep a record of your check numbers, the missing number would tip you off immediately. Businesses also use prenumbered checks to avoid the unauthorized use of their bank accounts. In fact, prenumbered forms are used for all important documents such as purchase orders, receiving reports, invoices, and checks. To reduce errors, prenumbered forms should be as simple and easy to use as possible. Also, the documents should allow for authorized signatures. For example, credit sales slips should be signed by the customer to clearly establish who made the purchase, reducing the likelihood of unauthorized transactions.

Physical Control

Employees walk away with billions of dollars of business assets each year. To limit losses, companies should establish adequate physical control over valuable assets. For example, inventory should be kept in a storeroom and not released without proper authorization. Serial numbers on equipment should be recorded along with the name of the individual who is responsible for the equipment. Unannounced physical counts should be conducted randomly to verify the presence of company-owned equipment. Certificates of deposit and marketable securities should be kept in fireproof vaults. Access to these vaults should be limited to authorized personnel. These procedures protect the documents from fire and limit access to only those individuals who have the appropriate security clearance to handle the documents.

In addition to safeguarding assets, there should be physical control over the accounting records. The accounting journals, ledgers, and supporting documents should be kept in a fireproof safe. Only personnel responsible for recording transactions in the journals should have access to them. With limited access, there is less chance that someone will change the records to conceal fraud or embezzlement.

Performance Evaluations

Because few people can evaluate their own performance objectively, internal controls should include independent verification of employee performance. For example, someone other than the person who has control over inventory should take a physical count of inventory. Internal and external audits serve as independent verification of performance. Auditors should evaluate the effectiveness of the internal control system as well as verify the accuracy of the accounting records. In addition, the external auditors attest to the company's use of generally accepted accounting principles in the financial statements.

Limitations

A system of internal controls is designed to prevent or detect errors and fraud. However, no control system is foolproof. Internal controls can be circumvented by collusion among employees. Two or more employees working together can hide embezzlement by covering for each other. For example, if an embezzler goes on vacation, fraud will not be reported by a replacement who is in collusion with the embezzler. No system can prevent all fraud. However, a good system of internal controls minimizes illegal or unethical activities by reducing temptation and increasing the likelihood of early detection.

 CHECK YOURSELF 4.1

What are nine features of an internal control system?

Answer

The nine features follow.

1. Separating duties so that fraud or theft requires collusion.
2. Hiring and training competent employees.

3. Bonding employees to recover losses through insurance.

4. Requiring employees to be absent from their jobs so that their replacements can discover errors or fraudulent activity that might have occurred.

5. Establishing proper procedures for processing transactions.

6. Establishing clear lines of authority and responsibility.

7. Using prenumbered documents.

8. Implementing physical controls such as locking cash in a safe.

9. Conducting performance evaluations through independent internal and external audits.

ACCOUNTING FOR CASH

For financial reporting purposes, **cash** generally includes currency and other items that are payable *on demand,* such as checks, money orders, bank drafts, and certain savings accounts. Savings accounts that impose substantial penalties for early withdrawal should be classified as *investments* rather than cash. Postdated checks or IOUs represent *receivables* and should not be included in cash. As illustrated in Exhibit 4.1, most companies combine currency and other payable on demand items in a single balance sheet account with varying titles.

Companies must maintain a sufficient amount of cash to pay employees, suppliers, and other creditors. When a company fails to pay its legal obligations, its creditors can force the company into bankruptcy. Even so, management should avoid accumulating more cash than is needed. The failure to invest excess cash in earning assets reduces profitability. Cash inflows and outflows must be managed to prevent a shortage or surplus of cash.

Controlling Cash

Controlling cash, more than any other asset, requires strict adherence to internal control procedures. Cash has universal appeal. A relatively small suitcase filled with high-denomination currency can represent significant value. Furthermore, the rightful owner of currency is difficult to prove. In most cases, possession constitutes ownership. As a result, cash is highly susceptible to theft and must be carefully protected. Cash is most susceptible to embezzlement when it is received or disbursed. The following controls should be employed to reduce the likelihood of theft.

Cash Receipts

A record of all cash collections should be prepared immediately upon receipt. The amount of cash on hand should be counted regularly. Missing amounts of money can be detected by comparing the actual cash on hand with the book balance. Employees who receive cash should give customers a copy of a written receipt. Customers usually review their receipts to ensure they have gotten credit for the amount paid and call any errors to the receipts clerk's attention. This not only reduces errors but also provides a control on the clerk's honesty. Cash receipts should be deposited in a bank on a timely basis. Cash collected late in the day should be deposited in a night depository. Every effort should be made to minimize the amount of cash on hand. Keeping large amounts of cash on hand not only increases the risk of loss from theft but also places employees in danger of being harmed by criminals who may be tempted to rob the company.

Cash Payments

To effectively control cash, a company should make all disbursements using checks, thereby providing a record of cash payments. All checks should be prenumbered, and unused checks should be locked up. Using prenumbered checks allows companies to easily identify lost or stolen checks by comparing the numbers on unused and canceled checks with the numbers used for legitimate disbursements.

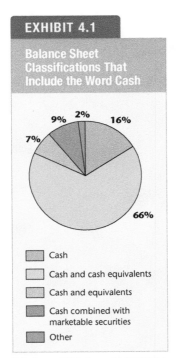

EXHIBIT 4.1

Balance Sheet Classifications That Include the Word Cash

- Cash
- Cash and cash equivalents
- Cash and equivalents
- Cash combined with marketable securities
- Other

Data Source: AICPA, *Accounting Trends and Techniques.*

136   Chapter 4

REALITY BYTES
THE COST OF PROTECTING CASH

Could you afford to buy a safe like the one shown here? The vault is only one of many expensive security devices used by banks to safeguard cash. By using checking accounts, companies are able to avoid many of the costs associated with keeping cash safe. In addition to providing physical control, checking accounts enable companies to maintain a written audit trail of cash receipts and payments. Checking accounts represent the most widely used internal control device in modern society. It is difficult to imagine a business operating without the use of checking accounts.

The duties of approving disbursements, signing checks, and recording transactions should be separated. If one person is authorized to approve, sign, and record checks, he or she could falsify supporting documents, write an unauthorized check, and record a cover-up transaction in the accounting records. By separating these duties, the check signer reviews the documentation provided by the approving individual before signing the check. Likewise, the recording clerk reviews the work of both the approving person and the check signer when the disbursement is recorded in the accounting records. Thus writing unauthorized checks requires trilevel collusion.

Supporting documents with authorized approval signatures should be required when checks are presented to the check signer. For example, a warehouse receiving order should be matched with a purchase order before a check is approved to pay a bill from a supplier. Before payments are approved, invoice amounts should be checked and payees verified as valid vendors. Matching supporting documents with proper authorization discourages employees from creating phony documents for a disbursement to a friend or fictitious business. Also, the approval process serves as a check on the accuracy of the work of all employees involved.

Supporting documents should be marked *Paid* when the check is signed. If the documents are not indelibly marked, they could be retrieved from the files and resubmitted for a duplicate, unauthorized payment. A payables clerk could collude with the payee to split extra cash paid out by submitting the same supporting documents for a second payment.

All spoiled and voided checks should be defaced and retained. If defaced checks are not retained, an employee could steal a check and then claim that it was written incorrectly and thrown away. The clerk could then use the stolen check to make an unauthorized payment.

Checking Account Documents

The previous section explained the need for businesses to use checking accounts. A description of four main types of forms associated with a bank checking account follows.

Signature Card

A bank **signature card** shows the bank account number and the signatures of the people authorized to sign checks. The card is retained in the bank's files. If a bank employee is unfamiliar with the signature on a check, he or she can refer to the signature card to verify the signature before cashing the check.

Deposit Ticket

Each deposit of cash or checks is accompanied by a **deposit ticket,** which normally identifies the account number and the name of the account. The depositor lists the individual amounts of currency, coins, and checks, as well as the total deposited, on the deposit ticket.

Bank Check

A written check affects three parties: (1) the person or business writing the check (the *payer*); (2) the bank on which the check is drawn; and (3) the person or business to whom the check is payable (the *payee*). Companies often write **checks** using multicopy, prenumbered forms, with the name of the issuing business preprinted on the face of each check. A remittance notice is usually attached to the check forms. This portion of the form provides the issuer space to record what the check is for (e.g., what invoices are being paid), the amount being disbursed, and the date of payment. When signed by the person whose signature is on the signature card, the check authorizes the bank to transfer the face amount of the check from the payer's account to the payee.

Bank Statement

Periodically, the bank sends the depositor a **bank statement.** The bank statement is presented from the bank's point of view. Checking accounts are liabilities to a bank because the bank is obligated to pay back the money that customers have deposited in their accounts. Therefore, in the bank's accounting records a customer's checking account has a *credit* balance. As a result, **bank statement debit memos** describe transactions that reduce the customer's account balance (the bank's liability). **Bank statement credit memos** describe activities that increase the customer's account balance (the bank's liability). Since a checking account is an asset (cash) to the depositor, a *bank statement debit memo* requires a *credit entry* to the cash account on the depositor's books. Likewise, when a bank tells you that it has credited your account, you will debit your cash account in response.

Bank statements normally report (a) the balance of the account at the beginning of the period; (b) additions for customer deposits made during the period; (c) other additions described in credit memos (e.g., for interest earned); (d) subtractions for the payment of checks drawn on the account during the period; (e) other subtractions described in debit memos (e.g., for service charges); (f) a running balance of the account; and (g) the balance of the account at the end of the period. The sample bank statement in Exhibit 4.2 on the next page illustrates these items. Normally, the canceled checks or copies of them are enclosed with the bank statement.

RECONCILING THE BANK ACCOUNT

Usually the ending balance reported on the bank statement differs from the balance in the depositor's cash account as of the same date. The discrepancy is normally attributable to timing differences. For example, a depositor deducts the amount of a check from its cash account when it writes the check. However, the bank does not deduct the amount of the check from the depositor's account until the payee presents it for payment, which may be days, weeks, or even months after the check is written. As a result, the balance on the depositor's books is lower than the balance on the bank's books. Companies prepare a **bank reconciliation** to explain the differences between the cash balance reported on the bank statement and the cash balance recorded in the depositor's accounting records.

LO 4-2

Prepare a bank reconciliation.

Determining True Cash Balance

A bank reconciliation normally begins with the cash balance reported by the bank which is called the **unadjusted bank balance.** The adjustments necessary to determine the amount of cash that the depositor actually owns as of the date of the bank statement are then added to and subtracted from the unadjusted bank balance. The final total is the **true cash balance.** The true cash balance is independently reached a second time by making adjustments to the **unadjusted book balance.** The bank account is

138   Chapter 4

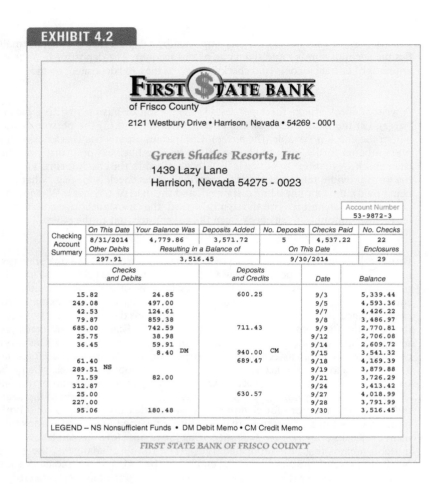

EXHIBIT 4.2

FIRST $ STATE BANK
of Frisco County

2121 Westbury Drive • Harrison, Nevada • 54269 - 0001

Green Shades Resorts, Inc
1439 Lazy Lane
Harrison, Nevada 54275 - 0023

Account Number
53-9872-3

Checking Account Summary	On This Date	Your Balance Was	Deposits Added	No. Deposits	Checks Paid	No. Checks
	8/31/2014	4,779.86	3,571.72	5	4,537.22	22
	Other Debits	Resulting in a Balance of			On This Date	Enclosures
	297.91	3,516.45			9/30/2014	29

Checks and Debits			Deposits and Credits	Date	Balance
15.82	24.85		600.25	9/3	5,339.44
249.08	497.00			9/5	4,593.36
42.53	124.61			9/7	4,426.22
79.87	859.38			9/8	3,486.97
685.00	742.59		711.43	9/9	2,770.81
25.75	38.98			9/12	2,706.08
36.45	59.91			9/14	2,609.72
	8.40 DM		940.00 CM	9/15	3,541.32
61.40			689.47	9/18	4,169.39
289.51 NS				9/19	3,879.88
71.59	82.00			9/21	3,726.29
312.87				9/24	3,413.42
25.00			630.57	9/27	4,018.99
227.00				9/28	3,791.99
95.06	180.48			9/30	3,516.45

LEGEND – NS Nonsufficient Funds • DM Debit Memo • CM Credit Memo

FIRST STATE BANK OF FRISCO COUNTY

reconciled when the true cash balance determined from the perspective of the unadjusted *bank* balance agrees with the true cash balance determined from the perspective of the unadjusted *book* balance. The procedures a company uses to determine the *true cash balance* from the two different perspectives are outlined here.

Adjustments to the Bank Balance

A typical format for determining the true cash balance beginning with the unadjusted bank balance is

> Unadjusted bank balance
> + Deposits in transit
> − Outstanding checks
> ─────────────────
> = True cash balance

Deposits in transit. Companies frequently leave deposits in the bank's night depository or make them on the day following the receipt of cash. Such deposits are called **deposits in transit.** Because these deposits have been recorded in the depositor's accounting records but have not yet been added to the depositor's account by the bank, they must be added to the unadjusted bank balance.

Outstanding checks. These are disbursements that have been properly recorded as cash deductions on the depositor's books. However, the bank has not deducted the amounts from the depositor's bank account because the checks have not yet been presented by the payee to the bank for payment; that is, the checks have not cleared the bank. **Outstanding checks** must be subtracted from the unadjusted bank balance to determine the true cash balance.

Adjustments to the Book Balance

A typical format for determining the true cash balance beginning with the unadjusted book balance is as follows.

```
Unadjusted book balance
+ Accounts receivable collections
+ Interest earned
− Bank service charges
− Non-sufficient-funds (NSF) checks
= True cash balance
```

Accounts receivable collections. To collect cash as quickly as possible, many companies have their customers send payments directly to the bank. The bank adds the collection directly to the depositor's account and notifies the depositor about the collection through a credit memo that is included on the bank statement. The depositor adds the amount of the cash collections to the unadjusted book balance in the process of determining the true cash balance.

Interest earned. Banks pay interest on certain checking accounts. The amount of the interest is added directly to the depositor's bank account. The bank notifies the depositor about the interest through a credit memo that is included on the bank statement. The depositor adds the amount of the interest revenue to the unadjusted book balance in the process of determining the true cash balance.

Service charges. Banks frequently charge depositors fees for services performed. They may also charge a penalty if the depositor fails to maintain a specified minimum cash balance throughout the period. Banks deduct such fees and penalties directly from the depositor's account and advise the depositor of the deduction through a debit memo that is included on the bank statement. The depositor deducts such **service charges** from the unadjusted book balance to determine the true cash balance.

Non-sufficient-funds (NSF) checks. **NSF checks** are checks that a company obtains from its customers and deposits in its checking account. However, when the checks are submitted to the customers' banks for payment, the banks refuse payment because there is insufficient money in the customers' accounts. When such checks are returned, the amounts of the checks are deducted from the company's bank account balance. The company is advised of NSF checks through debit memos that appear on the bank statement. The depositor deducts the amounts of the NSF checks from the unadjusted book balance in the process of determining the true cash balance.

Correction of Errors

In the course of reconciling the bank statement with the cash account, the depositor may discover errors in the bank's records, the depositor's records, or both. If an error is found on the bank statement, an adjustment for it is made to the unadjusted bank balance to determine the true cash balance, and the bank should be notified immediately to correct its records. Errors made by the depositor require adjustments to the book balance to arrive at the true cash balance.

Certified Checks

A **certified check** is guaranteed for payment by a bank. Whereas a regular check is deducted from the customer's account when it is presented for payment, a certified check is deducted from the customer's account when the bank certifies that the check is good.

Certified checks, therefore, *have* been deducted by the bank in determining the unadjusted bank balance, whether they have cleared the bank or remain outstanding as of the date of the bank statement. Since certified checks are deducted both from bank and depositor records immediately, they do not cause differences between the depositor and bank balances. As a result, certified checks are not included in a bank reconciliation.

Illustrating a Bank Reconciliation

The following example illustrates preparing the bank reconciliation for Green Shades Resorts, Inc. (GSRI). The bank statement for GSRI is displayed in Exhibit 4.2. Exhibit 4.3 illustrates the completed bank reconciliation. The items on the reconciliation are described below.

Adjustments to the Bank Balance

As of September 30, 2014, the bank statement showed an unadjusted balance of $3,516.45. A review of the bank statement disclosed three adjustments that had to be made to the unadjusted bank balance to determine GSRI's true cash balance.

1. Comparing the deposits on the bank statement with deposits recorded in GSRI's accounting records indicated there was $724.11 of deposits in transit.
2. An examination of the returned checks disclosed that the bank had erroneously deducted a $25 check written by Green Valley Resorts from GSRI's bank account. This amount must be added back to the unadjusted bank balance to determine the true cash balance.
3. The checks returned with the bank statement were sorted and compared to the cash records. Three checks with amounts totaling $235.25 were outstanding.

After these adjustment are made GSRI's true cash balance is determined to be $4,030.31.

EXHIBIT 4.3

GREEN SHADES RESORTS, INC.
Bank Reconciliation
September 30, 2014

Unadjusted bank balance, September 30, 2014	$3,516.45
Add: Deposits in transit	724.11
Bank error: Check drawn on Green Valley Resorts charged to GSRI	25.00
Less: Outstanding checks	

Check No.	Date	Amount
639	Sept. 18	$ 13.75
646	Sept. 20	29.00
672	Sept. 27	192.50

Total	(235.25)
True cash balance, September 30, 2014	$4,030.31
Unadjusted book balance, September 30, 2014	$3,361.22
Add: Receivable collected by bank	940.00
Error made by accountant (Check no. 633 recorded as $63.45 instead of $36.45)	27.00
Less: Bank service charges	(8.40)
NSF check	(289.51)
True cash balance, September 30, 2014	$4,030.31

Adjustments to the Book Balance

As indicated in Exhibit 4.3, GSRI's unadjusted book balance as of September 30, 2014, was $3,361.22. This balance differs from GSRI's true cash balance because of four unrecorded accounting events:

1. The bank collected a $940 account receivable for GSRI.
2. GSRI's accountant made a $27 recording error.
3. The bank charged GSRI an $8.40 service fee.
4. GSRI had deposited a $289.51 check from a customer who did not have sufficient funds to cover the check.

Two of these four adjustments increase the unadjusted cash balance. The other two decrease the unadjusted cash balance. After the adjustments have been recorded, the cash account reflects the true cash balance of $4,030.31 ($3,361.22 unadjusted cash balance + $940.00 receivable collection + $27.00 recording error − $8.40 service charge − $289.51 NSF check). Because the true balance determined from the perspective of the bank statement agrees with the true balance determined from the perspective of GSRI's books, the bank statement has been successfully reconciled with the accounting records.

Updating GSRI's Accounting Records

Each of the adjustments to the book balance must be recorded in GSRI's financial records. The effects of each adjustment on the financial statements are as follows.

ADJUSTMENT 1 *Recording the $940 receivable collection increases cash and reduces accounts receivable.*

The event is an asset exchange transaction. The effect of the collection on GSRI's financial statements is

Assets			=	Liab.	+	Equity	Rev.	−	Exp.	=	Net Inc.	Cash Flow	
Cash	+	Accts. Rec.											
940	+	(940)	=	NA	+	NA	NA	−	NA	=	NA	940	OA

ADJUSTMENT 2 *Assume the $27 recording error occurred because GSRI's accountant accidentally transposed two numbers when recording check no. 633 for utilities expense.*

The check was written to pay utilities expense of $36.45 but was recorded as a $63.45 disbursement. Since cash payments are overstated by $27.00 ($63.45 − $36.45), this amount must be added back to GSRI's cash balance and deducted from the utilities expense account, which increases net income. The effects on the financial statements are

Assets	=	Liab.	+	Equity	Rev.	−	Exp.	=	Net Inc.	Cash Flow	
Cash	=			Ret. Earn.							
27	=	NA	+	27	NA	−	(27)	=	27	27	OA

ADJUSTMENT 3   *The $8.40 service charge is an expense that reduces assets, stockholders' equity, net income, and cash.*

The effects are

Assets	=	Liab.	+	Equity	Rev.	−	Exp.	=	Net Inc.	Cash Flow
Cash	=			Ret. Earn.						
(8.40)	=	NA	+	(8.40)	NA	−	8.40	=	(8.40)	(8.40) OA

ADJUSTMENT 4   *The $289.51 NSF check reduces GSRI's cash balance.*

When it originally accepted the customer's check, GSRI increased its cash account. Because there is not enough money in the customer's bank account to pay the check, GSRI didn't actually receive cash so GSRI must reduce its cash account. GSRI will still try to collect the money from the customer. In the meantime, it will show the amount of the NSF check as an account receivable. The adjusting entry to record the NSF check is an asset exchange transaction. Cash decreases and accounts receivable increases. The effect on GSRI's financial statements is

Assets			=	Liab.	+	Equity	Rev.	−	Exp.	=	Net Inc.	Cash Flow
Cash	+	Accts. Rec.										
(289.51)	+	289.51	=	NA	+	NA	NA	−	NA	=	NA	(289.51) OA

Answers to The Curious Accountant

As this chapter explains, separation of duties is one of the primary features of a good system of internal controls. However, separation of duties is not designed to detect fraud at the very top level of management. Mr. Madoff ran BMI with almost complete control; he had no boss.

Even with a good system of internal controls, there is always some level of trust required in business. Mr. Madoff had an excellent reputation in the investment community. He had even been the president of the NASDAQ. His investors trusted him and assumed they could depend on his independent auditor to detect any major problems with the way BMI was investing, or not investing, their money.

On March 12, 2009, the 70-year-old Mr. Madoff pled guilty to 11 felony charges. He entered his guilty pleas without the benefit of a plea bargain, and will spend the remainder of his life in prison. In 2012, Peter Madoff, Bernard's 67-year-old brother, pled guilty to several crimes related to the scandal, including falsifying documents. In December 2012, he was sentenced to 10 years in prison.

Federal prosecutors accused BMI's auditor, David Friehling, with improperly auditing BMI's books. On March 18, 2009, he also was arrested and charged with falsely certifying BMI's financial statements. He pled guilty to several charges related to the fraud and is cooperating with federal prosecutors. His sentencing has been scheduled and postponed several times pending the outcome of his cooperation.

Prison terms and financial fines are not the only price people pay as a result of their fraud. On Saturday, December 11, 2010, exactly two years after Bernard Madoff's arrest, his oldest son committed suicide. His death was attributed to personal problems related to his father's scandal. In November of 2012, the 23-year-old son of David Friehling also committed suicide.

> ☑ **CHECK YOURSELF 4.2**
>
> The following information was drawn from Reliance Company's October bank statement. The unadjusted bank balance on October 31 was $2,300. The statement showed that the bank had collected a $200 account receivable for Reliance. The statement also included $20 of bank service charges for October and a $100 check payable to Reliance that was returned NSF. A comparison of the bank statement with company accounting records indicates that there was a $500 deposit in transit and $1,800 of checks outstanding at the end of the month. Based on this information, determine the true cash balance on October 31.
>
> **Answer**   Since the unadjusted book balance is not given, start with the unadjusted bank balance to determine the true cash balance. The collection of the receivable, the bank service charges, and the NSF check are already recognized in the unadjusted bank balance, so these items are not used to determine the true cash balance. Determine the true cash balance by adding the deposit in transit to and subtracting the outstanding checks from the unadjusted bank balance. The true cash balance is $1,000 ($2,300 unadjusted bank balance + $500 deposit in transit − $1,800 outstanding checks).

IMPORTANCE OF ETHICS

The chapter began with a discussion of the importance of internal control systems in preventing accounting scandals. After the Enron and WorldCom scandals and the passage of the Sarbanes-Oxley Act, much more attention has been paid to establishing effective internal control systems. However, despite this increase in legislation and awareness, accounting scandals continue to occur. In 2008, Lehman Brothers declared bankruptcy after it was discovered that the company had kept more than $50 billion in loans off the balance sheet by classifying them as sales. Several months later, Bernie Madoff used a Ponzi scheme to leave his investors with more than $21.2 billion in cash losses. These examples illustrate that legislation alone will not prevent accounting scandals. To prevent a scandal it is necessary to develop a culture that fosters and promotes ethical conduct.

LO 4-3

Discuss the role of ethics in the accounting profession.

The accountant's role in society requires trust and credibility. Accounting information is worthless if the accountant is not trustworthy. Similarly, tax and consulting advice is useless if it comes from an incompetent person. The high ethical standards required by the profession state "a certified public accountant assumes an obligation of self-discipline above and beyond requirements of laws and regulations." The **American Institute of Certified Public Accountants** requires its members to comply with the **Code of Professional Conduct.** Section I of the Code includes six articles that are summarized in Exhibit 4.4. The importance of ethical conduct is universally recognized across a broad spectrum of accounting organizations. The Institute of Management Accountants requires its members to follow a set of Standards of Ethical Conduct. The Institute of Internal Auditors also requires its members to subscribe to the organization's Code of Ethics.

Common Features of Criminal and Ethical Misconduct

Unfortunately, it takes more than a code of conduct to stop fraud. People frequently engage in activities that they know are unethical or even criminal. The auditing profession has identified three elements that are typically present when fraud occurs.

1. The availability of an opportunity.
2. The existence of some form of pressure leading to an incentive.
3. The capacity to rationalize.

EXHIBIT 4.4

Articles of AICPA Code of Professional Conduct

Article I Responsibilities
In carrying out their responsibilities as professionals, members should exercise sensitive professional and moral judgments in all their activities.

Article II The Public Interest
Members should accept the obligation to act in a way that will serve the public interest, honor the public trust, and demonstrate commitment to professionalism.

Article III Integrity
To maintain and broaden public confidence, members should perform all professional responsibilities with the highest sense of integrity.

Article IV Objectivity and Independence
A member should maintain objectivity and be free of conflicts of interest in discharging professional responsibilities. A member in public practice should be independent in fact and appearance when providing auditing and other attestation services.

Article V Due Care
A member should observe the profession's technical and ethical standards, strive continually to improve competence and the quality of services, and discharge professional responsibility to the best of the member's ability.

Article VI Scope and Nature of Services
A member in public practice should observe the principles of the Code of Professional Conduct in determining the scope and nature of services to be provided.

The three elements are frequently arranged in the shape of a triangle as shown in Exhibit 4.5.

Opportunity is shown at the head to the triangle because without opportunity fraud could not exist. The most effective way to reduce opportunities for ethical or criminal misconduct is to implement an effective set of internal controls. *Internal controls* are policies and procedures that a business implements to reduce opportunities

---

EXHIBIT 4.5

The Fraud Triangle

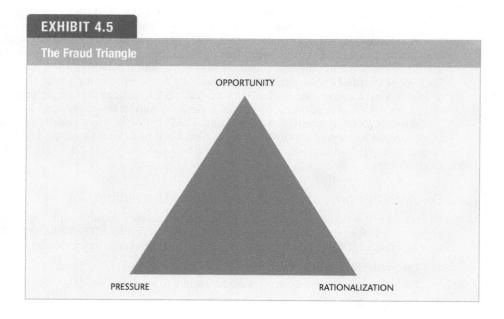

for fraud and to assure that its objectives will be accomplished. Specific controls are tailored to meet the individual needs of particular businesses. For example, banks use elaborate vaults to protect cash and safety deposit boxes, but universities have little use for this type of equipment. Even so, many of the same procedures are used by a wide variety of businesses. The internal control policies and procedures that have gained widespread acceptance are discussed in a subsequent chapter.

Only a few employees turn to the dark side even when internal control is weak and opportunities abound. So, what causes one person to commit fraud and another to remain honest? The second element of the fraud triangle recognizes **pressure** as a key ingredient of misconduct. A manager who is told "either make the numbers or you are fired" is more likely to cheat than one who is told to "tell it like it is." Pressure can come from a variety of sources.

- Personal vices such as drug addiction, gambling, and promiscuity.
- Intimidation from superiors.
- Personal debt from credit cards, consumer and mortgage loans, or poor investments.
- Family expectations to provide a standard of living that is beyond one's capabilities.
- Business failure caused by poor decision making or temporary factors such as a poor economy.
- Loyalty or trying to be agreeable.

The third and final element of the fraud triangle is **rationalization.** Few individuals think of themselves as evil. They develop rationalizations to justify their misconduct. Common rationalizations include the following.

- Everybody does it.
- They are not paying me enough. I'm only taking what I deserve.
- I'm only borrowing the money. I'll pay it back.
- The company can afford it. Look what they are paying the officers.
- I'm taking what my family needs to live like everyone else.

Most people are able to resist pressure and the tendency to rationalize ethical or legal misconduct. However, some people will yield to temptation. What can accountants do to protect themselves and their companies from unscrupulous characters? The answer lies in personal integrity. The best indicator of personal integrity is past performance. Accordingly, companies must exercise due care in performing appropriate background investigations before hiring people to fill positions of trust.

Ethical misconduct is a serious offense in the accounting profession. A single mistake can destroy an accounting career. If you commit a white-collar crime, you normally lose the opportunity to hold a white-collar job. Second chances are rarely granted; it is extremely important that you learn how to recognize and avoid the common features of ethical misconduct. To help you prepare for the real-world situations you are likely to encounter, we include ethical dilemmas in the end-of-chapter materials. When working with these dilemmas, try to identify the (1) opportunity, (2) pressure, and (3) rationalization associated with the particular ethical situation described. If you are not an ethical person, accounting is not the career for you.

ROLE OF THE INDEPENDENT AUDITOR

As previously explained, financial statements are prepared in accordance with certain rules called *generally accepted accounting principles (GAAP)*. Thus, when General Electric publishes its financial statements, it is saying, "here are our financial statements prepared according to GAAP." How can a financial analyst know that a company really did follow GAAP? Analysts and other statement users rely on **audits** conducted by **certified public accountants (CPAs).**

LO 4-4

Describe the auditor's role in financial reporting.

The primary roles of an independent auditor (CPA) are summarized below:

1. Conducts a financial audit (a detailed examination of a company's financial statements and underlying accounting records).

2. Assumes both legal and professional responsibilities to the public as well as to the company paying the auditor.

3. Determines if financial statements are *materially* correct rather than *absolutely* correct.

4. Presents conclusions in an audit report that includes an opinion as to whether the statements are prepared in conformity with GAAP. In rare cases, the auditor issues a disclaimer.

5. Maintains professional confidentiality of client records. The auditor is not, however, exempt from legal obligations such as testifying in court.

The Financial Statement Audit

What is an audit? There are several types of audits. The type most relevant to this course is a **financial statement audit,** often referred to as simply a financial audit. The financial audit is a detailed examination of a company's financial statements and the documents that support those statements. It also tests the reliability of the accounting system used to produce the financial reports. A financial audit is conducted by an **independent auditor.**

The term *independent auditor* typically refers to a *firm* of certified public accountants. CPAs are licensed by state governments to provide services to the public. They are to be as independent of the companies they audit as is reasonably possible. To help assure independence, CPAs may not be employees of the companies they audit. Further, they cannot have investments in the companies they audit. Although CPAs are paid by the companies they audit, the audit fee may not be based on the outcome of the audit.

Although the independent auditors are chosen by, paid by, and can be fired by their client companies, the auditors are primarily responsible to *the public.* In fact, auditors have a legal responsibility to those members of the public who have a financial interest in the company being audited. If investors in a company lose money, they sometimes sue the independent auditors in an attempt to recover their losses, especially if the losses were related to financial failure. A lawsuit against auditors will succeed only if the auditors failed in their professional responsibilities when conducting the audit. Auditors are not responsible for the success or failure of a company. Instead, they are responsible for the appropriate reporting of that success or failure. While recent debacles such as Bernard Madoff Investments produce spectacular headlines, auditors are actually not sued very often, considering the number of audits they perform.

Materiality and Financial Audits

Auditors do not guarantee that financial statements are absolutely correct—only that they are free from *material* misstatements. This is where things get a little fuzzy. What is a *material misstatement*? The concept of materiality is very subjective. If ExxonMobil inadvertently overstated its sales by $1 million, would this be material? In 2012, ExxonMobil had approximately $453 billion of sales! A $1 million error in computing sales at ExxonMobil is like a $1 error in computing the pay of a person who makes $453,000 per year—not material at all! An error, or other reporting problem, is **material** if knowing about it would influence the decisions of an *average prudent investor.*

Financial audits are not directed toward the discovery of fraud. Auditors are, however, responsible for providing *reasonable assurance* that statements are free from material misstatements, whether caused by errors or fraud. Also, auditors are responsible for evaluating whether internal control procedures are in place to help prevent material misstatements due to fraud. If fraud is widespread in a company, normal audit procedures should detect it.

Accounting majors take at least one and often two or more courses in auditing to understand how to conduct an audit. An explanation of auditing techniques is beyond the scope of this course, but at least be aware that auditors do not review how the company accounted for every transaction. Along with other methods, auditors use statistics to choose representative samples of transactions to examine.

Types of Audit Opinions

Once an audit is complete, the auditors present their conclusions in a report that includes an *audit opinion*. There are three basic types of audit opinions.

An **unqualified opinion,** despite its negative-sounding name, is the most favorable opinion auditors can express. It means the auditor believes the financial statements are in compliance with GAAP without qualification, reservation, or exception. Most audits result in unqualified opinions because companies correct any reporting deficiencies the auditors find before the financial statements are released.

The most negative report an auditor can issue is an **adverse opinion.** An adverse opinion means that one or more departures from GAAP are so material that the financial statements do not present a fair picture of the company's status. The auditor's report explains the unacceptable accounting practice(s) that resulted in the adverse opinion being issued. Adverse opinions are very rare because public companies are required by law to follow GAAP.

A **qualified opinion** falls between an unqualified and an adverse opinion. A qualified opinion means that for the most part, the company's financial statements are in compliance with GAAP, but the auditors have reservations about something in the statements. The auditors' report explains why the opinion is qualified. A qualified opinion usually does not imply a serious accounting problem, but users should read the auditors' report and draw their own conclusions.

If an auditor is unable to perform the audit procedures necessary to determine whether the statements are prepared in accordance with GAAP, the auditor cannot issue an opinion on the financial statements. Instead, the auditor issues a **disclaimer of opinion.** A disclaimer means that the auditor is unable to obtain enough information to confirm compliance with GAAP.

Regardless of the type of report they issue, auditors are only expressing their judgment about whether the financial statements present a fair picture of a company. They do not provide opinions regarding the investment quality of a company.

The ultimate responsibility for financial statements rests with the executives of the reporting company. Just like auditors, managers can be sued by investors who believe they lost money due to improper financial reporting. This is one reason all business persons should understand accounting fundamentals.

Confidentiality

The **confidentiality** rules in the AICPA's code of ethics for CPAs prohibits auditors from *voluntarily disclosing* information they have acquired as a result of their accountant-client relationships. However, accountants may be required to testify in a court of law. In general, federal law does not recognize an accountant-client privilege as it does with attorneys and clergy. Some federal courts have taken exception to this position, especially as it applies to tax cases. State law varies with respect to accountant-client privilege. Furthermore, if auditors terminate a client relationship because of ethical or legal disagreements and they are subsequently contacted by a successor auditor, they may be required to inform the successor of the reasons for the termination. In addition, auditors must consider the particular circumstances of a case when assessing the appropriateness of disclosing confidential information. Given the diverse legal positions governing accountant-client confidentiality, auditors should seek legal counsel prior to disclosing any information obtained in an accountant-client relationship.

To illustrate, assume that Joe Smith, CPA, discovers that his client Jane Doe is misrepresenting information reported in her financial statements. Smith tries to convince Doe to correct the misrepresentations, but she refuses to do so. Smith is required by the code of ethics to terminate his relationship with Doe. However, Smith is not permitted to disclose Doe's dishonest reporting practices unless he is called on to testify in a legal hearing or to respond to an inquiry by Doe's successor accountant.

With respect to the discovery of significant fraud, the auditor is required to inform management at least one level above the position of the employee who is engaged in the fraud and to notify the board of directors of the company. Suppose that Joe Smith, CPA, discovers that Jane Doe, employee of Western Company, is embezzling money from Western. Smith is required to inform Doe's supervisor and to notify Western's board of directors. However, Smith is prohibited from publicly disclosing the fraud.

<< A Look Back

The policies and procedures used to provide reasonable assurance that the objectives of an enterprise will be accomplished are called *internal controls*. While the mechanics of internal control systems vary from company to company, the more prevalent features include the following.

1. *Separation of duties.* Whenever possible, the functions of authorization, recording, and custody should be exercised by different individuals.

2. *Quality of employees.* Employees should be qualified to competently perform the duties that are assigned to them. Companies must establish hiring practices to screen out unqualified candidates. Furthermore, procedures should be established to ensure that employees receive appropriate training to maintain their competence.

3. *Bonded employees.* Employees in sensitive positions should be covered by a fidelity bond that provides insurance to reimburse losses due to illegal actions committed by employees.

4. *Required absences.* Employees should be required to take extended absences from their jobs so that they are not always present to hide unscrupulous or illegal activities.

5. *Procedures manual.* To promote compliance, the procedures for processing transactions should be clearly described in a manual.

6. *Authority and responsibility.* To motivate employees and promote effective control, clear lines of authority and responsibility should be established.

7. *Prenumbered documents.* Prenumbered documents minimize the likelihood of missing or duplicate documents. Prenumbered forms should be used for all important documents such as purchase orders, receiving reports, invoices, and checks.

8. *Physical control.* Locks, fences, security personnel, and other physical devices should be employed to safeguard assets.

9. *Performance evaluations.* Because few people can evaluate their own performance objectively, independent performance evaluations should be performed. Substandard performance will likely persist unless employees are encouraged to take corrective action.

Because cash is such an important business asset and because it is tempting to steal, much of the discussion of internal controls in this chapter focused on cash controls. Special procedures should be employed to control the receipts and payments of cash. One of the most common control policies is to use *checking accounts* for all payments except petty cash disbursements.

A *bank reconciliation* should be prepared each month to explain differences between the bank statement and a company's internal accounting records. A common reconciliation format determines the true cash balance based on both bank and book records. Items that typically appear on a bank reconciliation include the following:

Unadjusted bank balance	xxx	Unadjusted book balance	xxx
Add		Add	
Deposits in transit	xxx	Interest revenue	xxx
		Collection of receivables	xxx
Subtract		Subtract	
Outstanding checks	xxx	Bank service charges	xxx
		NSF checks	xxx
True cash balance	xxx	True cash balance	xxx

Agreement of the two true cash balances provides evidence that accounting for cash transactions has been accurate.

The chapter discussed the importance of ethics in the accounting profession. The *American Institute of Public Accountants* requires all of its members to comply with the *Code of Professional Conduct.* Situations where *opportunity, pressure,* and *rationalization* exist can lead employees to conduct unethical acts, which, in cases like Enron, have destroyed the organization. Finally, the chapter discussed the auditor's role in financial reporting, including the materiality concept and the types of audit opinions that may be issued.

A Look Forward

The next chapter focuses on more specific issues related to accounts receivables and inventory. Accounting for receivables and payables was introduced in Chapter 2, using relatively simple illustrations. For example, we assumed that customers who purchased services on account always paid their bills. In real business practice, some customers do not pay their bills. Among other topics, Chapter 5 examines how companies account for uncollectible accounts receivable.

Accounting for inventory was discussed in Chapter 3. However, we assumed that all inventory items were purchased at the same price. This is unrealistic given that the price of goods is constantly changing. Chapter 5 discusses how to account for inventory items that are purchased at different times and different prices.

 Video lectures and accompanying self-assessment quizzes are available for all learning objectives through McGraw-Hill *Connect® Accounting.*

SELF-STUDY REVIEW PROBLEM

The following information pertains to Terry's Pest Control Company (TPCC) for July:

1. The unadjusted bank balance at July 31 was $870.
2. The bank statement included the following items:
   (a) A $60 credit memo for interest earned by TPCC.
   (b) A $200 NSF check made payable to TPCC.
   (c) A $110 debit memo for bank service charges.
3. The unadjusted book balance at July 31 was $1,400.

4. A comparison of the bank statement with company accounting records disclosed the following:

   (a) A $400 deposit in transit at July 31.

   (b) Outstanding checks totaling $120 at the end of the month.

Required

Prepare a bank reconciliation.

Solution

TERRY'S PEST CONTROL COMPANY
Bank Reconciliation
July 31

Unadjusted bank balance	$ 870
Add: Deposits in transit	400
Less: Outstanding checks	(120)
True cash balance	$1,150
Unadjusted book balance	$1,400
Add: Interest revenue	60
Less: NSF check	(200)
Less: Bank service charges	(110)
True cash balance	$1,150

KEY TERMS

Adverse opinion 147

American Institute of
  Certified Public
  Accountants 143

Audits 145

Authority manual 133

Bank reconciliation 137

Bank statement 137

Bank statement credit
  memo 137

Bank statement debit
  memo 137

Cash 135

Certified check 139

Certified public accountants
  (CPAs) 145

Checks 137

Code of Professional
  Conduct 143

Confidentiality 147

Deposits in transit 138

Deposit ticket 137

Disclaimer of opinion 147

Fidelity bond 133

Financial statement
  audit 146

General authority 133

Independent auditor 146

Internal controls 132

Material 146

Non-sufficient-funds (NSF)
  checks 139

Opportunity 144

Outstanding checks 139

Pressure 145

Procedures manual 133

Qualified opinion 147

Rationalization 145

Separation of duties 132

Service charges 139

Signature card 136

Specific authorizations 133

True cash balance 137

Unadjusted bank
  balance 137

Unadjusted book
  balance 137

Unqualified opinion 147

QUESTIONS

1. What motivated Congress to pass the Sarbanes-Oxley Act (SOX) of 2002?

2. Define the term *internal control*.

3. Explain the relationship between SOX and COSO.

4. Name and briefly define the five components of COSO's internal control framework.

5. Explain how COSO's *Enterprise Risk Management—An Integrated Framework* project relates to COSO's *Internal Control—An Integrated Framework* project.

6. List several control activities of an effective internal control system.

7. What is meant by *separation of duties*? Give an illustration.

8. What are the attributes of a high-quality employee?

9. What is a fidelity bond? Explain its purpose.

10. Why is it important that every employee periodically take a leave of absence or vacation?

11. What are the purpose and importance of a procedures manual?

12. What is the difference between specific and general authorizations?

13. Why should documents (checks, invoices, receipts) be prenumbered?

14. What procedures are important in the physical

control of assets and accounting records?

15. What is the purpose of independent verification of performance?

16. What items are considered cash?

17. Why is cash more susceptible to theft or embezzlement than other assets?

18. Giving written copies of receipts to customers can help prevent what type of illegal acts?

19. What procedures can help to protect cash receipts?

20. What procedures can help protect cash disbursements?

21. What effect does a debit memo in a bank statement have on the Cash account? What effect does a credit memo in a bank statement have on the Cash account?

22. What information is normally included in a bank statement?

23. Why might a bank statement reflect a balance that is larger than the balance recorded in the depositor's books? What could cause the bank balance to be smaller than the book balance?

24. What is the purpose of a bank reconciliation?

25. What is an outstanding check?

26. What is a deposit in transit?

27. What is a certified check?

28. How is an NSF check accounted for in the accounting records?

29. Name and comment on the three elements of the fraud triangle.

30. What are the six articles of ethical conduct set out under section I of the AICPA's Code of Professional Conduct?

MULTIPLE-CHOICE QUESTIONS

Multiple-choice questions are provided on the text website at www.mhhe.com/edmondssurvey4e.

EXERCISES

connect | ACCOUNTING   All applicable Exercises are available with McGraw-Hill's *Connect® Accounting.*

Exercise 4-1   *SOX and COSO's internal control frameworks*   LO 4-1

Required

a. Explain what the acronym SOX refers to.
b. Define the acronym COSO and explain how it relates to SOX.
c. Name and briefly define the five components of COSO's internal control framework.
d. Define the acronym ERM and explain how it relates to COSO's internal control framework.

Exercise 4-2   *Control activities of a strong internal control system*   LO 4-1

Required

List and describe nine control activities of a strong internal control system discussed in this chapter.

Exercise 4-3   *Internal controls for small businesses*   LO 4-1

Dick Haney is opening a new business that will sell sporting goods. It will initially be a small operation, and he is concerned about the security of his assets. He will not be able to be at the business all of the time and will have to rely on his employees and internal control procedures to ensure that transactions are properly accounted for and assets are safeguarded. He will have a store manager and two other employees who will be sales personnel and stock personnel and who will also perform any other duties necessary. Dick will be in the business on a regular basis. He has come to you for advice.

Required

Write a memo to Dick outlining the procedures that he should implement to ensure that his store assets are protected and that the financial transactions are properly recorded.

Exercise 4-4   *Internal controls for cash*   LO 4-1

Required

List and discuss effective internal control procedures that apply to cash.

LO 4-1

Exercise 4-5   *Internal controls to prevent theft*

Rhonda Cox worked as the parts manager for State Line Automobiles, a local automobile deal-ership. Rhonda was very dedicated and never missed a day of work. Since State Line was a small operation, she was the only employee in the parts department. Her duties consisted of ordering parts for stock and as needed for repairs, receiving the parts and checking them in, distributing them as needed to the shop or to customers for purchase, and keeping track of and taking the year-end inventory of parts. State Line decided to expand and needed to secure additional financing. The local bank agreed to a loan contingent on an audit of the dealership. One require-ment of the audit was to oversee the inventory count of both automobiles and parts on hand. Rhonda was clearly nervous, explaining that she had just inventoried all parts in the parts department. She supplied the auditors with a detailed list. The inventory showed parts on hand worth $225,000. The auditors decided they needed to verify a substantial part of the inventory. When the auditors began their counts, a pattern began to develop. Each type of part seemed to be one or two items short when the actual count was taken. This raised more concern. Although Rhonda assured the auditors the parts were just misplaced, the auditors continued the count. After completing the count of parts on hand, the auditors could document only $155,000 of actual parts. Suddenly, Rhonda quit her job and moved to another state.

Required

a. What do you suppose caused the discrepancy between the actual count and the count that Rhonda had supplied?

b. What procedures could be put into place to prevent this type of problem?

LO 4-1

Exercise 4-6   *Internal control procedures to prevent embezzlement*

Jane Jones was in charge of the returns department at The Software Company. She was respon-sible for evaluating returned merchandise. She sent merchandise that was reusable back to the warehouse, where it was restocked in inventory. Jones was also responsible for taking the merchandise that she determined to be defective to the city dump for disposal. She had agreed to buy a tax planning program for one of her friends at a discount through her contacts at work. That is when the idea came to her. She could simply classify one of the reusable returns as defec-tive and bring it home instead of taking it to the dump. She did so and made a quick $150. She was happy, and her friend was ecstatic; he was able to buy a $400 software package for only $150. He told his friends about the deal, and soon Jones had a regular set of customers. She was caught when a retail store owner complained to the marketing manager that his pricing strategy was being undercut by The Software Company's direct sales to the public. The marketing manager was suspicious because The Software Company had no direct marketing program. When the outside sales were ultimately traced back to Jones, the company discovered that it had lost over $10,000 in sales revenue because of her criminal activity.

Required

Identify an internal control procedure that could have prevented the company's losses. Explain how the procedure would have stopped the embezzlement.

LO 4-2

Exercise 4-7   *Treatment of NSF check*

Montgomery Stationery's bank statement contained a $260 NSF check that one of its customers had written to pay for supplies purchased.

Required

a. Show the effects of recognizing the NSF check on the financial statements by recording the appropriate amounts in a horizontal statements model like the following one:

Assets		= Liab.	+ Equity	Rev.	− Exp.	= Net Inc.	Cash Flow
Cash +	Accts. Rec.						

b. Is the recognition of the NSF check on Montgomery's books an asset source, use, or exchange transaction?

c. Suppose the customer redeems the check by giving Montgomery $290 cash in exchange for the bad check. The additional $30 was a service fee charged by Montgomery. Show the effects on the financial statements in the horizontal statements model in Requirement *a*.

d. Is the receipt of cash referenced in Requirement *c* an asset source, use, or exchange transaction?

Exercise 4-8   *Adjustments to the balance per books*   LO 4-2

Required

Identify which of the following items are added to or subtracted from the unadjusted *book balance* to arrive at the true cash balance. Distinguish the additions from the subtractions by placing a + beside the items that are added to the unadjusted book balance and a − beside those that are subtracted from it. The first item is recorded as an example.

Reconciling Items	Book Balance Adjusted?	Added or Subtracted?
Charge for checks	Yes	−
NSF check from customer		
Note receivable collected by the bank		
Outstanding checks		
Credit memo		
Interest revenue		
Deposits in transit		
Debit memo		
Service charge		

Exercise 4-9   *Adjustments to the balance per bank*   LO 4-2

Required

Identify which of the following items are added to or subtracted from the unadjusted *bank balance* to arrive at the true cash balance. Distinguish the additions from the subtractions by placing a + beside the items that are added to the unadjusted bank balance and a − beside those that are subtracted from it. The first item is recorded as an example.

Reconciling Items	Bank Balance Adjusted?	Added or Subtracted?
Certified checks	No	NA
Petty cash voucher		
NSF check from customer		
Interest revenue		
Bank service charge		
Outstanding checks		
Deposits in transit		
Debit memo		
Credit memo		

Exercise 4-10   *Adjusting the cash account*   LO 4-2

As of May 31, 2014, the bank statement showed an ending balance of $26,100. The unadjusted Cash account balance was $27,350. The following information is available:

1. Deposit in transit, $6,981.
2. Credit memo in bank statement for interest earned in May, $36.
3. Outstanding check, $5,720.
4. Debit memo for service charge, $25.

Required

Determine the true cash balance by preparing a bank reconciliation as of May 31, 2014, using the preceding information.

Exercise 4-11   *Determining the true cash balance, starting with the unadjusted bank balance*

The following information is available for Sharder Company for the month of June:

1. The unadjusted balance per the bank statement on June 30 was $71,230.
2. Deposits in transit on June 30 were $2,350.
3. A debit memo was included with the bank statement for a service charge of $25.
4. A $5,611 check written in June had not been paid by the bank.
5. The bank statement included a $930 credit memo for the collection of a note. The principal of the note was $900, and the interest collected amounted to $30.

Required

Determine the true cash balance as of June 30. (*Hint:* It is not necessary to use all of the preceding items to determine the true balance.)

Exercise 4-12   *Determining the true cash balance, starting with the unadjusted book balance*

Henderson Company had an unadjusted cash balance of $7,215 as of May 31. The company's bank statement, also dated May 31, included a $68 NSF check written by one of Henderson's customers. There were $750 in outstanding checks and $930 in deposits in transit as of May 31. According to the bank statement, service charges were $50, and the bank collected a $500 note receivable for Henderson. The bank statement also showed $13 of interest revenue earned by Henderson.

Required

Determine the true cash balance as of May 31. (*Hint:* It is not necessary to use all of the preceding items to determine the true balance.)

Exercise 4-13   *AICPA Code of Professional Conduct*

Mark Miller owns and operates Miller Enterprises. Mark's sister, Jessica, is the independent public accountant for Miller Enterprises. Jessica worked for Miller Enterprises for five years before she started her independent CPA practice. Mark considered hiring a different accounting firm but ultimately decided that no one knew his business as well as his sister.

Required

Use the AICPA Code of Professional Conduct to evaluate the appropriateness of Jessica's client relationship with Miller Enterprises.

Exercise 4-14   *AICPA Code of Professional Conduct*

Raula Kato discovered a material reporting error in the accounting records of Sampoon, Inc. (SI), during the annual audit. The error was so significant that it will certainly have an adverse effect on the price of the client's stock, which is actively traded on the Western stock exchange. After talking to his close friend and president of SI, Kato agreed to withhold the information until the president had time to sell his SI stock. Kato leaked the information to his parents so that they could sell their shares of stock as well. The reporting matter was a relatively complex issue that involved recently issued reporting standards. Kato told himself that if he were caught he would simply plead ignorance. He would simply say that he did not have time to keep up with the rapidly changing standards and he would be off the hook.

Required

a. Write a memo that identifies specific articles of the AICPA Code of Professional Conduct that were violated by Kato.
b. Would pleading ignorance relieve Kato from his audit responsibilities?

Exercise 4-15   *Fraud triangle*   LO 4-3

Jacob Perry is a CPA with a secret. His secret is that he gambles on sports. Jacob knows that his profession disapproves of gambling, but considers the professional standards to be misguided in his case. Jacob really doesn't consider his bets to be gambling because he spends a lot of time studying sports facts. He believes that he is simply making educated decisions based on facts. He argues that using sports facts to place bets is no different than using accounting information to buy stock.

Required

Use the fraud triangle as a basis to comment on Jacob Perry's gambling activities.

Exercise 4-16   *Materiality and the auditor*   LO 4-4

Melissa Moore is an auditor. Her work at two companies disclosed inappropriate recognition of revenue. Both cases involved dollar amounts in the $200,000 range. In one case, Moore considered the item material and required her client to restate earnings. In the other case, Moore dismissed the misstatement as being immaterial.

Required

Write a memo that explains how a $200,000 misstatement of revenue is acceptable for one company but unacceptable for a different company.

PROBLEMS

 connect **All applicable Problems are available with McGraw-Hill's** *Connect® Accounting.*

Problem 4-17   *Types of audit reports*   LO 4-4

Ellen Norman is a partner of a regional accounting firm. Ms. Norman was hired by a client to audit the company's books. After extensive work, Ms. Norman determined that she was unable to perform the appropriate audit procedures.

Required

a. Name the type of audit report that Ms. Norman should issue with respect to the work that she did accomplish.

b. If Ms. Norman had been able to perform the necessary audit procedures, there are three types of audit reports that she could have issued depending on the outcome of the audit. Name and describe these three types of audit reports.

Problem 4-18   *Using internal controls to restrict illegal or unethical behavior*   LO 4-1

Required

For each of the following fraudulent acts, describe one or more internal control procedures that could have prevented (or helped prevent) the problems.

a. Nina Wells, the administrative assistant in charge of payroll, created a fictitious employee, wrote weekly checks to the fictitious employee, and then personally cashed the checks for her own benefit.

b. Noel Rand, the receiving manager of Southern Lumber, created a fictitious supplier named F&M Building Supply. F&M regularly billed Southern Lumber for supplies purchased. Rand had printed shipping slips and billing invoices with the name of the fictitious company and opened a post office box as the mailing address. Rand simply prepared a receiving report and submitted it for payment to the accounts payable department. The accounts payable clerk then paid the invoice when it was received because Rand acknowledged receipt of the supplies.

c. Patty Smith works at a local hobby shop and usually operates the cash register. She has developed a way to give discounts to her friends. When they come by, she rings a lower price or does not charge the friend for some of the material purchased. At first, Smith thought she would get caught, but no one seemed to notice. Indeed, she has become so sure that there is no way for the owner to find out that she has started taking home some supplies for her own personal use.

Problem 4-19 *Preparing a bank reconciliation*

Hank Brock owns a card shop, Four Aces. The following cash information is available for the month of August 2014.

As of August 31, the bank statement shows a balance of $15,320. The August 31 unadjusted balance in the Cash account of Four Aces is $13,910. A review of the bank statement revealed the following information:

1. A deposit of $4,295 on August 31, 2014, does not appear on the August bank statement.
2. It was discovered that a check to pay for baseball cards was correctly written and paid by the bank for $3,650 but was recorded on the books as $4,400.
3. When checks written during the month were compared with those paid by the bank, three checks amounting to $5,030 were found to be outstanding.
4. A debit memo for $75 was included in the bank statement for the purchase of a new supply of checks.

Required

Prepare a bank reconciliation at the end of August showing the true cash balance.

Problem 4-20 *Missing information in a bank reconciliation*

The following data apply to Larry's Auto Supply Inc. for May 2014:

1. Balance per the bank on May 31, $8,250.
2. Deposits in transit not recorded by the bank, $1,230.
3. Bank error; check written by L7 Auto Supply was charged to Larry's Auto Supply's account, $720.
4. The following checks written and recorded by Larry's Auto Supply were not included in the bank statement:

3013	$ 420
3054	650
3056	1,830

5. Note collected by the bank, $400.
6. Service charge for collection of note, $15.
7. The bookkeeper recorded a check written for $230 to pay for the May utilities expense as $430 in the cash disbursements journal.
8. Bank service charge in addition to the note collection fee, $35.
9. Customer checks returned by the bank as NSF, $275.

Required

Determine the amount of the unadjusted cash balance per Larry's Auto Supply's books.

Problem 4-21 *Adjustments to the cash account based on the bank reconciliation*

Required

Determine whether the following items included in Sung Company's bank reconciliation will require adjusting or correcting entries on Sung's books.

a. Service charges of $30 for the month of January were listed on the bank statement.
b. The bank charged a $350 check drawn on Yung Restaurant to Sung's account. The check was included in Sung's bank statement.
c. A check of $62 was returned to the bank because of insufficient funds and was noted on the bank statement. Sung received the check from a customer and thought that it was good when it was deposited into the account.

d. A $982 deposit was recorded by the bank as $928.

e. Four checks totaling $725 written during the month of January were not included with the January bank statement.

f. A $65 check written to Office Max for office supplies was recorded in the general journal as $56.

g. The bank statement indicated that the bank had collected a $450 note for Sung.

h. Sung recorded $700 of receipts on January 31, 2014, which was deposited in the night depository of the bank. These deposits were not included in the bank statement.

Problem 4-22 *Bank reconciliation and adjustments to the cash account*

LO 4-2

The following information is available for Sunset Valley Hotel for July 2014:

CHECK FIGURE
a. True Cash Balance, July 31, 2014: $16,234

Bank Statement

STATE BANK

Bolta Vista, NV 10001

Sunset Valley Hotel 10 Main Street Bolta Vista, NV 10001	Account number 12-4567 July 31, 2014

Beginning balance 6/30/2014	$ 9,031
Total deposits and other credits	29,800
Total checks and other debits	23,902
Ending balance 7/31/2014	14,929

Checks and Debits		Deposits and Credits		
Check No.	Amount	Date		Amount
✓ 2350	$3,761	July	1	$1,102
2351	1,643	July	10	6,498
2352	8,000	July	15	4,929
2354	2,894	July	21	6,174
2355	1,401	July	26	5,963
2357	6,187	July	30	2,084
DM	16	CM		3,050

The following is a list of checks and deposits recorded on the books of the Sunset Valley Hotel for July 2014:

Date		Check No.	Amount of Check	Date		Amount of Deposit
July	2	2351	$1,643	July	8	$6,498
July	4	2352	8,000	July	14	4,929
July	10	2353	1,500	July	21	6,174
July	10	2354	2,894	July	26	5,963
July	15	2355	1,401	July	29	2,084
July	20	2356	745	July	30	3,550
July	22	2357	6,187			

Other Information

1. Check no. 2350 was outstanding from June.
2. The credit memo was for collection of notes receivable.
3. All checks were paid at the correct amount.
4. The debit memo was for printed checks.
5. The June 30 bank reconciliation showed a deposit in transit of $1,102.
6. The unadjusted Cash account balance at July 31 was $13,200.

Required

a. Prepare the bank reconciliation for Sunset Valley Hotel at the end of July.

b. Explain how the adjustments described above affect the cash account.

LO 4-1, 4-2

CHECK FIGURE

a. True Cash Balance, May 31, 2014: $21,650

Problem 4-23   *Bank reconciliation and internal control*

Following is a bank reconciliation for Pizza Express for May 31, 2014:

	Cash Account	Bank Statement
Balance as of 5/31/2014	$25,000	$22,000
Deposit in transit		4,250
Outstanding checks		(465)
Note collected by bank	1,815	
Bank service charge	(30)	
Automatic payment on loan	(1,000)	
Adjusted cash balance as of 5/31/2014	$25,785	$25,785

Because of limited funds, Pizza Express employed only one accountant who was responsible for receiving cash, recording receipts and disbursements, preparing deposits, and preparing the bank reconciliation. The accountant left the company on June 8, 2014, after preparing the May 31 bank reconciliation. His replacement compared the checks returned with the bank statement to the cash disbursements journal and found the total of outstanding checks to be $4,600.

Required

a. Prepare a corrected bank reconciliation.

b. What is the total amount of cash missing, and how was the difference between the "true cash" per the bank and the "true cash" per the books hidden on the reconciliation prepared by the former employee?

c. What could Pizza Express do to avoid cash theft in the future?

LO 4-3

Problem 4-24   *Fraud Triangle*

Robert Stroup is an accountant with a shady past. Suffice it to say that he owes some very unsavory characters a lot of money. Despite his past, Robert works hard at keeping up a strong professional image. He is a manager at Smith and Associates, a fast-growing CPA firm. Robert is highly regarded around the office because he is a strong producer of client revenue. Indeed, on several occasions he exceeded his authority in establishing prices with clients. This is typically a partner's job but who could criticize Robert, who is most certainly bringing in the business. Indeed, Robert is so good that he is able to pull off the following scheme. He bills clients at inflated rates and then reports the ordinary rate to his accounting firm. Say, for example, the normal charge for a job is $2,500. Robert will smooth talk the client, then charge him $3,000. He reports the normal charge of $2,500 to his firm and keeps the extra $500 for himself. He knows it isn't exactly right. Even so, his firm gets its regular charges and the client willingly pays for the services rendered. He thinks to himself, as he pockets his ill-gotten gains, who is getting hurt anyway?

Required

The text discusses three common features (conditions) that motivate ethical misconduct. Identify and explain each of the three features as they appear in the above scenario.

LO 4-4

Problem 4-25   *Confidentiality and the auditor*

West Aston discovered a significant fraud in the accounting records of a high profile client. The story has been broadcast on national airways. Aston was unable to resolve his remaining concerns with the company's management team and ultimately resigned from the audit engagement.

Aston knows that he will be asked by several interested parties, including his friends and relatives, the successor auditor, and prosecuting attorneys in a court of law, to tell what he knows. He has asked you for advice.

Required

Write a memo that explains Aston's disclosure responsibilities to each of the interested parties.

Problem 4-26   *Auditor responsibilities*   LO 4-4

You have probably heard it is unwise to bite the hand that feeds you. Independent auditors are chosen by, paid by, and can be fired by the companies they audit. What keeps the auditor independent? In other words, what stops an auditor from blindly following the orders of a client?

Required

Write a memo that explains the reporting responsibilities of an independent auditor.

ANALYZE, THINK, COMMUNICATE

ATC 4-1   Business Application Case   *Understanding real-world annual reports*

Use the Target Corporation's Form 10-K to answer the following questions related to Target's 2012 fiscal year (year ended February 2, 2013). Target's Form 10-K is available on the company's website or through the SEC's EDGAR database. Appendix A provides instructions for using the EDGAR database.

Required

a. Instead of "Cash," the company's balance sheet uses the account name "Cash and cash equivalents." How does the company define cash equivalents?

b. The annual report has two reports in which management is clearly identified as having responsibility for the company's financial reporting and internal controls. What are the names of these reports and on what pages are they located?

ATC 4-2   Group Assignment   *Bank reconciliations*

The following cash and bank information is available for three companies on June 30, 2014.

Cash and Adjustment Information	Peach Co.	Apple Co.	Pear Co.
Unadjusted cash balance per books, 6/30	$45,620	$32,450	$23,467
Outstanding checks	1,345	2,478	2,540
Service charge	50	75	35
Balance per bank statement, 6/30	48,632	37,176	24,894
Credit memo for collection of notes receivable	4,500	5,600	3,800
NSF check	325	145	90
Deposits in transit	2,500	3,200	4,800
Credit memo for interest earned	42	68	12

Required

a. Organize the class into three sections and divide each section into groups of three to five students. Assign Peach Co. to section 1, Apple Co. to section 2, and Pear Co. to section 3.

Group Tasks

(1) Prepare a bank reconciliation for the company assigned to your group.

(2) Select a representative from a group in each section to put the bank reconciliation on the board.

Class Discussion:

b. Discuss the cause of the difference between the unadjusted cash balance and the ending balance for the bank statement. Also, discuss types of adjustment that are commonly made to the bank balance and types of adjustment that are commonly made to the unadjusted book balance.

ATC 4-3 Research Assignment *Investigating cash and management issues at Smucker's*

Using the most current Form 10-K available on EDGAR, or the company's website, answer the following questions about the J. M. Smucker Company. Instructions for using EDGAR are in Appendix A. *Note: In some years the financial statements, footnotes, etc., portion of Smucker's annual report have been located at the end of the Form 10-K, in or just after "Item 15."*

Required

a. Instead of "Cash," the company's balance sheet uses the account name "Cash and cash equivalents." How does the company define cash equivalents?

b. The annual report has two reports in which management clearly acknowledges its responsibility for the company's financial reporting and internal controls. What are the names of these reports and on what pages are they located?

ATC 4-4 Writing Assignment *Internal control procedures*

Sarah Johnson was a trusted employee of Evergreen Trust Bank. She was involved in everything. She worked as a teller, she accounted for the cash at the other teller windows, and she recorded many of the transactions in the accounting records. She was so loyal that she never would take a day off, even when she was really too sick to work. She routinely worked late to see that all the day's work was posted into the accounting records. She would never take even a day's vacation because they might need her at the bank. Adam and Jammie, CPAs, were hired to perform an audit, the first complete audit that had been done in several years. Johnson seemed somewhat upset by the upcoming audit. She said that everything had been properly accounted for and that the audit was a needless expense. When Adam and Jammie examined some of the bank's internal control procedures, it discovered problems. In fact, as the audit progressed, it became apparent that a large amount of cash was missing. Numerous adjustments had been made to customer accounts with credit memorandums, and many of the transactions had been posted several days late. In addition, there were numerous cash payments for "office expenses." When the audit was complete, it was determined that more than $100,000 of funds was missing or improperly accounted for. All fingers pointed to Johnson. The bank's president, who was a close friend of Johnson, was bewildered. How could this type of thing happen at this bank?

Required

Prepare a written memo to the bank president, outlining the procedures that should be followed to prevent this type of problem in the future.

ATC 4-5 Ethical Dilemma *I need just a little extra money*

John Riley, a certified public accountant, has worked for the past eight years as a payroll clerk for Southeast Industries, a small furniture manufacturing firm in the Northeast. John recently experienced unfortunate circumstances. His teenage son required major surgery and the medical bills not covered by John's insurance have financially strained John's family.

John works hard and is a model employee. Although he received regular performance raises during his first few years with Southeast, John's wages have not increased in three years. John asked his supervisor, Bill Jameson, for a raise. Bill agreed that John deserved a raise, but told him he could not currently approve one because of sluggish sales.

A disappointed John returned to his duties while the financial pressures in his life continued. Two weeks later, Larry Tyler, an assembly worker at Southwest, quit over a dispute with management. John conceived an idea. John's duties included not only processing employee terminations but also approving time cards before paychecks were issued and then distributing the paychecks to firm personnel. John decided to delay processing Mr. Tyler's termination, to forge timecards for Larry Tyler for the next few weeks, and to cash the checks himself. Since he distributed paychecks, no one would find out, and John reasoned that he was really entitled to the extra money anyway. In fact, no one did discover his maneuver and John stopped the practice after three weeks.

Required

a. Does John's scheme affect Southeast's balance sheet? Explain your answer.

b. Review the AICPA's Articles of Professional Conduct and comment on any of the standards that have been violated.

c. Identify the three elements of unethical and criminal conduct recognized in the fraud triangle.

CHAPTER 5

Accounting for Receivables and Inventory Cost Flow

LEARNING OBJECTIVES

After you have mastered the material in this chapter, you will be able to:

LO 5-1   Explain how the allowance method of accounting for uncollectible accounts affects financial statements.

LO 5-2   Use the percent of revenue method to estimate the uncollectible accounts expense.

LO 5-3   Use the percent of receivables method to estimate the uncollectible accounts expense.

LO 5-4   Explain how accounting for notes receivable and accrued interest affects financial statements.

LO 5-5   Explain how accounting for credit card sales affects financial statements.

LO 5-6   Explain how different inventory cost flow methods (specific identification, FIFO, LIFO, and weighted average) affect financial statements.

 Video lectures and accompanying self-assessment quizzes are available for all learning objectives through McGraw-Hill Connect® Accounting.

CHAPTER OPENING

Many people buy on impulse. If they must wait, the desire to buy wanes. To take advantage of impulse buyers, most merchandising companies offer customers credit because it increases their sales. A disadvantage of this strategy occurs when some customers are unable or unwilling to pay their bills. Nevertheless, the widespread availability of credit suggests that the advantages of increased sales outweigh the disadvantages of some uncollectible accounts.

When a company allows a customer to "buy now and pay later," the company's right to collect cash in the future is called an **account receivable.** Typically, amounts due from individual accounts receivable are relatively small and the collection period is short. Most accounts receivable are collected within 30 days. When a longer credit term is needed or when a receivable is large, the seller usually requires the buyer to issue a note reflecting a credit agreement between the parties. The note specifies the maturity date, interest rate, and other credit terms. Receivables evidenced by such notes are called **notes receivable.** Accounts and notes receivable are reported as assets on the balance sheet.

The Curious Accountant

Lockheed Martin develops and maintains various types of technology related to security. Its biggest customer, by far, is the U.S. government for whom it provides aeronautics and space-system products and services. In 2012, 82 percent of its revenue came from sales to the U.S. government, and another 17 percent came from sales to governments of other countries. Suppose the U.S. government contracted with Lockheed Martin Corporation to provide management services related to a governmental hardware and software system, and that the cost of these services will be $10 million per month. Assume the government offers to pay for the services on the day they are provided (a cash purchase) or 30 days later (a purchase on account).

Assume that Lockheed Martin is absolutely sure the government will pay its account when due. Do you think the company should care whether the government pays for the services upon delivery or 30 days later? Why? (Answer on page 165.)

ALLOWANCE METHOD OF ACCOUNTING FOR UNCOLLECTIBLE ACCOUNTS

LO 5-1

Explain how the allowance method of accounting for uncollectible accounts affects financial statements.

Most companies do not expect to collect the full amount (face value) of their accounts receivable. Even carefully screened credit customers sometimes don't pay their bills. The **net realizable value** of accounts receivable represents the amount of receivables a company estimates it will actually collect. The net realizable value is the *face value* less an *allowance for doubtful accounts*.

The **allowance for doubtful accounts** represents a company's estimate of the amount of uncollectible receivables. To illustrate, assume a company with total accounts receivable of $50,000 estimates that $2,000 of its receivables will not be collected. The net realizable value of receivables is computed as follows.

Accounts receivable	$50,000
Less: Allowance for doubtful accounts	(2,000)
Net realizable value of receivables	$48,000

A company cannot know today, of course, the exact amount of the receivables it will not be able to collect in the future. The *allowance for doubtful accounts* and the *net realizable value* are necessarily *estimated amounts*. The net realizable value, however, more closely measures the cash that will ultimately be collected than does the face value. To avoid overstating assets, companies usually report receivables on their balance sheets at the net realizable value.

Reporting accounts receivable in the financial statements at net realizable value is commonly called the **allowance method of accounting for uncollectible accounts.** The following section illustrates using the allowance method for Allen's Tutoring Services (ATS).

Accounting Events Affecting the 2014 Period

Allen's Tutoring Services is a small company that provides tutoring services to college students. Allen's started operations on January 1, 2014. During 2014, Allen's experienced three types of accounting events. These events are discussed below.

EVENT 1   Revenue Recognition
Allen's Tutoring Services recognized $14,000 of service revenue earned on account during 2014.

This is an asset source transaction. Allen's Tutoring Services obtained assets (accounts receivable) by providing services to customers. Both assets and stockholders' equity (retained earnings) increase. The event increases revenue and net income. Cash flow is not affected. These effects follow.

Event No.	Assets	=	Liab.	+	Equity	Rev.	−	Exp.	=	Net Inc.	Cash Flow
	Accts. Rec.	=			Ret. Earn.						
1	14,000	=	NA	+	14,000	14,000	−	NA	=	14,000	NA

EVENT 2   Collection of Receivables
Allen's Tutoring Services collected $12,500 cash from accounts receivable in 2014.

This event is an asset exchange transaction. The asset cash increases; the asset accounts receivable decreases. Total assets remains unchanged. Net income is not affected

Answers to The Curious Accountant

Lockheed Martin would definitely prefer to make the sale to the government in cash rather than on account. Even though it may be certain to collect its accounts receivable, the sooner the company gets its cash the sooner the cash can be reinvested.

The interest cost related to a small account receivable of $50 that takes 30 days to collect may seem immaterial; at 6 percent the lost interest amounts to $.25. However, when one considers that Lockheed Martin had approximately $6.6 billion of accounts receivable on December 31, 2012, and took an average of 51 days to collect them, the cost of financing receivables for a real-world company becomes apparent. At 6 percent the cost of waiting 51 days to collect $6.6 billion of cash is $55.3 million ($6.6 billion × .06 × 51/365). For a full year, the cost to Lockheed Martin would be $396 million ($6.6 billion × .06). In 2012 the weighted-average interest rate on Lockheed Martin's debt was approximately 6 percent.

because the revenue was recognized in the previous transaction. The cash inflow is reported in the operating activities section of the statement of cash flows.

Event No.	Assets			=	Liab.	+	Equity	Rev.	−	Exp.	=	Net Inc.	Cash Flow
	Cash	+	Accts. Rec.										
2	12,500	+	(12,500)	=	NA	+	NA	NA	−	NA	=	NA	12,500 OA

Accounting for Uncollectible Accounts Expense

EVENT 3 Recognizing Uncollectible Accounts Expense

Allen's Tutoring Services recognized uncollectible accounts expense for accounts expected to be uncollectible in the future.

The year-end balance in the Accounts Receivable account is $1,500 ($14,000 of revenue on account − $12,500 of collections). Although Allen's Tutoring Services has the legal right to receive this $1,500 in 2015, the company is not likely to collect the entire amount because some of its customers may not pay the amounts due. Allen's will not know the actual amount of uncollectible accounts until some future time when the customers default (fail to pay). However, the company can *estimate* the amount of receivables that will be uncollectible.

Suppose Allen's Tutoring Services estimates that $75 of the receivables is uncollectible. To improve financial reporting, the company can recognize the estimated expense in 2014. In this way, uncollectible accounts expense and the related revenue will be recognized in the same accounting period (2014). Recognizing an estimated expense is more useful than recognizing no expense. The *matching* of revenues and expenses is improved and the statements are, therefore, more accurate.

The estimated amount of **uncollectible accounts expense** is recognized in a year-end adjusting entry. The adjusting entry reduces the book value of total assets, reduces stockholders' equity (retained earnings), and reduces the amount of reported net income. The statement of cash flows is not affected. The effects of recognizing uncollectible accounts expense are shown here.

Event No.	Assets			=	Liab.	+	Equity	Rev.	–	Exp.	=	Net Inc.	Cash Flow
	Accts. Rec.	–	Allow.	=		+	Ret. Earn.						
3	NA	–	75	=	NA	+	(75)	NA	–	75	=	(75)	NA

Instead of decreasing the receivables account directly, the asset reduction is recorded in the **contra asset account,** Allowance for Doubtful Accounts. Recall that the contra account is subtracted from the accounts receivable balance to determine the net realizable value of receivables, as follows for ATS.

Accounts receivable	$1,500
Less: Allowance for doubtful accounts	(75)
Net realizable value of receivables	$1,425

Generally accepted accounting principles require disclosure of both the net realizable value and the amount of the allowance account. Many companies disclose these amounts directly in the balance sheet in a manner similar to that shown in the text box above. Other companies disclose this information in the footnotes to the financial statements.

Financial Statements

The financial statements for Allen's Tutoring Services' 2014 accounting period are shown in Exhibit 5.1. As previously indicated, estimating uncollectible accounts improves the usefulness of the 2014 financial statements in two ways. First, the balance sheet reports the amount of cash ($1,500 − $75 = $1,425) the company actually expects to collect (net realizable value of accounts receivable). Second, the income statement provides a clearer picture of managerial performance because it better *matches* the uncollectible accounts expense with the revenue it helped produce. The statements in Exhibit 5.1 show that the cash flow from operating activities ($12,500)

EXHIBIT 5.1

Financial Statements for 2014

Income Statement		Balance Sheet			Statement of Cash Flows	
Service revenue	$14,000	Assets			Operating Activities	
Uncollectible accts. exp.	(75)	Cash		$12,500	Inflow from customers	$12,500
Net income	$13,925	Accounts receivable	$1,500		Investing Activities	0
		Less: Allowance	(75)		Financing Activities	0
		Net realizable value		1,425	Net change in cash	12,500
		Total assets		$13,925	Plus: Beginning cash balance	0
		Stockholders' equity			Ending cash balance	$12,500
		Retained earnings		$13,925		

CHECK YOURSELF 5.1

Pamlico Inc. began operations on January 1, 2015. During 2015, it earned $400,000 of revenue on account. The company collected $370,000 of accounts receivable. At the end of the year, Pamlico estimates uncollectible accounts expense will be 1 percent of sales. Based on this information alone, what is the net realizable value of accounts receivable as of December 31, 2015?

Answer   Accounts receivable at year-end are $30,000 ($400,000 sales on account − $370,000 collection of receivables). The amount in the allowance for doubtful accounts would be $4,000 ($400,000 credit sales × 0.01). The net realizable value of accounts receivable is therefore $26,000 ($30,000 − $4,000).

differs from net income ($13,925). The statement of cash flows reports only cash collections, whereas the income statement reports revenues earned on account less the estimated amount of uncollectible accounts expense.

Accounting Events Affecting the 2015 Period

To further illustrate accounting for uncollectible accounts, we discuss six accounting events affecting Allen's Tutoring Services during 2015.

Accounting for Write-Off of Uncollectible Accounts Receivable
EVENT 1   Write-Off of Uncollectible Accounts Receivable
Allen's Tutoring Services wrote off $70 of uncollectible accounts receivable.

This is an asset exchange transaction. The amount of the uncollectible accounts is removed from the Accounts Receivable account and from the Allowance for Doubtful Accounts account. Because the balances in both the Accounts Receivable and the Allowance accounts decrease, the net realizable value of receivables—and therefore total assets—remains unchanged. The write-off does not affect the income statement. Because the uncollectible accounts expense was recognized in the previous year, the expense would be double counted if it were recognized again at the time an uncollectible account is written off. Finally, the statement of cash flows is not affected by the write-off. These effects are shown in the following statements model.

Event No.	Assets			=	Liab.	+	Equity	Rev.	−	Exp.	=	Net Inc.	Cash Flow
	Accts. Rec.	−	Allow.										
1	(70)	−	(70)	=	NA	+	NA	NA	−	NA	=	NA	NA

The computation of the *net realizable value,* before and after the write-off, is shown below.

	Before Write-Off	After Write-Off
Accounts receivable	$1,500	$1,430
Less: Allowance for doubtful accounts	(75)	(5)
Net realizable value	$1,425	$1,425

EVENT 2   Revenue Recognition
Allen's Tutoring Services provided $10,000 of tutoring services on account during 2015.

Assets (accounts receivable) and stockholders' equity (retained earnings) increase. Recognizing revenue increases net income. Cash flow is not affected. These effects are illustrated below.

Event No.	Assets	=	Liab.	+	Equity	Rev.	−	Exp.	=	Net Inc.	Cash Flow
	Accts. Rec.	=			Ret. Earn.						
2	10,000	=	NA	+	10,000	10,000	−	NA	=	10,000	NA

EVENT 3   Collection of Accounts Receivable
Allen's Tutoring Services collected $8,430 cash from accounts receivable.

The balance in the Cash account increases, and the balance in the Accounts Receivable account decreases. Total assets are unaffected. Net income is not affected because revenue was recognized previously. The cash inflow is reported in the operating activities section of the statement of cash flows.

Event No.	Assets			=	Liab.	+	Equity	Rev.	−	Exp.	=	Net Inc.	Cash Flow
	Cash	+	Accts. Rec.										
3	8,430	+	(8,430)	=	NA	+	NA	NA	−	NA	=	NA	8,430 OA

Accounting for Recovery of an Uncollectible Account Receivable

EVENT 4   Recovery of an Uncollectible Account: Reinstate Receivable
Allen's Tutoring Services recovered a receivable that it had previously written off.

Occasionally, a company receives payment from a customer whose account was previously written off. In such cases, the customer's account should be reinstated and the cash received should be recorded the same way as any other collection on account. The account receivable is reinstated because a complete record of the customer's payment history may be useful if the customer requests credit again at some future date. To illustrate, assume that Allen's Tutoring Services received a $10 cash payment from a customer whose account had previously been written off. The first step is to **reinstate** the account receivable by reversing the previous write-off. The balances in the Accounts Receivable and the Allowance accounts increase. Since Allowance is a contra asset account, the increase in it offsets the increase in the Accounts Receivable account, and total assets are unchanged. Net income and cash flow are unaffected. These effects are shown here.

Event No.	Assets			=	Liab.	+	Equity	Rev.	−	Exp.	=	Net Inc.	Cash Flow
	Accts. Rec.	−	Allow.										
4	10	−	10	=	NA	+	NA	NA	−	NA	=	NA	NA

EVENT 5   Recovery of an Uncollectible Account: Collection of Receivable
Allen's Tutoring Services recorded collection of the reinstated receivable.

The collection of $10 is recorded like any other collection of a receivable account. Cash increases, and accounts receivable decreases.

Event No.	Assets			=	Liab.	+	Equity	Rev.	−	Exp.	=	Net Inc.	Cash Flow
	Cash	+	Accts. Rec.										
5	10	+	(10)	=	NA	+	NA	NA	−	NA	=	NA	10 OA

ESTIMATING UNCOLLECTIBLE ACCOUNTS EXPENSE USING THE PERCENT OF REVENUE (SALES) METHOD

Companies recognize the estimated amount of uncollectible accounts expense in a period-end adjusting entry. Since Allen's Tutoring Service began operations in 2014, it had no previous credit history upon which to base its estimate. After consulting trade publications and experienced people in the same industry, ATS made an educated guess as to the amount of expense it should recognize for its first year. In its second year of operation, however, ATS can use its first-year experience as a starting point for estimating the second year (2015) uncollectible accounts expense.

At the end of 2014 ATS estimated uncollectible accounts expense to be $75 on service revenue of $14,000. In 2015 ATS actually wrote off $70 of which $10 was later recovered. ATS therefore experienced actual uncollectible accounts of $60 on service revenue of $14,000 for an uncollectible accounts rate of approximately .43 percent of service revenue. ATS could apply this percentage to the 2015 service revenue to estimate the 2015 uncollectible accounts expense. In practice, many companies determine the percentage estimate of uncollectible accounts on a three- or five-year moving average.

Companies adjust the historical percentage for anticipated future circumstances. For example, they reduce it if they adopt more rigorous approval standards for new credit applicants. Alternatively, they may increase the percentage if economic forecasts signal an economic downturn that would make future defaults more likely. A company will also increase the percentage if it has specific knowledge one or more of its customers is financially distressed. Multiplying the service revenue by the percentage estimate of uncollectible accounts is commonly called the **percent of revenue method** of estimating uncollectible accounts expense.

LO 5-2

 Use the percent of revenue method to estimate the uncollectible accounts expense.

EVENT 6   Adjustment for Recognition of Uncollectible Accounts Expense
Using the percent of revenue method, Allen's Tutoring Services recognized uncollectible accounts expense for 2015.

ATS must record this adjustment as of December 31, 2015, to update its accounting records before preparing the 2015 financial statements. After reviewing its credit history, economic forecasts, and correspondence with customers, management estimates uncollectible accounts expense to be 1.35 percent of service revenue, or $135 ($10,000 service revenue × .0135). Recognizing the $135 uncollectible accounts expense decreases both assets (net realizable of receivables) and stockholders' equity (retained earnings). The expense recognition decreases net income. The statement of cash flows is not affected. The financial statements are affected as shown here.

Event No.	Assets			=	Liab.	+	Equity	Rev.	−	Exp.	=	Net Inc.	Cash Flow
	Accts. Rec.	−	Allow.	=			Ret. Earn.						
6	NA	−	135	=	NA	+	(135)	NA	−	135	=	(135)	NA

Analysis of Financial Statements

Exhibit 5.2 displays the 2015 financial statements. The amount of uncollectible accounts expense ($135) differs from the ending balance of the Allowance account ($150). The balance in the Allowance account was $15 before the 2015 adjusting entry for

170   Chapter 5

EXHIBIT 5.2

Financial Statements for 2015

Income Statement		Balance Sheet			Statement of Cash Flows	
Service revenue	$10,000	Assets			Operating Activities	
Uncollectible accts. exp.	(135)	Cash		$20,940	Inflow from customers	$ 8,440
Net income	$ 9,865	Accounts receivable	$3,000		Investing Activities	0
		Less: Allowance	(150)		Financing Activities	0
		Net realizable value		2,850	Net change in cash	8,440
		Total assets		$23,790	Plus: Beginning cash balance	12,500
		Stockholders' equity			Ending cash balance	$20,940
		Retained earnings		$23,790		

uncollectible accounts expense was recorded. At the end of 2014, Allen's Tutoring Services estimated there would be $75 of uncollectible accounts as a result of 2014 revenue earned on account. Actual write-offs, however, amounted to $70 and $10 of that amount was recovered, indicating the actual uncollectible accounts expense for 2014 was only $60. Hindsight shows the expense for 2014 was overstated by $15. However, if no estimate had been made, the amount of uncollectible accounts expense would have been understated by $60. In some accounting periods estimated uncollectible accounts expense will likely be overstated; in others it may be understated. The allowance method cannot produce perfect results, but it does improve the accuracy of the financial statements.

Because no dividends were paid, retained earnings at the end of 2015 equals the December 31, 2014, retained earnings plus 2015 net income (that is, $13,925 + $9,865 = $23,790). Again, the cash flow from operating activities ($8,440) differs from net income ($9,865) because the statement of cash flows does not include the effects of revenues earned on account and the recognition of uncollectible accounts expense.

☑ CHECK YOURSELF 5.2

Maher Company had beginning balances in Accounts Receivable and Allowance for Doubtful Accounts of $24,200 and $2,000, respectively. During the accounting period Maher earned $230,000 of revenue on account and collected $232,500 of cash from receivables. The company also wrote off $1,950 of uncollectible accounts during the period. Maher estimates uncollectible accounts expense will be 1 percent of credit sales. Based on this information, what is the net realizable value of receivables at the end of the period?

Answer   The balance in the Accounts Receivable account is $19,750 ($24,200 + $230,000 − $232,500 − $1,950). The amount of uncollectible accounts expense for the period is $2,300 ($230,000 × 0.01). The balance in Allowance for Doubtful Accounts is $2,350 ($2,000 − $1,950 + $2,300). The net realizable value of receivables is therefore $17,400 ($19,750 − $2,350).

ESTIMATING UNCOLLECTIBLE ACCOUNTS EXPENSE USING THE PERCENT OF RECEIVABLES METHOD

LO 5-3

Use the percent of receivables method to estimate the uncollectible accounts expense.

As an alternative to the percent of revenue method, which focuses on estimating the *expense* of uncollectible accounts, companies may estimate the amount of the adjusting entry to record uncollectible accounts expense using the **percent of receivables method.** The percent of receivables method focuses on estimating the most accurate amount for the balance sheet *Allowance for Doubtful Accounts* account.

EXHIBIT 5.3

PYRAMID CORPORATION
Accounts Receivable Aging Schedule
December 31, 2015

Customer Name	Total Balance	Current	Number of Days Past Due			
			0–30	31–60	61–90	Over 90
J. Davis	$ 6,700	$ 6,700				
B. Diamond	4,800	2,100	$ 2,700			
K. Eppy	9,400	9,400				
B. Gilman	2,200				$1,000	$1,200
A. Kelly	7,300	7,300				
L. Niel	8,600	1,000	6,000	$ 1,600		
L. Platt	4,600			4,600		
J. Turner	5,500			3,000	2,000	500
H. Zachry	6,900		3,000	3,900		
Total	$56,000	$26,500	$11,700	$13,100	$3,000	$1,700

The longer an account receivable remains outstanding, the less likely it is to be collected. Companies using the percent of receivables method typically determine the age of their individual accounts receivable accounts as part of estimating the allowance for doubtful accounts. An **aging of accounts receivable** schedule classifies all receivables by their due date. Exhibit 5.3 shows an aging schedule for Pyramid Corporation as of December 31, 2015.

A company estimates the required Allowance for Doubtful Accounts balance by applying different percentages to each category in the aging schedule. The percentage for each category is based on a company's previous collection experience for each of the categories. The percentages become progressively higher as the accounts become older. Exhibit 5.4 illustrates computing the allowance balance Pyramid Corporation requires.

The computations in Exhibit 5.4 mean the *ending balance* in the Allowance for Doubtful Accounts account should be $3,760. This balance represents the amount Pyramid will subtract from total accounts receivable to determine the net realizable value of receivables. To determine the amount of the adjusting entry to recognize uncollectible accounts expense, Pyramid must take into account any existing balance in the allowance account *before* recording the adjustment. For example, if Pyramid Corporation had a $500 balance in the Allowance account before the year-end adjustment, the

EXHIBIT 5.4

Balance Required in the Allowance for Doubtful Accounts at December 31, 2015

Number of Days Past Due	Receivables Amount	Percentage Likely to Be Uncollectible	Required Allowance Account Balance
Current	$26,500	.01	$ 265
0–30	11,700	.05	585
31–60	13,100	.10	1,310
61–90	3,000	.25	750
Over 90	1,700	.50	850
Total	$56,000		$3,760

adjusting entry would need to add $3,260 ($3,760 − $500) to the account. The effects on the financial statements are shown below.

Assets			= Liab.	+	Equity	Rev.	−	Exp.	=	Net Inc.	Cash Flow
Accts. Rec.	−	Allow.	=		Ret. Earn.						
NA	−	3,260	= NA	+	(3,260)	NA	−	3,260	=	3,260	NA

Matching Revenues and Expenses versus Asset Measurement

The *percent of revenue* method, with its focus on determining the uncollectible accounts expense, is often called the income statement approach. The *percent of receivables* method, focused on determining the best estimate of the allowance balance, is frequently called the balance sheet approach. Which estimating method is better? In any given year, the results will vary slightly between approaches. In the long run, however, the percentages used in either approach are based on a company's actual history of uncollectible accounts. Accountants routinely revise their estimates as more data become available, using hindsight to determine if the percentages should be increased or decreased. Either approach provides acceptable results.

ACCOUNTING FOR NOTES RECEIVABLE (PROMISSORY NOTES)

LO 5-4

Explain how accounting for notes receivable and accrued interest affects financial statements.

Companies typically do not charge their customers interest on accounts receivable that are not past due. When a company extends credit for a long time or when the amount of credit it extends is large, however, the cost of granting free credit and the potential for disputes about payment terms both increase. To address these concerns, the parties frequently enter into a credit agreement, the terms of which are legally documented in a **promissory note.**

To illustrate, assume Allen's Tutoring Services (ATS) loans some of its idle cash to an individual, Stanford Cummings, so Cummings can buy a car. ATS and Cummings agree that Cummings will repay the money borrowed plus interest at the end of one year. They also agree that ATS will hold the title to the car to secure the debt. Exhibit 5.5 illustrates a promissory note that outlines this credit agreement. For ATS, the credit arrangement represents a *note receivable.*

EXHIBIT 5.5

Promissory Note

Promissory Note

$15,000 (3)   *November 1, 2014*
Amount   **Date**

For consideration received, Stanford Cummings **hereby promises to pay to the order of:**

Allen's Tutoring Services (2)

Fifteen thousand and no/100   **Dollars**

payable on   October 31, 2015 (5)

plus interest thereon at the rate of 6 **percent per year.** (4)

Collateral Description   Automobile title (6)

Signature   *Stanford Cummings* (1)

Features of this note are discussed below. Each feature is cross-referenced with a number that corresponds to an item on the promissory note in Exhibit 5.5. Locate each feature in Exhibit 5.5 and read the corresponding description of the feature below.

1. Maker—The person responsible for making payment on the due date is the **maker** of the note. The maker may also be called the *borrower* or *debtor.*

2. Payee—The person to whom the note is made payable is the **payee.** The payee may also be called the *creditor* or *lender.* The payee loans money to the maker and expects the return of the principal and the interest due.

3. Principal—The amount of money loaned by the payee to the maker of the note is the **principal.**

4. Interest—The economic benefit earned by the payee for loaning the principal to the maker is **interest,** which is normally expressed as an annual percentage of the principal amount. For example, a note with a 6 percent interest rate requires interest payments equal to 6 percent of the principal amount every year the loan is outstanding.

5. Maturity Date—The date on which the maker must repay the principal and make the final interest payment to the payee is the **maturity date.**

6. Collateral—Assets belonging to the maker that are assigned as security to ensure that the principal and interest will be paid when due are called **collateral.** In this example, if Cummings fails to pay ATS the amount due, ownership of the car Cummings purchased will be transferred to ATS.

How Accounting for Notes Receivable Affects Financial Statements

We illustrate accounting for notes receivable using the credit agreement evidenced by the promissory note in Exhibit 5.5. Allen's Tutoring Services engaged in many transactions during 2014; we discuss here only transactions directly related to the note receivable.

EVENT 1 Loan of Money

The note shows that ATS loaned $15,000 to Stanford Cummings on November 1, 2014. This event is an asset exchange. The asset account Cash decreases and the asset account Notes Receivable increases. The income statement is not affected. The statement of cash flows shows a cash outflow for investing activities. The effects on the financial statements are shown below.

	Assets				=	Liab.	+	Equity	Rev.	−	Exp.	=	Net Inc.	Cash Flow
Date	Cash	+	Notes Rec.	+	Int. Rec.	=			Ret. Earn.						
11/01/12	(15,000)	+	15,000	+	NA	=	NA	+	NA	NA	−	NA	=	NA	(15,000) IA

EVENT 2 Accrual of Interest

For ATS, loaning money to the maker of the note, Stanford Cummings, represents investing in the note receivable. Cummings will repay the principal ($15,000) plus interest of 6 percent of the principal amount ($0.06 \times \$15,000 = \$900$), or a total of $15,900, on October 31, 2015, one year from the date he borrowed the money from ATS.

Conceptually, lenders *earn* interest continually even though they do not *collect* cash payment for it every day. Each day, the amount of interest due, called **accrued interest,** is greater than the day before. Companies would find it highly impractical to attempt to record (recognize) accrued interest continually as the amount due increased.

Businesses typically solve the record-keeping problem by only recording accrued interest when it is time to prepare financial statements or when it is due. At such times, the accounts are *adjusted* to reflect the amount of interest currently due. For example, ATS recorded the asset exchange immediately upon investing in the note receivable on November 1, 2014. ATS did not, however, recognize any interest earned on the note until the balance sheet date, December 31, 2014. At year-end ATS made an entry to recognize the interest it had earned during the previous two months (November 1 through December 31). This entry is an **adjusting entry** because it adjusts (updates) the account balances prior to preparing financial statements.

ATS computed the amount of accrued interest by multiplying the principal amount of the note by the annual interest rate and by the length of time for which the note has been outstanding.

Principal × Annual interest rate × Time outstanding = Interest revenue

$15,000 ×   0.06   ×   (2/12)   = $150

ATS recognized the $150 of interest revenue in 2014 although ATS will not collect the cash until 2015. This practice illustrates the **matching concept.** Interest revenue is recognized in (matched with) the period in which it is earned regardless of when the related cash is collected. The adjustment is an asset source transaction. The asset account Interest Receivable increases, and the stockholders' equity account Retained Earnings increases. The income statement reflects an increase in revenue and net income. The statement of cash flows is not affected because ATS will not collect cash until the maturity date (October 31, 2015). The effects on the financial statements are shown below.

	Assets				=	Liab.	+	Equity	Rev.	–	Exp.	=	Net Inc.	Cash Flow
Date	Cash	+	Notes Rec.	+	Int. Rec.	=			Ret. Earn.					
12/31/12	NA	+	NA	+	150	=	NA	+	150	150	–	NA	=	150	NA

EVENT 3   Collection of Principal and Interest on the Maturity Date

ATS collected $15,900 cash on the maturity date. The collection included $15,000 for the principal plus $900 for the interest. Recall that ATS previously accrued interest in the December 31, 2014, adjusting entry for the two months in 2014 that the note was outstanding. Since year-end, ATS has earned an additional 10 months of interest revenue. ATS must recognize this interest revenue before recording the cash collection. The amount of interest earned in 2015 is computed as follows.

Principal × Annual interest rate × Time outstanding = Interest revenue

$15,000 ×   0.06   ×   (10/12)   = $750

The effects on the financial statements are shown below.

	Assets				=	Liab.	+	Equity	Rev.	–	Exp.	=	Net Inc.	Cash Flow
Date	Cash	+	Notes Rec.	+	Int. Rec.	=			Ret. Earn.					
10/31/13	NA	+	NA	+	750	=	NA	+	750	750	–	NA	=	750	NA

The total amount of accrued interest is now $900 ($150 accrued in 2014 plus $750 accrued in 2015). The $15,900 cash collection is an asset exchange transaction. The asset account Cash increases and two asset accounts, Notes Receivable and Interest Receivable, decrease. The income statement is not affected. The statement of cash flows shows a $15,000 inflow from investing activities (recovery of principal) and a $900 inflow from operating activities (interest collection). The effects on the financial statements are shown below.

Date	Assets					=	Liab.	+	Equity	Rev.	−	Exp.	=	Net Inc.	Cash Flow	
	Cash	+	Notes Rec.	+	Int. Rec.	=			Ret. Earn.							
10/31/13	15,900	+	(15,000)	+	(900)	=	NA	+	NA	NA	−	NA	=	NA	15,000	IA
															900	OA

Financial Statements

The financial statements reveal key differences between the timing of revenue recognition and the exchange of cash. These differences are highlighted below.

	2014	2015	Total
Interest revenue recognized	$150	$750	$900
Cash inflow from operating activities	0	900	900

Accrual accounting calls for recognizing revenue in the period in which it is earned regardless of when cash is collected.

Income Statement

Although generally accepted accounting principles require reporting receipts of or payments for interest on the statement of cash flows as operating activities, they do not specify how to classify interest on the income statement. In fact, companies traditionally report interest on the income statement as a nonoperating item. Interest is therefore frequently reported in two different categories within the same set of financial statements.

Balance Sheet

As with other assets, companies report interest receivable and notes receivable on the balance sheet in order of their liquidity. **Liquidity** refers to how quickly assets are expected to be converted to cash during normal operations. In the preceding example, ATS expects to convert its accounts receivable to cash before it collects the interest receivable and note receivable. Companies commonly report interest and notes receivable after accounts receivable. Exhibit 5.6 shows a partial balance sheet for Southern Company to illustrate the presentation of receivables.

EXHIBIT 5.6

Typical Balance Sheet Presentation of Receivables

SOUTHERN COMPANY
Partial Balance Sheet
As of December 31, 2014

Cash		$xxxx
Accounts receivable	$xxxx	
Less: Allowance for doubtful accounts	(xxxx)	
Net realizable value of accounts receivable		xxxx
Interest receivable		xxxx
Notes receivable		xxxx

☑️ **CHECK YOURSELF 5.3**

On October 1, 2014, Mei Company accepted a promissory note for a loan it made to the Asia Pacific Company. The note had a $24,000 principal amount, a four-month term, and an annual interest rate of 4 percent. Determine the amount of interest revenue and the cash inflow from operating activities Mei will report in its 2014 and 2015 financial statements.

Answer   The computation of accrued interest revenue is shown below. The interest rate is stated in annual terms even though the term of the note is only four months. Interest rates are commonly expressed as an annual percentage regardless of the term of the note. The *time outstanding* in the following formulas is therefore expressed as a fraction of a year. Mei charged annual interest of 4 percent, but the note was outstanding for only 3/12 of a year in 2014 and 1/12 of a year in 2015.

2014
Principal × Annual interest rate × Time outstanding = Interest revenue
$24,000 ×   0.04   ×   (3/12)   = $240

2015
Principal × Annual interest rate × Time outstanding = Interest revenue
$24,000 ×   0.04   ×   (1/12)   = $80

In 2014, Mei's cash inflow from interest will be zero.
   In 2015, Mei will report a $320 ($240 + $80) cash inflow from operating activities for interest.

ACCOUNTING FOR CREDIT CARD SALES

LO 5-5

 Explain how accounting for credit card sales affects financial statements.

Maintaining accounts and notes receivable is expensive. In addition to uncollectible accounts expense, companies extending credit to their customers incur considerable costs for such clerical tasks as running background checks and maintaining customer records. Many businesses find it more efficient to accept third-party credit cards instead of offering credit directly to their customers. Credit card companies service the merchant's credit sales for a fee that typically ranges between 2 and 8 percent of gross sales.

The credit card company provides customers with plastic cards that permit cardholders to charge purchases at various retail outlets. When a sale takes place, the seller records the transaction on a receipt the customer signs. The receipt is forwarded to the credit card company, which immediately pays the merchant.

The credit card company deducts its service fee from the gross amount of the sale and pays the merchant the net balance (gross amount of sale less credit card fee) in cash. The credit card company collects the gross sale amount directly from the customer. The merchant avoids the risk of uncollectible accounts as well as the cost of maintaining customer credit records. To illustrate, assume that Allen's Tutoring Service experiences the following events.

EVENT 1   Recognition of Revenue and Expense on Credit Card Sales
ATS accepts a credit card payment for $1,000 of services rendered.

Assume the credit card company charges a 5 percent fee for handling the transaction ($1,000 × 0.05 = $50). ATS's income increases by the amount of revenue ($1,000) and decreases by the amount of the credit card expense ($50). Net income increases by $950. The event increases an asset, accounts receivable, due from the credit card company, and stockholders' equity (retained earnings) by $950 ($1,000 revenue − $50 credit card expense). Cash flow is not affected. These effects are shown here.

Event No.	Assets	=	Liab.	+	Equity	Rev.	−	Exp.	=	Net Inc.	Cash Flow
	Accts. Rec. =				Ret. Earn.						
1	950	=	NA	+	950	1,000	−	50	=	950	NA

EVENT 2 Collection of Credit Card Receivable
The collection of the receivable due from the credit card company is recorded like any other receivable collection.

When ATS collects the net amount of $950 ($1,000 − $50) from the credit card company, one asset account (Cash) increases and another asset account (Accounts Receivable) decreases. Total assets are not affected. The income statement is not affected. A $950 cash inflow is reported in the operating activities section of the statement of cash flows. These effects are illustrated below.

Event No.	Assets			=	Liab.	+	Equity	Rev.	−	Exp.	=	Net Inc.	Cash Flow
	Cash	+	Accts. Rec.										
2	950	+	(950)	=	NA	+	NA	NA	−	NA	=	NA	950 OA

As mentioned earlier, two costs of extending credit to customers are bad debts expense and record-keeping costs. These costs can be significant. Large companies spend literally millions of dollars to buy the equipment and pay the staff necessary to operate entire departments devoted to managing accounts receivable. Further, there is an implicit interest charge associated with extending credit. When a customer is permitted to delay payment, the creditor forgoes the opportunity to invest the amount the customer owes.

INVENTORY COST FLOW METHODS

In Chapter 3, we used the simplifying assumption that identical inventory items cost the same amount. In practice, businesses often pay different amounts for identical items. Suppose The Mountain Bike Company (TMBC) sells high-end Model 201 helmets. Even though all Model 201 helmets are identical, the price TMBC pays for each helmet frequently changes.

Explain how different inventory cost flow methods (specific identification, FIFO, LIFO, and weighted average) affect financial statements.

Assume TMBC purchases one Model 201 helmet at a cost of $100. Two weeks later, TMBC purchases a second Model 201 helmet. Because the supplier has raised prices, the second helmet costs $110. If TMBC sells one of its two helmets, should it record $100 or $110 as cost of goods sold? The following section of this chapter discusses several acceptable alternative methods for determining the amount of cost of goods sold under generally accepted accounting principles.

Recall that when goods are sold, product costs flow (are transferred) from the Inventory account to the Cost of Goods Sold account. Four acceptable methods for determining the amount of cost to transfer are (1) specific identification; (2) first-in, first-out (FIFO); (3) last-in, first-out (LIFO); and (4) weighted average.

Specific Identification

Suppose TMBC tags inventory items so that it can identify which one is sold at the time of sale. TMBC could then charge the actual cost of the specific item sold to cost of goods sold. Recall that the first inventory item TMBC purchased cost $100 and the second item cost $110. Using **specific identification,** cost of goods sold would be $100 if the first item purchased were sold or $110 if the second item purchased were sold.

When a company's inventory consists of many low-priced, high-turnover goods, the record keeping necessary to use specific identification isn't practical. Imagine the difficulty of recording the cost of each specific food item in a grocery store. Another disadvantage of the specific identification method is the opportunity for managers to manipulate the income statement. For example, TMBC can report a lower cost of goods sold by selling the first instead of the second item. Specific identification is, however, frequently used for high-priced, low-turnover inventory items such as automobiles. For big-ticket items like cars, customer demands for specific products limit management's ability to select which merchandise is sold and volume is low enough to manage the record keeping.

First-In, First-Out (FIFO)

The **first-in, first-out (FIFO) cost flow method** requires that the cost of the items purchased *first* be assigned to cost of goods sold. Using FIFO, TMBC's cost of goods sold is $100.

Last-In, First-Out (LIFO)

The **last-in, first-out (LIFO) cost flow method** requires that the cost of the items purchased *last* be charged to cost of goods sold. Using LIFO, TMBC's cost of goods sold is $110.

Weighted Average

To use the **weighted-average cost flow method,** first calculate the average cost per unit by dividing the *total cost* of the inventory available by the *total number* of units available. In the case of TMBC, the average cost per unit of the inventory is $105 ([$100 + $110] ÷ 2). Cost of goods sold is then calculated by multiplying the average cost per unit by the number of units sold. Using weighted average, TMBC's cost of goods sold is $105 ($105 × 1).

Physical Flow

The preceding discussion pertains to the flow of *costs* through the accounting records, *not* the actual **physical flow of goods.** Goods usually move physically on a FIFO basis, which means that the first items of merchandise acquired by a company (first-in) are the first items sold to its customers (first-out). The inventory items on hand at the end of the accounting period are typically the last items in (the most recently acquired goods). If companies did not sell their oldest inventory items first, inventories would include dated, less marketable merchandise. *Cost flow,* however, can differ from *physical flow.* For example, a company may use LIFO or weighted average for financial reporting even if its goods flow physically on a FIFO basis.

EFFECT OF COST FLOW ON FINANCIAL STATEMENTS

Effect on Income Statement

The cost flow method a company uses can significantly affect the gross margin reported in the income statement. To demonstrate, assume that TMBC sold the inventory item discussed previously for $120. The amounts of gross margin using the FIFO, LIFO, and weighted-average cost flow assumptions are shown in the following table.

	FIFO	LIFO	Weighted Average
Sales	$120	$120	$120
Cost of goods sold	(100)	(110)	(105)
Gross margin	$ 20	$ 10	$ 15

Even though the physical flow is assumed to be identical for each method, the gross margin reported under FIFO is double the amount reported under LIFO. Companies experiencing identical economic events (same units of inventory purchased and sold) can report significantly different results in their financial statements. Meaningful financial analysis requires an understanding of financial reporting practices.

Effect on Balance Sheet

Because total product costs are allocated between cost of goods sold and ending inventory, the cost flow method a company uses affects its balance sheet as well as its income statement. Because FIFO transfers the first cost to the income statement, it leaves the last cost on the balance sheet. Similarly, by transferring the last cost to the income statement, LIFO leaves the first cost in ending inventory. The weighted-average method bases both cost of goods sold and ending inventory on the average cost per unit. To illustrate, the ending inventory TMBC would report on the balance sheet using each of the three cost flow methods is shown in the following table.

	FIFO	LIFO	Weighted Average
Ending inventory	$110	$100	$105

EXHIBIT 5.7

Use of Inventory Cost Flow Methods

Other 4%
Average 19%
FIFO 42%
LIFO 35%

Data Source: AICPA, *Accounting Trends and Techniques.*

The FIFO, LIFO, and weighted-average methods are all used extensively in business practice. The same company may even use one cost flow method for some of its products and different cost flow methods for other products. Exhibit 5.7 illustrates the relative use of the different cost flow methods among U.S. companies.

✓ CHECK YOURSELF 5.4

Nash Office Supply (NOS) purchased two Model 303 copiers at different times. The first copier purchased cost $400 and the second copier purchased cost $450. NOS sold one of the copiers for $600. Determine the gross margin on the sale and the ending inventory balance assuming NOS accounts for inventory using (1) FIFO, (2) LIFO, and (3) weighted average.

Answer

	FIFO	LIFO	Weighted Average
Sales	$600	$600	$600
Cost of goods sold	(400)	(450)	(425)
Gross margin	$200	$150	$175
Ending inventory	$450	$400	$425

Multiple Layers with Multiple Quantities

The previous example illustrates different **inventory cost flow methods** using only two cost layers ($100 and $110) with only one unit of inventory in each layer. Actual business inventories are considerably more complex. Most real-world inventories are composed of multiple cost layers with different quantities of inventory in each layer. The underlying allocation concepts, however, remain unchanged.

For example, a different inventory item The Mountain Bike Company (TMBC) carries in its stores is a bike called the Eraser. TMBC's beginning inventory and two purchases of Eraser bikes are described below.

Jan. 1	Beginning inventory	10 units @ $200	=	$ 2,000
Mar. 18	First purchase	20 units @ $220	=	4,400
Aug. 21	Second purchase	25 units @ $250	=	6,250
Total cost of the 55 bikes available for sale				$12,650

The accounting records for the period show that TMBC paid cash for all Eraser bike purchases and that it sold 43 bikes at a cash price of $350 each.

Allocating Cost of Goods Available for Sale

The following discussion shows how to determine the cost of goods sold and ending inventory amounts under FIFO, LIFO, and weighted average. We show all three methods to demonstrate how they affect the financial statements differently; TMBC would actually use only one of the methods.

Regardless of the cost flow method chosen, TMBC must allocate the cost of goods available for sale ($12,650) between cost of goods sold and ending inventory. The amounts assigned to each category will differ depending on TMBC's cost flow method. Computations for each method are shown below.

FIFO Inventory Cost Flow

Recall that TMBC sold 43 Eraser bikes during the accounting period. The FIFO method transfers to the Cost of Goods Sold account the *cost of the first 43 bikes* TMBC had available to sell. The first 43 bikes acquired by TMBC were the 10 bikes in the beginning inventory (these were purchased in the prior period) plus the 20 bikes purchased in March and 13 of the bikes purchased in August. The expense recognized for the cost of these bikes ($9,650) is computed as follows.

Jan. 1	Beginning inventory	10 units @ $200	=	$2,000
Mar. 18	First purchase	20 units @ $220	=	4,400
Aug. 21	Second purchase	13 units @ $250	=	3,250
Total cost of the 43 bikes sold				$9,650

Because TMBC had 55 bikes available for sale it would have 12 bikes (55 available − 43 sold) in ending inventory. The cost assigned to these 12 bikes (the ending balance in the Inventory account) equals the cost of goods available for sale minus the cost of goods sold as shown below.

Cost of goods available for sale	$12,650
Cost of goods sold	(9,650)
Ending inventory balance	$ 3,000

We show the allocation of the cost of goods available for sale between cost of goods sold and ending inventory graphically below.

LIFO Inventory Cost Flow

Under LIFO, the cost of goods sold is the cost of the last 43 bikes acquired by TMBC, computed as follows.

Aug. 21	Second purchase	25 units @ $250	=	$ 6,250
Mar. 18	First purchase	18 units @ $220	=	3,960
Total cost of the 43 bikes sold				$10,210

The LIFO cost of the 12 bikes in ending inventory is computed as shown below.

Cost of goods available for sale	$12,650
Cost of goods sold	(10,210)
Ending inventory balance	$ 2,440

We show the allocation of the cost of goods available for sale between cost of goods sold and ending inventory graphically below.

Weighted-Average Cost Flow

The weighted-average cost per unit is determined by dividing the *total cost of goods available for sale* by the *total number of units* available for sale. For TMBC, the weighted-average cost per unit is $230 ($12,650 ÷ 55). The weighted-average cost of goods sold is determined by multiplying the average cost per unit by the number of units sold ($230 × 43 = $9,890). The cost assigned to the 12 bikes in ending inventory is $2,760 (12 × $230).

We show the allocation of the cost of goods available for sale between cost of goods sold and ending inventory graphically below.

Effect of Cost Flow on Financial Statements

Exhibit 5.8 displays partial financial statements for The Mountain Bike Company (TMBC). This exhibit includes only information pertaining to the Eraser bikes inventory item described above. Other financial statement data are omitted.

EXHIBIT 5.8			

TMBC COMPANY
Comparative Financial Statements
Partial Income Statements

	FIFO	LIFO	Weighted Average
Sales	$15,050	$15,050	$15,050
Cost of goods sold	(9,650)	(10,210)	(9,890)
Gross margin	5,400	4,840	5,160

Partial Balance Sheets

	FIFO	LIFO	Weighted Average
Assets			
Cash	$ xx	$ xx	$ xx
Accounts receivable	xx	xx	xx
Inventory	3,000	2,440	2,760

Partial Statements of Cash Flows

	FIFO	LIFO	Weighted Average
Operating Activities			
Cash inflow from customers	$15,050	$15,050	$15,050
Cash outflow for inventory	(10,650)	(10,650)	(10,650)

Recall that assets are reported on the balance sheet in order of liquidity (how quickly they are expected to be converted to cash). Because companies frequently sell inventory on account, inventory is less liquid than accounts receivable. As a result, companies commonly report inventory below accounts receivable on the balance sheet.

Exhibit 5.8 demonstrates that the amounts reported for gross margin on the income statement and inventory on the balance sheet differ significantly. The cash flow from operating activities on the statement of cash flows, however, is identical under all three methods. Regardless of cost flow reporting method, TMBC paid $10,650 cash ($4,400 first purchase + $6,250 second purchase) to purchase inventory and received $15,050 cash for inventory sold.

The Impact of Income Tax

Based on the financial statement information in Exhibit 5.8, which cost flow method should TMBC use? Most people initially suggest FIFO because FIFO reports the highest gross margin and the largest balance in ending inventory. However, other factors are relevant. FIFO produces the highest gross margin; it also produces the highest net income and the highest income tax expense. In contrast, LIFO results in recognizing the lowest gross margin, lowest net income, and the lowest income tax expense.

Will investors favor a company with more assets and higher net income or one with lower tax expense? Recognize that specific identification, FIFO, LIFO, and weighted average are *different methods of reporting the same information.* TMBC experienced only one set of events pertaining to Eraser bikes. Exhibit 5.8 reports those same events three different ways. However, if the FIFO reporting method causes TMBC to pay more taxes than the LIFO method, using FIFO will cause a real reduction in the value of the company. Paying more money in taxes leaves less money in the company. Knowledgeable investors would be more attracted to TMBC if it uses LIFO because the lower tax payments allow the company to keep more value in the business.

Research suggests that, as a group, investors are knowledgeable. They make investment decisions based on economic substance regardless of how information is reported in financial statements.

The Income Statement versus the Tax Return

In some instances companies may use one accounting method for financial reporting and a different method to compute income taxes (the tax return must explain any differences). With respect to LIFO, however, the Internal Revenue Service requires that companies using LIFO for income tax purposes must also use LIFO for financial reporting. A company could not, therefore, get both the lower tax benefit provided by LIFO and the financial reporting advantage offered under FIFO.

Inflation versus Deflation

Our illustration assumes an inflationary environment (rising inventory prices). In a deflationary environment, the impact of using LIFO versus FIFO is reversed. LIFO produces tax advantages in an inflationary environment, while FIFO produces tax advantages in a deflationary environment. Companies operating in the computer industry where prices are falling would obtain a tax advantage by using FIFO. In contrast, companies that sell medical supplies in an inflationary environment would obtain a tax advantage by using LIFO.

Full Disclosure and Consistency

Generally accepted accounting principles allow each company to choose the inventory cost flow method best suited to its reporting needs. Because results can vary considerably among methods, however, the GAAP principle of **full disclosure** requires that financial statements disclose the method chosen. In addition, so that a company's financial statements are comparable from year to year, the GAAP principle of **consistency** generally requires that companies use the same cost flow method each period. The limited exceptions to the consistency principle are described in more advanced accounting courses.

 CHECK YOURSELF 5.5

The following information was drawn from the inventory records of Fields, Inc.

Beginning inventory	200 units @ $20
First purchase	400 units @ $22
Second purchase	600 units @ $24

Assume that Fields sold 900 units of inventory.

1. Determine the amount of cost of goods sold using FIFO.
2. Would using LIFO produce a higher or lower amount of cost of goods sold? Why?

Answer

1. Cost of goods sold using FIFO

Beginning inventory	200 units @ $20	=	$ 4,000
First purchase	400 units @ $22	=	8,800
Second purchase	300 units @ $24	=	7,200
Total cost of goods sold			$20,000

2. The inventory records reflect an inflationary environment of steadily rising prices. Since LIFO charges the latest costs (in this case the highest costs) to the income statement, using LIFO would produce a higher amount of cost of goods sold than would using FIFO.

---

184   Chapter 5

REALITY BYTES

To avoid spoilage or obsolescence, most companies use the first-in, first-out (FIFO) approach for the flow of physical goods. The older goods (first units purchased) are sold before the newer goods are sold. For example, Kroger's and other food stores stack older merchandise at the front of the shelf where customers are more likely to pick it up first. As a result, merchandise is sold before it becomes dated. However, when timing is not an issue, convenience may dictate the use of the last-in, first-out (LIFO) method. Examples of products that frequently move on a LIFO basis include rock, gravel, dirt, or other nonwasting assets. Indeed, rock, gravel, and dirt are normally stored in piles that are unprotected from weather. New inventory is simply piled on top of the old. Inventory that is sold is taken from the top of the pile because it is convenient to do so. Accordingly, the last inventory purchased is the first inventory sold. For example, Vulcan Materials Co., which claims to be the nation's largest producer of construction aggregates (stone and gravel), uses LIFO. Regardless of whether the flow of physical goods occurs on a LIFO or FIFO basis, costs can flow differently. The flow of inventory through the physical facility is a separate issue from the flow of costs through the accounting system.

FOCUS ON INTERNATIONAL ISSUES

LIFO IN OTHER COUNTRIES

This chapter introduced a rather strange inventory cost flow assumption called LIFO. As explained, the primary advantage of LIFO is to reduce a company's income taxes. Given the choice, companies that use LIFO to reduce their taxes would probably prefer to use another method when preparing their GAAP–based financial statements, but the IRS does not permit this. Thus, they are left with no choice but to use the seemingly counterintuitive LIFO assumption for GAAP as well as tax reporting.

What happens in countries other than the United States? International Financial Reporting Standards (IFRS) do not allow the use of LIFO. Most industrialized nations are now using IFRS. You can see the impact of this disparity if you review the annual report of a U.S. company that uses LIFO *and* has significant operations in other countries. Very often it will explain that LIFO is used to calculate inventory (and cost of goods sold) for domestic operations, but another method is used for activities outside the United States.

For example, here is an excerpt from General Electric's 2012 Form 10-K, Note 1.

All inventories are stated at the lower of cost or realizable values. Cost for a significant portion of GE U.S. inventories is determined on a last-in, first-out (LIFO) basis. Cost of other GE inventories is determined on a first-in, first-out (FIFO) basis. LIFO was used for 37% and 38% of GE inventories at December 31, 2012 and 2011, respectively.

If the company has its headquarters in the United States, why not simply use LIFO in its foreign operations? In addition to having to prepare financial statements for the United States, the company probably has to prepare statements for its local operations using the reporting standards of the local country.

Prior to the establishment of IFRS each country was responsible for issuing its own, local GAAP. Even then, most countries did not allow for the use of LIFO.

A Look Back

We first introduced accounting for receivables in Chapter 2. This chapter presented additional complexities related to accounts receivable, such as the *allowance method of accounting for uncollectible accounts.* The allowance method improves matching of expenses with revenues. It also provides a more accurate measure of the value of accounts receivable on the balance sheet.

Under the allowance method, estimated uncollectible accounts expense is recorded in an adjusting entry at the end of the period in which a company has made credit sales. There are two methods commonly used to estimate the amount of uncollectible accounts expense: the percent of revenue method and the percent of receivables method. With the percent of revenue method, uncollectible accounts expense is measured as a percent of the period's sales. With the percent of receivables method, a company analyzes its accounts receivable at the end of the period, usually classifying them by age, to estimate the amount of the accounts receivable balance that is likely to be uncollectible. The balance in the Allowance for Doubtful Accounts account is then adjusted to equal the estimated amount of uncollectible accounts. Uncollectible accounts expense decreases the net realizable value of receivables (accounts receivable − allowance for doubtful accounts), stockholders' equity, and net income.

The allowance method of accounting for uncollectible accounts is conceptually superior to the *direct write-off method,* in which uncollectible accounts expense is recognized when an account is determined to be uncollectible. The direct write-off method fails to match revenues with expenses and overstates accounts receivable on the balance sheet. It is easier to use, however, and is permitted by generally accepted accounting principles if the amount of uncollectible accounts expense is immaterial.

The chapter also introduced notes receivable and accounting for *accrued interest.* When the term of a promissory note extends over more than one accounting period, companies must record adjusting entries to recognize interest in the appropriate accounting period, even if the cash exchange of interest occurs in a different accounting period.

We also discussed accounting for credit card sales, a vehicle that shifts uncollectible accounts expense to the credit card issuer. Many companies find the benefits of accepting major credit cards to be worth the credit card expense consequently incurred. Finally, we addressed the costs of making credit sales. In addition to uncollectible accounts expense, interest is a major cost of financing receivables.

This chapter also discussed the inventory cost flow methods of first-in, first-out (FIFO); last-in, first-out (LIFO); weighted average; and specific identification. Under FIFO, the cost of the items purchased first is reported on the income statement, and the cost of the items purchased last is reported on the balance sheet. Under the weighted-average method, the average cost of inventory is reported on both the income statement and the balance sheet. Finally, under specific identification the actual cost of goods is reported on the income statement and the balance sheet.

A Look Forward

Chapter 6 discusses accounting for long-term assets such as buildings and equipment. As with inventory cost flow, GAAP allows companies to use different accounting methods to report on similar types of business events. Life would be easier for accounting students if all companies used the same accounting methods. However, the business world is complex. For the foreseeable future, people are likely to continue to have diverse views as to the best way to account for a variety of business transactions. To function effectively in today's business environment, it is important for you to be able to recognize differences in reporting practices.

186 Chapter 5

 Video lectures and accompanying self-assessment quizzes are available for all learning objectives through McGraw-Hill *Connect® Accounting.*

SELF-STUDY REVIEW PROBLEM 1

During 2014 Calico Company experienced the following accounting events.

1. Provided $120,000 of services on account.
2. Collected $85,000 cash from accounts receivable.
3. Wrote off $1,800 of accounts receivable that were uncollectible.
4. Loaned $3,000 to an individual, Emma Gardner, in exchange for a note receivable.
5. Paid $90,500 cash for operating expenses.
6. Estimated that uncollectible accounts expense would be 2 percent of revenue earned on account. Recorded the year-end adjusting entry.
7. Recorded the year-end adjusting entry for accrued interest on the note receivable (see Event 4). Calico made the loan on August 1. It had a six-month term and a 6 percent rate of interest.

Calico's ledger balances on January 1, 2014, were as follows.

| Event No. | Assets | | | | | | | | | = | Liab. | + | Equity | | |
	Cash	+	Accts. Rec.	−	Allow.	+	Notes Rec.	+	Int. Rec.	=		+	Com. Stk.	+	Ret. Earn.
Bal.	12,000		18,000		2,200	+	NA	+	NA	=	NA	+	20,000	+	7,800

Required

a. Record the 2014 events in ledger accounts using the horizontal format shown above.
b. Determine net income for 2014.
c. Determine net cash flow from operating activities for 2014.
d. Determine the net realizable value of accounts receivable at December 31, 2014.
e. What amount of interest revenue will Calico recognize on its note receivable in 2015?

Solution to Requirement a.

| Event No. | Assets | | | | | | | | | = | Liab. | + | Equity | | |
	Cash	+	Accts. Rec.	−	Allow.	+	Notes Rec.	+	Int. Rec.	=		+	Com. Stk.	+	Ret. Earn.
Bal.	12,000	+	18,000	−	2,200	+	NA	+	NA	=	NA	+	20,000	+	7,800
1	NA	+	120,000	−	NA	+	NA	+	NA	=	NA	+	NA	+	120,000
2	85,000	+	(85,000)	−	NA	+	NA	+	NA	=	NA	+	NA	+	NA
3	NA	+	(1,800)	−	(1,800)	+	NA	+	NA	=	NA	+	NA	+	NA
4	(3,000)	+	NA	−	NA	+	3,000	+	NA	=	NA	+	NA	+	NA
5	(90,500)	+	NA	−	NA	+	NA	+	NA	=	NA	+	NA	+	(90,500)
6	NA	+	NA	−	2,400	+	NA	+	NA	=	NA	+	NA	+	(2,400)
7	NA	+	NA	−	NA	+	NA	+	75*	=	NA	+	NA	+	75
Totals	3,500	+	51,200	−	2,800	+	3,000	+	75	=	NA	+	20,000	+	34,975

*$3,000 × .06 × 5/12 = $75.

Solution to Requirements b–e.

b. Net income is $27,175 ($120,000 − $90,500 − $2,400 + $75).
c. Net cash flow from operating activities is an outflow of $5,500 ($85,000 − $90,500).
d. The net realizable value of accounts receivable is $48,400 ($51,200 − $2,800).
e. In 2015, Calico will recognize interest revenue for one month: $3,000 × .06 × 1/12 = $15.

Video lectures and accompanying self-assessment quizzes are available for all learning objectives through McGraw-Hill *Connect® Accounting*.

SELF-STUDY REVIEW PROBLEM 2

Erie Jewelers sells gold earrings. Its beginning inventory of Model 407 gold earrings consisted of 100 pairs of earrings at $50 per pair. Erie purchased two batches of Model 407 earrings during the year. The first batch purchased consisted of 150 pairs at $53 per pair; the second batch consisted of 200 pairs at $56 per pair. During the year, Erie sold 375 pairs of Model 407 earrings.

Required

Determine the amount of product cost Erie would allocate to cost of goods sold and ending inventory assuming that Erie uses (a) FIFO, (b) LIFO, and (c) weighted average.

Solution to Requirements *a–c*

Goods Available for Sale				
Beginning inventory	100	@	$50 =	$ 5,000
First purchase	150	@	53 =	7,950
Second purchase	200	@	56 =	11,200
Goods available for sale	450			$24,150

a. FIFO

Cost of Goods Sold	Pairs		Cost per Pair		Cost of Goods Sold
From beginning inventory	100	@	$50	=	$ 5,000
From first purchase	150	@	53	=	7,950
From second purchase	125	@	56	=	7,000
Total pairs sold	375				$19,950

Ending inventory = Goods available for sale − Cost of goods sold
Ending inventory = $24,150 − $19,950 = $4,200

b. LIFO

Cost of Goods Sold	Pairs		Cost per Pair		Cost of Goods Sold
From second purchase	200	@	$56	=	$11,200
From first purchase	150	@	53	=	7,950
From beginning inventory	25	@	50	=	1,250
Total pairs sold	375				$20,400

Ending inventory = Goods available for sale − Cost of goods sold
Ending inventory = $24,150 − $20,400 = $3,750

c. Weighted average

Goods available for sale ÷ Total pairs = Cost per pair
$24,150   ÷   450   = $53.6667

Cost of goods sold   375 units @ $53.6667 = $20,125
Ending inventory   75 units @ $53.6667 = $4,025

KEY TERMS

Account receivable 162	Consistency 183	Maker 173	Principal 173
Accrued interest 173	Contra asset account 166	Matching concept 174	Promissory note 172
Adjusting entry 174	First-in, first-out (FIFO) cost	Maturity date 173	Reinstate 168
Aging of accounts	flow method 178	Net realizable value 164	Specific identification 178
receivable 171	Full disclosure 183	Notes receivable 165	Uncollectible accounts
Allowance for doubtful	Interest 173	Payee 173	expense 165
accounts 164	Inventory cost flow	Percent of receivables	Weighted-average cost flow
Allowance method of	methods 180	method 170	method 178
accounting for uncollectible	Last-in, first-out (LIFO) cost	Percent of revenue	
accounts 164	flow method 178	method 169	
Collateral 173	Liquidity 175	Physical flow of goods 178	

QUESTIONS

1. What is the difference between accounts receivable and notes receivable?

2. What is the *net realizable value* of receivables?

3. What type of account is the Allowance for Doubtful Accounts?

4. What are two ways in which estimating uncollectible accounts improves the accuracy of the financial statements?

5. When using the allowance method, why is uncollectible accounts expense an estimated amount?

6. What is the most common format for reporting accounts receivable on the balance sheet? What information does this method provide beyond showing only the net amount?

7. Why is it necessary to reinstate a previously written off account receivable before the collection is recorded?

8. What are some factors considered in estimating the amount of uncollectible accounts receivable?

9. What is the effect on the accounting equation of recognizing uncollectible accounts expense?

10. What is the effect on the accounting equation of writing off an uncollectible account receivable when the allowance method is used?

11. How does the recovery of a previously written-off account affect the income statement when the allowance method is used? How does the recovery of a previously written-off account affect the statement of cash flows when the allowance method is used?

12. What is the advantage of using the allowance method of accounting for uncollectible accounts?

13. How do companies determine the percentage estimate of uncollectible accounts when using the percent of revenue method?

14. What is an advantage of using the percent of receivables method of estimating uncollectible accounts expense?

15. What is "aging of accounts receivable"?

16. What is a promissory note?

17. Define the following terms:
   a. Maker
   b. Payee
   c. Principal

   d. Interest
   e. Maturity date
   f. Collateral

18. What is the formula for computing interest revenue?

19. What is accrued interest?

20. How does the accrual of interest revenue or expense illustrate the matching concept?

21. Assets are listed on the balance sheet in the order of their liquidity. Explain this statement.

22. When is an adjusting entry for accrued interest generally recorded?

23. Assume that on July 1, 2014, Big Corp. loaned Little Corp. $12,000 for a period of one year at 6 percent interest. What amount of interest revenue will Big report for 2014? What amount of cash will Big receive upon maturity of the note?

24. In which section of the statement of cash flows will Big report the cash collected in Question 23?

25. Why is it generally beneficial for a business to accept major credit cards as payment for goods and services even when the fee charged by the credit card company is substantial?

26. What types of costs do businesses avoid when they accept major credit cards as compared with handling credit sales themselves?

27. Name and describe the four cost flow methods discussed in this chapter.

28. What are some advantages and disadvantages of the specific identification method of accounting for inventory?

29. What are some advantages and disadvantages of using the FIFO method of inventory valuation?

30. What are some advantages and disadvantages of using the LIFO method of inventory valuation?

31. In an inflationary period, which inventory cost flow method will produce the highest net income? Explain.

32. In an inflationary period, which inventory cost flow method will produce the largest amount of total assets on the balance sheet? Explain.

33. What is the difference between the flow of costs and the physical flow of goods?

34. Does the choice of cost flow method (FIFO, LIFO, or weighted average) affect the statement of cash flows? Explain.

35. Assume that Key Co. purchased 1,000 units of merchandise in its first year of operations for $25 per unit. The company sold 850 units for

$40. What is the amount of cost of goods sold using FIFO? LIFO? Weighted average?

36. Assume that Key Co. purchased 1,500 units of merchandise in its second year of operation for $27 per unit. Its beginning inventory was determined in Question 35.

Assuming that 1,500 units are sold, what is the amount of cost of goods sold using FIFO? LIFO? Weighted average?

37. Refer to Questions 35 and 36. Which method might be preferable for financial statements? For income tax reporting? Explain.

38. In an inflationary period, which cost flow method, FIFO or LIFO, produces the larger cash flow? Explain.

39. Which inventory cost flow method produces the highest net income in a deflationary period?

MULTIPLE-CHOICE QUESTIONS

Multiple-choice questions are provided on the text website at www.mhhe.com/edmondssurvey4e.

EXERCISES

  All applicable Exercises are available with McGraw-Hill's
Connect® Accounting.

Exercise 5-1   *Accounting for bad debts: Allowance method*   LO 5-1

Michelle's Accounting Service began operation on January 1, 2014. The company experienced the following events for its first year of operations:

Events Affecting 2014:

1. Provided $96,000 of accounting services on account.
2. Collected $80,000 cash from accounts receivable.
3. Paid salaries of $32,000 for the year.
4. Adjusted the accounts to reflect management's expectations that uncollectible accounts expense would be $1,600.

Required

a. Organize the transaction data in accounts under on accounting equation.
b. Prepare an income statement, a balance sheet, and a statement of cash flows for 2014.

Exercise 5-2   *Analysis of financial statement effects of accounting for uncollectible*   LO 5-1
      accounts under the allowance method

Businesses using the allowance method for the recognition of uncollectible accounts expense commonly experience four accounting events.

1. Recognition of revenue on account.
2. Collection of cash from accounts receivable.
3. Recognition of uncollectible accounts expense through a year-end adjusting entry.
4. Write-off of uncollectible accounts.

Required

Show the effect of each event on the elements of the financial statements, using a horizontal statements model like the one shown here. Use the following coding scheme to record your answers: increase is +, decrease is −, not affected is NA. In the cash flow column, indicate whether the item is an operating activity (OA), investing activity (IA), or financing activity (FA). The first transaction is entered as an example.

Event No.	Assets	=	Liab.	+	Equity	Rev.	−	Exp.	=	Net Inc.	Cash Flow
1	+		NA		+	+		NA		+	NA

LO 5-1

Exercise 5-3   *Analyzing account balances for a company using the allowance method of accounting for uncollectible accounts*

The following account balances come from the records of King Company:

	Beginning Balance	Ending Balance
Accounts Receivable	$4,000	$4,500
Allowance for Doubtful Accounts	150	250

During the accounting period, King recorded $21,000 of service revenue on account. The company also wrote off a $180 account receivable.

Required

a. Determine the amount of cash collected from receivables.

b. Determine the amount of uncollectible accounts expense recognized during the period.

LO 5-2

Exercise 5-4   *Effect of recognizing uncollectible accounts expense on financial statements: Percent of revenue allowance method*

Bulldog Auto Service was started on January 1, 2014. The company experienced the following events during its first two years of operation:

Events Affecting 2014

1. Provided $45,000 of repair services on account.
2. Collected $32,000 cash from accounts receivable.
3. Adjusted the accounting records to reflect the estimate that uncollectible accounts expense would be 1 percent of the service revenue on account.

Events Affecting 2015

1. Wrote off a $320 account receivable that was determined to be uncollectible.
2. Provided $65,000 of repair services on account.
3. Collected $66,000 cash from accounts receivable.
4. Adjusted the accounting records to reflect the estimate that uncollectible accounts expense would be 1 percent of the service revenue on account.

Required

a. Organize the transaction data in accounts under an accounting equation.

b. Determine the following amounts:
    (1) Net income for 2014.
    (2) Net cash flow from operating activities for 2014.
    (3) Balance of accounts receivable at the end of 2014.
    (4) Net realizable value of accounts receivable at the end of 2014.

c. Repeat Requirement *b* for the 2015 accounting period.

Exercise 5-5 *Analyzing financial statement effects of accounting for uncollectible accounts using the percent of revenue allowance method*

LO 5-2

Pate Bros. uses the allowance method to account for uncollectible accounts expense. Pate experienced the following four events in 2014:

1. Recognized $68,000 of revenue on account.
2. Collected $62,000 cash from accounts receivable.
3. Determined that $500 of accounts receivable were not collectible and wrote them off.
4. Recognized uncollectible accounts expense for the year. Pate estimates that uncollectible accounts expense will be 2 percent of its sales.

Required

Show the effect of each of these events on the elements of the financial statements, using a horizontal statements model like the following one. Use + for increase, − for decrease, and NA for not affected. In the Cash Flow column, indicate whether the item is an operating activity (OA), investing activity (IA), or financing activity (FA).

Event No.	Assets				=	Liab.	+	Equity	Rev.	−	Exp.	=	Net Inc.	Cash Flow
	Cash	+	Accts. Rec.	−	Allow.	=			Ret. Earn.					

Exercise 5-6 *Effect of recovering a receivable previously written off*

LO 5-1, 5-2

The accounts receivable balance for Don's Shoe Repair at December 31, 2014, was $76,000. Also on that date, the balance in Allowance for Doubtful Accounts was $3,200. During 2015, $2,900 of accounts receivable were written off as uncollectible. In addition, Don's Shoe Repair unexpectedly collected $200 of receivables that had been written off in a previous accounting period. Sales on account during 2015 were $210,000, and cash collections from receivables were $215,000. Uncollectible accounts expense was estimated to be 1 percent of the sales on account for the period.

Required

a. Organize the information in accounts under an accounting equation.
b. Based on the preceding information, compute (after year-end adjustment):
   (1) Balance of Allowance for Doubtful Accounts at December 31, 2015. *2,600*
   (2) Balance of Accounts Receivable at December 31, 2015. *081100*
   (3) Net realizable value of Accounts Receivable at December 31, 2015.
c. What amount of uncollectible accounts expense will Don's Shoe Repair report for 2015?
d. Explain how the $200 recovery of receivables affected the accounting equation.

Exercise 5-7 *Accounting for uncollectible accounts: Percent of revenue allowance method*

LO 5-2

Bing Auto Parts sells new and used auto parts. Although a majority of its sales are cash sales, it makes a significant amount of credit sales. During 2014, its first year of operations, Bing Auto Parts experienced the following:

Sales on account	$320,000
Cash sales	680,000
Collections of accounts receivable	295,000
Uncollectible accounts charged off during the year	1,400

Required

Assume that Bing Auto Parts uses the allowance method of accounting for uncollectible accounts and estimates that 1 percent of its sales on account will not be collected. Answer the following questions:

a. What is the Accounts Receivable balance at December 31, 2014?

b. What is the ending balance of Allowance for Doubtful Accounts at December 31, 2014, after all entries and adjusting entries are posted?

c. What is the amount of uncollectible accounts expense for 2014?

d. What is the net realizable value of accounts receivable at December 31, 2014?

LO 5-2

Exercise 5-8   *Determining account balances: Allowance method of accounting for uncollectible accounts*

During the first year of operation, 2014, Clayton Repair Co. recognized $500,000 of service revenue on account. At the end of 2014, the accounts receivable balance was $72,000. For this first year in business, the owner believes uncollectible accounts expense will be about 1 percent of sales on account.

Required

a. What amount of cash did Clayton collect from accounts receivable during 2014?

b. Assuming Clayton uses the allowance method to account for uncollectible accounts, what amount should Clayton record as uncollectible accounts expense for 2014?

c. What is the net realizable value of receivables at the end of 2014?

d. Show the effects of the above transactions on the financial statements by recording the appropriate amounts in a horizontal statements model like the one shown here. In the Cash Flow column, indicate whether the item is an operating activity (OA), investing activity (IA), or financing activity (FA). Use NA for not affected.

Assets			=	Liab.	+	Equity	Rev.	–	Exp.	=	Net Inc.	Cash Flow
Cash	+	Accts. Rec.	–	Allow.								

LO 5-3

Exercise 5-9   *Accounting for uncollectible accounts: Percent of receivables allowance method*

Tyler Service Co. experienced the following transactions for 2014, its first year of operations:

1. Provided $86,000 of services on account.

2. Collected $72,000 cash from accounts receivable.

3. Paid $39,000 of salaries expense for the year.

4. Tyler adjusted the accounts using the following information from an accounts receivable aging schedule:

Number of Days Past Due	Amount	Percent Likely to Be Uncollectible	Allowance Balance
Current	$7,500	.01	
0–30	2,000	.05	
31–60	1,500	.10	
61–90	1,000	.30	
Over 90 days	2,000	.50	

Required

a. Organize the information in accounts under an accounting equation.

b. Prepare the income statement for Tyler Service Co. for 2014.

c. What is the net realizable value of the accounts receivable at December 31, 2014?

Exercise 5-10 *Effect of recognizing uncollectible accounts on the financial statements: Percent of receivables allowance method* LO 5-3

Faello Inc. experienced the following events for the first two years of its operations:

2014:

1. Provided $80,000 of services on account.
2. Provided $22,000 of services and received cash.
3. Collected $65,000 cash from accounts receivable.
4. Paid $24,000 of salaries expense for the year.
5. Adjusted the accounting records to reflect uncollectible accounts expense for the year. Faello estimates that 5 percent of the ending accounts receivable balance will be uncollectible.

2015:

1. Wrote off an uncollectible account of $620.
2. Provided $95,000 of services on account.
3. Provided $15,000 of services and collected cash.
4. Collected $90,000 cash from accounts receivable.
5. Paid $35,000 of salaries expense for the year.
6. Adjusted the accounts to reflect uncollectible accounts expense for the year. Faello estimates that 5 percent of the ending accounts receivable balance will be uncollectible.

Required

a. Organize the transaction data in accounts under an accounting equation.
b. Prepare the income statement, statement of changes in stockholders' equity, balance sheet, and statement of cash flows for 2014.
c. What is the net realizable value of the accounts receivable at December 31, 2014?
d. Repeat Requirements *a, b,* and *c* for 2015.

Exercise 5-11 *Accounting for notes receivable* LO 5-4

Poole Enterprises loaned $30,000 to Boyd Co. on September 1, 2014, for one year at 6 percent interest.

Required

Show the effects of the following transactions in a horizontal statements model like the one shown below.

(1) The loan to Boyd Co.
(2) The adjusting entry at December 31, 2014.
(3) The adjusting entry and collection of the note on September 1, 2015.

	Assets			=	Liab.	+	Equity	Rev.	−	Exp.	=	Net Inc.	Cash Flow
Date	Cash	+	Notes Rec.	+	Int. Rec.	=			Ret. Earn.				

Exercise 5-12 *Notes receivable—accrued interest* LO 5-4

On March 1, 2014, Peppers Deli loaned $18,000 to Simms Supply for one year at 5 percent interest.

Required

Answer the following questions.

a. What is Peppers interest income for 2014?
b. What is Peppers total amount of receivables at December 31, 2014?
c. What amounts will be reported on Peppers 2014 statement of cash flows?
d. What is Peppers interest income for 2015?
e. What is the total amount of cash that Peppers will collect in 2015 from Simms Supply?

f. What amounts will be reported on Peppers's 2015 statement of cash flows?

g. What is the total amount of interest Peppers Deli earned from the loan to Simms Supply?

LO 5-2, 5-4

Exercise 5-13 *Comprehensive single-cycle problem*

The following post-closing trial balance was drawn from the accounts of Hardwood Timber Co. as of December 31, 2013:

	Debit	Credit
Cash	$16,000	
Accounts receivable	18,000	
Allowance for doubtful accounts		$ 2,000
Inventory	25,000	
Accounts payable		9,200
Common stock		30,000
Retained earnings		17,800
Totals	$59,000	$59,000

Transactions for 2014

1. Acquired an additional $20,000 cash from the issue of common stock.
2. Purchased $80,000 of inventory on account.
3. Sold inventory that cost $61,000 for $98,000. Sales were made on account.
4. Wrote off $1,500 of uncollectible accounts.
5. On September 1, Hardwood loaned $10,000 to Pine Co. The note had a 6 percent interest rate and a one-year term.
6. Paid $24,500 cash for salaries expense.
7. Collected $99,000 cash from accounts receivable.
8. Paid $78,000 cash on accounts payable.
9. Paid a $5,000 cash dividend to the stockholders.
10. Estimated uncollectible accounts expense to be 1 percent of sales on account.
11. Recorded the accrued interest at December 31, 2014.

Required

a. Organize the transaction data in accounts under an accounting equation.

b. Prepare an income statement, a statement of changes in stockholders' equity, a balance sheet, and a statement of cash flows for 2014.

LO 5-5

Exercise 5-14 *Effect of credit card sales on financial statements*

Superior Carpet Cleaning provided $76,000 of services during 2014, its first year of operations. All customers paid for the services with major credit cards. Superior submitted the credit card receipts to the credit card company immediately. The credit card company paid Superior cash in the amount of face value less a 3 percent service charge.

Required

a. Record the credit card sales and the subsequent collection of accounts receivable in a horizontal statements model like the one shown below. In the Cash Flow column, indicate whether the item is an operating activity (OA), investing activity (IA), or financing activity (FA). Use NA to indicate that an element is not affected by the event.

Assets		=	Liab.	+	Equity	Rev.	−	Exp.	=	Net Inc.	Cash Flow
Cash	+ Accts. Rec.										

b. Answer the following questions:

   (1) What is the amount of total assets at the end of the accounting period?

   (2) What is the amount of revenue reported on the income statement?

   (3) What is the amount of cash flow from operating activities reported on the statement of cash flows?

   (4) Why would Superior Carpet Cleaning accept credit cards instead of providing credit directly to its customers? In other words, why would Superior be willing to pay 3 percent of sales to have the credit card company handle its sales on account?

Exercise 5-15   *Recording credit card sales*   LO 5-5

Cassell Company accepted credit cards in payment for $8,650 of services performed during March 2014. The credit card company charged Cassell a 4 percent service fee. The credit card company paid Cassell as soon as it received the invoices.

Required

Based on this information alone, what is the amount of net income earned during the month of March?

Exercise 5-16   *Effect of inventory cost flow assumption on financial statements*   LO 5-6

Required

For each of the following situations, fill in the blank with *FIFO, LIFO*, or *weighted average:*

a. _____ would produce the highest amount of net income in an inflationary environment.

b. _____ would produce the highest amount of assets in an inflationary environment.

c. _____ would produce the lowest amount of net income in a deflationary environment.

d. _____ would produce the same unit cost for assets and cost of goods sold in an inflationary environment.

e. _____ would produce the lowest amount of net income in an inflationary environment.

f. _____ would produce an asset value that was the same regardless of whether the environment was inflationary or deflationary.

g. _____ would produce the lowest amount of assets in an inflationary environment.

h. _____ would produce the highest amount of assets in a deflationary environment.

Exercise 5-17   *Allocating product cost between cost of goods sold and ending inventory*   LO 5-6

Adams Co. started the year with no inventory. During the year, it purchased two identical inventory items at different times. The first purchase cost $950 and the other, $1,250. Adams sold one of the items during the year.

Required

Based on this information, how much product cost would be allocated to cost of goods sold and ending inventory on the year-end financial statements, assuming use of

a. FIFO?

b. LIFO?

c. Weighted average?

Exercise 5-18   *Allocating product cost between cost of goods sold and ending inventory: Multiple purchases*   LO 5-6

Suggs Company sells coffee makers used in business offices. Its beginning inventory of coffee makers was 400 units at $50 per unit. During the year, Suggs made two batch purchases of coffee makers. The first was a 500-unit purchase at $55 per unit; the second was a 600-unit purchase at $58 per unit. During the period, Suggs sold 1,200 coffee makers.

Required

Determine the amount of product costs that would be allocated to cost of goods sold and ending inventory, assuming that Suggs uses

a. FIFO.
b. LIFO.
c. Weighted average.

LO 5-6

Exercise 5-19   *Effect of inventory cost flow (FIFO, LIFO, and weighted average) on gross margin*

The following information pertains to Baxter Company for 2014.

Beginning inventory	90 units @ $15
Units purchased	320 units @ $19

Ending inventory consisted of 40 units. Baxter sold 310 units at $30 each. All purchases and sales were made with cash.

Required

a. Compute the gross margin for Baxter Company using the following cost flow assumptions: (1) FIFO, (2) LIFO, and (3) weighted average.
b. What is the dollar amount of difference in net income between using FIFO versus LIFO? (Ignore income tax considerations.)
c. Determine the cash flow from operating activities, using each of the three cost flow assumptions listed in Requirement *a*. Ignore the effect of income taxes. Explain why these cash flows have no differences.

LO 5-6

Exercise 5-20   *Effect of inventory cost flow on ending inventory balance and gross margin*

Dugan Sales had the following transactions for jackets in 2014, its first year of operations:

Jan. 20	Purchased 80 units @ $15	=	$1,200
Apr. 21	Purchased 420 units @ $16	=	6,720
July 25	Purchased 250 units @ $20	=	5,000
Sept. 19	Purchased 150 units @ $22	=	3,300

During the year, Dugan Sales sold 830 jackets for $40 each.

900 units   16,220 CGS

70 EI

Required

a. Compute the amount of ending inventory Dugan would report on the balance sheet, assuming the following cost flow assumptions: (1) FIFO, (2) LIFO, and (3) weighted average.
b. Compute the difference in gross margin between the FIFO and LIFO cost flow assumptions.

LO 5-6

Exercise 5-21   *Income tax effect of shifting from FIFO to LIFO*

The following information pertains to the inventory of the Windjammer Company:

Jan. 1	Beginning Inventory	300 units @ $25
Apr. 1	Purchased	2,800 units @ $30
Oct. 1	Purchased	1,000 units @ $32

During the year, Windjammer sold 3,500 units of inventory at $50 per unit and incurred $21,000 of operating expenses. Windjammer currently uses the FIFO method but is considering a change to LIFO. All transactions are cash transactions. Assume a 30 percent income tax rate. Windjammer started the period with cash of $36,000, inventory of $7,500, common stock of $20,000, and retained earnings of $23,500.

Required

a. Prepare income statements using FIFO and LIFO.

b. Determine the amount of income taxes Windjammer would save if it changed cost flow methods.

c. Determine the cash flow from operating activities under FIFO and LIFO.

d. Explain why cash flow from operating activities is lower under FIFO when that cost flow method produced the higher gross margin.

Exercise 5-22   *Effect of FIFO versus LIFO on income tax expense*   LO 5-6

Garden Gifts Inc. had cash sales of $112,500 for 2014, its first year of operation. On April 2, the company purchased 150 units of inventory at $180 per unit. On September 1, an additional 200 units were purchased for $200 per unit. The company had 50 units on hand at the end of the year. The company's income tax rate is 40 percent. All transactions are cash transactions.

Required

a. The preceding paragraph describes five accounting events: (1) a sales transaction, (2) the first purchase of inventory, (3) the second purchase of inventory, (4) the recognition of cost of goods sold expense, and (5) the payment of income tax expense. Record the amounts of each event in horizontal statements models like the following ones, assuming first a FIFO and then a LIFO cost flow.

		Effect of Events on Financial Statements										
			Panel 1: FIFO Cost Flow									
Event No.			**Balance Sheet**					**Income Statement**				**Statement of Cash Flows**
	Cash	+	Inventory	=	C. Stk.	+	Ret. Earn.	Rev.	−	Exp.	=	Net Inc.	
				Panel 2: LIFO Cost Flow									
Event No.			**Balance Sheet**					**Income Statement**				**Statement of Cash Flows**
	Cash	+	Inventory	=	C. Stk.	+	Ret. Earn.	Rev.	−	Exp.	=	Net Inc.	

b. Compute net income using FIFO.

c. Compute net income using LIFO.

d. Explain the difference, if any, in the amount of income tax expense incurred using the two cost flow assumptions.

e. How does the use of the FIFO versus the LIFO cost flow assumptions affect the statement of cash flows?

PROBLEMS

 connect All applicable Problems are available with McGraw-Hill's
|ACCOUNTING *Connect® Accounting.*

Problem 5-23   *Accounting for uncollectible accounts—two cycles using the percent of revenue allowance method*   LO 5-2

The following transactions apply to Expert Consulting for 2014, the first year of operation:

1. Recognized $70,000 of service revenue earned on account.

2. Collected $62,000 from accounts receivable.

3. Adjusted accounts to recognize uncollectible accounts expense. Expert uses the allowance method of accounting for uncollectible accounts and estimates that uncollectible accounts expense will be 2 percent of sales on account.

CHECK FIGURES
c. Ending Accounts Receivable, 2014: $8,000
d. Net Income, 2015: $31,966

5. Paid $190,000 on accounts payable.
6. Paid $46,000 of salaries expense for the year.
7. Paid other operating expenses of $62,000.
8. Frankel adjusted the accounts using the following information from an accounts receivable aging schedule.

Number of Days Past Due	Amount	Percent Likely to Be Uncollectible	Allowance Balance
Current	$15,700	.01	
0–30	8,500	.05	
31–60	4,000	.10	
61–90	2,600	.20	
Over 90 days	1,200	.50	

Required

a. Organize the transaction data in accounts under an accounting equation.
b. Prepare the income statement, statement of changes in stockholders' equity, balance sheet, and statement of cash flows for Frankel Inc. for 2014.
c. What is the net realizable value of the accounts receivable at December 31, 2014?

Problem 5-26 *Determination of account balances—percent of receivables allowance method of accounting for uncollectible accounts*

LO 5-2

CHECK FIGURE
c. Net Realizable Value: $44,448

During the first year of operation, 2014, Ferrell's Appliance recognized $261,000 of service revenue on account. At the end of 2014, the accounts receivable balance was $46,300. Even though this is his first year in business, the owner believes he will collect all but about 4 percent of the ending balance.

Required

a. What amount of cash was collected by Ferrell's during 2014?
b. Assuming the use of an allowance system to account for uncollectible accounts, what amount should Ferrell record as uncollectible accounts expense in 2014?
c. What is the net realizable value of receivables at the end of 2014?
d. Show the effect of the above transactions on the financial statements by recording the appropriate amounts in a horizontal statements model like the one shown here. When you record amounts in the Cash Flow column, indicate whether the item is an operating activity (OA), investing activity (IA), or financing activity (FA). The letters NA indicate that an element is not affected by the event.

Assets			=	Liab.	+	Equity	Rev.	−	Exp.	=	Net Inc.	Cash Flow
Cash	+	Accts. Rec.	−	Allow.								

Problem 5-27 *Accounting for notes receivable and uncollectible accounts using the percent of sales allowance method*

LO 5-2, 5-4

CHECK FIGURE
b. Net Income: $26,560

The following transactions apply to Brooks Co. for 2014, its first year of operations.

1. Issued $60,000 of common stock for cash.
2. Provided $74,000 of services on account.
3. Collected $62,000 cash from accounts receivable.
4. Loaned $15,000 to Horne Co. on October 1, 2014. The note had a one-year term to maturity and an 8 percent interest rate.
5. Paid $47,000 of salaries expense for the year.
6. Paid a $2,500 dividend to the stockholders.
7. Recorded the accrued interest on December 31, 2014 (see item 4).
8. Uncollectible accounts expense is estimated to be 1 percent of service revenue on account.

Required

a. Show the effects of the above transactions in a horizontal statements model like the one shown below.

	Assets					Equity		Rev. — Exp. = Net Inc.	Cash Flows
Event	Cash +	Accts. Rec. — Allow. for Doubtful Accts.	+ Notes Rec.	+ Int. Rec.	=	Com. Stk.	+ Ret. Earn.		

b. Prepare the income statement, balance sheet, and statement of cash flows for 2014.

LO 5-1, 5-4

Problem 5-28　*Multistep income statement and balance sheet*

Required

Use the following information to prepare a multistep income statement and a classified balance sheet for Webb Equipment Co. for 2014. (*Hint:* Some of the items will *not* appear on either statement, and ending retained earnings must be calculated.)

Salaries expense	$ 61,200	Interest receivable (short term)	$ 2,100
Common stock	70,000	Beginning retained earnings	120,100
Notes receivable (long term)	15,000	Operating expenses	45,000
Allowance for doubtful accounts	6,500	Cash flow from investing activities	(91,600)
Accumulated depreciation	12,000	Prepaid rent	16,100
Notes payable (long term)	26,000	Land	45,000
Salvage value of equipment	6,000	Cash	16,700
Interest payable (short term)	1,900	Inventory	105,000
Uncollectible accounts expense	9,600	Accounts payable	48,000
Supplies	4,500	Interest expense	1,300
Office equipment	47,000	Salaries payable	14,500
Interest revenue	12,000	Unearned revenue	42,000
Sales revenue	350,000	Cost of goods sold	225,000
Dividends	10,000	Accounts receivable	92,000
Rent expense	7,500		

LO 5-2, 5-4

Problem 5-29　*Missing information*

The following information comes from the accounts of Sawyer Company:

Account Title	Beginning Balance	Ending Balance
Accounts Receivable	$36,000	$32,000
Allowance for Doubtful Accounts	2,000	2,200
Notes Receivable	50,000	50,000
Interest Receivable	2,000	5,000

Required

a. There were $160,000 in sales on account during the accounting period. Write-offs of uncollectible accounts were $1,200. What was the amount of cash collected from accounts receivable? What amount of uncollectible accounts expense was reported on the income statement? What was the net realizable value of receivables at the end of the accounting period?

b. The note has a 6 percent interest rate and 24 months to maturity. What amount of interest revenue was recognized during the period? How much cash was collected for interest?

Problem 5-30   *Accounting for credit card sales and uncollectible accounts: Percent of receivables allowance method*   LO 5-3, 5-5

Iupe Supply Company had the following transactions in 2014:

1. Acquired $50,000 cash from the issue of common stock.
2. Purchased $120,000 of merchandise for cash in 2014.
3. Sold merchandise that cost $95,000 for $180,000 during the year under the following terms:

$ 50,000	Cash sales
115,000	Credit card sales (The credit card company charges a 3 percent service fee.)
15,000	Sales on account

4. Collected all the amount receivable from the credit card company.
5. Collected $11,300 of accounts receivable.
6. Paid selling and administrative expenses of $51,500.
7. Determined that 5 percent of the ending accounts receivable balance would be uncollectible.

Required

a. Record the above events in a horizontal statements model like the following one. When you record amounts in the Cash Flow column, indicate whether the item is an operating activity (OA), an investing activity (IA), or a financing activity (FA). The letters NA indicate that an element is not affected by the event.

Event	Balance Sheet										Income Statement					Statemt. of Cash Flows
	Assets						=	Equity			Rev.	−	Exp.	=	Net Inc.	
	Cash	+	Accts. Rec.	−	Allow	+	Mdse. Inv.	=	Com. Stk.	+	Ret. Earn.					

b. Prepare an income statement, a statement of changes in stockholders' equity, a balance sheet, and a statement of cash flows for 2014.

Problem 5-31   *Effect of transactions on the elements of financial statements*   LO 5-1, 5-4, 5-5

Required

Identify each of the following independent transactions as asset source (AS), asset use (AU), asset exchange (AE), or claims exchange (CE). Also explain how each event affects assets, liabilities, stockholders' equity, net income, and cash flow by placing a + for increase, − for decrease, or NA for not affected under each of the categories. The first event is recorded as an example.

Event	Type of Event	Assets	Liabilities	Common Stock	Retained Earnings	Net Income	Cash Flow
a	AS/AU	+/−	NA	NA	+	+	NA

a. Sold merchandise at a price above cost. Accepted payment by credit card. The credit card company charges a service fee. The receipts have not yet been forwarded to the credit card company.
b. Sold land for cash at its cost.
c. Paid cash to satisfy salaries payable.
d. Submitted receipts to the credit card company (see *a* above) and collected cash.

e. Loaned Carl Maddox cash. The loan had a 5 percent interest rate and a one-year term to maturity.

f. Paid cash to creditors on accounts payable.

g. Accrued three months' interest on the note receivable (see *e* above).

h. Provided services for cash.

i. Paid cash for salaries expense.

j. Provided services on account.

k. Wrote off an uncollectible account (use direct write-off method).

l. Collected cash from customers paying their accounts.

m. Recovered an uncollectible account that was previously written off (assume direct write-off method was used).

n. Paid cash for land.

o. Paid cash for other operating expenses.

LO 5-2, 5-4, 5-5

CHECK FIGURES
Net Income: $77,175
Total Assets: $223,925

Problem 5-32 *Comprehensive accounting cycle problem (uses percent of revenue allowance method)*

The following trial balance was prepared for Village Cycle Sales and Service on December 31, 2013, after the closing entries were posted:

Account Title	Debit	Credit
Cash	$ 46,200	
Accounts Receivable	21,300	
Allowance for Doubtful Accounts		$ 1,350
Inventory	85,600	
Accounts Payable		28,000
Common Stock		80,000
Retained Earnings		43,750
Totals	$153,100	$153,100

Village Cycle had the following transactions in 2014:

1. Purchased merchandise on account for $260,000.

2. Sold merchandise that cost $243,000 on account for $340,000.

3. Performed $80,000 of services for cash.

4. Sold merchandise for $60,000 to credit card customers. The merchandise cost $41,250. The credit card company charges a 5 percent fee.

5. Collected $348,000 cash from accounts receivable.

6. Paid $265,000 cash on accounts payable.

7. Paid $115,000 cash for selling and administrative expenses.

8. Collected cash for the full amount due from the credit card company (see item 4).

9. Loaned $50,000 to Lee Supply. The note had a 9 percent interest rate and a one-year term to maturity.

10. Wrote off $830 of accounts as uncollectible.

11. Made the following adjusting entries:

    (a) Recorded three months' interest on the note at December 31, 2014 (see item 9).

    (b) Estimated uncollectible accounts expense to be .5 percent of sales on account.

Required

a. Organize the transaction data in accounts under an accounting equation.

b. Prepare an income statement, a statement of changes in stockholders' equity, a balance sheet, and a statement of cash flows for 2014.

Problem 5-33   *Effect of different inventory cost flow methods on financial statements*   LO 5-6

The accounting records of Carrol's Lamp Shop reflected the following balances as of January 1, 2014:

CHECK FIGURES
a. Cost of Goods Sold—FIFO: $58,800
b. Net Income—LIFO: $21,000

Cash	$90,500
Beginning inventory	28,000 (200 units @ $140)
Common stock	40,000
Retained earnings	78,500

The following five transactions occurred in 2014:

1. First purchase (cash)   120 units @ $150
2. Second purchase (cash)   140 units @ $160
3. Sales (all cash)   400 units @ $320
4. Paid $40,000 cash for salaries expense.
5. Paid cash for income tax at the rate of 25 percent of income before taxes.

Required

a. Compute the cost of goods sold and ending inventory, assuming (1) FIFO cost flow, (2) LIFO cost flow, and (3) weighted-average cost flow.

b. Use a vertical model to prepare the 2014 income statement, balance sheet, and statement of cash flows under FIFO, LIFO, and weighted average. (*Hint:* Record the events under an accounting equation before preparing the statements.)

ANALYZE, THINK, COMMUNICATE

ATC 5-1   Business Application Case   *Understanding real-world annual reports*

Use the Target Corporation's Form 10-K to answer the following questions related to Target's 2012 fiscal year (year ended February 2, 2013). Target's Form 10-K is available on the company's website or through the SEC's EDGAR database. Appendix A provides instructions for using the EDGAR database. Round answers to one decimal place.

Required

a. What percentage of Target's total assets was comprised of credit card receivables?

b. Approximately what percentage of credit card receivables did the company think will not be collected in 2012 and 2013?

c. What is Target's policy regarding when to write off credit card receivables?

d. What percentage of Target's total assets was comprised of inventory?

e. What cost flow method did Target use to account for its inventory?

f. Target had arrangements with some of its vendors such that it does not purchase or pay for merchandise inventory until the merchandise is sold to outside customers. Was the cost of these goods ever included in the Inventory account?

ATC 5-2   Group Assignment   *Inventory cost flow*

The accounting records of Robin Co. showed the following balances at January 1, 2014:

Cash	$30,000
Beginning inventory (100 units @ $50, 70 units @ $55)	8,850
Common stock	20,000
Retained earnings	18,850

Transactions for 2014 were as follows:

Purchased 100 units @ $54 per unit.
Purchased 250 units @ $58 per unit.
Sold 220 units @ $80 per unit.
Sold 200 units @ $90 per unit.
Paid operating expenses of $3,200.
Paid income tax expense. The income tax rate is 30%.

Required

a. Organize the class into three sections, and divide each section into groups of three to five students. Assign each section one of the cost flow methods, FIFO, LIFO, or weighted average. The company uses the perpetual inventory system.

Group Tasks

Determine the amount of ending inventory, cost of goods sold, gross margin, and net income after income tax for the cost flow method assigned to your section. Also prepare an income statement using that cost flow assumption.

Class Discussion

b. Have a representative of each section put its income statement on the board. Discuss the effect that each cost flow method has on assets (ending inventory), net income, and cash flows. Which method is preferred for tax reporting? For financial reporting? What restrictions are placed on the use of LIFO for tax reporting?

ATC 5-3   Research Assignment   *Analyzing two real-world companies' accounts receivable*

Using the most current annual reports or the Forms 10-K for Starbucks, the world's largest coffee houses, and Whirlpool, which manufactures appliances, complete the requirements below. To obtain the Forms 10-K, use either the EDGAR system following the instructions in Appendix A or the companies' websites. The annual reports can be found on the companies' websites.

Required

a. For each company, compute accounts receivable as a percentage of revenue. Show your computations.
b. Which company appears to be making more of its sales on account? Explain your answer.
c. Try to provide a logical explanation as to why one of these companies is making more of its sales on account than the other.

ATC 5-4   Writing Assignment   *Cost of charge sales*

Paul Smith is opening a plumbing supply store in University City. He plans to sell plumbing parts and materials to both wholesale and retail customers. Since contractors (wholesale customers) prefer to buy parts and materials and pay at the end of the month, Paul expects he will have to offer charge accounts. He plans to offer charge sales to the wholesale customers only and to require retail customers to pay with either cash or credit cards. Paul wondered what expenses his business would incur relative to the charge sales and the credit cards.

Required

a. What issues will Paul need to consider if he allows wholesale customers to buy plumbing supplies on account?
b. Write a memo to Paul Smith outlining the potential cost of accepting charge customers. Discuss the difference between the allowance method for uncollectible accounts and the direct write-off method. Also discuss the cost of accepting credit cards.

ATC 5-5   Ethical Dilemma   *How bad can it be?*

Alonzo Saunders owns a small training services company that is experiencing growing pains. The company has grown rapidly by offering liberal credit terms to its customers. Although his competitors require payment for services within 30 days, Saunders permits his customers to delay payment for up to 90 days. Saunders's customers thereby have time to fully evaluate the training that employees receive before they must pay for that training. Saunders guarantees satisfaction. If a customer is unhappy, the customer does not have to pay. Saunders works with reputable companies, provides top-quality training, and rarely encounters dissatisfied customers.

The long collection period, however, has created a cash flow problem. Saunders has a $100,000 accounts receivable balance, but needs cash to pay current bills. He has recently negotiated a loan agreement with National Bank of Brighton County that should solve his cash flow problems. The loan agreement requires that Saunders pledge the accounts receivable as collateral for the loan. The bank agreed to loan Saunders 70 percent of the receivables balance, thereby giving him access to $70,000 cash. Saunders is satisfied with this arrangement because he estimates he needs approximately $60,000.

On the day Saunders was to execute the loan agreement, he heard a rumor that his biggest customer was experiencing financial problems and might declare bankruptcy. The customer owed Saunders $45,000. Saunders promptly called the customer's chief accountant and learned "off the record" that the rumor was true. The accountant told Saunders that the company's net worth was negative and most of its assets were pledged as collateral for bank loans. In his opinion, Saunders was unlikely to collect the balance due. Saunders's immediate concern was the impact the circumstances would have on his loan agreement with the bank.

Saunders uses the direct write-off method to recognize uncollectible accounts expense. Removing the $45,000 receivable from the collateral pool would leave only $55,000 of receivables, reducing the available credit to $38,500 ($55,000 × 0.70). Even worse, recognizing the uncollectible accounts expense would so adversely affect his income statement that the bank might further reduce the available credit by reducing the percentage of receivables allowed under the loan agreement. Saunders will have to attest to the quality of the receivables at the date of the loan but reasons that since the information he obtained about the possible bankruptcy was "off the record" he is under no obligation to recognize the uncollectible accounts expense until the receivable is officially uncollectible.

Required

a. How are income and assets affected by the decision not to act on the bankruptcy information?

b. Review the AICPA's Articles of Professional Conduct (see Chapter 4) and comment on any of the standards that would be violated by the actions Saunders is contemplating.

c. How do the elements of the fraud triangle (see Chapter 4) apply to this case?

CHAPTER 6

Accounting for Long-Term Operational Assets

LEARNING OBJECTIVES

After you have mastered the material in this chapter, you will be able to:

LO 6-1	Identify different types of long-term operational assets.
LO 6-2	Determine the cost of long-term operational assets.
LO 6-3	Explain how different depreciation methods affect financial statements.
LO 6-4	Determine how gains and losses on disposals of long-term operational assets affect financial statements.
LO 6-5	Show how revising estimates affects financial statements.
LO 6-6	Explain how continuing expenditures for operational assets affect financial statements.
LO 6-7	Explain how expense recognition for natural resources (depletion) affects financial statements.
LO 6-8	Explain how expense recognition for intangible assets (amortization) affects financial statements.
LO 6-9	Explain how expense recognition choices and industry characteristics affect financial performance measures.

 Video lectures and accompanying self-assessment quizzes are available for all learning objectives through McGraw-Hill Connect® Accounting.

CHAPTER OPENING

Companies use assets to produce revenue. Some assets, like inventory or office supplies, are called **current assets** because they are used relatively quickly (within a single accounting period). Other assets, like equipment or buildings, are used for extended periods of time (two or more accounting periods). These assets are called **long-term operational assets.**[1] Accounting for long-term assets raises several questions. For example, what is the cost of the asset? Is it

[1]Classifying assets as current versus long term is explained in more detail in Chapter 7.

the list price only or should the cost of transportation, transit insurance, setup, and so on be added to the list price? Should the cost of a long-term asset be recognized as expense in the period the asset is purchased or should the cost be expensed over the useful life of the asset? What happens in the accounting records when a long-term asset is retired from use? This chapter answers these questions. It explains accounting for long-term operational assets from the date of purchase through the date of disposal.

The Curious Accountant

Most companies have various types of long-term assets that they use to operate their business. Common types of long-term assets include buildings, machinery, and equipment. But there are other types as well. A major category of long-term assets for a mining company is the mineral reserves from which they extract ore.

Freeport-McMoRan Copper & Gold, Inc. (referred to as FCX) is one of the largest mining operations in the world. It produces copper, gold, and molybdenum from 12 major mines located on four continents. As of December 31, 2012, it owned proven mineral reserves that cost $4.6 billion, and buildings, machinery, and equipment that cost $16.7 billion.

How do you think the way a mining company uses its buildings and equipment differs from the way it uses its mineral reserves, and how will these differences affect the way these assets are accounted for? (Answer on page 211.)

208   Chapter 6

TANGIBLE VERSUS INTANGIBLE ASSETS

LO 6-1

Identify different types of long-term operational assets.

Long-term assets may be tangible or intangible. **Tangible assets** have a physical presence; they can be seen and touched. Tangible assets include equipment, machinery, natural resources, and land. In contrast, intangible assets have no physical form. Although they may be represented by physical documents, **intangible assets** are, in fact, rights or privileges. They cannot be seen or touched. For example, a patent represents an exclusive legal *privilege* to produce and sell a particular product. It protects inventors by making it illegal for others to profit by copying their inventions. Although a patent may be represented by legal documents, the privilege is the actual asset. Because the privilege cannot be seen or touched, the patent is an intangible asset.

Tangible Long-Term Assets

Tangible long-term assets are classified as (1) property, plant, and equipment; (2) natural resources; or (3) land.

Property, Plant, and Equipment

Property, plant, and equipment is sometimes called *plant assets* or *fixed assets.* Examples of property, plant, and equipment include furniture, cash registers, machinery, delivery trucks, computers, mechanical robots, and buildings. The level of detail used to account for these assets varies. One company may include all office equipment in one account, whereas another company might divide office equipment into computers, desks, chairs, and so on. The term used to recognize expense for property, plant, and equipment is **depreciation.**

Natural Resources

Mineral deposits, oil and gas reserves, timber stands, coal mines, and stone quarries are examples of **natural resources.** Conceptually, natural resources are inventories. When sold, the cost of these assets is frequently expensed as *cost of goods sold.* Although inventories are usually classified as short-term assets, natural resources are normally classified as long term because the resource deposits generally have long lives. For example, it may take decades to extract all of the diamonds from a diamond mine. The term used to recognize expense for natural resources is **depletion.**

Land

Land is classified separately from other property because land is not subject to depreciation or depletion. Land has an infinite life. It is not worn out or consumed as it is used. When buildings or natural resources are purchased simultaneously with land, the amount paid must be divided between the land and the other assets because of the nondepreciable nature of the land.

Intangible Assets

Intangible assets fall into two categories, those with *identifiable useful lives* and those with *indefinite useful lives.*

Intangible Assets with Identifiable Useful Lives

Intangible assets with identifiable useful lives include patents and copyrights. These assets may become obsolete (a patent may become worthless if new technology provides a superior product) or may reach the end of their legal lives. The term used when recognizing expense for intangible assets with identifiable useful lives is called **amortization.**

Intangible Assets with Indefinite Useful Lives

The benefits of some intangible assets may extend so far into the future that their useful lives cannot be estimated. For how many years will the Coca-Cola trademark attract customers? When will the value of a McDonald's franchise end? There are no answers to these questions. Intangible assets such as renewable franchises, trademarks, and goodwill have indefinite useful lives. The costs of such assets are not expensed unless the value of the assets becomes impaired.

DETERMINING THE COST OF LONG-TERM ASSETS

The **historical cost concept** requires that an asset be recorded at the amount paid for it. This amount includes the purchase price plus any costs necessary to get the asset in the location and condition for its intended use. Common cost components are:

LO 6-2

Determine the cost of long-term operational assets.

- **Buildings:** (1) purchase price, (2) sales taxes, (3) title search and transfer document costs, (4) realtor's and attorney's fees, and (5) remodeling costs.
- **Land:** (1) purchase price, (2) sales taxes, (3) title search and transfer document costs, (4) realtor's and attorney's fees, (5) costs for removal of old buildings, and (6) grading costs.
- **Equipment:** (1) purchase price (less discounts), (2) sales taxes, (3) delivery costs, (4) installation costs, and (5) costs to adapt for intended use.

The cost of an asset does not include payments for fines, damages, and so on that could have been avoided.

☑ CHECK YOURSELF 6.1

Sheridan Construction Company purchased a new bulldozer that had a $260,000 list price. The seller agreed to allow a 4 percent cash discount in exchange for immediate payment. The bulldozer was delivered FOB shipping point at a cost of $1,200. Sheridan hired a new employee to operate the dozer for an annual salary of $36,000. The employee was trained to operate the dozer for a one-time training fee of $800. The cost of the company's theft insurance policy increased by $300 per year as a result of adding the dozer to the policy. The dozer had a five-year useful life and an expected salvage value of $26,000. Determine the asset's cost.

Answer

List price	$260,000
Less: Cash discount ($260,000 × 0.04)	(10,400)
Shipping cost	1,200
Training cost	800
Total asset cost (amount capitalized)	$251,600

Basket Purchase Allocation

Acquiring a group of assets in a single transaction is known as a **basket purchase.** The total price of a basket purchase must be allocated among the assets acquired. Accountants commonly allocate the purchase price using the **relative fair market value method.** To illustrate, assume that Beatty Company purchased land and a building for $240,000 cash. A real estate appraiser determined the fair market value of each asset to be

Building	$270,000
Land	90,000
Total	$360,000

The appraisal indicates that the land is worth 25 percent ($90,000 ÷ $360,000) of the total value and the building is worth 75 percent ($270,000 ÷ $360,000). Using these percentages, the actual purchase price is allocated as follows.

Building	0.75 × $240,000 =	$180,000
Land	0.25 × $240,000 =	60,000
Total		$240,000

METHODS OF RECOGNIZING DEPRECIATION EXPENSE

LO 6-3

Explain how different depreciation methods affect financial statements.

The life cycle of an operational asset involves (1) acquiring the funds to buy the asset, (2) purchasing the asset, (3) using the asset, and (4) retiring (disposing of) the asset. These stages are illustrated in Exhibit 6.1. The stages involving (1) acquiring funds and (2) purchasing assets have been discussed previously. This section of the chapter describes how accountants recognize the *use* of assets (Stage 3). As they are used, assets suffer from wear and tear called *depreciation.* Ultimately, assets depreciate to the point that they are no longer useful in the process of earning revenue. This process usually takes several years. The amount of an asset's cost that is allocated to expense during an accounting period is called **depreciation expense.**

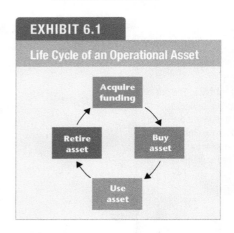

EXHIBIT 6.1

Life Cycle of an Operational Asset

An asset that is fully depreciated by one company may still be useful to another company. For example, a rental car that is no longer useful to Hertz may still be useful to a local delivery company. As a result, companies are frequently able to sell their fully depreciated assets to other companies or individuals. The expected market value of a fully depreciated asset is called its **salvage value.** The total amount of depreciation a company recognizes for an asset, its **depreciable cost,** is the difference between its original cost and its salvage value.

For example, assume a company purchases an asset for $5,000. The company expects to use the asset for 5 years (the **estimated useful life**) and then to sell it for $1,000 (salvage value). The depreciable cost of the asset is $4,000 ($5,000 − $1,000). The portion of the depreciable cost ($4,000) that represents its annual usage is recognized as depreciation expense.

Accountants must exercise judgment to estimate the amount of depreciation expense to recognize each period. For example, suppose you own a personal computer. You know how much the computer cost, and you know you will eventually need to replace it. How would you determine the amount the computer depreciates each year you use it? Businesses may use any of several acceptable methods to estimate the amount of depreciation expense to recognize each year.

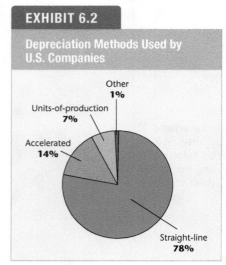

EXHIBIT 6.2

Depreciation Methods Used by U.S. Companies

Other **1%**
Units-of-production **7%**
Accelerated **14%**
Straight-line **78%**

Data Source: AICPA, *Accounting Trends and Techniques.*

The method used to recognize depreciation expense should match the asset's usage pattern. More expense should be recognized in periods when the asset is used more and less in periods when the asset is used less. Because assets are used to produce revenue, matching expense recognition with asset usage also matches expense recognition with revenue recognition. Three alternative methods for recognizing depreciation expense are (1) straight-line, (2) double-declining-balance, and (3) units-of-production.

The *straight-line* method produces the same amount of depreciation expense each accounting period. *Double-declining-balance,* an accelerated method, produces more depreciation expense in the early years of an asset's life, with a declining amount of expense in later years. *Units-of-production* produces varying amounts of depreciation expense in different accounting periods (more in some accounting periods and less in others). Exhibit 6.2 shows the relative use of different depreciation methods by U.S. companies.

Answers to The Curious Accountant

As assets lose their productive capacity, either from being used or due to obsolescence, the asset account is reduced and an expense account is increased. Assets such as buildings and equipment may decline faster if they are used, but, due to obsolescence, they usually continue to decline even if they are not used. For this reason, a time-based depreciation method, such as straight-line or double-declining-balance, is almost always used for buildings and more often than not for equipment. In contrast, a mineral reserve does not lose its capacity unless ore is extracted. After all, the gold the FCX is mining today has been in the earth for millions of years. For this reason, companies typically use the units-of-production method to calculate depletion on mineral reserves. In both cases, the objective should be to achieve the best matching of expenses incurred with the revenues they generate.

Dryden Enterprises Illustration

To illustrate the different depreciation methods, consider a van purchased by Dryden Enterprises. Dryden plans to use the van as rental property. The van had a list price of $23,500. Dryden obtained a 10 percent cash discount from the dealer. The van was delivered FOB shipping point, and Dryden paid an additional $250 for transportation costs. Dryden also paid $2,600 for a custom accessory package to increase the van's appeal as a rental vehicle. The cost of the van is computed as follows.

List price	$23,500	
Less: Cash discount	(2,350)	$23,500 × 0.10
Plus: Transportation costs	250	
Plus: Cost of customization	2,600	
Total	$24,000	

The van has an estimated *salvage value* of $4,000 and an *estimated useful life* of four years. The following section examines three different patterns of expense recognition for this van.

Straight-Line Depreciation

The first scenario assumes the van is used evenly over its four-year life. The revenue from renting the van is assumed to be $8,000 per year. The matching concept calls for the expense recognition pattern to match the revenue stream. Because the same amount of revenue is recognized in each accounting period, Dryden should use **straight-line depreciation** because it produces equal amounts of depreciation expense each year.

Life Cycle Phase 1

The first phase of the asset life cycle is to acquire funds to purchase the asset. Assume Dryden acquired $25,000 cash on January 1, 2014, by issuing common stock. The effects on the financial statements follow.

Assets				=	Equity			Rev.	−	Exp.	=	Net Inc.	Cash Flow
Cash	+	Van	− Acc. Dep.	=	Com. Stk.	+	Ret. Earn.						
25,000	+	NA	− NA	=	25,000	+	NA	NA	−	NA	=	NA	25,000 FA

212   Chapter 6

Life Cycle Phase 2

The second phase of the life cycle is to purchase the van. Assume Dryden bought the van on January 1, 2014, using funds from the stock issue. The cost of the van, previously computed, was $24,000 cash. The effects on the financial statements are:

Assets					=	Equity			Rev.	–	Exp.	=	Net Inc.	Cash Flow
Cash	+	Van	–	Acc. Dep.	=	Com. Stk.	+	Ret. Earn.						
(24,000)	+	24,000	–	NA	=	NA	+	NA	NA	–	NA	=	NA	(24,000) IA

Life Cycle Phase 3

Dryden used the van by renting it to customers. The rent revenue each year is $8,000 cash. The effects on the financial statements are shown next.

Assets					=	Equity			Rev.	–	Exp.	=	Net Inc.	Cash Flow
Cash	+	Van	–	Acc. Dep.	=	Com. Stk.	+	Ret. Earn.						
8,000	+	NA	–	NA	=	NA	+	8,000	8,000	–	NA	=	8,000	8,000 OA

Although illustrated only once, these effects occur four times—once for each year Dryden earns revenue by renting the van.

At the end of each year, Dryden adjusts its accounts to recognize depreciation expense. The amount of depreciation recognized using the straight-line method is calculated as follows.

$$(\text{Asset cost} - \text{Salvage value}) \div \text{Useful life} = \text{Depreciation expense}$$

$$(\$24{,}000 - \$4{,}000) \quad \div \quad 4 \text{ years} \quad = \quad \$5{,}000 \text{ per year}$$

Recognizing depreciation expense is an asset use transaction that reduces assets and equity. The asset reduction is reported using a **contra asset account** called **Accumulated Depreciation.** Recognizing depreciation expense *does not affect cash flow.* The entire cash outflow for this asset occurred in January 2014 when Dryden purchased the van. Depreciation reflects *using* tangible assets, not spending cash to purchase them. The effects on the financial statements are as follows.

Assets					=	Equity			Rev.	–	Exp.	=	Net Inc.	Cash Flow
Cash	+	Van	–	Acc. Dep.	=	Com. Stk.	+	Ret. Earn.						
NA	+	NA	–	5,000	=	NA	+	(5,000)	NA	–	5,000	=	(5,000)	NA

The Depreciation *Expense* account, like other expense accounts, is closed to the Retained Earnings account at the end of each year. The *Accumulated* Depreciation account, in contrast, increases each year, *accumulating* the total amount of depreciation recognized on the asset to date.

LO 6-4

Determine how gains and losses on disposals of long-term operational assets affect financial statements.

Life Cycle Phase 4

The final stage in the life cycle of a tangible asset is its disposal and removal from the company's records. Dryden retired the van from service on January 1, 2018, selling it for $4,500 cash. The van's **book value** (cost − accumulated depreciation) when it was sold was $4,000 ($24,000 cost − $20,000 accumulated depreciation), so Dryden recognized a $500 gain ($4,500 − $4,000) on the sale.

Gains are *like* revenues in that they increase assets or decrease liabilities. Gains are *unlike* revenues in that gains result from peripheral (incidental) transactions rather than routine operating activities. Dryden is not in the business of selling vans. Dryden's normal business activity is renting vans. Because selling vans is incidental to Dryden's normal operations, gains are reported separately, after operating income, on the income statement.

If Dryden had sold the asset for less than book value, the company would have recognized a loss on the asset disposal. Losses are similar to expenses in that they decrease assets or increase liabilities. However, like gains, losses result from peripheral transactions. Losses are reported as nonoperating items on the income statement.

The effects of the asset disposal on the financial statements are shown next.

Assets				=	Equity			Rev. or Gain	−	Exp. or Loss	=	Net Inc.	Cash Flow
Cash	+	Van	−	Acc. Dep.	=	Com. Stk.	+	Ret. Earn.					
4,500	+	(24,000)	−	(20,000)	=	NA	+	500	500	−	NA	=	500	4,500 IA

Although the gain reported on the 2018 income statement is $500, the cash inflow from selling the van is $4,500. Gains and losses are not reported on the statement of cash flows. Instead they are included in the total amount of cash collected from the sale of the asset. In this case, the entire $4,500 is shown in the cash flow from investing activities section of the 2018 statement of cash flows.

Financial Statements

Exhibit 6.3 displays a vertical statements model that shows the financial results for the Dryden illustration from 2014 through 2018. Study the exhibit until you understand how all the figures were derived. The amount of depreciation expense ($5,000) reported on the income statement is constant each year from 2014 through 2017. The amount of accumulated depreciation reported on the balance sheet grows from $5,000 to $10,000, to $15,000, and finally to $20,000. The Accumulated Depreciation account is a *contra asset account* that is subtracted from the Van account in determining total assets.

Study the timing differences between cash flow and net income. Dryden spent $24,000 cash to acquire the van. Over the van's life cycle, Dryden collected $36,500 [($8,000 revenue × 4 years = $32,000) plus ($4,500 from the asset disposal) = $36,500]. The $12,500 difference between the cash collected and the cash paid ($36,500 − $24,000) equals the total net income earned during the van's life cycle.

Although the amounts are the same, the timing of the cash flows and the income recognition are different. For example, in 2014 there was a $24,000 cash outflow to purchase the van and an $8,000 cash inflow from customers. In contrast, the income statement reports net income of $3,000. In 2018, Dryden reported a $500 gain on the asset disposal, but the amount of operating income and the cash flow from operating activities is zero for that year. The gain is only indirectly related to cash flows. The $4,500 of cash received on disposal is reported as a cash inflow from investing activities. Because gains and losses result from peripheral transactions, they do not affect operating income or cash flow from operating activities.

Double-Declining-Balance Depreciation

For the second scenario, assume demand for the van is strong when it is new, but fewer people rent the van as it ages. As a result, the van produces smaller amounts of revenue

EXHIBIT 6.3	Financial Statements under Straight-Line Depreciation

DRYDEN ENTERPRISES
Financial Statements

	2014	2015	2016	2017	2018
Income Statements					
Rent revenue	$ 8,000	$ 8,000	$ 8,000	$ 8,000	$ 0
Depreciation expense	(5,000)	(5,000)	(5,000)	(5,000)	0
Operating income	3,000	3,000	3,000	3,000	0
Gain on sale of van	0	0	0	0	500
Net income	$ 3,000	$ 3,000	$ 3,000	$ 3,000	$ 500
Balance Sheets					
Assets					
Cash	$ 9,000	$17,000	$25,000	$33,000	$37,500
Van	24,000	24,000	24,000	24,000	0
Accumulated depreciation	(5,000)	(10,000)	(15,000)	(20,000)	0
Total assets	$28,000	$31,000	$34,000	$37,000	$37,500
Stockholders' equity					
Common stock	$25,000	$25,000	$25,000	$25,000	$25,000
Retained earnings	3,000	6,000	9,000	12,000	12,500
Total stockholders' equity	$28,000	$31,000	$34,000	$37,000	$37,500
Statements of Cash Flows					
Operating Activities					
Inflow from customers	$ 8,000	$ 8,000	$ 8,000	$ 8,000	$ 0
Investing Activities					
Outflow to purchase van	(24,000)				
Inflow from sale of van					4,500
Financing Activities					
Inflow from stock issue	25,000				
Net Change in Cash	9,000	8,000	8,000	8,000	4,500
Beginning cash balance	0	9,000	17,000	25,000	33,000
Ending cash balance	$ 9,000	$17,000	$25,000	$33,000	$37,500

as time goes by. To match expenses with revenues, it is reasonable to recognize more depreciation expense in the van's early years and less as it ages.

Double-declining-balance depreciation produces a large amount of depreciation in the first year of an asset's life and progressively smaller levels of expense in each succeeding year. Because the double-declining-balance method recognizes depreciation expense more rapidly than the straight-line method does, it is called an **accelerated depreciation method.** Depreciation expense recognized using double-declining-balance is computed in three steps.

1. *Determine the straight-line rate.* Divide one by the asset's useful life. Because the estimated useful life of Dryden's van is four years, the straight-line rate is 25 percent $(1 \div 4)$ per year.
2. *Determine the double-declining-balance rate.* Multiply the straight-line rate by 2 (*double* the rate). The double-declining-balance rate for the van is 50 percent (25 percent × 2).

3. *Determine the depreciation expense.* Multiply the double-declining-balance rate by the book value of the asset *at the beginning of the period* (recall that book value is historical cost minus *accumulated depreciation*). The following table shows the amount of depreciation expense Dryden will recognize over the van's useful life (2014–2017).

Year	Book Value at Beginning of Period	×	Double the Straight-Line Rate	=	Annual Depreciation Expense	
2014	($24,000 − $ 0) ×		0.50	=	$12,000	
2015	(24,000 − 12,000) ×		0.50	=	6,000	
2016	(24,000 − 18,000) ×		0.50	=	~~3,000~~	2,000
2017	(24,000 − 20,000) ×		0.50	=	~~2,000~~	0

Regardless of the depreciation method used, *an asset cannot be depreciated below its salvage value.* This restriction affects depreciation computations for the third and fourth years. Because the van had a cost of $24,000 and a salvage value of $4,000, the total amount of depreciable cost (historical cost − salvage value) is $20,000 ($24,000 − $4,000). Because $18,000 ($12,000 + $6,000) of the depreciable cost is recognized in the first two years, only $2,000 ($20,000 − $18,000) remains to be recognized after the second year. Depreciation expense recognized in the third year is therefore $2,000 even though double-declining-balance computations suggest that $3,000 should be recognized. Similarly, zero depreciation expense is recognized in the fourth year even though the computations indicate a $2,000 charge.

 CHECK YOURSELF 6.2

Olds Company purchased an asset that cost $36,000 on January 1, 2016. The asset had an expected useful life of five years and an estimated salvage value of $5,000. Assuming Olds uses the double-declining-balance method, determine the amount of depreciation expense and the amount of accumulated depreciation Olds would report on the 2018 financial statements.

Answer

Year	Book Value at Beginning of Period	×	Double the Straight-Line Rate*	=	Annual Depreciation Expense
2016	($36,000 − $ 0)	×	0.40	=	$14,400
2017	(36,000 − 14,400)	×	0.40	=	8,640
2018	(36,000 − 23,040)	×	0.40	=	5,184
Total accumulated depreciation at December 31, 2018					$28,224

*Double-declining-balance rate = 2 × Straight-line rate = 2 × (1 ÷ 5 years) = 0.40

Effects on the Financial Statements

Exhibit 6.4 displays financial statements for the life of the asset assuming Dryden uses double-declining-balance depreciation. The illustration assumes a cash revenue stream of $15,000, $9,000, $5,000, and $3,000 for the years 2014, 2015, 2016, and 2017, respectively. Trace the depreciation expense from the table above to the income statements. Reported depreciation expense is greater in the earlier years and smaller in the later years of the asset's life.

EXHIBIT 6.4	Financial Statements under Double-Declining-Balance Depreciation

DRYDEN ENTERPRISES
Financial Statements

	2014	2015	2016	2017	2018
Income Statements					
Rent revenue	$15,000	$ 9,000	$ 5,000	$ 3,000	$ 0
Depreciation expense	(12,000)	(6,000)	(2,000)	0	0
Operating income	3,000	3,000	3,000	3,000	0
Gain on sale of van	0	0	0	0	500
Net income	$ 3,000	$ 3,000	$ 3,000	$ 3,000	$ 500
Balance Sheets					
Assets					
Cash	$16,000	$25,000	$30,000	$33,000	$37,500
Van	24,000	24,000	24,000	24,000	0
Accumulated depreciation	(12,000)	(18,000)	(20,000)	(20,000)	0
Total assets	$28,000	$31,000	$34,000	$37,000	$37,500
Stockholders' equity					
Common stock	$25,000	$25,000	$25,000	$25,000	$25,000
Retained earnings	3,000	6,000	9,000	12,000	12,500
Total stockholders' equity	$28,000	$31,000	$34,000	$37,000	$37,500
Statements of Cash Flows					
Operating Activities					
Inflow from customers	$15,000	$ 9,000	$ 5,000	$ 3,000	$ 0
Investing Activities					
Outflow to purchase van	(24,000)				
Inflow from sale of van					4,500
Financing Activities					
Inflow from stock issue	25,000				
Net Change in Cash	16,000	9,000	5,000	3,000	4,500
Beginning cash balance	0	16,000	25,000	30,000	33,000
Ending cash balance	$16,000	$25,000	$30,000	$33,000	$37,500

The double-declining-balance method smooths the amount of net income reported over the asset's useful life. In the early years, when heavy asset use produces higher revenue, depreciation expense is also higher. Similarly, in the later years, lower levels of revenue are matched with lower levels of depreciation expense. Net income is constant at $3,000 per year.

The depreciation method a company uses *does not* affect how it acquires the financing, invests the funds, and retires the asset. For Dryden's van, the accounting effects of these life cycle phases are the same as under the straight-line approach. Similarly, the *recording procedures* are not affected by the depreciation method. Different depreciation methods affect only the amount of depreciation expense recorded each year, not which accounts are used.

Units-of-Production Depreciation

Suppose rental demand for Dryden's van depends on general economic conditions. In a robust economy, travel increases, and demand for renting vans is high. In a stagnant economy, demand for van rentals declines. In such circumstances, revenues fluctuate from year to year. To accomplish the matching objective, depreciation should also fluctuate from year to year. A method of depreciation known as **units-of-production depreciation** accomplishes this goal by basing depreciation expense on actual asset usage.

Computing depreciation expense using units-of-production begins with identifying a measure of the asset's productive capacity. For example, the number of miles Dryden expects its van to be driven may be a reasonable measure of its productive capacity. If the depreciable asset were a saw, an appropriate measure of productive capacity could be the number of board feet the saw was expected to cut during its useful life. In other words, the basis for measuring production depends on the nature of the depreciable asset.

To illustrate computing depreciation using the units-of-production depreciation method, assume that Dryden measures productive capacity based on the total number of miles the van will be driven over its useful life. Assume Dryden estimates this productive capacity to be 100,000 miles. The first step in determining depreciation expense is to compute the cost per unit of production. For Dryden's van, this amount is total depreciable cost (historical cost − salvage value) divided by total units of expected productive capacity (100,000 miles). The depreciation cost per mile is therefore $0.20 ([$24,000 cost − $4,000 salvage] ÷ 100,000 miles). Annual depreciation expense is computed by multiplying the cost per mile by the number of miles driven. Odometer readings indicate the van was driven 40,000 miles, 20,000 miles, 30,000 miles, and 15,000 miles in 2014, 2015, 2016, and 2017, respectively. Dryden developed the following schedule of depreciation charges.

Year	Cost per Mile (a)	Miles Driven (b)	Depreciation Expense (a × b)
2014	$.20	40,000	$8,000
2015	.20	20,000	4,000
2016	.20	30,000	6,000
2017	.20	15,000	~~3,000~~ 2,000

As pointed out in the discussion of the double-declining-balance method, an asset cannot be depreciated below its salvage value. Because $18,000 of the $20,000 ($24,000 cost − $4,000 salvage) depreciable cost is recognized in the first three years of using the van, only $2,000 ($20,000 − $18,000) remains to be charged to depreciation in the fourth year, even though the depreciation computations suggest the charge should be $3,000. As the preceding table indicates, the general formula for computing units-of-production depreciation is

$$\frac{\text{Cost} - \text{Salvage value}}{\text{Total estimated units of production}} \times \begin{array}{c} \text{Units of production} \\ \text{in current} \\ \text{year} \end{array} = \begin{array}{c} \text{Annual} \\ \text{depreciation} \\ \text{expense} \end{array}$$

Exhibit 6.5 displays financial statements that assume Dryden uses units-of-production depreciation. The exhibit assumes a cash revenue stream of $11,000, $7,000, $9,000, and $5,000 for 2014, 2015, 2016, and 2017, respectively. Trace the depreciation expense from the schedule above to the income statements. Depreciation expense is greater in years the van is driven more and smaller in years the van is driven less, providing a reasonable matching of depreciation expense with revenue produced. Net income is again constant at $3,000 per year.

Comparing the Depreciation Methods

The total amount of depreciation expense Dryden recognized using each of the three methods was $20,000 ($24,000 cost − $4,000 salvage value). The different methods affect the *timing*, but not the *total amount*, of expense recognized. The different methods simply assign the $20,000 to different accounting periods. Exhibit 6.6

EXHIBIT 6.5	Financial Statements under Units-of-Production Depreciation

DRYDEN ENTERPRISES
Financial Statements

	2014	2015	2016	2017	2018
Income Statements					
Rent revenue	$11,000	$ 7,000	$ 9,000	$ 5,000	$ 0
Depreciation expense	(8,000)	(4,000)	(6,000)	(2,000)	0
Operating income	3,000	3,000	3,000	3,000	0
Gain on sale of van	0	0	0	0	500
Net income	$ 3,000	$ 3,000	$ 3,000	$ 3,000	$ 500
Balance Sheets					
Assets					
Cash	$12,000	$19,000	$28,000	$33,000	$37,500
Van	24,000	24,000	24,000	24,000	0
Accumulated depreciation	(8,000)	(12,000)	(18,000)	(20,000)	0
Total assets	$28,000	$31,000	$34,000	$37,000	$37,500
Stockholders' equity					
Common stock	$25,000	$25,000	$25,000	$25,000	$25,000
Retained earnings	3,000	6,000	9,000	12,000	12,500
Total stockholders' equity	$28,000	$31,000	$34,000	$37,000	$37,500
Statements of Cash Flows					
Operating Activities					
Inflow from customers	$11,000	$ 7,000	$ 9,000	$ 5,000	$ 0
Investing Activities					
Outflow to purchase van	(24,000)				
Inflow from sale of van					4,500
Financing Activities					
Inflow from stock issue	25,000				
Net Change in Cash	12,000	7,000	9,000	5,000	4,500
Beginning cash balance	0	12,000	19,000	28,000	33,000
Ending cash balance	$12,000	$19,000	$28,000	$33,000	$37,500

EXHIBIT 6.6

Depreciation Expense under Different Depreciation Methods

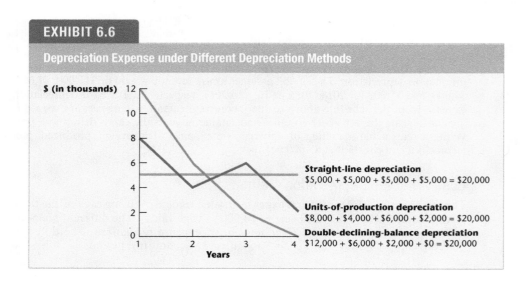

Straight-line depreciation
$5,000 + $5,000 + $5,000 + $5,000 = $20,000

Units-of-production depreciation
$8,000 + $4,000 + $6,000 + $2,000 = $20,000

Double-declining-balance depreciation
$12,000 + $6,000 + $2,000 + $0 = $20,000

presents graphically the differences among the three depreciation methods discussed above. A company should use the method that most closely matches expenses with revenues.

REVISION OF ESTIMATES

In order to report useful financial information on a timely basis, accountants must make many estimates of future results, such as the salvage value and useful life of depreciable assets and uncollectible accounts expense. Estimates are frequently revised when new information surfaces. Because revisions of estimates are common, generally accepted accounting principles call for incorporating the revised information into present and future calculations. Prior reports are not corrected.

LO 6-5

Show how revising estimates affects financial statements.

To illustrate, assume that McGraw Company purchased a machine on January 1, 2016, for $50,000. McGraw estimated the machine would have a useful life of 8 years and a salvage value of $3,000. Using the straight-line method, McGraw determined the annual depreciation charge as follows:

$$(\$50,000 - \$3,000) \div 8 \text{ years} = \$5,875 \text{ per year}$$

At the beginning of the fifth year, accumulated depreciation on the machine is $23,500 ($5,875 × 4). The machine's book value is $26,500 ($50,000 − $23,500). At this point, what happens if McGraw changes its estimates of useful life or the salvage value? Consider the following revision examples independently of each other.

Revision of Life

Assume McGraw revises the expected life to 14, rather than 8, years. The machine's *remaining* life would then be 10 more years instead of 4 more years. Assume salvage value remains $3,000. Depreciation for each remaining year is:

$$(\$26,500 \text{ book value} - \$3,000 \text{ salvage}) \div 10\text{-year remaining life} = \$2,350$$

Revision of Salvage

Alternatively, assume the original expected life remained 8 years, but McGraw revised its estimate of salvage value to $6,000. Depreciation for each of the remaining four years would be

$$(\$26,500 \text{ book value} - \$6,000 \text{ salvage}) \div 4\text{-year remaining life} = \$5,125$$

The revised amounts are determined for the full year, regardless of when McGraw revised its estimates. For example, if McGraw decides to change the estimated useful life on October 1, 2021, the change would be effective as of January 1, 2021. The year-end adjusting entry for depreciation would include a full year's depreciation calculated on the basis of the revised estimated useful life.

CONTINUING EXPENDITURES FOR PLANT ASSETS

Most plant assets require additional expenditures for maintenance or improvement during their useful lives. Accountants must determine if these expenditures should be expensed or capitalized (recorded as assets).

LO 6-6

Explain how continuing expenditures for operational assets affect financial statements.

Costs That Are Expensed

The costs of routine maintenance and minor repairs that are incurred to *keep* an asset in good working order are expensed in the period in which they are incurred. Because they reduce net income when incurred, accountants often call repair and maintenance costs **revenue expenditures** (companies subtract them from revenue).

With respect to the previous example, assume McGraw spent $500 for routine lubrication and to replace minor parts. The effects on the financial statements follow.

Assets	=	Equity			Rev.	−	Exp.	=	Net Inc.	Cash Flow
Cash	=	Com. Stk.	+	Ret. Earn.						
(500)	=	NA	+	(500)	NA	−	500	=	(500)	(500) OA

Costs That Are Capitalized

Substantial amounts spent to improve the quality or extend the life of an asset are described as **capital expenditures.** Capital expenditures are accounted for in one of two ways, depending on whether the cost incurred *improves the quality* or *extends the life* of the asset.

Improving Quality

Expenditures such as adding air conditioning to an existing building or installing a trailer hitch on a vehicle improve the quality of service these assets provide. If a capital expenditure improves an asset's quality, the amount is added to the historical cost of the asset. The additional cost is expensed through higher depreciation charges over the asset's remaining useful life.

To demonstrate, return to the McGraw Company example. Recall that the machine originally cost $50,000, had an estimated salvage of $3,000, and had a predicted life of 8 years. Recall further that accumulated depreciation at the beginning of the fifth year is $23,500 ($5,875 × 4) so the book value is $26,500 ($50,000 − $23,500). Assume McGraw makes a major expenditure of $4,000 in the machine's fifth year to improve its productive capacity. The effects on the financial statements follow.

Assets					=	Equity			Rev.	−	Exp.	=	Net Inc.	Cash Flow
Cash	+	Mach.	−	Acc. Dep.	=	Com. Stk.	+	Ret. Earn.						
(4,000)	+	4,000	−	NA	=	NA	+	NA	NA	−	NA	=	NA	(4,000) IA

After recording the expenditure, the machine account balance is $54,000 and the asset's book value is $30,500 ($54,000 − $23,500). The depreciation charges for each of the remaining four years are

$$(\$30,500 \text{ book value} - \$3,000 \text{ salvage}) \div 4\text{-year remaining life} = \$6,875$$

Extending Life

Expenditures such as replacing the roof of an existing building or putting a new engine in an old vehicle extend the useful life of these assets. If a capital expenditure extends the life of an asset rather than improving the asset's quality of service, accountants view the expenditure as canceling some of the depreciation previously charged to expense. The event is still an asset exchange; cash decreases, and the book value of the machine increases. However, the increase in the book value of the machine results from reducing the balance in the contra asset account, Accumulated Depreciation.

To illustrate, assume that instead of increasing productive capacity, McGraw's $4,000 expenditure had extended the useful life of the machine by two years. The effects of the expenditure on the financial statements follow.

Assets					=	Equity			Rev.	−	Exp.	=	Net Inc.	Cash Flow
Cash	+	Mach.	−	Acc. Dep.	=	Com. Stk.	+	Ret. Earn.						
(4,000)	+	NA	−	(4,000)	=	NA	+	NA	NA	−	NA	=	NA	(4,000) IA

After the expenditure is recognized, the book value is the same as if the $4,000 had been added to the Machine account ($50,000 cost − $19,500 adjusted balance in Accumulated Depreciation = $30,500). Depreciation expense for each of the remaining six years follows.

($30,500 book value − $3,000 salvage) ÷ 6-year remaining life = $4,583

☑ CHECK YOURSELF 6.3

On January 1, 2016, Dager Inc. purchased an asset that cost $18,000. It had a five-year useful life and a $3,000 salvage value. Dager uses straight-line depreciation. On January 1, 2018, it incurred a $1,200 cost related to the asset. With respect to this asset, determine the amount of expense and accumulated depreciation Dager would report in the 2018 financial statements under each of the following assumptions.

1. The $1,200 cost was incurred to repair damage resulting from an accident.
2. The $1,200 cost improved the operating capacity of the asset. The total useful life and salvage value remained unchanged.
3. The $1,200 cost extended the useful life of the asset by one year. The salvage value remained unchanged.

Answer

1. Dager would report the $1,200 repair cost as an expense. Dager would also report depreciation expense of $3,000 ([$18,000 − $3,000] ÷ 5). Total expenses related to this asset in 2018 would be $4,200 ($1,200 repair expense + $3,000 depreciation expense). Accumulated depreciation at the end of 2018 would be $9,000 ($3,000 depreciation expense × 3 years).

2. The $1,200 cost would be capitalized in the asset account, increasing both the book value of the asset and the annual depreciation expense.

	After Effects of Capital Improvement
Amount in asset account ($18,000 + $1,200)	$19,200
Less: Salvage value	(3,000)
Accumulated depreciation on January 1, 2018	(6,000)
Remaining depreciable cost before recording 2018 depreciation	$10,200
Depreciation for 2018 ($10,200 ÷ 3 years)	$ 3,400
Accumulated depreciation at December 31, 2018 ($6,000 + $3,400)	$ 9,400

3. The $1,200 cost would be subtracted from the Accumulated Depreciation account, increasing the book value of the asset. The remaining useful life would increase to four years, which would decrease the depreciation expense.

	After Effects of Capital Improvement
Amount in asset account	$18,000
Less: Salvage value	(3,000)
Accumulated depreciation on January 1, 2018 ($6,000 − $1,200)	(4,800)
Remaining depreciable cost before recording 2018 depreciation	$10,200
Depreciation for 2018 ($10,200 ÷ 4 years)	$ 2,550
Accumulated depreciation at December 31, 2018 ($4,800 + $2,550)	$ 7,350

NATURAL RESOURCES

LO 6-7

Explain how expense recognition for natural resources (depletion) affects financial statements.

The cost of natural resources includes not only the purchase price but also related items such as the cost of exploration, geographic surveys, and estimates. The process of expensing natural resources is commonly called depletion.[2] The most common method used to calculate depletion is units-of-production.

To illustrate, assume Apex Coal Mining paid $4,000,000 cash to purchase a mine with an estimated 16,000,000 tons of coal. The unit depletion charge is

$$\$4,000,000 \div 16,000,000 \text{ tons} = \$0.25 \text{ per ton}$$

If Apex mines 360,000 tons of coal in the first year, the depletion charge is:

$$360,000 \text{ tons} \times \$0.25 \text{ per ton} = \$90,000$$

The depletion of a natural resource has the same effect on the accounting equation as other expense recognition events. Assets (in this case, a *coal mine*) and stockholders' equity decrease. The depletion expense reduces net income. The effects on the financial statements follow.

Assets			=	Equity			Rev.	−	Exp.	=	Net Inc.	Cash Flow
Cash	+	Coal Mine	=	Com. Stk.	+	Ret. Earn.						
(4,000,000)	+	4,000,000	=	NA	+	NA	NA	−	NA	=	NA	(4,000,000) IA
NA	+	(90,000)	=	NA	+	(90,000)	NA	−	90,000	=	(90,000)	NA

INTANGIBLE ASSETS

LO 6-8

Explain how expense recognition for intangible assets (amortization) affects financial statements.

Intangible assets provide rights, privileges, and special opportunities to businesses. Common intangible assets include trademarks, patents, copyrights, franchises, and goodwill. Some of the unique characteristics of these intangible assets are described in the following sections.

Trademarks

A **trademark** is a name or symbol that identifies a company or a product. Familiar trademarks include the Polo emblem, the name *Coca-Cola*, and the Nike slogan, "Just do it." Trademarks are registered with the federal government and have an indefinite legal lifetime.

The costs incurred to design, purchase, or defend a trademark are capitalized in an asset account called Trademarks. Companies want their trademarks to become familiar but also face the risk of a trademark being used as the generic name for a product. To protect a trademark, companies in this predicament spend large sums on legal fees and extensive advertising programs to educate consumers. Well-known trademarks that have been subject to this problem include Coke, Xerox, Kleenex, and Vaseline.

Patents

A **patent** grants its owner an exclusive legal right to produce and sell a product that has one or more unique features. Patents issued by the U.S. Patent Office have a legal life of 20 years. Companies may obtain patents through purchase, lease, or internal development. The costs capitalized in the Patent account are usually limited to the purchase price and legal fees to obtain and defend the patent. The research and development

[2]In practice, the depletion charge is considered a product cost and allocated between inventory and cost of goods sold. This text uses the simplifying assumption that all resources are sold in the same accounting period in which they are extracted. The full depletion charge is therefore expensed in the period in which the resources are extracted.

FOCUS ON INTERNATIONAL ISSUES

As you have learned, U.S. GAAP requires companies to use historical cost when accounting for property, plant, and equipment (PPE). Once a company begins depreciating its buildings and equipment, expenses increase (due to depreciation expense), which causes net income and retained earnings to decrease. This, of course, ignores the revenue the company hopes to generate by using the asset.

Under IFRS a company has two options regarding accounting of PPE. First, it can use a historical cost accounting method that is virtually identical to that required by U.S. GAAP. Second, it can use the "revaluation model," which reports PPE at its fair value. There can be different ways of determining fair value, but the preferred approach is to base fair value on a market-based appraisal, performed by professional appraisers. These revaluations must be conducted frequently enough that the fair value of an asset is not materially different from its recorded book value.

Basically, the revaluation model works as follows. The company periodically compares the current book value of its PPE to the fair value at that same date. This fair value relates to the value of the used asset, not the amount required to replace it with a new asset. If the fair value of an asset is higher than its currently recorded book value, the recorded amount for the asset is increased, which increases total assets. However, the increase in the asset's fair value is *not* reported on the company's income statement, as would a gain from selling the asset. Rather, the increase is reported in a special section of stockholders' equity, which balances the increase that was recorded for assets. However, if the new fair value is *lower* than the asset's current book value, the decrease is charged to net income, as well as to assets. This is another example of the conservatism principle at work. Not surprisingly, there are exceptions to these rules. Once a new fair value is established, future depreciation expense is based on these values.

One concern might be that companies, hoping to manipulate earnings, would pick and choose some assets to account for under historical costs and others to account for under the revaluation model. This is not permitted. Although a company does not have to use a single method for all its assets, it must use a single method for all the assets in a given class of assets. For example, historical costs could be used for all factory equipment, and the revaluation model used for all its buildings.

As significant as the difference between the historical cost method and the fair value approach might be, the majority of companies continue to use historical costs. Professors H.B. Christensen and V. Nikolaev conducted a study of the use of revaluation accounting for nonfinancial assets by companies in Germany and the United Kingdom. Their research found that only 3.2 percent of the 1,539 companies surveyed used the revaluation model for property, plant, and equipment.*

*Source: Christensen, H.B. and Nikolaev, V., "Who Uses Fair Value Accounting for Nonfinancial Assets after IFRS Adoption?" The University of Chicago Booth School of Business Working Paper No. 09-12, February 2009.

costs that are incurred to develop patentable products are usually expensed in the period in which they are incurred.

Copyrights

A **copyright** protects writings, musical compositions, works of art, and other intellectual property for the exclusive benefit of the creator or persons assigned the right by the creator. The cost of a copyright includes the purchase price and any legal costs associated with obtaining and defending the copyright. Copyrights granted by the federal government extend for the life of the creator plus 70 years. A radio commercial could legally use a Bach composition as background music; it could not, however, use the theme song from the movie, *The Matrix,* without obtaining permission from the copyright owner. The cost of a copyright is often expensed early because future royalties may be uncertain.

Franchises

Franchises grant exclusive rights to sell products or perform services in certain geographic areas. Franchises may be granted by governments or private businesses.

224   Chapter 6

REALITY BYTES

For its fiscal year ended April 30, 2010, Jackson-Hewitt Tax Services, Inc. wrote off $274 million of its $419 million of goodwill due to "goodwill impairment." Without this write-off, the company would have reported positive earnings before taxes of $2.7 million. Because of the write-off, it reported a negative loss before taxes of $271.4 million. Below is an excerpt from the notes to its financial statements explaining the goodwill impairment.

GOODWILL AND OTHER INTANGIBLE ASSETS

Goodwill is the excess of the purchase price over the fair value assigned to the net assets acquired in a business combination. Goodwill is not amortized, but instead is subject to periodic testing for impairment. The Company assesses goodwill for impairment by comparing the carrying values of its reporting units to their estimated fair values. . . .

Due to the loss of approximately 50% of the Company's RAL [*refund anticipation loans*] program in the third quarter of fiscal 2010, the Company concluded that a goodwill impairment triggering event had occurred. . . .

Significant management judgment is required in assessing whether goodwill is impaired.

Franchises granted by governments include federal broadcasting licenses. Private business franchises include fast-food restaurant chains and brand labels such as Healthy Choice. The legal and useful lives of a franchise are frequently difficult to determine. Judgment is often crucial to establishing the estimated useful life for franchises.

Goodwill

Goodwill is the value attributable to favorable factors such as reputation, location, and superior products. Consider the most popular restaurant in your town. If the owner sells the restaurant, do you think the purchase price would be simply the total value of the chairs, tables, kitchen equipment, and building? Certainly not, because much of the restaurant's value lies in its popularity; in other words, its ability to generate a high return is based on the goodwill (reputation) of the business.

Calculating goodwill can be complex; here we present a simple example to illustrate how it is determined. Suppose the accounting records of a restaurant named Bendigo's show

$$\text{Assets} \ = \ \text{Liabilities} \ + \ \text{Stockholders' Equity}$$
$$\$200,000 = \ \$50,000 \ + \ \ \ \ \ \ \$150,000$$

Assume a buyer agrees to purchase the restaurant by paying the owner $300,000 cash and assuming the existing liabilities. In other words, the restaurant is purchased at a price of $350,000 ($300,000 cash + $50,000 assumed liabilities). Now assume that the assets of the business (tables, chairs, kitchen equipment, etc.) have a fair market value of only $280,000. Why would the buyer pay $350,000 to purchase assets with a market value of $280,000? Obviously, the buyer is purchasing more than just the assets. The buyer is purchasing the business's goodwill. The amount of the goodwill is the difference between the purchase price and the fair market value of the assets. In this case, the goodwill is $70,000 ($350,000 − $280,000). The effects of the purchase on the financial statements of the buyer follow.

Assets				=	Liab.	+	Equity		Rev.	−	Exp.	=	Net Inc.		Cash Flow	
Cash	+	Rest. Assets	+	Goodwill												
(300,000)	+	280,000	+	70,000	=	50,000	+	NA		NA	−	NA	=	NA		(300,000)	IA

The fair market value of the restaurant assets represents the historical cost to the new owner. It becomes the basis for future depreciation charges.

EXPENSE RECOGNITION FOR INTANGIBLE ASSETS

As mentioned earlier, intangible assets fall into two categories, those with *identifiable useful lives* and those with *indefinite useful lives.* Expense recognition for intangible assets depends on which classification applies.

Expensing Intangible Assets with Identifiable Useful Lives

The costs of intangible assets with identifiable useful lives are normally expensed on a straight-line basis using a process called *amortization.* An intangible asset should be amortized over the shorter of two possible time periods: (1) its legal life or (2) its useful life.

To illustrate, assume that Flowers Industries purchased a newly granted patent for $44,000 cash. Although the patent has a legal life of 20 years, Flowers estimates that it will be useful for only 11 years. The annual amortization charge is therefore $4,000 ($44,000 ÷ 11 years). The effects on the financial statements follow.

Assets			=	Equity			Rev.	−	Exp.	=	Net Inc.	Cash Flow	
Cash	+	Patent	=	Com. Stk.	+	Ret. Earn.							
(44,000)	+	44,000	=	NA	+	NA	NA	−	NA	=	NA	(44,000)	IA
NA	+	(4,000)	=	NA	+	(4,000)	NA	−	4,000	=	(4,000)	NA	

Impairment Losses for Intangible Assets with Indefinite Useful Lives

Intangible assets with indefinite useful lives must be tested for impairment annually. The impairment test consists of comparing the fair value of the intangible asset to its carrying value (book value). If the fair value is less than the book value, an impairment loss must be recognized.

To illustrate, return to the example of the Bendigo's restaurant purchase. Recall that the buyer of Bendigo's paid $70,000 for goodwill. Assume the restaurant experiences a significant decline in revenue because many of its former regular customers are dissatisfied with the food prepared by the new chef. Suppose the decline in revenue is so substantial that the new owner believes the Bendigo's name is permanently impaired. The owner decides to hire a different chef and change the name of the restaurant. In this case, the business has suffered a permanent decline in value of goodwill. The company must recognize an impairment loss.

The restaurant's name has lost its value, but the owner believes the location continues to provide the opportunity to produce above-average earnings. Some, but not all, of the goodwill has been lost. Assume the fair value of the remaining goodwill is determined to be $40,000. The impairment loss to recognize is $30,000 ($70,000 − $40,000). The loss reduces the intangible asset (goodwill), stockholder's equity (retained earnings), and net income. The statement of cash flows would not be affected. The effects on the financial statements follow.

Assets	=	Liab.	+	Equity	Rev.	−	Exp./Loss	=	Net Inc.	Cash Flow
Goodwill	=			Ret. Earn.						
(30,000)	=	NA	+	(30,000)	NA	−	30,000	=	(30,000)	NA

BALANCE SHEET PRESENTATION

This chapter has explained accounting for the acquisition, expense recognition, and disposal of a wide range of long-term assets. Exhibit 6.7 illustrates typical balance sheet presentation of many of the assets discussed.

EXHIBIT 6.7

Balance Sheet Presentation of Operational Assets

Partial Balance Sheet			
Long-Term Assets			
Plant and equipment			
Buildings	$4,000,000		
Less: Accumulated depreciation	(2,500,000)	$1,500,000	
Equipment	1,750,000		
Less: Accumulated depreciation	(1,200,000)	550,000	
Total plant and equipment			$2,050,000
Land			850,000
Natural resources			
Mineral deposits (Less: Depletion)		2,100,000	
Oil reserves (Less: Depletion)		890,000	
Total natural resources			2,990,000
Intangibles			
Patents (Less: Amortization)		38,000	
Goodwill		175,000	
Total intangible assets			213,000
Total long-term assets			$6,103,000

EFFECT OF JUDGMENT AND ESTIMATION

LO 6-9

Explain how expense recognition choices and industry characteristics affect financial performance measures.

Managers may have differing opinions about which allocation method (straight-line, accelerated, or units-of-production) best matches expenses with revenues. As a result, one company may use straight-line depreciation while another company in similar circumstances uses double-declining-balance. Because the allocation method a company uses affects the amount of expense it recognizes, analysts reviewing financial statements must consider the accounting procedures companies use in preparing the statements.

Assume that two companies, Alpha and Zeta, experience identical economic events in 2015 and 2016. Both generate revenue of $50,000 and incur cost of goods sold of $30,000 during each year. In 2015, each company pays $20,000 for an asset with an expected useful life of five years and no salvage value. How will the companies' financial statements differ if one uses straight-line depreciation and the other uses the double-declining-balance method? To answer this question, first compute the depreciation expense for both companies for 2015 and 2016.

If Alpha Company uses the straight-line method, depreciation for 2015 and 2016 is

$$(\text{Cost} - \text{Salvage}) \div \text{Useful life} = \text{Depreciation expense per year}$$

$$(\$20,000 - \$0) \div 5 \text{ years} = \$4,000$$

In contrast, if Zeta Company uses the double-declining-balance method, Zeta recognizes the following amounts of depreciation expense for 2015 and 2016.

	(Cost − Accumulated Depreciation)	×	2 × (Straight-Line Rate)	=	Depreciation Expense
2015	($20,000 − $ 0)	×	[2 × (1 ÷ 5)]	=	$8,000
2016	($20,000 − $8,000)	×	[2 × (1 ÷ 5)]	=	$4,800

Based on these computations, the income statements for the two companies are:

Income Statements				
	2015		**2016**	
	Alpha Co.	Zeta Co.	Alpha Co.	Zeta Co.
Sales	$50,000	$50,000	$50,000	$50,000
Cost of goods sold	(30,000)	(30,000)	(30,000)	(30,000)
Gross margin	20,000	20,000	20,000	20,000
Depreciation expense	(4,000)	(8,000)	(4,000)	(4,800)
Net income	$16,000	$12,000	$16,000	$15,200

The relevant sections of the balance sheets are

Plant Assets				
	2015		**2016**	
	Alpha Co.	Zeta Co.	Alpha Co.	Zeta Co.
Assets	$20,000	$20,000	$20,000	$20,000
Accumulated depreciation	(4,000)	(8,000)	(8,000)	(12,800)
Book value	$16,000	$12,000	$12,000	$ 7,200

The depreciation method is not the only aspect of expense recognition that can vary between companies. Companies may also make different assumptions about the useful lives and salvage values of long-term operational assets. Thus, even if the same depreciation method is used, depreciation expense may still differ.

Because the depreciation method and the underlying assumptions regarding useful life and salvage value affect the determination of depreciation expense, they also affect the amounts of net income, retained earnings, and total assets.

To promote meaningful analysis, public companies are required to disclose all significant accounting policies used to prepare their financial statements. This disclosure is usually provided in the notes that accompany the financial statements.

EFFECT OF INDUSTRY CHARACTERISTICS

As indicated in previous chapters, industry characteristics affect financial performance measures. For example, companies in manufacturing industries invest heavily in machinery while insurance companies rely more on human capital. Manufacturing companies therefore have relatively higher depreciation charges than insurance companies. To illustrate how the type of industry affects financial reporting, examine Exhibit 6.8. This exhibit compares the ratio of sales to property, plant, and equipment for two companies in each of three different industries.

EXHIBIT 6.8

Industry Data Reflecting the Use of Long-Term Tangible Assets

Industry	Company	Sales ÷ Property, Plant, and Equipment
Cable Companies	Comcast Corporation	2.30
	Verizon Communications	1.31
Airlines	Alaska Air Group	1.29
	Southwest Airlines	1.34
Employment Agencies	Kelly Services	60.63
	Manpower, Inc.	111.89

The table indicates that for every $1.00 invested in property, plant, and equipment, Kelly Services produced $60.63 of sales. In contrast, Verizon Communications and Alaska Air Group produced only $1.31 and $1.29, respectively, for each $1.00 they invested in operational assets. Does this mean the management of Kelly is doing a better job than the management of Verizon Communications or Alaska Air Group? Not necessarily. It means that these companies operate in different economic environments. In other words, it takes significantly more equipment to operate a cable company or an airline than it takes to operate an employment agency.

 ## A Look Back

This chapter explains that the primary objective of recognizing depreciation is to match the cost of a long-term tangible asset with the revenues the asset is expected to generate. The matching concept also applies to natural resources (depletion) and intangible assets (amortization). The chapter explains how alternative methods can be used to account for the same event (e.g., straight-line versus double-declining-balance depreciation). Companies experiencing exactly the same business events could produce different financial statements. The alternative accounting methods for depreciating, depleting, or amortizing assets include the (1) straight-line, (2) double-declining-balance, and (3) units-of-production methods.

The *straight-line method* produces equal amounts of expense in each accounting period. The amount of the expense recognized is determined using the formula [(cost − salvage) ÷ number of years of useful life]. The *double-declining-balance method* produces proportionately larger amounts of expense in the early years of an asset's useful life and increasingly smaller amounts of expense in the later years of the asset's useful life. The formula for calculating double-declining-balance depreciation is [book value at beginning of period × (2 × the straight-line rate)]. The *units-of-production method* produces expense in direct proportion to the number of units produced during an accounting period. The formula for the amount of expense recognized each period is [(cost − salvage) ÷ total estimated units of production = allocation rate × units of production in current accounting period].

This chapter showed how to account for *changes in estimates* such as the useful life or the salvage value of a depreciable asset. Changes in estimates do not affect the amount of depreciation recognized previously. Instead, the remaining book value of the asset is expensed over its remaining useful life.

After an asset has been placed into service, companies typically incur further costs for maintenance, quality improvement, and extensions of useful life. *Maintenance costs* are expensed in the period in which they are incurred. *Costs that improve the quality* of an asset are added to the cost of the asset, increasing the book value and the amount of future depreciation charges. *Costs that extend the useful life* of an asset are subtracted from the asset's Accumulated Depreciation account thereby increasing the book value of the asset.

A Look Forward

In Chapter 7 we move from the assets section of the balance sheet to issues in accounting for liabilities.

 Video lectures and accompanying self-assessment quizzes are available for all learning objectives through McGraw-Hill *Connect*® *Accounting*.

SELF-STUDY REVIEW PROBLEM

The following information pertains to a machine purchased by Bakersfield Company on January 1, 2016.

Purchase price	$ 63,000
Delivery cost	$ 2,000
Installation charge	$ 3,000
Estimated useful life	8 years
Estimated units the machine will produce	130,000
Estimated salvage value	$ 3,000

The machine produced 14,400 units during 2016 and 17,000 units during 2017.

Required

Determine the depreciation expense Bakersfield would report for 2016 and 2017 using each of the following methods.

a. Straight-line.
b. Double-declining-balance.
c. Units-of-production.

Solution to Requirements a–c.

a. Straight-line

Purchase price	$63,000
Delivery cost	2,000
Installation charge	3,000
Total cost of machine	68,000
Less: Salvage value	(3,000)
	$65,000 ÷ 8 = $8,125 Depreciation per year
2016	$ 8,125
2017	$ 8,125

b. Double-declining-balance

Year	Cost	−	Accumulated Depreciation at Beginning of Year	×	2 × S-L Rate	=	Annual Depreciation
2016	$68,000	−	$ 0	×	(2 × 0.125)	=	$17,000
2017	68,000	−	17,000	×	(2 × 0.125)	=	12,750

   c. Units-of-production

     (1) (Cost − Salvage value) ÷ Estimated units of production = Depreciation cost per unit produced

$$\frac{\$68,000 - \$3,000}{130,000} = \$0.50 \text{ per unit}$$

     (2) Cost per unit × Annual units produced = Annual depreciation expense

       2016 $0.50 × 14,400 = $7,200

       2017   0.50 × 17,000 = 8,500

KEY TERMS

Accelerated depreciation method 214	Current assets 206	Goodwill 224	Relative fair market value method 209
Accumulated Depreciation 212	Depletion 208	Historical cost concept 209	Revenue expenditures 219
Amortization 208	Depreciable cost 210	Intangible assets 208	Salvage value 210
Basket purchase 209	Depreciation 208	Long-term operational assets 206	Straight-line depreciation 211
Book value 212	Depreciation expense 210	Natural resources 208	Tangible assets 208
Capital expenditures 220	Double-declining-balance depreciation 214	Patent 222	Trademark 222
Contra asset account 212	Estimated useful life 210	Property, plant, and equipment 208	Units-of-production depreciation 217
Copyright 223	Franchise 223		

QUESTIONS

1. What is the difference between the functions of long-term operational assets and investments?

2. What is the difference between tangible and intangible assets? Give an example of each.

3. What is the difference between goodwill and specifically identifiable intangible assets?

4. Define *depreciation*. What kind of asset depreciates?

5. Why are natural resources called *wasting assets*?

6. Is land a depreciable asset? Why or why not?

7. Define *amortization*. What kind of assets are *amortized*?

8. Explain the historical cost concept as it applies to long-term operational assets. Why is the book value of an asset likely to be different from the current market value of the asset?

9. What different kinds of expenditures might be included in the recorded cost of a building?

10. What is a basket purchase of assets? When a basket purchase is made, how is cost assigned to individual assets?

11. What are the stages in the life cycle of a long-term operational asset?

12. Explain straight-line, units-of-production, and double-declining-balance depreciation. When is it appropriate to use each of these depreciation methods?

13. What effect does the recognition of depreciation expense have on total assets? On total equity?

14. Does the recognition of depreciation expense affect cash flows? Why or why not?

15. MalMax purchased a depreciable asset. What would be the difference in total assets at the end of the first year if MalMax chooses straight-line depreciation versus double-declining-balance depreciation?

16. John Smith mistakenly expensed the cost of a long-term tangible fixed asset. Specifically, he charged the cost of a truck to a delivery expense account. How will this error affect the income statement and the balance sheet in the year in which the mistake is made?

17. What is *salvage value*?

18. What type of account (classification) is Accumulated Depreciation?

19. How is the book value of an asset determined?

20. Why is depreciation that has been recognized over the life of an asset shown in a contra account? Why not just reduce the asset account?

21. Assume that a piece of equipment cost $5,000 and had accumulated depreciation of $3,000. What is the book value of the equipment? Is the book value equal to the fair market value of the equipment? Explain.

22. Why would a company choose to depreciate one piece of equipment using the double-declining-balance method and another piece of equipment using straight-line depreciation?

23. Why may it be necessary to revise the estimated life of a plant asset? When the estimated life is revised, does it affect the amount of depreciation per year? Why or why not?

24. How are capital expenditures made to improve the

quality of a capital asset accounted for? Would the answer change if the expenditure extended the life of the asset but did not improve quality? Explain.

25. When a long-term operational asset is sold at a

gain, how is the balance sheet affected? Is the statement of cash flows affected? If so, how?

26. Define *depletion*. What is the most commonly used method of computing depletion?

27. List several common intangible assets. How is the life determined that is to be used to compute amortization?

28. List some differences between U.S. GAAP and GAAP of other countries

with respect to amortization and accounting for intangibles.

29. How can judgment and estimation affect information reported in the financial statements?

MULTIPLE-CHOICE QUESTIONS

Multiple-choice questions are provided on the text website at www.mhhe.com/edmondssurvey4e.

EXERCISES

≡ connect | ACCOUNTING   All applicable Exercises are available with McGraw-Hill's *Connect® Accounting.*

Unless specifically included, ignore income tax considerations in all exercises and problems.

Exercise 6-1   *Long-term operational assets used in a business*   LO 6-1

Required

Give some examples of long-term operational assets that each of the following companies is likely to own: *(a)* Freds, *(b)* Princess Cruise Lines, *(c)* Southwest Airlines, and *(d)* Harley-Davidson Co.

Exercise 6-2   *Identifying long-term operational assets*   LO 6-1

Required

Which of the following items should be classified as long-term operational assets?

a. Inventory C
b. Patent L
c. Tract of timber L
d. Land L
e. Computer L
f. Goodwill L

g. Cash C
h. Buildings L
i. Production machinery L
j. Accounts receivable C
k. Prepaid rent C
l. Franchise L

Exercise 6-3   *Classifying tangible and intangible assets*   LO 6-1

Required

Identify each of the following long-term operational assets as either tangible (T) or intangible (I).

a. 18-wheel truck T
b. Timber T
c. Log loader T
d. Dental chair T
e. Goodwill I
f. Computer software I

g. Retail store building T
h. Shelving for inventory T
i. Trademark I
j. Gas well T
k. Drilling rig T
l. FCC license for TV station I

Exercise 6-4   *Determining the cost of an asset*   LO 6-2

Louisiana Logging Co. purchased an electronic saw to cut various types and sizes of logs. The saw had a list price of $160,000. The seller agreed to allow a 5 percent discount because

232   Chapter 6

Louisiana paid cash. Delivery terms were FOB shipping point. Freight cost amounted to $3,200. Louisiana had to hire an individual to operate the saw. Louisiana had to build a special platform to mount the saw. The cost of the platform was $2,500. The saw operator was paid an annual salary of $50,000. The cost of the company's theft insurance policy increased by $1,800 per year as a result of acquiring the saw. The saw had a five-year useful life and an expected salvage value of $25,000.

Required

Determine the amount to be capitalized in the asset account for the purchase of the saw.

LO 6-2

Exercise 6-5   *Allocating costs on the basis of relative market values*

Carolina Company purchased a building and the land on which the building is situated for a total cost of $800,000 cash. The land was appraised at $300,000 and the building at $700,000.

Required

a. What is the accounting term for this type of acquisition?
b. Determine the amount of the purchase cost to allocate to the land and the amount to allocate to the building.
c. Would the company recognize a gain on the purchase? Why or why not?
d. Record the purchase in a statements model like the following one.

Assets	= Liab. + Equity	Rev. − Exp. = Net Inc.	Cash Flow
Cash + Land + Building			

LO 6-2

Exercise 6-6   *Allocating costs for a basket purchase*

Sneathen Company purchased a restaurant building, land, and equipment for $600,000 cash. The appraised value of the assets was as follows:

Land	$200,000
Building	480,000
Equipment	120,000
Total	$800,000

Required

a. Compute the amount to be recorded on the books for each of the assets.
b. Record the purchase in a horizontal statements model like the following one.

Assets	= Liab. + Equity	Rev. − Exp. = Net Inc.	Cash Flow
Cash + Land + Building + Equip.			

LO 6-3

Exercise 6-7   *Effect of depreciation on the accounting equation and financial statements*

The following events apply to The Ice Cream Parlor for the 2014 fiscal year:

1. The company started when it acquired $20,000 cash from the issue of common stock.
2. Purchased a new ice cream machine that cost $20,000 cash.
3. Earned $36,000 in cash revenue.
4. Paid $21,000 cash for salaries expense.
5. Paid $6,000 cash for operating expenses.

6. Adjusted the records to reflect the use of the ice cream machine. The machine, purchased on January 1, 2014, has an expected useful life of five years and an estimated salvage value of $5,000. Use straight-line depreciation. The adjusting entry was made as of December 31, 2014.

Required

a. Record the above transactions in a horizontal statements model like the following one.

Event	Balance Sheet							Income Statement				Statemt. of Cash Flows
	Assets				=	Equity		Rev.	− Exp.	= Net Inc.		
	Cash	+ Equip.	− A. Depr.	=		Com. Stock	+ Ret. Earn.					

b. What amount of depreciation expense would The Ice Cream Parlor report on the 2014 income statement?

c. What amount of accumulated depreciation would The Ice Cream Parlor report on the December 31, 2014, balance sheet?

d. Would the cash flow from operating activities be affected by depreciation in 2014?

Exercise 6-8 *Effect of double-declining-balance depreciation on financial statements*   LO 6-3

Posey Company started operations by acquiring $120,000 cash from the issue of common stock. On January 1, 2014, the company purchased equipment that cost $110,000 cash. The equipment had an expected useful life of five years and an estimated salvage value of $10,000. Posey Company earned $85,000 and $72,000 of cash revenue during 2014 and 2015, respectively. Posey Company uses double-declining-balance depreciation.

Required

a. Record the above transactions in a horizontal statements model like the following one.

Event	Balance Sheet							Income Statement				Statemt. of Cash Flows
	Assets				=	Equity		Rev.	− Exp.	= Net Inc.		
	Cash	+ Equip.	− A. Depr.	=		Com. Stock	+ Ret. Earn.					

b. Prepare income statements, balance sheets, and statements of cash flows for 2014 and 2015. Use a vertical statements format.

Exercise 6-9 *Computing and recording straight-line versus double-declining-balance depreciation*   LO 6-3

At the beginning of 2014, Metal Manufacturing purchased a new computerized drill press for $75,000. It is expected to have a five-year life and a $15,000 salvage value.

Required

a. Compute the depreciation for each of the five years, assuming that the company uses
   (1) Straight-line depreciation.
   (2) Double-declining-balance depreciation.

b. Record the purchase of the drill press and the depreciation expense for the first year under the straight-line and double-declining-balance methods in a financial statements model like the following one:

Assets				=	Equity	Rev.	− Exp.	= Net Inc.	Cash Flow
Cash	+ Drill Press	− Acc. Dep.	=		Ret. Earn				

LO 6-3, 6-4

Exercise 6-10   *Double-declining-balance and units-of-production depreciation: Gain or loss on disposal*

Graphics Service Co. purchased a new color copier at the beginning of 2014 for $47,000. The copier is expected to have a five-year useful life and a $7,000 salvage value. The expected copy production was estimated at 2,000,000 copies. Actual copy production for the five years was as follows:

2014	560,000
2015	490,000
2016	430,000
2017	350,000
2018	210,000
Total	2,040,000

The copier was sold at the end of 2018 for $7,600.

Required

a. Compute the depreciation expense for each of the five years, using double-declining-balance depreciation.

b. Compute the depreciation expense for each of the five years, using units-of-production depreciation. (Round cost per unit to three decimal places.)

c. Calculate the amount of gain or loss from the sale of the asset under each of the depreciation methods.

LO 6-3, 6-4

Exercise 6-11   *Events related to the acquisition, use, and disposal of a tangible plant asset: Straight-line depreciation*

Sam's Subs purchased a delivery van on January 1, 2014, for $35,000. In addition, Sam's paid sales tax and title fees of $1,500 for the van. The van is expected to have a four-year life and a salvage value of $6,500.

Required

a. Using the straight-line method, compute the depreciation expense for 2014 and 2015.

b. Assume the van was sold on January 1, 2017, for $21,000. Determine the amount of gain or loss that would be recognized on the asset disposal.

LO 6-4

Exercise 6-12   *Effect of the disposal of plant assets on the financial statements*

A plant asset with a cost of $50,000 and accumulated depreciation of $44,000 is sold for $10,000.

Required

a. What is the book value of the asset at the time of sale?

b. What is the amount of gain or loss on the disposal?

c. How would the sale affect net income (increase, decrease, no effect) and by how much?

d. How would the sale affect the amount of total assets shown on the balance sheet (increase, decrease, no effect) and by how much?

e. How would the event affect the statement of cash flows (inflow, outflow, no effect) and in what section?

LO 6-4

Exercise 6-13   *Effect of gains and losses on the accounting equation and financial statements*

On January 1, 2014, Liken Enterprises purchased a parcel of land for $20,000 cash. At the time of purchase, the company planned to use the land for future expansion. In 2015, Liken Enterprises changed its plans and sold the land.

Required

a. Assume that the land was sold for $22,500 in 2015.
   (1) Show the effect of the sale on the accounting equation.
   (2) What amount would Liken report on the income statement related to the sale of the land?
   (3) What amount would Liken report on the statement of cash flows related to the sale of the land?

b. Assume that the land was sold for $18,500 in 2015.
   (1) Show the effect of the sale on the accounting equation.
   (2) What amount would Liken report on the income statement related to the sale of the land?
   (3) What amount would Liken report on the statement of cash flows related to the sale of the land?

Exercise 6-14 *Revision of estimated useful life*

LO 6-5

On January 1, 2014, Muoy Machining Co. purchased a compressor and related installation equipment for $72,500. The equipment had a three-year estimated life with a $12,500 salvage value. Straight-line depreciation was used. At the beginning of 2016, Muoy revised the expected life of the asset to four years rather than three years. The salvage value was revised to $2,500.

Required

Compute the depreciation expense for each of the four years.

Exercise 6-15 *Distinguishing between revenue expenditures and capital expenditures*

LO 6-6

Houston's Shredding Service has just completed a minor repair on a shredding machine. The repair cost was $1,900, and the book value prior to the repair was $6,000. In addition, the company spent $12,000 to replace the roof on a building. The new roof extended the life of the building by five years. Prior to the roof replacement, the general ledger reflected the Building account at $110,000 and related Accumulated Depreciation account at $30,000.

Required

After the work was completed, what book value should Houston's report on the balance sheet for the shredding machine and the building?

Exercise 6-16 *Effect of revenue expenditures versus capital expenditures on financial statements*

LO 6-6

Apac Construction Company purchased a forklift for $150,000 cash. It had an estimated useful life of four years and a $10,000 salvage value. At the beginning of the third year of use, the company spent an additional $9,000 that was related to the forklift. The company's financial condition just prior to this expenditure is shown in the following statements model:

Assets			=	Equity			Rev.	−	Exp.	=	Net Inc.	Cash Flow
Cash	+	Forklift	Acc. Depr.	=	Com. Stk.	+	Ret. Earn.						
15,000	+	150,000	70,000	=	45,000	+	50,000	NA	−	NA	=	NA	NA

Required

Record the $9,000 expenditure in the statements model under each of the following *independent* assumptions:

a. The expenditure was for routine maintenance.
b. The expenditure extended the forklift's life.
c. The expenditure improved the forklift's operating capacity.

LO 6-6

Exercise 6-17   *Effect of revenue expenditures versus capital expenditures on financial statements*

On January 1, 2014, Plains Power Company overhauled four turbine engines that generate power for customers. The overhaul resulted in a slight increase in the capacity of the engines to produce power. Such overhauls occur regularly at two-year intervals and have been treated as maintenance expense in the past. Management is considering whether to capitalize this year's $22,000 cash cost in the Engine asset account or to expense it as a maintenance expense. Assume that the engines have a remaining useful life of two years and no expected salvage value. Assume straight-line depreciation.

Required

a. Determine the amount of additional depreciation expense Plains would recognize in 2014 and 2015 if the cost were capitalized in the Engine account.

b. Determine the amount of expense Plains would recognize in 2014 and 2015 if the cost were recognized as maintenance expense.

c. Determine the effect of the overhaul on cash flow from operating activities for 2014 and 2015 if the cost were capitalized and expensed through depreciation charges.

d. Determine the effect of the overhaul on cash flow from operating activities for 2014 and 2015 if the cost were recognized as maintenance expense.

LO 6-7

Exercise 6-18   *Computing and recording depletion expense*

Tishimingo Sand and Gravel paid $800,000 to acquire 1,200,000 cubic yards of sand reserves. The following statements model reflects Tishimingo's financial condition just prior to purchasing the sand reserves. The company extracted 650,000 cubic yards of sand in year 1 and 450,000 cubic yards in year 2.

Assets			=	Equity			Rev.	−	Exp.	=	Net Inc.	Cash Flow
Cash	+	Sand Res.	=	Com. Stk.	+	Ret. Earn.						
900,000	+	NA	=	900,000	+	NA	NA	−	NA	=	NA	NA

Required

a. Compute the depletion charge per unit.

b. Record the acquisition of the sand reserves and the depletion expense for years 1 and 2 in a financial statements model like the preceding one.

LO 6-8

Exercise 6-19   *Computing and recording the amortization of intangibles*

Pacart Manufacturing paid cash to acquire the assets of an existing company. Among the assets acquired were the following items:

Patent with 5 remaining years of legal life	$48,000
Goodwill	35,000

Pacart's financial condition just prior to the purchase of these assets is shown in the following statements model:

Assets					=	Liab.	+	Equity	Rev.	−	Exp.	=	Net Inc.	Cash Flow
Cash	+	Patent	+	Goodwill										
94,000	+	NA	+	NA	=	NA	+	94,000	NA	−	NA	=	NA	NA

Required

a. Compute the annual amortization expense for these items if applicable.

b. Record the purchase of the intangible assets and the related amortization expense for year 1 in a horizontal statements model like the preceding one.

Exercise 6-20   *Computing and recording goodwill*   LO 6-8

Bill Yeates acquired the business Sun Supply Co. for $275,000 cash and assumed all liabilities at the date of acquisition. Sun's books showed tangible assets of $250,000, liabilities of $10,000, and equity of $240,000. An appraiser assessed the fair market value of the tangible assets at $265,000 at the date of acquisition. Yeates's financial condition just prior to the acquisition is shown in the following statements model:

Assets					=	Liab.	+	Equity	Rev.	−	Exp.	=	Net Inc.	Cash Flow
Cash	+	Assets	+	Goodwill										
450,000	+	NA	+	NA	=	NA	+	450,000	NA	−	NA	=	NA	NA

Required

a. Compute the amount of goodwill purchased.

b. Record the purchase in a financial statements model like the preceding one.

Exercise 6-21   *Performing ratio analysis using real-world data*   LO 6-9

American Greetings Corporation manufactures and sells greeting cards and related items such as gift wrapping paper. CSX Corporation is one of the largest railway networks in the nation. The following data were taken from one of the companies' December 28, 2012, annual report and from the other's February 29, 2012, annual report. Revealing which data relate to which company was intentionally omitted. For one company, the dollar amounts are in thousands, while for the other they are in millions.

	Company 1	Company 2
Sales	$1,695,144	$11,756
Depreciation costs	34,210	1,059
Net earnings	57,198	1,859
Current assets	640,959	2,801
Property, plant, and equipment	277,597	24,974
Total assets	1,549,464	30,571

Required

a. Calculate depreciation costs as a percentage of sales for each company.

b. Calculate property, plant, and equipment as a percentage of total assets for each company.

c. Based on the information now available to you, decide which data relate to which company. Explain the rationale for your decision.

d. Which company appears to be using its assets most efficiently? Explain your answer.

PROBLEMS

 All applicable Problems are available with McGraw-Hill's
Connect® Accounting.

Problem 6-22   *Accounting for acquisition of assets including a basket purchase*   LO 6-2

Shay Company made several purchases of long-term assets in 2014. The details of each purchase are presented here.

238   Chapter 6

New Office Equipment

1. List price: $50,000; terms: 1/10, n/30; paid within the discount period.
2. Transportation-in: $1,200.
3. Installation: $1,000.
4. Cost to repair damage during unloading: $700.
5. Routine maintenance cost after eight months: $240.

Basket Purchase of Office Furniture, Copier, Computers, and Laser Printers for $70,000 with Fair Market Values

1. Office furniture, $48,000.
2. Copier, $12,000.
3. Computers and printers, $20,000.

Land for New Headquarters with Old Barn Torn Down

1. Purchase price, $100,000.
2. Demolition of barn, $7,000.
3. Lumber sold from old barn, $2,000.
4. Grading in preparation for new building, $11,000.
5. Construction of new building, $310,000.

Required

In each of these cases, determine the amount of cost to be capitalized in the asset accounts.

LO 6-3

Problem 6-23   *Calculating depreciation expense using four different methods*

Weir Service Company purchased a copier on January 1, 2014, for $25,000 and paid an additional $500 for delivery charges. The copier was estimated to have a life of four years or 1,000,000 copies. Salvage was estimated at $1,500. The copier produced 250,000 copies in 2014 and 270,000 copies in 2015.

Required

Compute the amount of depreciation expense for the copier for calendar years 2014 and 2015, using these methods:

a. Straight-line.
b. Units-of-production.
c. Double-declining-balance.

LO 6-3

Problem 6-24   *Determining the effect of depreciation expense on financial statements*

Three different companies each purchased a machine on January 1, 2014, for $64,000. Each machine was expected to last five years or 200,000 hours. Salvage value was estimated to be $4,000. All three machines were operated for 50,000 hours in 2014, 55,000 hours in 2015, 40,000 hours in 2016, 44,000 hours in 2017, and 31,000 hours in 2018. Each of the three companies earned $30,000 of cash revenue during each of the five years. Company A uses straight-line depreciation, company B uses double-declining-balance depreciation, and company C uses units-of-production depreciation.

Required

Answer each of the following questions. Ignore the effects of income taxes.

a. Which company will report the highest amount of net income for 2014?
b. Which company will report the lowest amount of net income for 2016?
c. Which company will report the highest book value on the December 31, 2016, balance sheet?

d. Which company will report the highest amount of retained earnings on the December 31, 2017, balance sheet?

e. Which company will report the lowest amount of cash flow from operating activities on the 2016 statement of cash flows?

Problem 6-25 *Accounting for depreciation over multiple accounting cycles: Straight-line depreciation*

LO 6-3, 6-4

CHECK FIGURES
Net Income, 2014: $500
Total Assets, 2017: $42,500

Zhao Company began operations when it acquired $40,000 cash from the issue of common stock on January 1, 2014. The cash acquired was immediately used to purchase equipment for $40,000 that had a $4,000 salvage value and an expected useful life of four years. The equipment was used to produce the following revenue stream (assume all revenue transactions are for cash). At the beginning of the fifth year, the equipment was sold for $4,500 cash. Zhao uses straight-line depreciation.

	2014	2015	2016	2017	2018
Revenue	$9,500	$10,000	$10,500	$8,500	$0

Required

Prepare income statements, statements of changes in stockholders' equity, balance sheets, and statements of cash flows for each of the five years.

Problem 6-26 *Effect of straight-line versus double-declining-balance depreciation on the recognition of expense and gains or losses*

LO 6-3, 6-4

CHECK FIGURES
a. Depreciation Expense, Year 2: $8,000
b. Depreciation Expense, Year 2: $10,800

One Day Laundry Services purchased a new steam press on January 1, for $42,000. It is expected to have a five-year useful life and a $2,000 salvage value. One Day expects to use the steam press more extensively in the early years of its life.

Required

a. Calculate the depreciation expense for each of the five years, assuming the use of straight-line depreciation.

b. Calculate the depreciation expense for each of the five years, assuming the use of double-declining-balance depreciation.

c. Would the choice of one depreciation method over another produce a different amount of cash flow for any year? Why or why not?

d. Assume that One Day Laundry Services sold the steam press at the end of the third year for $22,000. Compute the amount of gain or loss using each depreciation method.

Problem 6-27 *Computing and recording units-of-production depreciation*

LO 6-3, 6-4

Renner Corporation purchased a delivery van for $28,500 in 2014. The firm's financial condition immediately prior to the purchase is shown in the following horizontal statements model:

Assets			=	Equity			Rev.	−	Exp.	=	Net Inc.	Cash Flow
Cash	+	Book Value of Van	=	Com. Stk.	+	Ret. Earn.						
50,000	+	NA	=	50,000	+	NA	NA	−	NA	=	NA	NA

The van was expected to have a useful life of 200,000 miles and a salvage value of $2,500. Actual mileage was as follows:

CHECK FIGURES
a. Depreciation Expense, 2014: $7,800
c. Gain on Sale: $950

2014	60,000
2015	50,000
2016	55,000

Required

a. Compute the depreciation for each of the three years, assuming the use of units-of-production depreciation.

b. Assume that Renner earns $26,000 of cash revenue during 2014. Record the purchase of the van and the recognition of the revenue and the depreciation expense for the first year in a financial statements model like the preceding one.

c. Assume that Renner sold the van at the end of the third year for $8,000. Calculate the amount of gain or loss from the sale.

LO 6-2, 6-3, 6-5, 6-6

CHECK FIGURES
b. Net Income, 2014: $48,520
Total Assets, 2016: $242,591

Problem 6-28   *Purchase and use of tangible asset: Three accounting cycles, double-declining-balance depreciation*

The following transactions pertain to Engineering Solutions Inc. Assume the transactions for the purchase of the computer and any capital improvements occur on January 1 each year.

2014

1. Acquired $80,000 cash from the issue of common stock.
2. Purchased a computer system for $35,000. It has an estimated useful life of five years and a $5,000 salvage value.
3. Paid $2,450 sales tax on the computer system.
4. Collected $65,000 in fees from clients.
5. Paid $1,500 in fees to service the computers.
6. Recorded double-declining-balance depreciation on the computer system for 2014.

2015

1. Paid $1,000 for repairs to the computer system.
2. Bought off-site backup services to maintain the computer system, $1,500.
3. Collected $68,000 in fees from clients.
4. Paid $1,500 in fees to service the computers.
5. Recorded double-declining-balance depreciation for 2015.

2016

1. Paid $6,000 to upgrade the computer system, which extended the total life of the system to six years. The salvage value did not change.
2. Paid $1,200 in fees to service the computers.
3. Collected $70,000 in fees from clients.
4. Recorded double-declining-balance depreciation for 2016.

Required

a. Record the above transactions in a horizontal statements model like the following one.

Event	Balance Sheet							Income Statement				Statemt. of Cash Flows
	Assets				=	Equity		Rev.	− Exp.	=	Net Inc.	
	Cash	+ Equip.	−	A. Depr.	=	Com. Stock	+ Ret. Earn.					

b. Use a vertical model to present financial statements for 2014, 2015, and 2016.

Problem 6-29   *Recording continuing expenditures for plant assets*   LO 6-3, 6-4, 6-5, 6-6

Seaside Inc. recorded the following transactions over the life of a piece of equipment purchased in 2014:

CHECK FIGURES
b. 2016 Depreciation Expense:
   $8,333
d. Loss on Sale: $2,916

Jan. 1, 2014	Purchased the equipment for $38,000 cash. The equipment is estimated to have a five-year life and $3,000 salvage value and was to be depreciated using the straight-line method.
Dec. 31, 2014	Recorded depreciation expense for 2014.
May 5, 2015	Undertook routine repairs costing $900.
Dec. 31, 2015	Recorded depreciation expense for 2015.
Jan. 1, 2016	Made an adjustment costing $4,000 to the equipment. It improved the quality of the output but did not affect the life and salvage value estimates.
Dec. 31, 2016	Recorded depreciation expense for 2016.
Mar. 1, 2017	Incurred $410 cost to oil and clean the equipment.
Dec. 31, 2017	Recorded depreciation expense for 2017.
Jan. 1, 2018	Had the equipment completely overhauled at a cost of $9,000. The overhaul was estimated to extend the total life to seven years and revised the salvage value to $2,500.
Dec. 31, 2018	Recorded depreciation expense for 2018.
July 1, 2019	Sold the equipment for $8,500 cash.

Required

a. Use a horizontal statements model like the following one to show the effects of these transactions on the elements of the financial statements. Use + for increase, − for decrease, and NA for not affected. The first event is recorded as an example.

Date	Assets	=	Liabilities	+	Equity	Net Inc.	Cash Flow
Jan. 1, 2011	+ −		NA		NA	NA	− IA

b. Determine the amount of depreciation expense Seaside will report on the income statements for the years 2014 through 2018.
c. Determine the book value (cost − accumulated depreciation) Seaside will report on the balance sheets at the end of the years 2014 through 2018.
d. Determine the amount of the gain or loss Seaside will report on the disposal of the equipment on July 1, 2019.

Problem 6-30   *Accounting for depletion*   LO 6-7

Cohen Exploration Corporation engages in the exploration and development of many types of natural resources. In the last two years, the company has engaged in the following activities:

CHECK FIGURES
a. Coal Mine Depletion, 2014:
   $204,000
b. Total Natural Resources:
   $2,126,030

Jan. 1, 2014	Purchased a coal mine estimated to contain 300,000 tons of coal for $900,000.
July 1, 2014	Purchased for $2,000,000 a tract of timber estimated to yield 3,000,000 board feet of lumber and to have a residual land value of $200,000.
Feb. 1, 2014	Purchased a silver mine estimated to contain 30,000 tons of silver for $850,000.
Aug. 1, 2014	Purchased for $875,000 oil reserves estimated to contain 270,000 barrels of oil, of which 20,000 would be unprofitable to pump.

Required

a. Determine the amount of depletion expense that would be recognized on the 2014 income statement for each of the four reserves, assuming 68,000 tons of coal, 1,200,000 board feet of lumber, 9,000 tons of silver, and 80,000 barrels of oil are extracted.
b. Prepare the portion of the December 31, 2014, balance sheet that reports natural resources.

242   Chapter 6

Problem 6-31   *Accounting for continuing expenditures*

Bird Manufacturing paid $62,000 to purchase a computerized assembly machine on January 1, 2014. The machine had an estimated life of eight years and a $2,000 salvage value. Bird's financial condition as of January 1, 2017, is shown in the following financial statements model. Bird uses the straight-line method for depreciation.

Assets				=	Equity			Rev.	−	Exp.	=	Net Inc.	Cash Flow
Cash	+	Mach.	−	Acc. Dep.	=	Com. Stk.	+	Ret. Earn.					
15,000	+	62,000	−	22,500	=	10,500	+	44,000	NA	−	NA	=	NA	NA

Bird Manufacturing made the following expenditures on the computerized assembly machine in 2017.

Jan. 2   Added an overdrive mechanism for $8,000 that would improve the overall quality of the performance of the machine but would not extend its life. The salvage value was revised to $2,500.

Aug. 1   Performed routine maintenance, $1,250.

Oct. 2   Replaced some computer chips (considered routine), $800.

Dec. 31   Recognized 2017 depreciation expense.

Required

Record the 2017 transactions in a statements model like the preceding one.

Problem 6-32   *Accounting for intangible assets*

Cafe Olé Company acquired a fast-food restaurant for $1,500,000. The fair market values of the assets acquired were as follows. No liabilities were assumed.

Equipment	$380,000
Land	200,000
Building	680,000
Franchise (5-year life)	120,000

Required

Calculate the amount of goodwill purchased.

Problem 6-33   *Accounting for goodwill*

Tri-State Co. acquired the assets of Riley Co. for $1,200,000 in 2014. The estimated fair market value of the assets at the acquisition date was $1,000,000. Goodwill of $200,000 was recorded at acquisition. In 2015, because of negative publicity, one-half of the goodwill acquired from Riley Co. was judged to be permanently impaired.

Required

Explain how the recognition of the impairment of the goodwill will affect the 2015 balance sheet, income statement, and statement of cash flows.

Problem 6-34   *Performing ratio analysis using real-world data*

Companies in the coal mining business use a lot of property, plant, and equipment. Not only is there the significant investment they must make in the equipment used to extract and process the coal, but they must also purchase the rights to the coal reserves themselves.

Goodyear Tire & Rubber Company, Inc. is the largest tire manufacturer in North America. Cloud Peak Energy Corporation claims to be the largest private-sector coal company in the world. The following information was taken from these companies' December 31, 2012, annual reports. All dollar amounts are in millions.

	Cloud Peak Energy, Inc.	Goodyear Tire
Sales	$1,517	$20,992
Depreciation and depletion costs	95	684
Property, plant, and equipment (net of accumulated depreciation)	1,678	6,956
Total assets	2,351	16,973
Depreciation method	Straight-line or units of production	Straight-line
Estimated life of assets:		
Buildings	5 to 25 years	5 to 45 years
Machinery and equipment	3 to 20 years	3 to 30 years

Required

a. Calculate depreciation costs as a percentage of sales for each company.

b. Calculate buildings, property, plant, and equipment as a percentage of total assets for each company.

c. Based only on the percentages calculated in Requirements a and b, which company appears to be using its assets most efficiently? Explain your answer.

d. Identify some of the problems a financial analyst encounters when trying to compare the used of long-term assets of Cloud Peak versus Goodyear.

ANALYZE, THINK, COMMUNICATE

ATC 6-1   Business Applications Case   *Understanding real-world annual reports*

Required

Use the Target Corporation's Form 10-K to answer the following questions related to Target's 2012 fiscal year (year ended February 2, 2013). Target's Form 10-K is available on the company's website or through the SEC's EDGAR database. Appendix A provides instructions for using the EDGAR database.

a. What method of depreciation does Target use?

b. What types of intangible assets does Target have?

c. What are the estimated lives that Target uses for the various types of long-term assets?

d. As of February 2, 2013, what is the original cost of Target's: Land; Buildings and improvements; and Fixtures and equipment (see the footnotes)?

e. What was Target's depreciation expense and amortization expense for 2012 (see the footnotes)?

ATC 6-2   Group Assignment   *Different depreciation methods*

Sweet's Bakery makes cakes, pies, and other pastries that it sells to local grocery stores. The company experienced the following transactions during 2014.

1. Started business by acquiring $60,000 cash from the issue of common stock.
2. Purchased bakery equipment for $46,000 with a four-year life and a $6,000 salvage value.
3. Had cash sales in 2014 amounting to $42,000.
4. Paid $8,200 of cash for supplies which were all used during the year to make baked goods.
5. Paid other operating expenses of $12,000 for 2014.

Required

a. Organize the class into two sections and divide each section into groups of three to five students. Assign each section a depreciation method: straight-line or double-declining-balance.

Group Task

Prepare an income statement and a balance sheet using the preceding information and the depreciation method assigned to your group.

Class Discussion

b. Have a representative of each section put its income statement on the board. Are there differences in net income? How will these differences in the amount of depreciation expense change over the life of the equipment?

ATC 6-3　Research Assignment　*Comparing Microsoft's and Intel's operational assets*

Companies in different industries often use different proportions of current versus long-term assets to accomplish their business objective. The technology revolution resulting from the silicon microchip has often been led by two well-known companies: Microsoft and Intel. Although often thought of together, these companies are really very different. Using either the most current Forms 10-K or annual reports for Microsoft Corporation and Intel Corporation, complete the requirements below. To obtain the Forms 10-K, use either the EDGAR system following the instructions in Appendix A or the company's website. Microsoft's annual report is available on its website; Intel's annual report is its Form 10-K.

Required

a. Fill in the missing data in the following table. The percentages must be computed; they are not included in the companies' 10-Ks. (*Note:* The percentages for current assets and property, plant, and equipment will not sum to 100.)

	Current Assets		Property, Plant, and Equipment		Total Assets	
Microsoft						
Dollar Amount	$ _____		$ _____		$ _____	
% of Total Assets		_____ %		_____ %		100%
Intel						
Dollar Amount	$ _____		$ _____		$ _____	
% of Total Assets		_____ %		_____ %		100%

b. Briefly explain why these two companies have different percentages of their assets in current assets versus property, plant, and equipment.

ATC 6-4　Writing Assignment　*Impact of historical cost on asset presentation on the balance sheet*

Assume that you are examining the balance sheets of two companies and note the following information.

	Company A	Company B
Equipment	$1,130,000	$900,000
Accumulated Depreciation	(730,000)	(500,000)
Book Value	$ 400,000	$400,000

Maxie Smith, a student who has had no accounting courses, remarks that Company A and Company B have the same amount of equipment.

Required

In a short paragraph, explain to Maxie that the two companies do not have equal amounts of equipment. You may want to include in your discussion comments regarding the possible age of each company's equipment, the impact of the historical cost concept on balance sheet information, and the impact of different depreciation methods on book value.

ATC 6-5   Ethical Dilemma   *What's an expense?*

Several years ago, Wilson Blowhard founded a communications company. The company became successful and grew by expanding its customer base and acquiring some of its competitors. In fact, most of its growth resulted from acquiring other companies. Mr. Blowhard is adamant about continuing the company's growth and increasing its net worth. To achieve these goals, the business's net income must continue to increase at a rapid pace.

If the company's net worth continues to rise, Mr. Blowhard plans to sell the company and retire. He is, therefore, focused on improving the company's profit any way he can.

In the communications business, companies often use the lines of other communications companies. This line usage is a significant operating expense for Mr. Blowhard's company. Generally accepted accounting principles require operating costs like line use to be expensed as they are incurred each year. Each dollar of line cost reduces net income by a dollar.

After reviewing the company's operations, Mr. Blowhard concluded that the company did not currently need all of the line use it was paying for. It was really paying the owner of the lines now so that the line use would be available in the future for all of Mr. Blowhard's expected new customers. Mr. Blowhard instructed his accountant to capitalize all of the line cost charges and depreciate them over 10 years. The accountant reluctantly followed Mr. Blowhard's instructions and the company's net income for the current year showed a significant increase over the prior year's net income. Mr. Blowhard had found a way to report continued growth in the company's net income and increase the value of the company.

Required

a. How does Mr. Blowhard's scheme affect the amount of income that the company would otherwise report in its financial statements and how does the scheme affect the company's balance sheet? Explain your answer.

b. Review the AICPA's Articles of Professional Conduct (see Chapter 4) and comment on any of the standards that were violated.

c. Review the fraud triangle discussed in Chapter 4 and comment on the features of the fraud triangle that are evident in this case.

CHAPTER 7

Accounting for Liabilities

LEARNING OBJECTIVES

After you have mastered the material in this chapter, you will be able to:

LO 7-1   Show how notes payable and related interest expense affect financial statements.

LO 7-2   Show how sales tax liabilities affect financial statements.

LO 7-3   Define contingent liabilities and explain how they are reported in financial statements.

LO 7-4   Explain how warranty obligations affect financial statements.

LO 7-5   Show how installment notes affect financial statements.

LO 7-6   Show how a line of credit affects financial statements.

LO 7-7   Explain how to account for bonds issued at face value and their related interest costs.

LO 7-8   Use the straight-line method to amortize bond discounts and premiums.

LO 7-9   Distinguish between current and noncurrent assets and liabilities.

LO 7-10   Prepare a classified balance sheet.

LO 7-11   Use the effective interest rate method to amortize bond discounts and premiums. (Appendix)

 Video lectures and accompanying self-assessment quizzes are available for all learning objectives through McGraw-Hill Connect® Accounting.

CHAPTER OPENING

Chapter 2 discussed several types of liabilities with known amounts due, including accounts payable, salaries payable, and unearned revenue. This chapter introduces other liabilities with known amounts due: notes payable, sales taxes payable, lines of credit, and bond liabilities. We also discuss a contingent liability called warranties payable. We begin with a discussion of current liabilities, those that are payable within one year or the operating cycle, whichever is longer.

The Curious Accountant

For its 2012 fiscal year Hewlett-Packard Company reported a net loss of $12.7 billion. The company had $8.8 billion of interest expense in 2012.

With such huge losses on its income statement, do you think Hewlett-Packard was able to make the interest payments on its debt? If so, how? (Answer on page 255.)

ACCOUNTING FOR CURRENT LIABILITIES

Accounting for Notes Payable

LO 7-1

Show how notes payable and related interest expense affect financial statements.

Our discussion of promissory notes in Chapter 5 focused on the payee, the company with a note receivable on its books. In this chapter we focus on the maker of the note, the company with a note payable on its books. Because the maker of the note issues (gives) the note to the payee, the maker is sometimes called the **issuer.**

To illustrate, assume that on September 1, 2014, Herrera Supply Company (HSC) borrowed $90,000 from the National Bank. As evidence of the debt, Herrera issued a **note payable** that had a one-year term and an annual interest rate of 9 percent.

Issuing the note is an asset source transaction. The asset account Cash increases and the liability account Notes Payable increases. The income statement is not affected. The statement of cash flows shows a $90,000 cash inflow from financing activities. The effects on the financial statements are as follows.

	Assets	=	Liabilities			+	Stockholders' Equity			Rev.	−	Exp.	=	Net Inc.	Cash Flow	
Date	Cash	=	Notes Pay.	+	Int. Pay.	+	Com. Stk.	+	Ret. Earn.							
09/01/12	90,000	=	90,000	+	NA	+	NA	+	NA	NA	−	NA	=	NA	90,000	FA

On December 31, 2014, HSC would recognize four months (September 1 through December 31) of accrued interest expense. The accrued interest is $2,700 [$90,000 × 0.09 × (4 ÷ 12)]. Recognizing the accrued interest expense increases the liability account Interest Payable and decreases retained earnings. It is a claims exchange event. The income statement would report interest expense although HSC had not paid any cash for interest in 2014. The effects on the financial statements are as follows.

	Assets	=	Liabilities			+	Stockholders' Equity			Rev.	−	Exp.	=	Net Inc.	Cash Flow
Date	Cash	=	Notes Pay.	+	Int. Pay.	+	Com. Stk.	+	Ret. Earn.						
12/31/12	NA	=	NA	+	2,700	+	NA	+	(2,700)	NA	−	2,700	=	(2,700)	NA

HSC would record three events on August 31, 2015 (the maturity date). The first event recognizes $5,400 of interest expense that accrued in 2015 from January 1 through August 31 [$90,000 × 0.09 × (8 ÷ 12)]. The effects on the financial statements are as follows.

	Assets	=	Liabilities			+	Stockholders' Equity			Rev.	−	Exp.	=	Net Inc.	Cash Flow
Date	Cash	=	Notes Pay.	+	Int. Pay.	+	Com. Stk.	+	Ret. Earn.						
08/31/13	NA	=	NA	+	5,400	+	NA	+	(5,400)	NA	−	5,400	=	(5,400)	NA

The second event recognizes HSC's cash payment for interest on August 31, 2015. This event is an asset use transaction that reduces both the Cash and Interest Payable accounts for the total amount of interest due, $8,100 [$90,000 × 0.09 × (12 ÷ 12)]. The interest payment includes the four months' interest accrued in 2014 and the eight months accrued in 2015 ($2,700 + $5,400 = $8,100). There is no effect on the income statement because HSC recognized the interest expense in two previous journal entries.

The statement of cash flows would report an $8,100 cash outflow from operating activities. The effects on the financial statements follow.

	Assets	=	Liabilities			+	Stockholders' Equity			Rev.	−	Exp.	=	Net Inc.	Cash Flow
Date	Cash	=	Notes Pay.	+	Int. Pay.	+	Com. Stk.	+	Ret. Earn.						
08/31/13	(8,100)	=	NA	+	(8,100)	+	NA	+	NA	NA	−	NA	=	NA	(8,100)　OA

The third event on August 31, 2015, reflects repaying the principal. This event is an asset use transaction. The Cash account and the Notes Payable account each decrease by $90,000. There is no effect on the income statement. The statement of cash flows would show a $90,000 cash outflow from financing activities. Recall that paying interest is classified as an operating activity even though repaying the principal is a financing activity. The effects on the financial statements are as follows.

	Assets	=	Liabilities			+	Stockholders' Equity			Rev.	−	Exp.	=	Net Inc.	Cash Flow
Date	Cash	=	Notes Pay.	+	Int. Pay.	+	Com. Stk.	+	Ret. Earn.						
08/31/13	(90,000)	=	(90,000)	+	NA	+	NA	+	NA	NA	−	NA	=	NA	(90,000)　FA

☑ CHECK YOURSELF 7.1

On October 1, 2014, Mellon Company issued an interest-bearing note payable to Better Banks Inc. The note had a $24,000 principal amount, a four-month term, and an annual interest rate of 4 percent. Determine the amount of interest expense and the cash outflow from operating activities Mellon will report in its 2014 and 2015 financial statements.

Answer　The computation of accrued interest expense is shown below. Unless otherwise specified, the interest rate is stated in annual terms even though the term of the note is only four months. Interest rates are commonly expressed as an annual percentage regardless of the term of the note. The *time outstanding* in the following formulas is therefore expressed as a fraction of a year. Mellon paid interest at an annual rate of 4 percent, but the note was outstanding for only 3/12 of a year in 2014 and 1/12 of a year in 2015.

2014

Principal × Annual interest rate × Time outstanding = Interest expense

$24,000 × 0.04 × (3/12) = $240

2015

Principal × Annual interest rate × Time outstanding = Interest expense

$24,000 × 0.04 × (1/12) = $80

Mellon will report a $320 ($240 + $80) cash outflow from operating activities for interest in 2015.

Accounting for Sales Tax

Most states require retail companies to collect a sales tax on items sold to their customers. The retailer collects the tax from its customers and remits the tax to the state at regular intervals. The retailer has a current liability for the amount of sales tax collected but not yet paid to the state.

Show how sales tax liabilities affect financial statements.

250   Chapter 7

To illustrate, assume Herrera Supply Company (HSC) sells merchandise to a customer for $2,000 cash plus tax in a state where the sales tax rate is 6 percent. The effects on the financial statements are shown below.[1]

Assets =	Liab.	+		Equity		Rev.	−	Exp.	=	Net Inc.	Cash Flow	
Cash =	Sales Tax Pay.	+	Com. Stk.	+	Ret. Earn.							
2,120 =	120	+	NA	+	2,000	2,000	−	NA	=	2,000	2,120	OA

Remitting the tax (paying cash to the tax authority) is an asset use transaction. Both the Cash account and the Sales Tax Payable account decrease. The effects on the financial statements are as follows.

Assets =	Liab.	+		Equity		Rev.	−	Exp.	=	Net Inc.	Cash Flow	
Cash =	Sales Tax Pay.	+	Com. Stk.	+	Ret. Earn.							
(120) =	(120)	+	NA	+	NA	NA	−	NA	=	NA	(120)	OA

Contingent Liabilities

LO 7-3

Define contingent liabilities and explain how they are reported in financial statements.

A **contingent liability** is a potential obligation arising from a past event. The amount or existence of the obligation depends on some future event. A pending lawsuit, for example, is a contingent liability. Depending on the outcome, a defendant company could be required to pay a large monetary settlement or could be relieved of any obligation. Generally accepted accounting principles require that companies classify contingent liabilities into three different categories depending on the likelihood of their becoming actual liabilities. The categories and the accounting for each are described below.

1. If the likelihood of a future obligation arising is *probable* (likely) and its amount can be *reasonably estimated,* a liability is recognized in the financial statements. Contingent liabilities in this category include warranties, vacation pay, and sick leave.

2. If the likelihood of a future obligation arising is *reasonably possible* but not likely or if it is probable but *cannot be reasonably estimated,* no liability is reported on the balance sheet. The potential liability is, however, disclosed in the notes to the financial statements. Contingent liabilities in this category include legal challenges, environmental damages, and government investigations.

3. If the likelihood of a future obligation arising is *remote,* no liability need be recognized in the financial statements or disclosed in the notes to the statements.[2]

Determining whether a contingent liability is probable, reasonably possible, or remote requires professional judgment. Even seasoned accountants seek the advice of attorneys, engineers, insurance agents, and government regulators before classifying significant contingent liabilities. Professional judgment is also required to distinguish between contingent liabilities and **general uncertainties.** All businesses face uncertainties such as competition and damage from floods or storms. Such uncertainties are not contingent liabilities, however, because they do not arise from past events.

---

[1]The entry to record cost of goods sold for this sale is intentionally omitted.

[2]Companies may, if desired, voluntarily disclose contingent liabilities classified as remote.

EXHIBIT 7.1

Reporting Contingent Liabilities

Exhibit 7.1 summarizes the three categories of contingent liabilities and the accounting for each category.

Warranty Obligations

To attract customers, many companies guarantee their products or services. Such guarantees are called **warranties.** Warranties take many forms. Usually, they extend for a specified period of time. Within this period, the seller promises to replace or repair defective products without charge. Although the amount and timing of warranty obligations are uncertain, warranties usually represent liabilities that must be reported in the financial statements.

To illustrate accounting for warranty obligations, assume Herrera Supply Company (HSC) had cash of $2,000, inventory of $6,000, common stock of $5,000, and retained earnings of $3,000 on January 1, 2014. The 2014 accounting period is affected by three accounting events: (1) sale of merchandise under warranty; (2) recognition of warranty obligations to customers who purchased the merchandise; and (3) settlement of a customer's warranty claim.

EVENT 1 Sale of Merchandise
HSC sold for $7,000 cash merchandise that had cost $4,000.

In the following statements model, revenue from the sale is referenced as 1a and the cost of the sale as 1b. The effects of the sales transaction on the financial statements are shown below.

LO 7-4

 Explain how warranty obligations affect financial statements.

Event No.	Assets			=	Liab.	+	Equity	Rev.	−	Exp.	=	Net Inc.	Cash Flow
	Cash	+	Inventory	=			Ret. Earn.						
1a	7,000	+	NA	=	NA	+	7,000	7,000	−	NA	=	7,000	7,000 OA
1b	NA	+	(4,000)	=	NA	+	(4,000)	NA	−	4,000	=	(4,000)	NA

EVENT 2   Recognition of Warranty Expense

HSC guaranteed the merchandise sold in Event 1 to be free from defects for one year following the date of sale.

Although the exact amount of future warranty claims is unknown, HSC must inform financial statement users of the company's obligation. HSC must estimate the amount of the warranty liability and report the estimate in the 2014 financial statements. Assume the warranty obligation is estimated to be $100. Recognizing this obligation increases liabilities (warranties payable) and reduces stockholders' equity (retained earnings). Recognizing the warranty expense reduces net income. The statement of cash flows is not affected when the obligation and the corresponding expense are recognized. The effects on the financial statements follow.

Event No.	Assets	=	Liab.	+	Equity	Rev.	−	Exp.	=	Net Inc.	Cash Flow
			Warr. Pay.	+	Ret. Earn.						
2	NA	=	100	+	(100)	NA	−	100	=	(100)	NA

EVENT 3   Settlement of Warranty Obligation

HSC paid $40 cash to repair defective merchandise returned by a customer.

The cash payment for the repair is not an expense. Warranty expense was recognized in the period in which the sale was made. The payment reduces an asset (cash) and a liability (warranties payable). The income statement is not affected by the repairs payment. However, there is a $40 cash outflow reported in the operating activities section of the statement of cash flows. The effects on the financial statements follow.

Event No.	Assets	=	Liab.	+	Equity	Rev.	−	Exp.	=	Net Inc.	Cash Flow
	Cash	=	Warr. Pay.	+	Ret. Earn.						
3	(40)	=	(40)	+	NA	NA	−	NA	=	NA	(40) OA

Financial Statements

The financial statements for HSC's 2014 accounting period are shown in Exhibit 7.2.

EXHIBIT 7.2

Financial Statements for 2014

Income Statement		Balance Sheet		Statement of Cash Flows	
Sales revenue	$7,000	Assets		**Operating Activities**	
Cost of goods sold	(4,000)	Cash	$ 8,960	Inflow from customers	$7,000
Gross margin	3,000	Inventory	2,000	Outflow for warranty	(40)
Warranty expense	(100)	Total assets	$10,960	Net inflow from	
Net income	$2,900	Liabilities		operating activities	6,960
		Warranties payable	$ 60	**Investing Activities**	0
		Stockholders' equity		**Financing Activities**	0
		Common stock	5,000	Net change in cash	6,960
		Retained earnings	5,900	Plus: Beginning cash balance	2,000
		Total liab. and stockholders' equity	$10,960	Ending cash balance	$8,960

REALITY BYTES

Many of the items we purchase come with a manufacturer's warranty, but companies that sell electronics and electrical appliances often offer to sell you an extended warranty that provides protection after the manufacturer's warranty has expired. Why do they offer this option to customers, and how do these warranties differ from the standard manufactures' warranties?

Companies such as Best Buy offer to sell customers extended warranties because they make a significant profit on them. If you buy an extended warranty from Best Buy, the retailer is not actually the one who is promising to repair your product; that will be done by a third party. Best Buy simply receives a commission for selling the warranty. In 2012 such commissions accounted for 2.7 percent of the company's total revenues, and since it had to incur very little expense to earn these revenues, they are mostly profit.

The typical manufacturer's warranty, as you have learned in this chapter, is an expense recognized at the time of the sale. However, companies that provide extended warranties must recognize the warranty revenue over the life of the warranty, not immediately upon sale. Remember, this is referring to the third-party warranty provider, not Best Buy. Since Best Buy is simply earning a commission from selling the warranty, it gets to recognize all of the revenue at the time of the sale.

☑ CHECK YOURSELF 7.2

Flotation Systems, Inc. (FSI) began operations in 2014. Its sales were $360,000 in 2014 and $410,000 in 2015. FSI estimates the cost of its one-year product warranty will be 2 percent of sales. Actual cash payments for warranty claims amounted to $5,400 during 2014 and $8,500 during 2015. Determine the amount of warranty expense that FSI would report on its 2014 and 2015 year-end income statements. Also, determine the amount of warranties payable FSI would report on its 2014 and 2015 year-end balance sheet.

Answer   FSI would report Warranty Expense on the December 31, 2014, income statement of $7,200 ($360,000 × .02). Warranty Expense on the December 31, 2015, income statement is $8,200 ($410,000 × .02).

FSI would report Warranties Payable on the December 31, 2014, balance sheet of $1,800 ($7,200 − $5,400). Warranties Payable on the December 31, 2015, balance sheet is $1,500 ($1,800 + $8,200 − $8,500).

ACCOUNTING FOR LONG-TERM DEBT

Most businesses finance their investing activities with long-term debt. Recall that current liabilities mature within one year or a company's operating cycle, whichever is longer. Other liabilities are **long-term liabilities.** Long-term debt agreements vary with respect to requirements for paying interest charges and repaying principal (the amount borrowed). Interest payments may be due monthly, annually, at some other interval, or at the maturity date. Interest charges may be based on a **fixed interest rate** that remains constant during the term of the loan or may be based on a **variable interest rate** that fluctuates up or down during the loan period.

Principal repayment is generally required either in one lump sum at the maturity date or in installments that are spread over the life of the loan. For example, each

254   Chapter 7

monthly payment on your car loan probably includes both paying interest and repaying some of the principal. Repaying a portion of the principal with regular payments that also include interest is often called loan **amortization.**[3] This section explains accounting for interest and principal with respect to the major forms of long-term debt financing.

Installment Notes Payable

LO 7-5

Show how installment notes affect financial statements.

Loans that require payments of principal and interest at regular intervals (amortizing loans) are typically represented by **installment notes.** The terms of installment notes usually range from two to five years. To illustrate accounting for installment notes, assume Blair Company was started on January 1, 2014, when it borrowed $100,000 cash from the National Bank. In exchange for the money, Blair issued the bank a five-year installment note with a 9 percent fixed interest rate. The effects on the financial statements are as follows.

	Assets	=	Liab.	+		Equity			Rev.	−	Exp.	=	Net Inc.	Cash Flow	
Date	Cash	=	Note Pay.	+	Com. Stk.	+	Ret. Earn.								
2012 Jan. 1	100,000	=	100,000	+	NA	+	NA		NA	−	NA	=	NA	100,000	FA

The loan agreement required Blair to pay five equal installments of $25,709[4] on December 31 of each year from 2014 through 2018. Exhibit 7.3 shows the allocation of each payment between principal and interest. When Blair pays the final installment, both the principal and interest will be paid in full. The amounts shown in Exhibit 7.3 are computed as follows.

1. The Interest Expense (Column D) is computed by multiplying the Principal Balance on Jan. 1 (Column B) by the interest rate. For example, interest expense for 2014 is $100,000 × .09 = $9,000; for 2015 it is $83,291 × .09 = $7,496; and so on.

EXHIBIT 7.3

Amortization Schedule for Installment Note Payable

Accounting Period Column A	Principal Balance on Jan. 1 Column B	Cash Payment on Dec. 31 Column C	Interest Expense Column D	Principal Repayment Column E	Principal Balance on Dec. 31 Column F
2014	$100,000	$25,709	$9,000	$16,709	$83,291
2015	83,291	25,709	7,496	18,213	65,078
2016	65,078	25,709	5,857	19,852	45,226
2017	45,226	25,709	4,070	21,639	23,587
2018	23,587	25,710*	2,123	23,587	0

*All computations are rounded to the nearest dollar. To fully liquidate the liability, the final payment is one dollar more than the others because of rounding differences.

[3]In Chapter 6 the term *amortization* described the expense recognized when the *cost of an intangible asset* is systematically allocated to expense over the useful life of the asset. This chapter shows that the term amortization refers more broadly to a variety of allocation processes. Here it means the systematic process of allocating the *principal repayment* over the life of a loan.

[4]The amount of the annual payment is determined using the present value concepts presented in a later chapter. Usually the lender (bank or other financial institution) calculates the amount of the payment for the customer. In this chapter we provide the amount of the annual payment.

Answers to The Curious Accountant

Hewlett-Packard Company (HP) was able to make its interest payments in 2012 for two reasons. (1) Interest is paid with cash, not accrued earnings. Many of the expenses on the company's income statement did not require the use of cash. The company's statement of cash flows shows that net cash flow from operating activities, *after making interest payments,* was a positive $10.6 billion in 2012, which is much better than the $12.7 billion it reported as a net loss. (2) The net loss the company incurred was *after* interest expense had been deducted. The capacity of operations to support interest payments is measured by the amount of earnings before interest deductions. For example, look at the 2014 income statement for Blair Company in Exhibit 7.4. This statement shows only $3,000 of net income, but $12,000 of cash revenue was available for the payment of interest. Similarly, H-P's 2012 net loss is not an indication of the company's ability to pay interest in the short run.

2. The Principal Repayment (Column E) is computed by subtracting the Interest Expense (Column D) from the Cash Payment on Dec. 31 (Column C). For example, the Principal Repayment for 2014 is $25,709 − $9,000 = $16,709; for 2015 it is $25,709 − $7,496 = $18,213; and so on.

3. The Principal Balance on Dec. 31 (Column F) is computed by subtracting the Principal Repayment (Column E) from the Principal Balance on Jan. 1 (Column B). For example, the Principal Balance on Dec. 31 for 2014 is $100,000 − $16,709 = $83,291; on December 31, 2015, the principal balance is $83,291 − $18,213 = $65,078; and so on. The Principal Balance on Dec. 31 (ending balance) for 2014 ($83,291) is also the Principal Balance on Jan. 1 (beginning balance) for 2015; the principal balance on December 31, 2015, is the principal balance on January 1, 2016; and so on.

Although the amounts for interest expense and principal repayment differ each year, the effects of the annual payment on the financial statements are the same. On the balance sheet, assets (cash) decrease by the total amount of the payment; liabilities (note payable) decrease by the amount of the principal repayment; and stockholders' equity (retained earnings) decreases by the amount of interest expense. Net income decreases from recognizing interest expense. On the statement of cash flows, the portion of the cash payment applied to interest is reported in the operating activities section and the portion applied to principal is reported in the financing activities section. The effects on the financial statements are as follows.

	Assets	=	Liab.	+		Equity		Rev.	−	Exp.	=	Net Inc.	Cash Flow	
Date	Cash	=	Note Pay.	+	Com. Stk.	+	Ret. Earn.							
2012 Dec. 31	(25,709)	=	(16,709)	+	NA	+	(9,000)	NA	−	9,000	=	(9,000)	(9,000) OA (16,709) FA	

Exhibit 7.4 displays income statements, balance sheets, and statements of cash flows for Blair Company for the accounting periods 2014 through 2018. The illustration assumes that Blair earned $12,000 of rent revenue each year. Because some

EXHIBIT 7.4

BLAIR COMPANY
Financial Statements

	2014	2015	2016	2017	2018
Income Statements					
Rent revenue	$ 12,000	$12,000	$12,000	$12,000	$12,000
Interest expense	(9,000)	(7,496)	(5,857)	(4,070)	(2,123)
Net income	$ 3,000	$ 4,504	$ 6,143	$ 7,930	$ 9,877
Balance Sheets					
Assets					
Cash	$ 86,291	$72,582	$58,873	$45,164	$31,454
Liabilities					
Note payable	$ 83,291	$65,078	$45,226	$23,587	$ 0
Stockholders' equity					
Retained earnings	3,000	7,504	13,647	21,577	31,454
Total liabilities and stk. equity	$ 86,291	$72,582	$58,873	$45,164	$31,454
Statements of Cash Flows					
Operating Activities					
Inflow from customers	$ 12,000	$12,000	$12,000	$12,000	$12,000
Outflow for interest	(9,000)	(7,496)	(5,857)	(4,070)	(2,123)
Investing Activities	0	0	0	0	0
Financing Activities					
Inflow from note issue	100,000	0	0	0	0
Outflow to repay note	(16,709)	(18,213)	(19,852)	(21,639)	(23,587)
Net change in cash	86,291	(13,709)	(13,709)	(13,709)	(13,710)
Plus: Beginning cash balance	0	86,291	72,582	58,873	45,164
Ending cash balance	$ 86,291	$72,582	$58,873	$45,164	$31,454

of the principal is repaid each year, the note payable amount reported on the balance sheet and the amount of the interest expense on the income statement both decline each year.

 CHECK YOURSELF 7.3

On January 1, 2014, Krueger Company issued a $50,000 installment note to State Bank. The note had a 10-year term and an 8 percent interest rate. Krueger agreed to repay the principal and interest in 10 annual payments of $7,451.47 at the end of each year. Determine the amount of principal and interest Krueger paid during the first and second year that the note was outstanding.

Answer

Accounting Period	Principal Balance January 1 A	Cash Payment December 31 B	Applied to Interest C = A × 0.08	Applied to Principal B − C
2014	$50,000.00	$7,451.47	$4,000.00	$3,451.47
2015	46,548.53	7,451.47	3,723.88	3,727.59

Line of Credit

A **line of credit** enables a company to borrow or repay funds as needed. For example, a business may borrow $50,000 one month and make a partial repayment of $10,000 the next month. Credit agreements usually specify a limit on the amount that can be borrowed. Exhibit 7.5 shows that credit agreements are widely used.

Interest rates on lines of credit normally vary with fluctuations in some designated interest rate benchmark such as the rate paid on U.S. Treasury bills. For example, a company may pay 4 percent interest one month and 4.5 percent the next month, even if the principal balance remains constant.

Lines of credit typically have one-year terms. Although they are classified on the balance sheet as short-term liabilities, lines of credit are frequently extended indefinitely by simply renewing the credit agreement.

To illustrate accounting for a line of credit, assume Lagoon Company owns a wholesale jet-ski distributorship. In the spring, Lagoon borrows money using a line of credit to finance building up its inventory. Lagoon repays the loan over the summer months using cash generated from jet-ski sales. Borrowing or repaying events occur on the first of the month. Interest payments occur at the end of each month. Exhibit 7.6 presents all 2015 line of credit events.

Each borrowing event (March 1, April 1, and May 1) is an asset source transaction. Both cash and the line of credit liability increase. Each repayment (June 1, July 1, and August 1) is an asset use transaction. Both cash and the line of credit liability decrease. Each month's interest expense recognition and payment is an asset use transaction. Assets (cash) and stockholders' equity (retained earnings) decrease, as does net income. The effects of the events on the financial statements are shown in Exhibit 7.7.

Show how a line of credit affects financial statements.

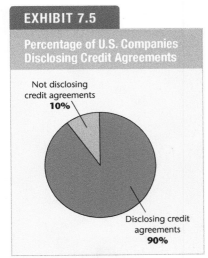

EXHIBIT 7.5

Percentage of U.S. Companies Disclosing Credit Agreements

Not disclosing credit agreements
10%

Disclosing credit agreements
90%

Data Source: AICPA, *Accounting Trends and Techniques.*

EXHIBIT 7.6

Summary of 2015 Line of Credit Events

Date	Amount Borrowed (Repaid)	Loan Balance at End of Month	Effective Interest Rate per Month (%)	Interest Expense (rounded to nearest $1)
Mar. 1	$20,000	$ 20,000	0.09 ÷ 12	$150
Apr. 1	30,000	50,000	0.09 ÷ 12	375
May 1	50,000	100,000	0.105 ÷ 12	875
June 1	(10,000)	90,000	0.10 ÷ 12	750
July 1	(40,000)	50,000	0.09 ÷ 12	375
Aug. 1	(50,000)	0	0.09 ÷ 12	0

Bond Liabilities

Many companies borrow money directly from the public by selling **bond certificates,** otherwise called *issuing* bonds. Bond certificates describe a company's obligation to pay interest and to repay the principal. The seller, or **issuer,** of a bond is the borrower; the buyer of a bond, or **bondholder,** is the lender.

From the issuer's point of view, a bond represents an obligation to pay a sum of money to the bondholder on the bond's maturity date. The amount due at maturity is the **face value** of the bond. Most bonds also require the issuer to make cash interest

LO 7-7

Explain how to account for bonds issued at face value and their related interest costs.

EXHIBIT 7.7

Date		Assets	=	Liabilities	+	Equity	Rev.	−	Exp.	=	Net Inc.	Cash Flow	
Mar.	1	20,000	=	20,000	+	NA	NA	−	NA	=	NA	20,000	FA
	31	(150)	=	NA	+	(150)	NA	−	150	=	(150)	(150)	OA
Apr.	1	30,000	=	30,000	+	NA	NA	−	NA	=	NA	30,000	FA
	30	(375)	=	NA	+	(375)	NA	−	375	=	(375)	(375)	OA
May	1	50,000	=	50,000	+	NA	NA	−	NA	=	NA	50,000	FA
	31	(875)	=	NA	+	(875)	NA	−	875	=	(875)	(875)	OA
June	1	(10,000)	=	(10,000)	+	NA	NA	−	NA	=	NA	(10,000)	FA
	30	(750)	=	NA	+	(750)	NA	−	750	=	(750)	(750)	OA
July	1	(40,000)	=	(40,000)	+	NA	NA	−	NA	=	NA	(40,000)	FA
	31	(375)	=	NA	+	(375)	NA	−	375	=	(375)	(375)	OA
Aug.	1	(50,000)	=	(50,000)	+	NA	NA	−	NA	=	NA	(50,000)	FA
	31	NA	=	NA	+	NA	NA	−	NA	=	NA	NA	

payments based on a **stated interest rate** at regular intervals over the life of the bond. Exhibit 7.8 shows a typical bond certificate.

EXHIBIT 7.8

Bond Certificate

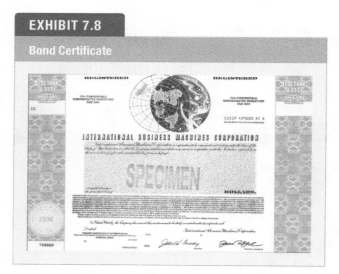

Advantages of Issuing Bonds

Bond financing offers companies the following advantages.

1. Bonds usually have longer terms than notes issued to banks. While typical bank loan terms range from 2 to 5 years, bonds normally have 20-year terms to maturity. Longer terms to maturity allow companies to implement long-term strategic plans without having to worry about frequent refinancing arrangements.

2. Bond interest rates may be lower than bank interest rates. Banks earn profits by borrowing money from the public (depositors) at low interest rates, then loaning that money to companies at higher rates. By issuing bonds directly to the public, companies can pay lower interest costs by eliminating the middle man (banks).

Bonds Issued at Face Value

Assume Marsha Mason needs cash in order to seize a business opportunity. Mason knows of a company seeking a plot of land on which to store its inventory of crushed stone. Mason also knows of a suitable tract of land she could purchase for $100,000. The company has agreed to lease the land it needs from Mason for $12,000 per year. Mason lacks the funds to buy the land.

Some of Mason's friends recently complained about the low interest rates banks were paying on certificates of deposit. Mason suggested that her friends invest in bonds instead of CDs. She offered to sell them bonds with a 9 percent stated interest rate. The terms specified in the bond agreement Mason drafted included making interest payments in cash on December 31 of each year, a five-year term to maturity, and pledging the land as collateral for the bonds.[5] Her friends were favorably impressed, and Mason issued the bonds to them in exchange for cash on January 1, 2014.

Mason used the bond proceeds to purchase the land and immediately contracted to lease it for five years. On December 31, 2018, the maturity date of the bonds, Mason sold the land for its $100,000 book value and used the proceeds from the sale to repay the bond liability.

Mason's business venture involved six distinct accounting events.

1. Received $100,000 cash from issuing five-year bonds at face value.
2. Invested proceeds from the bond issue to purchase land for $100,000 cash.
3. Earned $12,000 cash revenue annually from leasing the land.
4. Paid $9,000 annual interest on December 31 of each year.
5. Sold the land for $100,000 cash.
6. Repaid the bond principal to bondholders.

Effect of Events on Financial Statements

EVENT 1   Issue Bonds for Cash

Issuing bonds is an asset source transaction.

Assets (cash) and liabilities (bonds payable) increase. Net income is not affected. The $100,000 cash inflow is reported in the financing activities section of the statement of cash flows. These effects are shown here.

Assets	=	Liab.	+	Equity	Rev.	−	Exp.	=	Net Inc.	Cash Flow	
Cash	=	Bonds Pay.									
100,000	=	100,000	+	NA	NA	−	NA	=	NA	100,000	FA

EVENT 2   Investment in Land

Paying $100,000 cash to purchase land is an asset exchange transaction.

The asset cash decreases and the asset land increases. The income statement is not affected. The cash outflow is reported in the investing activities section of the statement of cash flows. These effects are illustrated below.

Assets			=	Liab.	+	Equity	Rev.	−	Exp.	=	Net Inc.	Cash Flow	
Cash	+	Land											
(100,000)	+	100,000	=	NA	+	NA	NA	−	NA	=	NA	(100,000)	IA

EVENT 3   Revenue Recognition

Recognizing $12,000 cash revenue from renting the property is an asset source transaction.

This event is repeated each year from 2014 through 2018. The event increases assets and stockholders' equity. Recognizing revenue increases net income. The cash inflow is reported in the operating activities section of the statement of cash flows. These effects follow.

Assets	=	Liab.	+	Equity	Rev.	−	Exp.	=	Net Inc.	Cash Flow	
Cash	=			Ret. Earn.							
12,000	=	NA	+	12,000	12,000	−	NA	=	12,000	12,000	OA

[5]In practice, bonds are usually issued for much larger sums of money, often hundreds of millions of dollars. Also, terms to maturity are normally long, with 20 years being common. Using such large amounts for such long terms is unnecessarily cumbersome for instructional purposes. The effects of bond issues can be illustrated efficiently by using smaller amounts of debt with shorter maturities, as assumed in the case of Marsha Mason.

EVENT 4   Expense Recognition
Mason's $9,000 ($100,000 × 0.09) cash payment represents interest expense.

This event is also repeated each year from 2014 through 2018. The interest payment is an asset use transaction. Cash and stockholders' equity (retained earnings) decrease. The expense recognition decreases net income. The cash outflow is reported in the operating activities section of the statement of cash flows. These effects follow.

Assets	=	Liab.	+	Equity	Rev.	−	Exp.	=	Net Inc.	Cash Flow
Cash	=			Ret. Earn.						
(9,000)	=	NA	+	(9,000)	NA	−	9,000	=	(9,000)	(9,000) OA

EVENT 5   Sale of Investment in Land
Selling the land for cash equal to its $100,000 book value is an asset exchange transaction.

Cash increases and land decreases. Because there was no gain or loss on the sale, the income statement is not affected. The cash inflow is reported in the investing activities section of the statement of cash flows. These effects follow.

Assets			=	Liab.	+	Equity	Rev.	−	Exp.	=	Net Inc.	Cash Flow
Cash	+	Land										
100,000	+	(100,000)	=	NA	+	NA	NA	−	NA	=	NA	100,000 IA

EVENT 6   Payoff of Bond Liability
Repaying the face value of the bond liability is an asset use transaction.

Cash and bonds payable decrease. The income statement is not affected. The cash outflow is reported in the financing activities section of the statement of cash flows.

Assets	=	Liab.	+	Equity	Rev.	−	Exp.	=	Net Inc.	Cash Flow
Cash	=	Bonds Pay.								
(100,000)	=	(100,000)	+	NA	NA	−	NA	=	NA	(100,000) FA

Financial Statements

Exhibit 7.9 displays Mason Company's financial statements. For simplicity, the income statement does not distinguish between operating and nonoperating items. Rent revenue and interest expense are constant across all accounting periods, so Mason recognizes $3,000 of net income in each accounting period. On the balance sheet, cash increases by $3,000 each year because cash revenue exceeds cash paid for interest. Land remains constant each year at its $100,000 historical cost until it is sold in 2018. Similarly, the bonds payable liability is reported at $100,000 from the date the bonds were issued in 2014 until they are paid off on December 31, 2018.

Compare Blair Company's income statements in Exhibit 7.4 with Mason Company's income statements in Exhibit 7.9. Both Blair and Mason borrowed $100,000 cash at a 9 percent stated interest rate for five-year terms. Blair, however, repaid its liability

EXHIBIT 7.9

Mason Company Financial Statements

	Bonds Issued at Face Value				
	2014	2015	2016	2017	2018
Income Statements					
Rent revenue	$ 12,000	$ 12,000	$ 12,000	$ 12,000	$ 12,000
Interest expense	(9,000)	(9,000)	(9,000)	(9,000)	(9,000)
Net income	$ 3,000	$ 3,000	$ 3,000	$ 3,000	$ 3,000
Balance Sheets					
Assets					
Cash	$ 3,000	$ 6,000	$ 9,000	$ 12,000	$ 15,000
Land	100,000	100,000	100,000	100,000	0
Total assets	$103,000	$106,000	$109,000	$112,000	$ 15,000
Liabilities					
Bonds payable	$100,000	$100,000	$100,000	$100,000	$ 0
Stockholders' equity					
Retained earnings	3,000	6,000	9,000	12,000	15,000
Total liabilities and					
stockholders' equity	$103,000	$106,000	$109,000	$112,000	$ 15,000
Statements of Cash Flows					
Operating Activities					
Inflow from customers	$ 12,000	$ 12,000	$ 12,000	$ 12,000	$ 12,000
Outflow for interest	(9,000)	(9,000)	(9,000)	(9,000)	(9,000)
Investing Activities					
Outflow to purchase land	(100,000)				
Inflow from sale of land					100,000
Financing Activities					
Inflow from bond issue	100,000				
Outflow to repay bond liab.					(100,000)
Net change in cash	3,000	3,000	3,000	3,000	3,000
Plus: Beginning cash balance	0	3,000	6,000	9,000	12,000
Ending cash balance	$ 3,000	$ 6,000	$ 9,000	$ 12,000	$ 15,000

under the terms of an installment note while Mason did not repay any principal until the end of the five-year bond term. Because Blair repaid part of the principal balance on the installment loan each year, Blair's interest expense declined each year. The interest expense on Mason's bond liability, however, remained constant because the full principal amount was outstanding for the entire five-year bond term.

Effect of Semiannual Interest Payments

The previous examples assumed that interest payments were made annually. In practice, most bond agreements call for interest to be paid semiannually, which means that interest is paid in cash twice each year. If Marsha Mason's bond certificate had stipulated semiannual interest payments, her company would have paid $4,500 ($100,000 × 0.09 = $9,000 ÷ 2 = $4,500) cash to bondholders for interest on June 30 and December 31 of each year.

AMORTIZATION USING THE STRAIGHT-LINE METHOD

LO 7-8

Use the straight-line method to amortize bond discounts and premiums.

Bonds Issued at a Discount

Return to the Mason Company illustration with one change. Assume Mason's bond certificates have a 9 percent stated rate of interest printed on them. Suppose Mason's friends find they can buy bonds from another entrepreneur willing to pay a higher rate of interest. They explain to Mason that business decisions cannot be made on the basis of friendship. Mason provides a counteroffer. There is no time to change the bond certificates, so Mason offers to accept $95,000 for the bonds today and still repay the full face value of $100,000 at the maturity date. The $5,000 difference is called a **bond discount.** Mason's friends agree to buy the bonds for $95,000.

Effective Interest Rate

The bond discount increases the interest Mason must pay. First, Mason must still make the annual cash payments described in the bond agreement. In other words, Mason must pay cash of $9,000 (.09 × $100,000) annually even though she actually borrowed only $95,000. Second, Mason will have to pay back $5,000 more than she received ($100,000 − $95,000). The extra $5,000 (bond discount) is additional interest. Although the $5,000 of additional interest is not paid until maturity, when spread over the life of the bond, it amounts to $1,000 of additional interest expense per year.

The actual rate of interest that Mason must pay is called the **effective interest rate.** A rough estimate of the effective interest rate for the discounted Mason bonds is 10.5 percent [($9,000 annual stated interest + $1,000 annual amortization of the discount) ÷ $95,000 amount borrowed]. Selling the bonds at a $5,000 discount permits Mason to raise the 9 percent stated rate of interest to an effective rate of roughly 10.5 percent. Deeper discounts would raise the effective rate even higher. More shallow discounts would reduce the effective rate of interest. Mason can set the effective rate of interest to any level desired by adjusting the amount of the discount.

Bond Prices

It is common business practice to use discounts to raise the effective rate of interest above the stated rate. Bonds frequently sell for less than face value. Bond prices are normally expressed *as a percentage of the face value.* For example, Mason's discounted bonds sold for 95, meaning the bonds sold at 95 percent of face value ($100,000 × .95 = $95,000). Amounts of less than 1 percentage point are usually expressed as a fraction. Therefore, a bond priced at 98 3/4 sells for 98.75 percent of face value.

Financial Statement Effects

To illustrate accounting for bonds issued at a discount, return to the Mason Company example using the assumption the bonds are issued for 95 instead of face value. We examine the same six events using this revised assumption. This revision changes some amounts reported on the financial statements. For example, Event 1 in year 2014 reflects receiving $95,000 cash from the bond issue. Because Mason had only $95,000 available to invest in land, the illustration assumes that Mason acquired a less desirable piece of property which generated only $11,400 of rent revenue per year.

EVENT 1   Bonds with a face value of $100,000 are issued at 95.

Because Mason must pay the face value at maturity, the $100,000 face value of the bonds is recorded in the Bonds Payable account. The $5,000 discount is recorded in a separate contra liability account called **Discount on Bonds Payable.** As shown below, the contra account is subtracted from the face value to determine the **carrying value** (book value) of the bond liability on January 1, 2014.

Bonds payable	$100,000
Less: Discount on bonds payable	(5,000)
Carrying value	$ 95,000

The bond issue is an asset source transaction. Both assets and total liabilities increase by $95,000. Net income is not affected. The cash inflow is reported in the financing activities section of the statement of cash flows. The effects on the financial statements are shown here.

Assets	=	Liabilities	+	Equity	Rev.	–	Exp.	=	Net Inc.	Cash Flow
Cash	=	Carrying Value of Bond Liability	+	Equity						
95,000	=	95,000	+	NA	NA	–	NA	=	NA	95,000 FA

EVENT 2   Paid $95,000 cash to purchase land.

The asset cash decreases and the asset land increases. The income statement is not affected. The cash outflow is reported in the investing activities section of the statement of cash flows. The effects on the financial statements are shown here.

Assets			=	Liab.	+	Equity	Rev.	–	Exp.	=	Net Inc.	Cash Flow
Cash	+	Land										
(95,000)	+	95,000	=	NA	+	NA	NA	–	NA	=	NA	(95,000) IA

EVENT 3   Recognized $11,400 cash revenue from renting the land.

This event is repeated each year from 2014 through 2018. The event is an asset source transaction that increases assets and stockholders' equity. Recognizing revenue increases net income. The cash inflow is reported in the operating activities section of the statement of cash flows. The effects on the financial statements are shown here.

Assets	=	Liab.	+	Equity	Rev.	–	Exp.	=	Net Inc.	Cash Flow
Cash	=			Ret. Earn.						
11,400	=	NA	+	11,400	11,400	–	NA	=	11,400	11,400 OA

EVENT 4   Recognized interest expense. The interest cost of borrowing has two components: the $9,000 paid in cash each year and the $5,000 discount paid at maturity.

Using **straight-line amortization,** the amount of the discount recognized as expense in each accounting period is $1,000 ($5,000 discount ÷ 5 years). Mason will therefore recognize $10,000 of interest expense each year ($9,000 at the stated interest rate plus

$1,000 amortization of the bond discount). On the balance sheet, the asset cash decreases by $9,000, the carrying value of the bond liability increases by $1,000 (through a decrease in the bond discount), and retained earnings (interest expense) decreases by $10,000. The effects on the financial statements are shown here.

Assets	=	Liabilities	+	Equity	Rev.	−	Exp.	=	Net Inc.	Cash Flow
Cash	=	Carrying Value of Bond Liability	+	Ret. Earn.						
(9,000)	=	1,000	+	(10,000)	NA	−	10,000	=	(10,000)	(9,000) OA

EVENT 5   Sold the land for cash equal to its $95,000 book value.

Cash increases and land decreases. Because there was no gain or loss on the sale, the income statement is not affected. The cash inflow is reported in the investing activities section of the statement of cash flows. The effects on the financial statements are shown here.

Assets			=	Liab.	+	Equity	Rev.	−	Exp.	=	Net Inc.	Cash Flow
Cash	+	Land										
95,000	+	(95,000)	=	NA	+	NA	NA	−	NA	=	NA	95,000 IA

EVENT 6   Paid the bond liability.

Cash and bonds payable decrease. The income statement is not affected. For reporting purposes, the cash outflow is separated into two parts on the statement of cash flows: $95,000 of the cash outflow is reported in the financing activities section because it represents repaying the principal amount borrowed; the remaining $5,000 cash outflow is reported in the operating activities section because it represents the interest arising from issuing the bonds at a discount. In practice, the amount of the discount is frequently immaterial and is combined in the financing activities section with the principal repayment. The effects on the financial statements are shown here.

Assets	=	Liab.	+	Equity	Rev.	−	Exp.	=	Net Inc.	Cash Flow
Cash	=	Bonds Pay.								
(100,000)	=	(100,000)	+	NA	NA	−	NA	=	NA	(95,000) FA (5,000) OA

Financial Statements

Exhibit 7.10 displays Mason Company's financial statements assuming the bonds were issued at a discount. Contrast the net income reported in Exhibit 7.10 (bonds issued at a discount) with the net income reported in Exhibit 7.9 (bonds sold at face value). Two factors cause the net income in Exhibit 7.10 to be lower. First, because the bonds were sold at a discount, Mason Company had less money to spend on its land investment. It bought less desirable land which generated less revenue. Second, the effective interest rate was higher than the stated rate, resulting in higher interest expense. Lower revenues coupled with higher expenses result in less profitability.

On the balance sheet, the carrying value of the bond liability increases each year until the maturity date, December 31, 2018, when it is equal to the $100,000 face value of the bonds (the amount Mason is obligated to pay). Because Mason did not pay any

EXHIBIT 7.10

Mason Company Financial Statements

Bonds Issued at a Discount

	2014	2015	2016	2017	2018
Income Statements					
Rent revenue	$ 11,400	$ 11,400	$ 11,400	$ 11,400	$ 11,400
Interest expense	(10,000)	(10,000)	(10,000)	(10,000)	(10,000)
Net income	$ 1,400	$ 1,400	$ 1,400	$ 1,400	$ 1,400
Balance Sheets					
Assets					
Cash	$ 2,400	$ 4,800	$ 7,200	$ 9,600	$ 7,000
Land	95,000	95,000	95,000	95,000	0
Total assets	$ 97,400	$ 99,800	$102,200	$104,600	$ 7,000
Liabilities					
Bonds payable	$100,000	$100,000	$100,000	$100,000	$ 0
Discount on bonds payable	(4,000)	(3,000)	(2,000)	(1,000)	0
Carrying value of bond liab.	96,000	97,000	98,000	99,000	0
Stockholders' equity					
Retained earnings	1,400	2,800	4,200	5,600	7,000
Total liabilities and stockholders' equity	$ 97,400	$ 99,800	$102,200	$104,600	$ 7,000
Statements of Cash Flows					
Operating Activities					
Inflow from customers	$ 11,400	$ 11,400	$ 11,400	$ 11,400	$ 11,400
Outflow for interest	(9,000)	(9,000)	(9,000)	(9,000)	(14,000)
Investing Activities					
Outflow to purchase land	(95,000)				
Inflow from sale of land					95,000
Financing Activities					
Inflow from bond issue	95,000				
Outflow to repay bond liab.					(95,000)
Net change in cash	2,400	2,400	2,400	2,400	(2,600)
Plus: Beginning cash balance	0	2,400	4,800	7,200	9,600
Ending cash balance	$ 2,400	$ 4,800	$ 7,200	$ 9,600	$ 7,000

dividends, the retained earnings of $7,000 on December 31, 2018, is equal to the total amount of net income reported over the five-year period ($1,400 × 5). All earnings were retained in the business.

Several factors account for the differences between net income and cash flow. First, although $10,000 of interest expense is reported on each income statement, only $9,000 of cash was paid for interest each year until 2018, when $14,000 was paid for interest ($9,000 based on the stated rate + $5,000 for discount). The $1,000 difference between interest expense and cash paid for interest in 2014, 2015, 2016, and 2017 results from amortizing the bond discount. The cash outflow for the interest related to the discount is included in the $100,000 payment made at maturity on December 31, 2018. Even though $14,000 of cash is paid for interest in 2018, only $10,000 is recognized as interest expense on the income statement that year. Although the total increase in cash over the five-year life of the business ($7,000) is equal to the total net income reported for the same period, there are significant timing differences between when the interest expense is recognized and when the cash outflows occur to pay for it.

☑ CHECK YOURSELF 7.4

On January 1, 2014, Moffett Company issued bonds with a $600,000 face value at 98. The bonds had a 9 percent annual interest rate and a 10-year term. Interest is payable in cash on December 31 of each year. What amount of interest expense will Moffett report on the 2016 income statement? What carrying value for bonds payable will Moffett report on the December 31, 2016, balance sheet?

Answer   The bonds were issued at a $12,000 ($600,000 × 0.02) discount. The discount will be amortized over the 10-year life at the rate of $1,200 ($12,000 ÷ 10 years) per year. The amount of interest expense for 2016 is $55,200 ($600,000 × .09 = $54,000 annual cash interest + $1,200 discount amortization).

The carrying value of the bond liability is equal to the face value less the unamortized discount. By the end of 2016, $3,600 of the discount will have been amortized ($1,200 × 3 years = $3,600). The unamortized discount as of December 31, 2016, will be $8,400 ($12,000 − $3,600). The carrying value of the bond liability as of December 31, 2016, will be $591,600 ($600,000 − $8,400).

Bonds Issued at a Premium

When bonds are sold for more than their face value, the difference between the amount received and the face value is called a **bond premium.** Bond premiums reduce the effective interest rate. For example, assume Mason Company issued its 9 percent bonds at 105, receiving $105,000 cash on the issue date. The company is still only required to repay the $100,000 face value of the bonds at the maturity date. The $5,000 difference between the amount received and the amount repaid at maturity reduces the total amount of interest expense. The premium is recorded in a separate liability account called **Premium on Bonds Payable.** This account is reported on the balance sheet as an addition to Bonds Payable, increasing the carrying value of the bond liability. On the issue date, the bond liability would be reported on the balance sheet as follows:

Bonds payable	$100,000
Plus: Premium on bonds payable	5,000
Carrying value	$105,000

The entire $105,000 cash inflow is reported in the financing activities section of the statement of cash flows even though the $5,000 premium is conceptually an operating activities cash flow because it pertains to interest. In practice, premiums are usually so small they are immaterial and the entire cash inflow is normally classified as a financing activity. The effects on the financial statements are shown here.

Date	Assets	=	Liabilities	+	Equity	Rev.	−	Exp.	=	Net Inc.	Cash Flow
	Cash	=	Carrying Value of Bond Liability								
Jan. 1	105,000	=	105,000	+	NA	NA	−	NA	=	NA	105,000 FA
Dec. 31	(9,000)		(1,000)		(8,000)			8,000		(8,000)	9,000 OA

The Market Rate of Interest

When a bond is issued, the effective interest rate is determined by current market conditions. Market conditions are influenced by many factors such as the state of the economy, government policy, and the law of supply and demand. These conditions are collectively reflected in the **market rate of interest.** The *effective rate of interest* investors are willing to accept *for a particular bond* equals the *market rate of interest* for other investments with similar levels of risk at the time the bond is issued. When the market rate of interest is higher than the stated rate of interest, bonds will sell at a discount so as to increase the effective rate of interest to the market rate. When the market rate is lower than the stated rate, bonds will sell at a premium so as to reduce the effective rate to the market rate.

SECURITY FOR LOAN AGREEMENTS

In general, large loans with long terms to maturity pose more risk to lenders (creditors) than small loans with short terms. To reduce the risk that they won't get paid, lenders frequently require borrowers (debtors) to pledge designated assets as **collateral** for loans. For example, when a bank makes a car loan, it usually retains legal title to the car until the loan is fully repaid. If the borrower fails to make the monthly payments, the bank repossesses the car, sells it to someone else, and uses the proceeds to pay the original owner's debt. Similarly, assets like accounts receivable, inventory, equipment, buildings, and land may be pledged as collateral for business loans.

In addition to requiring collateral, creditors often obtain additional protection by including **restrictive covenants** in loan agreements. Such covenants may restrict additional borrowing, limit dividend payments, or restrict salary increases. If the loan restrictions are violated, the borrower is in default and the loan balance is due immediately.

Finally, creditors often ask key personnel to provide copies of their personal tax returns and financial statements. The financial condition of key executives is important because they may be asked to pledge personal property as collateral for business loans, particularly for small businesses.

CURRENT VERSUS NONCURRENT

Because meeting obligations on time is critical to business survival, financial analysts and creditors are interested in whether companies will have enough money available to pay bills when they are due. Most businesses provide information about their bill-paying ability by classifying their assets and liabilities according to liquidity. The more quickly an asset is converted to cash or consumed, the more *liquid* it is. Assets are usually divided into two major classifications: *current* and *noncurrent*. Current items are also referred to as *short term* and noncurrent items as *long term*.

A **current (short-term) asset** is expected to be converted to cash or consumed within one year or an operating cycle, whichever is longer. An **operating cycle** is defined as the average time it takes a business to convert cash to inventory, inventory to accounts receivable, and accounts receivable back to cash. For most businesses, the operating cycle is less than one year. As a result, the one-year rule normally prevails with respect to classifying assets as current. The current assets section of a balance sheet typically includes the following items.

LO 7-9

Distinguish between current and noncurrent assets and liabilities.

> Current Assets
> Cash
> Marketable securities
> Accounts receivable
> Short-term notes receivable
> Interest receivable
> Inventory
> Supplies
> Prepaid items

Given the definition of current assets, it seems reasonable to assume that **current (short-term) liabilities** would be those due within one year or an operating cycle, whichever is longer. This assumption is usually correct. However, an exception is made for long-term renewable debt. For example, consider a liability that was issued with a 20-year term to maturity. After 19 years, the liability becomes due within one year and is, therefore, a current liability. Even so, the liability will be classified as long term if the company plans to issue new long-term debt and to use the proceeds from that debt to repay the maturing liability. This situation is described as *refinancing short-term debt on a long-term basis.* In general, if a business does not plan to use any of its current assets to repay a debt, that debt is listed as long term even if it is due within one year. The current liabilities section of a balance sheet typically includes the following items.

LO 7-10

 Prepare a classified balance sheet.

Current Liabilities
Accounts payable
Short-term notes payable
Wages payable
Taxes payable
Interest payable

Balance sheets that distinguish between current and noncurrent items are called **classified balance sheets.** To enhance the usefulness of accounting information, most real-world balance sheets are classified. Exhibit 7.11 displays an example of a classified balance sheet.

EXHIBIT 7.11

LIMBAUGH COMPANY
Classified Balance Sheet
As of December 31, 2014

Assets			
Current Assets			
Cash		$ 20,000	
Accounts receivable		35,000	
Inventory		230,000	
Prepaid rent		3,600	
Total current assets			$288,600
Property, Plant, and Equipment			
Office equipment	$ 80,000		
Less: Accumulated depreciation	(25,000)	55,000	
Building	340,000		
Less: Accumulated depreciation	(40,000)	300,000	
Land		120,000	
Total property, plant, and equipment			475,000
Total assets			$763,600

Liabilities and Stockholders' Equity			
Current Liabilities			
Accounts payable		$ 32,000	
Notes payable		120,000	
Salaries payable		32,000	
Unearned revenue		9,800	
Total current liabilities			$193,800
Long-Term Liabilities			
Note payable			100,000
Total liabilities			293,800
Stockholders' Equity			
Common stock		200,000	
Retained earnings		269,800	469,800
Total liabilities and stockholders' equity			$763,600

FOCUS ON INTERNATIONAL ISSUES

WHY ARE THESE BALANCE SHEETS BACKWARD?

As discussed in earlier chapters, most industrialized countries require companies to use international financial accounting standards (IFRS), which are similar to the GAAP used in the United States. The globalization of accounting standards should, therefore, make it easier to read a company's annual report regardless of its country or origin. However, there are still language differences between companies; German companies prepare their financial reports using IFRS, but in German, while the UK companies use English.

Suppose language is not an issue. For example, companies in the United States, England, and even India, prepare their annual reports in English. Thus, one would expect to find few differences between financial reports prepared by companies in these countries. However, if a person who learned accounting in the United States looks at the balance sheet of a U.K. company he or she might think the statement is a bit "backwards," and if he or she reviews the balance sheet of an Indian company they may find it to be upside down.

Like U.S. companies, U.K. companies report assets at the top, or left, of the balance sheet, and liabilities and stockholders' equity on the bottom or right. However, unlike the United States, U.K. companies typically show long-term assets before current assets. Even more different are balance sheets of Indian companies, which begin with stockholders' equity and then liabilities at the top or left, and then show assets on the bottom or right. Like the U.K. statements, those in India show long-term assets before current assets. Realize that most of the accounting rules established by IFRS or U.S. GAAP deal with measurement issues. Assets can be measured using the same rules, but be disclosed in different manners. IFRS require companies to classify assets and liabilities as current versus noncurrent, but the order in which these categories are listed on the balance sheet is not specified.

For an example of a financial statement for a U.K. company, go to www.itvplc.com. Click on "Investors" and then "Reports and results." For an example of an Indian company's annual report, go to www.tatamotors.com. Highlight on "Investors," then "Reports & Filings," and then "Annual Reports" under "Reports and Filings."

A Look Back

Chapter 7 discussed accounting for current liabilities and long-term debt. Current liabilities are obligations due within one year or the company's operating cycle, whichever is longer. The chapter expanded the discussion of promissory notes begun in Chapter 5. Chapter 5 introduced accounting for the note payee, the lender; Chapter 7 discussed accounting for the note maker (issuer), the borrower. Notes payable and related interest payable are reported as liabilities on the balance sheet. Chapter 7 also discussed accounting for the contingent liability and warranty obligations.

Long-term notes payable mature in two to five years and usually require payments that include a return of principal plus interest. *Lines of credit* enable companies to borrow limited amounts on an as-needed basis. Although lines of credit normally have one-year terms, companies frequently renew them, extending the effective maturity date to the intermediate range of five or more years. Interest on a line of credit is normally paid monthly. Long-term debt financing for more than 10 years usually requires issuing *bonds*.

A Look Forward

A company seeking long-term financing might choose to use debt, such as the types of bonds or term loans that were discussed in this chapter. Owners' equity is another source of long-term financing. Several equity alternatives are available, depending on the type of business organization the owners choose to establish. For example, a company could be organized as a sole proprietorship, partnership, or corporation. Chapter 8 presents accounting issues related to equity transactions for each of these types of business structures.

APPENDIX

Amortization Using the Effective Interest Rate Method

LO 7-11

Use the effective interest rate method to amortize bond discounts and premiums.

To this point we have demonstrated the straight-line method for amortizing bond discounts and premiums. While this method is easy to understand, it is inaccurate because it does not show the correct amount of interest expense incurred during each accounting period. To illustrate, return to the case of Mason Company demonstrated in Exhibit 7.10 (page 265). Recall that the exhibit shows the effects of accounting for a $100,000 face value bond with a 9 percent stated rate of interest that was issued at a price of 95. The carrying value of the bond liability on the January 1, 2014, issue date was $95,000. The bond discount was amortized using the straight-line method.

Recall that the straight-line method amortizes the discount equally over the life of the bond. Specifically, there is a $5,000 discount that is amortized over a five-year life resulting in a $1,000 amortization per year. As the discount is amortized the bond liability (carrying value of the bond) increases. Specifically, the carrying value of the bond liability shown in Exhibit 7.10 increases as follows:

Accounting Period	2014	2015	2016	2017
Carrying value as of December 31	$96,000	$97,000	$98,000	$99,000

While the carrying value of the bond liability increases steadily, the straight-line method recognizes the same amount of interest expense ($9,000 stated rate of interest + $1,000 discount amortization = $10,000 interest expense) per year. This straight-line recognition pattern is irrational because the amount of interest expense recognized should increase as the carrying value of the bond liability increases. A more accurate recognition pattern can be accomplished by using an approach called the **effective interest rate method.**

Amortizing Bond Discounts

The effective interest rate is determined by the price that the buyer of a bond is willing to pay on the issue date. In the case of Mason Company the issue price of $95,000 for bonds with a $100,000 face value, a 9 percent stated rate of interest, and a five-year term produces an effective interest rate of approximately 10.33 percent.[6] Since the effective interest rate is based on the market price of the bonds on the day of issue, it is sometimes called *the market rate of interest.*

Interest recognition under the effective interest method is accomplished as follows:

1. Determine the cash payment for interest by multiplying the stated rate of interest times the face value of the bonds.

2. Determine the amount of interest expense by multiplying the effective rate of interest times the carrying value of the bond liability.

---

[6]In practice the effective rate of interest is calculated using software programs, interest formulas, or interest tables.

EXHIBIT 7.12

Amortization Schedule for Bond Discount

	(A) Cash Payment	(B) Interest Expense	(C) Discount Amortization	(D) Carrying Value
January 1, 2014				$ 95,000
December 31, 2014	$ 9,000	$ 9,814	$ 814	95,814
December 31, 2015	9,000	9,898	898	96,712
December 31, 2016	9,000	9,990	990	97,702
December 31, 2017	9,000	10,093	1,093	98,795
December 31, 2018	9,000	10,205	1,205	100,000
Totals	$45,000	$50,000	$5,000	

(A) Stated rate of interest times the face value of the bonds ($100,000 × .09).
(B) Effective interest rate times the carrying value at the beginning of the period. For the 2014 accounting period the amount is $9,814 ($95,000 × .1033).
(C) Interest Expense − Cash Payment. For 2014 the discount amortization is $814 ($9,814 − $9,000 = $814).
(D) Carrying value at beginning of period plus portion of discount amortized. For the accounting period ending December 31, 2014, the amount is $95,814 ($95,000 + $814).

3. Determine the amount of the amortization of the bond discount by subtracting the cash payment from the interest expense.

4. Update the carrying value of the liability by adding the amount of the discount amortization to the amount of the carrying value at the beginning of the accounting period.

Applying these procedures to the Mason Company illustration produces the amortization schedule shown in Exhibit 7.12.

The recognition of interest expense at the end of each accounting period has the following effects on the financial statements. On the balance sheet, assets decrease, liabilities increase, and retained earnings decrease. On the income statement, expenses increase and net income decreases. There is a cash outflow in the operating activities of the statement of cash flows. The effects on the financial statements are shown here.

Assets	=	Liabilities	+	Equity	Rev.	−	Exp.	=	Net Inc.	Cash Flow
Cash	=	Carrying Value of Bond Liab.	+	Ret. Earn.						
(9,000)	=	814	+	(9,814)	NA	−	9,814	=	(9,814)	(9,000) OA

Exhibit 7.13 shows the financial statements for Mason Company for 2014 through 2018. The statements assume the same events as described as those used to construct Exhibit 7.10 (page 265). These events are summarized below:

1. Mason issues a $100,000 face value bond with a 9 percent stated rate of interest. The bond has a 5-year term and is issued at a price of 95. Annual interest is paid with cash on December 31 of each year.

2. Mason uses the proceeds from the bond issue to purchase land.

3. Leasing the land produces rent revenue of $11,400 cash per year.

4. On the maturity date of the bond, the land is sold and the proceeds from the sale are used to repay the bond liability.

EXHIBIT 7.13

Financial Statements

Under the Assumption that Bonds Are Issued at a Discount

	2014	2015	2016	2017	2018
Income Statements					
Rent revenue	$ 11,400	$ 11,400	$ 11,400	$ 11,400	$ 11,400
Interest expense	(9,814)	(9,898)	(9,990)	(10,093)	(10,205)
Net income	$ 1,586	$ 1,502	$ 1,410	$ 1,307	$ 1,195
Balance Sheets					
Assets:					
Cash	$ 2,400	$ 4,800	$ 7,200	$ 9,600	$ 7,000
Land	95,000	95,000	95,000	95,000	0
Total assets	$ 97,400	$ 99,800	$102,200	$104,600	$ 7,000
Liabilities					
Bond payable	$100,000	$100,000	$100,000	$100,000	$ 0
Discount on bonds payable	(4,186)	(3,288)	(2,298)	(1,205)	0
Carrying value of bond liab.	95,814	96,712	97,702	98,795	0
Equity					
Retained earnings	1,586	3,088	4,498	5,805	7,000
Total liabilities and equity	$ 97,400	$ 99,800	$102,200	$104,600	$ 7,000
Statements of Cash Flows					
Operating Activities					
Inflow from customers	$ 11,400	$ 11,400	$ 11,400	$ 11,400	$ 11,400
Outflow for interest	(9,000)	(9,000)	(9,000)	(9,000)	(14,000)
Investing Activities					
Outflow to purchase land	(95,000)				
Inflow from sale of land					95,000
Financing Activities					
Inflow from bond issue	95,000				
Outflow to repay bond liab.					(95,000)
Net change in cash	2,400	2,400	4,800	7,200	(2,600)
Beginning cash balance	0	2,400	2,400	2,400	9,600
Ending cash balance	$ 2,400	$ 4,800	$ 7,200	$ 9,600	$ 7,000

The only difference between the two exhibits is that Exhibit 7.10 was constructed assuming that the bond discount was amortized using the straight-line method while Exhibit 7.13 assumes that the discount was amortized using the effective interest rate method.

Notice that interest expense under the effective interest rate method (Exhibit 7.13) increases each year while interest expense under the straight-line method (Exhibit 7.10, page 265) remains constant for all years. This result occurs because the effective interest rate method amortizes increasingly larger amounts of the discount (see Column C of Exhibit 7.12) as the carrying value of the bond liability increases. In contrast, the straight-line method amortized the bond discount at a constant rate of $1,000 per year over the life of the bond. Even so, total amount of interest expense recognized over the life of the bond is the same ($50,000) under both methods. Since the effective interest rate method matches the interest expense with the carrying value of the bond liability, it is the theoretically preferred approach. Indeed, accounting standards require the use

EXHIBIT 7.14

Amortization Schedule for Bond Premium

	(A) Cash Payment	(B) Interest Expense	(C) Premium Amortization	(D) Carrying Value
January 1, 2014				$107,985
December 31, 2014	$10,000	$ 8,639	$1,361	106,624
December 31, 2015	10,000	8,530	1,470	105,154
December 31, 2016	10,000	8,413	1,587	103,567
December 31, 2017	10,000	8,285	1,715	101,852
December 31, 2018	10,000	8,148	1,852	100,000
Totals	$50,000	$42,015	$7,985	

(A) Stated rate of interest times the face value of the bonds ($100,000 × .10).
(B) Effective interest times the carrying value at the beginning of the period. For the 2014 accounting period the amount is $8,639 ($107,985 × .08).
(C) Cash Payment − Interest Expense. For 2014 the premium amortization is $1,361 ($10,000 − $8,639 = $1,361).
(D) Carrying value at beginning of period minus the portion of premium amortized. For the accounting period ending December 31, 2014, the amount is $106,624 ($107,985 − 1,361).

of the effective interest rate method when the differences between it and the straight-line method are material.

The amortization of the discount affects the carrying value of the bond as well as the amount of interest expense. Under the effective interest method the rate of growth of the carrying value of the bond increases as the maturity date approaches. In contrast, under the straight-line method the rate of growth of the carrying value of the bond remains constant at $1,000 per year throughout the life of the bond.

Finally, notice that cash flow is not affected by the method of amortization. The exact same cash flow consequences occur under both the straight-line (Exhibit 7.10) and the effective interest rate method (Exhibit 7.13).

Amortizing Bond Premiums

Bond premiums can also be amortized using the effective interest rate method. To illustrate, assume United Company issued a $100,000 face value bond with a 10 percent stated rate of interest. The bond had a 5-year term. The bond was issued at a price of $107,985. The effective rate of interest is 8 percent. United's accountant prepared the amortization schedule shown in Exhibit 7.14.

The recognition of interest expense at the end of each accounting period has the following effects on the financial statements. On the balance sheet assets decrease, liabilities decrease, and retained earnings decrease. On the income statement expenses increase and net income decreases. There is a cash outflow in the operating activities of the statement of cash flows. The effects on the financial statements are shown here.

Assets	=	Liabilities	+	Equity	Rev.	−	Exp.	=	Net Inc.	Cash Flow	
Cash	=	Carrying Value of Bond Liab.	+	Ret. Earn.							
(10,000)	=	(1,361)	+	(8,639)	NA	−	8,639	=	(8,639)	(8,639) (1,361)	OA FA

274 Chapter 7

 Video lectures and accompanying self-assessment quizzes are available for all learning objectives through McGraw-Hill *Connect® Accounting.*

SELF-STUDY REVIEW PROBLEM

Perfect Picture Inc. (PPI) experienced the following transactions during 2015. The transactions are summarized (transaction data pertain to the full year) and limited to those that affect the company's current liabilities.

1. PPI had cash sales of $820,000. The state requires that PPI charge customers an 8 percent sales tax (ignore cost of goods sold).
2. PPI paid the state sales tax authority $63,000.
3. On March 1, PPI issued a note payable to the County Bank. PPI received $50,000 cash (principal balance). The note had a one-year term and a 6 percent annual interest rate.
4. On December 31, PPI recognized accrued interest on the note issued in Event 3.
5. On December 31, PPI recognized warranty expense at the rate of 3 percent of sales.
6. PPI paid $22,000 cash to settle warranty claims.
7. On January 1, 2014, PPI issued a $100,000 installment note. The note had a 10-year term and an 8 percent interest rate. PPI agreed to repay the principal and interest in 10 annual interest payments of $14,902.94 at the end of each year. While the note was issued in 2014, the effects of interest appear in the 2015 balance sheet.

Required

Prepare the liabilities section of the December 31, 2015, balance sheet.

Solution

PERFECT PICTURE INC. Partial Balance Sheet December 31, 2015	
Current Liabilities	
Sales tax payable	$ 2,600
Notes payable	50,000
Interest payable	2,500
Warranties payable	2,600
Installment note payable	85,642
Total liabilities	$143,342

Explanations for amounts shown in the balance sheet:

1. Sales Tax Payable: $820,000 × 0.08 = $65,600 Amount Due − $63,000 Amount Paid = $2,600 Liability as of December 31, 2015.
2. Note Payable: $50,000 Borrowed with no repayment.
3. Interest Payable: $50,000 × 0.06 × 10/12 = $2,500.
4. Warranty Payable: $820,000 × 0.03 = $24,600 Estimated Warranty Liability − $22,000 Cash Paid to Settle Warranty Claims = $2,600 Remaining Liability.
5. Installment Note Payable:

Accounting Period	Principal Bal. January 1 A	Cash Payment December 31 B	Applied to Interest C = A × 0.08	Applied to Principal B − C
2014	$100,000.00	$14,902.94	$8,000.00	$6,902.94
2015	93,097.06	14,902.94	7,447.76	7,455.18
2016*	85,641.88			

*The amount due on December 31, 2015, is the same as the amount due on January 1, 2016. The amount shown on the balance sheet has been rounded to the nearest dollar.

KEY TERMS

Amortization 254
Bond certificates 257
Bond discount 262
Bond premium 266
Bondholder 257
Carrying value 263
Classified balance sheets 268
Collateral 267
Contingent liability 250

Current (short-term)
   asset 267
Current (short-term)
   liabilities 267
Discount on Bonds
   Payable 262
Effective interest rate 262
Effective interest rate
   method 270

Face value 257
Fixed interest rate 253
General uncertainties 250
Installment notes 254
Issuer 248, 257
Line of credit 257
Long-term liabilities 253
Market rate of interest 266
Note payable 248

Operating cycle 267
Premium on Bonds
   Payable 266
Restrictive covenants 267
Stated interest rate 258
Straight-line
   amortization 263
Variable interest rate 253
Warranties 251

QUESTIONS

1. What type of transaction is a cash payment to creditors? How does this type of transaction affect the accounting equation?

2. What is a current liability? Distinguish between a current liability and a long-term debt.

3. How does recording accrued interest affect the accounting equation?

4. Who is the maker of a note payable?

5. How does the going concern assumption discussed in Chapter 1 affect the way liabilities are reported in the financial statements?

6. Why is it necessary to make an adjustment at the end of the accounting period for unpaid interest on a note payable?

7. Assume that on October 1, 2014, Big Company borrowed $10,000 from the local bank at 6 percent interest. The note is due on October 1, 2015. How much interest does Big pay in 2014? How much interest does Big pay in 2015? What amount of cash does Big pay back in 2015?

8. When a business collects sales tax from customers,

is it revenue? Why or why not?

9. What is a contingent liability?

10. List the three categories of contingent liabilities.

11. Are contingent liabilities recorded on a company's books? Explain.

12. What is the difference in accounting procedures for a liability that is probable and estimable and one that is reasonably possible but not estimable?

13. What type of liabilities are not recorded on a company's books?

14. What does the term *warranty* mean?

15. What effect does recognizing future warranty obligations have on the balance sheet? On the income statement?

16. When is warranty cost reported on the statement of cash flows?

17. What is the difference between classification of a note as short term or long term?

18. At the beginning of year 1, B Co. has a note payable of $72,000 that calls for an annual payment of $16,246, which includes both principal and

interest. If the interest rate is 8 percent, what is the amount of interest expense in year 1 and in year 2? What is the balance of the note at the end of year 2?

19. What is the purpose of a line of credit for a business? Why would a company choose to obtain a line of credit instead of issuing bonds?

20. What are the primary sources of debt financing for most large companies?

21. What are some advantages of issuing bonds versus borrowing from a bank?

22. What are some disadvantages of issuing bonds?

23. Why can a company usually issue bonds at a lower interest rate than the company would pay if the funds were borrowed from a bank?

24. If Roc Co. issued $100,000 of 5 percent, 10-year bonds at the face amount, what is the effect of the issuance of the bonds on the financial statements? What amount of interest expense will Roc Co. recognize each year?

25. What mechanism is used to adjust the stated

interest rate to the market rate of interest?

26. When the effective interest rate is higher than the stated interest rate on a bond issue, will the bond sell at a discount or premium? Why?

27. What type of transaction is the issuance of bonds by a company?

28. What factors may cause the effective interest rate and the stated interest rate to be different?

29. If a bond is selling at 97½, how much cash will the company receive from the sale of a $1,000 bond?

30. How is the carrying value of a bond computed?

31. Gay Co. has a balance in the Bonds Payable account of $25,000 and a balance in the Discount on Bonds Payable account of $5,200. What is the carrying value of the bonds? What is the total amount of the liability?

32. When the effective interest rate is higher than the stated interest rate, will interest expense be higher or lower than the amount of interest paid?

33. What is a classified balance sheet?

 ## MULTIPLE-CHOICE QUESTIONS

Multiple-choice questions are provided on the text website at www.mhhe.com/edmondssurvey4e.

EXERCISES

≣ connect All applicable Exercises are available with McGraw-Hill's
|ACCOUNTING *Connect® Accounting.*

LO 7-1

Exercise 7-1   *Recognizing accrued interest expense*

Harveys Corporation borrowed $60,000 from the bank on November 1, 2014. The note had a 6 percent annual rate of interest and matured on April 30, 2015. Interest and principal were paid in cash on the maturity date.

Required

a. What amount of interest expense was paid in cash in 2014?
b. What amount of interest expense was reported on the 2014 income statement?
c. What amount of total liabilities was reported on the December 31, 2014, balance sheet?
d. What total amount of cash was paid to the bank on April 30, 2015, for principal and interest?
e. What amount of interest expense was reported on the 2015 income statement?

LO 7-1

Exercise 7-2   *Effects of recognizing accrued interest on financial statements*

R.T. Jackson started Jackson Company on January 1, 2014. The company experienced the following events during its first year of operation:

1. Earned $3,000 of cash revenue for performing services.
2. Borrowed $4,800 cash from the bank.
3. Adjusted the accounting records to recognize accrued interest expense on the bank note. The note, issued on August 1, 2014, had a one-year term and a 6 percent annual interest rate.

Required

a. What is the amount of interest expense in 2014?
b. What amount of cash was paid for interest in 2014?
c. Use a horizontal statements model to show how each event affects the balance sheet, income statement, and statement of cash flows. Indicate whether the event increases (I), decreases (D), or does not affect (NA) each element of the financial statements. In the Cash Flows column, designate the cash flows as operating activities (OA), investing activities (IA), or financing activities (FA). The first transaction has been recorded as an example.

Event No.	Balance Sheet											Income Statement					Statement of Cash Flows
	Cash	=	Notes Pay.	+	Int. Pay.	+	Com. Stk.	+	Ret. Earn.			Rev.	−	Exp.	=	Net Inc.	
1	I	=	NA	+	NA	+	NA	+	I			I	−	NA	=	I	I OA

LO 7-2

Exercise 7-3   *Recording sales tax expense*

The Rebel Book Store sells books and other supplies to students in a state where the sales tax rate is 7 percent. The Rebel Book Store engaged in the following transactions for 2014. Sales tax of 7 percent is collected on all sales.

1. Book sales, not including sales tax, for 2014 amounted to $215,000 cash.
2. Cash sales of miscellaneous items in 2014 were $160,000, not including tax.
3. Cost of goods sold amounted to $195,000 for the year.
4. Paid $95,000 in operating expenses for the year.
5. Paid the sales tax collected to the state agency.

Required

a. What is the total amount of sales tax the Rebel Book Store collected and paid for the year?
b. What is the Rebel Book Store's net income for the year?

Exercise 7-4 *Recognizing sales tax payable*

The following selected transactions apply to Easy Stop for November and December 2014. November was the first month of operations. Sales tax is collected at the time of sale but is not paid to the state sales tax agency until the following month.

1. Cash sales for November 2014 were $85,000 plus sales tax of 8 percent.
2. Easy Stop paid the November sales tax to the state agency on December 10, 2014.
3. Cash sales for December 2014 were $98,000 plus sales tax of 8 percent.

Required

a. Show the effect of the above transactions on a statements model like the one shown below.

Assets =	Liabilities	+	Equity		Income Statement			
Cash =	Sales Tax Pay.	+	Com. Stk. +	Ret. Earn.	Rev. −	Exp. =	Net Inc.	Cash Flow

b. What was the total amount of sales tax paid in 2014?
c. What was the total amount of sales tax collected in 2014?
d. What is the amount of the sales tax liability as of December 31, 2014?
e. On which financial statement will the sales tax liability appear?

Exercise 7-5 *Contingent liabilities*

The following legal situations apply to Dabney Corp. for 2014:

1. A customer slipped and fell on a slick floor while shopping in the retail store. The customer has filed a $5 million lawsuit against the company. Dabney's attorney knows that the company will have to pay some damages but is reasonably certain that the suit can be settled for $750,000.
2. The EPA has assessed a fine against Dabney of $250,000 for hazardous emissions from one of its manufacturing plants. The EPA had previously issued a warning to Dabney and required Dabney to make repairs within six months. Dabney began to make the repairs, but was not able to complete them within the six-month period. Because Dabney has started the repairs, Dabney's attorney thinks the fine will be reduced to $100,000. He is approximately 80 percent certain that he can negotiate the fine reduction because of the repair work that has been completed.
3. One of Dabney's largest manufacturing facilities is located in "tornado alley." Property is routinely damaged by storms. Dabney estimates it may have property damage of as much as $400,000 this coming year.

Required

a. Discuss the various categories of contingent liabilities.
b. For each item above determine the correct accounting treatment.

Exercise 7-6 *Effect of warranties on income and cash flow*

To support himself while attending school, Devon James sold computers to other students. During the year Devon purchased computers for $150,000 and sold them for $280,000 cash. He provided his customers with a one-year warranty against defects in parts and labor. Based on industry standards, he estimated that warranty claims would amount to 5 percent of sales. During the year he paid $1,545 cash to replace a defective hard drive.

Required

a. Prepare an income statement and a statement of cash flows for James's first year of operation.
b. Explain the difference between net income and the amount of cash flow from operating activities.

278   Chapter 7

LO 7-4

Exercise 7-7 *Effect of warranty obligations and payments on financial statements*

The Wolf Appliance Co. provides a 120-day parts-and-labor warranty on all merchandise it sells. Wolf estimates the warranty expense for the current period to be $2,450. During the period a customer returned a product that cost $1,950 to repair.

Required

a. Show the effects of these transactions on the financial statements using a horizontal statements model like the example shown here. Use a + to indicate increase, a − for decrease, and NA for not affected. In the Cash Flow column, indicate whether the item is an operating activity (OA), investing activity (IA), or financing activity (FA).

Assets	=	Liab.	+	Equity	Rev.	−	Exp.	=	Net Inc.	Cash Flow

b. Discuss the advantage of estimating the amount of warranty expense.

LO 7-5

Exercise 7-8 *How credit terms affect financial statements*

Dodson Co. is planning to finance an expansion of its operations by borrowing $120,000. City Bank has agreed to loan Dodson the funds. Dodson has two repayment options: (1) to issue a note with the principal due in 10 years and with interest payable annually or (2) to issue a note to repay $12,000 of the principal each year along with the annual interest based on the unpaid principal balance. Assume the interest rate is 8 percent for each option.

Required

a. What amount of interest will Dodson pay in year 1
  (1) Under option 1?
  (2) Under option 2?
b. What amount of interest will Dodson pay in year 2
  (1) Under option 1?
  (2) Under option 2?
c. Explain the advantage of each option.

LO 7-5

Exercise 7-9 *Amortization schedule for an installment note*

On January 1, 2014, Hatch Co. borrowed $100,000 cash from First Bank by issuing a four-year, 6 percent note. The principal and interest are to be paid by making annual payments in the amount of $28,859. Payments are to be made December 31 of each year, beginning December 31, 2014.

Required

Prepare an amortization schedule for the interest and principal payments for the four-year period.

LO 7-5

Exercise 7-10 *Financial statement effects of an installment note*

Jay Mills started a business by issuing a $60,000 face value note to State National Bank on January 1, 2015. The note had a 6 percent annual rate of interest and a 10-year term. Payments of $8,152 are to be made each December 31 for 10 years.

Required

a. What portion of the December 31, 2014, payment is applied to
  (1) Interest expense?
  (2) Principal?
b. What is the principal balance on January 1, 2015?
c. What portion of the December 31, 2015, payment is applied to
  (1) Interest expense?
  (2) Principal?

Exercise 7-11   *Amortization of a long-term loan*

LO 7-5

A partial amortization schedule for a five-year note payable that Holly Co. issued on January 1, 2014, is shown here:

Accounting Period	Principal Balance January 1	Cash Payment	Applied to Interest	Applied to Principal
2014	$50,000	$11,549	$2,500	$8,959 9049
2015	41,041 40,951	11,549	2,052 2048	9,497 9501

Required

a. What rate of interest is Holly Co. paying on the note?

b. Using a financial statements model like the one shown below, record the appropriate amounts for the following two events.

  (1) January 1, 2014, issue of the note payable.

  (2) December 31, 2015, payment on the note payable.

Event No.	Assets	=	Liab.	+	Equity	Rev.	−	Exp.	=	Net Inc.	Cash Flow
1											

c. If the company earned $75,000 cash revenue and paid $35,000 in cash expenses in addition to the interest in 2014, what is the amount of each of the following?

  (1) Net income for 2014.

  (2) Cash flow from operating activities for 2014.

  (3) Cash flow from financing activities for 2014.

d. What is the amount of interest expense on this loan for 2015?

Exercise 7-12   *Effect of a line of credit on financial statements*

LO 7-6

Sims Company has a line of credit with Bay Bank. Sims can borrow up to $400,000 at any time over the course of the 2014 calendar year. The following table shows the prime rate expressed as an annual percentage along with the amounts borrowed and repaid during 2014. Sims agreed to pay interest at an annual rate equal to 1 percent above the bank's prime rate. Funds are borrowed or repaid on the first day of each month. Interest is payable in cash on the last day of the month. The interest rate is applied to the outstanding monthly balance. For example, Sims pays 6 percent (5 percent + 1 percent) annual interest on $60,000 for the month of January.

Month	Amount Borrowed or (Repaid)	Prime Rate for the Month
January	$60,000	5%
February	40,000	5
March	(30,000)	6
April through October	No change	No change
November	(20,000)	6
December	(10,000)	5

Required

Show the effects of these transactions on the financial statements using a horizontal statements model like the one shown here. Use a + to indicate increase, a − for decrease, and NA for not affected. In the Cash Flow column, indicate whether the item is an operating activity (OA), investing activity (IA), or financing activity (FA).

Assets	=	Liabilities	+	Equity	Rev.	−	Exp.	=	Net Inc.	Cash Flow

What is the total amount of interest expense paid for 2014?

LO 7-7

Exercise 7-13   *Two complete accounting cycles: Bonds issued at face value with annual interest*

Chapman Company issued $400,000 of 20-year, 6 percent bonds on January 1, 2014. The bonds were issued at face value. Interest is payable in cash on December 31 of each year. Chapman immediately invested the proceeds from the bond issue in land. The land was leased for an annual $60,000 of cash revenue, which was collected on December 31 of each year, beginning December 31, 2014.

Required

a. Organize the transaction data in accounts under the accounting equation.

b. Prepare the income statement, balance sheet, and statement of cash flows for 2014 and 2015.

LO 7-7

Exercise 7-14   *Annual versus semiannual interest for bonds issued at face value*

Ellis Co. issued bonds with a face value of $150,000 on January 1, 2014. The bonds had a 6 percent stated rate of interest and a five-year term. The bonds were issued at face value.

Required

a. What total amount of interest will Ellis pay in 2014 if bond interest is paid annually each December 31?

b. What total amount of interest will Ellis pay in 2014 if bond interest is paid semiannually each June 30 and December 31?

c. Write a memo explaining which option Ellis would prefer.

LO 7-8

Exercise 7-15   *Stated rate of interest versus the market rate of interest*

Required

Indicate whether a bond will sell at a premium (P), discount (D), or face value (F) for each of the following conditions:

a. _____ The market rate of interest is higher than the stated rate.

b. _____ The stated rate of interest is higher than the market rate.

c. _____ The stated rate of interest is less than the market rate.

d. _____ The market rate of interest is equal to the stated rate.

e. _____ The market rate of interest is less than the stated rate.

LO 7-8

Exercise 7-16   *Straight-line amortization of a bond discount*

Brock Company issued $300,000 face value of bonds on January 1, 2014. The bonds had a 6 percent stated rate of interest and a 10-year term. Interest is paid in cash annually, beginning December 31, 2014. The bonds were issued at 98.

Required

a. Use a financial statements model like the one shown below to demonstrate how (1) the January 1, 2014, bond issue and (2) the December 31, 2014, recognition of interest expense, including the amortization of the discount and the cash payment, affects the company's financial statements. Use + for increase, − for decrease, and NA for not affected.

Event No.	Assets	=	Liab.	+	Equity	Rev.	−	Exp.	=	Net Inc.	Cash Flow
1											

b. Determine the amount of interest expense reported on the 2014 income statement.

c. Determine the carrying value (face value less discount or plus premium) of the bond liability as of December 31, 2014.

d. Determine the amount of interest expense reported on the 2015 income statement.

e. Determine the carrying value (face value less discount or plus premium) of the bond liability as of December 31, 2015.

Exercise 7-17   *Determining cash receipts from bond issues*   LO 7-8

Required

Compute the cash proceeds from bond issues under the following terms. For each case, indicate whether the bonds sold at a premium or discount:

a. Few, Inc., issued $400,000 of 8-year, 8 percent bonds at 101.

b. Files Co. issued $250,000 of 4-year, 6 percent bonds at 98.

c. Fry Co. issued $300,000 of 10-year, 7 percent bonds at 102¼.

d. Ford, Inc., issued $200,000 of 5-year, 6 percent bonds at 97½.

Exercise 7-18   *Determining the amount of bond premiums and discounts*   LO 7-8

Required

For each of the following situations, calculate the amount of bond discount or premium, if any:

a. Wolfe Co. issued $120,000 of 6 percent bonds at 101.

b. Riley, Inc., issued $80,000 of 10-year, 8 percent bonds at 98.

c. Rais, Inc., issued $200,000 of 15-year, 9 percent bonds at 102¼.

d. Beaux Co. issued $400,000 of 20-year, 8 percent bonds at 99¾.

Exercise 7-19   *Identifying bond premiums and discounts*   LO 7-8

Required

In each of the following situations, state whether the bonds will sell at a premium or discount:

a. Addy issued $400,000 of bonds with a stated interest rate of 7 percent. At the time of issue, the market rate of interest for similar investments was 6 percent.

b. Rigsby issued $200,000 of bonds with a stated interest rate of 6 percent. At the time of issue, the market rate of interest for similar investments was 8 percent.

c. Sanders Inc., issued callable bonds with a stated interest rate of 6 percent. The bonds were callable at 102. At the date of issue, the market rate of interest was 7 percent for similar investments.

Exercise 7-20   *Straight-line amortization of a bond premium*   LO 7-8

Asmus Company issued $300,000 face value of bonds on January 1, 2014. The bonds had a 6 percent stated rate of interest and a 10-year term. Interest is paid in cash annually, beginning December 31, 2014. The bonds were issued at 101½.

Required

a. Use a financial statements model like the one shown below to demonstrate how (1) the January 1, 2014, bond issue and (2) the December 31, 2014, recognition of interest expense, including the amortization of the premium and the cash payment, affects the company's financial statements. Use + for increase, − for decrease, and NA for not affected.

Event No.	Assets	=	Liab.	+	Equity	Rev.	−	Exp.	=	Net Inc.	Cash Flow
1											

282   Chapter 7

b. Determine the carrying value (face value less discount or plus premium) of the bond liability as of December 31, 2014.

c. Determine the amount of interest expense reported on the 2014 income statement.

d. Determine the carrying value of the bond liability as of December 31, 2015.

e. Determine the amount of interest expense reported on the 2015 income statement.

LO 7-2, 7-4, 7-9

Exercise 7-21 *Current liabilities*

The following transactions apply to Midsouth Equipment Sales Corp. for 2014:

1. The business was started when Midsouth received $60,000 from the issue of common stock.
2. Purchased $160,000 of merchandise on account.
3. Sold merchandise for $220,000 cash (not including sales tax). Sales tax of 8 percent is collected when the merchandise is sold. The merchandise had a cost of $140,000.
4. Provided a six-month warranty on the merchandise sold. Based on industry estimates, the warranty claims would amount to 4 percent of merchandise sales.
5. Paid the sales tax to the state agency on $180,000 of the sales.
6. On September 1, 2014, borrowed $40,000 from the local bank. The note had a 6 percent interest rate and matures on March 1, 2015.
7. Paid $6,600 for warranty repairs during the year.
8. Paid operating expenses of $61,000 for the year.
9. Paid $145,000 of accounts payable.
10. Recorded accrued interest at the end of the year.

Required

a. Record the above transactions in a horizontal statements model like the following one.

	Balance Sheet										Income Statement			Statemt. of Cash Flows
Event	Assets	=	Liabilities						+	Equity	Rev.	− Exp.	= Net Inc.	
	Cash + Mdse. Inv.		Acct. Pay.	+ Sales Tax Pay.	+ War. Pay.	+ Int. Pay.	+ Notes Pay.	+ Com. Stock	+ Ret. Earn.					

b. Prepare the income statement, balance sheet, and statement of cash flows for 2014.

c. What is the total amount of current liabilities at December 31, 2014?

LO 7-10

Exercise 7-22 *Preparing a classified balance sheet*

Required

Use the following information to prepare a classified balance sheet for Blackmon Co. at the end of 2014:

Accounts receivable	$36,200
Accounts payable	12,400
Cash	29,650
Common stock	50,000
Long-term notes payable	45,500
Merchandise inventory	38,300
Office equipment	36,400
Retained earnings	36,250
Prepaid insurance	3,600

LO 7-11

Exercise 7-23 *Effective interest amortization of a bond discount*

On January 1, 2014, Carrolton Condo Association issued bonds with a face value of $250,000, a stated rate of interest of 8 percent, and a 10-year term to maturity. Interest is payable in cash on

December 31 of each year. The effective rate of interest was 10 percent at the time the bonds were issued. The bonds sold for $219,277. Carrolton used the effective interest rate method to amortize bond discount.

Required

a. Determine the amount of the discount on the day of issue.
b. Determine the amount of interest expense recognized on December 31, 2014.
c. Determine the carrying value of the bond liability on December 31, 2014.

Exercise 7-24   *Effective interest amortization of a bond discount*

LO 7-11

On January 1, 2014, Seaside Enterprises issued bonds with a face value of $60,000, a stated rate of interest of 8 percent, and a five-year term to maturity. Interest is payable in cash on December 31 of each year. The effective rate of interest was 9 percent at the time the bonds were issued. The bonds sold for $57,666. Seaside used the effective interest rate method to amortize bond discount.

Required

a. Prepare an amortization table as shown below:

	Cash Payment	Interest Expense	Discount Amortization	Carrying Value
January 1, 2014				57,666
December 31, 2014	4,800	5,190	390	58,056
December 31, 2015	?	?	?	?
December 31, 2016	?	?	?	?
December 31, 2017	?	?	?	?
December 31, 2018	?	?	?	?
Totals	24,000	26,334	2,334	

b. What item(s) in the table would appear on the 2015 balance sheet?
c. What item(s) in the table would appear on the 2015 income statement?
d. What item(s) in the table would appear on the 2015 statement of cash flows?

Exercise 7-25   *Effective interest versus straight-line amortization*

LO 7-11

On January 1, 2014, Purvis and Associates issued bonds with a face value of $800,000, a stated rate of interest of 8 percent, and a 20-year term to maturity. Interest is payable in cash on December 31 of each year. The effective rate of interest was 9 percent at the time the bonds were issued.

Required

Write a brief memo explaining whether the effective interest rate method or the straight-line method will produce the highest amount of interest expense recognized on the 2014 income statement.

PROBLEMS

 All applicable Problems are available with McGraw-Hill's
Connect® Accounting.

Problem 7-26   *Effect of accrued interest on financial statements*

LO 7-1

Powell Co. borrowed $20,000 from the local bank on April 1, 2014, when the company was started. The note had an 8 percent annual interest rate and a one-year term to maturity. Powell Co. recognized $54,000 of revenue on account in 2014 and $65,000 of revenue on account in 2015. Cash collections from accounts receivable were $46,000 in 2014 and $63,000 in 2015. Powell Co. paid $27,000 of salaries expense in 2014 and $36,000 of salaries expense in 2015. Powell Co. paid the loan and interest at the maturity date.

CHECK FIGURES
b. $19,000
i. $54,400

Required

a. Organize the information in accounts under an accounting equation.
b. What amount of net cash flow from operating activities would be reported on the 2014 cash flow statement?
c. What amount of interest expense would be reported on the 2014 income statement?
d. What amount of total liabilities would be reported on the December 31, 2014, balance sheet?
e. What amount of retained earnings would be reported on the December 31, 2014, balance sheet?
f. What amount of cash flow from financing activities would be reported on the 2014 statement of cash flows?
g. What amount of interest expense would be reported on the 2015 income statement?
h. What amount of cash flows from operating activities would be reported on the 2015 cash flow statement?
i. What amount of assets would be reported on the December 31, 2015, balance sheet?

LO 7-3

Problem 7-27 *Contingent liabilities*

Required

How should each of the following situations be reported in the financial statements?

a. It has been determined that one of the company's products has caused a safety hazard. It is considered probable that liabilities have been incurred and a reasonable estimate of the amount can be made.
b. A company warehouse is located in a section of the city that has routinely flooded in the past. Consequently the company can no longer find a source of insurance for the warehouse. No flood has yet occurred this year.
c. Because of newly passed legislation, a company will have to upgrade its facilities over the next two years. Significant expenditures will occur, but at this time the amount has not been determined.

LO 7-1, 7-2, 7-4

CHECK FIGURE
Total Current Liabilities: $54,695

Problem 7-28 *Current liabilities*

The following selected transactions were taken from the books of Aliceville Company for 2014:

1. On March 1, 2014, borrowed $60,000 cash from the local bank. The note had a 6 percent interest rate and was due on September 1, 2014.
2. Cash sales for the year amounted to $240,000 plus sales tax at the rate of 7 percent.
3. Aliceville provides a 90-day warranty on the merchandise sold. The warranty expense is estimated to be 2 percent of sales.
4. Paid the sales tax to the state sales tax agency on $200,000 of the sales.
5. Paid the note due on September 1 and the related interest.
6. On October 1, 2014, borrowed $50,000 cash from the local bank. The note had a 7 percent interest rate and a one-year term to maturity.
7. Paid $3,800 in warranty repairs.
8. A customer has filed a lawsuit against Aliceville for $150,000 for breach of contract. The company attorney does not believe the suit has merit.

Required

a. Answer the following questions:
   (1) What amount of cash did Aliceville pay for interest during the year?
   (2) What amount of interest expense is reported on Aliceville's income statement for the year?
   (3) What is the amount of warranty expense for the year?
b. Prepare the current liabilities section of the balance sheet at December 31, 2014.
c. Show the effect of these transactions on the financial statements using a horizontal statements model like the one shown here. Use a + to indicate increase, a − for decrease, and NA for not affected. In the Cash Flow column, indicate whether the item is an operating activity

(OA), investing activity (IA), or financing activity (FA). The first transaction is recorded as an example.

Assets	=	Liabilities	+	Equity	Rev.	−	Exp.	=	Net Inc.	Cash Flow
+		+		NA	NA		NA		NA	+ FA

Problem 7-29   *Accounting for short-term debt and sales tax—two accounting cycles*

LO 7-1, 7-2, 7-3, 7-4

The following transactions apply to Ocktoc Co. for 2014, its first year of operations:

1. Received $50,000 cash from the issue of a short-term note with a 5 percent interest rate and a one-year maturity. The note was made on April 1, 2014.
2. Received $140,000 cash plus applicable sales tax from performing services. The services are subject to a sales tax rate of 6 percent.
3. Paid $84,000 cash for other operating expenses during the year.
4. Paid the sales tax due on $110,000 of the service revenue for the year. Sales tax on the balance of the revenue is not due until 2015.
5. Recognized the accrued interest at December 31, 2014.

The following transactions apply to Ocktoc Co. for 2015:

1. Paid the balance of the sales tax due for 2015.
2. Received $155,000 cash plus applicable sales tax from performing services. The services are subject to a sales tax rate of 6 percent.
3. Repaid the principal of the note and applicable interest on April 1, 2015.
4. Paid $96,000 of other operating expenses during the year.
5. Paid the sales tax due on $135,000 of the service revenue. The sales tax on the balance of the revenue is not due until 2016.

Required

a. Organize the transaction data in accounts under an accounting equation.
b. Prepare an income statement, a statement of changes in stockholders' equity, a balance sheet, and a statement of cash flow for 2014 and 2015.

Problem 7-30   *Effect of an installment note on financial statements*

LO 7-5

On January 1, 2014, Mixon Co. borrowed cash from First City Bank by issuing a $90,000 face value, three-year term note that had a 7 percent annual interest rate. The note is to be repaid by making annual cash payments of $34,295 that include both interest and principal on December 31 of each year. Mixon used the proceeds from the loan to purchase land that generated rental revenues of $45,000 cash per year.

Required

a. Prepare an amortization schedule for the three-year period.
b. Organize the information in accounts under an accounting equation.
c. Prepare an income statement, a balance sheet, and a statement of cash flows for each of the three years.
d. Does cash outflow from operating activities remain constant or change each year? Explain.

Problem 7-31   *Accounting for an installment note payable*

LO 7-5

The following transactions apply to Stegall Co. for 2014, its first year of operations.

1. Received $200,000 cash in exchange for issuance of common stock.
2. Secured a $400,000, 10-year installment loan from First Bank. The interest rate was 6 percent and annual payments are $54,348.
3. Purchased land for $120,000.

286   Chapter 7

4. Provided services for $240,000 cash.

5. Paid other operating expenses of $170,000.

6. Paid the annual payment on the loan.

Required

a. Organize the transaction data in accounts under an accounting equation.

b. Prepare an income statement and balance sheet for 2014.

c. What is the interest expense for 2015? 2016?

LO 7-6

CHECK FIGURE
a. Interest Expense for April: $1,050

Problem 7-32   *Accounting for a line of credit*

Sea Marine Co. uses a line of credit to help finance its inventory purchases. Sea Marine sells boats and equipment and uses the line of credit to build inventory for its peak sales months, which tend to be clustered in the summer months. Account balances at the beginning of 2014 were as follows.

Cash	$150,000
Inventory	175,000
Common stock	200,000
Retained earnings	125,000

Sea Marine experienced the following transactions for April, May, and June, 2014.

1. April 1, 2014, obtained approval for a line of credit of up to $550,000. Funds are to be obtained or repaid on the first day of each month. The interest rate is the bank prime rate plus 1 percent.

2. April 1, 2014, borrowed $210,000 on the line of credit. The bank's prime interest rate is 5 percent for January.

3. April 15, purchased inventory on account, $180,000.

4. April 31, paid other operating expenses of $96,000.

5. In April, sold inventory for $325,000 on account. The inventory had cost $200,000.

6. April 30, paid the interest due on the line of credit.

7. May 1, borrowed $170,000 on the line of credit. The bank's prime rate is 6 percent for May.

8. May 1, paid the accounts payable from transaction 3.

9. May 10, collected $312,000 of the sales on account.

10. May 20, purchased inventory on account, $265,000.

11. May sales on account were $425,000. The inventory had cost $230,000.

12. May 31, paid the interest due on the line of credit.

13. June 1, repaid $130,000 on the line of credit. The bank's prime rate is 6 percent for June.

14. June 5, paid $250,000 of the accounts payable.

15. June 10, collected $430,000 from accounts receivable.

16. June 20, purchased inventory on account, $245,000.

17. June sales on account were $465,000. The inventory had cost $220,000.

18. June 31, paid the interest due on the line of credit.

Required

a. What is the amount of interest expense for April? May? June?

b. What amount of cash was paid for interest in April? May? June?

LO 7-6

Problem 7-33   *Effect of a line of credit on financial statements*

Melvin Company has a line of credit with Bay Bank. Melvin can borrow up to $500,000 at any time over the course of the 2014 calendar year. The following table shows the prime rate expressed as an annual percentage along with the amounts borrowed and repaid during 2014.

Melvin agreed to pay interest at an annual rate equal to 1 percent above the bank's prime rate. Funds are borrowed or repaid on the first day of each month. Interest is payable in cash on the last day of the month. The interest rate is applied to the outstanding monthly balance. For example, Melvin pays 6 percent (5 percent + 1 percent) annual interest on $60,000 for the month of January.

Month	Amount Borrowed or (Repaid)	Prime Rate for the Month, %
January	$ 60,000	5
February	120,000	5
March	(50,000)	6
April through October	No change	No change
November	(30,000)	6
December	(50,000)	5

Melvin earned $54,000 of cash revenue during 2014.

Required

a. Organize the information in accounts under an accounting equation.
b. Prepare an income statement, balance sheet, and statement of cash flows for 2014.
c. Write a memo discussing the advantages to a business of arranging a line of credit.

Problem 7-34   *Effect of debt transactions on financial statements*

LO 7-1, 7-6, 7-7

Required

Show the effect of each of the following independent accounting events on the financial statements using a horizontal statements model like the following one. Use + for increase, − for decrease, and NA for not affected. The first event is recorded as an example.

Event No.	Assets	=	Liab.	+	Equity	Rev.	−	Exp.	=	Net Inc.	Cash Flow
a	+		+		NA	NA		NA		NA	+ FA

a. Borrowed funds using a line of credit.
b. Made an interest payment for funds that had been borrowed against a line of credit.
c. Issued a bond at face value.
d. Made an interest payment on a bond that had been issued at face value.
e. Made a cash payment on a note payable for both interest and principal.

Problem 7-35   *Straight-line amortization of a bond discount*

LO 7-8

Brown Co. was formed when it acquired cash from the issue of common stock. The company then issued bonds at a discount on January 1, 2014. Interest is payable on December 31 with the first payment made December 31, 2014. On January 2, 2014, Brown Co. purchased a piece of land that produced rent revenue annually. The rent is collected on December 31 of each year, beginning December 31, 2014. At the end of the six-year period (January 1, 2020), the land was sold at a gain, and the bonds were paid off at face value. A summary of the transactions for each year follows:

2014

1. Acquired cash from the issue of common stock.
2. Issued six-year bonds.
3. Purchased land.

4. Received land rental income.
5. Recognized interest expense, including the amortization of the discount, and made the cash payment for interest on December 31.

2015–2019

6. Received land rental income.
7. Recognized interest expense, including the amortization of the discount, and made the cash payment for interest December 31.

2020

8. Sold the land at a gain.
9. Retired the bonds at face value.

Required

Identify each of these nine transactions as asset source (AS), asset use (AU), asset exchange (AE), or claims exchange (CE). Explain how each event affects assets, liabilities, equity, net income, and cash flow by placing a + for increase, − for decrease, or NA for not affected under each of the categories. In the Cash Flow column, indicate whether the item is an operating activity (OA), investing activity (IA), or financing activity (FA). The first event is recorded as an example.

Event No.	Type of Event	Assets	=	Liabilities	+	Common Stock	+	Retained Earnings	Net Income	Cash Flow
1	AS	+		NA		+		NA	NA	+ FA

LO 7-8

CHECK FIGURES
c. 2014 Interest Expense: $10,625
d. 2014 Interest Paid: $6,000

Problem 7-36 *Straight-line amortization of a bond discount*

During 2014 and 2015, Cook Co. completed the following transactions relating to its bond issue. The company's fiscal year ends on December 31.

2014

Mar. 1   Issued $200,000 of eight-year, 6 percent bonds for $194,000. The semiannual cash payment for interest is due on March 1 and September 1, beginning September 2014.

Sept. 1   Recognized interest expense including the amortization of the discount and made the semiannual cash payment for interest.

Dec. 31   Recognized accrued interest expense including the amortization of the discount.

2015

Mar. 1   Recognized interest expense including the amortization of the discount and made the semiannual cash payment for interest.

Sept. 1   Recognized interest expense including the amortization of the discount and made the semiannual cash payment for interest.

Dec. 31   Recognized accrued interest expense including the amortization of the discount.

Required

a. When the bonds were issued, was the market rate of interest more or less than the stated rate of interest? If the bonds had sold at face value, what amount of cash would Cook Co. have received?
b. Prepare the liabilities section of the balance sheet at December 31, 2014 and 2015.
c. Determine the amount of interest expense Cook would report on the income statements for 2014 and 2015.
d. Determine the amount of interest Cook would pay to the bondholders in 2014 and 2015.

Problem 7-37 *Multistep income statement and classified balance sheet*

LO 7-10

Required

Use the following information to prepare a multistep income statement and a classified balance sheet for Vernon Company for 2014. (*Hint:* Some of the items will *not* appear on either statement, and ending retained earnings must be calculated.)

Operating expenses	$ 45,000	Cash	$ 46,000
Land	75,000	Interest receivable (short term)	1,600
Accumulated depreciation	46,000	Cash flow from investing activities	(96,000)
Accounts payable	35,000	Allowance for doubtful accounts	14,000
Unearned revenue	27,000	Interest payable (short term)	6,000
Warranties payable (short term)	4,500	Sales revenue	900,000
Equipment	96,000	Uncollectible accounts expense	25,000
Notes payable (long term)	140,000	Interest expense	16,000
Salvage value of equipment	10,000	Accounts receivable	88,000
Dividends	15,000	Salaries payable	48,000
Warranty expense	7,200	Supplies	4,500
Beginning retained earnings	41,100	Prepaid rent	18,000
Interest revenue	4,200	Common stock	90,000
Gain on sale of equipment	7,000	Cost of goods sold	575,000
Inventory	126,000	Salaries expense	102,000
Notes receivable (short term)	12,500	Building	110,000

Problem 7-38 *Effective interest amortization for a bond premium (Appendix)*

LO 7-11

On January 1, 2014, Pitre Incorporated issued bonds with a face value of $120,000, a stated rate of interest of 8 percent, and a five-year term to maturity. Interest is payable in cash on December 31 of each year. The effective rate of interest was 7 percent at the time the bonds were issued. The bonds sold for $124,920. Pitre used the effective interest rate method to amortize bond discount.

Required

a. Prepare an amortization table as shown below:

	Cash Payment	Interest Expense	Premium Amortization	Carrying Value
January 1, 2014				124,920
December 31, 2014	9,600	8,744	856	124,064
December 31, 2015	?	?	?	?
December 31, 2016	?	?	?	?
December 31, 2017	?	?	?	?
December 31, 2018	?	?	?	?
Totals	48,000	43,080	4,920	

b. What item(s) in the table would appear on the 2015 balance sheet?
c. What item(s) in the table would appear on the 2015 income statement?
d. What item(s) in the table would appear on the 2015 statement of cash flows?

ANALYZE, THINK, COMMUNICATE

ATC 7-1 Business Application Case *Understanding real-world annual reports*

Use the Target Corporation's Form 10-K to answer the following questions related to Target's 2012 fiscal year (year ended February 2, 2013). Target's Form 10-K is available on the company's website or through the SEC's EDGAR database. Appendix A provides instructions for using the EDGAR database. You will need to read carefully the company's Consolidated Statements of Financial Position (balance sheets) as well as footnotes 16 through 19.

Target Corporation

290   Chapter 7

Required

a. What percentage of Target's assets was being financed with liabilities (versus shareholders' equity)?

b. How does Target account for bank overdrafts, and how much overdrafts did it have as of February 2, 2013?

c. What was the average interest rate that Target paid on its borrowings?

d. Target reported Accrued and Other Liabilities of $3,981 as of February 2, 2013. What was the largest subcategory of liabilities included in this account?

ATC 7-2   Group Assignment   *Missing information*

The following three companies issued the following bonds:

1. Lot, Inc., issued $100,000 of 8 percent, five-year bonds at 102¼ on January 1, 2014. Interest is payable annually on December 31.

2. Max, Inc., issued $100,000 of 8 percent, five-year bonds at 98 on January 1, 2014. Interest is payable annually on December 31.

3. Par, Inc., issued $100,000 of 8 percent, five-year bonds at 104 on January 1, 2014. Interest is payable annually on December 31.

Required

a. Organize the class into three sections and divide each section into groups of three to five students. Assign each of the sections one of the companies.

Group Tasks

(1) Compute the following amounts for your company (use straight-line amortization):
    (a) Cash proceeds from the bond issue.
    (b) Interest paid in 2014.
    (c) Interest expense for 2014.

(2) Prepare the liabilities section of the balance sheet as of December 31, 2014.

Class Discussion

b. Have a representative of each section put the liabilities section for its company on the board.

c. Is the amount of interest expense different for the three companies? Why or why not?

d. Is the amount of interest paid different for each of the companies? Why or why not?

e. Is the amount of total liabilities different for each of the companies? Why or why not?

ATC 7-3   Research Assignment   *Analyzing two real-world companies' use of liabilities*

Complete the requirements below using the most current annual reports or the Forms 10-K for Lowe's, a company that sells home-building supplies, and Dominion Resources, one of the nation's leading generators of energy. To obtain the Forms 10-K, use either the EDGAR system following the instructions in Appendix A or the companies' websites. The annual reports can be found on the companies' websites.

Required

a. Which of these two companies is using debt to finance its assets the most? Show your computations.

b. Provide a logical explanation as to why one of these companies uses more debt to finance its assets than the other.

c. Lowe's has some lines of credit type arrangements? How much money is available to Lowe's under these credit arrangements?

ATC 7-4   Writing Assignment   *Definition of elements of financial statements*

Putting "yum" on people's faces around the world is the mission of YUM Brands, Inc. Yum was spun off from PepsiCo in 1997. A spin-off occurs when a company separates its operations into two or more distinct companies. The company was originally composed of KFC, Pizza Hut, and Taco Bell and was operated as a part of PepsiCo prior to the spin-off. YUM's long-term debt in 2012 was $2.9 billion. YUM's net income before interest and taxes in 2012 was $1.69 million.

Required

a. If YUM's debt remains constant at $2.9 billion for 2013, how much interest will YUM incur in 2013, assuming the average interest rate is 6 percent?

b. Does the debt seem excessive compared with the amount of 2012 net income before interest and taxes? Explain.

c. Assuming YUM pays tax at the rate of 25 percent, what amount of tax will YUM pay in 2012?

d. Assume you are the president of the company. Write a memo to the shareholders explaining how YUM is able to meet its obligations and increase stockholders' equity.

ATC 7-5   Ethical Dilemma   *Sometimes debt is not debt*

David Sheridan was a well-respected CPA in his mid-fifties. After spending 10 years at a national accounting firm, he was hired by Global, Inc., a multinational corporation headquartered in the United States. He patiently worked his way up to the top of Global's accounting department, and in the early 1990s, took over as chief financial officer for the company. As the Internet began to explode, management at Global, Inc., decided to radically change the nature of its business to one of e-commerce. Two years after the transition, Internet commerce began to slow down, and Global was in dire need of cash in order to continue operations. Management turned to the accounting department.

Global, Inc., needed to borrow a substantial amount of money but couldn't afford to increase the amount of liabilities on the balance sheet for fear of the stock price dropping and banks becoming nervous and demanding repayment of existing loans. David discovered a way that would allow the company to raise the needed cash to continue operations without having to report the long-term notes payable on the balance sheet. Under an obscure rule, companies can set up separate legal organizations that do not have to be reported on the parent company's financial statements, if a third party contributes just 3 percent of the start-up capital. David called a friend, Brian Johnson, and asked him to participate in a business venture with Global. Brian agreed, and created a special purpose entity with Global named BrianCo. For his participation, Brian was awarded a substantial amount of valuable Global stock. Brian then went to a bank and used the stock as collateral to borrow a large sum of money for BrianCo. Then, Global sold some of its poor or underperforming assets to BrianCo for the cash that Brian borrowed. In the end, Global got rid of bad assets, received the proceeds of the long-term note payable, and did not have to show the liability on the balance sheet. Only the top executives and the accountants that worked closely with David knew of the scheme, and they planned to use this method only until the e-commerce portion of Global became profitable again.

Required

a. How did David's scheme affect the overall appearance of Global's financial statements? Why was this important to investors and creditors?

b. Review the AICPA's Articles of Professional Conduct (see Chapter 4) and comment on any of the standards that have been violated.

c. Name the features of the fraud triangle and explain how they materialize in this case.

CHAPTER 8

Proprietorships, Partnerships, and Corporations

LEARNING OBJECTIVES

After you have mastered the material in this chapter, you will be able to:

LO 8-1	Identify the primary characteristics of sole proprietorships, partnerships, and corporations.
LO 8-2	Analyze financial statements to identify the different types of business organizations.
LO 8-3	Explain the characteristics of major types of stock issued by corporations.
LO 8-4	Explain how to account for different types of stock issued by corporations.
LO 8-5	Show how treasury stock transactions affect a company's financial statements.
LO 8-6	Explain the effects of declaring and paying cash dividends on a company's financial statements.
LO 8-7	Explain the effects of stock dividends and stock splits on a company's financial statements.
LO 8-8	Show how the appropriation of retained earnings affects financial statements.
LO 8-9	Explain some uses of accounting information in making stock investment decisions.

 Video lectures and accompanying self-assessment quizzes are available for all learning objectives through McGraw-Hill Connect® Accounting.

CHAPTER OPENING

You want to start a business. How should you structure it? Should it be a sole proprietorship, partnership, or corporation? Each form of business structure presents advantages and disadvantages. For example, a sole proprietorship allows maximum independence and control while partnerships and corporations allow individuals to pool resources and talents with other people. This chapter discusses these and other features of the three primary forms of business structure.

The Curious Accountant

Imagine your rich uncle rewarded you for doing well in your first accounting course by giving you $10,000 to invest in the stock of one company. After reviewing many recent annual reports, you narrowed your choice to two companies with the following characteristics:

Mystery Company A: This company began operations in 2003, but did not begin selling its stock to the public until June 28, 2010. It has lost money every year it has been in existence, and by December 31, 2012, it had total lifetime losses of approximately $1 billion. Even so, its products have received lots of attention from the media and celebrities. At its current price of $35 you could buy 286 shares. A friend told you that a status-conscious person like you should at least buy this company's stock, since you cannot afford its products.

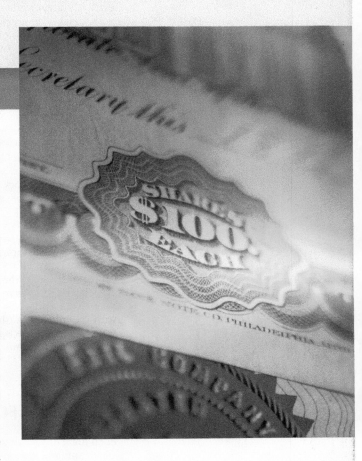

Mystery Company B: This company has been in existence since 1883 and has made a profit most years. In its 2012 fiscal year alone its net earnings were $1.5 billion, and it paid dividends of $267 million. Unlike Company A, Company B sells items that everyone needs and can afford. Its stock is selling for about $32 per share, so you can buy around 312 shares. Your friend said that buying this company's stock would be the most boring investment you would ever make.

The names of the real-world companies described above are disclosed later. Based on the information provided, which company's stock would you buy? (Answer on page 296.)

LO 8-1

Identify the primary characteristics of sole proprietorships, partnerships, and corporations.

FORMS OF BUSINESS ORGANIZATIONS

Sole proprietorships are owned by a single individual who is responsible for making business and profit distribution decisions. If you want to be the absolute master of your destiny, you should organize your business as a proprietorship. Establishing a sole proprietorship is usually as simple as obtaining a business license from local government authorities. Usually no legal ownership agreement is required.

Partnerships allow persons to share their talents, capital, and the risks and rewards of business ownership. Because two or more individuals share ownership, partnerships require clear agreements about how authority, risks, and profits will be shared. Prudent partners minimize misunderstandings by hiring attorneys to prepare a **partnership agreement** which defines the responsibilities of each partner and describes how income or losses will be divided. Because the measurement of income affects the distribution of profits, partnerships frequently hire accountants to ensure that records are maintained in accordance with generally accepted accounting principles (GAAP). Partnerships (and sole proprietorships) also may need professional advice to deal with tax issues.

A **corporation** is a separate legal entity created by the authority of a state government. The paperwork to start a corporation is complex. For most laypersons, engaging professional attorneys and accountants to assist with the paperwork is well worth the fees charged.

Each state has separate laws governing establishing corporations. Many states follow the standard provisions of the Model Business Corporation Act. All states require the initial application to provide **articles of incorporation,** which normally include the following information: (1) the corporation's name and proposed date of incorporation; (2) the purpose of the corporation; (3) the location of the business and its expected life (which can be *perpetuity,* meaning *endless*); (4) provisions for capital stock; and (5) the names and addresses of the members of the first board of directors, the individuals with the ultimate authority for operating the business. If the articles are in order, the state establishes the legal existence of the corporation by issuing a charter of incorporation. The charter and the articles are public documents.

ADVANTAGES AND DISADVANTAGES OF DIFFERENT FORMS OF BUSINESS ORGANIZATION

Each form of business organization presents a different combination of advantages and disadvantages. Persons wanting to start a business or invest in one should consider the characteristics of each type of business structure.

Regulation

Few laws specifically affect the operations of proprietorships and partnerships. Corporations, however, are usually heavily regulated. The extent of government regulation depends on the size and distribution of a company's ownership interests. Ownership interests in corporations are normally evidenced by **stock certificates.**

Ownership of corporations can be transferred from one individual to another through exchanging stock certificates. As long as the exchanges (buying and selling of shares of stock, often called *trading*) are limited to transactions between individuals, a company is defined as a **closely held corporation.** However, once a corporation reaches a certain size, it may list its stock on a stock exchange such as the New York Stock Exchange or the NASDAQ. Trading on a stock exchange is limited to the stockbrokers who are members of the exchange. These brokers represent buyers and sellers who are willing to pay the brokers commissions for exchanging stock certificates on their behalf. Although closely held corporations are relatively free from government regulation, companies whose stock is publicly traded on the exchanges by brokers are subject to extensive regulation.

The extensive regulation of trading on stock exchanges began in the 1930s. The stock market crash of 1929 and the subsequent Great Depression led Congress to pass the **Securities Act of 1933** and the **Securities Exchange Act of 1934** to regulate issuing stock and to govern the exchanges. The 1934 act also created the Securities and Exchange Commission (SEC) to enforce the securities laws. Congress gave the SEC legal authority to establish accounting principles for corporations that are registered on the exchanges. However, the SEC has generally deferred its rule-making authority to private sector accounting bodies such as the Financial Accounting Standards Board (FASB), effectively allowing the accounting profession to regulate itself.

A number of high-profile business failures around the turn of the last century raised questions about the effectiveness of self-regulation and the usefulness of audits to protect the public. The Sarbanes-Oxley Act of 2002 was adopted to address these concerns. The act creates a five-member Public Company Accounting Oversight Board (PCAOB) with the authority to set and enforce auditing, attestation, quality control, and ethics standards for auditors of public companies. The PCAOB is empowered to impose disciplinary and remedial sanctions for violations of its rules, securities laws, and professional auditing and accounting standards. Public corporations operate in a complex regulatory environment that requires the services of attorneys and professional accountants.

Double Taxation

Corporations pay income taxes on their earnings and then owners pay income taxes on distributions (dividends) received from corporations. As a result, distributed corporate profits are taxed twice—first when income is reported on the corporation's income tax return and a second time when distributions are reported on individual owners' tax returns. This phenomenon is commonly called **double taxation** and is a significant disadvantage of the corporate form of business organization.

To illustrate, assume Glide Corporation earns pretax income of $100,000. Glide is in a 30 percent tax bracket. The corporation itself will pay income tax of $30,000 ($100,000 × 0.30). If the corporation distributes the after-tax income of $70,000 ($100,000 − $30,000) to individual stockholders in 15 percent tax brackets, the $70,000 dividend will be reported on the individual tax returns, requiring tax payments of $10,500 ($70,000 × .15). Total income tax of $40,500 ($30,000 + $10,500) is due on $100,000 of earned income. In contrast, consider a proprietorship that is owned by an individual in a 30 percent tax bracket. If the proprietorship earns and distributes $100,000 profit, the total tax would be only $30,000 ($100,000 × .30).

Double taxation can be a burden for small companies. To reduce that burden, tax laws permit small closely held corporations to elect "S Corporation" status. S Corporations are taxed as proprietorships or partnerships. Also, many states have recently enacted laws permitting the formation of **limited liability companies (LLCs),** which offer many of the benefits of corporate ownership yet are in general taxed as partnerships. Because proprietorships and partnerships are not separate legal entities, company earnings are taxable to the owners rather than the company itself.

Limited Liability

Given the disadvantages of increased regulation and double taxation, why would anyone choose the corporate form of business structure over a partnership or proprietorship? A major reason is that the corporate form limits an investor's potential liability as an owner of a business venture. Because a corporation is legally separate from its owners, creditors cannot claim owners' personal assets as payment for the company's debts. Also, plaintiffs must sue the corporation, not its owners. The most that owners of a

Answers to The Curious Accountant

Mystery Company A is Tesla Motors, Inc., as of March 20, 2013. The company's original product was the Tesla Roadster. The Roadster is an electric-only sports car that can go from 0 to 60 miles per hour in under 4 seconds; reach a top speed of 125 MPH, and go up to 245 miles before having to recharge its batteries. It cost over $100,000. The company sold its first car in 2008, and had sold around 2,500 cars by the end of 2012, the year in which it ended production of the Roadster. In 2012 it began selling a second model of car named the Model S, 2,700 units of which had been sold by the end of that year. Tesla also supplies electric car components to Daimler and Toyota.

Mystery Company B is Kroger Company, as of March 20, 2013. Of course, only the future will tell which company will be the better investment.

corporation can lose is the amount they have invested in the company (the value of the company's stock).

Unlike corporate stockholders, the owners of proprietorships and partnerships are *personally liable* for actions they take in the name of their companies. In fact, partners are responsible not only for their own actions but also for those taken by any other partner on behalf of the partnership. The benefit of **limited liability** is one of the most significant reasons the corporate form of business organization is so popular.

Continuity

Unlike partnerships or proprietorships, which terminate with the departure of their owners, a corporation's life continues when a shareholder dies or sells his or her stock. Because of **continuity** of existence, many corporations formed in the 1800s still thrive today.

Transferability of Ownership

The **transferability** of corporate ownership is easy. An investor simply buys or sells stock to acquire or give up an ownership interest in a corporation. Hundreds of millions of shares of stock are bought and sold on the major stock exchanges each day.

Transferring the ownership of proprietorships is much more difficult. To sell an ownership interest in a proprietorship, the proprietor must find someone willing to purchase the entire business. Because most proprietors also run their businesses, transferring ownership also requires transferring management responsibilities. Consider the difference in selling $1 million of ExxonMobil stock versus selling a locally owned gas station. The stock could be sold on the New York Stock Exchange within minutes. In contrast, it could take years to find a buyer who is financially capable of and interested in owning and operating a gas station.

Transferring ownership in partnerships can also be difficult. As with proprietorships, ownership transfers may require a new partner to make a significant investment and accept management responsibilities in the business. Further, a new partner must accept and be accepted by the other partners. Personality conflicts and differences in management style can cause problems in transferring ownership interests in partnerships.

Management Structure

Partnerships and proprietorships are usually managed by their owners. Corporations, in contrast, have three tiers of management authority. The *owners* (**stockholders**) represent the highest level of organizational authority. The stockholders *elect* a **board of directors** to oversee company operations. The directors then *hire* professional executives to manage the company on a daily basis. Because large corporations can offer high salaries and challenging career opportunities, they can often attract superior managerial talent.

While the management structure used by corporations is generally effective, it sometimes complicates dismissing incompetent managers. The chief executive officer (CEO) is usually a member of the board of directors and is frequently influential in choosing other board members. The CEO is also in a position to reward loyal board members. As a result, board members may be reluctant to fire the CEO or other top executives even if the individuals are performing poorly. Corporations operating under such conditions are said to be experiencing **entrenched management.**

Ability to Raise Capital

Because corporations can have millions of owners (shareholders), they have the opportunity to raise huge amounts of capital. Few individuals have the financial means to build and operate a telecommunications network such as AT&T or a marketing distribution system such as Walmart. However, by pooling the resources of millions of owners through public stock and bond offerings, corporations generate the billions of dollars of capital needed for such massive investments. In contrast, the capital resources of proprietorships and partnerships are limited to a relatively small number of private owners. Although proprietorships and partnerships can also obtain resources by borrowing, the amount creditors are willing to lend them is usually limited by the size of the owners' net worth.

APPEARANCE OF CAPITAL STRUCTURE IN FINANCIAL STATEMENTS

The ownership interest (equity) in a business is composed of two elements: (1) owner/investor contributions and (2) retained earnings. The way these two elements are reported in the financial statements differs for each type of business structure (proprietorship, partnership, or corporation).

Analyze financial statements to identify the different types of business organizations.

Presentation of Equity in Proprietorships

Owner contributions and retained earnings are combined in a single capital account on the balance sheets of proprietorships. To illustrate, assume that Worthington Sole Proprietorship was started on January 1, 2014, when it acquired a $5,000 capital contribution from its owner, Phil Worthington. During the first year of operation, the company generated $4,000 of cash revenues, incurred $2,500 of cash expenses, and distributed $1,000 cash to the owner. Exhibit 8.1 displays 2012 financial statements for Worthington's company. Note on the *capital statement* that distributions are called **withdrawals.** Verify that the $5,500 balance in the capital account on the balance sheet includes the $5,000 owner contribution and the retained earnings of $500 ($1,500 net income − $1,000 withdrawal).

EXHIBIT 8.1

WORTHINGTON SOLE PROPRIETORSHIP
Financial Statements
As of December 31, 2014

Income Statement		Capital Statement		Balance Sheet	
Revenue	$4,000	Beginning capital balance	$ 0	Assets	
Expenses	2,500	Plus: Investment by owner	5,000	Cash	$5,500
Net income	$1,500	Plus: Net income	1,500	Equity	
		Less: Withdrawal by owner	(1,000)	Worthington, capital	$5,500
		Ending capital balance	$5,500		

☑ **CHECK YOURSELF 8.1**

Weiss Company was started on January 1, 2014, when it acquired $50,000 cash from its owner(s). During 2014 the company earned $72,000 of net income. Explain how the equity section of Weiss's December 31, 2014, balance sheet would differ if the company were a proprietorship versus a corporation.

Answer *Proprietorship* records combine capital acquisitions from the owner and earnings from operating the business in a single capital account. In contrast, *corporation* records separate capital acquisitions from the owners and earnings from operating the business. If Weiss were a proprietorship, the equity section of the year-end balance sheet would report a single capital component of $122,000. If Weiss were a corporation, the equity section would report two separate equity components, most likely common stock of $50,000 and retained earnings of $72,000.

Presentation of Equity in Partnerships

The financial statement format for reporting partnership equity is similar to that used for proprietorships. Contributed capital and retained earnings are combined. However, a separate capital account is maintained for each partner in the business to reflect each partner's ownership interest.

To illustrate, assume that Sara Slater and Jill Johnson formed a partnership on January 1, 2014. The partnership acquired $2,000 of capital from Slater and $4,000 from Johnson. The partnership agreement called for each partner to receive an annual distribution equal to 10 percent of her capital contribution. Any further earnings were to be retained in the business and divided equally between the partners. During 2014, the company earned $5,000 of cash revenue and incurred $3,000 of cash expenses, for net income of $2,000 ($5,000 − $3,000). As specified by the partnership agreement, Slater received a $200 ($2,000 × 0.10) cash withdrawal and Johnson received $400 ($4,000 × 0.10). The remaining $1,400 ($2,000 − $200 − $400) of income was retained in the business and divided equally, adding $700 to each partner's capital account.

Exhibit 8.2 displays financial statements for the Slater and Johnson partnership. Again, note that distributions are called *withdrawals*. Also find on the balance sheet a *separate capital account* for each partner. Each capital account includes the amount of the partner's contributed capital plus her proportionate share of the retained earnings.

EXHIBIT 8.2

SLATER AND JOHNSON PARTNERSHIP
Financial Statements
As of December 31, 2014

Income Statement		Capital Statement		Balance Sheet	
Revenue	$5,000	Beginning capital balance	$ 0	Assets	
Expenses	3,000	Plus: Investment by owners	6,000	Cash	$7,400
Net income	$2,000	Plus: Net income	2,000	Equity	
		Less: Withdrawal by owners	(600)	Slater, capital	$2,700
		Ending capital balance	$7,400	Johnson, capital	4,700
				Total capital	$7,400

Presentation of Equity in Corporations

Corporations have more complex capital structures than proprietorships and partnerships. Explanations of some of the more common features of corporate capital structures and transactions follow.

CHARACTERISTICS OF CAPITAL STOCK

Stock issued by corporations may have a variety of different characteristics. For example, a company may issue different classes of stock that grant owners different rights and privileges. Also, the number of shares a corporation can legally issue may differ from the number it actually has issued. Further, a corporation can even buy back its own stock. Finally, a corporation may assign different values to the stock it issues. Accounting for corporate equity transactions is discussed in the next section of the text.

LO 8-3

Explain the characteristics of major types of stock issued by corporations.

Par Value

Many states require assigning a **par value** to stock. Historically, par value represented the maximum liability of the investors. Par value multiplied by the number of shares of stock issued represents the minimum amount of assets that must be retained in the company as protection for creditors. This amount is known as **legal capital.** To ensure that the amount of legal capital is maintained in a corporation, many states require that purchasers pay at least the par value for a share of stock initially purchased from a corporation. To minimize the amount of assets that owners must maintain in the business, many corporations issue stock with very low par values, often $1 or less. Therefore, *legal capital* as defined by par value has come to have very little relevance to investors or creditors. As a result, many states allow corporations to issue no-par stock.

Stated Value

No-par stock may have a stated value. Like par value, **stated value** is an arbitrary amount assigned by the board of directors to the stock. It also has little relevance to investors and creditors. Stock with a par value and stock with a stated value are accounted for exactly the same way. When stock has no par or stated value, accounting for it is slightly different. These accounting differences are illustrated later in this chapter.

Other Valuation Terminology

The price an investor must pay to purchase a share of stock is the **market value.** The sales price of a share of stock may be more or less than the par value. Another term analysts frequently associate with stock is *book value.* **Book value per share** is calculated by dividing total stockholders' equity (assets − liabilities) by the number of shares of stock owned by investors. Book value per share differs from market value per share because equity is measured in historical dollars and market value reflects investors' estimates of a company's current value.

Stock: Authorized, Issued, and Outstanding

As part of the regulatory function, states approve the maximum number of shares of stock corporations are legally permitted to issue. This maximum number is called **authorized stock.** Authorized stock that has been sold to the public is called **issued stock.** When a corporation buys back some of its issued stock from the public, the repurchased stock is called **treasury stock.** Treasury stock is still considered to be issued stock, but it is no longer outstanding. **Outstanding stock** (total issued stock minus treasury stock) is stock owned by investors outside the corporation. For example, assume a company that is authorized to issue 150 shares of stock issues 100 shares to investors,

FOCUS ON INTERNATIONAL ISSUES

PICKY, PICKY, PICKY ...

Considering the almost countless number of differences that could exist between U.S. GAAP and IFRS, it is not surprising that some of those that do exist relate to very specific issues. Consider the case of the timing of stock splits.

Assume a company that ends its fiscal year on December 31, 2014, declares a 2-for-1 stock split on January 15, 2015, before it has issued its 2014 annual report. Should the company apply the effects of the stock split retroactively to its 2014 financial statements, or begin showing the effects of the split on its 2015 statements? Under U.S. GAAP the split must be applied retroactively to the 2014 statements since they had not been issued at the time of the split. Under IFRS the 2014 statements would not show the effects of the split, but the 2015 statements would. By the way, an event that occurs between a company's fiscal year-end and the date its annual report is released is called a *subsequent event* by accountants.

Obviously no one can know every GAAP rule, much less all of the differences between GAAP and IFRS. This is why it is important to learn how to find answers to specific accounting questions as well as to develop an understanding of the basic accounting rules. Most important, if you are not sure you know the answer, do not assume you do.

and then buys back 20 shares of treasury stock. There are 150 shares authorized, 100 shares issued, and 80 shares outstanding.

Classes of Stock

The corporate charter defines the number of shares of stock authorized, the par value or stated value (if any), and the classes of stock that a corporation can issue. Most stock issued is either *common* or *preferred*.

Common Stock

All corporations issue **common stock.** Common stockholders bear the highest risk of losing their investment if a company is forced to liquidate. On the other hand, they reap the greatest rewards when a corporation prospers. Common stockholders generally enjoy several rights, including: (1) the right to buy and sell stock, (2) the right to share in the distribution of profits, (3) the right to share in the distribution of corporate assets in the case of liquidation, (4) the right to vote on significant matters that affect the corporate charter, and (5) the right to participate in the election of directors.

Preferred Stock

Many corporations issue **preferred stock** in addition to common stock. Holders of preferred stock receive certain privileges relative to holders of common stock. In exchange for special privileges in some areas, preferred stockholders give up rights in other areas. Preferred stockholders usually have no voting rights and the amount of their dividends is usually limited. Preferences granted to preferred stockholders include the following.

1. *Preference as to assets.* Preferred stock often has a liquidation value. In case of bankruptcy, preferred stockholders must be paid the liquidation value before any assets are distributed to common stockholders. However, preferred stockholder claims still fall behind creditor claims.

2. *Preference as to dividends.* Preferred shareholders are frequently guaranteed the right to receive dividends before common stockholders. The amount of the preferred dividend is normally stated on the stock certificate. It may be stated as a

dollar value (say, $5) per share or as a percentage of the par value. Most preferred stock has **cumulative dividends,** meaning that if a corporation is unable to pay the preferred dividend in any year, the dividend is not lost but begins to accumulate. Cumulative dividends that have not been paid are called **dividends in arrears.** When a company pays dividends, any preferred stock arrearages must be paid before any other dividends are paid. Noncumulative preferred stock is not often issued because preferred stock is much less attractive if missed dividends do not accumulate.

To illustrate the effects of preferred dividends, consider Dillion, Incorporated, which has the following shares of stock outstanding.

Preferred stock, 4%, $10 par, 10,000 shares
Common stock, $10 par, 20,000 shares

Assume the preferred stock dividend has not been paid for two years. If Dillion pays $22,000 in dividends, how much will each class of stock receive? It depends on whether the preferred stock is cumulative.

Allocation of Distribution for Cumulative Preferred Stock		
	To Preferred	**To Common**
Dividends in arrears	$ 8,000	$ 0
Current year's dividends	4,000	10,000
Total distribution	$12,000	$10,000

Allocation of Distribution for Noncumulative Preferred Stock		
	To Preferred	**To Common**
Dividends in arrears	$ 0	$ 0
Current year's dividends	4,000	18,000
Total distribution	$4,000	$18,000

The total annual dividend on the preferred stock is $4,000 (0.04 × $10 par × 10,000 shares). If the preferred stock is cumulative, the $8,000 in arrears must be paid first. Then $4,000 for the current year's dividend is paid next. The remaining $10,000 goes to common stockholders. If the preferred stock is noncumulative, the $8,000 of dividends from past periods is ignored. This year's $4,000 preferred dividend is paid first, with the remaining $18,000 going to common.

Other features of preferred stock may include the right to participate in distributions beyond the established amount of the preferred dividend, the right to convert preferred stock to common stock or to bonds, and the potential for having the preferred stock called (repurchased) by the corporation. Detailed discussion of these topics is left to more advanced courses. Exhibit 8.3 indicates that roughly 25 percent of U.S. companies have preferred shares outstanding.

EXHIBIT 8.3

Presence of Preferred Stock in the Capital Structure of U.S. Companies

With preferred stock
25%

Without preferred stock
75%

Data Source: AICPA, *Accounting Trends and Techniques,* 2006.

ACCOUNTING FOR STOCK TRANSACTIONS ON THE DAY OF ISSUE

LO 8-4

Explain how to account for different types of stock issued by corporations.

Issuing stock with a par or stated value is accounted for differently from issuing no-par stock. For stock with either a par or stated value, the total amount acquired from the owners is divided between two separate equity accounts. The amount of the par or stated value is recorded in the stock account. Any amount received above the par or stated value is recorded in an account called **Paid-in Capital in Excess of Par** (or **Stated**) **Value.**

Issuing Par Value Stock

To illustrate the issue of common stock with a par value, assume that Nelson Incorporated is authorized to issue 250 shares of common stock. During 2014, Nelson issued 100 shares of $10 par common stock for $22 per share. The event increases assets and stockholders' equity by $2,200 ($22 × 100 shares). The increase in stockholders' equity is divided into two parts, $1,000 of par value ($10 per share × 100 shares) and $1,200 ($2,200 − $1,000) received in excess of par value. The income statement is not affected. The $2,200 cash inflow is reported in the financing activities section of the statement of cash flows. The effects on the financial statements follow.

Assets	=	Liab.	+	Equity			Rev.	−	Exp.	=	Net Inc.	Cash Flow	
Cash	=			Com. Stk.	+	PIC in Excess							
2,200	=	NA	+	1,000	+	1,200	NA	−	NA	=	NA	2,200	FA

The *legal capital* of the corporation is $1,000, the total par value of the issued common stock. The number of shares issued can be easily verified by dividing the total amount in the common stock account by the par value ($1,000 ÷ $10 = 100 shares).

Stock Classification

Assume Nelson Incorporated obtains authorization to issue 400 shares of Class B, $20 par value common stock. The company issues 150 shares of this stock at $25 per share. The event increases assets and stockholders' equity by $3,750 ($25 × 150 shares). The increase in stockholders' equity is divided into two parts, $3,000 of par value ($20 per share × 150 shares) and $750 ($3,750 − $3,000) received in excess of par value. The income statement is not affected. The $3,750 cash inflow is reported in the financing activities section of the statement of cash flows. The effects on the financial statements follow.

Assets	=	Liab.	+	Equity			Rev.	−	Exp.	=	Net Inc.	Cash Flow	
Cash	=			Com. Stk.	+	PIC in Excess							
3,750	=	NA	+	3,000	+	750	NA	−	NA	=	NA	3,750	FA

As the preceding event suggests, companies can issue numerous classes of common stock. The specific rights and privileges for each class are described in the individual stock certificates.

Stock Issued at Stated Value

Assume Nelson is authorized to issue 300 shares of a third class of stock, 7 percent cumulative preferred stock with a stated value of $10 per share. Nelson issued 100 shares of the preferred stock at a price of $22 per share. The effects on the financial statements are identical to those described for the issue of the $10 par value common stock.

Assets	=	Liab.	+		Equity			Rev.	−	Exp.	=	Net Inc.		Cash Flow	
Cash	=			Pfd. Stk.	+	PIC in Excess									
2,200	=	NA	+	1,000	+	1,200		NA	−	NA	=	NA		2,200	FA

Stock Issued with No Par Value

Assume that Nelson Incorporated is authorized to issue 150 shares of a fourth class of stock. This stock is no-par common stock. Nelson issues 100 shares of this no-par stock at $22 per share. The entire amount received ($22 × 100 = $2,200) is recorded in the stock account. The effects on the financial statements follow.

Assets	=	Liab.	+		Equity			Rev.	−	Exp.	=	Net Inc.		Cash Flow	
Cash	=			Com. Stk.	+	PIC in Excess									
2,200	=	NA	+	2,200	+	NA		NA	−	NA	=	NA		2,200	FA

Financial Statement Presentation

Exhibit 8.4 displays Nelson Incorporated's balance sheet after the four stock issuances described above. The exhibit assumes that Nelson earned and retained $5,000 of cash income during 2014. The stock accounts are presented first, followed by the paid-in capital in excess of par (or stated) value accounts. A wide variety of reporting formats is used in practice. For example, another popular format is to group accounts by stock class, with the paid-in capital in excess accounts listed with their associated stock accounts. Alternatively, many companies combine the different classes of stock into a single amount and provide the detailed information in notes to the financial statements.

EXHIBIT 8.4

NELSON INCORPORATED
Balance Sheet
As of December 31, 2014

Assets	
Cash	$15,350
Stockholders' equity	
Preferred stock, $10 stated value, 7% cumulative,	
300 shares authorized, 100 issued and outstanding	$ 1,000
Common stock, $10 par value, 250 shares authorized,	
100 issued and outstanding	1,000
Common stock, class B, $20 par value, 400 shares	
authorized, 150 issued and outstanding	3,000
Common stock, no par, 150 shares authorized,	
100 issued and outstanding	2,200
Paid-in capital in excess of stated value—preferred	1,200
Paid-in capital in excess of par value—common	1,200
Paid-in capital in excess of par value—class B common	750
Total paid-in capital	10,350
Retained earnings	5,000
Total stockholders' equity	$15,350

304   Chapter 8

STOCKHOLDERS' EQUITY TRANSACTIONS AFTER THE DAY OF ISSUE

Treasury Stock

When a company buys its own stock, the stock purchased is called *treasury stock*. Why would a company buy its own stock? Common reasons include (1) to have stock available to give employees pursuant to stock option plans, (2) to accumulate stock in preparation for a merger or business combination, (3) to reduce the number of shares outstanding in order to increase earnings per share, (4) to keep the price of the stock high when it appears to be falling, and (5) to avoid a hostile takeover (removing shares from the open market reduces the opportunity for outsiders to obtain enough voting shares to gain control of the company).

Conceptually, purchasing treasury stock is the reverse of issuing stock. When a business issues stock, the assets and equity of the business increase. When a business buys treasury stock, the assets and equity of the business decrease. To illustrate, return to the Nelson Incorporated example. Assume that in 2015 Nelson paid $20 per share to buy back 50 shares of the $10 par value common stock that it originally issued at $22 per share. The purchase of treasury stock is an asset use transaction. Assets and stockholders' equity decrease by the cost of the purchase ($20 × 50 shares = $1,000). The income statement is not affected. The cash outflow is reported in the financing activities section of the statement of cash flows. The effects on the financial statements follow.

Assets	=	Liab.	+	Equity			Rev.	−	Exp.	=	Net Inc.	Cash Flow
Cash	=			Other Equity Accts.	−	Treasury Stk.						
(1,000)	=	NA	+	NA	−	1,000	NA	−	NA	=	NA	(1,000) FA

The Treasury Stock account is a contra equity account. It is deducted from the other equity accounts in determining total stockholders' equity. In this example, the Treasury Stock account contains the full amount paid ($1,000). The original issue price and the par value of the stock have no effect on the Treasury Stock account. Recognizing the full amount paid in the treasury stock account is called the **cost method of accounting for treasury stock** transactions. Although other methods could be used, the cost method is the most common.

Assume Nelson reissues 30 shares of treasury stock at a price of $25 per share. As with any other stock issue, the sale of treasury stock is an asset source transaction. In this case, assets and stockholders' equity increase by $750 ($25 × 30 shares). The income statement is not affected. The cash inflow is reported in the financing activities section of the statement of cash flows. The effects on the financial statements follow.

Assets	=	Liab.	+	Equity					Rev.	−	Exp.	=	Net Inc.	Cash Flow
Cash	=			Other Equity Accounts	−	Treasury Stock	+	PIC from Treasury Stk.						
750	=	NA	+	NA	−	(600)	+	150	NA	−	NA	=	NA	750 FA

The decrease in the Treasury Stock account increases stockholders' equity. The $150 difference between the cost of the treasury stock ($20 per share × 30 shares = $600) and the sales price ($750) is *not* reported as a gain. The sale of treasury stock is a capital acquisition, not a revenue transaction. The $150 is additional paid-in capital. *Corporations do not recognize gains or losses on the sale of treasury stock.*

After selling 30 shares of treasury stock, 20 shares remain in Nelson's possession. These shares cost $20 each, so the balance in the Treasury Stock account is now $400 ($20 × 20 shares). Treasury stock is reported on the balance sheet directly below retained earnings. Although this placement suggests that treasury stock reduces retained earnings, the reduction actually applies to the entire stockholders' equity section. Exhibit 8.5 on page 308 shows the presentation of treasury stock in the balance sheet.

 CHECK YOURSELF 8.2

On January 1, 2014, Janell Company's Common Stock account balance was $20,000. On April 1, 2014, Janell paid $12,000 cash to purchase some of its own stock. Janell resold this stock on October 1, 2014, for $14,500. What is the effect on the company's cash and stockholders' equity from both the April 1 purchase and the October 1 resale of the stock?

Answer   The April 1 purchase would reduce both cash and stockholders' equity by $12,000. The treasury stock transaction represents a return of invested capital to those owners who sold stock back to the company.

The sale of the treasury stock on October 1 would increase both cash and stockholders' equity by $14,500. The difference between the sales price of the treasury stock and its cost ($14,500 − $12,000) represents additional paid-in capital from treasury stock transactions. The stockholders' equity section of the balance sheet would include Common Stock, $20,000, and Additional Paid-in Capital from Treasury Stock Transactions, $2,500.

Cash Dividend

Cash dividends are affected by three significant dates: *the declaration date, the date of record,* and *the payment date.* Assume that on October 15, 2015, the board of Nelson Incorporated declared a 7 percent cash dividend on the 100 outstanding shares of its $10 stated value preferred stock. The dividend will be paid to stockholders of record as of November 15, 2015. The cash payment will be made on December 15, 2015.

LO 8-6

 Explain the effects of declaring and paying cash dividends on a company's financial statements.

Declaration Date

Although corporations are not required to declare dividends, they are legally obligated to pay dividends once they have been declared. They must recognize a liability on the **declaration date** (in this case, October 15, 2015). The increase in liabilities is accompanied by a decrease in retained earnings. The income statement and statement of cash flows are not affected. The effects on the financial statements of *declaring* the $70 (0.07 × $10 × 100 shares) dividend follow.

Assets	=	Liab.	+		Equity		Rev.	−	Exp.	=	Net Inc.	Cash Flow
Cash	=	Div. Pay.	+	Com. Stk.	+	Ret. Earn.						
NA	=	70	+	NA	+	(70)	NA	−	NA	=	NA	NA

Date of Record

Cash dividends are paid to investors who owned the preferred stock on the **date of record** (in this case November 15, 2015). Any stock sold after the date of record but

306   Chapter 8

REALITY BYTES

As you have learned, dividends, unlike interest on bonds, do not have to be paid. In fact, a company's board of directors must vote to pay dividends before they can be paid. Even so, once a company establishes a practice of paying a dividend of a given amount each period, usually quarterly, the company is reluctant to not pay the dividend. The amount of dividends that companies pay, relative to their earnings, varies widely.

Large, well-established companies usually do pay dividends, while young, growing companies often do not. Consider the 30 companies that make up the Dow Jones Industrials Average group. In 2012, 29 of these companies paid dividends. The only one that did not was General Motors, and it was still trying to repay money it received from the U.S. government during the recession of 2008–2009. Of the remaining 29 companies, UnitedHealth Group paid the lowest percentage of its earnings out in dividends (14.8 percent). At the other extreme, in 2012 Verizon Communications paid $5.98 of dividends for every $1.00 it had in earnings. The average percentage of earnings paid out as dividends for all 30 companies in the Dow was 60.9 percent.

For comparison, consider two large, relatively young, technology companies: Google and Facebook. Although both of these companies have had positive earnings in recent years—Google alone had $10.7 billion of earnings in 2012—neither has ever paid a dividend to its common shareholders. They are using their cash to grow their businesses, often by purchasing other companies.

before the payment date (in this case December 15, 2015) is traded **ex-dividend,** meaning the buyer will not receive the upcoming dividend. The date of record is merely a cutoff date. It does not affect the financial statements.

Payment Date

Nelson actually paid the cash dividend on the **payment date.** This event has the same effect as paying any other liability. Assets (cash) and liabilities (dividends payable) both decrease. The income statement is not affected. The cash outflow is reported in the financing activities section of the statement of cash flows. The effects of the cash payment on the financial statements follow.

Assets	=	Liab.	+		Equity			Rev.	−	Exp.	=	Net Inc.	Cash Flow
Cash	=	Div. Pay.	+	Com. Stk.	+	Ret. Earn.							
(70)	=	(70)	+	NA	+	NA		NA	−	NA	=	NA	(70) FA

Stock Dividend

Dividends are not always paid in cash. Companies sometimes choose to issue **stock dividends,** wherein they distribute additional shares of stock to the stockholders. To illustrate, assume that Nelson Incorporated decided to issue a 10 percent stock dividend on its class B, $20 par value common stock. Because dividends apply to outstanding shares only, Nelson will issue 15 (150 outstanding shares × 0.10) additional shares of class B stock.

Assume the new shares are distributed when the market value of the stock is $30 per share. As a result of the stock dividend, Nelson will transfer $450 ($30 × 15 new shares) from retained earnings to paid-in capital.[1] The stock dividend is an equity exchange

---

[1]The accounting here applies to small stock dividends. Accounting for large stock dividends is explained in a more advanced course.

transaction. The income statement and statement of cash flows are not affected. The effects of the stock dividend on the financial statements follow.

Assets	=	Liab.	+	Equity						Rev.	−	Exp.	=	Net Inc.	Cash Flow
				Com. Stk.	+	PIC in Excess	+	Ret. Earn.							
NA	=	NA	+	300	+	150	+	(450)		NA	−	NA	=	NA	NA

Stock dividends have no effect on assets. They merely increase the number of shares of stock outstanding. Because a greater number of shares represents the same ownership interest in the same amount of assets, the market value per share of a company's stock normally declines when a stock dividend is distributed. A lower market price makes the stock more affordable and may increase demand for the stock, which benefits both the company and its stockholders.

Stock Split

A corporation may also reduce the market price of its stock through a **stock split.** A stock split replaces existing shares with a greater number of new shares. Any par or stated value of the stock is proportionately reduced to reflect the new number of shares outstanding. For example, assume Nelson Incorporated declared a 2-for-1 stock split on the 165 outstanding shares (150 originally issued + 15 shares distributed in a stock dividend) of its $20 par value, class B common stock. Nelson notes in the accounting records that the 165 old $20 par shares are replaced with 330 new $10 par shares. Investors who owned the 165 shares of old common stock would now own 330 shares of the new common stock.

Stock splits have no effect on the dollar amounts of assets, liabilities, and stockholders' equity. They only affect the number of shares of stock outstanding. In Nelson's case, the ownership interest that was previously represented by 165 shares of stock is now represented by 330 shares. Because twice as many shares now represent the same ownership interest, the market value per share should be one-half as much as it was prior to the split. However, as with a stock dividend, the lower market price will probably stimulate demand for the stock. As a result, doubling the number of shares will likely reduce the market price to slightly more than one-half of the pre-split value. For example, if the stock were selling for $30 per share before the 2-for-1 split, it might sell for $15.50 after the split.

Appropriation of Retained Earnings

The board of directors may restrict the amount of retained earnings available to distribute as dividends. The restriction may be required by credit agreements, or it may be discretionary. A retained earnings restriction, often called an *appropriation,* is an equity exchange event. It transfers a portion of existing retained earnings to **Appropriated Retained Earnings.** Total retained earnings remains unchanged. To illustrate, assume that Nelson appropriates $1,000 of retained earnings for future expansion. The income statement and the statement of cash flows are not affected. The effects on the financial statements of appropriating $1,000 of retained earnings follow.

Show how the appropriation of retained earnings affects financial statements.

Assets	=	Liab.	+	Equity						Rev.	−	Exp.	=	Net Inc.	Cash Flow
				Com. Stk.	+	Ret. Earn.	+	App. Ret. Earn.							
NA	=	NA	+	NA	+	(1,000)	+	1,000		NA	−	NA	=	NA	NA

FINANCIAL STATEMENT PRESENTATION

The 2014 and 2015 events for Nelson Incorporated are summarized below. Events 1 through 8 are cash transactions. The results of the 2014 transactions (nos. 1–5) are reflected in Exhibit 8.4. The results of the 2015 transactions (nos. 6–9) are shown in Exhibit 8.5.

1. Issued 100 shares of $10 par value common stock at a market price of $22 per share.
2. Issued 150 shares of class B, $20 par value common stock at a market price of $25 per share.
3. Issued 100 shares of $10 stated value, 7 percent cumulative preferred stock at a market price of $22 per share.
4. Issued 100 shares of no-par common stock at a market price of $22 per share.
5. Earned and retained $5,000 cash from operations.
6. Purchased 50 shares of $10 par value common stock as treasury stock at a market price of $20 per share.
7. Sold 30 shares of treasury stock at a market price of $25 per share.
8. Declared and paid a $70 cash dividend on the preferred stock.
9. Issued a 10 percent stock dividend on the 150 shares of outstanding class B, $20 par value common stock (15 additional shares). The additional shares were issued when the market price of the stock was $30 per share. There are 165 (150 + 15) class B common shares outstanding after the stock dividend.
10. Issued a 2-for-1 stock split on the 165 shares of class B, $20 par value common stock. After this transaction, there are 330 shares outstanding of the class B common stock with a $10 par value.
11. Appropriated $1,000 of retained earnings.

EXHIBIT 8.5

NELSON INCORPORATED
Balance Sheet
As of December 31, 2015

Assets		
Cash		$21,030
Stockholders' equity		
Preferred stock, $10 stated value, 7% cumulative,		
300 shares authorized, 100 issued and outstanding	$1,000	
Common stock, $10 par value, 250 shares authorized,		
100 issued, and 80 outstanding	1,000	
Common stock, class B, $10 par, 800 shares authorized,		
330 issued and outstanding	3,300	
Common stock, no par, 150 shares authorized,		
100 issued and outstanding	2,200	
Paid-in capital in excess of stated value—preferred	1,200	
Paid-in capital in excess of par value—common	1,200	
Paid-in capital in excess of par value—class B common	900	
Paid-in capital in excess of cost of treasury stock	150	
Total paid-in capital		$10,950
Retained earnings		
Appropriated	1,000	
Unappropriated	9,480	
Total retained earnings		10,480
Less: Treasury stock, 20 shares @ $20 per share		(400)
Total stockholders' equity		$21,030

The illustration assumes that Nelson earned net income of $6,000 in 2015. The ending retained earnings balance is determined as follows: Beginning Balance $5,000 − $70 Cash Dividend − $450 Stock Dividend + $6,000 Net Income = $10,480.

INVESTING IN CAPITAL STOCK

Stockholders may benefit in two ways when a company generates earnings. The company may distribute the earnings directly to the stockholders in the form of dividends. Alternatively, the company may retain some or all of the earnings to finance growth and increase its potential for future earnings. If the company retains earnings, the market value of its stock should increase to reflect its greater earnings prospects. How can analysts use financial reporting to help assess the potential for dividend payments or growth in market value?

Explain some uses of accounting information in making stock investment decisions.

Receiving Dividends

Is a company likely to pay dividends in the future? The financial statements can help answer this question. They show if dividends were paid in the past. Companies with a history of paying dividends usually continue to pay dividends. Also, to pay dividends in the future, a company must have sufficient cash and retained earnings. These amounts are reported on the balance sheet and the statement of cash flows.

Increasing the Price of Stock

Is the market value (price) of a company's stock likely to increase? Increases in a company's stock price occur when investors believe the company's earnings will grow. Financial statements provide information that is useful in predicting the prospects for earnings growth. Here also, a company's earnings history is an indicator of its growth potential. However, because published financial statements report historical information, investors must recognize their limitations. Investors want to know about the future. Stock prices are therefore influenced more by forecasts than by history.

For example:

■ On February 12, 2013, Blue Nile, Inc., announced that earnings for the fourth quarter of 2012 were 30 percent higher than they had been for the same quarter of 2011. In reaction to this seemingly good news, the price of Blue Nile's stock *fell* by almost 7 percent. Why did the stock market respond in this way? Because financial analysts who follow the company closely had expected the company's fourth quarter earnings to be 21 percent higher than they were.

■ On February 12, 2013, Avon Products, Inc., announced that earnings for the fourth quarter of 2012 were about 5 percent lower than they had been for the fourth quarter of 2011. The stock market's reaction to the news was to *increase* the price of Avon's stock by a little over 23 percent. The market reacted this way because even though earnings were down from the previous year, they were 37 percent higher than analysts had expected them to be.

In each case, investors reacted to the potential for earnings growth rather than the historical earnings reports. Because investors find forecasted statements more relevant to decision making than historical financial statements, most companies provide forecasts in addition to historical financial statements.

The value of a company's stock is also influenced by nonfinancial information that financial statements cannot provide. For example, suppose ExxonMobil announced in the middle of its fiscal year that it had just discovered substantial oil reserves on property to which it held drilling rights. Consider the following questions:

■ What would happen to the price of ExxonMobil's stock on the day of the announcement?

■ What would happen to ExxonMobil's financial statements on that day?

The price of ExxonMobil's stock would almost certainly increase as soon as the discovery was made public. However, nothing would happen to its financial statements on that day. There would probably be very little effect on its financial statements for that year. Only after the company begins to develop the oil field and sell the oil will its financial statements reflect the discovery. Changes in financial statements tend to lag behind the announcements companies make regarding their earnings potential.

Stock prices are also affected by general economic conditions and consumer confidence as well as the performance measures reported in financial statements. For example, the stock prices of virtually all companies declined sharply immediately after the September 11, 2001, terrorist attacks on the World Trade Center and the Pentagon. Historically based financial statements are of little benefit in predicting general economic conditions or changes in consumer confidence.

Exercising Control through Stock Ownership

The more influence an investor has over the operations of a company, the more the investor can benefit from owning stock in the company. For example, consider a power company that needs coal to produce electricity. The power company may purchase some common stock in a coal mining company to ensure a stable supply of coal. What percentage of the mining company's stock must the power company acquire to exercise significant influence over the mining company? The answer depends on how many investors own stock in the mining company and how the number of shares is distributed among the stockholders.

The greater its number of stockholders, the more *widely held* a company is. If stock ownership is concentrated in the hands of a few persons, a company is *closely held.* Widely held companies can generally be controlled with smaller percentages of ownership than closely held companies. Consider a company in which no existing investor owns more than 1 percent of the voting stock. A new investor who acquires a 5 percent interest would immediately become, by far, the largest shareholder and would likely be able to significantly influence board decisions. In contrast, consider a closely held company in which one current shareholder owns 51 percent of the company's stock. Even if another investor acquired the remaining 49 percent of the company, that investor could not control the company.

Financial statements contain some, but not all, of the information needed to help an investor determine ownership levels necessary to permit control. For example, the financial statements disclose the total number of shares of stock outstanding, but they normally contain little information about the number of shareholders and even less information about any relationships between shareholders. Relationships between shareholders are critically important because related shareholders, whether bound by family or business interests, might exercise control by voting as a block. For publicly traded companies, information about the number of shareholders and the identity of some large shareholders is disclosed in reports filed with the Securities and Exchange Commission.

<< A Look Back

Starting a business requires obtaining financing; it takes money to make money. Although some money may be borrowed, lenders are unlikely to make loans to businesses that lack some degree of owner financing. Equity financing is therefore critical to virtually all profit-oriented businesses. This chapter has examined some of the issues related to accounting for equity transactions.

The idea that a business must obtain financing from its owners was one of the first events presented in this textbook. This chapter discussed the advantages and disadvantages of organizing a business as a sole proprietorship versus a partnership versus a corporation. These advantages and disadvantages include the following.

1. *Double taxation*—Income of corporations is subject to double taxation, but that of proprietorships and partnerships is not.

2. *Regulation*—Corporations are subject to more regulation than are proprietorships and partnerships.

3. *Limited liability*—An investor's personal assets are not at risk as a result of owning corporate securities. The investor's liability is limited to the amount of the investment. In general, proprietorships and partnerships do not offer limited liability. However, laws in some states permit the formation of limited liability companies, which operate like proprietorships and partnerships yet place some limits on the personal liability of their owners.

4. *Continuity*—Proprietorships and partnerships dissolve when one of the owners leaves the business. Corporations are separate legal entities that continue to exist regardless of changes in ownership.

5. *Transferability*—Ownership interests in corporations are easier to transfer than those of proprietorships or partnerships.

6. *Management structure*—Corporations are more likely to have independent professional managers than are proprietorships or partnerships.

7. *Ability to raise capital*—Because they can be owned by millions of investors, corporations have the opportunity to raise more capital than proprietorships or partnerships.

Corporations issue different classes of common stock and preferred stock as evidence of ownership interests. In general, *common stock* provides the widest range of privileges including the right to vote and participate in earnings. *Preferred stockholders* usually give up the right to vote in exchange for preferences such as the right to receive dividends or assets upon liquidation before common stockholders. Stock may have a *par value* or *stated value*, which relates to legal requirements governing the amount of capital that must be maintained in the corporation. Corporations may also issue *no-par stock*, avoiding some of the legal requirements that pertain to par or stated value stock.

Stock that a company issues and then repurchases is called *treasury stock*. Purchasing treasury stock reduces total assets and stockholders' equity. Reselling treasury stock represents a capital acquisition. The difference between the reissue price and the cost of the treasury stock is recorded directly in the equity accounts. Treasury stock transactions do not result in gains or losses on the income statement.

Companies may issue *stock splits* or *stock dividends*. These transactions increase the number of shares of stock without changing the net assets of a company. The per share market value usually drops when a company issues stock splits or dividends.

A Look Forward

Financial statement analysis is so important that Chapter 9 is devoted solely to a detailed discussion of this subject. The chapter covers vertical analysis (analyzing relationships within a specific statement) and horizontal analysis (analyzing relationships across accounting periods). Finally, the chapter discusses limitations associated with financial statement analysis.

312   Chapter 8

 Video lectures and accompanying self-assessment quizzes are available for all learning objectives through McGraw-Hill *Connect®* *Accounting*.

SELF-STUDY REVIEW PROBLEM

Edwards Inc. experienced the following events:

1. Issued common stock for cash.
2. Declared a cash dividend.
3. Issued noncumulative preferred stock for cash.
4. Appropriated retained earnings.
5. Distributed a stock dividend.
6. Paid cash to purchase treasury stock.
7. Distributed a 2-for-1 stock split.
8. Issued cumulative preferred stock for cash.
9. Paid a cash dividend that had previously been declared.
10. Sold treasury stock for cash at a higher amount than the cost of the treasury stock.

Required

Show the effect of each event on the elements of the financial statements using a horizontal statements model like the one shown here. Use + for increase, − for decrease, and NA for not affected. In the Cash Flow column, indicate whether the item is an operating activity (OA), investing activity (IA), or a financing activity (FA). The first transaction is entered as an example.

Event	Assets	=	Liab.	+	Equity	Rev.	−	Exp.	=	Net Inc.	Cash Flow
1	+		NA		+	NA		NA		NA	+ FA

Solution to Self-Study Review Problem

Event	Assets	=	Liab.	+	Equity	Rev.	−	Exp.	=	Net Inc.	Cash Flow
1	+		NA		+	NA		NA		NA	+ FA
2	NA		+		−	NA		NA		NA	NA
3	+		NA		+	NA		NA		NA	+ FA
4	NA		NA		− +	NA		NA		NA	NA
5	NA		NA		− +	NA		NA		NA	NA
6	−		NA		−	NA		NA		NA	− FA
7	NA		NA		NA	NA		NA		NA	NA
8	+		NA		+	NA		NA		NA	+ FA
9	−		−		NA	NA		NA		NA	− FA
10	+		NA		+	NA		NA		NA	+ FA

KEY TERMS

QUESTIONS

1. What are the three major forms of business organizations? Describe each.

2. How are sole proprietorships formed?

3. Discuss the purpose of a partnership agreement. Is such an agreement necessary for partnership formation?

4. What is meant by the phrase *separate legal entity*? To which type of business organization does it apply?

5. What is the purpose of the articles of incorporation? What information do they provide?

6. What is the function of the stock certificate?

7. What prompted Congress to pass the Securities Act of 1933 and the Securities Exchange Act of 1934? What is the purpose of these laws?

8. What are the advantages and disadvantages of the corporate form of business organization?

9. What is a limited liability company? Discuss its advantages and disadvantages.

10. How does the term *double taxation* apply to corporations? Give an example of double taxation.

11. What is the difference between contributed capital and retained earnings for a corporation?

12. What are the similarities and differences in the equity structure of a sole proprietorship, a partnership, and a corporation?

13. Why is it easier for a corporation to raise large amounts of capital than it is for a partnership?

14. What is the meaning of each of the following terms with respect to the corporate form of organization?
    (a) Legal capital
    (b) Par value of stock
    (c) Stated value of stock
    (d) Market value of stock
    (e) Book value of stock
    (f) Authorized shares of stock
    (g) Issued stock
    (h) Outstanding stock
    (i) Treasury stock
    (j) Common stock
    (k) Preferred stock
    (l) Dividends

15. What is the difference between cumulative preferred stock and noncumulative preferred stock?

16. What is no-par stock? How is it recorded in the accounting records?

17. Assume that Best Co. has issued and outstanding 1,000 shares of $100 par value, 10 percent, cumulative preferred stock. What is the dividend per share? If the preferred dividend is two years in arrears, what total amount of dividends must be paid before the common shareholders can receive any dividends?

18. If Best Co. issued 10,000 shares of $20 par value common stock for $30 per share, what amount is added to the Common Stock account? What amount of cash is received?

19. What is the difference between par value stock and stated value stock?

20. Why might a company repurchase its own stock?

21. What effect does the purchase of treasury stock have on the equity of a company?

22. Assume that Day Company repurchased 1,000 of its own shares for $30 per share and sold the shares two weeks later for $35 per share. What is the amount of gain on the sale? How is it reported on the balance sheet? What type of account is Treasury Stock?

23. What is the importance of the declaration date, record date, and payment date in conjunction with corporate dividends?

24. What is the difference between a stock dividend and a stock split?

25. Why would a company choose to distribute a stock dividend instead of a cash dividend?

26. What is the primary reason that a company would declare a stock split?

27. If Best Co. had 10,000 shares of $20 par value common stock outstanding and declared a 5-for-1 stock split, how many shares would then be outstanding and what would be their par value after the split?

28. When a company appropriates retained earnings, does the company set aside cash for a specific use? Explain.

29. What is the largest source of financing for most U.S. businesses?

30. What is meant by *equity financing*? What is meant by *debt financing*?

31. What is a widely held corporation? What is a closely held corporation?

32. What are some reasons that a corporation might not pay dividends?

MULTIPLE-CHOICE QUESTIONS

Multiple-choice questions are provided on the text website at www.mhhe.com/edmondssurvey4e.

314 Chapter 8

EXERCISES

≣ connect | ACCOUNTING
All applicable Exercises are available with McGraw-Hill's *Connect® Accounting.*

LO 8-1, 8-2

Exercise 8-1 *Effect of accounting events on the financial statements of a sole proprietorship*

A sole proprietorship was started on January 1, 2014, when it received $30,000 cash from Alex Ard, the owner. During 2014, the company earned $50,000 in cash revenues and paid $22,300 in cash expenses. Ard withdrew $10,000 cash from the business during 2014.

Required

Prepare the income statement, capital statement (statement of changes in equity), balance sheet, and statement of cash flows for Ard's 2014 fiscal year.

LO 8-1, 8-2

Exercise 8-2 *Effect of accounting events on the financial statements of a partnership*

Drake Cushing and Shawn Tadlock started the CT partnership on January 1, 2014. The business acquired $70,000 cash from Cushing and $140,000 from Tadlock. During 2014, the partnership earned $75,000 in cash revenues and paid $39,000 for cash expenses. Cushing withdrew $2,000 cash from the business, and Tadlock withdrew $4,000 cash. The net income was allocated to the capital accounts of the two partners in proportion to the amounts of their original investments in the business.

Required

Prepare the income statement, capital statement, balance sheet, and statement of cash flows for the CT partnership for the 2014 fiscal year.

LO 8-1, 8-2

Exercise 8-3 *Effect of accounting events on the financial statements of a corporation*

Bozeman Corporation was started with the issue of 10,000 shares of $10 par common stock for cash on January 1, 2014. The stock was issued at a market price of $16 per share. During 2014, the company earned $71,000 in cash revenues and paid $46,500 for cash expenses. Also a $5,000 cash dividend was paid to the stockholders.

Required

Prepare the income statement, statement of changes in stockholders' equity, balance sheet, and statement of cash flows for Bozeman Corporation's 2014 fiscal year.

LO 8-4

Exercise 8-4 *Effect of issuing common stock on the balance sheet*

Newly formed Electronics Services Corporation has 100,000 shares of $10 par common stock authorized. On March 1, 2014, Electronics Services issued 20,000 shares of the stock for $12 per share. On May 2 the company issued an additional 30,000 shares for $15 per share. Electronics Services was not affected by other events during 2014.

Required

a. Record the transactions in a horizontal statements model like the following one. In the Cash Flow column, indicate whether the item is an operating activity (OA), investing activity (IA), or financing activity (FA). Use NA to indicate that an element was not affected by the event.

Assets	=	Liab.	+		Equity		Rev.	−	Exp.	=	Net Inc.	Cash Flow
Cash	=		+	Com. Stk.	+	Paid-in Excess						

b. Determine the amount Electronics Services would report for common stock on the December 31, 2014, balance sheet.

c. Determine the amount Electronics Services would report for paid-in capital in excess of par.

d. What is the total amount of capital contributed by the owners?

e. What amount of total assets would Electronics Services report on the December 31, 2014, balance sheet?

Exercise 8-5 *Recording and reporting common and preferred stock transactions*

LO 8-4

Goldman Inc. was organized on June 1, 2014. It was authorized to issue 500,000 shares of $10 par common stock and 100,000 shares of 4 percent cumulative class A preferred stock. The class A stock had a stated value of $50 per share. The following stock transactions pertain to Goldman Inc.:

1. Issued 40,000 shares of common stock for $16 per share.
2. Issued 20,000 shares of the class A preferred stock for $52 per share.
3. Issued 60,000 shares of common stock for $20 per share.

Required

Prepare the stockholders' equity section of the balance sheet immediately after these transactions have been recognized.

Exercise 8-6 *Effect of no-par common and par preferred stock on the horizontal statements model*

LO 8-4

Bailey Corporation issued 10,000 shares of no-par common stock for $25 per share. Bailey also issued 3,000 shares of $40 par, 6 percent noncumulative preferred stock at $42 per share.

Required

Record these events in a horizontal statements model like the following one. In the cash flow column, indicate whether the item is an operating activity (OA), investing activity (IA), or financing activity (FA). Use NA to indicate that an element was not affected by the event.

Assets =	Equity			Rev. − Exp. = Net Inc.	Cash Flow
Cash =	Pfd. Stk. +	Com. Stk. +	PIC in Excess		

Exercise 8-7 *Issuing stock for assets other than cash*

LO 8-4

Hammond Corporation was formed when it issued shares of common stock to two of its shareholders. Hammond issued 10,000 shares of $5 par common stock to P. Coldwell in exchange for $80,000 cash (the issue price was $8 per share). Hammond also issued 3,500 shares of stock to M. Roberts in exchange for a one-year-old delivery van on the same day. Roberts had originally paid $39,000 for the van.

Required

a. What was the market value of the delivery van on the date of the stock issue?

b. Show the effect of the two stock issues on Hammond's books in a horizontal statements model like the following one. In the Cash Flow column, indicate whether the item is an operating activity (OA), investing activity (IA), or financing activity (FA). Use NA to indicate that an element was not affected by the event.

Assets =		Equity		Rev. − Exp. = Net Inc.	Cash Flow
Cash + Van =	Com. Stk. +	PIC in Excess			

Exercise 8-8 *Treasury stock transactions*

LO 8-5

Moore Corporation repurchased 4,000 shares of its own stock for $30 per share. The stock has a par of $10 per share. A month later Moore resold 2,500 shares of the treasury stock for $35 per share.

Required

What is the balance of the Treasury Stock account after these transactions are recognized?

LO 8-5

Exercise 8-9   *Recording and reporting treasury stock transactions*

The following information pertains to Wise Corp. at January 1, 2014:

Common stock, $10 par, 50,000 shares authorized, 3,000 shares issued and outstanding	$30,000
Paid-in capital in excess of par, common stock	12,000
Retained earnings	46,000

Wise Corp. completed the following transactions during 2014:

1. Issued 2,000 shares of $10 par common stock for $16 per share.
2. Repurchased 500 shares of its own common stock for $18 per share.
3. Resold 120 shares of treasury stock for $20 per share.

Required

a. How many shares of common stock were outstanding at the end of the period?
b. How many shares of common stock had been issued at the end of the period?
c. Organize the transactions data in accounts under the accounting equation.
d. Prepare the stockholders' equity section of the balance sheet reflecting these transactions. Include the number of shares authorized, issued, and outstanding in the description of the common stock.

LO 8-6

Exercise 8-10   *Effect of cash dividends on financial statements*

On October 1, 2014, Daster Corporation declared a $50,000 cash dividend to be paid on December 15 to shareholders of record on November 1.

Required

Record the events occurring on October 1 and December 15 in a horizontal statements model like the following one. In the Cash Flow column, indicate whether the item is an operating activity (OA), investing activity (IA), or financing activity (FA).

Date	Assets	=	Liab.	+	Com. Stock	+	Ret. Earn.		Rev.	−	Exp.	=	Net Inc.		Cash Flow

LO 8-6

Exercise 8-11   *Accounting for cumulative preferred dividends*

When Higdon Corporation was organized in January 2014, it immediately issued 10,000 shares of $50 par, 5 percent, cumulative preferred stock and 15,000 shares of $10 par common stock. The company's earnings history is as follows: 2014, net loss of $18,000; 2015, net income of $110,000; 2016, net income of $90,000. The corporation did not pay a dividend in 2014.

Required

a. How much is the dividend arrearage as of January 1, 2014?
b. Assume that the board of directors declares a $65,000 cash dividend at the end of 2015 (remember that the 2014 and 2015 preferred dividends are due). How will the dividend be divided between the preferred and common stockholders?

Exercise 8-12   *Cash dividends for preferred and common shareholders*

J&J Corporation had the following stock issued and outstanding at January 1, 2014:

1. 200,000 shares of $10 par common stock.
2. 8,000 shares of $100 par, 4 percent, noncumulative preferred stock.

On May 10, J&J Corporation declared the annual cash dividend on its 8,000 shares of preferred stock and a $.50 per share dividend for the common shareholders. The dividends will be paid on June 15 to the shareholders of record on May 30.

Required

Determine the total amount of dividends to be paid to the preferred shareholders and common shareholders.

Exercise 8-13   *Cash dividends: Common and preferred stock*

Yan Corp. had the following stock issued and outstanding at January 1, 2014:

1. 60,000 shares of no-par common stock.
2. 15,000 shares of $100 par, 4 percent, cumulative preferred stock. (Dividends are in arrears for one year, 2013.)

On February 1, 2014, Yan declared a $150,000 cash dividend to be paid March 31 to shareholders of record on March 10.

Required

What amount of dividends will be paid to the preferred shareholders versus the common shareholders?

Exercise 8-14   *Accounting for stock dividends*

Tidwell Corporation issued a 4 percent stock dividend on 20,000 shares of its $10 par common stock. At the time of the dividend, the market value of the stock was $30 per share.

Required

a. Compute the amount of the stock dividend.
b. Show the effects of the stock dividend on the financial statements using a horizontal statements model like the following one.

Assets	=	Liab.	+	Com. Stk.	+	PIC in Excess	+	Ret. Earn.	Rev.	−	Exp.	=	Net Inc.	Cash Flow

Exercise 8-15   *Determining the effects of stock splits on the accounting records*

The market value of Dylan Corporation's common stock had become excessively high. The stock was currently selling for $240 per share. To reduce the market price of the common stock, Dylan declared a 3-for-1 stock split for the 200,000 outstanding shares of its $10 par common stock.

Required

a. How will Dylan Corporation's books be affected by the stock split?
b. Determine the number of common shares outstanding and the par value after the split.
c. Explain how the market value of the stock will be affected by the stock split.

Exercise 8-16   *Corporate announcements*

Super Drugs (one of the three largest drug makers) just reported that its 2014 third-quarter profits are essentially the same as the 2013 third-quarter profits. In addition to this announcement, the same day, Super Drugs also announced that the Food and Drug Administration has just approved a new drug used to treat high blood pressure that Super Drugs developed. This new drug has been shown to be extremely effective and has few or no side effects. It will also be less expensive than the other drugs currently on the market.

Required

Using the above information, answer the following questions:

a. What do you think will happen to the stock price of Super Drugs on the day these two announcements are made? Explain your answer.
b. How will the balance sheet be affected on that day by the above announcements?
c. How will the income statement be affected on that day by the above announcements?
d. How will the statement of cash flows be affected on that day by the above announcements?

318 Chapter 8

PROBLEMS

 All applicable Problems are available with McGraw-Hill's *Connect® Accounting.*

LO 8-1

Problem 8-17 *Different forms of business organization*

Shawn Bates was working to establish a business enterprise with four of his wealthy friends. Each of the five individuals would receive a 20 percent ownership interest in the company. A primary goal of establishing the enterprise was to minimize the amount of income taxes paid. Assume that the five investors are in a 35 percent personal tax bracket and that the corporate tax rate is 25 percent. Also assume that the new company is expected to earn $200,000 of cash income before taxes during its first year of operation. All earnings are expected to be immediately distributed to the owners.

Required

Calculate the amount of after-tax cash flow available to each investor if the business is established as a partnership versus a corporation. Write a memo explaining the advantages and disadvantages of these two forms of business organization. Explain why a limited liability company may be a better choice than either a partnership or a corporation.

LO 8-1, 8-2

CHECK FIGURES
a. Net Income: $24,000
b. Sue Moore Capital: $78,100

Problem 8-18 *Effect of business structure on financial statements*

Auto Spa Company was started on January 1, 2014, when the owners invested $120,000 cash in the business. During 2014, the company earned cash revenues of $80,000 and incurred cash expenses of $56,000. The company also paid cash distributions of $5,000.

Required

Prepare a 2014 income statement, capital statement (statement of changes in equity), balance sheet, and statement of cash flows using each of the following assumptions. (Consider each assumption separately.)

a. Auto Spa is a sole proprietorship owned by B. Burns.

b. Auto Spa is a partnership with two partners, Sue Moore and Jim Pounds. Moore invested $72,000 and Pounds invested $48,000 of the $120,000 cash that was used to start the business. Pounds was expected to assume the vast majority of the responsibility for operating the business. The partnership agreement called for Pounds to receive 60 percent of the profits and Moore the remaining 40 percent. With regard to the $5,000 distribution, Pounds withdrew $1,500 from the business and Moore withdrew $3,500.

c. Auto Spa is a corporation. The owners were issued 10,000 shares of $10 par common stock when they invested the $120,000 cash in the business.

LO 8-5

CHECK FIGURES
Total Paid-In Capital: $653,600
Total Stockholders' Equity:
$792,600

Problem 8-19 *Recording and reporting treasury stock transactions*

Quality Corporation reports the following information in its January 1, 2014, balance sheet:

Stockholders' equity	
Common stock, $10 par value, 100,000 shares authorized, 50,000 shares issued and outstanding	$500,000
Paid-in capital in excess of par value	150,000
Retained earnings	120,000
Total stockholders' equity	$770,000

During 2014, Quality was affected by the following accounting events:

1. Purchased 2,000 shares of treasury stock at $15 per share.
2. Reissued 1,200 shares of treasury stock at $18 per share.
3. Earned $72,000 of cash revenues.
4. Paid $41,000 of cash operating expenses.

Required

Prepare the stockholders' equity section of the year-end balance sheet.

Problem 8-20   *Recording and reporting stock transactions and cash dividends across*
two accounting cycles

LO 8-4, 8-5, 8-6

CHECK FIGURES
b. Preferred Stock, 2014: $160,000
c. Common Shares Outstanding,
   2015: 44,000

Malard Corporation was authorized to issue 100,000 shares of $8 par common stock and 50,000 shares of $80 par, 4 percent, cumulative preferred stock. Malard Corporation completed the following transactions during its first two years of operation:

2014

Jan.   2   Issued 25,000 shares of $8 par common stock for $10 per share.
      15   Issued 2,000 shares of $80 par preferred stock for $90 per share.
Feb. 14   Issued 20,000 shares of $8 par common stock for $12 per share.
Dec. 31   During the year, earned $280,000 of cash revenues and paid $165,000 of cash operating expenses.
      31   Declared the cash dividend on outstanding shares of preferred stock for 2014. The dividend will be paid on January 31 to stockholders of record on January 15, 2015.
      31   Closed revenue, expense, and dividend accounts to the retained earnings account.

2015

Jan. 31   Paid the cash dividend declared on December 31, 2014.
Mar.   1   Issued 4,000 shares of $80 par preferred stock for $92 per share.
June   1   Purchased 1,000 shares of common stock as treasury stock at $14 per share.
Dec. 31   During the year, earned $185,000 of cash revenues and paid $110,000 of cash operating expenses.
      31   Declared the dividend on the preferred stock and a $1.00 per share dividend on the common stock.
      31   Closed revenue, expense, and dividend accounts to the retained earnings account.

Required

a. Organize the transaction data in accounts under an accounting equation.
b. Prepare the stockholders' equity section of the balance sheet at December 31, 2014.
c. Prepare the balance sheet at December 31, 2015.

Problem 8-21   *Recording and reporting treasury stock transactions*

LO 8-5, 8-6, 8-8

CHECK FIGURE
b. Total Paid-In Capital: $411,200

Prairie Corp. completed the following transactions in 2014, the first year of operation:

1. Issued 15,000 shares of $10 par common stock at par.
2. Issued 5,000 shares of $50 stated value preferred stock at $52 per share.
3. Purchased 800 shares of common stock as treasury stock for $12 per share.
4. Declared a 5 percent cash dividend on preferred stock.
5. Sold 300 shares of treasury stock for $16 per share.
6. Paid the cash dividend on preferred stock that was declared in Event 4.
7. Earned revenue of $80,000 and incurred operating expenses of $48,000.
8. Appropriated $6,000 of retained earnings.

Required

a. Organize the transaction in accounts under an accounting equation.
b. Prepare the stockholders' equity section of the balance sheet as of December 31, 2014.

Problem 8-22   *Recording and reporting stock dividends*

LO 8-4, 8-6, 8-7

CHECK FIGURES
b. Total Paid-In Capital: $1,084,500
b. Retained Earnings: $8,500

Concord Corp. completed the following transactions in 2014, the first year of operation:

1. Issued 30,000 shares of $10 par common stock for $15 per share.
2. Issued 6,000 shares of $100 par, 5 percent, preferred stock at $101 per share.
3. Paid the annual cash dividend to preferred shareholders.
4. Issued a 5 percent stock dividend on the common stock. The market value at the dividend declaration date was $19 per share.
5. Later that year, issued a 2-for-1 split on the 31,500 shares of outstanding common stock.
6. Earned $165,000 of cash revenues and paid $98,000 of cash operating expenses.

Required

a. Record each of these events in a horizontal statements model like the following one. In the Cash Flow column, indicate whether the item is an operating activity (OA), investing activity (IA), or financing activity (FA). Use NA to indicate that an element is not affected by the event.

Assets = Liab. +	Equity					Rev. − Exp. = Net Inc.	Cash Flow
	Pfd. Stk. + Com. Stk. +	PIC in Excess PS +	PIC in Excess CS +	Ret. Earn.			

b. Prepare the stockholders' equity section of the balance sheet at the end of 2014.

LO 8-4, 8-7

Problem 8-23 *Analyzing the stockholders' equity section of the balance sheet*

The stockholders' equity section of the balance sheet for Gator Company at December 31, 2014, is as follows:

Stockholders' Equity		
Paid-in capital		
Preferred stock, ? par value, 5% cumulative,		
100,000 shares authorized, 40,000 shares issued		
and outstanding	$400,000	
Common stock, $20 stated value, 150,000 shares		
authorized, 40,000 shares issued and ? outstanding	800,000	
Paid-in capital in excess of par—Preferred	30,000	
Paid-in capital in excess of stated value—Common	100,000	
Total paid-in capital		$1,330,000
Retained earnings		250,000
Treasury stock, 2,000 shares		(25,000)
Total stockholders' equity		$1,555,000

Note: The market value per share of the common stock is $40, and the market value per share of the preferred stock is $12.

Required

a. What is the par value per share of the preferred stock?

b. What is the dividend per share on the preferred stock?

c. What is the number of common stock shares outstanding?

d. What was the average issue price per share (price for which the stock was issued) of the common stock?

e. Explain the difference between the average issue price and the market price of the common stock.

f. If Gator declared a 2-for-1 stock split on the common stock, how many shares would be outstanding after the split? What amount would be transferred from the Retained Earnings account because of the stock split? Theoretically, what would be the market price of the common stock immediately after the stock split?

LO 8-4, 8-5, 8-6, 8-7, 8-8

Problem 8-24 *Effects of equity transactions on financial statements*

The following events were experienced by Baskin, Inc.:

1. Issued cumulative preferred stock.
2. Issued common stock for cash.
3. Issued noncumulative preferred stock.
4. Paid cash to purchase treasury stock.
5. Sold treasury stock for an amount of cash that was more than the cost of the treasury stock.
6. Declared a cash dividend.
7. Declared a 2-for-1 stock split on the common stock.
8. Distributed a stock dividend.

9. Appropriated retained earnings.

10. Paid a cash dividend that was previously declared.

Required

Show the effect of each event on the elements of the financial statements using a horizontal statements model like the following one. Use + for increase, − for decrease, and NA for not affected. In the Cash Flow column indicate whether the item is an operating activity (OA), investing activity (IA), or financing activity (FA). The first transaction is entered as an example.

Event No.	Assets	=	Liab.	+	Equity	Rev.	−	Exp.	=	Net Inc.	Cash Flow
1	+		NA		+	NA		NA		NA	+ FA

ANALYZE, THINK, COMMUNICATE

ATC 8-1   Business Applications Case   *Understanding real-world annual reports*

Use the Target Corporation's Form 10-K to answer the following questions related to Target's 2012 fiscal year (year ended February 2, 2013). Target's Form 10-K is available on the company's website or through the SEC's EDGAR database. Appendix A provides instructions for using the EDGAR database.

Required

a. What is the par value per share of Target's stock?

b. How many shares of Target's common stock were *outstanding* as of February 2, 2013?

c. Target's annual report provides some details about the company's executive officers. How many are identified? What is their minimum, maximum, and average age? How many are females?

d. Target's balance sheet does not show a balance for treasury stock. Does this mean the company has not repurchased any of its own stock? Explain.

ATC 8-2   Group Assignment   *Missing information*

Listed here are the stockholders' equity sections of three public companies for years ending in 2012 and 2011:

	2012	2011
Wendy's/Arby's Group (in thousands)		
Stockholders' equity		
Common stock, ?? stated value per share, authorized:		
1,500,000; 470,424 shares issued	$ 47,042	$ 47,042
Capital in excess of stated value	2,782,765	2,779,871
Retained earnings	(467,007)	(434,999)
Acc. other comp. income (loss)	5,981	102
Treasury stock, at cost: 78,051 in 2012 and 80,700 in 2011	(382,926)	(395,947)
Coca-Cola (in millions)		
Stockholders' equity		
Common stock, ?? par value per share, authorized:		
11,200; issued: 7,040 shares in 2012 and 2011	1,760	1,760
Capital surplus	11,379	10,332
Reinvested earnings	58,045	53,621
Acc. other comp. inc. (loss)	(3,385)	(2,774)
Treasury stock, at cost: 2,571 in 2012 and 2,514 in 2011	(35,009)	(31,304)
Harley-Davidson (in thousands)		
Stockholders' equity		
Common stock, ?? par value per share, authorized: 800,000;		
issued: 341,266 in 2012 and 339,107 shares in 2011	3,412	3,391
Additional paid-in capital	1,066,069	968,392
Retained earnings	7,306,424	6,824,180
Acc. other comp. inc. (loss)	(607,678)	(476,733)
Treasury stock, at cost: 115,166 for 2012 and 108,567 for 2011	(5,210,604)	(4,898,974)

Required

a. Divide the class in three sections and divide each section into groups of three to five students. Assign each section one of the companies.

Group Tasks

Based on the company assigned to your group, answer the following questions.

b. What is the per-share par or stated value of the common stock in 2012?

c. What was the average issue price of the common stock for each year?

d. How many shares of stock are outstanding at the end of each year?

e. What is the average cost per share of the treasury stock for 2012?

f. Do the data suggest that your company was profitable in 2012?

g. Can you determine the amount of net income from the information given? What is missing?

h. What is the total stockholders' equity of your company for each year?

Class Discussion

i. Have each group select a representative to present the information about its company. Compare the share issue price and the par or stated value of the companies.

j. Compare the average issue price to the current market price for each of the companies. Speculate about what might cause the difference.

ATC 8-3   Research Assignment   *Analyzing Skechers' equity structure*

Using either Skechers USA, Inc. most current Form 10-K or the company's annual report, answer the questions below. To obtain the Form 10-K use either the EDGAR system following the instructions in Appendix A or the company's website. The company's annual report is available on its website.

Required

a. What is the *book value* of Skechers' stockholders' equity that is shown on the company's balance sheet?

b. What is the par value of Skechers common stock?

c. Does Skechers have any treasury stock? If so, how many shares of treasury stock does the company hold?

d. Why does the stock of a company such as a Skechers have a market value that is higher than its book value?

ATC 8-4   Writing Assignment   *Comparison of organizational forms*

Jim Baku and Scott Hanson are thinking about opening a new restaurant. Baku has extensive marketing experience but does not know that much about food preparation. However, Hanson is an excellent chef. Both will work in the business, but Baku will provide most of the funds necessary to start the business. At this time, they cannot decide whether to operate the business as a partnership or a corporation.

Required

Prepare a written memo to Baku and Hanson describing the advantages and disadvantages of each organizational form. Also, from the limited information provided, recommend the organizational form you think they should use.

ATC 8-5   Ethical Dilemma   *Bad news versus very bad news*

Louise Stinson, the chief financial officer of Bostonian Corporation, was on her way to the president's office. She was carrying the latest round of bad news. There would be no executive bonuses this year. Corporate profits were down. Indeed, if the latest projections held true, the company would report a small loss on the year-end income statement. Executive bonuses were tied to corporate profits. The executive compensation plan provided for 10 percent of net earnings to be set aside for bonuses. No profits meant no bonuses. While things looked bleak, Stinson had a plan that might help soften the blow.

After informing the company president of the earnings forecast, Stinson made the following suggestion: Because the company was going to report a loss anyway, why not report a big loss? She reasoned that the directors and stockholders would not be much more angry if the company reported a large loss than if it reported a small one. There were several questionable assets that could be written down in the current year. This would increase the current year's loss but would reduce expenses in subsequent accounting periods. For example, the company was carrying damaged inventory that was estimated to have a value of $2,500,000. If this estimate were revised to $500,000, the company would have to recognize a $2,000,000 loss in the current year. However, next year when the goods were sold, the expense for cost of goods sold would be $2,000,000 less and profits would be higher by that amount. Although the directors would be angry this year, they would certainly be happy next year. The strategy would also have the benefit of adding $200,000 to next year's executive bonus pool ($2,000,000 × 0.10). Furthermore, it could not hurt this year's bonus pool since there would be no pool this year because the company is going to report a loss.

Some of the other items that Stinson is considering include (1) converting from straight-line to accelerated depreciation, (2) increasing the percentage of receivables estimated to be uncollectible in the current year and lowering the percentage in the following year, and (3) raising the percentage of estimated warranty claims in the current period and lowering it in the following period. Finally, Stinson notes that two of the company's department stores have been experiencing losses. The company could sell these stores this year and thereby improve earnings next year. Stinson admits that the sale would result in significant losses this year, but she smiles as she thinks of next year's bonus check.

Required

a. Explain how each of the three numbered strategies for increasing the amount of the current year's loss would affect the stockholders' equity section of the balance sheet in the current year. How would the other elements of the balance sheet be affected?

b. If Stinson's strategy were effectively implemented, how would it affect the stockholders' equity in subsequent accounting periods?

c. Comment on the ethical implications of running the company for the sake of management (maximization of bonuses) versus the maximization of return to stockholders.

d. Formulate a bonus plan that will motivate managers to maximize the value of the firm instead of motivating them to manipulate the reporting process.

e. How would Stinson's strategy of overstating the amount of the reported loss in the current year affect the company's current P/E ratio?

CHAPTER 9

Financial Statement Analysis

LEARNING OBJECTIVES

After you have mastered the material in this chapter, you will be able to:

LO 9-1 Differentiate between horizontal and vertical analysis.

LO 9-2 Calculate ratios for assessing a company's liquidity.

LO 9-3 Calculate ratios for assessing a company's solvency.

LO 9-4 Calculate ratios for assessing company management's effectiveness.

LO 9-5 Calculate ratios for assessing a company's position in the stock market.

 Video lectures and accompanying self-assessment quizzes are available for all learning objectives through McGraw-Hill Connect® Accounting.

CHAPTER OPENING

Expressing financial statement information in the form of ratios enhances its usefulness. Ratios permit comparisons over time and among companies, highlighting similarities, differences, and trends. Proficiency with common financial statement analysis techniques benefits both internal and external users. Before beginning detailed explanations of numerous ratios and percentages, however, we consider factors relevant to communicating useful information.

The Curious Accountant

Quest Software, Inc., " . . . designs, develops, markets, distributes, and supports enterprise systems management software products. . . . Quest is an 'Independent Software Vendor,' or 'ISV,' a company whose products are designed to support or to interact or interoperate with other vendors' software or hardware platforms." On March 9, 2012, Insight Venture Partners, a private investment firm, offered to buy Quest for $2 billion by offering $23 per share for its outstanding stock. At the time, Quest's balance sheet showed total owners' equity of $880 million, less than one-half the price offered by Insight Venture Partners. Two months later, Quest announced that it had received additional offers for the company, and on May 26 the company announced that Dell, Inc., had tentatively offered a price as much as $2.26 billion. By June 1, these negotiations had failed, but on June 14, a third, unnamed, bidder had offered $2.15 billion. Five days later the original bidder, Insight Venture Partners, raised its offering price to $2.17 billion. On June 25, Dell raised its offering price to $2.32 billion. On July 2, it was announced that Dell had won the bidding war for Quest, agreeing to pay $2.36 billion for the company.

Why would Dell be so anxious to buy Quest that it would raise the price it was willing to pay for the company by 18 percent over its original offer? What types of analysis would the company use to make this decision? (Answers on page 329.)

FACTORS IN COMMUNICATING USEFUL INFORMATION

The primary objective of accounting is to provide information useful for decision making. To provide information that supports this objective, accountants must consider the intended users, the types of decisions users make with financial statement information, and available means of analyzing the information.

The Users

Users of financial statement information include managers, creditors, stockholders, potential investors, and regulatory agencies. These individuals and organizations use financial statements for different purposes and bring varying levels of sophistication to understanding business activities. For example, investors range from private individuals who know little about financial statements to large investment brokers and institutional investors capable of using complex statistical analysis techniques. At what level of user knowledge should financial statements be aimed? Condensing and reporting complex business transactions at a level easily understood by nonprofessional investors is increasingly difficult. Current reporting standards target users that have a reasonably informed knowledge of business, though that level of sophistication is difficult to define.

The Types of Decisions

Just as the knowledge level of potential users varies, the information needs of users varies, depending on the decision at hand. A supplier considering whether or not to sell goods on account to a particular company wants to evaluate the likelihood of getting paid; a potential investor in that company wants to predict the likelihood of increases in the market value of the company's common stock. Financial statements, however, are designed for general purposes; they are not aimed at any specific user group. Some disclosed information, therefore, may be irrelevant to some users but vital to others. Users must employ different forms of analysis to identify information most relevant to a particular decision.

Financial statements can provide only highly summarized economic information. The costs to a company of providing excessively detailed information would be prohibitive. In addition, too much detail leads to **information overload,** the problem of having so much data that important information becomes obscured by trivial information. Users faced with reams of data may become so frustrated attempting to use it that they lose the value of *key* information that is provided.

Information Analysis

Because of the diversity of users, their different levels of knowledge, the varying information needs for particular decisions, and the general nature of financial statements, a variety of analysis techniques has been developed. In the following sections, we explain several common methods of analysis. The choice of method depends on which technique appears to provide the most relevant information in a given situation.

METHODS OF ANALYSIS

LO 9-1

Differentiate between horizontal and vertical analysis.

Financial statement analysis should focus primarily on isolating information useful for making a particular decision. The information required can take many forms but usually involves comparisons, such as comparing changes in the same item for the same company over a number of years, comparing key relationships within the same year, or comparing the operations of several different companies in the same industry. This chapter discusses three categories of analysis methods: horizontal, vertical, and ratio. Exhibits 9.1 and 9.2 present comparative financial statements for Milavec Company. We refer to these statements in the examples of analysis techniques.

EXHIBIT 9.1		
MILAVEC COMPANY		
Income Statements and Statements of Retained Earnings For the Years Ending December 31		
	2015	2014
Sales	$900,000	$800,000
Cost of goods sold		
Beginning inventory	43,000	40,000
Purchases	637,000	483,000
Goods available for sale	680,000	523,000
Ending inventory	70,000	43,000
Cost of goods sold	610,000	480,000
Gross margin	290,000	320,000
Operating expenses	248,000	280,000
Income before taxes	42,000	40,000
Income taxes	17,000	18,000
Net income	25,000	22,000
Plus: Retained earnings, beginning balance	137,000	130,000
Less: Dividends	0	15,000
Retained earnings, ending balance	$162,000	$137,000

EXHIBIT 9.2		
MILAVEC COMPANY		
Balance Sheets As of December 31		
	2015	2014
Assets		
Cash	$ 20,000	$ 17,000
Marketable securities	20,000	22,000
Notes receivable	4,000	3,000
Accounts receivable	50,000	56,000
Merchandise inventory	70,000	43,000
Prepaid expenses	4,000	4,000
Property, plant, and equipment (net)	340,000	310,000
Total assets	$508,000	$455,000
Liabilities and Stockholders' Equity		
Accounts payable	$ 40,000	$ 38,000
Salaries payable	2,000	3,000
Taxes payable	4,000	2,000
Bonds payable, 8%	100,000	100,000
Preferred stock, 6%, $100 par, cumulative	50,000	50,000
Common stock, $10 par	150,000	125,000
Retained earnings	162,000	137,000
Total liabilities and stockholders' equity	$508,000	$455,000

Horizontal Analysis

Horizontal analysis, also called **trend analysis,** refers to studying the behavior of individual financial statement items over several accounting periods. These periods may be several quarters within the same fiscal year or they may be several different years. The analysis of a given item may focus on trends in the absolute dollar amount of the item or trends in percentages. For example, a user may observe that revenue increased from one period to the next by $42 million (an absolute dollar amount) or that it increased by a percentage such as 15 percent.

Absolute Amounts

The **absolute amounts** of particular financial statement items have many uses. Various national economic statistics, such as gross domestic product and the amount spent to replace productive capacity, are derived by combining absolute amounts reported by businesses. Financial statement users with expertise in particular industries might evaluate amounts reported for research and development costs to judge whether a company is spending excessively or conservatively. Users are particularly concerned with how amounts change over time. For example, a user might compare a pharmaceutical company's revenue before and after the patent expired on one of its drugs.

Comparing only absolute amounts has drawbacks, however, because *materiality* levels differ from company to company or even from year to year for a given company. The **materiality** of information refers to its relative importance. An item is considered material if knowledge of it would influence the decision of a reasonably informed user. Generally accepted accounting principles permit companies to account for *immaterial* items in the most convenient way, regardless of technical accounting rules. For example, companies may expense, rather than capitalize and depreciate, relatively inexpensive long-term assets like pencil sharpeners or waste baskets even if the assets have useful lives of many years. The concept of materiality, which has both quantitative and qualitative aspects, underlies all accounting principles.

It is difficult to judge the materiality of an absolute financial statement amount without considering the size of the company reporting it. For reporting purposes, Exxon Corporation's financial statements are rounded to the nearest million dollars. For Exxon, a $400,000 increase in sales is not material. For a small company, however, $400,000 could represent total sales, a highly material amount. Meaningful comparisons between the two companies' operating performance are impossible using only absolute amounts. Users can surmount these difficulties with percentage analysis.

Percentage Analysis

Percentage analysis involves computing the percentage relationship between two amounts. In horizontal percentage analysis, a financial statement item is expressed as a percentage of the previous balance for the same item. Percentage analysis sidesteps the materiality problems of comparing different size companies by measuring changes in percentages rather than absolute amounts. Each change is converted to a percentage of the base year. Exhibit 9.3 presents a condensed version of Milavec's income statement with horizontal percentages for each item.

The percentage changes disclose that, even though Milavec's net income increased slightly more than sales, products may be underpriced. Cost of goods sold increased much more than sales, resulting in a lower gross margin. Users would also want to investigate why operating expenses decreased substantially despite the increase in sales.

Whether basing their analyses on absolute amounts, percentages, or ratios, users must avoid drawing overly simplistic conclusions about the reasons for the results. Numerical relationships flag conditions requiring further study. Recall that a change that appears favorable on the surface may not necessarily be a good sign. Users must evaluate the underlying reasons for the change.

EXHIBIT 9.3			
MILAVEC COMPANY			
Comparative Income Statements			
For the Years Ending December 31			
	2015	2014	Percentage Difference
Sales	$900,000	$800,000	+12.5%*
Cost of goods sold	610,000	480,000	+27.1
Gross margin	290,000	320,000	−9.4
Operating expenses	248,000	280,000	−11.4
Income before taxes	42,000	40,000	+5.0
Income taxes	17,000	18,000	−5.6
Net income	$ 25,000	$ 22,000	+13.6

*($900,000 − $800,000) ÷ $800,000; all changes expressed as percentages of previous totals.

☑ **CHECK YOURSELF 9.1**

The following information was drawn from the annual reports of two retail companies (amounts are shown in millions). One company is an upscale department store; the other is a discount store. Based on this limited information, identify which company is the upscale department store.

	Jenkins Co.	Horn's, Inc.
Sales	$325	$680
Cost of goods sold	130	408
Gross margin	$195	$272

Answer Jenkins's gross margin represents 60 percent ($195 ÷ $325) of sales. Horn's gross margin represents 40 percent ($272 ÷ $680) of sales. Since an upscale department store would have higher margins than a discount store, the data suggest that Jenkins is the upscale department store.

Obviously, Dell, Inc., agreed to acquire Quest because it believed it could make a profit on the investment. A major reason Dell wanted to buy Quest was its desire to continue to expand its business beyond making and selling computer hardware and into software and computer services. How do companies decide what another company is worth, and how could Dell and Insight Venture Partners have such different opinions about the value of an investment? Valuing a potential investment is the result of extensive financial analysis, which we discuss in this chapter, and capital budgeting techniques, which were discussed in Chapter 16. As you have seen in these chapters, such decision making is based on estimates about future events. Predicting the future is imperfect, no matter how well-trained the forecaster might be.

Does this mean that financial analysis is useless? No. Assume you were planning to drive across the United States. Would you prefer to take the trip with a map or without? Obviously you would prefer to have a map or GPS, even though you know neither device is perfect. Just as five different financial analysts looking at the same data may calculate five different amounts they think a company is worth, five individuals planning a trip from Key West, Florida, to Anchorage, Alaska, could look at the same map and decide on five different ways to get there. It is only after the trips have been completed that we can say which person made the best decision.

Source: Quest Software, Inc., news releases.

When comparing more than two periods, analysts use either of two basic approaches: (1) choosing one base year from which to calculate all increases or decreases or (2) calculating each period's percentage change from the preceding figure. To illustrate, assume Milavec's sales for 2012 through 2015 are as follows:

	2015	2014	2013	2012
Sales	$900,000	$800,000	$750,000	$600,000
Increase over 2012 sales	50.0%	33.3%	25.0%	—
Increase over preceding year	12.5%	6.7%	25.0%	—

Analysis discloses that Milavec's 2015 sales represented a 50 percent increase over 2012 sales, and a large increase (25 percent) occurred in 2013. From 2013 to 2014, sales increased only 6.7 percent but in the following year, sales increased much more (12.5 percent).

Vertical Analysis

Vertical analysis uses percentages to compare individual components of financial statements to a key statement figure. Horizontal analysis compares items over many time periods; vertical analysis compares many items within the same time period.

Vertical Analysis of the Income Statement

Vertical analysis of an income statement (also called a *common size* income statement) involves converting each income statement component to a percentage of sales. Although vertical analysis suggests examining only one period, it is useful to compare common size income statements for several years. Exhibit 9.4 presents Milavec's income statements, along with vertical percentages, for 2015 and 2014. This analysis discloses that cost of goods sold increased significantly as a percentage of sales. Operating expenses and income taxes, however, decreased in relation to sales. Each of these observations indicates a need for more analysis regarding possible trends for future profits.

EXHIBIT 9.4

MILAVEC COMPANY
Vertical Analysis of Comparative Income Statements

	2015		2014	
	Amount	Percentage* of Sales	Amount	Percentage* of Sales
Sales	$900,000	100.0%	$800,000	100.0%
Cost of goods sold	610,000	67.8	480,000	60.0
Gross margin	290,000	32.2	320,000	40.0
Operating expenses	248,000	27.6	280,000	35.0
Income before taxes	42,000	4.7	40,000	5.0
Income taxes	17,000	1.9	18,000	2.3
Net income	$ 25,000	2.8%	$ 22,000	2.8%

*Percentages may not add exactly due to rounding.

Vertical Analysis of the Balance Sheet

Vertical analysis of the balance sheet involves converting each balance sheet component to a percentage of total assets. The vertical analysis of Milavec's balance sheets in Exhibit 9.5 discloses few large percentage changes from the preceding year. Even small individual percentage changes, however, may represent substantial dollar increases. For example, inventory constituted 9.5 percent of total assets in 2014 and 13.8 percent in 2015. While this appears to be a small increase, it actually represents a 62.8 percent increase in the inventory account balance [($70,000 − $43,000) ÷ $43,000] from 2014 to 2015. Careful analysis requires considering changes in both percentages *and* absolute amounts.

RATIO ANALYSIS

Ratio analysis involves studying various relationships between different items reported in a set of financial statements. For example, net earnings (net income) reported on the income statement may be compared to total assets reported on the balance sheet. Analysts calculate many different ratios for a wide variety of purposes. The remainder of this chapter is devoted to discussing some of the more commonly used ratios.

Objectives of Ratio Analysis

As suggested earlier, various users approach financial statement analysis with many different objectives. Creditors are interested in whether a company will be able to repay its debts on time. Both creditors and stockholders are concerned with how the company is financed, whether through debt, equity, or earnings. Stockholders and potential investors analyze past earnings performance and dividend policy for

EXHIBIT 9.5

MILAVEC COMPANY Vertical Analysis of Comparative Balance Sheets				
	2015	Percentage* of Total	2014	Percentage* of Total
Assets				
Cash	$ 20,000	3.9%	$ 17,000	3.7%
Marketable securities	20,000	3.9	22,000	4.8
Notes receivable	4,000	0.8	3,000	0.7
Accounts receivable	50,000	9.8	56,000	12.3
Merchandise inventory	70,000	13.8	43,000	9.5
Prepaid expenses	4,000	0.8	4,000	0.9
Total current assets	168,000	33.1	145,000	31.9
Property, plant, and equipment	340,000	66.9	310,000	68.1
Total assets	$508,000	100.0%	$455,000	100.0%
Liabilities and Stockholders' Equity				
Accounts payable	$ 40,000	7.9%	$ 38,000	8.4%
Salaries payable	2,000	0.4	3,000	0.7
Taxes payable	4,000	0.8	2,000	0.4
Total current liabilities	46,000	9.1	43,000	9.5
Bonds payable, 8%	100,000	19.7	100,000	22.0
Total liabilities	146,000	28.7	143,000	31.4
Preferred stock 6%, $100 par	50,000	9.8	50,000	11.0
Common stock, $10 par	150,000	29.5	125,000	27.5
Retained earnings	162,000	31.9	137,000	30.1
Total stockholders' equity	362,000	71.3	312,000	68.6
Total liabilities and stockholders' equity	$508,000	100.0%	$455,000	100.0%

*Percentages may not add exactly due to rounding.

clues to the future value of their investments. In addition to using internally generated data to analyze operations, company managers find much information prepared for external purposes useful for examining past operations and planning future policies. Although many of these objectives are interrelated, it is convenient to group ratios into categories such as measures of debt-paying ability and measures of profitability.

MEASURES OF DEBT-PAYING ABILITY

Liquidity Ratios

Liquidity ratios indicate a company's ability to pay short-term debts. They focus on current assets and current liabilities. The examples in the following section use the financial statement information reported by Milavec Company.

LO 9-2

 Calculate ratios for assessing a company's liquidity.

Working Capital

Working capital is current assets minus current liabilities. Current assets include assets most likely to be converted into cash in the current operating period. Current liabilities represent debts that must be satisfied in the current period. Working capital therefore measures the excess funds the company will have available for operations, excluding any new funds it generates during the year. Think of working capital as the cushion against short-term debt-paying problems. Working capital at the end of 2015 and 2014 for Milavec Company was as follows.

	2015	2014
Current assets	$168,000	$145,000
− Current liabilities	46,000	43,000
Working capital	$122,000	$102,000

Milavec's working capital increased from 2014 to 2015, but the numbers themselves say little. Whether $122,000 is sufficient or not depends on such factors as the industry in which Milavec operates, its size, and the maturity dates of its current obligations. We can see, however, that the increase in working capital is primarily due to the increase in inventories.

Current Ratio

Working capital is an absolute amount. Its usefulness is limited by the materiality difficulties discussed earlier. It is hard to draw meaningful conclusions from comparing Milavec's working capital of $122,000 with another company that also has working capital of $122,000. By expressing the relationship between current assets and current liabilities as a ratio, however, we have a more useful measure of the company's debt-paying ability relative to other companies. The **current ratio,** also called the **working capital ratio,** is calculated as follows.

$$\text{Current ratio} = \frac{\text{Current assets}}{\text{Current liabilities}}$$

To illustrate using the current ratio for comparisons, consider Milavec's current position relative to that of Laroque's, a larger firm with current assets of $500,000 and current liabilities of $378,000.

	Milavec	Laroque
Current assets (a)	$168,000	$500,000
− Current liabilities (b)	46,000	378,000
Working capital	$122,000	$122,000
Current ratio (a ÷ b)	3.65:1	1.32:1

The current ratio is expressed as the number of dollars of current assets for each dollar of current liabilities. In the above example, both companies have the same amount of working capital. Milavec, however, appears to have a much stronger working capital position. Any conclusions from this analysis must take into account the circumstances of the particular companies; there is no single ideal current ratio that suits all companies. In recent years, the average current ratio of the nonfinancial companies that constitute the Dow Jones Industrial Average was around 1.38:1. The individual company ratios, however, ranged from .65:1 to 2.60:1. A current ratio can be too high. Money invested in factories and developing new products is usually more profitable than money held as large cash balances or invested in inventory.

Quick Ratio

The **quick ratio,** also known as the **acid-test ratio,** is a conservative variation of the current ratio. The quick ratio measures a company's *immediate* debt-paying ability.

Only cash, receivables, and current marketable securities (*quick assets*) are included in the numerator. Less liquid current assets, such as inventories and prepaid expenses, are omitted. Inventories may take several months to sell; prepaid expenses reduce otherwise necessary expenditures but do not lead eventually to cash receipts. The quick ratio is computed as follows.

$$\text{Quick ratio} = \frac{\text{Quick assets}}{\text{Current liabilities}}$$

Milavec Company's current ratios and quick ratios for 2015 and 2014 follow.

	2015	2014
Current ratio	168,000 ÷ 46,000	145,000 ÷ 43,000
	3.65:1	3.37:1
Quick ratio	94,000 ÷ 46,000	98,000 ÷ 43,000
	2.04:1	2.28:1

The decrease in the quick ratio from 2014 to 2015 reflects both a decrease in quick assets and an increase in current liabilities. The result indicates that the company is less liquid (has less ability to pay its short-term debt) in 2015 than it was in 2014.

Accounts Receivable Ratios

Offering customers credit plays an enormous role in generating revenue, but it also increases expenses and delays cash receipts. To minimize bad debts expense and collect cash for use in current operations, companies want to collect receivables as quickly as possible without losing customers. Two relationships are often examined to assess a company's collection record: *accounts receivable turnover* and *average days to collect receivables (average collection period)*.

Accounts receivable turnover is calculated as follows.

$$\text{Accounts receivable turnover} = \frac{\text{Net credit sales}}{\text{Average accounts receivable}}$$

Net credit sales refers to total sales on account less sales discounts and returns. When most sales are credit sales or when a breakdown of total sales between cash sales and credit sales is not available, the analyst must use total sales in the numerator. The denominator is based on *net accounts receivable* (receivables after subtracting the allowance for doubtful accounts). Since the numerator represents a whole period, it is preferable to use average receivables in the denominator if possible. When comparative statements are available, the average can be based on the beginning and ending balances. Milavec Company's accounts receivable turnover is computed as follows.

	2015	2014
Net sales (assume all on account) (a)	$900,000	$800,000
Beginning receivables (b)	$ 56,000	$ 55,000*
Ending receivables (c)	50,000	56,000
Average receivables (d) = (b + c) ÷ 2	$ 53,000	$ 55,500
Accounts receivable turnover (a ÷ d)	16.98	14.41

*The beginning receivables balance was drawn from the 2013 financial statements, which are not included in the illustration.

The 2015 accounts receivable turnover of 16.98 indicates Milavec collected its average receivables almost 17 times that year. The higher the turnover, the faster the collections. A company can have cash flow problems and lose substantial purchasing power if resources are tied up in receivables for long periods.

Average days to collect receivables is calculated as follows.

$$\text{Average days to collect receivables} = \frac{365 \text{ days}}{\text{Accounts receivable turnover}}$$

This ratio offers another way to look at turnover by showing the number of days, on average, it takes to collect a receivable. If receivables were collected 16.98 times in 2015, the average collection period was 21 days, $365 \div 16.98$ (the number of days in the year divided by accounts receivable turnover). For 2014, it took an average of 25 days ($365 \div 14.41$) to collect a receivable.

Although the collection period improved, no other conclusions can be reached without considering the industry, Milavec's past performance, and the general economic environment. In recent years, the average time to collect accounts receivable for the 26 nonfinancial companies that make up the Dow Jones Industrial Average was around 39 days. (Financial firms are excluded because, by the nature of their business, they have very long collection periods.)

Inventory Ratios

A fine line exists between having too much and too little inventory in stock. Too little inventory can result in lost sales and costly production delays. Too much inventory can use needed space, increase financing and insurance costs, and become obsolete. To help analyze how efficiently a company manages inventory, we use two ratios similar to those used in analyzing accounts receivable.

Inventory turnover indicates the number of times, on average, that inventory is totally replaced during the year. The relationship is computed as follows.

$$\text{Inventory turnover} = \frac{\text{Cost of goods sold}}{\text{Average inventory}}$$

The average inventory is usually based on the beginning and ending balances that are shown in the financial statements. Inventory turnover for Milavec was as follows.

	2015	2014
Cost of goods sold (a)	$610,000	$480,000
Beginning inventory (b)	$ 43,000	$ 40,000*
Ending inventory (c)	70,000	43,000
Average inventory (d) = (b + c) ÷ 2	$ 56,500	$ 41,500
Inventory turnover (a ÷ d)	10.80	11.57

*The beginning inventory balance was drawn from the company's 2013 financial statements, which are not included in the illustration.

Generally, a higher turnover indicates that merchandise is being handled more efficiently. Trying to compare firms in different industries, however, can be misleading. Inventory turnover for grocery stores and many retail outlets is high. Because of the nature of the goods being sold, inventory turnover is much lower for appliance and jewelry stores. We look at this issue in more detail when we discuss return on investment.

Average days to sell inventory is determined by dividing the number of days in the year by the inventory turnover as follows.

$$\text{Average days to sell inventory} = \frac{365 \text{ days}}{\text{Inventory turnover}}$$

The result approximates the number of days the firm could sell inventory without purchasing more. For Milavec, this figure was 34 days in 2015 (365 ÷ 10.80) and 32 days in 2014 (365 ÷ 11.57). In recent years it took around 80 days, on average, for the companies in the Dow Jones Industrial Average that have inventory to sell their inventory. The time it took individual companies to sell their inventory varied by industry, ranging from 7 days to 252 days.

Solvency Ratios

Solvency ratios are used to analyze a company's long-term debt-paying ability and its financing structure. Creditors are concerned with a company's ability to satisfy outstanding obligations. The larger a company's liability percentage, the greater the risk that the company could fall behind or default on debt payments. Stockholders, too, are concerned about a company's solvency. If a company is unable to pay its debts, the owners could lose their investment. Each user group desires that company financing choices minimize its investment risk, whether the investment is in debt or stockholders' equity.

 Calculate ratios for assessing a company's solvency.

Debt Ratios

The following ratios represent two different ways to express the same relationship. Both are frequently used.

Debt to assets ratio.   This ratio measures the percentage of a company's assets that are financed by debt.

Debt to equity ratio.   As used in this ratio, *equity* means stockholders' equity. The debt to equity ratio compares creditor financing to owner financing. It is expressed as the dollar amount of liabilities for each dollar of stockholders' equity.

These ratios are calculated as follows.

$$\text{Debt to assets} = \frac{\text{Total liabilities}}{\text{Total assets}}$$

$$\text{Debt to equity} = \frac{\text{Total liabilities}}{\text{Total stockholders' equity}}$$

Applying these formulas to Milavec Company's results produces the following.

	2015	2014
Total liabilities (a)	$146,000	$143,000
Total stockholders' equity (b)	362,000	312,000
Total equities (Liabilities + Stockholders' equity) (c)	$508,000	$455,000
Debt to assets (a ÷ c)	29%	31%
Debt to equity ratio (a ÷ b)	0.40:1	0.46:1

Each year, less than one-third of the company's assets were financed with debt. The amount of liabilities per dollar of stockholders' equity declined by 0.06. It is difficult to judge whether the reduced percentage of liabilities is favorable. In general, a lower level of liabilities provides greater security because the likelihood of bankruptcy is reduced. Perhaps, however, the company is financially strong enough to incur more liabilities and benefit from financial leverage. The 26 nonfinancial companies that make up the Dow Jones Industrial Average report around 42 percent of their assets, on average, are financed through borrowing. The debt to asset ratios of these companies ranged from 10 percent to 79 percent.

Number of Times Interest Is Earned

This ratio measures the burden a company's interest payments represent. Users often consider times interest is earned along with the debt ratios when evaluating financial risk. The numerator of this ratio uses *earnings before interest and taxes (EBIT)*, rather than net earnings, because the amount of earnings *before* interest and income taxes is available for paying interest.

$$\text{Number of times interest is earned} = \frac{\text{Earnings before interest and taxes expense}}{\text{Interest expense}}$$

Dividing EBIT by interest expense indicates how many times the company could have made its interest payments. Obviously, interest is paid only once, but the more times it *could* be paid, the bigger the company's safety net. Although interest is paid from cash, not accrual earnings, it is standard practice to base this ratio on accrual-based EBIT, not a cash-based amount. For Milavec, this calculation is as follows.

	2015	2014
Income before taxes	$42,000	$40,000
Interest expense (b)	8,000	8,000*
Income before taxes and interest (a)	$50,000	$48,000
Times interest earned (a ÷ b)	6.25 times	6 times

*Interest on bonds: $100,000 × .08 = $8,000.

Any expense or dividend payment can be analyzed this way. Another frequently used calculation is the number of times the preferred dividend is earned. In that case, the numerator is net income (after taxes) and the denominator is the amount of the annual preferred dividend.

✓ CHECK YOURSELF 9.2

Selected data for Riverside Corporation and Academy Company follow (amounts are shown in millions).

	Riverside Corporation	Academy Company
Total liabilities (a)	$650	$450
Stockholders' equity (b)	300	400
Total liabilities + Stockholders' equity (c)	$950	$850
Interest expense (d)	$ 65	$ 45
Income before taxes (e)	140	130
Income before taxes and interest (f)	$205	$175

Based on this information alone, which company would likely obtain the less favorable interest rate on additional debt financing?

Answer   Interest rates vary with risk levels. Companies with less solvency (long-term debt-paying ability) generally must pay higher interest rates to obtain financing. Two solvency measures for the two companies follow. Recall:

Total assets = Liabilities + Stockholders' equity

	Riverside Corporation	Academy Company
Debt to assets ratio (a ÷ c)	68.4%	52.9%
Times interest earned (f ÷ d)	3.15 times	3.89 times

Since Riverside has a higher percentage of debt and a lower times interest earned ratio, the data suggest that Riverside is less solvent than Academy. Riverside would therefore likely have to pay a higher interest rate to obtain additional financing.

Plant Assets to Long-Term Liabilities

Companies often pledge plant assets as collateral for long-term liabilities. Financial statement users may analyze a firm's ability to obtain long-term financing on the strength of its asset base. Effective financial management principles dictate that asset purchases should be financed over a time span about equal to the expected lives of the assets. Short-term assets should be financed with short-term liabilities; the current ratio, introduced earlier, indicates how well a company manages current debt. Long-lived assets should be financed with long-term liabilities, and the *plant assets to long-term liabilities* ratio suggests how well long-term debt is managed. It is calculated as follows.

$$\text{Plant assets to long-term liabilities} = \frac{\text{Net plant assets}}{\text{Long-term liabilities}}$$

For Milavec Company, these ratios follow.

	2015	2014
Net plant assets (a)	$340,000	$310,000
Bonds payable (b)	100,000	100,000
Plant assets to long-term liabilities (a ÷ b)	3.4:1	3.1:1

MEASURES OF PROFITABILITY

Profitability refers to a company's ability to generate earnings. Both management and external users employ **profitability ratios** to assess a company's success in generating profits and how these profits are used to reward investors. Some of the many ratios available to measure different aspects of profitability are discussed in the following two sections.

LO 9-4

Calculate ratios for assessing company management's effectiveness.

Measures of Managerial Effectiveness

The most common ratios used to evaluate managerial effectiveness measure what percentage of sales results in earnings and how productive assets are in generating those sales. As mentioned earlier, the *absolute amount* of sales or earnings means little without also considering company size.

Net Margin (or Return on Sales)

Gross margin and *gross profit* are alternate terms for the amount remaining after subtracting the expense cost of goods sold from sales. **Net margin,** sometimes called *operating margin, profit margin,* or the *return on sales ratio,* describes the percent of each sales dollar remaining after subtracting other expenses as well as cost of goods sold. Net margin can be calculated in several ways; some of the more common methods only subtract normal operating expenses or all expenses other than income tax expense. For simplicity, our calculation uses net income (we subtract all expenses). Net income divided by net sales expresses net income (earnings) as a percentage of sales, as follows.

$$\text{Net margin} = \frac{\text{Net income}}{\text{Net sales}}$$

For Milavec Company, the net margins for 2015 and 2014 were as follows.

	2015	2014
Net income (a)	$ 25,000	$ 22,000
Net sales (b)	900,000	800,000
Net margin (a ÷ b)	2.78%	2.75%

338   Chapter 9

Milavec has maintained approximately the same net margin. Obviously, the larger the percentage, the better; a meaningful interpretation, however, requires analyzing the company's history and comparing the net margin to other companies in the same industry. The average net margin for the 26 nonfinancial companies that make up the Dow Jones Industrial Average has been around 12 percent in recent years; some companies, such as Microsoft with 33 percent, have been much higher than the average. Of course, if a company has a net loss, its net margin for that year will be negative.

Asset Turnover Ratio

The **asset turnover ratio** (sometimes called *turnover of assets ratio*) measures how many sales dollars were generated for each dollar of assets invested. As with many ratios used in financial statement analysis, users may define the numerator and denominator of this ratio in different ways. For example, they may use total assets or only include operating assets. Since the numerator represents a whole period, it is preferable to use average assets in the denominator if possible, especially if the amount of assets changed significantly during the year. We use average total assets in our illustration.

$$\text{Asset turnover} = \frac{\text{Net sales}}{\text{Average total assets}}$$

For Milavec, the asset turnover ratios were as follows.

	2015	2014
Net sales (a)	$900,000	$800,000
Beginning assets (b)	$455,000	$420,000*
Ending assets (c)	508,000	455,000
Average assets (d) = (b + c) ÷ 2	$481,500	$437,500
Asset turnover (a ÷ d)	1.87	1.83

*The beginning asset balance was drawn from the 2013 financial statements, which are not included in the illustration.

As with most ratios, the implications of a given asset turnover ratio are affected by other considerations. Asset turnover will be high in an industry that requires only minimal investment to operate, such as real estate sales companies. On the other hand, industries that require large investments in plant and machinery, like the auto industry, are likely to have lower asset turnover ratios. The asset turnover ratios of the nonfinancial companies that make up the Dow Jones Industrial Average have averaged around 0.85 in recent years. This means that annual sales have averaged 85 percent of their assets.

Return on Investment

Return on investment (ROI), also called **return on assets** or *earning power,* is the ratio of wealth generated (net income) to the amount invested (average total assets) to generate the wealth. ROI can be calculated as follows.[1]

$$\text{ROI} = \frac{\text{Net income}}{\text{Average total assets}}$$

---

[1]Detailed coverage of the return on investment ratio is provided in Chapter 15. As discussed in that chapter, companies frequently manipulate the formula to improve managerial motivation and performance. For example, instead of using net income, companies frequently use operating income because net income may be affected by items that are not controllable by management such as loss on a plant closing, storm damage, and so on.

For Milavec, ROI was as follows.

2015

$25,000 ÷ $481,500* = 5.19%

2014

$22,000 ÷ $437,500* = 5.03%

*The computation of average assets is shown above.

In general, higher ROIs suggest better performance. The return on investment ratios of the large nonfinancial companies that make up the Dow Jones Industrial Average have averaged around 9 percent in recent years. These data suggest that Milavec is performing below average, and therefore signals a need for further evaluation that would lead to improved performance.

Return on Equity

Return on equity (ROE) is often used to measure the profitability of the stockholders' investment. ROE is usually higher than ROI because of financial leverage. Financial leverage refers to using debt financing to increase the assets available to a business beyond the amount of assets financed by owners. As long as a company's ROI exceeds its cost of borrowing (interest expense), the owners will earn a higher return on their investment in the company by using borrowed money. For example, if a company borrows money at 8 percent and invests it at 10 percent, the owners will enjoy a return that is higher than 10 percent. ROE is computed as follows.

$$ROE = \frac{Net\ income}{Average\ total\ stockholders'\ equity}$$

	2015	2014
Net income (a)	$ 25,000	$ 22,000
Preferred stock, 6%, $100 par, cumulative	50,000	50,000
Common stock, $10 par	150,000	125,000
Retained earnings	162,000	137,000
Ending stockholders' equity (b)	$362,000	$312,000
Beginning stockholders' equity (c)	$312,000	$268,000*
Average stockholders' equity (d) = (b + c) ÷ 2	$337,000	$290,000
ROE (a ÷ b)	7.4%	7.6%

*The 2014 beginning stockholders' equity balance was drawn from the 2013 financial statements, which are not included in the illustration.

The slight decrease in ROE is due primarily to the increase in common stock. The effect of the increase in total stockholders' equity offsets the effect of the increase in earnings. It is interesting to note that Milavec's ROEs of 7.6 percent and 7.4 percent are low in relation to real-world companies that make up the Dow Jones Industrial Average. Recently, the average ROE for the these companies was 30 percent. One contribution factor explaining this difference is that most companies in the DOW are more highly leveraged.

Stock Market Ratios

Existing and potential investors in a company's stock use many common ratios to analyze and compare the earnings and dividends of different size companies in different industries. Purchasers of stock can profit in two ways: through receiving dividends and

LO 9-5

Calculate ratios for assessing a company's position in the stock market.

through increases in stock value. Investors consider both dividends and overall earnings performance as indicators of the value of the stock they own.

Earnings per Share

Perhaps the most frequently quoted measure of earnings performance is **earnings per share (EPS).** EPS calculations are among the most complex in accounting, and more advanced textbooks devote entire chapters to the subject. At this level, we use the following basic formula.

$$\text{Earnings per share} = \frac{\text{Net earnings available for common stock}}{\text{Average number of outstanding common shares}}$$

EPS pertains to shares of *common stock.* Limiting the numerator to earnings available for common stock eliminates the annual preferred dividend (0.06 × $50,000 = $3,000) from the calculation. Exhibit 9.1 shows that Milavec did not pay the preferred dividends in 2015. Since the preferred stock is cumulative, however, the preferred dividend is in arrears and not available to the common stockholders. The number of common shares outstanding is determined by dividing the book value of the common stock by its par value per share ($150,000 ÷ $10 = 15,000 for 2015 and $125,000 ÷ $10 = 12,500 for 2014). Using these data, Milavec's 2015 EPS is calculated as follows.

$$\frac{\$25,000\ \text{(net income)} - \$3,000\ \text{(preferred dividend)}}{(15,000 + 12,500)/2\ \text{(average outstanding common shares)}} = \$1.60\ \text{per share}$$

Investors attribute a great deal of importance to EPS figures. The amounts used in calculating EPS, however, have limitations. Many accounting choices, assumptions, and estimates underlie net income computations, including alternative depreciation methods, different inventory cost flow assumptions, and estimates of future bad debt or warranty expenses, to name only a few. The denominator is also inexact because various factors (discussed in advanced accounting courses) affect the number of shares to include. Numerous opportunities therefore exist to manipulate EPS figures. Prudent investors consider these variables in deciding how much weight to attach to earnings per share.

Book Value

Book value per share is another frequently quoted measure of a share of stock. It is calculated as follows.

$$\text{Book value per share} = \frac{\text{Stockholders' equity} - \text{Preferred stock}}{\text{Outstanding common shares}}$$

Instead of describing the numerator as stockholders' equity, we could have used assets minus liabilities, the algebraic computation of a company's "net worth." Net worth is a misnomer. A company's accounting records reflect book values, not worth. Because assets are recorded at historical costs and different methods are used to transfer asset costs to expense, the book value of assets after deducting liabilities is difficult to interpret. Nevertheless, investors use the term *book value per share* frequently. Book value per share for 2015 is calculated as follows.

$$\frac{\$362,000 - \$50,000}{15,000\ \text{shares}} = \$20.80\ \text{per share}$$

Price-Earnings Ratio

The **price-earnings ratio,** or *P/E ratio,* compares the earnings per share of a company to the market price for a share of the company's stock. Assume Avalanche Company and Brushfire Company each report earnings per share of $3.60. For the same year, Cyclone Company reports EPS of $4.10. Based on these data alone, Cyclone stock may seem to be the best investment. Suppose, however, that the price for one share of stock in each company is $43.20, $36.00, and $51.25, respectively. Which stock would you buy? Cyclone's stock price is the highest, but so is its EPS. The P/E ratio provides a common base of comparison.

$$\text{Price-earnings ratio} = \frac{\text{Market price per share}}{\text{Earnings per share}}$$

The P/E ratios for the three companies are:

Avalanche	Brushfire	Cyclone
12.0	10.0	12.5

Brushfire might initially seem to be the best buy for your money. Yet there must be some reason that Cyclone's stock is selling at 12½ times earnings. In general, a higher P/E ratio indicates the market is more optimistic about a company's growth potential than it is about a company with a lower P/E ratio. The market price of a company's stock reflects judgments about both the company's current results and expectations about future results. Investors cannot make informed use of these ratios for investment decisions without examining the reasons behind the ratios. In early February 2013, when the Dow Jones Industrial Average was around 14,000 points, the average P/E ratio for the companies in the Dow Jones Industrial Average was around 15.

Dividend Yield

There are two ways to profit from a stock investment. One, investors can sell the stock for more than they paid to purchase it (if the stock price rises). Two, the company that issued the stock can pay cash dividends to the shareholders. Most investors view rising stock prices as the primary reward for investing in stock. The importance of receiving dividends, however, should not be overlooked. Evaluating dividend payments is more complex than simply comparing the dividends per share paid by one company to the dividends per share paid by another company. Receiving a $1 dividend on a share purchased for $10 is a much better return than receiving a $1.50 dividend on stock bought for $100. Computing the **dividend yield** simplifies comparing dividend payments. Dividend yield measures dividends received as a percentage of a stock's market price.

$$\text{Dividend yield} = \frac{\text{Dividends per share}}{\text{Market price per share}}$$

To illustrate, consider Dragonfly, Inc., and Elk Company. The information for calculating dividend yield follows.

	Dragonfly	Elk
Dividends per share (a)	$ 1.80	$ 3.00
Market price per share (b)	40.00	75.00
Dividend yield (a ÷ b)	4.5%	4.0%

Even though the dividend per share paid by Elk Company is higher, the yield is lower (4.0 percent versus 4.5 percent) because Elk's stock price is so high. The dividend yields for the companies included in the Dow Jones Industrial Average were averaging around 2.5 percent in February of 2013.

Other Ratios

Investors can also use a wide array of other ratios to analyze profitability. Most *profitability ratios* use the same reasoning. For example, you can calculate the *yield* of a variety of financial investments. Yield is determined by dividing the amount of the return (the dividend or interest earned) by the amount of the investment. The dividend yield explained above could be calculated for either common or preferred stock.

Investors could measure the earnings yield by calculating earnings per share as a percentage of market price. Yield on a bond can be calculated the same way: interest received divided by the price of the bond.

The specific ratios presented in this chapter are summarized in Exhibit 9.6.

EXHIBIT 9.6

Summary of Key Relationships

Liquidity Ratios	1. Working capital	Current assets − Current liabilities
	2. Current ratio	Current assets ÷ Current liabilities
	3. Quick (acid-test) ratio	(Current assets − Inventory − Prepaids) ÷ Current liabilities
	4. Accounts receivable turnover	Net credit sales ÷ Average receivables
	5. Average days to collect receivables	365 ÷ Accounts receivable turnover
	6. Inventory turnover	Cost of goods sold ÷ Average inventory
	7. Average days to sell inventory	365 ÷ Inventory turnover
Solvency Ratios	8. Debt to assets ratio	Total liabilities ÷ Total assets
	9. Debt to equity ratio	Total liabilities ÷ Total stockholders' equity
	10. Number of times interest is earned	Earnings before interest and taxes ÷ Interest expense
	11. Plant assets to long-term liabilities	Net plant assets ÷ Long-term liabilities
Profitability Ratios	12. Net margin	Net income ÷ Net sales
	13. Asset turnover	Net sales ÷ Average total assets
	14. Return on investment (also: return on assets)	Net income ÷ Average total assets
	15. Return on equity	Net income ÷ Average total stockholders' equity
Stock Market Ratios	16. Earnings per share	Net earnings available for common stock ÷ Average outstanding common shares
	17. Book value per share	(Stockholders' equity − Preferred rights) ÷ Outstanding common shares
	18. Price-earnings ratio	Market price per share ÷ Earnings per share
	19. Dividend yield	Dividends per share ÷ Market price per share

LIMITATIONS OF FINANCIAL STATEMENT ANALYSIS

Analyzing financial statements is analogous to choosing a new car. Each car is different, and prospective buyers must evaluate and weigh myriad features: gas mileage, engine size, manufacturer's reputation, color, accessories, and price, to name a few. Just as it is difficult to compare a Toyota minivan to a Ferrari sports car, so it is difficult to compare a small textile firm to a giant oil company. To make a meaningful assessment, the potential car buyer must focus on key data that can be comparably expressed for each car, such as gas mileage. The superior gas mileage of the minivan may pale in comparison to the thrill of driving the sports car, but the price of buying and operating the sports car may be the characteristic that determines the ultimate choice.

External users can rely on financial statement analysis only as a general guide to the potential of a business. They should resist placing too much weight on any particular figure or trend. Many factors must be considered simultaneously before making any judgments. Furthermore, the analysis techniques discussed in this chapter are all based on historical information. Future events and unanticipated changes in conditions will also influence a company's operating results.

Different Industries

Different industries may be affected by unique social policies, special accounting procedures, or other individual industry attributes. Ratios of companies in different industries are not comparable without considering industry characteristics. A high debt to assets ratio is more acceptable in some industries than others. Even within an industry,

REALITY BYTES

The single most important source of financial information is a company's annual report, but decision makers should also consider other sources. Interested persons can access quarterly and annual reports through the SEC's EDGAR database and often from company websites as well. Many companies will provide printed versions of these reports upon request. Companies also post information on their websites that is not included in their annual reports. For example, some automobile companies provide very detailed production data through their corporate websites.

Users can frequently obtain information useful in analyzing a particular company from independent sources as well as from the company itself. For example, the websites of popular news services, such as CNN (www.money.cnn.com) and CNBC (www.moneycentral.msn.com) provide archived news stories and independent financial information about many companies. The websites of brokerage houses like www.schwab.com offer free financial information about companies. Finally, libraries often subscribe to independent services that evaluate companies as potential investments. One example worth reviewing is *Value Line Investment Survey.*

a particular business may require more or less working capital than the industry average. If so, the working capital and quick ratios would mean little compared to those of other firms, but may still be useful for trend analysis.

Because of industry-specific factors, most professional analysts specialize in one, or only a few, industries. Financial institutions such as brokerage houses, banks, and insurance companies typically employ financial analysts who specialize in areas such as mineral or oil extraction, chemicals, banking, retail, insurance, bond markets, or automobile manufacturing.

Changing Economic Environment

When comparing firms, analysts must be alert to changes in general economic trends from year to year. Significant changes in fuel costs and interest rates in recent years make old rule-of-thumb guidelines for evaluating these factors obsolete. In addition, the presence or absence of inflation affects business prospects.

Accounting Principles

Financial statement analysis is only as reliable as the data on which it is based. Although most firms follow generally accepted accounting principles, a wide variety of acceptable accounting methods is available from which to choose, including different inventory and depreciation methods, different schedules for recognizing revenue, and different ways to account for oil and gas exploration costs. Analyzing statements of companies that seem identical may produce noncomparable ratios if the companies have used different accounting methods. Analysts may seek to improve comparability by trying to recast different companies' financial statements as if the same accounting methods had been applied.

Accrual accounting requires the use of many estimates; bad debt expense, warranty expense, asset lives, and salvage value are just a few. The reliability of the resulting financial reports depends on the expertise and integrity of the persons who make the estimates.

The quality and usefulness of accounting information are influenced by underlying accounting concepts. Two particular concepts, *conservatism* and *historical cost,* have a tremendous impact on financial reporting. Conservatism dictates recognizing estimated losses as soon as they occur, but gain recognition is almost always deferred until the gains are actually realized. Conservatism produces a negative bias in financial statements. There are persuasive arguments for the conservatism principle, but users should be alert to distortions it may cause in accounting information.

The pervasive use of the historical cost concept is probably the greatest single cause of distorted financial statement analysis results. The historical cost of an asset does not represent its current value. The asset purchased in 2001 for $10,000 is not comparable in value to the asset purchased in 2015 for $10,000 because of changes in the value of the dollar. Using historical cost produces financial statements that report dollars with differing purchasing power in the same statement. Combining these differing dollar values is akin to adding miles to kilometers. To get the most from analyzing financial statements, users should be cognizant of these limitations.

☑ CHECK YOURSELF 9.3

The return on equity for Gup Company and Hunn Company is 23.4 percent and 17 percent, respectively. Does this mean Gup Company is better managed than Hunn Company?

Answer   No single ratio can adequately measure management performance. Even analyzing a wide range of ratios provides only limited insight. Any useful interpretation requires the analyst to recognize the limitations of ratio analysis. For example, ratio norms typically differ between industries and may be affected by temporary economic factors. In addition, companies' use of different accounting practices and procedures produces different ratio results even when underlying circumstances are comparable.

‹‹ A Look Back

Financial statement analysis involves many factors, among them user characteristics, information needs for particular types of decisions, and how financial information is analyzed. Analytical techniques include *horizontal, vertical,* and *ratio analysis.* Users commonly calculate ratios to measure a company's liquidity, solvency, and profitability. The specific ratios presented in this chapter are summarized in Exhibit 9.6. Although ratios are easy to calculate and provide useful insights into business operations, when interpreting analytical results, users should consider limitations resulting from differing industry characteristics, differing economic conditions, and the fundamental accounting principles used to produce reported financial information.

›› A Look Forward

This chapter concludes the *financial* accounting portion of the text. Beginning with Chapter 10, we introduce various tools from a branch of the field called *managerial* accounting. Managerial accounting focuses on meeting the accounting information needs of decision makers inside, rather than outside, a company. In addition to financial statement data, inside users require detailed, forward-looking information that includes nonfinancial as well as financial components. We begin with a chapter that discusses the value management accounting adds to the decision-making process.

Video lectures and accompanying self-assessment quizzes are available for all learning
objectives through McGraw-Hill *Connect® Accounting.*

SELF-STUDY REVIEW PROBLEM

Financial statements for Stallings Company follow.

Income Statements for the Years Ended December 31	2015	2014
Revenues		
Net sales	$315,000	$259,000
Expenses		
Cost of goods sold	(189,000)	(154,000)
Selling, general, and administrative expenses	(54,000)	(46,000)
Interest expense	(4,000)	(4,500)
Income before taxes	68,000	54,500
Income tax expense (40%)	(27,200)	(21,800)
Net income	$ 40,800	$ 32,700

Balance Sheets As of December 31	2015	2014
Assets		
Current assets		
Cash	$ 6,500	$ 11,500
Accounts receivable	51,000	49,000
Inventories	155,000	147,500
Total current assets	212,500	208,000
Plant and equipment (net)	187,500	177,000
Total assets	$400,000	$385,000
Liabilities and Stockholders' Equity		
Liabilities		
Current liabilities		
Accounts payable	$ 60,000	$ 81,500
Other	25,000	22,500
Total current liabilities	85,000	104,000
Bonds payable	100,000	100,000
Total liabilities	185,000	204,000
Stockholders' equity		
Common stock (50,000 shares, $3 par)	150,000	150,000
Paid-in capital in excess of par	20,000	20,000
Retained earnings	45,000	11,000
Total stockholders' equity	215,000	181,000
Total liabilities and stockholders' equity	$400,000	$385,000

Required

a. Use horizontal analysis to determine which expense item increased by the highest percentage from 2014 to 2015.

b. Use vertical analysis to determine whether the inventory balance is a higher percentage of total assets in 2014 or 2015.

c. Calculate the following ratios for 2014 and 2015. When data limitations prohibit computing averages, use year-end balances in your calculations.

(1) Net margin

(2) Return on investment

(3) Return on equity

(4) Earnings per share

(5) Price-earnings ratio (market price per share at the end of 2015 and 2014 was $12.04 and $8.86, respectively)

(6) Book value per share of common stock

(7) Times interest earned

(8) Working capital

(9) Current ratio

(10) Acid-test ratio

(11) Accounts receivable turnover

(12) Inventory turnover

(13) Debt to equity

Solution to Requirement a

Income tax expense increased by the greatest percentage. Computations follow.

Cost of goods sold ($189,000 − $154,000) ÷ $154,000 = 22.73%

General, selling, and administrative ($54,000 − $46,000) ÷ $46,000 = 17.39%

Interest expense decreased.

Income tax expense ($27,200 − $21,800) ÷ $21,800 = 24.77%

Solution to Requirement b

2014: $147,500 ÷ $385,000 = 38.31%

2015: $155,000 ÷ $400,000 = 38.75%

Inventory is slightly larger relative to total assets in 2015.

Solution to Requirement c

		2015	2014
1.	$\dfrac{\text{Net income}}{\text{Net sales}}$	$\dfrac{\$40,800}{\$315,000} = 12.95\%$	$\dfrac{\$32,700}{\$259,000} = 12.63\%$
2.	$\dfrac{\text{Net income}}{\text{Average total assets}}$	$\dfrac{\$40,800}{\$392,500} = 10.39\%$	$\dfrac{\$32,700}{\$385,000} = 8.49\%$
3.	$\dfrac{\text{Net income}}{\text{Average total stockholders' equity}}$	$\dfrac{\$40,800}{\$198,000} = 20.61\%$	$\dfrac{\$32,700}{\$181,000} = 18.07\%$
4.	$\dfrac{\text{Net income}}{\text{Average common shares outstanding}}$	$\dfrac{\$40,800}{50,000 \text{ shares}} = \$0.816$	$\dfrac{\$32,700}{50,000 \text{ shares}} = \$0.654$
5.	$\dfrac{\text{Market price per share}}{\text{Earnings per share}}$	$\dfrac{\$12.04}{\$0.816} = 14.75 \text{ times}$	$\dfrac{\$8.86}{\$0.654} = 13.55 \text{ times}$
6.	$\dfrac{\text{Stockholders' equity} - \text{Preferred stock}}{\text{Outstanding common shares}}$	$\dfrac{\$215,000}{50,000 \text{ shares}} = \$4.30$	$\dfrac{\$181,000}{50,000 \text{ shares}} = \$3.62$
7.	$\dfrac{\text{Net income} + \text{Taxes} + \text{Interest expense}}{\text{Interest expense}}$	$\dfrac{\$40,800 + \$27,200 + \$4,000}{\$4,000} = 18 \text{ times}$	$\dfrac{\$32,700 + \$21,800 + \$4,500}{\$4,500} = 13.1 \text{ times}$
8.	Current assets − Current liabilities	$\$212,500 - \$85,000 = \$127,500$	$\$208,000 - \$104,000 = \$104,000$
9.	$\dfrac{\text{Current assets}}{\text{Current liabilities}}$	$\dfrac{\$212,500}{\$85,000} = 2.5{:}1$	$\dfrac{\$208,000}{\$104,000} = 2{:}1$
10.	$\dfrac{\text{Quick assets}}{\text{Current liabilities}}$	$\dfrac{\$57,500}{\$85,000} = 0.68{:}1$	$\dfrac{\$60,500}{\$104,000} = 0.58{:}1$
11.	$\dfrac{\text{Net credit sales}}{\text{Average accounts receivable}}$	$\dfrac{\$315,000}{\$50,000} = 6.3 \text{ times}$	$\dfrac{\$259,000}{\$49,000} = 5.29 \text{ times}$
12.	$\dfrac{\text{Cost of goods sold}}{\text{Average inventory}}$	$\dfrac{\$189,000}{\$151,250} = 1.25 \text{ times}$	$\dfrac{\$154,000}{\$147,500} = 1.04 \text{ times}$
13.	$\dfrac{\text{Total liabilities}}{\text{Total stockholders' equity}}$	$\dfrac{\$185,000}{\$215,000} = 86.05\%$	$\dfrac{\$204,000}{\$181,000} = 112.71\%$

KEY TERMS

Absolute amounts 327	Book value per share 340	Liquidity ratios 331	Return on equity 339
Accounts receivable	Current ratio 332	Materiality 327	Return on investment 338
turnover 333	Debt to assets ratio 335	Net margin 337	Solvency ratios 335
Acid-test ratio 332	Debt to equity ratio 335	Percentage analysis 328	Trend analysis 327
Asset turnover ratio 338	Dividend yield 341	Price-earnings ratio 340	Vertical analysis 329
Average days to collect	Earnings per share 340	Profitability ratios 337	Working capital 331
receivables 334	Horizontal analysis 327	Quick ratio 332	Working capital ratio 332
Average days to sell	Information overload 326	Ratio analysis 330	
inventory 334	Inventory turnover 334	Return on assets 338	

QUESTIONS

1. Why are ratios and trends used in financial analysis?
2. What do the terms *liquidity* and *solvency* mean?
3. What is apparent from a horizontal presentation of financial statement information? A vertical presentation?
4. What is the significance of inventory turnover, and how is it calculated?

5. What is the difference between the current ratio and the quick ratio? What does each measure?
6. Why are absolute amounts of limited use when comparing companies?
7. What is the difference between return on investment and return on equity?

8. Which ratios are used to measure long-term debt-paying ability? How is each calculated?
9. What are some limitations of the earnings per share figure?
10. What is the formula for calculating return on investment (ROI)?
11. What is information overload?

12. What is the price-earnings ratio? Explain the difference between it and the dividend yield.
13. What environmental factors must be considered in analyzing companies?
14. How do accounting principles affect financial statement analysis?

MULTIPLE-CHOICE QUESTIONS

Multiple-choice questions are provided on the text website at www.mhhe.com/edmondssurvey4e.

EXERCISES

 All applicable Exercises are available with McGraw-Hill *Connect® Accounting.*

Exercise 9-1 *Horizontal analysis*   LO 9-1

Hall Corporation reported the following operating results for two consecutive years.

	2014	2013	Percentage Change
Sales	$1,000,000	$800,000	
Cost of goods sold	630,000	500,000	
Gross margin	$ 370,000	$300,000	
Operating expenses	190,000	125,000	
Income before taxes	$ 180,000	$175,000	
Income taxes	50,000	40,000	
Net income	$ 130,000	$135,000	

Required

a. Compute the percentage changes in Hall Corporation's income statement components between the two years. Round percentages to one decimal point.
b. Comment on apparent trends revealed by the percentage changes computed in Requirement *a*.

348   Chapter 9

LO 9-1

Exercise 9-2   *Vertical analysis*

Jordan Company reported the following operating results for two consecutive years.

2014	Amount	Percent of Sales
Sales	$1,600,000	
Cost of goods sold	900,000	
Gross margin on sales	700,000	
Operating expenses	200,000	
Income before taxes	500,000	
Income taxes	100,000	
Net income	$ 400,000	

2015	Amount	Percent of Sales
Sales	$2,000,000	
Cost of goods sold	1,180,000	
Gross margin on sales	820,000	
Operating expenses	240,000	
Income before taxes	580,000	
Income taxes	120,000	
Net income	$ 460,000	

Required

Express each income statement component for each of the two years as a percent of sales. Round percentages to one decimal point.

LO 9-1

Exercise 9-3   *Horizontal and vertical analysis*

Income statements for Gaidar Company for 2014 and 2015 follow.

	2015	2014
Sales	$300,000	$250,000
Cost of goods sold	192,000	150,000
Selling expenses	30,000	24,000
Administrative expenses	15,000	20,000
Interest expense	6,000	8,000
Total expenses	$243,000	$202,000
Income before taxes	57,000	48,000
Income taxes expense	14,000	12,000
Net income	$ 43,000	$ 36,000

Required

Round all percentages to one decimal point.

a. Perform a horizontal analysis, showing the percentage change in each income statement component between 2014 and 2015.

b. Perform a vertical analysis, showing each income statement component as a percent of sales for each year.

LO 9-2

Exercise 9-4   *Inventory turnover*

Selected financial information for Wilson Company for 2015 follows.

Sales	$1,600,000
Cost of goods sold	1,000,000
Merchandise inventory	
Beginning of year	75,000
End of year	85,000

Required

Assuming that the merchandise inventory buildup was relatively constant, how many times did the merchandise inventory turn over during 2015?

Exercise 9-5   Current ratio   LO 9-2

Elsea Corporation wrote off an $800 uncollectible account receivable against the $24,000 balance in its allowance account.

Required

Explain the effect of the write-off on Elsea's current ratio.

Exercise 9-6   Working capital and current ratio   LO 9-2

On June 30, 2014, Freeman Company's total current assets were $800,000 and its total current liabilities were $400,000. On July 1, 2014, Freeman issued a short-term note to a bank for $80,000 cash.

Required

a. Compute Freeman's working capital before and after issuing the note.
b. Compute Freeman's current ratio before and after issuing the note. Round ratios to two decimal points.

Exercise 9-7   Working capital and current ratio   LO 9-2

On June 30, 2014, Freeman Company's total current assets were $800,000 and its total current liabilities were $400,000. On July 1, 2014, Freeman issued a long-term note to a bank for $80,000 cash.

Required

Round computations to one decimal point.

a. Compute Freeman's working capital before and after issuing the note.
b. Compute Freeman's current ratio before and after issuing the note.

Exercise 9-8   Ratio analysis   LO 9-2, 9-3

The balance sheet for Bukin Corporation follows.

Current assets	$ 300,000
Long-term assets (net)	950,000
Total assets	$1,250,000
Current liabilities	$ 200,000
Long-term liabilities	600,000
Total liabilities	800,000
Common stock and retained earnings	450,000
Total liabilities and stockholders' equity	$1,250,000

Required

Compute the following. Round ratios to one decimal point.

Working capital	✓ _____
Current ratio	✓ _____
Debt to assets ratio	_____
Debt to equity ratio	_____

Exercise 9-9   Comprehensive analysis   LO 9-2, 9-3

The December 31, 2015, balance sheet for Satine Corporation is presented here. These are the only accounts on Satine's balance sheet. Amounts indicated by question marks (?) can be calculated using the following additional information.

Assets	
Cash	$ 25,000
Accounts receivable (net)	?
Inventory	?
Property, plant, and equipment (net)	294,000
	$432,000
Liabilities and Stockholders' Equity	
Accounts payable (trade)	$?
Income taxes payable (current)	25,000
Long-term debt	?
Common stock	300,000
Retained earnings	?
	$?
Additional Information	
Current ratio (at year end)	1.5 to 1.0
Total liabilities ÷ Total stockholders' equity	80%
Gross margin percent	30%
Inventory turnover (Cost of goods sold ÷ Ending inventory)	10.5 times
Gross margin for 2015	$ 315,000

Required

Determine the following.

a. The balance in trade accounts payable as of December 31, 2015.

b. The balance in retained earnings as of December 31, 2015.

c. The balance in the inventory account as of December 31, 2015. (Assume that the level of inventory did not change from last year.)

LO 9-3

Exercise 9-10   *Number of times interest earned*

The following data come from the financial records of Adams Corporation for 2014.

Sales	$720,000
Interest expense	6,000
Income tax expense	12,000
Net income	42,000

Required

How many times was interest earned in 2014?

LO 9-2, 9-4

Exercise 9-11   *Accounts receivable turnover, inventory turnover, and net margin*

Selected data from Komar Company follow.

Balance Sheet As of December 31		
	2014	2013
Accounts receivable	$500,000	$450,000
Allowance for doubtful accounts	(20,000)	(16,000)
Net accounts receivable	$480,000	$434,000
Inventories, lower of cost or market	$600,000	$525,000

	Income Statement for the Years Ended December 31	
	2014	**2013**
Net credit sales	$2,000,000	$1,760,000
Net cash sales	400,000	320,000
Net sales	2,400,000	2,080,000
Cost of goods sold	1,600,000	1,440,000
Selling, general, and administrative expenses	240,000	216,000
Other expenses	40,000	24,000
Total operating expenses	$1,880,000	$1,680,000

Required

Compute the following and round computations to two decimal points.

a. The accounts receivable turnover for 2014.
b. The inventory turnover for 2014.
c. The net margin for 2013.

Exercise 9-12   *Ratio analysis*

LO 9-5

During 2014, Desny Corporation reported after-tax net income of $3,890,000. During the year, the number of shares of stock outstanding remained constant at 10,000 of $100 par, 9 percent preferred stock and 400,000 shares of common stock. The company's total stockholders' equity is $20,000,000 at December 31, 2014. Desny Corporation's common stock was selling at $52 per share at the end of its fiscal year. All dividends for the year have been paid, including $4.80 per share to common stockholders.

Required

Compute the following by rounding to two decimal points.

a. Earnings per share
b. Book value per share of common stock
c. Price-earnings ratio
d. Dividend yield

Exercise 9-13   *Ratio analysis*

LO 9-2, 9-3, 9-4, 9-5

Compute the specified ratios using Faustin Company's balance sheet for 2014.

Assets	
Cash	$ 18,000
Marketable securities	12,000
Accounts receivable	25,000
Inventory	22,000
Property and equipment	160,000
Accumulated depreciation	(37,000)
Total assets	$200,000
Liabilities and Stockholders' Equity	
Accounts payable	$ 11,500
Current notes payable	3,500
Mortgage payable	4,000
Bonds payable	21,500
Common stock	100,000
Retained earnings	59,500
Total liabilities and stockholders' equity	$200,000

352   Chapter 9

The average number of common stock shares outstanding during 2014 was 880 shares. Net income for the year was $20,000.

Required

Compute each of the following and round computations to two decimal points.

a. Current ratio
b. Earnings per share
c. Quick (acid-test) ratio
d. Return on investment
e. Return on equity
f. Debt to equity ratio

LO 9-2, 9-3, 9-4, 9-5

Exercise 9-14   *Ratio analysis*

Required

Match each of the following ratios with the formula used to compute it.

_____ **1.** Working capital	**a.**	Net income ÷ Average total stockholders' equity
_____ **2.** Current ratio	**b.**	Cost of goods sold ÷ Average inventory
_____ **3.** Quick ratio	**c.**	Current assets − Current liabilities
_____ **4.** Accounts receivable turnover	**d.**	365 ÷ Inventory turnover
_____ **5.** Average days to collect	**e.**	Net income ÷ Average total assets
_____ **6.** Inventory turnover	**f.**	(Net income − Preferred dividends) ÷ Average outstanding common shares
_____ **7.** Average days to sell inventory	**g.**	(Current assets − Inventory − Prepaid expenses) ÷ Current liabilities
_____ **8.** Debt to assets ratio	**h.**	Total liabilities ÷ Total assets
_____ **9.** Debt to equity ratio	**i.**	365 ÷ Accounts receivable turnover
_____ **10.** Return on investment	**j.**	Total liabilities ÷ Total stockholders' equity
_____ **11.** Return on equity	**k.**	Net credit sales ÷ Average accounts receivables
_____ **12.** Earnings per share	**l.**	Current assets ÷ Current liabilities

LO 9-2, 9-3, 9-4, 9-5

Exercise 9-15   *Comprehensive analysis*

Required

Indicate the effect of each of the following transactions on (1) the current ratio, (2) working capital, (3) stockholders' equity, (4) book value per share of common stock, and (5) retained earnings. Assume that the current ratio is greater than 1:1.

a. Collected account receivable.
b. Wrote off account receivable.
c. Converted a short-term note payable to a long-term payable.
d. Purchased inventory on account.
e. Declared cash dividend.
f. Sold merchandise on account at a profit.
g. Issued stock dividend.
h. Paid account payable.
i. Sold building at a loss.

PROBLEMS

 All applicable Problems are available with McGraw-Hill *Connect® Accounting*.

LO 9-1

Problem 9-16   *Vertical analysis*

The following percentages apply to Safin Company for 2014 and 2015.

	2015	2014
Sales	100.0%	100.0%
Cost of goods sold	61.0	64.0
Gross margin	39.0	36.0
Selling and administrative expense	26.5	20.5
Interest expense	2.5	2.0
Total expenses	29.0	22.5
Income before taxes	10.0	13.5
Income tax expense	5.5	7.0
Net income	4.5%	6.5%

Required

Assuming that sales were $400,000 in 2014 and $480,000 in 2015, prepare income statements for the two years.

Problem 9-17   *Horizontal analysis*

LO 9-1

Financial statements for Revnik Company follow.

REVNIK COMPANY
Balance Sheets
As of December 31

	2015	2014
Assets		
Current assets		
Cash	$ 16,000	$ 12,000
Marketable securities	20,000	6,000
Accounts receivable (net)	54,000	46,000
Inventories	135,000	143,000
Prepaid items	25,000	10,000
Total current assets	250,000	217,000
Investments	27,000	20,000
Plant (net)	270,000	255,000
Land	29,000	24,000
Total assets	$576,000	$516,000
Liabilities and Stockholders' Equity		
Liabilities		
Current liabilities		
Notes payable	$ 17,000	$ 6,000
Accounts payable	113,800	100,000
Salaries payable	21,000	15,000
Total current liabilities	151,800	121,000
Noncurrent liabilities		
Bonds payable	100,000	100,000
Other	32,000	27,000
Total noncurrent liabilities	132,000	127,000
Total liabilities	283,800	248,000
Stockholders' equity		
Preferred stock, (par value $10, 4% cumulative, non-participating; 8,000 shares authorized and issued)	80,000	80,000
Common stock (No par; 50,000 shares authorized; 10,000 shares issued)	80,000	80,000
Retained earnings	132,200	108,000
Total stockholders' equity	292,200	268,000
Total liabilities and stockholders' equity	$576,000	$516,000

REVNIK COMPANY
Statements of Income and Retained Earnings
For the Years Ended December 31

	2015	2014
Revenues		
Sales (net)	$230,000	$210,000
Other revenues	8,000	5,000
Total revenues	238,000	215,000
Expenses		
Cost of goods sold	120,000	103,000
Selling, general, and administrative	55,000	50,000
Interest expense	8,000	7,200
Income tax expense	23,000	22,000
Total expenses	206,000	182,200
Net earnings (net income)	32,000	32,800
Retained earnings, January 1	108,000	83,000
Less: Preferred stock dividends	3,200	3,200
Common stock dividends	4,600	4,600
Retained earnings, December 31	$132,200	$108,000

Required

Prepare a horizontal analysis of the balance sheet and income statement for 2015 and 2014. Round percentages to one decimal point.

LO 9-1

Problem 9-18   *Vertical analysis*

CHECK FIGURE
2015 Retained earnings: 22.95%

Required

Use the financial statements for Revnik Company from Problem 9-17 to perform a vertical analysis of both the balance sheets and income statements for 2015 and 2014. Round computations to two decimal points.

LO 9-2

Problem 9-19   *Effect of transactions on current ratio and working capital*

Wowk Manufacturing has a current ratio of 3:1 on December 31, 2014. Indicate whether each of the following transactions would increase (+), decrease (−), or have no effect (NA) on Wowk's current ratio and its working capital.

Required

a. Paid cash for a trademark.
b. Wrote off an uncollectible account receivable.
c. Sold equipment for cash.
d. Sold merchandise at a profit (cash).
e. Declared a cash dividend.
f. Purchased inventory on account.
g. Scrapped a fully depreciated machine (no gain or loss).
h. Issued a stock dividend.
i. Purchased a machine with a long-term note.
j. Paid a previously declared cash dividend.
k. Collected accounts receivable.
l. Invested in current marketable securities.

Problem 9-20   *Supply missing balance sheet numbers*

LO 9-2, 9-3

The bookkeeper for Rakov's Country Music Bar left this incomplete balance sheet. Rakov's working capital is $180,000 and its debt to assets ratio is 40 percent.

CHECK FIGURES
D: $675,000
F: $195,000

Assets	
Current assets	
Cash	$ 42,000
Accounts receivable	84,000
Inventory	(A)
Prepaid expenses	18,000
Total current assets	(B)
Long-term assets	
Building	(C)
Less: Accumulated depreciation	(78,000)
Total long-term assets	420,000
Total assets	$ (D)
Liabilities and Stockholders' Equity	
Liabilities	
Current liabilities	
Accounts payable	$ (E)
Notes payable	24,000
Income tax payable	21,000
Total current liabilities	75,000
Long-term liabilities	
Mortgage payable	(F)
Total liabilities	(G)
Stockholders' equity	
Common stock	210,000
Retained earnings	(H)
Total stockholders' equity	(I)
Total liabilities and stockholders' equity	$ (J)

Required

Complete the balance sheet by supplying the missing amounts.

Problem 9-21   *Ratio analysis*

LO 9-5

Selected data for Putin Company for 2014 and additional information on industry averages follow.

Earnings (net income)		$ 195,600
Preferred stock (13,200 shares at $50 par, 4%)		$ 660,000
Common stock (45,000 shares no par, market value $56)		510,000
Retained earnings		562,500
		$1,732,500
Less: Treasury stock		
Preferred (1,800 shares)	$54,000	
Common (1,800 shares)	24,000	78,000
Total stockholders' equity		$1,654,500

CHECK FIGURE
a. Earnings per share: $4

Industry averages	
Earnings per share	$5.20
Price-earnings ratio	9.50
Return on equity	11.20%

Required

a. Calculate and compare Putin Company's ratios with the industry averages.

b. Discuss factors you would consider in deciding whether to invest in the company.

LO 9-3, 9-4, 9-5

CHECK FIGURES
a. 2014: 13.33 times
c. 2014: 7.58 times

Problem 9-22   *Ratio analysis*

Sokov Company's income statement information follows.

	2014	2013
Net sales	$480,000	$320,000
Income before interest and taxes	120,000	98,000
Net income after taxes	81,000	72,000
Interest expense	9,000	8,000
Stockholders' equity, December 31 (2012: $200,000)	300,000	240,000
Common stock, December 31	240,000	200,000

The average number of shares outstanding was 9,600 for 2014 and 8,000 for 2013.

Required

Compute the following ratios for Sokov for 2014 and 2013 and round the computation to two decimal points.

a. Number of times interest was earned.

b. Earnings per share based on the average number of shares outstanding.

c. Price-earnings ratio (market prices: 2014, $64 per share; 2013, $78 per share).

d. Return on average equity.

e. Net margin.

LO 9-2, 9-3, 9-4, 9-5

CHECK FIGURES
d. 2015: $0.72
k. 2014: 5.47 times

Problem 9-23   *Ratio analysis*

The following financial statements apply to Robin Company.

	2015	2014
Revenues		
Net sales	$210,000	$175,000
Other revenues	4,000	5,000
Total revenues	214,000	180,000
Expenses		
Cost of goods sold	126,000	103,000
Selling expenses	21,000	19,000
General and administrative expenses	11,000	10,000
Interest expense	3,000	3,000
Income tax expense	21,000	18,000
Total expenses	182,000	153,000
Earnings from continuing operations before extraordinary items	32,000	27,000
Extraordinary gain (net of $3,000 tax)	4,000	0
Net income	$ 36,000	$ 27,000

continued

	2015	2014
Assets		
Current assets		
Cash	$ 4,000	$ 8,000
Marketable securities	1,000	1,000
Accounts receivable	35,000	32,000
Inventories	100,000	96,000
Prepaid expenses	3,000	2,000
Total current assets	143,000	139,000
Plant and equipment (net)	105,000	105,000
Intangibles	20,000	0
Total assets	$268,000	$244,000
Liabilities and Stockholders' Equity		
Liabilities		
Current liabilities		
Accounts payable	$ 40,000	$ 54,000
Other	17,000	15,000
Total current liabilities	57,000	69,000
Bonds payable	66,000	67,000
Total liabilities	123,000	136,000
Stockholders' equity		
Common stock (50,000 shares)	115,000	115,000
Retained earnings	30,000	(7,000)
Total stockholders' equity	145,000	108,000
Total liabilities and stockholders' equity	$268,000	$244,000

Required

Calculate the following ratios for 2014 and 2015. When data limitations prohibit computing averages, use year-end balances in your calculations. Round computations to two decimal points.

a. Net margin

b. Return on investment

c. Return on equity

d. Earnings per share

e. Price-earnings ratio (market prices at the end of 2014 and 2015 were $5.94 and $4.77, respectively)

f. Book value per share of common stock

g. Times interest earned

h. Working capital

i. Current ratio

j. Quick (acid-test) ratio

k. Accounts receivable turnover

l. Inventory turnover

m. Debt to equity ratio

n. Debt to assets ratio

Problem 9-24   *Ratio analysis*

Required

Use the financial statements for Revnik Company from Problem 9-17 to calculate the following ratios for 2015 and 2014 by rounding computations to two decimal points.

a. Working capital

b. Current ratio

LO 9-2, 9-3, 9-4, 9-5

CHECK FIGURES
k. 2015: 2.0:1
p. 2014: $2.96

c. Quick ratio

d. Receivables turnover (beginning receivables at January 1, 2014, were $47,000)

e. Average days to collect accounts receivable

f. Inventory turnover (beginning inventory at January 1, 2014, was $140,000)

g. Number of days to sell inventory

h. Debt to assets ratio

i. Debt to equity ratio

j. Number of times interest was earned

k. Plant assets to long-term debt

l. Net margin

m. Turnover of assets (Use the total assets of 2013 as the average total assets to compute the 2013 figure.)

n. Return on investment (Use the total assets of 2013 as the average total assets to compute the 2013 figure.)

o. Return on equity (Use the total stockholders' equity of 2014 as the average stockholders' equity to compute the 2014 figure.)

p. Earnings per share

q. Book value per share of common stock

r. Price-earnings ratio (market price per share: 2014, $11.75; 2015, $12.50)

s. Dividend yield on common stock

ANALYZE, THINK, COMMUNICATE

ATC 9-1   Business Applications Case   *Analyzing Costco and Walmart*

The following information relates to Costco Wholesale Corporation and Wal-Mart Stores, Inc., for their 2012 and 2011 fiscal years.

COSTCO WHOLESALE CORPORATION Selected Financial Information (Amounts in millions, except per share amounts)		
	September 2, 2012	August 28, 2011
Total current assets	$13,526	$13,706
Merchandise inventory	7,096	6,638
Property and equipment, net of depreciation	12,961	12,432
Total assets	27,140	26,761
Total current liabilities	12,260	12,050
Total long-term liabilities	2,362	2,138
Total liabilities	14,622	14,188
Total shareholders' equity	12,518	12,573
Revenue	99,137	88,915
Cost of goods sold	86,823	77,739
Gross profit	12,314	11,176
Operating income	2,759	2,439
Earnings from continuing operations before income tax expense	2,767	2,383
Income tax expense	1,000	841
Net earnings	1,767	1,542
Basic earnings per share	$ 3.94	$ 3.35

WAL-MART STORES, INC.		
Selected Financial Information		
(Amounts in millions except per share data)		
	January 31, 2012	January 31, 2011
Total current assets	$ 54,975	$ 51,893
Merchandise inventory	40,714	36,318
Property and equipment, net of depreciation	112,324	107,878
Total assets	193,406	180,663
Total current liabilities	62,300	58,484
Total long-term liabilities	55,345	50,932
Total liabilities	117,645	109,416
Total stockholders' equity	75,761	71,247
Revenues	446,950	421,849
Cost of goods sold	335,127	315,287
Gross profit	111,823	106,562
Operating income	26,558	25,542
Earnings from continuing operations before income taxes	24,398	23,538
Income tax expense	7,944	7,579
Net earnings	16,387	16,993
Basic earnings per share	$ 4.56	$ 4.20

Required

a. Compute the following ratios for the companies' 2012 fiscal years:

(1) Current ratio.

(2) Average days to sell inventory. (Use average inventory.)

(3) Debt to assets ratio.

(4) Return on investment. (Use average assets and use "earnings from continuing operations" rather than "net earnings.")

(5) Gross margin percentage.

(6) Asset turnover. (Use average assets.)

(7) Return on sales. (Use "earnings from continuing operations" rather than "net earnings.")

(8) Plant assets to long-term debt ratio.

b. Which company appears to be more profitable? Explain your answer and identify which ratio(s) from Requirement *a* you used to reach your conclusion.

c. Which company appears to have the higher level of financial risk? Explain your answer and identify which ratio(s) from Requirement *a* you used to reach your conclusion.

d. Which company appears to be charging higher prices for its goods? Explain your answer and identify which ratio(s) from Requirement *a* you used to reach your conclusion.

e. Which company appears to be the more efficient at using its assets? Explain your answer and identify which ratio(s) from Requirement *a* you used to reach your conclusion.

ATC 9-2 Group Assignment *Ratios and basic logic*

Presented here are selected data from the 10-K reports of four companies for their 2011 fiscal years. The four companies, in alphabetical order, are:

Advanced Micro Devices, a company that manufactures semiconductors.

AT&T, Inc., a large telecommunications company.

Deere & Company, a company that manufactures heavy equipment for construction and farming.

Pfizer, Inc., a pharmaceutical company.

The data for the companies, presented in the order of the amount of their sales in millions of dollars, are as follows:

	A	B	C	D
Sales	$126,723	$ 67,425	$29,466	$6,568
Cost of goods sold	57,374	15,085	21,919	3,628
Net income	3,944	10,009	2,800	491
Inventory	0	7,769	4,371	476
Accounts receivable	13,606	13,608	19,924	919
Total assets	270,344	188,002	48,207	4,954

Required

a. Divide the class into groups of four or five students per group and then organize the groups into four sections. Assign Task 1 to the first section of groups, Task 2 to the second section, Task 3 to the third section, and Task 4 to the fourth section.

Group Tasks

(1) Assume that you represent AT&T. Identify the set of financial data (Column A, B, C, or D) that relates to your company.

(2) Assume that you represent Advanced Micro Devices. Identify the set of financial data (Column A, B, C, or D) that relates to your company.

(3) Assume that you represent Deere & Co. Identify the set of financial data (Column A, B, C, or D) that relates to your company.

(4) Assume that you represent Pfizer. Identify the set of financial data (Column A, B, C, or D) that relates to your company.

Hint: In addition to the ratios presented in this chapter, you might also find it useful to compute a ratio from the first course of accounting, the gross margin percentage (Gross margin ÷ Sales).

b. Select a representative from each section. Have the representative explain the rationale for the group's selection. The explanation should include a set of ratios that support the group's conclusion.

ATC 9-3   Research Assignment   *Analyzing InBev's acquisition of Anheuser-Busch*

In 2008, the world's largest beer brewery, Anheuser-Busch, merged with the world's second largest brewery, InBev. The new company, headquartered in the Netherlands, is named Anheuser-Busch InBev NV. To complete the requirements below, you will need to obtain Anheuser-Busch InBev's financial statements for 2007 and 2011. Obtain these as follows:

■ Go to the company's website at www.ab-inbev.com.

■ Click on the "Investors" link.

■ Click on the "Reports and Publications" link.

■ Click on the "Annual and HY reports" link.

■ Click on the years of report desired, 2007 and 2011.

■ Click on the "Financial Reports" link.

The information in the 2007 financial statements is for InBev without Anheuser-Busch, and the information for 2011 is for the merged companies. Be careful when extracting data from the balance sheets because they are in reverse order of statements for companies in the United States. For example, InBev lists its noncurrent assets before current assets. Also note that the 2011 data are in dollars and the 2007 data are in euros. There is no need to convert the data to a common currency for this assignment since you will be asked to calculate ratios for each year separately.

Required

a. Compute the following ratios for 2011 and 2007. To make the computations simpler, use end-of-year amounts for total assets and total equity rather than averages. Show your calculations.

Gross margin percentage	Net margin
Return on investment	Return on equity
Current ratio	Debt to assets ratio

b. Based on the ratios computed in Requirement *a*, comment on the apparent effects of InBev's merger with Anheuser-Busch. Assume any significant change in these ratios was the result of the acquisition.

c. Based on this limited analysis, does it appear that the effects of the merger were good or bad for InBev?

ATC 9-4   Writing Assignment   *Identifying companies based on financial statement information*

The following ratios are for four companies in different industries. Some of these ratios have been discussed in the textbook and others have not, but their names explain how the ratio was computed. These data are for the companies' 2011 fiscal years. The four sets of ratios, presented randomly, are as follows:

	Company 1	Company 2	Company 3	Company 4
Current assets ÷ Total assets	19%	17%	17%	47%
Average days to sell inventory	9	10	55	114
Average days to collect receivables	25	3	37	122
Return on assets	27%	32%	5%	6%
Gross profit ÷ Sales	58%	25%	42%	24%
Asset turnover	1.62	1.54	0.28	0.70
Sales ÷ Number of full-time employees	$32,485	$53,853	$230,341	$458,773

The four companies to which these ratios relate, listed in alphabetical order, are:

Caterpillar, Inc., a company that manufactures heavy construction equipment.

Denny's Corporation, which operated over 1,685 restaurants as of December 31, 2011.

Molson Coors Brewing, Inc., a company that produces beer and related products.

Weight Watchers International, Inc., a company that provides weight-loss services and products.

Required

Determine which company should be matched with each set of ratios. Write a memorandum explaining the rationale for your decisions.

ATC 9-5   Ethical Dilemma   *Making the ratios look good*

J. Talbot is the accounting manager for Kolla Waste Disposal Corporation. Kolla is having its worst financial year since its inception. The company is expected to report a net loss. In the midst of such bad news, Ms. Talbot surprised the company president, Mr. Winston, by suggesting that the company write off approximately 25 percent of its garbage trucks. Mr. Winston responded by noting that the trucks could still be operated for another two or three years. Ms. Talbot replied, "We may use them for two or three more years, but you couldn't sell them on the street if you had to. Who wants to buy a bunch of old garbage trucks, and besides, it will make next year's financials so sweet. No one will care about the additional write-off this year. We are already showing a loss. Who will care if we lose a little bit more?"

Required

a. How will the write-off affect the following year's return on assets ratio?

b. How will the write-off affect the asset and income growth percentages?

c. Would writing off the garbage trucks violate any of the standards of ethical professional practice shown in Exhibit 4.4 of Chapter 4?

d. Explain how the components of the fraud triangle relate to this case.

CHAPTER 10

An Introduction to Management Accounting

LEARNING OBJECTIVES

After you have mastered the material in this chapter, you will be able to:

LO 10-1	Distinguish between managerial and financial accounting.
LO 10-2	Identify the cost of manufacturing a product and show how these costs affect financial statements.
LO 10-3	Prepare a schedule of cost of goods manufactured and sold.
LO 10-4	Show how just-in-time inventory can increase profitability.
LO 10-5	Identify the standards contained in IMA's Statement of Ethical Professional Practice.
LO 10-6	Identify emerging trends in accounting (Appendix).

 Video lectures and accompanying self-assessment quizzes are available for all learning objectives through McGraw-Hill Connect® Accounting.

CHAPTER OPENING

Andy Grove, Senior Advisor to Executive Management of Intel Corporation, is credited with the motto, "Only the paranoid survive." Mr. Grove describes a wide variety of concerns that make him paranoid. Specifically, he declares:

> I worry about products getting screwed up, and I worry about products getting introduced prematurely. I worry about factories not performing well, and I worry about having too many factories. I worry about hiring the right people, and I worry about morale slacking off. And, of course, I worry about competitors. I worry about other people figuring out how to do what we do better or cheaper, and displacing us with our customers.

Do Intel's historically based financial statements contain the information Mr. Grove needs? No. **Financial accounting** is not designed to satisfy all the information needs of business managers. Its scope is limited to the needs of external users such as investors and creditors. The field of accounting designed to meet the needs of internal users is called **managerial accounting.**

The Curious Accountant

Earlier in this course of accounting, you learned how retailers, such as Target, account for the cost of equipment that lasts more than one year. Recall that the equipment was recorded as an asset when purchased, and then it was depreciated over its expected useful life. The depreciation charge reduced the company's assets and increased its expenses. This approach was justified under the matching principle, which seeks to recognize costs as expenses in the same period that the cost (resource) is used to generate revenue.

Is depreciation always shown as an expense on the income statement? The answer may surprise you. Consider the following scenario. Bose Corporation manufactures the headphones that it sells to Target. In order to produce the headphones, Bose had to purchase a robotic machine that it expects can be used to produce 100,000 headphones.

Do you think Bose should account for depreciation on its manufacturing equipment the same way Target accounts for depreciation on its registers at the checkout counters? If not, how should Bose account for its depreciation? Remember the matching principle when thinking of your answer. (Answer on page 373.)

DIFFERENCES BETWEEN MANAGERIAL AND FINANCIAL ACCOUNTING

LO 10-1

Distinguish between managerial and financial accounting.

While the information needs of internal and external users overlap, the needs of managers generally differ from those of investors or creditors. Some distinguishing characteristics are discussed in the following section.

Users and Types of Information

Financial accounting provides information used primarily by investors, creditors, and others *outside* a business. In contrast, managerial accounting focuses on information used by executives, managers, and employees who work *inside* the business. These two user groups need different types of information.

Internal users need information to *plan, direct,* and *control* business operations. The nature of information needed is related to an employee's job level. Lower level employees use nonfinancial information such as work schedules, store hours, and customer service policies. Moving up the organizational ladder, financial information becomes increasingly important. Middle managers use a blend of financial and nonfinancial information, while senior executives concentrate on financial data. To a lesser degree, senior executives also use general economic data and nonfinancial operating information. For example, an executive may consider the growth rate of the economy before deciding to expand the company's workforce.

External users (investors and creditors) have greater needs for general economic information than do internal users. For example, an investor debating whether to purchase stock versus bond securities might be more interested in government tax policy than financial statement data. Exhibit 10.1 summarizes the information needs of different user groups.

Level of Aggregation

External users generally desire *global information* that reflects the performance of a company as a whole. For example, an investor is not so much interested in the performance of a particular Sears store as she is in the performance of Sears Roebuck Company versus that of JC Penney Company. In contrast, internal users focus on detailed information about specific subunits of the company. To meet the needs of the different user groups, financial accounting data are more aggregated than managerial accounting data.

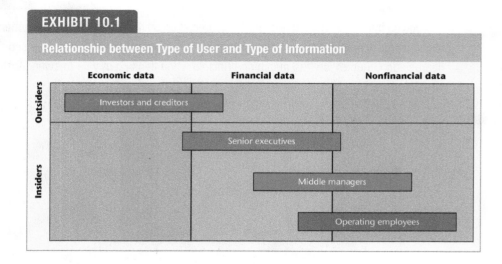

EXHIBIT 10.1

Relationship between Type of User and Type of Information

Regulation

Financial accounting is designed to generate information for the general public. In an effort to protect the public interest, Congress established the **Securities and Exchange Commission (SEC)** and gave it authority to regulate public financial reporting practices. The SEC has delegated much of its authority for developing accounting rules to the private sector **Financial Accounting Standards Board (FASB),** thereby allowing the accounting profession considerable influence over financial accounting reports. The FASB supports a broad base of pronouncements and practices known as **generally accepted accounting principles (GAAP).** GAAP severely restricts the accounting procedures and practices permitted in published financial statements.

Beyond financial statement data, much of the information generated by management accounting systems is proprietary information not available to the public. Since this information is not distributed to the public, it need not be regulated to protect the public interest. Management accounting is restricted only by the **value-added principle.** Management accountants are free to engage in any information gathering and reporting activity so long as the activity adds value in excess of its cost. For example, management accountants are free to provide forecasted information to internal users. In contrast, financial accounting as prescribed by GAAP does not permit forecasting.

Information Characteristics

While financial accounting is characterized by its objectivity, reliability, consistency, and historical nature, managerial accounting is more concerned with relevance and timeliness. Managerial accounting uses more estimates and fewer facts than financial accounting. Financial accounting reports what happened yesterday; managerial accounting reports what is expected to happen tomorrow.

Time Horizon and Reporting Frequency

Financial accounting information is reported periodically, normally at the end of a year. Management cannot wait until the end of the year to discover problems. Planning, controlling, and directing require immediate attention. Managerial accounting information is delivered on a continuous basis.

Exhibit 10.2 summarizes significant differences between financial and managerial accounting.

PRODUCT COSTING IN MANUFACTURING COMPANIES

A major focus for managerial accountants is determining **product cost.**[1] Managers need to know the cost of their products for a variety of reasons. For example, **cost-plus pricing** is a common business practice.[2] **Product costing** is also used to control business operations. It is useful in answering questions such as: Are costs higher or lower than expected? Who is responsible for the variances between expected and actual costs? What actions can be taken to control the variances?

LO 10-2

Identify the cost of manufacturing a product and show how these costs affect financial statements.

Components of Product Cost

A company normally incurs three types of costs when making products. Specifically, the company must pay for (1) the *materials* used to make the products, (2) the *labor*

---

[1]This text uses the term *product* in a generic sense to mean both goods and services.

[2]Other pricing strategies will be introduced in subsequent chapters.

EXHIBIT 10.2

Comparative Features of Managerial versus Financial Accounting Information

Features	Managerial Accounting	Financial Accounting
Users	Insiders, including executives, managers, and operators	Outsiders, including investors, creditors, government agencies, analysts, and reporters
Information type	Economic and physical data as well as financial data	Financial data
Level of aggregation	Local information on subunits of the organization	Global information on the company as a whole
Regulation	No regulation, limited only by the value-added principle	Regulation by SEC, FASB, and other determiners of GAAP
Information characteristics	Estimates that promote relevance and enable timeliness	Factual information that is characterized by objectivity, reliability, consistency, and accuracy
Time horizon	Past, present, and future	Past only, historically based
Reporting frequency	Continuous reporting	Delayed, with emphasis on annual reports

expended by the employees who transform the materials into products, and (3) the *overhead* (other resources such as utilities and equipment consumed in the process of making the products). If the company stores its products, the costs of the materials, labor, and overhead used in making the products are maintained in an inventory account until the products are sold. For a detailed explanation of how product costs flow through the financial statements, refer to the following example of Tabor Manufacturing Company.

Tabor Manufacturing Company

Tabor Manufacturing Company makes wooden tables. The company spent $1,000 cash to build four tables: $390 for materials, $470 for a carpenter's labor, and $140 for tools used in making the tables. How much is Tabor's expense? The answer is zero. The $1,000 cash has been converted into products (four tables). The cash payments for materials, labor, and tools (overhead) were *asset exchange* transactions. One asset (cash) decreased while another asset (tables) increased. Tabor will not recognize any expense until the tables are sold; in the meantime, the cost of the tables is held in an asset account called *Finished Goods Inventory.* Exhibit 10.3 illustrates how cash is transformed into inventory.

Average Cost per Unit

How much did each table made by Tabor cost? The *actual* cost of each of the four tables likely differs. The carpenter probably spent a little more time on some of the tables than others. Material and tool usage probably varied from table to table. Determining the exact cost of each table is virtually impossible. Minute details such as a second of labor time cannot be effectively measured. Even if Tabor could determine the exact cost of each table, the information would be of little use. Minor differences in the cost per table would make no difference in pricing or other decisions management needs to make. Accountants therefore normally calculate cost per unit as an *average*. In the case of Tabor Manufacturing, the **average cost** per table is $250 ($1,000 ÷ 4 units). Unless otherwise stated, assume *cost per unit* means *average cost per unit.*

EXHIBIT 10.3

Transforming the Asset Cash into the Asset Finished Goods Inventory

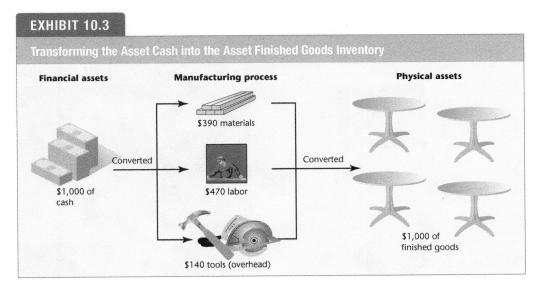

Financial assets   **Manufacturing process**   **Physical assets**

$390 materials

$1,000 of cash   Converted   Converted

$470 labor

$140 tools (overhead)

$1,000 of finished goods

✓ CHECK YOURSELF 10.1

All boxes of General Mills' Total Raisin Bran cereal are priced at exactly the same amount in your local grocery store. Does this mean that the actual cost of making each box of cereal was exactly the same?

Answer   No, making each box would not cost exactly the same amount. For example, some boxes contain slightly more or less cereal than other boxes. Accordingly, some boxes cost slightly more or less to make than others do. General Mills uses average cost rather than actual cost to develop its pricing strategy.

Costs Can Be Assets or Expenses

It might seem odd that wages paid to production workers are recorded as inventory instead of being expensed. Remember, however, that expenses are assets used in the process of *earning revenue*. The cash paid to production workers is not used to produce revenue. Instead, the cash is used to produce inventory. Revenue will be earned when the inventory is used (sold). So long as the inventory remains on hand, all product costs (materials, labor, and overhead) remain in an inventory account.

When a table is sold, the average cost of the table is transferred from the Inventory account to the Cost of Goods Sold (expense) account. If some tables remain unsold at the end of the accounting period, part of the *product cost* is reported as an asset (inventory) on the balance sheet while the other part is reported as an expense (cost of goods sold) on the income statement.

Costs that are not classified as product costs are normally expensed in the period in which they are incurred. These costs include *general operating costs, selling and administrative costs, interest costs,* and the *cost of income taxes*.

To illustrate, return to the Tabor Manufacturing example. Recall that Tabor made four tables at an average cost per unit of $250. Assume Tabor pays an employee who sells three of the tables a $200 sales commission. The sales commission is expensed immediately. The total product cost for the three tables (3 tables × $250 each = $750) is expensed on the income statement as cost of goods sold. The portion of the total

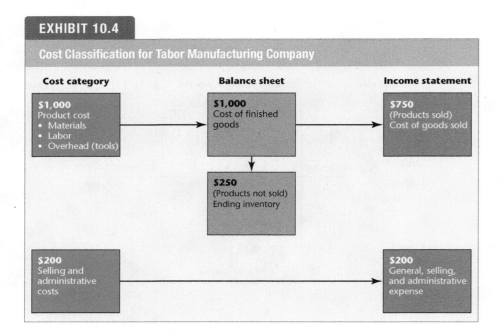

EXHIBIT 10.4

Cost Classification for Tabor Manufacturing Company

Cost category	Balance sheet	Income statement
$1,000 Product cost • Materials • Labor • Overhead (tools)	**$1,000** Cost of finished goods	**$750** (Products sold) Cost of goods sold
	$250 (Products not sold) Ending inventory	
$200 Selling and administrative costs		**$200** General, selling, and administrative expense

product cost remaining in inventory is $250 (1 table × $250). Exhibit 10.4 shows the relationship between the costs incurred and the expenses recognized for Tabor Manufacturing Company.

Effect of Product Costs on Financial Statements

We illustrate accounting for product costs in manufacturing companies with Patillo Manufacturing Company, a producer of ceramic pottery. Patillo, started on January 1, 2016, experienced the following accounting events during its first year of operations.[3] *Assume that all transactions except 6, 8, and 10 are cash transactions.*

1. Acquired $15,000 cash by issuing common stock.
2. Paid $2,000 for materials that were used to make products. All products started were completed during the period.
3. Paid $1,200 for salaries of selling and administrative employees.
4. Paid $3,000 for wages of production workers.
5. Paid $2,800 for furniture used in selling and administrative offices.
6. Recognized depreciation on the office furniture purchased in Event 5. The furniture was acquired on January 1, had a $400 estimated salvage value, and a four-year useful life. The annual depreciation charge is $600 [($2,800 − $400) ÷ 4].
7. Paid $4,500 for manufacturing equipment.
8. Recognized depreciation on the equipment purchased in Event 7. The equipment was acquired on January 1, had a $1,500 estimated salvage value, and a three-year useful life. The annual depreciation charge is $1,000 [($4,500 − $1,500) ÷ 3].
9. Sold inventory to customers for $7,500 cash.
10. The inventory sold in Event 9 cost $4,000 to make.

[3]This illustration assumes that all inventory started during the period was completed during the period. Patillo therefore uses only one inventory account, Finished Goods Inventory. Many manufacturing companies normally have three categories of inventory on hand at the end of an accounting period: Raw Materials Inventory, Work in Process Inventory (inventory of partially completed units), and Finished Goods Inventory.

EXHIBIT 10.5

Effect of Product versus Selling and Administrative Costs on Financial Statements

Event No.	Cash	+	Inventory	+	Office Furn.*	+	Manuf. Equip.*	=	Com. Stk.	+	Ret. Earn.	Rev.	−	Exp.	=	Net Inc.	Cash Flow	
					Assets				**Equity**									
1	15,000							=	15,000								15,000	FA
2	(2,000)	+	2,000														(2,000)	OA
3	(1,200)							=			(1,200)		−	1,200	=	(1,200)	(1,200)	OA
4	(3,000)	+	3,000														(3,000)	OA
5	(2,800)	+			2,800												(2,800)	IA
6					(600)			=			(600)		−	600	=	(600)		
7	(4,500)	+					4,500										(4,500)	IA
8			1,000	+			(1,000)											
9	7,500							=			7,500	7,500			=	7,500	7,500	OA
10			(4,000)					=			(4,000)		−	4,000	=	(4,000)		
Totals	9,000	+	2,000	+	2,200	+	3,500	=	15,000	+	1,700	7,500	−	5,800	=	1,700	9,000	NC

*Negative amounts in these columns represent accumulated depreciation.

The effects of these transactions on the balance sheet, income statement, and statement of cash flows are shown in Exhibit 10.5. Study each row in this exhibit, paying particular attention to how similar costs such as salaries for selling and administrative personnel and wages for production workers have radically different effects on the financial statements. The example illustrates the three elements of product costs— materials (Event 2), labor (Event 4), and overhead (Event 8). These events are discussed in more detail below.

Materials Costs (Event 2)

Materials used to make products are usually called **raw materials.** The cost of raw materials is first recorded in an asset account (Inventory). The cost is then transferred from the Inventory account to the Cost of Goods Sold account at the time the goods are sold. Remember that materials cost is only one component of total manufacturing costs. When inventory is sold, the combined cost of materials, labor, and overhead is expensed as *cost of goods sold.* The costs of materials that can be easily and conveniently traced to products are called **direct raw materials** costs.

Labor Costs (Event 4)

The salaries paid to selling and administrative employees (Event 3) and the wages paid to production workers (Event 4) are accounted for differently. Salaries paid to selling and administrative employees are expensed immediately, but the cost of production wages is added to inventory. Production wages are expensed as part of cost of goods sold at the time the inventory is sold. Labor costs that can be easily and conveniently traced to products are called **direct labor** costs. The cost flow of wages for production employees versus salaries for selling and administrative personnel is shown in Exhibit 10.6.

Overhead Costs (Event 8)

Although depreciation cost totaled $1,600 ($600 on office furniture and $1,000 on manufacturing equipment), only the $600 of depreciation on the office furniture is expensed directly on the income statement. The depreciation on the manufacturing equipment is

EXHIBIT 10.6

Flow of Labor Costs

Labor costs	Balance sheet	Income statement
Production wages	Inventory	Cost of goods sold
Selling and administrative salaries		Salaries expense

EXHIBIT 10.7

Flow of Depreciation Costs

Overhead cost	Balance sheet	Income statement
Depreciation on manufacturing equipment	Inventory	Cost of goods sold
Depreciation on office furniture		Depreciation expense

split between the income statement (cost of goods sold) and the balance sheet (inventory). The depreciation cost flow for the manufacturing equipment versus the office furniture is shown in Exhibit 10.7.

Total Product Cost. A summary of Patillo Manufacturing's total product cost is shown in Exhibit 10.8.

Financial Statements

The income statement, balance sheet, and statement of cash flows for Patillo Manufacturing are displayed in Exhibit 10.9.

Product Costs. The $4,000 cost of goods sold reported on the income statement includes a portion of the materials, labor, and overhead costs incurred by Patillo during the year. Similarly, the $2,000 of finished goods inventory on the balance sheet includes

EXHIBIT 10.8

Schedule of Inventory Costs

Materials	$ 2,000
Labor	3,000
Manufacturing overhead*	1,000
Total product costs	6,000
Less: Cost of goods sold	(4,000)
Ending inventory balance	$ 2,000

*Depreciation [($4,500 − $1,500) ÷ 3]

EXHIBIT 10.9

PATILLO MANUFACTURING COMPANY
Financial Statements

Income Statement for 2016

Sales revenue	$ 7,500
Cost of goods sold	(4,000)
Gross margin	3,500
G, S, & A expenses	
Salaries expense	(1,200)
Depreciation expense—office furniture	(600)
Net income	$ 1,700

Balance Sheet as of December 31, 2016

Cash		$ 9,000
Finished goods inventory		2,000
Office furniture	$2,800	
Accumulated depreciation	(600)	
Book value		2,200
Manufacturing equipment	4,500	
Accumulated depreciation	(1,000)	
Book value		3,500
Total assets		$16,700
Stockholders' equity		
Common stock		$15,000
Retained earnings		1,700
Total stockholders' equity		$16,700

Statement of Cash Flows for 2016

Operating Activities	
Inflow from revenue	$ 7,500
Outflow for inventory	(5,000)
Outflow for S&A salaries	(1,200)
Net inflow from operating activities	1,300
Investing Activities	
Outflow for equipment and furniture	(7,300)
Financing Activities	
Inflow from stock issue	15,000
Net change in cash	9,000
Beginning cash balance	-0-
Ending cash balance	$ 9,000

materials, labor, and overhead costs. These product costs will be recognized as an expense in the next accounting period when the goods are sold. Initially classifying a cost as a product cost delays, but does not eliminate, its recognition as an expense. All product costs are ultimately recognized as an expense (cost of goods sold). Cost classification does not affect cash flow. Cash inflows and outflows are recognized in the period that cash is collected or paid regardless of whether the cost is recorded as an asset or is expensed.

Selling, General, and Administrative Costs. Selling, general, and administrative costs (SG&A) are normally expensed *in the period* in which they are incurred. Because of this recognition pattern, nonproduct expenses are sometimes called **period costs.** In Patillo's case, the salaries expense for selling and administrative employees and the depreciation on office furniture are period costs reported directly on the income statement.

Overhead Costs: A Closer Look

Costs such as depreciation on manufacturing equipment cannot be easily traced to products. Suppose that Patillo Manufacturing makes both tables and chairs. What part of the depreciation is caused by manufacturing tables versus manufacturing chairs? Similarly, suppose a production supervisor oversees employees who work on both tables and chairs. How much of the supervisor's salary relates to tables and how much to chairs? Likewise, the cost of glue used in the production department would be difficult to trace to tables versus chairs. You could count the drops of glue used on each product, but the information would not be useful enough to merit the time and money spent collecting the data.

Costs that cannot be traced to products and services in a *cost-effective* manner are called **indirect costs.** The indirect costs incurred to make products are called **manufacturing overhead.** Some of the items commonly included in manufacturing overhead are indirect materials, indirect labor, factory utilities, rent of manufacturing facilities, and depreciation on manufacturing assets.

CHECK YOURSELF 10.2

Lawson Manufacturing Company paid production workers wages of $100,000. It incurred materials costs of $120,000 and manufacturing overhead costs of $160,000. Selling and administrative salaries were $80,000. Lawson started and completed 1,000 units of product and sold 800 of these units. The company sets sales prices at $220 above the average per-unit production cost. Based on this information alone, determine the amount of gross margin and net income. What is Lawson's pricing strategy called?

Answer   Total product cost is $380,000 ($100,000 labor + $120,000 materials + $160,000 overhead). Cost per unit is $380 ($380,000 ÷ 1,000 units). The sales price per unit is $600 ($380 + $220). Cost of goods sold is $304,000 ($380 × 800 units). Sales revenue is $480,000 ($600 × 800 units). Gross margin is $176,000 ($480,000 revenue − $304,000 cost of goods sold). Net income is $96,000 ($176,000 gross margin − $80,000 selling and administrative salaries). Lawson's pricing strategy is called *cost-plus* pricing.

Since indirect costs cannot be effectively traced to products, they are normally assigned to products using **cost allocation,** a process of dividing a total cost into parts and assigning the parts to relevant cost objects. To illustrate, suppose that production workers spend an eight-hour day making a chair and a table. The chair requires two hours to complete and the table requires six hours. Now suppose that $120 of utilities cost is consumed during the day. How much of the $120 should be assigned to each piece of furniture? The utility cost cannot be directly traced to each specific piece of furniture, but the piece of furniture that required more labor also likely consumed more of the utility cost. Using this line of reasoning, it is rational to allocate the utility cost to the two pieces of furniture based on *direct labor hours* at a rate of $15 per hour ($120 ÷ 8 hours). The chair would be assigned $30 ($15 per hour × 2 hours) of the utility cost and the table would be assigned the remaining $90 ($15 × 6 hours) of utility cost. The allocation of the utility cost is shown in Exhibit 10.10.

We discuss the details of cost allocation in a later chapter. For now, recognize that overhead costs are normally allocated to products rather than traced directly to them.

Manufacturing Product Cost Summary

As explained, the cost of a product made by a manufacturing company is normally composed of three categories: direct materials, direct labor, and manufacturing overhead. Relevant information about these three cost components is summarized in Exhibit 10.11.

EXHIBIT 10.10

Cost Allocation

Answers to The Curious Accountant

As you have seen, accounting for depreciation related to manufacturing assets is different from accounting for depreciation for nonmanufacturing assets. Depreciation on the checkout equipment at Target is recorded as depreciation expense. Depreciation on manufacturing equipment at Bose is considered a product cost. It is included first as a part of the cost of inventory and eventually as a part of the expense, cost of goods sold. Recording depreciation on manufacturing equipment as an inventory cost is simply another example of the matching principle, because the cost does not become an expense until revenue from the product sale is recognized.

EXHIBIT 10.11

Components of Manufacturing Product Cost

Component 1—Direct Raw Materials
Sometimes called *raw materials*. In addition to basic resources such as wood or metals, it can include manufactured parts. For example, engines, glass, and car tires can be considered as raw materials for an automotive manufacturer. If the amount of a material in a product is known, it can usually be classified as a direct material. The cost of direct materials can be easily traced to specific products.

Component 2—Direct Labor
The cost of wages paid to factory workers involved in hands-on contact with the products being manufactured. If the amount of time employees worked on a product can be determined, this cost can usually be classified as direct labor. Like direct materials, labor costs must be easily traced to a specific product in order to be classified as a direct cost.

Component 3—Manufacturing Overhead
Costs that cannot be easily traced to specific products. Accordingly, these costs are called *indirect costs*. They can include but are not limited to the following:

1. Indirect materials such as glue, nails, paper, and oil. Indeed, note that indirect materials used in the production process may not appear in the finished product. An example is a chemical solvent used to clean products during the production process but not a component material found in the final product.
2. Indirect labor such as the cost of salaries paid to production supervisors, inspectors, and maintenance personnel.
3. Rental cost for manufacturing facilities and equipment.
4. Utility costs.
5. Depreciation.
6. Security.
7. The cost of preparing equipment for the manufacturing process (i.e., setup costs).
8. Maintenance cost for the manufacturing facility and equipment.

SCHEDULE OF COST OF GOODS MANUFACTURED AND SOLD

To this point, we assumed all inventory started during an accounting period was also completed during that accounting period. All product costs (materials, labor, and manufacturing overhead) were either in inventory or expensed as cost of goods sold. At the end of an accounting period, however, most real-world companies have raw materials on hand, and manufacturing companies are likely to have in inventory items

LO 10-3

Prepare a schedule of cost of goods manufactured and sold.

that have been started but are not completed. Most manufacturing companies accumulate product costs in three distinct inventory accounts: (1) **Raw Materials Inventory,** which includes lumber, metals, paints, and chemicals that will be used to make the company's products; (2) **Work in Process Inventory,** which includes partially completed products; and (3) **Finished Goods Inventory,** which includes completed products that are ready for sale.

The cost of materials is first recorded in the Raw Materials Inventory account. The cost of materials placed in production is then transferred from the Raw Materials Inventory account to the Work in Process Inventory account. The costs of labor and overhead are added to the Work in Process Inventory account. The cost of the goods completed during the period is transferred from the Work in Process Inventory account to the Finished Goods Inventory account. The cost of the goods that are sold during the accounting period is transferred from the Finished Goods Inventory account to the Cost of Goods Sold account. The balances that remain in the Raw Materials, Work in Process, and Finished Goods Inventory accounts are reported on the balance sheet. The amount of product cost transferred to the Cost of Goods Sold account is expensed on the income statement. Exhibit 10.12 shows the flow of manufacturing costs through the accounting records.

To help managers analyze manufacturing costs, companies frequently summarize product cost information in a report called a **schedule of cost of goods manufactured and sold.** To illustrate, assume that in 2017 Patillo Manufacturing Company purchased $37,950 of raw materials inventory. During 2017 Patillo used $37,000 of raw materials, incurred $34,600 of labor costs, and $26,700 of overhead costs in the process of making inventory. Also, during 2017 the company completed work on products that cost $94,600. Recall that Patillo had zero balances in its Raw Materials and Work in Process Inventory accounts at the end of 2016. It had a $2,000 balance in its Finished Goods Inventory account at the end of 2016. The 2016 ending balance becomes the 2017 beginning balance for finished goods. The 2017 ending balances for the inventory accounts were as follows: Raw Materials Inventory, $950; Work in Process Inventory, $3,700; Finished Goods Inventory, $3,200. Finally, during 2017 Patillo had sales revenue of $153,000. Patillo's schedule of cost of goods manufactured and sold for 2017 is shown in Exhibit 10.13.

The $93,400 of cost of goods sold would appear on Patillo's 2017 income statement. A partial income statement for Patillo is shown in Exhibit 10.14.

EXHIBIT 10.12

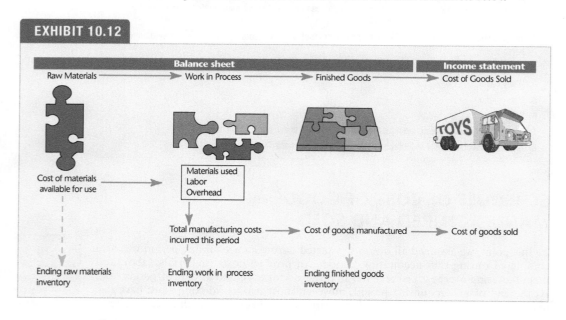

EXHIBIT 10.13

PATILLO MANUFACTURING COMPANY
Schedule of Cost of Goods Manufactured and Sold
For the Year Ended December 31, 2017

Beginning raw materials Inventory	$ 0
Plus: Raw materials purchases	37,950
Less: Ending raw materials inventory	(950)
Raw materials used	37,000
Labor	34,600
Overhead	26,700
Total manufacturing costs	98,300
Plus: Beginning work in process inventory	0
Total work in process inventory	98,300
Less: Ending work in process inventory	(3,700)
Cost of goods manufactured	94,600
Plus: Beginning finished goods inventory	2,000
Cost of goods available for sale	96,600
Less: Ending finished goods inventory	(3,200)
Cost of goods sold	$93,400

EXHIBIT 10.14

PATILLO MANUFACTURING COMPANY
Income Statement
For the Year Ended December 31, 2017

Sales revenue	$153,000
Cost of goods sold	(93,400)
Gross margin	$ 59,600

Upstream and Downstream Costs

Most companies incur product-related costs before and after, as well as during, the manufacturing process. For example, Ford Motor Company incurs significant research and development costs prior to mass producing a new car model. These **upstream costs** occur before the manufacturing process begins. Similarly, companies normally incur significant costs after the manufacturing process is complete. Examples of **downstream costs** include transportation, advertising, sales commissions, and bad debts. While upstream and downstream costs are not considered to be product costs for financial reporting purposes, profitability analysis requires that they be considered in cost-plus pricing decisions. To be profitable, a company must recover the total cost of developing, producing, and delivering its products to customers.

Product Costing in Service and Merchandising Companies

Companies are frequently classified as being service, merchandising, or manufacturing businesses. As the name implies, service organizations provide services, rather than physical products, to consumers. For example, St. Jude Children's Hospital provides treatment programs aimed at healing patient diseases. Other common service providers include public accountants, lawyers, restaurants, dry cleaning establishments, and lawn care companies. Merchandising businesses are sometimes called retail or wholesale companies; they sell goods other companies make. The Home Depot, Inc., Costco Wholesale Corporation, and Best Buy Co., Inc., are merchandising companies. Manufacturing companies make the goods they sell to their customers. Toyota Motor Corporation, Texaco, Inc., and American Standard Companies, Inc., are manufacturing businesses.

How do manufacturing companies differ from service and merchandising businesses? Do service and merchandising companies incur materials, labor, and overhead costs? Yes. For example, Ernst & Young, a large accounting firm, must pay employees (labor costs), use office supplies (material costs), and incur utilities, depreciation, and so on (overhead costs) in the process of conducting audits. *The primary difference between manufacturing entities and service companies is that the products provided by service companies are consumed immediately.* In contrast, products made by manufacturing companies can be held in the form of inventory until they are sold to consumers. Similarly, most labor and overhead costs incurred by merchandising companies result from providing assistance to customers. These costs are normally treated as selling, general, and administrative expenses rather than accumulated in inventory accounts. Indeed, merchandising companies are often viewed as service companies rather than considered a separate business category.

The important point to remember is that all business managers are expected to control costs, improve quality, and increase productivity. Like managers of manufacturing companies, managers of service and merchandising businesses can benefit from the analysis of the cost of satisfying their customers. For example, Wendy's, a service company, can benefit from knowing how much a hamburger costs in the same manner that Bayer Corporation, a manufacturing company, benefits from knowing the cost of a bottle of aspirin.

CHECK YOURSELF 10.3

The cost of making a Burger King hamburger includes the cost of materials, labor, and overhead. Does this mean that Burger King is a manufacturing company?

Answer   No, Burger King is not a manufacturing company. It is a service company because its products are consumed immediately. In contrast, there may be a considerable delay between the time the product of a manufacturing company is made and the time it is consumed. For example, it could be several months between the time Ford Motor Company makes an Explorer and the time the Explorer is ultimately sold to a customer. The primary difference between service and manufacturing companies is that manufacturing companies have inventories of products and service companies do not.

JUST-IN-TIME INVENTORY

LO 10-4

Show how just-in-time inventory can increase profitability.

Companies attempt to minimize the amount of inventory they maintain because of the high cost of holding it. Many **inventory holding costs** are obvious: financing, warehouse space, supervision, theft, damage, and obsolescence. Other costs are hidden: diminished motivation, sloppy work, inattentive attitudes, and increased production time.

Many businesses have been able to simultaneously reduce their inventory holding costs and increase customer satisfaction by making products available **just in time (JIT)** for customer consumption. For example, hamburgers that are cooked to order are fresher and more individualized than those that are prepared in advance and stored until a customer places an order. Many fast-food restaurants have discovered that JIT systems lead not only to greater customer satisfaction but also to lower costs through reduced waste.

Just-in-Time Illustration

To illustrate the benefits of a JIT system, consider Paula Elliot, a student at a large urban university. She helps support herself by selling flowers. Three days each week, Paula drives to a florist, purchases 25 single-stem roses, returns to the school, and sells the flowers to individuals from a location on a local street corner. She pays $2 per rose and sells each one for $3. Some days she does not have enough flowers to meet customer demand. Other days, she must discard one or two unsold flowers; she believes quality is important and refuses to sell flowers that are not fresh. During May, she purchased 300 roses and sold 280. She calculated her driving cost to be $45. Exhibit 10.15 displays Paula's May income statement.

EXHIBIT 10.15

Income Statement for May

Sales revenue (280 units × $3 per unit)	$840
Cost of goods sold (280 units × $2 per unit)	(560)
Gross margin	280
Driving expense	(45)
Excess inventory waste (20 units × 2)	(40)
Net income	$195

EXHIBIT 10.16

Income Statement for June

Sales revenue (310 units × $3 per unit)	$930
Cost of goods sold (310 units × $2 per unit)	(620)
Gross margin	310
Driving expense	0
Net income	$310

After studying just-in-time inventory systems in her managerial accounting class, Paula decided to apply the concepts to her small business. She *reengineered* her distribution system by purchasing her flowers from a florist within walking distance of her sales location. She had considered purchasing from this florist earlier but had rejected the idea because the florist's regular selling price of $2.25 per rose was too high. After learning about *most-favored customer status,* she developed a strategy to get a price reduction. By guaranteeing that she would buy at least 30 roses per week, she was able to convince the local florist to match her current cost of $2.00 per rose. The local florist agreed that she could make purchases in batches of any size so long as the total amounted to at least 30 per week. Under this arrangement, Paula was able to buy roses *just in time* to meet customer demand. Each day she purchased a small number of flowers. When she ran out, she simply returned to the florist for additional ones.

The JIT system also enabled Paula to eliminate the cost of the *nonvalue-added activity* of driving to her former florist. Customer satisfaction actually improved because no one was ever turned away because of the lack of inventory. In June, Paula was able to buy and sell 310 roses with no waste and no driving expense. The June income statement is shown in Exhibit 10.16.

At Ford Motor Company's plant in Valencia, Spain, suppliers feed parts such as these bumpers just in time and in the right order directly to the assembly line.

Paula was ecstatic about her $115 increase in profitability ($310 in June − $195 in May = $115 increase), but she was puzzled about the exact reasons for the change. She had saved $40 (20 flowers × $2 each) by avoiding waste and eliminated $45 of driving expenses. These two factors explained only $85 ($40 waste + $45 driving expense) of the $115 increase. What had caused the remaining $30 ($115 − $85) increase in profitability? Paula asked her accounting professor to help her identify the remaining $30 difference.

The professor explained that May sales had suffered from *lost opportunities.* Recall that under the earlier inventory system, Paula had to turn away some prospective customers because she sold out of flowers before all customers were served. Sales increased from 280 roses in May to 310 roses in June. A likely explanation for the 30 unit difference (310 − 280) is that customers who would have purchased flowers in May were unable to do so because of a lack of availability. May's sales suffered from the lost opportunity to earn a gross margin of $1 per flower on 30 roses, a $30 **opportunity cost.** This opportunity cost is the missing link in explaining the profitability difference between May and June. The total $115 difference consists of (1) $40 savings from waste elimination, (2) $45 savings from eliminating driving expense, and (3) opportunity cost of $30. The subject of opportunity cost has widespread application and is discussed in more depth in subsequent chapters of the text.

> ☑ **CHECK YOURSELF 10.4**
>
> A strike at a General Motors brake plant caused an almost immediate shutdown of many of the company's assembly plants. What could have caused such a rapid and widespread shutdown?
>
> **Answer**   A rapid and widespread shutdown could have occurred because General Motors uses a just-in-time inventory system. With a just-in-time inventory system, there is no stockpile of inventory to draw on when strikes or other forces disrupt inventory deliveries. This illustrates a potential negative effect of using a just-in-time inventory system.

STATEMENT OF ETHICAL PROFESSIONAL PRACTICE

LO 10-5

Identify the standards contained in IMA's Statement of Ethical Professional Practice.

There are several conflicts of interest management accountants might face. It is tempting to misclassify a cost if doing so will significantly increase a manager's bonus. Management accountants must be prepared not only to make difficult choices between legitimate alternatives but also to face conflicts of a more troubling nature, such as pressure to:

1. Undertake duties they have not been trained to perform competently.
2. Disclose confidential information.
3. Compromise their integrity through falsification, embezzlement, bribery, and so on.
4. Issue biased, misleading, or incomplete reports.

To provide management accountants with guidance for ethical conduct, the Institute of Management Accountants (IMA) issued a *Statement of Ethical Professional Practice,* which is shown in Exhibit 10.17. Management accountants are also frequently required to abide by organizational codes of ethics. Failure to adhere to professional and organizational ethical standards can lead to personal disgrace, loss of employment, or imprisonment.

FOCUS ON INTERNATIONAL ISSUES

FINANCIAL ACCOUNTING VERSUS MANAGERIAL ACCOUNTING—AN INTERNATIONAL PERSPECTIVE

This chapter has already explained some of the conceptual differences between financial and managerial accounting, but these differences have implications for international businesses as well. With respect to financial accounting, publicly traded companies in most countries must follow the generally accepted accounting principles (GAAP) for their country, but these rules can vary from country to country. Generally, companies that are audited under the auditing standards of the United States follow the standards established by the Financial Accounting Standards Board. Most companies located outside of the United States follow the standards established by the International Accounting Standards Board (IASB). For example, the United States is one of very few countries whose GAAP allow the use of the LIFO inventory cost flow assumption.

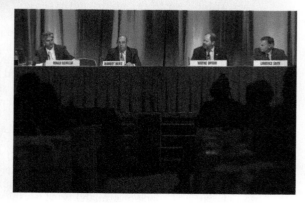

Conversely, most of the managerial accounting concepts introduced in this course can be used by businesses in any country. For example, while accrual-based earnings can differ depending on whether a company uses U.S. GAAP or IFRS, cash flow will not. As you will learn, managerial accounting decisions often focus on cash flow versus accrual-based income. Therefore, managerial accounting concepts are more universal than financial accounting rules.

EXHIBIT 10.17

Statement of Ethical Professional Practice

Members of IMA shall behave ethically. A commitment to ethical professional practice includes overarching principles that express our values, and standards that guide our conduct. IMA's overarching ethical principles include: Honesty, Fairness, Objectivity, and Responsibility. Members shall act in accordance with these principles and shall encourage others within their organizations to adhere to them. A member's failure to comply with the following standards may result in disciplinary action.

Competence Each member has a responsibility to
- Maintain an appropriate level of professional expertise by continually developing knowledge and skills.
- Perform professional duties in accordance with relevant laws, regulations, and technical standards.
- Provide decision support information and recommendations that are accurate, clear, concise, and timely.
- Recognize and communicate professional limitations or other constraints that would preclude responsible judgment or successful performance of an activity.

Confidentiality Each member has a responsibility to
- Keep information confidential except when disclosure is authorized or legally required.
- Inform all relevant parties regarding appropriate use of confidential information. Monitor subordinates' activities to ensure compliance.
- Refrain from using confidential information for unethical or illegal advantage.

Integrity Each member has a responsibility to
- Mitigate actual conflicts of interest and avoid apparent conflicts of interest. Advise all parties of any potential conflicts.
- Refrain from engaging in any conduct that would prejudice carrying out duties ethically.
- Abstain from engaging in or supporting any activity that might discredit the profession.

Credibility Each member has a responsibility to
- Communicate information fairly and objectively.
- Disclose all relevant information that could reasonably be expected to influence an intended user's understanding of the reports, analyses, or recommendations.
- Disclose delays or deficiencies in information, timeliness, processing, or internal controls in conformance with organization policy and/or applicable law.

Resolution of Ethical Conflict In applying these standards, you may encounter problems identifying unethical behavior or resolving an ethical conflict. When faced with ethical issues, follow your organization's established policies on the resolution of such conflict. If these policies do not resolve the ethical conflict, consider the following courses of action:
- Discuss the issue with your immediate supervisor except when it appears that the supervisor is involved. In that case, present the issue to the next level. If you cannot achieve a satisfactory resolution, submit the issue to the next management level. Communication of such problems to authorities or individuals not employed or engaged by the organization is not considered appropriate, unless you believe there is a clear violation of the law.
- Clarify relevant ethical issues by initiating a confidential discussion with an IMA Ethics Counselor or other impartial advisor to obtain a better understanding of possible courses of action.
- Consult your own attorney as to legal obligations and rights concerning the ethical conflict.

REALITY BYTES

Unethical behavior occurs in all types of organizations. In its *2011 National Business Ethics Survey,* the Ethics Resource Center reported its findings of the occurrences and reporting of unethical behavior in American corporations based on a survey of over 4,600 employees.

Forty-five percent of those surveyed reported having observed unethical conduct during the past year. This was the lowest level reported in the 17 years the survey has been conducted. Sixty-five percent of those who said they had observed misconduct went on to report it to their employer. However, fear of retaliation for reporting misconduct was a concern. Of respondents who said they had reported misconduct at their companies, 22 percent said they had experienced some form of retaliation, such as being excluded from decision making.

The definition of ethical misconduct used in the study was quite broad. The five most frequently reported types of misconduct were: misuse of company time, abusive behavior, abusing company resources, lying to employees, and violating the company's policies for using the Internet.

For the complete *2011 National Business Ethics Survey,* go to www.ethics.org.

380   Chapter 10

 A Look Back

Managerial accounting focuses on the information needs of *internal* users, while *financial accounting* focuses on the information needs of *external* users. Managerial accounting uses economic, operating, and nonfinancial, as well as financial, data. Managerial accounting information is local (pertains to the company's subunits), is limited by cost/benefit considerations, is more concerned with relevance and timeliness, and is future-oriented. Financial accounting information, on the other hand, is more global than managerial accounting information. It supplies information that applies to the whole company. Financial accounting is regulated by numerous authorities, is characterized by objectivity, is focused on reliability and accuracy, and is historical in nature.

Both managerial and financial accounting are concerned with product costing. Financial accountants need product cost information to determine the amount of inventory reported on the balance sheet and the amount of cost of goods sold reported on the income statement. Managerial accountants need to know the cost of products for pricing decisions and for control and evaluation purposes. When determining unit product costs, managers use the average cost per unit. Determining the actual cost of each product requires an unreasonable amount of time and record keeping and it makes no difference in product pricing and product cost control decisions.

Product costs are the costs incurred to make products: the costs of direct materials, direct labor, and overhead. *Overhead costs* are product costs that cannot be cost effectively traced to a product; therefore, they are assigned to products using *cost allocation*. Overhead costs include indirect materials, indirect labor, depreciation, rent, and utilities for manufacturing facilities. Product costs are first accumulated in an asset account (Inventory). They are expensed as cost of goods sold in the period the inventory is sold. The difference between sales revenue and cost of goods sold is called *gross margin.*

Selling, general, and administrative costs are classified separately from product costs. They are subtracted from gross margin to determine net income. Selling, general, and administrative costs can be divided into two categories. Costs incurred before the manufacturing process begins (research and development costs) are *upstream costs.* Costs incurred after manufacturing is complete (transportation) are *downstream costs.*

Service companies, like manufacturing companies, incur materials, labor, and overhead costs, but the products provided by service companies are consumed immediately. Therefore, service company product costs are not accumulated in an Inventory account.

A *code of ethical conduct* is needed in the accounting profession because accountants hold positions of trust and face conflicts of interest. In recognition of the temptations that accountants face, the IMA has issued a *Statement of Ethical Professional Practice,* which provides accountants guidance in resisting temptations and in making difficult decisions.

Emerging trends such as *just-in-time inventory* and *activity-based management* are methods that many companies have used to reengineer their production and delivery systems to eliminate waste, reduce errors, and minimize costs. Activity-based management seeks to eliminate or reduce *nonvalue-added activities* and to create new *value-added activities.* Just-in-time inventory seeks to reduce inventory holding costs and to lower prices for customers by making inventory available just in time for customer consumption.

 A Look Forward

In addition to distinguishing costs by product versus SG&A classification, other classifications can be used to facilitate managerial decision making. In the next chapter, costs are classified according to the *behavior* they exhibit when the number of units of product increases or decreases (volume of activity changes). You will learn to distinguish between costs that vary with activity volume changes versus costs that remain fixed with activity volume changes. You will learn not only to recognize *cost behavior* but also how to use such recognition to evaluate business risk and opportunity.

APPENDIX

Emerging Trends in Managerial Accounting

Global competition has forced many companies to reengineer their production and delivery systems to eliminate waste, reduce errors, and minimize costs. A key ingredient of successful **reengineering** is benchmarking. **Benchmarking** involves identifying the **best practices** used by world-class competitors. By studying and mimicking these practices, a company uses benchmarking to implement highly effective and efficient operating methods. Best practices employed by world-class companies include total quality management (TQM), activity-based management (ABM), and value-added assessment.

Identify emerging trends in accounting.

Total Quality Management

To promote effective and efficient operations, many companies practice **total quality management (TQM).** TQM is a two-dimensional management philosophy using (1) a systematic problem-solving philosophy that encourages frontline workers to achieve *zero defects* and (2) an organizational commitment to achieving *customer satisfaction*. A key component of TQM is **continuous improvement,** an ongoing process through which employees strive to eliminate waste, reduce response time, minimize defects, and simplify the design and delivery of products and services to customers.

Activity-Based Management

Simple changes in perspective can have dramatic results. For example, imagine how realizing the world is round instead of flat changed the nature of travel. A recent change in perspective developing in management accounting is the realization that an organization cannot manage *costs*. Instead, it manages the *activities* that cause costs to be incurred. **Activities** represent the measures an organization takes to accomplish its goals.

The primary goal of all organizations is to provide products (goods and services) their customers *value*. The sequence of activities used to provide products is called a **value chain. Activity-based management** assesses the value chain to create new or refine existing **value-added activities** and to eliminate or reduce *nonvalue-added activities*. A value-added activity is any unit of work that contributes to a product's ability to satisfy customer needs. For example, cooking is an activity that adds value to food served to a hungry customer. **Nonvalue-added activities** are tasks undertaken that do not contribute to a product's ability to satisfy customer needs. Waiting for the oven to preheat so that food can be cooked does not add value. Most customers value cooked food, but they do not value waiting for it.

To illustrate, consider the value-added activities undertaken by a pizza restaurant. Begin with a customer who is hungry for pizza; certain activities must occur to satisfy that hunger. These activities are pictured in Exhibit 10.18. At a minimum, the restaurant must conduct research and development (devise a recipe), obtain raw materials (acquire the ingredients), manufacture the product (combine and bake the ingredients), market the product (advertise its availability), and deliver the product (transfer the pizza to the customer).

Businesses gain competitive advantages by adding activities that satisfy customer needs. For example, Domino's Pizza grew briskly by recognizing the value customers placed on the convenience of home pizza delivery. Alternatively, Little Caesar's has been highly successful by satisfying customers who value low prices. Other restaurants capitalize on customer values pertaining to taste, ambience, or location. Businesses can

EXHIBIT 10.18

Value Chain

| Conducting research and development | Obtaining materials | Manufacturing | Marketing | Delivering |

also gain competitive advantages by identifying and eliminating nonvalue-added activities, providing products of comparable quality at lower cost than competitors.

Value Chain Analysis across Companies

Comprehensive value chain analysis extends from obtaining raw materials to the ultimate disposition of finished products. It encompasses the activities performed not only by a particular organization but also by that organization's suppliers and those who service its finished products. For example, PepsiCo must be concerned with the activities of the company that supplies the containers for its soft drinks as well as the retail companies that sell its products. If cans of Pepsi fail to open properly, the customer is more likely to blame PepsiCo than the supplier of the cans. Comprehensive value chain analysis can lead to identifying and eliminating nonvalue-added activities that occur between companies. For example, container producers could be encouraged to build manufacturing facilities near Pepsi's bottling factories, eliminating the nonvalue-added activity of transporting empty containers from the manufacturer to the bottling facility. The resulting cost savings benefits customers by reducing costs without affecting quality.

 Video lectures and accompanying self-assessment quizzes are available for all learning objectives through McGraw-Hill *Connect®* *Accounting.*

SELF-STUDY REVIEW PROBLEM

Tuscan Manufacturing Company makes a unique headset for use with mobile phones. The company had the following amounts in its accounts at the beginning of 2015: Cash, $795,000; Raw Materials Inventory, $5,000; Work in Process Inventory, $11,000; Finished Goods Inventory, $39,000; Common Stock, $650,000; and Retained Earnings, $200,000. Tuscan experienced the following accounting events during 2015. Other than the adjusting entries for depreciation, assume that all transactions are cash transactions.

1. Paid $50,000 of research and development costs to create the headset.
2. Paid $139,000 for raw materials that will be used to make headsets.
3. Placed $141,000 of the raw materials cost into the process of manufacturing headsets.
4. Paid $82,200 for salaries of selling and administrative employees.
5. Paid $224,000 for wages of production workers.
6. Paid $48,000 to purchase furniture used in selling and administrative offices.
7. Recognized depreciation on the office furniture. The furniture was acquired January 1, 2015. It has an $8,000 salvage value and a four-year useful life. The amount of depreciation is computed as [(cost − salvage) ÷ useful life]. Specifically, ($48,000 − $8,000) ÷ 4 = $10,000.
8. Paid $65,000 to purchase manufacturing equipment.

9. Recognized depreciation on the manufacturing equipment. The equipment was acquired January 1, 2015. It has a $5,000 salvage value and a three-year useful life. The amount of depreciation is computed as [(cost − salvage) ÷ useful life]. Specifically, ($65,000 − $5,000) ÷ 3 = $20,000.

10. Paid $136,000 for rent and utility costs on the manufacturing facility.

11. Paid $41,000 for inventory holding expenses for completed headsets (rental of warehouse space, salaries of warehouse personnel, and other general storage costs).

12. Completed and transferred headsets that had a total cost of $520,000 from work in process inventory to finished goods.

13. Sold headsets for $738,200.

14. It cost Tuscan $517,400 to make the headsets sold in Event 13.

Required

a. Show how these events affect the balance sheet, income statement, and statement of cash flows by recording them in a horizontal financial statement model.

b. Explain why Tuscan's recognition of cost of goods sold expense had no impact on cash flow.

c. Prepare a schedule of costs of goods manufactured and sold, an income statement, and a balance sheet.

d. Distinguish between the product costs and the upstream and downstream costs that Tuscan incurred.

Solution to Requirement *a*

Event No.	Cash +	Raw Mat. Inv. +	WIP Inv. +	Finished Goods Inv. +	Office Furn.* +	Manuf. Equip.* =	Com. Stk. +	Ret. Earn.	Rev. −	Exp. = Net Inc.	Cash Flow
	795,000	5,000	11,000	39,000		= 650,000		200,000		=	
1	(50,000)					=		(50,000)	− 50,000 = (50,000)		(50,000) OA
2	(139,000)	139,000				=			=		(139,000) OA
3		(141,000)	141,000			=			=		
4	(82,200)					=		(82,200)	− 82,200 = (82,200)		(82,200) OA
5	(224,000)		224,000			=			=		(224,000) OA
6	(48,000)				48,000	=			=		(48,000) IA
7					(10,000)	=		(10,000)	− 10,000 = (10,000)		
8	(65,000)					65,000 =			=		(65,000) IA
9			20,000			(20,000) =			=		
10	(136,000)		136,000			=			=		(136,000) OA
11	(41,000)					=		(41,000)	− 41,000 = (41,000)		(41,000) OA
12			(520,000)	520,000		=			=		
13	738,200					=		738,200	738,200 = 738,200		738,200 OA
14				(517,400)		=		(517,400)	− 517,400 = (517,400)		
Totals	748,000 +	3,000 +	12,000 +	41,600 +	38,000 +	45,000 = 650,000 +		237,600	738,200 − 700,600 = 37,600		(47,000) NC

*Negative amounts in these columns represent accumulated depreciation.

Solution to Requirement *b*

Tuscan does not recognize a cash outflow at the time the goods are sold because the cash is paid when the materials, labor, and overhead are acquired.

Solution to Requirement c

TUSCAN MANUFACTURING COMPANY
Schedule of Cost of Goods Manufactured and Sold
For the Year Ended December 31, 2015

Beginning raw materials inventory	$ 5,000
Plus: Raw materials purchases	139,000
Less: Ending raw materials inventory	(3,000)
Raw materials used	141,000
Labor	224,000
Overhead	156,000
Total manufacturing costs	521,000
Plus: Beginning work in process inventory	11,000
Total work in process inventory	532,000
Less: Ending work in process inventory	(12,000)
Cost of goods manufactured	520,000
Plus: Beginning finished goods inventory	39,000
Cost of goods available for sale	559,000
Less: Ending finished goods inventory	(41,600)
Cost of goods sold	$517,400

TUSCAN MANUFACTURING COMPANY
Income Statement
For the Year Ended December 31, 2015

Sales revenue	$738,200
Cost of goods sold	(517,400)
Gross margin	220,800
Research and development expenses	(50,000)
Selling and administrative salary expense	(82,200)
Selling and administrative depreciation expense	(10,000)
Inventory holding expenses	(41,000)
Net Income	$ 37,600

TUSCAN MANUFACTURING COMPANY
Balance Sheet
As of December 31, 2015

Assets	
Cash	$748,000
Raw materials inventory	3,000
Work in process inventory	12,000
Finished goods inventory	41,600
Manufacturing equipment less accumulated depreciation	45,000
Office furniture less accumulated depreciation	38,000
Total assets	$887,600
Equity	
Common stock	$650,000
Retained earnings	237,600
Total stockholders' equity	$887,600

Solution to Requirement *d*

Inventory product costs for manufacturing companies focus on the costs necessary to make the product. The cost of research and development (Event 1) occurs before the inventory is made and is therefore an upstream cost, not an inventory (product) cost. The inventory holding costs (Event 11) are incurred after the inventory has been made and are therefore downstream costs, not product costs. Selling costs (included in Events 4 and 7) are normally incurred after products have been made and are therefore usually classified as downstream costs. Administrative costs (also included in Events 4 and 7) are not related to making products and are therefore not classified as product costs. Administrative costs may be incurred before, during, or after products are made, so they may be classified as either upstream or downstream costs. Only the costs of materials, labor, and overhead that are actually incurred for the purpose of making goods (Events 3, 5, 9, and 10) are classified as product costs.

KEY TERMS

Activities 381	Financial accounting 362	Manufacturing overhead 371	Securities and Exchange
Activity-based management	Financial Accounting	Nonvalue-added activities 381	Commission (SEC) 365
(ABM) 381	Standards Board	Opportunity cost 377	Selling, general, and
Average cost 366	(FASB) 365	Overhead 366	administrative costs 371
Benchmarking 381	Finished Goods Inventory 374	Period costs 371	Total quality management
Best practices 381	Generally acceptable	Product costing 365	(TQM) 381
Continuous improvement 381	accounting principles	Product costs 365	Upstream costs 375
Cost allocation 372	(GAAP) 365	Raw materials 369	Value-added activity 381
Cost-plus pricing 365	Indirect costs 371	Raw Materials Inventory 374	Value-added principle 365
Direct labor 369	Inventory holding costs 376	Reengineering 381	Value chain 381
Direct raw materials 369	Just in time (JIT) 376	Schedule of cost of goods	Work in Process Inventory 374
Downstream costs 375	Managerial accounting 362	manufactured and sold 374	

QUESTIONS

1. What are some differences between financial and managerial accounting?

2. What does the value-added principle mean as it applies to managerial accounting information? Give an example of value-added information that may be included in managerial accounting reports but is not shown in publicly reported financial statements.

3. How does product costing used in financial accounting differ from product costing used in managerial accounting?

4. What does the statement "costs can be assets or expenses" mean?

5. Why are the salaries of production workers accumulated in an inventory account instead of being directly expensed on the income statement?

6. How do product costs affect the financial statements? How does the classification of product cost (as an asset vs. an expense) affect net income?

7. What is an indirect cost? Provide examples of product costs that would be classified as indirect.

8. How does a product cost differ from a general, selling, and administrative cost? Give examples of each.

9. Why is cost classification important to managers?

10. What is cost allocation? Give an example of a cost that needs to be allocated.

11. What are some of the common ethical conflicts that accountants encounter?

12. What costs should be considered in determining the sales price of a product?

13. What is a just-in-time (JIT) inventory system? Name some inventory costs that can be eliminated or reduced by its use.

14. What are the two dimensions of a total quality management (TQM) program? Why is TQM being used in business practice? (Appendix)

15. How has the Institute of Management Accountants responded to the need for high standards of ethical conduct in the accounting profession?

16. What does the term *reengineering* mean? Name some reengineering practices. (Appendix)

17. What does the term *activity-based management* mean? (Appendix)

18. What is a value chain? (Appendix)

19. What do the terms *value-added activity* and *nonvalue-added activity* mean? Provide an example of each type of activity. (Appendix)

386 Chapter 10

MULTIPLE-CHOICE QUESTIONS

Multiple-choice questions are provided on the text website at www.mhhe.com/edmondssurvey4e.

EXERCISES

All applicable Exercises are available with McGraw-Hill *Connect® Accounting.*

LO 10-1

Exercise 10-1 *Identifying financial versus managerial accounting items*

Required

Indicate whether each of the following items is representative of managerial or of financial accounting.

a. Information is based on estimates that are bounded by relevance and timeliness.
b. Information is historically based and usually reported annually.
c. Information is local and pertains to subunits of the organization.
d. Information includes economic and nonfinancial data as well as financial data.
e. Information is global and pertains to the company as a whole.
f. Information is provided to insiders, including executives, managers, and employees.
g. Information is factual and is characterized by objectivity, reliability, consistency, and accuracy.
h. Information is reported continuously and has a current or future orientation.
i. Information is provided to outsiders, including investors, creditors, government agencies, analysts, and reporters.
j. Information is regulated by the SEC, FASB, and other sources of GAAP.

LO 10-2

Exercise 10-2 *Identifying product versus general, selling, and administrative costs*

Required

Indicate whether each of the following costs should be classified as a product cost or as a selling, general, and administrative cost.

a. Interest on the mortgage for the company's corporate headquarters.
b. Indirect labor used to manufacture inventory.
c. Attorney's fees paid to protect the company from frivolous lawsuits.
d. Research and development costs incurred to create new drugs for a pharmaceutical company.
e. The cost of secretarial supplies used in a doctor's office.
f. Depreciation on the office furniture of the company president.
g. Direct materials used in a manufacturing company.
h. Indirect materials used in a manufacturing company.
i. Salaries of employees working in the accounting department.
j. Commissions paid to sales staff.

LO 10-2

Exercise 10-3 *Classifying costs: Product or SG&A cost; asset or expense*

Required

Use the following format to classify each cost as a product cost or a selling, general, and administrative (SG&A) cost. Also indicate whether the cost would be recorded as an asset or an expense. The first item is shown as an example.

Cost Category	Product/SG&A	Asset/Expense
Utilities used in manufacturing facility	Product	Asset
Cars for sales staff		
Real estate tax levied on a factory		✓
General office supplies		
Raw materials used in the manufacturing process		
Cost to rent office equipment		
Wages of production workers		
Advertising costs		
Promotion costs		
Production supplies		
Depreciation on administration building		
Depreciation on manufacturing equipment		
Research and development costs		
Cost to set up manufacturing equipment		

Exercise 10-4 Identifying effect of product versus selling, general, and administrative costs on financial statements

LO 10-2

Required

Ames Corporation recognized accrued compensation cost. Use the following model to show how this event would affect the company's financial statements under the following two assumptions: (1) the compensation is for office personnel and (2) the compensation is for production workers. Use pluses or minuses to show the effect on each element. If an element is not affected, indicate so by placing the letters NA under the appropriate heading.

	Assets	=	Liab.	+	Equity	Rev.	−	Exp.	=	Net Inc.	Cash Flow
1.											
2.											

Exercise 10-5 Identify effect of product versus selling, general, and administrative costs on financial statements

LO 10-2

Required

Taft Industries recognized the annual cost of depreciation on its December 31, 2015, financial statements. Using the following horizontal financial statements model, indicate how this event affected the company's financial statements under the following two assumptions: (1) the depreciation was on office furniture and (2) the depreciation was on manufacturing equipment. Indicate whether the event increases (I), decreases (D), or has no effect (NA) on each element of the financial statements. Also, in the Cash Flow column, indicate whether the cash flow is for operating activities (OA), investing activities (IA), or financing activities (FA). (Note: Show accumulated depreciation as a decrease in the book value of the appropriate asset account.)

Event No.	Assets					Equity							
	Cash	+	Inventory	+	Manuf. Equip.	+	Office Furn.	=	Com. Stk.	+	Ret. Ear.	Rev. − Exp. = Net Inc.	Cash Flow
1.													
2.													

LO 10-2

Exercise 10-6 *Identifying product costs in a manufacturing company*

Jessica Hansen was talking to another accounting student, Adam Ruud. Upon discovering that the accounting department offered an upper-level course in cost measurement, Jessica remarked to Adam, "How difficult can it be? My parents own a toy store. All you have to do to figure out how much something costs is look at the invoice. Surely you don't need an entire course to teach you how to read an invoice."

Required

a. Identify the three main components of product cost for a manufacturing entity.

b. Explain why measuring product cost for a manufacturing entity is more complex than measuring product cost for a retail toy store.

c. Assume that Jessica's parents rent a store for $7,500 per month. Different types of toys use different amounts of store space. For example, displaying a bicycle requires more store space than displaying a deck of cards. Also, some toys remain on the shelf longer than others. Fad toys sell rapidly, but traditional toys sell more slowly. Under these circumstances, how would you determine the amount of rental cost required to display each type of toy? Identify two other costs incurred by a toy store that may be difficult to allocate to individual toys.

LO 10-2

Exercise 10-7 *Identifying product versus selling, general, and administrative costs*

A review of the accounting records of Spiller Manufacturing indicated that the company incurred the following payroll costs during the month of September.

1. Salary of the company president—$40,000.
2. Salary of the vice president of manufacturing—$25,000.
3. Salary of the chief financial officer—$20,000.
4. Salary of the vice president of marketing—$18,000.
5. Salaries of middle managers (department heads, production supervisors) in manufacturing plant—$196,000.
6. Wages of production workers—$938,000.
7. Salaries of administrative secretaries—$60,000.
8. Salaries of engineers and other personnel responsible for maintaining production equipment—$178,000.
9. Commissions paid to sales staff—$252,000.

Required

a. What amount of payroll cost would be classified as selling, general, and administrative expense?

b. Assuming that Spiller made 4,000 units of product and sold 3,600 of them during the month of September, determine the amount of payroll cost that would be included in cost of goods sold.

LO 10-2

Exercise 10-8 *Recording product versus selling, general, and administrative costs in a financial statements model*

Naoki Manufacturing experienced the following events during its first accounting period.

1. Recognized depreciation on manufacturing equipment.
2. Recognized depreciation on office furniture.
3. Recognized revenue from cash sale of products.
4. Recognized cost of goods sold from sale referenced in Event 3.
5. Acquired cash by issuing common stock.
6. Paid cash to purchase raw materials that were used to make products.
7. Paid wages to production workers.
8. Paid salaries to administrative staff.

Required

Use the following horizontal financial statements model to show how each event affects the balance sheet, income statement, and the statement of cash flows. Indicate whether the event increases (I), decreases (D), or has no effect (NA) on each element of the financial statements. Also, in the Cash Flow column, indicate whether the cash flow is for operating activities (OA), investing activities (IA), or financing activities (FA). The first transaction has been recorded as an example. (*Note:* Show accumulated depreciation as a decrease in the book value of the appropriate asset account.)

Event No.	Cash	+	Inventory	+	Manuf. Equip.	+	Office Furn.	=	Com. Stk.	+	Ret. Ear.	Rev.	−	Exp.	=	Net Inc.	Cash Flow
						Assets					**Equity**						
1.	NA		I		D		NA		NA		NA	NA		NA		NA	NA

Exercise 10-9   *Allocating product costs between ending inventory and cost of goods sold*   LO 10-2

Santiago Manufacturing Company began operations on January 1. During the year, it started and completed 2,000 units of product. The company incurred the following costs.

1. Raw materials purchased and used—$4,700.
2. Wages of production workers—$5,100.
3. Salaries of administrative and sales personnel—$2,600.
4. Depreciation on manufacturing equipment—$3,800.
5. Depreciation on administrative equipment—$1,900.

Santiago sold 1,650 units of product.

Required

a. Determine the total product cost for the year.
b. Determine the total cost of the ending inventory.
c. Determine the total of cost of goods sold.

Exercise 10-10   *Financial statement effects for manufacturing versus service organizations*   LO 10-2

The following financial statements model shows the effects of recognizing depreciation in two different circumstances. One circumstance represents recognizing depreciation on a machine used in a factory. The other circumstance recognizes depreciation on computers used in a consulting firm. The effects of each event have been recorded using the letter (I) for increase, (D) for decrease, and (NA) for no effect.

Event No.	Cash	+	Inventory	+	Equip.	=	Com. Stk.	+	Ret. Ear.	Rev.	−	Exp.	=	Net Inc.	Cash Flow
			Assets					**Equity**							
1.	NA		NA		D		NA		D	NA		I		D	NA
2.	NA		I		D		NA		NA	NA		NA		NA	NA

Required

a. Identify the event that represents depreciation on the computers.
b. Explain why recognizing depreciation on equipment used in a manufacturing company affects financial statements differently than recognizing depreciation on equipment used in a service organization.

LO 10-2

Exercise 10-11 *Identifying the effect of product versus selling, general, and administrative cost on the income statement*

Each of the following events describes acquiring an asset that requires a year-end adjusting entry.

1. Paid $27,000 cash on January 1 to purchase computer equipment to be used for administrative purposes. The equipment had an estimated expected useful life of five years and a $2,000 salvage value.
2. Paid $27,000 cash on January 1 to purchase manufacturing equipment. The equipment had an estimated expected useful life of five years and a $2,000 salvage value.
3. Paid $12,000 cash in advance on May 1 for a one-year rental contract on administrative offices.
4. Paid $12,000 cash in advance on May 1 for a one-year rental contract on manufacturing facilities.
5. Paid $2,000 cash to purchase supplies to be used by the marketing department. At the end of the year, $400 of supplies was still on hand.
6. Paid $2,000 cash to purchase supplies to be used in the manufacturing process. At the end of the year, $400 of supplies was still on hand.

Required

Explain how the adjusting entry affects the amount of net income shown on the year-end financial statements. Assume a December 31 annual closing date. Also, in the Cash Flow column, indicate whether the cash flow is for operating activities (OA), investing activities (IA), or financing activities (FA). The first event has been recorded as an example. Assume that any products that have been made have not been sold.

	Net Income	Cash Flow
Event No.	**Amount of Change**	**Amount of Change**
1. Adjusting entry	$(5,000)	NA

LO 10-3

Exercise 10-12 *Missing information in a schedule of cost of goods manufactured*

Required

Supply the missing information on the following schedule of cost of goods manufactured.

FISCHER CORPORATION
Schedule of Cost of Goods Manufactured
For the Year Ended December 31, 2014

Raw materials		
Beginning inventory	$?	
Plus: Purchases	120,000	
Raw materials available for use	$148,000	
Minus: Ending raw materials inventory	?	
Cost of direct raw materials used		$124,000
Direct labor		?
Manufacturing overhead		24,000
Total manufacturing costs		324,000
Plus: Beginning work in process inventory		?
Total work in process		?
Minus: Ending work in process inventory		46,000
Cost of goods manufactured		$320,000

Exercise 10-13 *Cost of goods manufactured and sold*

The following information pertains to Flaxman Manufacturing Company for March 2015. Assume actual overhead equaled applied overhead.

March 1	
Inventory balances	
Raw materials	$100,000
Work in process	120,000
Finished goods	78,000
March 31	
Inventory balances	
Raw materials	$ 60,000
Work in process	145,000
Finished goods	80,000
During March	
Costs of raw materials purchased	$120,000
Costs of direct labor	100,000
Costs of manufacturing overhead	63,000
Sales revenues	380,000

Required

a. Prepare a schedule of cost of goods manufactured and sold.

b. Calculate the amount of gross margin on the income statement.

Exercise 10-14 *Upstream and downstream costs*

During 2014, Welch Manufacturing Company incurred $67,000,000 of research and development (R&D) costs to create a long-life battery to use in computers. In accordance with FASB standards, the entire R&D cost was recognized as an expense in 2014. Manufacturing costs (direct materials, direct labor, and overhead) are expected to be $250 per unit. Packaging, shipping, and sales commissions are expected to be $50 per unit. Welch expects to sell 2,000,000 batteries before new research renders the battery design technologically obsolete. During 2014, Welch made 440,000 batteries and sold 400,000 of them.

Required

a. Identify the upstream and downstream costs.

b. Determine the 2014 amount of cost of goods sold and the ending inventory balance.

c. Determine the sales price assuming that Welch desires to earn a profit margin that is equal to 25 percent of the *total cost* of developing, making, and distributing the batteries.

d. Prepare an income statement for 2014. Use the sales price developed in Requirement *c.*

e. Why would Welch price the batteries at a level that would generate a loss for the 2014 accounting period?

Exercise 10-15 *Using JIT to minimize waste and lost opportunity*

Kate Connor, a teacher at Meadow Middle School, is in charge of ordering the T-shirts to be sold for the school's annual fund-raising project. The T-shirts are printed with a special Meadow School logo. In some years, the supply of T-shirts has been insufficient to satisfy the number of sales orders. In other years, T-shirts have been left over. Excess T-shirts are normally donated to some charitable organization. T-shirts cost the school $7 each and are normally sold for $15 each. Ms. Connor has decided to order 800 shirts.

Required

a. If the school receives actual sales orders for 725 shirts, what amount of profit will the school earn? What is the cost of waste due to excess inventory?

b. If the school receives actual sales orders for 825 shirts, what amount of profit will the school earn? What amount of opportunity cost will the school incur?

c. Explain how a JIT inventory system could maximize profitability by eliminating waste and opportunity cost.

LO 10-4

Exercise 10-16 *Using JIT to minimize holding costs*

Ray Pet Supplies purchases its inventory from a variety of suppliers, some of which require a six-week lead time before delivering the goods. To ensure that she has a sufficient supply of goods on hand, Ms. Jelavich, the owner, must maintain a large supply of inventory. The cost of this inventory averages $46,000. She usually finances the purchase of inventory and pays an 8 percent annual finance charge. Ms. Jelavich's accountant has suggested that she establish a relationship with a single large distributor who can satisfy all of her orders within a two-week time period. Given this quick turnaround time, she will be able to reduce her average inventory balance to $4,000. Ms. Jelavich also believes that she could save $5,600 per year by reducing phone bills, insurance, and warehouse rental space costs associated with ordering and maintaining the larger level of inventory.

Required

a. Is the new inventory system available to Ms. Jelavich a pure or approximate just-in-time system?

b. Based on the information provided, how much of Ms. Jelavich's inventory holding cost could be eliminated by taking the accountant's advice?

LO 10-5

Exercise 10-17 *Professional conduct and code of ethics*

In February 2006, former senator Warren Rudman of New Hampshire completed a 17-month investigation of an $11 billion accounting scandal at Fannie Mae (a major enterprise involved in home mortgage financing). The Rudman investigation concluded that Fannie Mae's CFO and controller used an accounting gimmick to manipulate financial statements in order to meet earnings-per-share (EPS) targets. Meeting the EPS targets triggered bonus payments for the executives. Fannie Mae's problems continued after 2006, and on September 8, 2008, it went into conservatorship under the control of the Federal Housing Financing Agency. The primary executives at the time of the Rudman investigation were replaced, and the enterprise reported a $59.8 billion loss in 2008. By June 2012, the federal government had spent $170 million to assist Fannie Mae as a result of mismanagement.

Required

Review the statement of ethical professional practice shown in Exhibit 10.17. Identify and comment on which of the ethical principles the CFO and controller violated.

LO 10-6

Exercise 10-18 *Value chain analysis (Appendix)*

Audiomax Company manufactures and sells high-quality audio speakers. The speakers are encased in solid walnut cabinets supplied by Serle Cabinet, Inc. Serle packages the speakers in durable moisture-proof boxes and ships them by truck to Audiomax's manufacturing facility, which is located 50 miles from the cabinet factory.

Required

Identify the nonvalue-added activities that occur between the companies described in the above scenario. Provide a logical explanation as to how these nonvalue-added activities could be eliminated.

PROBLEMS

 All applicable Problems are available with McGraw-Hill Connect® Accounting.

Problem 10-19   *Product versus selling, general, and administrative costs*

LO 10-2

CHECK FIGURES
a. Average cost per unit: $7.00
f. $120,600

Issa Manufacturing Company was started on January 1, 2014, when it acquired $78,000 cash by issuing common stock. Issa immediately purchased office furniture and manufacturing equipment costing $21,000 and $49,000, respectively. The office furniture had a seven-year useful life and a zero salvage value. The manufacturing equipment had a $4,000 salvage value and an expected useful life of five years. The company paid $12,000 for salaries of administrative personnel and $21,000 for wages to production personnel. Finally, the company paid $26,000 for raw materials that were used to make inventory. All inventory was started and completed during the year. Issa completed production on 8,000 units of product and sold 7,200 units at a price of $15 each in 2014. (Assume that all transactions are cash transactions.)

Required

a. Determine the total product cost and the average cost per unit of the inventory produced in 2014.
b. Determine the amount of cost of goods sold that would appear on the 2014 income statement.
c. Determine the amount of the ending inventory balance that would appear on the December 31, 2014, balance sheet.
d. Determine the amount of net income that would appear on the 2014 income statement.
e. Determine the amount of retained earnings that would appear on the December 31, 2014, balance sheet.
f. Determine the amount of total assets that would appear on the December 31, 2014, balance sheet.
g. Determine the amount of net cash flow from operating activities that would appear on the December 31, 2014 statement of cash flows.
h. Determine the amount of net cash flow from investing activities that would appear on the December 31, 2014 statement of cash flows.

Problem 10-20   *Effect of product versus period costs on financial statements*

LO 10-2

CHECK FIGURES
Cash balance: $67,400
Net income: $14,200

Gunn Manufacturing Company experienced the following accounting events during its first year of operation. With the exception of the adjusting entries for depreciation, assume that all transactions are cash transactions.

1. Acquired $80,000 cash by issuing common stock.
2. Paid $9,200 for the materials used to make its products, all of which were started and completed during the year.
3. Paid salaries of $3,800 to selling and administrative employees.
4. Paid wages of $12,000 to production workers.
5. Paid $9,600 for furniture used in selling and administrative offices. The furniture was acquired on January 1. It had a $1,600 estimated salvage value and a four-year useful life.
6. Paid $16,000 for manufacturing equipment. The equipment was acquired on January 1. It had a $1,000 estimated salvage value and a five-year useful life.
7. Sold inventory to customers for $38,000 that had cost $18,000 to make.

Required

Explain how these events would affect the balance sheet, income statement, and statement of cash flows by recording them in a horizontal financial statements model as indicated here. Also, in the Cash Flow column, indicate whether the cash flow is for operating activities

(OA), investing activities (IA), or financing activities (FA). The first event is recorded as an example.

	Financial Statements Model											
	Assets				**Equity**							
Event No.	Cash	+ Inventory	+ Manuf. Equip.*	+ Office Furn.*	= Com. Stk.	+ Ret. Ear.	Rev.	− Exp.	= Net Inc.	Cash Flow
1.	80,000				80,000					80,000 FA

*Record accumulated depreciation as negative amounts in these columns.

LO 10-2

CHECK FIGURES
Net income: $1,725
Total assets: $8,725

Problem 10-21 *Product versus selling, general, and administrative costs*

The following transactions pertain to 2015, the first-year operations of Bailey Company. All inventory was started and completed during 2015. Assume that all transactions are cash transactions.

1. Acquired $7,000 cash by issuing common stock.
2. Paid $2,800 for materials used to produce inventory.
3. Paid $1,900 to production workers.
4. Paid $1,300 rental fee for production equipment.
5. Paid $350 to administrative employees.
6. Paid $400 rental fee for administrative office equipment.
7. Produced 500 units of inventory of which 450 units were sold at a price of $17.50 each.

Required

Prepare an income statement, a balance sheet, and statement of cash flows.

LO 10-2

Problem 10-22 *Service versus manufacturing companies*

Lang Company began operations on January 1, 2014, by issuing common stock for $64,000 cash. During 2014, Lang received $95,000 cash from revenue and incurred costs that required $75,000 of cash payments.

Required

Prepare an income statement, a balance sheet, and a statement of cash flows for Lang Company for 2014, under each of the following independent scenarios.

CHECK FIGURES
a. Net income: $20,000
b. Total assets: $144,000
c. Net income: $57,000

a. Lang is a promoter of rock concerts. The $75,000 was paid to provide a rock concert that produced the revenue.
b. Lang is in the car rental business. The $75,000 was paid to purchase automobiles. The automobiles were purchased on January 1, 2014, and have five-year useful lives, with no expected salvage value. Lang uses straight-line depreciation. The revenue was generated by leasing the automobiles.
c. Lang is a manufacturing company. The $75,000 was paid to purchase the following items:
   (1) Paid $12,000 cash to purchase materials that were used to make products during the year.
   (2) Paid $22,000 cash for wages of factory workers who made products during the year.
   (3) Paid $5,000 cash for salaries of sales and administrative employees.
   (4) Paid $36,000 cash to purchase manufacturing equipment. The equipment was used solely to make products. It had a three-year life and a $6,000 salvage value. The company uses straightline depreciation.
   (5) During 2014, Lang started and completed 2,000 units of product. The revenue was earned when Lang sold 1,500 units of product to its customers.

d. Refer to Requirement *c*. Could Lang determine the actual cost of making the 500th unit of product? How likely is it that the actual cost of the 500th unit of product was exactly the same as the cost of producing the 501st unit of product? Explain why management may be more interested in average cost than in actual cost.

Problem 10-23 *Importance of cost classification*

LO 10-2

Naoki Manufacturing Company (NMC) was started when it acquired $50,000 by issuing common stock. During the first year of operations, the company incurred specifically identifiable product costs (materials, labor, and overhead) amounting to $30,000. NMC also incurred $24,000 of engineering design and planning costs. There was a debate regarding how the design and planning costs should be classified. Advocates of Option 1 believe that the costs should be classified as general, selling, and administrative costs. Advocates of Option 2 believe it is more appropriate to classify the design and planning costs as product costs. During the year, NMC made 4,000 units of product and sold 3,000 units at a price of $30 each. All transactions were cash transactions.

CHECK FIGURES
a. Option 1: NI = $43,500
   Option 2: Total
   assets = $99,500

Required

a. Prepare an income statement, a balance sheet, and a statement of cash flows under each of the two options.

b. Identify the option that results in financial statements that are more likely to leave a favorable impression on investors and creditors.

c. Assume that NMC provides an incentive bonus to the company president equal to 25 percent of net income. Compute the amount of the bonus under each of the two options. Identify the option that provides the president with the higher bonus.

d. Assume a 35 percent income tax rate. Determine the amount of income tax expense under each of the two options. Identify the option that minimizes the amount of the company's income tax expense.

e. Comment on the conflict of interest between the company president as determined in Requirement *c* and the owners of the company as indicated in Requirement *d*. Describe an incentive compensation plan that would avoid a conflict of interest between the president and the owners.

Problem 10-24 *Schedule of cost of goods manufactured and sold*

LO 10-3

Antioch Company makes eBook readers. The company had the following amounts at the beginning of 2014: Cash, $660,000; Raw Materials Inventory, $51,000; Work in Process Inventory, $18,000; Finished Goods Inventory, $43,000; Common Stock, $583,000; and Retained Earnings, $189,000. Antioch experienced the following accounting events during 2014. Other than the adjusting entries for depreciation, assume that all transactions are cash transactions.

1. Paid $23,000 of research and development costs.
2. Paid $47,000 for raw materials that will be used to make eBook readers.
3. Placed $83,000 of the raw materials cost into the process of manufacturing eBook readers.
4. Paid $60,000 for salaries of selling and administrative employees.
5. Paid $91,000 for wages of production workers.
6. Paid $90,000 to purchase equipment used in selling and administrative offices.
7. Recognized depreciation on the office equipment. The equipment was acquired on January, 1, 2014. It has a $10,000 salvage value and a five-year life. The amount of depreciation is computed as [(Cost − salvage) ÷ useful life]. Specifically, ($90,000 − $10,000) ÷ 5 = $16,000.
8. Paid $165,000 to purchase manufacturing equipment.
9. Recognized depreciation on the manufacturing equipment. The equipment was acquired on January 1, 2014. It has a $25,000 salvage value and a seven-year life. The amount of depreciation is computed as [(Cost − salvage) ÷ useful life]. Specifically, ($165,000 − $25,000) ÷ 7 = $20,000.
10. Paid $45,000 for rent and utility costs on the manufacturing facility.

11. Paid $70,000 for inventory holding expenses for completed eBook readers (rental of warehouse space, salaries of warehouse personnel, and other general storage cost).

12. Completed and transferred eBook readers that had total cost of $240,000 from work in process inventory to finished goods.

13. Sold 1,000 eBook readers for $420,000.

14. It cost Antioch $220,000 to make the eBook readers sold in Event 13.

Required

a. Show how these events affect the balance sheet, income statement, and statement of cash flows by recording them in a horizontal financial statements model.

b. Explain why Antioch's recognition of cost of goods sold had no impact on cash flow.

c. Prepare a schedule of cost of goods manufactured and sold, a formal income statement, and a balance sheet for the year.

d. Distinguish between the product costs and the upstream costs that Antioch incurred.

e. The company president believes that Antioch could save money by buying the inventory that it currently makes. The warehouse manager said that would not be a good idea because the purchase price of $230 per unit was above the $220 average cost per unit of making the product. Assuming the purchased inventory would be available on demand, explain how the company could be correct and why the production manager could be biased in his assessment of the option to buy the inventory.

LO 10-4

Problem 10-25   *Using JIT to reduce inventory holding costs*

Torre Manufacturing Company obtains its raw materials from a variety of suppliers. Torre's strategy is to obtain the best price by letting the suppliers know that it buys from the lowest bidder. Approximately four years ago, unexpected increases in demand resulted in materials shortages. Torre was unable to find the materials it needed even though it was willing to pay premium prices. Because of the lack of raw materials, Torre was forced to close its manufacturing facility for two weeks. Its president vowed that her company would never again be at the mercy of its suppliers. She immediately ordered her purchasing agent to perpetually maintain a one-month supply of raw materials. Compliance with the president's orders resulted in a raw materials inventory amounting to approximately $2,000,000. Warehouse rental and personnel costs to maintain the inventory amounted to $9,000 per month. Torre has a line of credit with a local bank that calls for a 10 percent annual rate of interest. Assume that Torre finances the raw materials inventory with the line of credit.

Required

a. Based on the information provided, determine the annual holding cost of the raw materials inventory.

b. Explain how a JIT system could reduce Torre's inventory holding cost.

c. Explain how most-favored customer status could enable Torre to establish a JIT inventory system without risking the raw materials shortages experienced in the past.

LO 10-4

Problem 10-26   *Using JIT to minimize waste and lost opportunity*

CMA Review, Inc., provides review courses twice each year for students studying to take the CMA exam. The cost of textbooks is included in the registration fee. Text material requires constant updating and is useful for only one course. To minimize printing costs and ensure availability of books on the first day of class, CMA Review has books printed and delivered to its offices two weeks in advance of the first class. To ensure that enough books are available, CMA Review normally orders 10 percent more than expected enrollment. Usually there is an oversupply and books are thrown away. However, demand occasionally exceeds expectations by more than 10 percent and there are too few books available for student use. CMA Review has been forced to turn away students because of a lack of textbooks. CMA Review expects to enroll approximately 110 students per course. The tuition fee is $1,500 per student. The cost of teachers is $36,000 per course, textbooks cost $80 each, and other operating expenses are estimated to be $40,000 per course.

Required

a. Prepare an income statement, assuming that 95 students enroll in a course. Determine the cost of waste associated with unused books.

b. Prepare an income statement, assuming that 115 students attempt to enroll in the course. Note that five students are turned away because of too few textbooks. Determine the amount of lost profit resulting from the inability to serve the five additional students.

c. Suppose that textbooks can be produced through a high-speed copying process that permits delivery *just in time* for class to start. The cost of books made using this process, however, is $90 each. Assume that all books must be made using the same production process. In other words, CMA Review cannot order some of the books using the regular copy process and the rest using the high-speed process. Prepare an income statement under the JIT system assuming that 95 students enroll in a course. Compare the income statement under JIT with the income statement prepared in Requirement *a*. Comment on how the JIT system would affect profitability.

d. Assume the same facts as in Requirement *c* with respect to a JIT system that enables immediate delivery of books at a cost of $90 each. Prepare an income statement under the JIT system, assuming that 115 students enroll in a course. Compare the income statement under JIT with the income statement prepared in Requirement *b*. Comment on how the JIT system would affect profitability.

e. Discuss the possible effect of the JIT system on the level of customer satisfaction.

Problem 10-27 *Value chain analysis (Appendix)*   LO 10-6

Vernon Company invented a new process for manufacturing ice cream. The ingredients are mixed in high-tech machinery that forms the product into small round beads. Like a bag of balls, the ice cream beads are surrounded by air pockets in packages. This design has numerous advantages. First, each bite of ice cream melts rapidly when placed in a person's mouth, creating a more flavorful sensation when compared to ordinary ice cream. Also, the air pockets mean that a typical serving includes a smaller amount of ice cream. This not only reduces materials cost but also provides the consumer with a low-calorie snack. A cup appears full of ice cream, but it is really half full of air. The consumer eats only half the ingredients that are contained in a typical cup of blended ice cream. Finally, the texture of the ice cream makes scooping it out of a large container a very easy task. The frustration of trying to get a spoon into a rock-solid package of blended ice cream has been eliminated. Vernon Company named the new product Sonic Cream.

Like many other ice cream producers, Vernon Company purchases its raw materials from a food wholesaler. The ingredients are mixed in Vernon's manufacturing plant. The packages of finished product are distributed to privately owned franchise ice cream shops that sell Sonic Cream directly to the public.

Vernon provides national advertising and is responsible for all research and development costs associated with making new flavors of Sonic Cream.

Required

a. Based on the information provided, draw a comprehensive value chain for Vernon Company that includes its suppliers and customers.

b. Identify the place in the chain where Vernon Company is exercising its opportunity to create added value beyond that currently being provided by its competitors.

ANALYZE, THINK, COMMUNICATE

ATC 10-1 Business Applications Case *Financial versus managerial accounting*

The following information was taken from Starbucks Corporation's 2011 and 2012 Form 10-Ks.

	Fiscal Year Ended	
	September 30, 2012	October 2, 2011
Number of global employees	160,000	149,000
Number of employees in the U.S.	120,000	112,000
Revenues (in millions)	$13,300	$11,700
Properties used for roasting warehouse and distribution	2,171,000 square feet	2,396,000 square feet
Total assets (in millions)	$8,219	$7,360
Company-owned stores	9,045	9,007
Net earnings (in millions)	$1,384	$1,246

Required

a. Explain whether each line of information in the table above would best be described as being primarily financial accounting or managerial accounting in nature.

b. Provide some additional examples of managerial and financial accounting information that could apply to Starbucks.

c. If you analyze only the data you identified as financial in nature, does it appear that Starbucks' 2012 fiscal year was better or worse than its 2011 fiscal year? Explain.

d. If you analyze only the data you identified as managerial in nature, does it appear that Starbucks' 2012 fiscal year was better or worse than its 2011 fiscal year? Explain.

e. Did Starbucks appear to be using its roasting and distribution facilities more efficiently or less efficiently in 2012 than in 2011?

ATC 10-2 Group Assignment *Product versus upstream and downstream costs*

Victor Holt, the accounting manager of Sexton, Inc., gathered the following information for 2014. Some of it can be used to construct an income statement for 2014. Ignore items that do not appear on an income statement. Some computation may be required. For example, the cost of manufacturing equipment would not appear on the income statement. However, the cost of manufacturing equipment is needed to compute the amount of depreciation. All units of product were started and completed in 2014.

1. Issued $864,000 of common stock.
2. Paid engineers in the product design department $10,000 for salaries that were accrued at the end of the previous year.
3. Incurred advertising expenses of $70,000.
4. Paid $720,000 for materials used to manufacture the company's product.
5. Incurred utility costs of $160,000. These costs were allocated to different departments on the basis of square footage of floor space. Mr. Holt identified three departments and determined the square footage of floor space for each department to be as shown in the table below.

Department	Square Footage
Research and development	10,000
Manufacturing	60,000
Selling and administrative	30,000
Total	100,000

6. Paid $880,000 for wages of production workers.
7. Paid cash of $658,000 for salaries of administrative personnel. There was $16,000 of accrued salaries owed to administrative personnel at the end of 2014. There was no beginning balance in the Salaries Payable account for administrative personnel.
8. Purchased manufacturing equipment two years ago at a cost of $10,000,000. The equipment had an eight-year useful life and a $2,000,000 salvage value.

9. Paid $390,000 cash to engineers in the product design department.

10. Paid a $258,000 cash dividend to owners.

11. Paid $80,000 to set up manufacturing equipment for production.

12. Paid a one-time $186,000 restructuring cost to redesign the production process to implement a just-in-time inventory system.

13. Prepaid the premium on a new insurance policy covering nonmanufacturing employees. The policy cost $72,000 and had a one-year term with an effective starting date of May 1. Four employees work in the research and development department and eight employees work in the selling and administrative department. Assume a December 31 closing date.

14. Made 69,400 units of product and sold 60,000 units at a price of $70 each.

Required

a. Divide the class into groups of four or five students per group, and then organize the groups into three sections. Assign Task 1 to the first section of groups, Task 2 to the second section of groups, and Task 3 to the third section of groups.

Group Tasks

(1) Identify the items that are classified as product costs and determine the amount of cost of goods sold reported on the 2014 income statement.

(2) Identify the items that are classified as upstream costs and determine the amount of upstream cost expensed on the 2014 income statement.

(3) Identify the items that are classified as downstream costs and determine the amount of downstream cost expensed on the 2014 income statement.

b. Have the class construct an income statement in the following manner. Select a member of one of the groups assigned Group Task (1), identifying the product costs. Have that person go to the board and list the costs included in the determination of cost of goods sold. Anyone in the other groups who disagrees with one of the classifications provided by the person at the board should voice an objection and explain why the item should be classified differently. The instructor should lead the class to a consensus on the disputed items. After the amount of cost of goods sold is determined, the student at the board constructs the part of the income statement showing the determination of gross margin. The exercise continues in a similar fashion with representatives from the other sections explaining the composition of the upstream and downstream costs. These items are added to the income statement started by the first group representative. The final result is a completed income statement.

ATC 10-3 Research Assignment *Identifying product costs at Snap-on Inc.*

Use the 2011 Form 10-K for Snap-on Inc. to complete the requirements below. To obtain the Form 10-K, you can use the EDGAR system following the instructions in Appendix A, at the back of this text, or it can be found under "Corporate Information" on the company's corporate website at www.snapon.com. Read carefully the following portions of the document:

■ "Products and Services" on page 5.

"Consolidated Statement of Earnings" on page 64.

The following parts of Note 1 on page 71:

- "Shipping and handling"
- "Advertising and promotion"

■ "Note 4: Inventories" on page 79.

■ "Note 5: Property and equipment" on page 79.

Required

a. Does the level of detail that Snap-on provides regarding costs incurred to manufacture its products suggest the company's financial statements are designed primarily to meet the needs of external or internal users?

b. Does Snap-on treat shipping and handling costs as product or period costs?

c. Does Snap-on treat advertising and promotion costs as product or period costs?

  d. Earlier in this course you learned about a class of inventory called merchandise inventory. What categories of inventory does Snap-on report in its annual report?

  e. What is the cost of the land owned by Snap-on? What is the cost of its machinery and equipment?

ATC 10-4   Writing Assignment   *Emerging practices in managerial accounting*

On April 14, 2012, Best Buy Company, Inc., issued a press release from which the following excerpt was taken:

> *April 14, 2012—Best Buy announced plans March 29, 2012, to close 50 U.S. stores as part of a number of key initiatives for this year. . . . This was not an easy decision to make. We chose these stores carefully, and are working to ensure the impact to our employees will be as minimal as possible, while serving all customers in a convenient and satisfying way. But we also recognize the impact this news has on the people who deserve respect for the contributions they have made to our business. . . . More broadly, our previously announced retail store actions are intended to increase points of presence, while decreasing overall square footage, for increased flexibility—including key store remodels with a new Connected Store format, while continuing to build out the successful Best Buy Mobile small format stores throughout the U.S. . . . We are committed to making it easier for customers to shop with us, whenever and wherever they want.*

The restructuring cost Best Buy $40 million and disrupted the lives of many of the company's employees.

Required

Assume that you are Best Buy's vice president of human relations. Write a letter to the employees who are affected by the restructuring. The letter should explain why it was necessary for the company to undertake the restructuring. Your explanation should refer to the ideas discussed in the section "Emerging Trends in Managerial Accounting" of this chapter (see Appendix).

ATC 10-5   Ethical Dilemma   *Product cost versus selling and administrative expense*

Emma Emerson is a proud woman with a problem. Her daughter has been accepted into a prestigious law school. While Ms. Emerson beams with pride, she is worried sick about how to pay for the school; she is a single parent who has worked hard to support herself and her three children. She had to go heavily into debt to finance her own education. Even though she now has a good job, family needs have continued to outpace her income and her debt burden is staggering. She knows she will be unable to borrow the money needed for her daughter's law school.

  Ms. Emerson is the chief financial officer (CFO) of a small manufacturing company. She has just accepted a new job offer. Indeed, she has not yet told her employer that she will be leaving in a month. She is concerned that her year-end incentive bonus may be affected if her boss learns of her plans to leave. She plans to inform the company immediately after receiving the bonus. She knows her behavior is less than honorable, but she believes that she has been underpaid for a long time. Her boss, a relative of the company's owner, makes twice what she makes and does half the work. Why should she care about leaving with a little extra cash? Indeed, she is considering an opportunity to boost the bonus.

  Ms. Emerson's bonus is based on a percentage of net income. Her company recently introduced a new product line that required substantial production start-up costs. Ms. Emerson is fully aware that GAAP requires these costs to be expensed in the current accounting period, but no one else in the company has the technical expertise to know exactly how the costs should be treated. She is considering misclassifying the start-up costs as product costs. If the costs are misclassified, net income will be significantly higher, resulting in a nice boost in her incentive bonus. By the time the auditors discover the misclassification, Ms. Emerson will have moved on to her new job. If the matter is brought to the attention of her new employer, she will simply plead ignorance. Considering her daughter's needs, Ms. Emerson decides to classify the start-up costs as product costs.

Required

a. Based on this information, indicate whether Ms. Emerson believes the number of units of product sold will be equal to, less than, or greater than the number of units made. Write a brief paragraph explaining the logic that supports your answer.

b. Explain how the misclassification could mislead an investor or creditor regarding the company's financial condition.

c. Explain how the misclassification could affect income taxes.

d. Review the Statement of Ethical Professional Practice shown in Exhibit 10.17 and identify at least two ethical principles that Ms. Emerson's misclassification of the start-up costs violated.

CHAPTER 11

Cost Behavior, Operating Leverage, and Profitability Analysis

LEARNING OBJECTIVES

After you have mastered the material in this chapter, you will be able to:

LO 11-1   Identify and describe fixed, variable, and mixed cost behavior.

LO 11-2   Demonstrate the effects of operating leverage on profitability.

LO 11-3   Prepare an income statement using the contribution margin approach.

LO 11-4   Calculate the magnitude of operating leverage.

LO 11-5   Determine the sales volume necessary to break even or to earn a desired profit.

LO 11-6   Calculate and interpret the margin of safety measure.

 Video lectures and accompanying self-assessment quizzes are available for all learning objectives through McGraw-Hill Connect® Accounting.

CHAPTER OPENING

Three college students are planning a vacation. One of them suggests inviting a fourth person along, remarking that four can travel for the same cost as three. Certainly, some costs will be the same whether three or four people go on the trip. For example, the hotel room costs $800 per week, regardless of whether three or four people stay in the room. In accounting terms, the cost of the hotel room is a **fixed cost.** The total amount of a fixed cost does not change when volume changes. The total hotel room cost is $800 whether 1, 2, 3, or 4 people use the room. In contrast, some costs vary in direct proportion with changes in volume. When volume increases, total variable cost increases; when volume decreases, total variable cost decreases. For example, the cost of tickets to a theme park is a **variable cost.** The total cost of tickets increases proportionately with each vaca-tioner who goes to the theme park. Cost behavior (fixed versus variable) can significantly impact profitability. This chapter explains cost behavior and ways it can be used to increase profitability.

The Curious Accountant

News flash! On April 16, 2012, Charles Schwab Company announced that its first quarter's revenues decreased 1.5 percent compared to the same quarter in 2011, yet its earnings had decreased by 19.8 percent. On April 19, 2012, Union Pacific Corporation announced that an increase in revenue of 14 percent for the just-ended quarter would cause its earnings to increase 35 percent compared to the same quarter in 2011. On April 18, 2012, Qualcomm, Inc., reported that its revenue for the quarter had increased by 28 percent compared to the previous year, but its earnings increased by 123 percent.

Can you explain why such relatively small changes in these companies' revenues resulted in such relatively large changes in their earnings or losses? In other words, if a company's sales increase 10 percent, why do its earnings not also increase 10 percent? (Answer on page 407.)

FIXED COST BEHAVIOR

LO 11-1

Identify and describe fixed, variable, and mixed cost behavior.

How much more will it cost to send one additional employee to a sales meeting? If more people buy our products, can we charge less? If sales increase by 10 percent, how will profits be affected? Managers seeking answers to such questions must consider **cost behavior.** Knowing how costs behave relative to the level of business activity enables managers to more effectively plan and control costs. To illustrate, consider the entertainment company Star Productions, Inc. (SPI).

SPI specializes in promoting rock concerts. It is considering paying a band $48,000 to play a concert. Obviously, SPI must sell enough tickets to cover this cost. In this example, the relevant activity base is the number of tickets sold. The cost of the band is a fixed cost because it does not change regardless of the number of tickets sold. Exhibit 11.1 illustrates the fixed cost behavior pattern, showing the *total cost* and the *cost per unit* at three different levels of activity.

Total versus *per-unit* fixed costs behave differently. The total cost for the band remains constant (fixed) at $48,000. In contrast, fixed cost per unit decreases as volume (number of tickets sold) increases. The term *fixed cost* is consistent with the behavior of *total cost.* Total fixed cost remains constant (fixed) when activity changes. However, there is a contradiction between the term *fixed cost per unit* and the *per-unit behavior pattern of a fixed cost.* Fixed cost per unit is *not* fixed. It changes with the number of tickets sold. This contradiction in terminology can cause untold confusion. Study carefully the fixed cost behavior patterns in Exhibit 11.2.

EXHIBIT 11.1

Fixed Cost Behavior

Number of tickets sold (a)	2,700	3,000	3,300
Total cost of band (b)	$48,000	$48,000	$48,000
Cost per ticket sold (b ÷ a)	$17.78	$16.00	$14.55

EXHIBIT 11.2

Fixed Cost Behavior

	When Activity Increases	When Activity Decreases
Total fixed cost	Remains constant	Remains constant
Fixed cost **per unit**	Decreases	Increases

The fixed cost data in Exhibit 11.1 help SPI's management decide whether to sponsor the concert. For example, the information influences potential pricing choices. The per-unit costs represent the minimum ticket prices required to cover the fixed cost at various levels of activity. SPI could compare these per-unit costs to the prices of competing entertainment events (such as the prices of movies, sporting events, or theater tickets). If the price is not competitive, tickets will not sell and the concert will lose money. Management must also consider the number of tickets to be sold. The volume data in Exhibit 11.1 can be compared to the band's track record of ticket sales at previous concerts. A proper analysis of these data can reduce the risk of undertaking an unprofitable venture.

OPERATING LEVERAGE

LO 11-2

Demonstrate the effects of operating leverage on profitability.

Heavy objects can be moved with little effort using *physical* leverage. Business managers apply **operating leverage** to magnify small changes in revenue into dramatic changes in profitability. The *lever* managers use to achieve disproportionate changes between revenue and profitability is fixed costs. The leverage relationships between revenue, fixed costs, and profitability are displayed in Exhibit 11.3.

When all costs are fixed, every sales dollar contributes one dollar toward the potential profitability of a project. Once sales dollars cover fixed costs, each

EXHIBIT 11.3

Operating Leverage

FOCUS ON INTERNATIONAL ISSUES

THE EFFECTS OF A TSUNAMI AND FIXED COSTS ON TOYOTA'S PERFORMANCE

On March 11, 2011, a major earthquake and tsunami hit a coastal area of Japan where automobile production facilities were located. Both Toyota and Honda were affected by these events, and both of these companies end their fiscal years on March 31. Presented below are data for Toyota Motor Corporation for the quarter ending on June 30, 2011, the first full quarter after the tsunami, and for the same quarter of 2010.

	Quarter Ended		Percentage
	June 30, 2011	June 30, 2010	Change
Sales in units	1,221,374	1,819,995	(32.9)
Sales in billions of yen	¥3,441.1	¥4,871.8	(29.4)
Operating income in billions of yen	(¥108.0)	¥211.7	(151.0)

As the data above reveal, Toyota's earnings declined much more than the decline in its sales. This is due to the fact that its fixed costs did not decrease when its sales declined. Fortunately for Toyota, a year later things had greatly improved. During the quarter ended June 30, 2012, Toyota sold 2,268,563 vehicles and its operating earnings were ¥353.1 billion.

One might think the impact of the tsunami would have been limited mostly to Toyota's operations in Japan. After all, Toyota manufactures about 72 percent of its vehicles in countries outside of Japan. However, like many modern international companies, Toyota's operations are integrated. Cars assembled in the United States rely on some parts that are produced in Japan, so effects of the Japanese tsunami were felt throughout the world.

---

additional sales dollar represents pure profit. As a result, a small change in sales volume can significantly affect profitability. To illustrate, assume SPI estimates it will sell 3,000 tickets for $18 each. A 10 percent difference in actual sales volume will produce a 90 percent difference in profitability. Examine the data in Exhibit 11.4 to verify this result.[1]

EXHIBIT 11.4

Effect of Operating Leverage on Profitability

Number of tickets sold	2,700	⇐ −10% ⇐	3,000	⇒ +10% ⇒	3,300
Sales revenue ($18 per ticket)	$ 48,600		$ 54,000		$ 59,400
Cost of band (fixed cost)	(48,000)		(48,000)		(48,000)
Gross margin	$ 600	⇐ −90% ⇐	$ 6,000	⇒ +90% ⇒	$ 11,400

Calculating Percentage Change

The percentages in Exhibit 11.4 are computed as follows:

$$(\text{Alternative measure} - \text{Base measure}) \div \text{Base measure} = \%\text{ change}$$

The base measure is the starting point. To illustrate, compute the percentage change in gross margin when moving from 3,000 units (base measure) to 3,300 units (the alternative measure).

$$(\text{Alternative measure} - \text{Base measure}) \div \text{Base measure} = \%\text{ change}$$

$$(\$11,400 - \$6,000) \div \$6,000 = 90\%$$

---

[1]Do not confuse operating leverage with financial leverage. Companies employ *financial leverage* when they use debt to profit from investing money at a higher rate of return than the rate they pay on borrowed money. Companies employ *operating leverage* when they use proportionately more fixed costs than variable costs to magnify the effect on earnings of changes in revenues.

The percentage *decline* in profitability is similarly computed:

$$(\text{Alternative measure} - \text{Base measure}) \div \text{Base measure} = \% \text{ change}$$

$$(\$600 - \$6{,}000) \div \$6{,}000 = (90\%)$$

Risk and Reward Assessment

Risk refers to the possibility that sacrifices may exceed benefits. A fixed cost represents a commitment to an economic sacrifice. It represents the ultimate risk of undertaking a particular business project. If SPI pays the band but nobody buys a ticket, the company will lose $48,000. SPI can avoid this risk by substituting *variable costs* for the *fixed cost.*

VARIABLE COST BEHAVIOR

To illustrate variable cost behavior, assume SPI arranges to pay the band $16 per ticket sold instead of a fixed $48,000. Exhibit 11.5 shows the total cost of the band and the cost per ticket sold at three different levels of activity.

EXHIBIT 11.5

Variable Cost Behavior

Number of tickets sold (a)	2,700	3,000	3,300
Total cost of band (b)	$43,200	$48,000	$52,800
Cost per ticket sold (b ÷ a)	$16	$16	$16

Since SPI will pay the band $16 for each ticket sold, the *total* variable cost increases in direct proportion to the number of tickets sold. If SPI sells one ticket, total band cost will be $16 (1 × $16); if SPI sells two tickets, total band cost will be $32 (2 × $16); and so on. The total cost of the band increases proportionately as ticket sales move from 2,700 to 3,000 to 3,300. The variable cost *per ticket* remains $16, however, regardless of whether the number of tickets sold is 1, 2, 3, or 3,000. The behavior of variable cost *per unit* is contradictory to the word *variable.* Variable cost per unit remains *constant* regardless of how many tickets are sold. Study carefully the variable cost behavior patterns in Exhibit 11.6.

EXHIBIT 11.6

Variable Cost Behavior

	When Activity Increases	When Activity Decreases
Total variable cost	Increases proportionately	Decreases proportionately
Variable cost **per unit**	Remains constant	Remains constant

Risk and Reward Assessment

Shifting the cost structure from fixed to variable enables SPI to avoid the fixed cost risk. Recall that under the fixed cost structure, SPI was locked into a $48,000 cost for the band regardless of how many tickets are sold. If no tickets are sold, SPI will have to report a $48,000 loss on its income statement. The risk of incurring this loss is eliminated by the variable cost structure that requires SPI to only pay the band $16 per ticket sold. If SPI sells zero tickets, then the cost of the band is zero. For each ticket sold, SPI earns a $2 profit ($18 ticket sales price − $16 fee paid to band).

Shifting the cost structure from fixed to variable reduces not only the level of risk but also the potential for profits. Managers cannot avoid the risk of fixed costs without also

EXHIBIT 11.7

Variable Cost Eliminates Operating Leverage

Number of tickets sold	2,700	⇐−10%⇐	3,000	⇒+10%⇒	3,300
Sales revenue ($18 per ticket)	$48,600		$ 54,000		$ 59,400
Cost of band ($16 variable cost)	(43,200)		(48,000)		(52,800)
Gross margin	$ 5,400	⇐−10%⇐	$ 6,000	⇒+10%⇒	$ 6,600

sacrificing the benefits. Variable costs do not offer operating leverage. Exhibit 11.7 shows that a variable cost structure produces a proportional relationship between sales and profitability. A 10 percent increase or decrease in sales results in a corresponding 10 percent increase or decrease in profitability.

 CHECK YOURSELF 11.1

Suppose that you are sponsoring a political rally at which Ralph Nader will speak. You estimate that approximately 2,000 people will buy tickets to hear Mr. Nader's speech. The tickets are expected to be priced at $12 each. Would you prefer a contract that agrees to pay Mr. Nader $10,000 or one that agrees to pay him $5 per ticket purchased?

Answer   Your answer would depend on how certain you are that 2,000 people will purchase tickets. If it were likely that many more than 2,000 tickets would be sold, you would be better off with a fixed cost structure, agreeing to pay Mr. Nader a flat fee of $10,000. If attendance numbers are highly uncertain, you would be better off with a variable cost structure, thereby guaranteeing a lower cost if fewer people buy tickets.

Answers to The Curious Accountant

The explanation for how a company's earnings can rise faster, as a percentage, than its revenue is operating leverage, and operating leverage is due entirely to fixed costs. As the chapter explains, when a company's output goes up, its fixed cost per unit goes down. As long as it can keep prices about the same, this lower unit cost will result in higher profit per unit sold. In real-world companies, the relationship between changing sales levels and changing earnings levels can be very complex, but the existence of fixed costs helps to explain why a 14 percent rise in revenue can cause a 35 percent rise in net earnings.

 CHECK YOURSELF 11.2

If both Kroger Food Stores and Delta Airlines were to experience a 5 percent increase in revenues, which company would be more likely to experience a higher percentage increase in net income?

Answer   Delta would be more likely to experience a higher percentage increase in net income because a large portion of its cost (e.g., employee salaries and depreciation) is fixed, while a large portion of Kroger's cost is variable (e.g., cost of goods sold).

AN INCOME STATEMENT UNDER THE CONTRIBUTION MARGIN APPROACH

LO 11-3

Prepare an income statement using the contribution margin approach.

The impact of cost structure on profitability is so significant that managerial accountants frequently construct income statements that classify costs according to their behavior patterns. Such income statements first subtract variable costs from revenue; the resulting subtotal is called the **contribution margin.** The contribution margin represents the amount available to cover fixed expenses and thereafter to provide company profits. Net income is computed by subtracting the fixed costs from the contribution margin. A contribution margin style income statement cannot be used for public reporting (GAAP prohibits its use in external financial reports), but it is widely used for internal reporting purposes. Exhibit 11.8 illustrates income statements prepared using the contribution margin approach.

EXHIBIT 11.8

Income Statements

	Company Name	
	Bragg	**Biltmore**
Variable cost per unit (a)	$ 6	$ 12
Sales revenue (10 units × $20)	$ 200	$ 200
Variable cost (10 units × a)	(60)	(120)
Contribution margin	140	80
Fixed cost	(120)	(60)
Net income	$ 20	$ 20

MEASURING OPERATING LEVERAGE USING CONTRIBUTION MARGIN

LO 11-4

Calculate the magnitude of operating leverage.

A contribution margin income statement allows managers to easily measure operating leverage. The magnitude of operating leverage can be determined as follows:

$$\text{Magnitude of operating leverage} = \frac{\text{Contribution margin}}{\text{Net income}}$$

Applying this formula to the income statement data reported for Bragg Company and Biltmore Company in Exhibit 11.8 produces the following measures.

Bragg Company:

$$\text{Magnitude of operating leverage} = \frac{\$140}{\$20} = 7$$

Biltmore Company:

$$\text{Magnitude of operating leverage} = \frac{\$80}{\$20} = 4$$

The computations show that Bragg is more highly leveraged than Biltmore. Bragg's change in profitability will be seven times greater than a given percentage change in revenue. In contrast, Biltmore's profits change by only four times the percentage change in revenue. For example, a 10 percent increase in revenue produces a 70 percent increase (10 percent × 7) in profitability for Bragg Company and a 40 percent increase (10 percent × 4) in profitability for Biltmore Company. The income statements in Exhibits 11.9 and 11.10 confirm these expectations.

EXHIBIT 11.9				EXHIBIT 11.10			
Comparative Income Statements for Bragg Company				**Comparative Income Statements for Biltmore Company**			
Units (a)	10		11	Units (a)	10		11
Sales revenue ($20 × a)	$ 200	⇒ +10% ⇒	$ 220	Sales revenue ($20 × a)	$ 200	⇒ +10% ⇒	$ 220
Variable cost ($6 × a)	(60)		(66)	Variable cost ($12 × a)	(120)		(132)
Contribution margin	140		154	Contribution margin	80		88
Fixed cost	(120)		(120)	Fixed cost	(60)		(60)
Net income	$ 20	⇒ +70% ⇒	$ 34	Net income	$ 20	⇒ +40% ⇒	$ 28

Operating leverage itself is neither good nor bad; it represents a strategy that can work to a company's advantage or disadvantage, depending on how it is used. The next section explains how managers can use operating leverage to create a competitive business advantage.

 CHECK YOURSELF 11.3

Boeing Company's 2012 10-K annual report filed with the Securities and Exchange Commission refers to "operating margins in our Commercial Airplanes business." Is Boeing referring to gross margins or contribution margins?

Answer Since the data come from the company's external annual report, the reference must be to gross margins (revenue − cost of goods sold), a product cost measure. The contribution margin (revenue − variable cost) is a measure used in internal reporting.

COST BEHAVIOR SUMMARIZED

The term *fixed* refers to the behavior of *total* fixed cost. The cost *per unit* of a fixed cost *varies inversely* with changes in the level of activity. As activity increases, fixed cost per unit decreases. As activity decreases, fixed cost per unit increases. These relationships are graphed in Exhibit 11.11.

The term *variable* refers to the behavior of *total* variable cost. Total variable cost increases or decreases proportionately with changes in the volume of activity. In contrast, variable cost *per unit* remains *fixed* at all levels of activity. These relationships are graphed in Exhibit 11.12.

The relationships between fixed and variable costs are summarized in the chart in Exhibit 11.13. Study these relationships thoroughly.

EXHIBIT 11.11

Graphical Presentation of Fixed Cost Behavior

EXHIBIT 11.12

Graphical Presentation of Variable Cost Behavior

EXHIBIT 11.13

Fixed and Variable Cost Behavior

When Activity Level Changes	Total Cost	Cost per Unit
Fixed costs	Remains constant	Changes *inversely*
Variable costs	Changes in direct proportion	Remains constant

Mixed Costs (Semivariable Costs)

Mixed costs (semivariable costs) include both fixed and variable components. For example, suppose Star Productions, Inc., has to pay-for janitorial services. The charge for these services includes a base fee of $1,000 plus $20 per hour required to do a cleanup. The $1,000 base fee is fixed. It is the same no matter how many hours it takes to accomplish the cleanup. In contrast, the $20 hourly cost is a variable cost because the total cost increases with each additional hour it takes to complete the cleanup. Since the total janitorial cost is composed of fixed and variable components, it is frequently called a mixed cost. It may also be called a semivariable cost.

Given the $1,000 base plus $20 per hour cost components, the total janitorial cost for any cleanup can be easily computed as shown below:

$$\text{Total cost} = \text{Fixed cost} + (\text{Variable cost per hour} \times \text{Number of hours})$$

If 60 hours are required to accomplish a cleanup, the total mixed cost is:

$$\text{Total cost} = \$1,000 + (\$20 \times 60) = \$2,200$$

If 90 hours are required to accomplish a cleanup, the total mixed cost is:

$$\text{Total cost} = \$1,000 + (\$20 \times 90) = \$2,800$$

Exhibit 11.14 illustrates a variety of mixed costs businesses commonly encounter.

EXHIBIT 11.14

Examples of Mixed Costs

Type of Cost	Fixed Cost Component(s)	Variable Cost Component(s)
Cost of sales staff	Monthly salary	Bonus based on sales volume
Truck rental	Monthly rental fee	Cost of gas, tires, and maintenance
Legal fees	Monthly retainer	Reimbursements to attorney for out-of-pocket costs (copying, postage, travel, filing fees)
Outpatient service cost	Salaries of doctors and nurses, depreciation of facility, utilities	Medical supplies such as bandages, sterilization solution, and paper products
Phone services	Monthly connection fee	Per-minute usage fee
LP gas utility cost	Container rental fee	Cost of gas consumed
Cable TV services	Monthly fee	Pay-per-view charges
Training cost	Instructor salary, facility cost	Textbooks, supplies
Shipping and handling	Salaries of employees who process packages	Boxes, packing supplies, tape, and other shipping supplies, postage
Inventory holding cost	Depreciation on inventory warehouse, salaries of employees managing inventory	Delivery costs, interest on funds borrowed to finance inventory, cost of supplies

The Relevant Range

Suppose SPI, the rock concert promoter mentioned earlier, must pay $5,000 to rent a concert hall with a seating capacity of 4,000 people. Is the cost of the concert hall fixed or variable? Since total cost remains unchanged regardless of whether one ticket, 4,000 tickets, or any number in between is sold, the cost is fixed relative to ticket sales. However, what if demand for tickets is significantly more than 4,000? In that case, SPI might rent a larger concert hall at a higher cost. In other words, *the cost is fixed only for a designated range of activity (1 to 4,000).*

A similar circumstance affects many variable costs. For example, a supplier may offer a volume discount to buyers who purchase more than a specified number of products. The point is that descriptions of cost behavior pertain to a specified range of activity. The range of activity over which the definitions of fixed and variable costs are valid is commonly called the **relevant range.**

Context-Sensitive Definitions of Fixed and Variable

The behavior pattern of a particular cost may be either fixed or variable, depending on the context. For example, the cost of the band was fixed at $48,000 when SPI was considering hiring it to play a single concert. Regardless of how many tickets SPI sold, the total band cost was $48,000. However, the band cost becomes variable if SPI decides to hire it to perform at a series of concerts. The total cost and the cost per concert for one, two, three, four, or five concerts are shown in Exhibit 11.15.

EXHIBIT 11.15					
Cost Behavior Relative to Number of Concerts					
Number of concerts (a)	1	2	3	4	5
Cost per concert (b)	$48,000	$48,000	$ 48,000	$ 48,000	$ 48,000
Total cost (a × b)	$48,000	$96,000	$144,000	$192,000	$240,000

In this context, the total cost of hiring the band increases proportionately with the number of concerts while cost per concert remains constant. The band cost is therefore variable. The same cost can behave as either a fixed cost or a variable cost, depending on the **activity base.** When identifying a cost as fixed or variable, first ask, fixed or variable *relative to what activity base?* The cost of the band is fixed relative to *the number of tickets sold for a specific concert;* it is variable relative to *the number of concerts produced.*

✓ CHECK YOURSELF 11.4

Is the compensation cost for managers of Pizza Hut Restaurants a fixed cost or a variable cost?

Answer   The answer depends on the context. For example, since a store manager's salary remains unchanged regardless of how many customers enter a particular restaurant, it can be classified as a fixed cost relative to the number of customers at a particular restaurant. However, the more restaurants that Pizza Hut operates, the higher the total managers' compensation cost will be. Accordingly, managers' salary cost would be classified as a variable cost relative to the number of restaurants opened.

LO 11-5

Determine the sales volume necessary to break even or to earn a desired profit.

DETERMINING THE BREAK-EVEN POINT

Bright Day Distributors sells nonprescription health food supplements including vitamins, herbs, and natural hormones in the northwestern United States. Bright Day recently obtained the rights to distribute the new herb mixture Delatine. Recent scientific research found that Delatine delayed aging in laboratory animals. The researchers hypothesized that the substance would have a similar effect on humans. Their theory could not be confirmed because of the relatively long human life span. The news media reported the research findings; as stories turned up on television and radio news, talk shows, and in magazines, demand for Delatine increased.

Bright Day plans to sell the Delatine product at a price of $36 per bottle. Delatine costs $24 per bottle. Bright Day's management team suspects that enthusiasm for Delatine will abate quickly as the news media shift to other subjects. To attract customers immediately, the product managers consider television advertising. The marketing manager suggests running a campaign of several hundred cable channel ads at an estimated cost of $60,000.

Bright Day's first concern is whether it can sell enough units to cover its costs. The president made this position clear when he said, "We don't want to lose money on this product. We have to sell at least enough units to break even." In accounting terms, the **break-even point** is where profit (income) equals zero. So how many bottles of Delatine must be sold to produce a profit of zero? The break-even point is commonly computed using either the *equation method,* the *contribution margin per unit method,* or the *contribution margin ratio method.* All three of these approaches produce the same result. They are merely different ways to arrive at the same conclusion.

Equation Method

The **equation method** begins by expressing the income statement as follows:

$$\text{Sales} - \text{Variable costs} - \text{Fixed costs} = \text{Profit (Net income)}$$

As previously stated, profit at the break-even point is zero. Therefore, the break-even point for Delatine is computed as follows:

$$\text{Sales} - \text{Variable costs} - \text{Fixed costs} = \text{Profit}$$
$$\$36N - \$24N - \$60{,}000 = \$0$$
$$\$12N = \$60{,}000$$
$$N = \$60{,}000 \div \$12$$
$$N = 5{,}000 \text{ Units}$$

Where:

N = Number of units
$36 = Sales price per unit
$24 = Variable cost per unit
$60,000 = Fixed costs

✓ CHECK YOURSELF 11.5

B-Shoc is an independent musician who is considering whether to independently produce and sell a CD. B-Shoc estimates fixed costs of $5,400 and variable costs of $2.00 per unit. The expected selling price is $8.00 per CD. Use the equation method to determine B-Shoc's break-even point.

Answer

$$\text{Sales} - \text{Variable costs} - \text{Fixed costs} = \text{Profit}$$

$$\$8N - \$2N - \$5{,}400 = \$0$$

$$\$6N = \$5{,}400$$

$$N = \$5{,}400 \div \$6$$

$$N = 900 \text{ Units (CDs)}$$

Where:

N = Number of units
$8 = Sales price per unit
$2 = Variable cost per unit
$5,400 = Fixed costs

Contribution Margin per Unit Method

Recall that the *total contribution margin* is the amount of sales minus total variable cost. The **contribution margin per unit** is the sales price per unit minus the variable cost per unit. Therefore, the contribution margin per unit for Delatine is:

Sales price per unit	$ 36
Less: Variable cost per unit	(24)
Contribution margin per unit	$ 12

For every bottle of Delatine it sells, Bright Day earns a $12 contribution margin. In other words, every time Bright Day sells a bottle of Delatine, it receives enough money ($24) to cover the variable cost of the bottle of Delatine and still has $12 left to go toward paying the fixed cost. Bright Day will reach the break-even point when it sells enough bottles of Delatine to cover its fixed costs. Therefore the break-even point can be determined as follows:

$$\text{Break-even point in units} = \frac{\text{Fixed costs}}{\text{Contribution margin per unit}}$$

$$\text{Break-even point in units} = \frac{\$60{,}000}{\$12}$$

$$\text{Break-even point in units} = 5{,}000 \text{ Units}$$

This result is the same as that determined under the equation method. Indeed, the contribution margin per unit method formula is an abbreviated version of the income statement formula used in the equation method. In other words, both methods are simply different derivations of the same formula. The proof is provided in the footnote below.[2]

---

[2]The formula for the *contribution margin per unit method* is (where N is the number of units at the break-even point):

N = Fixed costs ÷ Contribution margin per unit

The income statement formula for the *equation method* produces the same result as shown below (where N is the number of units at the break-even point):

Sales − Variable costs − Fixed costs = Profit
Sales price per unit (N) − Variable cost per unit (N) − Fixed costs = Profit
Contribution margin per unit (N) − Fixed costs = Profit
Contribution margin per unit (N) − Fixed costs = 0
Contribution margin per unit (N) = Fixed costs

N = Fixed costs ÷ Contribution margin per unit

Both the *equation method* and the *contribution margin per unit method* yield the amount of break-even sales measured *in units.* To determine the amount of break-even sales measured *in dollars,* multiply the number of units times the sales price per unit. For Delatine, the break-even point measured in dollars is $180,000 (5,000 units × $36 per unit). The following income statement confirms this result:

Sales revenue (5,000 units × $36)	$ 180,000
Total variable expenses (5,000 units × $24)	(120,000)
Total contribution margin (5,000 units × $12)	60,000
Fixed expenses	(60,000)
Net income	$ 0

Determining the Sales Volume Necessary to Reach a Desired Profit

Bright Day's president decides the ad campaign should produce a $40,000 profit. He asks the accountant to determine the sales volume that is required to achieve this level of profitability. Using the *equation method,* the sales volume in units required to attain the desired profit is computed as follows:

$$\text{Sales} - \text{Variable costs} - \text{Fixed costs} = \text{Profit}$$

$$\$36N - \$24N - \$60{,}000 = \$40{,}000$$

$$\$12N = \$60{,}000 + \$40{,}000$$

$$N = \$100{,}000 \div \$12$$

$$N = 8{,}333 \text{ Units}$$

Where:

N = Number of units

$36 = Sales price per unit

$24 = Variable cost per unit

$60,000 = Fixed costs

$40,000 = Desired profit

The accountant used the *contribution margin per unit method* to confirm these computations as follows:

$$\text{Sales volume in units} = \frac{\text{Fixed costs} + \text{Desired profit}}{\text{Contribution margin per unit}}$$

$$= \frac{\$60{,}000 + \$40{,}000}{\$12} = 8{,}333.33 \text{ Units}$$

The required volume in sales dollars is this number of units multiplied by the sales price per unit (8,333.33 units × $36 = $300,000). The following income statement confirms this result; all amounts are rounded to the nearest whole dollar.

Sales revenue (8,333.33 units × $36)	$ 300,000
Total variable expenses (8,333.33 units × $24)	(200,000)
Total contribution margin (8,333.33 units × $12)	100,000
Fixed expenses	(60,000)
Net income	$ 40,000

In practice, the company will not sell partial bottles of Delatine, so the accountant rounds 8,333.33 bottles to 8,334 whole units. For planning and decision making, managers frequently make decisions using approximate data. Accuracy is desirable, but it is not as important as relevance. Do not be concerned when computations do not produce whole numbers. Rounding and approximation are common characteristics of managerial accounting data.

REALITY BYTES

The relationship among the costs to produce goods, the volume of goods produced, the price charged for those goods, and the profit earned is relevant to all industries, but perhaps no industry demonstrates the effects of these relationships more dramatically than automobile manufacturing. The automobile industry is characterized by having a lot of fixed production costs for things such as buildings, equipment, and research and development, as well as financing costs associated with borrowed funds, such as interest expense on bonds.

In the 1980s, foreign automobile manufacturers began increasing their market share, thus decreasing the market share of domestic companies such as General Motors (GM). As GM's relative level of production fell, its fixed cost per unit increased. In response, GM and others tried to regain market share by lowering prices, largely through rebates. Unfortunately this did not work, so the lower prices, combined with the higher relative fixed costs, seriously eroded profits. These problems reached a crisis in 2008 and 2009, when GM sought financial help from the government and entered expedited bankruptcy proceedings.

What did GM hope to achieve by entering bankruptcy? Primarily it needed to lower its costs—especially its fixed costs. As a result of bankruptcy proceedings it was able to greatly reduce interest and principal payments on outstanding bonds (fixed costs), reduce the number of brands (fixed costs), shut down some plants (fixed costs), reduce health care costs to retirees (fixed costs), and reduce the number of dealers. While reducing the number of dealers did reduce some cost to the companies, it also reduced price competition among the dealers, which had the potential of allowing GM to charge more for its cars. All of these changes, it was hoped, would allow GM to return to profitability.

However, before a company can be profitable, it must break even. At one time, GM's break-even point was estimated to be around 16 million vehicles per year. GM's CEO until 2000, Rick Wagoner, had implemented changes that reduced the company's break-even point to 12 million units. On March 29, 2009, as a condition of receiving government financial support, the administration of President Barack Obama asked Mr. Wagoner to resign as GM's CEO. A fact perhaps overlooked by many amid the news coverage of Mr. Wagoner's resignation were reports that officials at the U.S. Treasury Department also asked the new leadership at GM to take steps to reduce the company's break-even point to 10 million units.

It would be a major achievement if GM were able to reduce its break-even point from 16 million units to 10 million units in the span of a few years. In 2008, GM sold only 8.8 million units, and its sales in the first quarter of 2009 were even lower than the same quarter of 2008, so even selling 10 million units was not a sure thing. Furthermore, it should be remembered that the objective of businesses is not simply to break even, but to make a profit.

Did the strategy work? As of December 31, 2011, the answer seems to be yes. The table below shows GM's results for the two years preceding and the two years following its bankruptcy. As the data show, the break-even level is now less than 10 million units.

	"New" GM		"Old" GM	
	2011	2010	2008	2007
Sales in units (thousands)	9,286	8,144	8,714	9,267
Sales in dollars (millions)	$150,276	$135,592	$148,979	$179,984
Operating income (millions)	$5,656	$5,108	($4,863)	($16,095)

CHECK YOURSELF 11.6

VolTech Company manufactures small engines that it sells for $130 each. Variable costs are $70 per unit. Fixed costs are expected to be $100,000. The management team has established a target profit of $188,000. Use the contribution margin per unit method to determine how many engines VolTech must sell to attain the target profit.

Answer

Contribution margin per unit approach:

$$\text{Sales volume in units} = \frac{\text{Fixed costs} + \text{Desired profit}}{\text{Contribution margin per unit}} = \frac{\$100,000 + \$188,000}{\$130 - \$70} = 4,800 \text{ Units}$$

CALCULATING THE MARGIN OF SAFETY

The final meeting of Bright Day's management team focused on the reliability of the data used to construct the CVP chart. The accountant called attention to the sales volume figures in the area of profitability. Recall that Bright Day must sell 4,375 bottles of Delatine to earn the desired profit. In dollars, budgeted sales are $122,500 (4,375 bottles × $28 per bottle). The accountant highlighted the large gap between these budgeted sales and break-even sales. The amount of this gap, called the *margin of safety,* can be measured in units or in sales dollars as shown here.

	In Units	In Dollars
Budgeted sales	4,375	$122,500
Break-even sales	(1,875)	(52,500)
Margin of safety	2,500	$ 70,000

The **margin of safety** measures the cushion between budgeted sales and the break-even point. It quantifies the amount by which actual sales can fall short of expectations before the company will begin to incur losses.

To help compare diverse products or companies of different sizes, the margin of safety can be expressed as a percentage. Divide the margin of safety by the budgeted sales volume[3] as shown here.

$$\text{Margin of safety} = \frac{\text{Budgeted sales} - \text{Break-even sales}}{\text{Budgeted sales}}$$

$$\text{Margin of safety} = \frac{\$122,500 - \$52,500}{\$122,500} = 57.14\%$$

This analysis suggests actual sales would have to fall short of expected sales by more than 57 percent before Bright Day would experience a loss on Delatine. The large margin of safety suggests the proposed radio advertising program to market bottles of 30 mg Delatine capsules has minimal risk. As a result, the project team recommends that Delatine be added to the company's line of products.

CHECK YOURSELF 11.7

Suppose that Bright Day is considering the possibility of selling a protein supplement that will cost Bright Day $5 per bottle. Bright Day believes that it can sell 4,000 bottles of the supplement for $25 per bottle. Fixed costs associated with selling the supplement are expected to be $42,000. Does the supplement have a wider margin of safety than Delatine?

Answer Calculate the break-even point for the protein supplement.

$$\text{Break-even volume in units} = \frac{\text{Fixed costs}}{\text{Contribution margin per unit}} = \frac{\$42,000}{\$25 - \$5} = 2,100 \text{ Units}$$

Calculate the margin of safety. Note that the margin of safety expressed as a percentage can be calculated using the number of units or sales dollars. Using either units or dollars yields the same percentage.

$$\text{Margin of safety} = \frac{\text{Budgeted sales} - \text{Break-even sales}}{\text{Budgeted sales}} = \frac{4,000 - 2,100}{4,000} = 47.5\%$$

The margin of safety for Delatine (57.14 percent) exceeds that for the protein supplement (47.5 percent). This suggests that Bright Day is less likely to incur losses selling Delatine than selling the supplement.

---

[3]The margin of safety percentage can be based on actual as well as budgeted sales. For example, an analyst could compare the margins of safety of two companies under current operating conditions by substituting actual sales for budgeted sales in the computation, as follows: [(Actual sales − Break-even sales) ÷ Actual sales].

A Look Back

To plan and control business operations effectively, managers need to understand how different costs behave in relation to changes in the volume of activity. Total *fixed cost* remains constant when activity changes. Fixed cost per unit decreases with increases in activity and increases with decreases in activity. In contrast, total *variable cost* increases proportionately with increases in activity and decreases proportionately with decreases in activity. Variable cost per unit remains constant regardless of activity levels. The definitions of fixed and variable costs have meaning only within the context of a specified range of activity (the relevant range) for a defined period of time. In addition, cost behavior depends on the relevant volume measure (a store manager's salary is fixed relative to the number of customers visiting a particular store but is variable relative to the number of stores operated). A mixed cost has both fixed and variable cost components.

Fixed costs allow companies to take advantage of *operating leverage.* With operating leverage, each additional sale decreases the cost per unit. This principle allows a small percentage change in volume of revenue to cause a significantly larger percentage change in profits. The *magnitude of operating leverage* can be determined by dividing the contribution margin by net income. When all costs are fixed and revenues have covered fixed costs, each additional dollar of revenue represents pure profit. Having a fixed cost structure (employing operating leverage) offers a company both risks and rewards. If sales volume increases, fixed costs do not increase, allowing profits to soar. Alternatively, if sales volume decreases, fixed costs do not decrease and profits decline significantly more than revenues. Companies with high variable costs in relation to fixed costs do not experience as great a level of operating leverage. Their costs increase or decrease in proportion to changes in revenue. These companies face less risk but fail to reap disproportionately higher profits when volume soars.

Under the contribution margin approach, variable costs are subtracted from revenue to determine the *contribution margin.* Fixed costs are then subtracted from the contribution margin to determine net income. The contribution margin represents the amount available to pay fixed costs and provide a profit. Although not permitted by GAAP for external reporting, many companies use the contribution margin format for internal reporting purposes.

The *break-even point* (the point where total revenue equals total cost) in units can be determined by dividing fixed costs by the contribution margin per unit. The break-even point in sales dollars can be determined by multiplying the number of break-even units by the sales price per unit. To determine sales in units to obtain a designated profit, the sum of fixed costs and desired profit is divided by the contribution margin per unit.

The *margin of safety* is the number of units or the amount of sales dollars by which actual sales can fall below expected sales before a loss is incurred. The margin of safety can also be expressed as a percentage to permit comparing different size companies. The margin of safety can be computed as a percentage by dividing the difference between budgeted sales and break-even sales by the amount of budgeted sales.

A Look Forward

The next chapter begins investigating cost measurement. Accountants seek to determine the cost of certain objects. A cost object may be a product, a service, a department, a customer, or any other thing for which the cost is being determined. Some costs can be directly traced to a cost object, while others are difficult to trace. Costs that are difficult to trace to cost objects are called *indirect costs,* or *overhead.* Indirect costs are assigned to cost objects through *cost allocation.* The next chapter introduces the basic concepts and procedures of cost allocation.

Video lectures and accompanying self-assessment quizzes are available for all learning objectives through McGraw-Hill *Connect®* *Accounting.*

SELF-STUDY REVIEW PROBLEM 1

Mensa Mountaineering Company (MMC) provides guided mountain climbing expeditions in the Rocky Mountains. Its only major expense is guide salaries; it pays each guide $4,800 per climbing expedition. MMC charges its customers $1,500 per expedition and expects to take five climbers on each expedition.

Part 1

Base your answers on the preceding information.

Required

a. Determine the total cost of guide salaries and the cost of guide salaries per climber assuming that four, five, or six climbers are included in a trip. Relative to the number of climbers in a single expedition, is the cost of guides a fixed or a variable cost?

b. Relative to the number of expeditions, is the cost of guides a fixed or a variable cost?

c. Determine the profit of an expedition assuming that five climbers are included in the trip.

d. Determine the profit assuming a 20 percent increase (six climbers total) in expedition revenue. What is the percentage change in profitability?

e. Determine the profit assuming a 20 percent decrease (four climbers total) in expedition revenue. What is the percentage change in profitability?

f. Explain why a 20 percent shift in revenue produces more than a 20 percent shift in profitability. What term describes this phenomenon?

Part 2

Assume that the guides offer to make the climbs for a percentage of expedition fees. Specifically, MMC will pay guides $960 per climber on the expedition. Assume also that the expedition fee charged to climbers remains at $1,500 per climber.

Required

g. Determine the total cost of guide salaries and the cost of guide salaries per climber assuming that four, five, or six climbers are included in a trip. Relative to the number of climbers in a single expedition, is the cost of guides a fixed or a variable cost?

h. Relative to the number of expeditions, is the cost of guides a fixed or a variable cost?

i. Determine the profit of an expedition assuming that five climbers are included in the trip.

j. Determine the profit assuming a 20 percent increase (six climbers total) in expedition revenue. What is the percentage change in profitability?

k. Determine the profit assuming a 20 percent decrease (four climbers total) in expedition revenue. What is the percentage change in profitability?

l. Explain why a 20 percent shift in revenue does not produce more than a 20 percent shift in profitability.

Solution to Part 1, Requirement *a*

Number of climbers (a)	4	5	6
Total cost of guide salaries (b)	$4,800	$4,800	$4,800
Cost per climber (b ÷ a)	1,200	960	800

Because the total cost remains constant (fixed) regardless of the number of climbers on a particular expedition, the cost is classified as fixed. Note that the cost per climber decreases as the number of climbers increases. This is the *per unit* behavior pattern of a fixed cost.

Solution to Part 1, Requirement *b*

Because the total cost of guide salaries changes proportionately each time the number of expeditions increases or decreases, the cost of salaries is variable relative to the number of expeditions.

Solution to Part 1, Requirements *c*, *d*, and *e*

Number of Climbers	4	Percentage Change	5	Percentage Change	6
Revenue ($1,500 per climber)	$6,000	⇐ (20%) ⇐	$7,500	⇒ +20% ⇒	$9,000
Cost of guide salaries (fixed)	4,800		4,800		4,800
Profit	$1,200	⇐ (55.6%) ⇐	$2,700	⇒ +55.6% ⇒	$4,200

Percentage change in revenue: ±$1,500 ÷ $7,500 = ±20%
Percentage change in profit: ±$1,500 ÷ $2,700 = ±55.6%

Solution to Part 1, Requirement *f*

Because the cost of guide salaries remains fixed while volume (number of climbers) changes, the change in profit, measured in absolute dollars, exactly matches the change in revenue. More specifically, each time MMC increases the number of climbers by one, revenue and profit increase by $1,500. Because the base figure for profit ($2,700) is lower than the base figure for revenue ($7,500), the percentage change in profit ($1,500 ÷ $2,700 = 55.6%) is higher than percentage change in revenue ($1,500 ÷ $7,500). This phenomenon is called *operating leverage.*

Solution for Part 2, Requirement *g*

Number of climbers (a)	4	5	6
Per climber cost of guide salaries (b)	$ 960	$ 960	$ 960
Cost per climber (b × a)	3,840	4,800	5,760

Because the total cost changes in proportion to changes in the number of climbers, the cost is classified as variable. Note that the cost per climber remains constant (stays the same) as the number of climbers increases or decreases. This is the *per unit* behavior pattern of a variable cost.

Solution for Part 2, Requirement *h*

Because the total cost of guide salaries changes proportionately with changes in the number of expeditions, the cost of salaries is also variable relative to the number of expeditions.

Solution for Part 2, Requirements *i*, *j*, and *k*

Number of Climbers	4	Percentage Change	5	Percentage Change	6
Revenue ($1,500 per climber)	$6,000	⇐ (20%) ⇐	$7,500	⇒ +20% ⇒	$9,000
Cost of guide salaries (variable)	3,840		4,800		5,760
Profit	$2,160	⇐ (20%) ⇐	$2,700	⇒ +20% ⇒	$3,240

Percentage change in revenue: ±$1,500 ÷ $7,500 = ±20%
Percentage change in profit: ±$540 ÷ $2,700 = ±20%

Solution for Part 2, Requirement *l*

Because the cost of guide salaries changes when volume (number of climbers) changes, the change in net income is proportionate to the change in revenue. More specifically, each time the number of climbers increases by one, revenue increases by $1,500 and net income increases by $540 ($1,500 − $960). Accordingly, the percentage change in net income will always equal the percentage change in revenue. This means that there is no operating leverage when all costs are variable.

Video lectures and accompanying self-assessment quizzes are available for all learning objectives through McGraw-Hill *Connect*® *Accounting*.

SELF-STUDY REVIEW PROBLEM 2

Sharp Company makes and sells pencil sharpeners. The variable cost of each sharpener is $20. The sharpeners are sold for $30 each. Fixed operating expenses amount to $40,000.

Required

a. Determine the break-even point in units and sales dollars.

b. Determine the sales volume in units and dollars that is required to attain a profit of $12,000. Verify your answer by preparing an income statement using the contribution margin format.

c. Determine the margin of safety between sales required to attain a profit of $12,000 and break-even sales.

Solution to Requirement *a*

Formula for Computing Break-even Point in Units

Sales − Variable costs − Fixed costs = Profit
Sales price per unit (N) − Variable cost per unit (N) − Fixed costs = Profit
Contribution margin per unit (N) − Fixed costs = Profit
N = (Fixed costs + Profit) ÷ Contribution margin per unit
N = ($40,000 + 0) ÷ ($30 − $20) = 4,000 Units

Break-even Point in Sales Dollars

Sales price	$ 30
× Number of units	4,000
Sales volume in dollars	$120,000

Solution to Requirement *b*

Formula for Computing Unit Sales Required to Attain Desired Profit

Sales − Variable costs − Fixed costs = Profit
Sales price per unit (N) − Variable cost per unit (N) − Fixed costs = Profit
Contribution margin per unit (N) − Fixed costs = Profit
N = (Fixed costs + Profit) ÷ Contribution margin per unit
N = ($40,000 + 12,000) ÷ ($30 − $20) = 5,200 Units

Sales Dollars Required to Attain Desired Profit

Sales price	$ 30
× Number of units	5,200
Sales volume in dollars	$156,000

Income Statement

Sales volume in units (a)	5,200
Sales revenue (a × $30)	$156,000
Variable costs (a × $20)	(104,000)
Contribution margin	52,000
Fixed costs	(40,000)
Net income	$ 12,000

Solution to Requirement *c*

Margin of Safety Computations	Units	Dollars
Budgeted sales	5,200	$156,000
Break-even sales	(4,000)	(120,000)
Margin of safety	1,200	$ 36,000

Percentage Computation

$$\frac{\text{Margin of safety in \$}}{\text{Budgeted sales}} = \frac{\$36,000}{\$156,000} = 23.08\%$$

KEY TERMS

Activity base 411
Break-even point 412
Contribution
   margin 408

Contribution margin
   per unit 413
Cost behavior 404
Equation method 412

Fixed cost 402
Margin of safety 416
Mixed costs (semivariable
   costs) 410

Operating leverage 404
Relevant range 411
Variable cost 402

QUESTIONS

1. Define *fixed cost* and *variable cost* and give an example of each.

2. How can knowing cost behavior relative to volume fluctuations affect decision making?

3. Define the term *operating leverage* and explain how it affects profits.

4. How is operating leverage calculated?

5. Explain the limitations of using operating leverage to predict profitability.

6. If volume is increasing, would a company benefit more from a pure variable or a pure fixed cost structure? Which cost structure would be advantageous if volume is decreasing?

7. Explain the risk and rewards to a company that result from having fixed costs.

8. Are companies with predominately fixed cost structures likely to be most profitable?

9. How is the relevant range of activity related to fixed and variable cost? Give an example of how the definitions of these costs become invalid when volume is outside the relevant range.

10. Which cost structure has the greater risk? Explain.

11. The president of Bright Corporation tells you that he sees a dim future for his company. He feels that his hands are tied because fixed costs are too high. He says that fixed costs do not change and therefore the situation is hopeless. Do you agree? Explain.

12. All costs are variable because if a business ceases operations, its costs fall to zero. Do you

agree with the statement? Explain.

13. Verna Salsbury tells you that she thinks the terms fixed cost and variable cost are confusing. She notes that fixed cost per unit changes when the number of units changes. Furthermore, variable cost per unit remains fixed regardless of how many units are produced. She concludes that the terminology seems to be backward. Explain why the terminology appears to be contradictory.

14. What does the term *break-even point* mean? Name the two ways it can be measured.

15. How does a contribution margin income statement differ from the income statement used in financial reporting?

16. If Company A has a projected margin of safety of

22 percent while Company B has a margin of safety of 52 percent, which company is at greater risk when actual sales are less than budgeted?

17. Mary Hartwell and Jane Jamail, college roommates, are considering the joint purchase of a computer that they can share to prepare class assignments. Ms. Hartwell wants a particular model that costs $2,000; Ms. Jamail prefers a more economical model that costs $1,500. In fact, Ms. Jamail is adamant about her position, refusing to contribute more than $750 toward the purchase. If Ms. Hartwell is also adamant about her position, should she accept Ms. Jamail's $750 offer and apply that amount toward the purchase of the more expensive computer?

MULTIPLE-CHOICE QUESTIONS

Multiple-choice questions are provided on the text website at www.mhhe.com/edmondssurvey4e.

EXERCISES

≣ connect All applicable Exercises are available with McGraw-Hill
|ACCOUNTING *Connect® Accounting.*

LO 11-1

Exercise 11-1 *Identifying cost behavior*

Molly's Restaurant, a fast-food restaurant company, operates a chain of restaurants across the nation. Each restaurant employs eight people; one is a manager paid a salary plus a bonus equal to 3 percent of sales. Other employees, two cooks, one dishwasher, and four waitresses, are paid salaries. Each manager is budgeted $3,000 per month for advertising costs.

Required

Classify each of the following costs incurred by Molly's Restaurant as fixed, variable, or mixed:

a. Manager's compensation relative to the number of customers.
b. Waitresses' salaries relative to the number of restaurants.
c. Advertising costs relative to the number of customers for a particular restaurant.
d. Rental costs relative to the number of restaurants.
e. Cooks' salaries at a particular location relative to the number of customers.
f. Cost of supplies (cups, plates, spoons, etc.) relative to the number of customers.

LO 11-1

Exercise 11-2 *Identifying cost behavior*

At the various activity levels shown, Yates Company incurred the following costs:

	Units Sold	20	40	60	80	100
a.	Total cost of shopping bags	$ 2.00	$ 4.00	$ 6.00	$ 8.00	$ 10.00
b.	Cost per unit of merchandise sold	90.00	90.00	90.00	90.00	90.00
c.	Rental cost per unit of merchandise sold	36.00	18.00	12.00	9.00	7.20
d.	Total phone expense	80.00	100.00	120.00	140.00	160.00
e.	Cost per unit of supplies	1.00	1.00	1.00	1.00	1.00
f.	Total insurance cost	480.00	480.00	480.00	480.00	480.00
g.	Total salary cost	1,200.00	1,600.00	2,000.00	2,400.00	2,800.00
h.	Total cost of goods sold	1,800.00	3,600.00	5,400.00	7,200.00	9,000.00
i.	Depreciation cost per unit	240.00	120.00	80.00	60.00	48.00
j.	Total rent cost	3,200.00	3,200.00	3,200.00	3,200.00	3,200.00

Required

Identify each of these costs as fixed, variable, or mixed.

LO 11-1

Exercise 11-3 *Determining fixed cost per unit*

Munoz Corporation incurs the following annual fixed costs:

Item	Cost
Depreciation	$ 75,000
Officers' salaries	160,000
Long-term lease	38,000
Property taxes	12,000

Required

Determine the total fixed cost per unit of production, assuming that Munoz produces 4,000, 4,500, or 5,000 units.

Exercise 11-4   *Determining total variable cost*

The following variable production costs apply to goods made by Raeburn Manufacturing Corporation:

Item	Cost per Unit
Materials	$ 8.00
Labor	3.50
Variable overhead	2.50
Total	$14.00

Required

Determine the total variable production cost, assuming that Raeburn makes 5,000, 15,000, or 25,000 units.

Exercise 11-5   *Fixed versus variable cost behavior*

Nasenko Company's cost and production data for two recent months included the following:

	March	April
Production (units)	200	400
Rent	$1,800	$1,800
Utilities	$ 600	$1,200

Required

a. Separately calculate the rental cost per unit and the utilities cost per unit for both March and April.
b. Identify which cost is variable and which is fixed. Explain your answer.

Exercise 11-6   *Fixed versus variable cost behavior*

Varina Trophies makes and sells trophies it distributes to little league ballplayers. The company normally produces and sells between 6,000 and 12,000 trophies per year. The following cost data apply to various activity levels:

Number of Trophies	6,000	8,000	10,000	12,000
Total costs incurred				
Fixed	$48,000			
Variable	48,000			
Total costs	$96,000			
Cost per unit				
Fixed	$ 8.00			
Variable	8.00			
Total cost per trophy	$ 16.00			

Required

a. Complete the preceding table by filling in the missing amounts for the levels of activity shown in the first row of the table. Round all cost-per-unit figures to the nearest whole penny.
b. Explain why the total cost per trophy decreases as the number of trophies increases.

LO 11-1

Exercise 11-7 *Graphing fixed cost behavior*

The following graph setups depict the dollar amount of fixed cost on the vertical axes and the level of activity on the horizontal axes:

Total fixed cost   **Fixed cost per unit**

Required

a. Draw a line that depicts the relationship between total fixed cost and the level of activity.

b. Draw a line that depicts the relationship between fixed cost per unit and the level of activity.

LO 11-1

Exercise 11-8 *Graphing variable cost behavior*

The following graph setups depict the dollar amount of variable cost on the vertical axes and the level of activity on the horizontal axes:

Total variable cost   **Variable cost per unit**

Required

a. Draw a line that depicts the relationship between total variable cost and the level of activity.

b. Draw a line that depicts the relationship between variable cost per unit and the level of activity.

LO 11-1

Exercise 11-9 *Mixed cost at different levels of activity*

Veasy Corporation paid one of its sales representatives $7,500 during the month of March. The rep is paid a base salary plus $25 per unit of product sold. During March, the rep sold 200 units.

Required

Calculate the total monthly cost of the sales representative's salary for each of the following months:

Month	April	May	June	July
Number of units sold	240	150	250	160
Total variable cost				
Total fixed cost				
Total salary cost				

Exercise 11-10   *Fixed versus variable cost behavior*

Moore Entertainment sponsors rock concerts. The company is considering a contract to hire a band at a cost of $105,000 per concert.

Required

a. What are the total band cost and the cost per person if concert attendance is 2,000, 2,500, 3,000, 3,500, or 4,000?

b. Is the cost of hiring the band a fixed or a variable cost?

c. Draw a graph and plot total cost and cost per unit if attendance is 2,000, 2,500, 3,000, 3,500, or 4,000.

d. Identify Moore's major business risks and explain how they can be minimized.

Exercise 11-11   *Fixed versus variable cost behavior*

Moore Entertainment sells souvenir T-shirts at each rock concert that it sponsors. The shirts cost $9 each. Any excess shirts can be returned to the manufacturer for a full refund of the purchase price. The sales price is $15 per shirt.

Required

a. What are the total cost of shirts and cost per shirt if sales amount to 2,000, 2,500, 3,000, 3,500, or 4,000?

b. Is the cost of T-shirts a fixed or a variable cost?

c. Draw a graph and plot total cost and cost per shirt if sales amount to 2,000, 2,500, 3,000, 3,500, or 4,000.

d. Comment on Moore's likelihood of incurring a loss due to its operating activities.

Exercise 11-12   *Using fixed cost as a competitive business strategy*

The following income statements illustrate different cost structures for two competing companies:

Income Statements		
	Company Name	
	Kent	Trent
Number of customers (a)	100	100
Sales revenue (a × $250)	$ 25,000	$ 25,000
Variable cost (a × $175)	N/A	(17,500)
Variable cost (a × $0)	0	N/A
Contribution margin	25,000	7,500
Fixed cost	(17,500)	0
Net income	$ 7,500	$ 7,500

Required

a. Reconstruct Kent's income statement, assuming that it serves 200 customers when it lures 100 customers away from Trent by lowering the sales price to $150 per customer.

b. Reconstruct Trent's income statement, assuming that it serves 200 customers when it lures 100 customers away from Kent by lowering the sales price to $150 per customer.

c. Explain why the price-cutting strategy increased Kent Company's profits but caused a net loss for Trent Company.

Exercise 11-13   *Prepare an income statement using the contribution margin approach*

AJ Manufacturing Company incurred $50,000 of fixed product cost and $40,000 of variable product cost during its first year of operation. Also during its first year, AJ incurred $16,000 of fixed selling and administrative costs and $13,000 of variable selling and administrative costs. The company sold all of the units it produced for $160,000.

Required

a. Prepare an income statement using the format required by generally accepted accounting Principles (GAAP).
b. Prepare an income statement using the contribution margin approach.
c. Explain why both statements have the same amount of net income.

LO 11-3

Exercise 11-14 *Determining contribution margin from incomplete cost data*

Estrada Corporation produced 300,000 watches that it sold for $35 each. The company determined that fixed manufacturing cost per unit was $14 per watch. The company reported a $2,700,000 gross margin on its income statement.

Required

Determine the variable cost per unit, the total variable cost, and the total contribution margin.

LO 11-3, 11-4

Exercise 11-15 *Using contribution margin format income statement to measure the magnitude of operating leverage*

The following income statement was drawn from the records of Butler Company, a merchandising firm:

BUTLER COMPANY	
Income Statement	
For the Year Ended December 31, 2014	
Sales revenue (2,000 units × $275)	$ 550,000
Cost of goods sold (2,000 units × $146)	(292,000)
Gross margin	258,000
Sales commissions (10% of sales)	(55,000)
Administrative salaries expense	(80,000)
Advertising expense	(38,000)
Depreciation expense	(50,000)
Shipping and handling expenses (2,000 units × $1.50)	(3,000)
Net income	$ 32,000

Required

a. Reconstruct the income statement using the contribution margin format.
b. Calculate the magnitude of operating leverage.
c. Use the measure of operating leverage to determine the amount of net income Butler will earn if sales increase by 10 percent.

LO 11-4

Exercise 11-16 *Assessing the magnitude of operating leverage*

The following income statement applies to Nagano Company for the current year:

Income Statement	
Sales revenue (250 units × $60)	$15,000
Variable cost (250 units × $36)	(9,000)
Contribution margin	6,000
Fixed costs	(2,000)
Net income	$ 4,000

Required

a. Use the contribution margin approach to calculate the magnitude of operating leverage.
b. Use the operating leverage measure computed in Requirement *a* to determine the amount of net income that Nagano Company will earn if it experiences a 10 percent increase in revenue. The sales price per unit is not affected.

c. Verify your answer to Requirement *b* by constructing an income statement based on a 10 percent increase in sales revenue. The sales price is not affected. Calculate the percentage change in net income for the two income statements.

Exercise 11-17   *Break-even point*

LO 11-5

Agassi Corporation sells products for $90 each that have variable costs of $60 per unit. Agassi's annual fixed cost is $450,000.

Required

Determine the break-even point in units and dollars.

Exercise 11-18   *Desired profit*

LO 11-5

Lindo Company incurs annual fixed costs of $80,000. Variable costs for Lindo's product are $40 per unit, and the sales price is $64 per unit. Lindo desires to earn an annual profit of $40,000.

Required

Determine the sales volume in dollars and units required to earn the desired profit.

Exercise 11-19   *Margin of safety*

LO 11-6

Information concerning a product produced by Ender Company appears here:

Sales price per unit	$200
Variable cost per unit	$80
Total annual fixed manufacturing and operating costs	$600,000

Required

Determine the following:

a. Contribution margin per unit.
b. Number of units that Ender must sell to break even.
c. Sales level in units that Ender must reach to earn a profit of $240,000.
d. Determine the margin of safety in units, sales dollars, and as a percentage. Round the percentage to one decimal place.

Exercise 11-20   *Margin of safety*

LO 11-6

Otto Company makes a product that sells for $5 per unit. The company pays $3 per unit for the variable costs of the product and incurs fixed costs of $50,000. Otto expects to sell 30,000 units of product.

Required

Determine Otto's margin of safety in units, sales dollars, and as a percentage. Round the percentage to one decimal place.

PROBLEMS

 All applicable Problems are available with McGraw-Hill
Connect® Accounting.

Problem 11-21   *Identifying cost behavior*

LO 11-1

Required

Identify the following costs as fixed or variable:

Costs related to plane trips between New York, New York, and Los Angeles, California, follow. Pilots are paid on a per-trip basis.

a. Pilots' salaries relative to the number of trips flown.
b. Depreciation relative to the number of planes in service.

    c. Cost of refreshments relative to the number of passengers.

    d. Pilots' salaries relative to the number of passengers on a particular trip.

    e. Cost of a maintenance check relative to the number of passengers on a particular trip.

    f. Fuel costs relative to the number of trips.

Guaranty National Bank operates several branch offices in grocery stores. Each branch employs a supervisor and two tellers. Costs related to Guaranty's branch operations follow.

    g. Tellers' salaries relative to the number of tellers in a particular district, which is composed of branches.

    h. Supplies cost relative to the number of transactions processed in a particular branch.

    i. Tellers' salaries relative to the number of customers served at a particular branch.

    j. Supervisors' salaries relative to the number of branches operated.

    k. Supervisors' salaries relative to the number of customers served in a particular branch.

    l. Facility rental costs relative to the size of customer deposits.

Costs related to operating a fast-food restaurant follow.

    m. Depreciation of equipment relative to the number of restaurants.

    n. Building rental cost relative to the number of customers served in a particular restaurant.

    o. Manager's salary of a particular store relative to the number of employees.

    p. Food cost relative to the number of customers.

    q. Utility cost relative to the number of restaurants in operation.

    r. Company president's salary relative to the number of restaurants in operation.

    s. Land costs relative to the number of hamburgers sold at a particular restaurant.

    t. Depreciation of equipment relative to the number of customers served at a particular restaurant.

LO 11-1

CHECK FIGURES
c. Total supplies cost for cleaning 30 houses: $150
d. Total cost for 20 houses: $2,200

Problem 11-22   *Cost behavior and averaging*

Kara Buchanan has decided to start Kara Cleaning, a residential housecleaning service company. She is able to rent cleaning equipment at a cost of $900 per month. Labor costs are expected to be $60 per house cleaned and supplies are expected to cost $5 per house.

Required

    a. Determine the total expected cost of equipment rental and the average expected cost of equipment rental per house cleaned, assuming that Kara Cleaning cleans 10, 20, or 30 houses during one month. Is the cost of equipment a fixed or a variable cost?

    b. Determine the total expected cost of labor and the average expected cost of labor per house cleaned, assuming that Kara Cleaning cleans 10, 20, or 30 houses during one month. Is the cost of labor a fixed or a variable cost?

    c. Determine the total expected cost of supplies and the average expected cost of supplies per house cleaned, assuming that Kara Cleaning cleans 10, 20, or 30 houses during one month. Is the cost of supplies a fixed or a variable cost?

    d. Determine the total expected cost of cleaning houses, assuming that Kara Cleaning cleans 10, 20, or 30 houses during one month.

    e. Determine the average expected cost per house, assuming that Kara Cleaning cleans 10, 20, or 30 houses during one month. Why does the cost per unit decrease as the number of houses increases?

    f. If Ms. Buchanan tells you that she prices her services at 25 percent above cost, would you assume that she means average or actual cost? Why?

LO 11-1

CHECK FIGURE
b. Average teller cost for 60,000 transactions: $1.60

Problem 11-23   *Context-sensitive nature of cost behavior classifications*

Atlantic Bank's start-up division establishes new branch banks. Each branch opens with three tellers. Total teller cost per branch is $96,000 per year. The three tellers combined can process up to 90,000 customer transactions per year. If a branch does not attain a volume of at least 60,000 transactions during its first year of operations, it is closed. If the demand for services exceeds 90,000 transactions, an additional teller is hired and the branch is transferred from the start-up division to regular operations.

Required

a. What is the relevant range of activity for new branch banks?

b. Determine the amount of teller cost in total and the average teller cost per transaction for a branch that processes 60,000, 70,000, 80,000, or 90,000 transactions. In this case (the activity base is the number of transactions for a specific branch), is the teller cost a fixed or a variable cost? Round year figures to 2 decimal points.

c. Determine the amount of teller cost in total and the average teller cost per branch for Atlantic Bank, assuming that the start-up division operates 10, 15, or 25 branches. In this case (the activity base is the number of branches), is the teller cost a fixed or a variable cost?

Problem 11-24   *Context-sensitive nature of cost behavior classifications*

Lisa Dunkley operates a sales booth in computer software trade shows, selling an accounting software package, *Abacus*. She purchases the package from a software company for $150 each. Booth space at the convention hall costs $8,000 per show.

LO 11-1

CHECK FIGURES
a. Average cost at
   400 units: $170
b. Average price at
   250 units: $227

Required

a. Sales at past trade shows have ranged between 200 and 400 software packages per show. Determine the average cost of sales per unit if Ms. Dunkley sells 200, 250, 300, 350, or 400 units of *Abacus* at a trade show. Use the following chart to organize your answer. Is the cost of booth space fixed or variable? Round your computation to 2 decimal points.

	Sales Volume in Units (a)				
	200	250	300	350	400
Total cost of software (a × $150)	$30,000				
Total cost of booth rental	8,000				
Total cost of sales (b)	$38,000				
Average cost per unit (b ÷ a)	$190.00				

b. If Ms. Dunkley wants to earn a $45 profit on each package of software she sells at a trade show, what price must she charge at sales volumes of 200, 250, 300, 350, or 400 units?

c. Record the total cost of booth space if Ms. Dunkley attends one, two, three, four, or five trade shows. Record your answers in the following chart. Is the cost of booth space fixed or variable relative to the number of shows attended?

	Number of Trade Shows Attended				
	1	2	3	4	5
Total cost of booth rental	$8,000				

d. Ms. Dunkley provides decorative shopping bags to customers who purchase software packages. Some customers take the bags; others do not. Some customers stuff more than one software package into a single bag. The number of bags varies in relation to the number of units sold, but the relationship is not proportional. Assume that Ms. Dunkley uses $30 of bags for every 50 software packages sold. What is the additional cost per unit sold? Is the cost fixed or variable?

Problem 11-25   *Effects of operating leverage on profitability*

LO 11-2

Rohr Training Services (RTS) provides instruction on the use of computer software for the employees of its corporate clients. It offers courses in the clients' offices on the clients' equipment. The only major expense RTS incurs is instructor salaries; it pays instructors $4,000 per course taught. RTS recently agreed to offer a course of instruction to the employees of Basemera Incorporated at a price of $600 per student. Basemera estimated that 20 students would attend the course.

Base your answers on the preceding information.

430   Chapter 11

Part 1:

Required

a. Relative to the number of students in a single course, is the cost of instruction a fixed or a variable cost?

b. Determine the profit, assuming that 20 students attend the course.

c. Determine the profit, assuming a 10 percent increase in enrollment (i.e., enrollment increases to 22 students). What is the percentage change in profitability?

d. Determine the profit, assuming a 10 percent decrease in enrollment (i.e., enrollment decreases to 18 students). What is the percentage change in profitability?

e. Explain why a 10 percent shift in enrollment produces more than a 10 percent shift in profitability. Use the term that identifies this phenomenon.

Part 2:

The instructor has offered to teach the course for a percentage of tuition fees. Specifically, she wants $360 per person attending the class. Assume that the tuition fee remains at $600 per student.

Required

f. Is the cost of instruction a fixed or a variable cost?

g. Determine the profit, assuming that 20 students take the course.

h. Determine the profit, assuming a 10 percent increase in enrollment (i.e., enrollment increases to 22 students). What is the percentage change in profitability?

i. Determine the profit, assuming a 10 percent decrease in enrollment (i.e., enrollment decreases to 18 students). What is the percentage change in profitability?

j. Explain why a 10 percent change in enrollment produces a proportional 10 percent change in profitability.

Part 3:

RTS sells a workbook with printed material unique to each course to each student who attends the course. Any workbooks that are not sold must be destroyed. Prior to the first class, RTS printed 20 copies of the books based on the client's estimate of the number of people who would attend the course. Each workbook costs $30 and is sold to course participants for $50. This cost includes a royalty fee paid to the author and the cost of duplication.

Required

k. Calculate the workbook cost in total and per student, assuming that 18, 20, or 22 students attempt to attend the course. Round your computation to 2 decimal points.

l. Classify the cost of workbooks as fixed or variable relative to the number of students attending the course.

m. Discuss the risk of holding inventory as it applies to the workbooks.

n. Explain how a just-in-time inventory system can reduce the cost and risk of holding inventory.

LO 11-2

Problem 11-26   *Effects of fixed and variable cost behavior on the risk and rewards of business opportunities*

Orlando and Diego Universities offer executive training courses to corporate clients. Orlando pays its instructors $4,600 per course taught. Diego pays its instructors $230 per student enrolled in the class. Both universities charge executives a $400 tuition fee per course attended.

Required

a. Prepare income statements for Orlando and Diego, assuming that 20 students attend a course.

b. Orlando University embarks on a strategy to entice students from Diego University by lowering its tuition to $220 per course. Prepare an income statement for Orlando assuming that the university is successful and enrolls 40 students in its course.

c. Diego University embarks on a strategy to entice students from Orlando University by lowering its tuition to $220 per course. Prepare an income statement for Diego, assuming that the university is successful and enrolls 40 students in its course.

d. Explain why the strategy described in Requirement *b* produced a profit but the same strategy described in Requirement *c* produced a loss.

e. Prepare income statements for Orlando and Diego Universities, assuming that 10 students attend a course, and assuming that both universities charge executives a $400 tuition fee per course attended.

f. It is always better to have fixed rather than variable cost. Explain why this statement is false.

g. It is always better to have variable rather than fixed cost. Explain why this statement is false.

Problem 11-27   *Analyzing operating leverage*

LO 11-4

Palvo Sorokin is a venture capitalist facing two alternative investment opportunities. He intends to invest $1 million in a start-up firm. He is nervous, however, about future economic volatility. He asks you to analyze the following financial data for the past year's operations of the two firms he is considering and give him some business advice.

	Company Name	
	Wood	Lake
Variable cost per unit (a)	$ 16.00	$ 8.00
Sales revenue (8,000 units × $25)	$200,000	$200,000
Variable cost (8,000 units × a)	(128,000)	(64,000)
Contribution margin	$ 72,000	$136,000
Fixed cost	(24,000)	(88,000)
Net income	$ 48,000	$ 48,000

Required

Round your figures to 2 decimal points in all required computation.

a. Use the contribution margin approach to compute the operating leverage for each firm.

b. If the economy expands in coming years, Wood and Lake will both enjoy a 10 percent per year increase in sales, assuming that the selling price remains unchanged. Compute the change in net income for each firm in *dollar amount* and in *percentage*. (*Note:* Since the number of units increases, both revenue and variable cost will increase.)

c. If the economy contracts in coming years, Wood and Lake will both suffer a 10 percent decrease in sales volume, assuming that the selling price remains unchanged. Compute the change in net income for each firm in *dollar amount* and in *percentage*. (*Note:* Since the number of units decreases, both total revenue and total variable cost will decrease.)

d. Write a memo to Palvo Sorokin with your analyses and advice.

CHECK FIGURES
b. % of change for Lake: 28.33
c. % of change for Wood: (15.00)

Problem 11-28   *Determining the break-even point and preparing a contribution margin income statement*

LO 11-3, 11-5

Lucent Manufacturing Company makes a product that it sells for $75 per unit. The company incurs variable manufacturing costs of $30 per unit. Variable selling expenses are $9 per unit, annual fixed manufacturing costs are $240,000, and fixed selling and administrative costs are $165,000 per year.

Required

Determine the break-even point in units and dollars using each of the following approaches:

a. Equation method.

b. Contribution margin per unit.

c. Confirm your results by preparing a contribution margin income statement for the break-even sales volume.

CHECK FIGURE
a. 11,250 units

Problem 11-29   *Margin of safety and operating leverage*

LO 11-4, 11-6

Carmon Company is considering the addition of a new product to its cosmetics line. The company has three distinctly different options: a skin cream, a bath oil, or a hair coloring gel.

432   Chapter 11

Relevant information and budgeted annual income statements for each of the products follow.

Relevant Information			
	Skin Cream	**Bath Oil**	**Color Gel**
Budgeted sales in units (a)	100,000	180,000	60,000
Expected sales price (b)	$7.00	$4.00	$10.00
Variable costs per unit (c)	$2.00	$1.00	$6.00
Income statements			
Sales revenue (a × b)	$ 700,000	$ 720,000	$ 600,000
Variable costs (a × c)	(200,000)	(180,000)	(360,000)
Contribution margin	500,000	540,000	240,000
Fixed costs	(420,000)	(480,000)	(100,000)
Net income	$ 80,000	$ 60,000	$ 140,000

Required

a. Determine the margin of safety as a percentage for each product. Round your figures to 2 decimal points.

b. Prepare revised income statements for each product, assuming a 20 percent increase in the budgeted sales volume.

c. For each product, determine the percentage change in net income that results from the 20 percent increase in sales. Which product has the highest operating leverage? Round your figures to 2 decimal points.

d. Assuming that management is pessimistic and risk averse, which product should the company add to its cosmetics line? Explain your answer.

e. Assuming that management is optimistic and risk aggressive, which product should the company add to its cosmetics line? Explain your answer.

ANALYZE, THINK, COMMUNICATE

ATC 11-1   Business Applications   *Operating leverage*

Description of Business for Merck & Co., Inc.

Merck & Co., Inc., is a global health care company that delivers innovative health solutions through its prescription medicines, vaccines, biologic therapies, animal health, and consumer care products, which it markets directly and through its joint ventures. The company's operations are principally managed on a products basis and are comprised of four operating segments, which are the Pharmaceutical, Animal Health, Consumer Care, and Alliances segments, and one reportable segment, which is the Pharmaceutical segment.

Merck & Company	2011	2010
Revenue	$48,047	$45,987
Operating earnings	7,334	1,653

Description of Business for Costco Wholesale Corporation

We at Costco Wholesale Corporation operate membership warehouses based on the concept that offering our members low prices on a limited selection of nationally branded and private-label products in a wide range of merchandise categories will produce high sales volumes and rapid inventory turnover. . . .

Because of our high sales volume and rapid inventory turnover, we generally sell inventory before we are required to pay many of our merchandise vendors, even though we take advantage of early payment discounts when available. To the extent that sales increase and inventory turnover becomes more rapid, a greater percentage of inventory is financed through payment terms provided by suppliers rather than by our working capital.

Costco Corporation	2011	2010
Revenue	$88,915	$77,946
Operating earnings	2,439	2,077

Required

a. Determine which company appears to have the higher operating leverage.

b. Write a paragraph or two explaining why the company you identified in Requirement *a* might be expected to have the higher operating leverage.

c. If revenues for both companies declined, which company do you think would likely experience the greater decline in operating earnings? Explain your answer.

ATC 11-2   Group Assignment   *Operating leverage*

The Parent Teacher Association (PTA) of Meadow High School is planning a fund-raising campaign. The PTA is considering the possibility of hiring Eric Logan, a world-renowned investment counselor, to address the public. Tickets would sell for $28 each. The school has agreed to let the PTA use Harville Auditorium at no cost. Mr. Logan is willing to accept one of two compensation arrangements. He will sign an agreement to receive a fixed fee of $10,000 regardless of the number of tickets sold. Alternatively, he will accept payment of $20 per ticket sold. In communities similar to that in which Meadow is located, Mr. Logan has drawn an audience of approximately 500 people.

Required

a. In front of the class, present a statement showing the expected net income assuming 500 people buy tickets.

b. The instructor will divide the class into groups and then organize the groups into four sections. The instructor will assign one of the following tasks to each section of groups.

Group Tasks

(1) Assume the PTA pays Mr. Logan a fixed fee of $10,000. Determine the amount of net income that the PTA will earn if ticket sales are 10 percent higher than expected. Calculate the percentage change in net income.

(2) Assume that the PTA pays Mr. Logan a fixed fee of $10,000. Determine the amount of net income that the PTA will earn if ticket sales are 10 percent lower than expected. Calculate the percentage change in net income.

(3) Assume that the PTA pays Mr. Logan $20 per ticket sold. Determine the amount of net income that the PTA will earn if ticket sales are 10 percent higher than expected. Calculate the percentage change in net income.

(4) Assume that the PTA pays Mr. Logan $20 per ticket sold. Determine the amount of net income that the PTA will earn if ticket sales are 10 percent lower than expected. Calculate the percentage change in net income.

c. Have each group select a spokesperson. Have one of the spokespersons in each section of groups go to the board and present the results of the analysis conducted in Requirement *b*. Resolve any discrepancies between the computations presented at the board and those developed by the other groups.

d. Draw conclusions regarding the risks and rewards associated with operating leverage. At a minimum, answer the following questions:

(1) Which type of cost structure (fixed or variable) produces the higher growth potential in profitability for a company?

(2) Which type of cost structure (fixed or variable) faces the higher risk of declining profitability for a company?

(3) Under what circumstances should a company seek to establish a fixed cost structure?

(4) Under what circumstances should a company seek to establish a variable cost structure?

ATC 11-3 Research Assignment *Fixed versus variable cost*

Use the 2011 Form 10-K for Black & Decker Corp. (B&D) (not Stanley Black & Decker) to complete the requirements below. To obtain the Form 10-K, you can use the EDGAR system (see Appendix A at the back of this text for instructions), or it can be found under "Investor Relations" on the company's corporate website at www.bdk.com. Be sure to read carefully the following portions of the document:

- "General Development of the Business" on pages 3–4.
- "Consolidated Statement of Operations" on page 65.

Required

a. Calculate the percentage increase in B&D's sales and its "earnings from continuing operations" from 2010 to 2011.

b. Would fixed costs or variable costs be more likely to explain why B&D's operating earnings increased by a bigger percentage than its sales?

c. On page 105, B&D reported that it incurred research and development costs of $147.2 million in 2011. If this cost is thought of in the context of the number of units of products sold, should it be considered as primarily fixed or variable in nature?

d. If the research and development costs are thought of in the context of the number of new products developed, should they be considered as primarily fixed or variable in nature?

ATC 11-4 Writing Assignment *Operating leverage, margin of safety, and cost behavior*

Early versions of cellular phones could do one thing—make and receive voice phone calls. Later versions were developed that could send and receive text messages, but due to their typing interface, performing this task was cumbersome. Then a company named Research in Motion (RIM) brought its BlackBerry phone to the market with an integrated keyboard that made typing text much easier. The BlackBerry became the phone of choice for users who wanted to send and receive e-mail messages via their cell phone, and its success soared.

Unfortunately for RIM, Apple Inc. began selling the iPhone to the world in June of 2007. The iPhone was not only capable of dealing with e-mail messages efficiently, but it also allowed users to search the Internet using a popular touchscreen interface. The popularity of RIM's BlackBerry began to decline. RIM's sales declined 14 percent in its 2012 fiscal year compared to its sales in 2011, but its operating earnings declined 32 percent.

Required

Write a memorandum that explains how a 14 percent decline in sales could cause a 32 percent decline in profits. Your memo should address the following:

a. An identification of the accounting concept involved.

b. A discussion of how various major types of costs incurred by RIM were likely affected by the decline in its sales.

c. The effect of the decline in sales on RIM's margin of safety.

ATC 11-5 Ethical Dilemma *Profitability versus social conscience (effects of cost behavior)*

Advances in biological technology have enabled two research companies, Bio Labs, Inc., and Scientific Associates, to develop an insect-resistant corn seed. Neither company is financially strong enough to develop the distribution channels necessary to bring the product to world markets. World Agra Distributors, Inc., has negotiated contracts with both companies for the exclusive right to market their seed. Bio Labs signed an agreement to receive an annual royalty of $1,000,000. In contrast, Scientific Associates chose an agreement that provides for a royalty of $0.50 per pound of seed sold. Both agreements have a 10-year term. During 2014, World Agra sold approximately 1,600,000 pounds of the Bio Labs, Inc., seed and 2,400,000 pounds of the Scientific Associates seed. Both types of seed were sold for $1.25 per pound. By the end of 2014, it was apparent that the seed developed by Scientific Associates was superior. Although insect infestation was virtually nonexistent for both types of seed, the seed developed by Scientific Associates produced corn that was sweeter and had consistently higher yields.

World Agra Distributors' chief financial officer, Roger Weatherstone, recently retired. To the astonishment of the annual planning committee, Mr. Weatherstone's replacement, Ray Borrough, adamantly recommended that the marketing department develop a major advertising campaign to promote the seed developed by Bio Labs, Inc. The planning committee reluctantly approved the recommendation. A $100,000 ad campaign was launched; the ads emphasized the ability of the Bio Labs seed to avoid insect infestation. The campaign was silent with respect to taste or crop yield. It did not mention the seed developed by Scientific Associates. World Agra's sales staff was instructed to push the Bio Labs seed and to sell the Scientific Associates seed only on customer demand. Although total sales remained relatively constant during 2015, sales of the Scientific Associates seed fell to approximately 1,300,000 pounds while sales of the Bio Labs, Inc., seed rose to 2,700,000 pounds.

Required

a. Determine the amount of increase or decrease in profitability experienced by World Agra in 2015 as a result of promoting the Bio Labs seed. Support your answer with appropriate commentary.

b. Did World Agra's customers in particular and society in general benefit or suffer from the decision to promote the Bio Labs seed?

c. Review the statement of ethical professional practice in Exhibit 10.17 of Chapter 10 and comment on whether Mr. Borrough's recommendation violated any of the standards in the code of ethical conduct.

d. Comment on your belief regarding the adequacy of the statement of ethical professional practice in terms of directing the conduct of management accountants.

CHAPTER 12

Cost Accumulation, Tracing, and Allocation

LEARNING OBJECTIVES

After you have mastered the material in this chapter, you will be able to:

LO 12-1   Identify cost objects and distinguish between direct costs versus indirect costs.

LO 12-2   Allocate indirect costs to cost objects.

LO 12-3   Identify the most appropriate cost driver.

LO 12-4   Recognize the effects of cost allocation on employee motivation.

 Video lectures and accompanying self-assessment quizzes are available for all learning objectives through McGraw-Hill Connect® Accounting.

CHAPTER OPENING

What does it cost? This is one of the questions most frequently asked by business managers. Managers must have reliable cost estimates to price products, evaluate performance, control operations, and prepare financial statements. As this discussion implies, managers need to know the cost of many different things. The things we are trying to determine the cost of are commonly called **cost objects.** For example, if we are trying to determine the cost of operating a department, that department is the cost object. Cost objects may be products, processes, departments, services, activities, and so on. This chapter explains techniques managerial accountants use to determine the cost of a variety of cost objects.

The Curious Accountant

A former patient of a California hospital complained about being charged $7 for a single aspirin tablet. After all, an entire bottle of 100 aspirins can be purchased at the local pharmacy store for around $2.

Can you think of any reasons, other than shameless profiteering, that a hospital would need to charge $7 for an aspirin? Remember that the hospital is not just selling the aspirin; it is also delivering it to the patient. (Answer on page 446.)

438   Chapter 12

DETERMINE THE COST OF COST OBJECTS

Accountants use **cost accumulation** to determine the cost of a particular object. Suppose the Atlanta Braves advertising manager wants to promote a Tuesday night ball game by offering free baseball caps to all children who attend. What would be the promotion cost? The team's accountant must *accumulate* many individual costs and add them together. For simplicity, consider only three cost components: (1) the cost of the caps, (2) the cost of advertising the promotion, and (3) the cost of an employee to work on the promotion.

Cost accumulation begins with identifying the cost objects. The primary cost object is the cost of the promotion. Three secondary cost objects are (1) the cost of caps, (2) the cost of advertising, and (3) the cost of labor. The costs of the secondary cost objects are combined to determine the cost of the primary cost object.

Determining the costs of the secondary cost objects requires identifying what *drives* those costs. A **cost driver** has a *cause-and-effect* relationship with a cost object. For example, the *number of caps* (cost driver) has an effect on the *cost of caps* (cost object). The *number of advertisements* is a cost driver for the *advertising cost* (cost object); the *number of labor hours* worked is a cost driver for the *labor cost* (cost object). Using the following assumptions about unit costs and cost drivers, the accumulated cost of the primary cost object (cost of the cap promotion) is:

Cost Object	Cost per Unit	×	Cost Driver	=	Total Cost of Object
Cost of caps	$ 2.50	×	4,000 Caps	=	$10,000
Cost of advertising	$100.00	×	50 Advertisements	=	5,000
Cost of labor	$ 8.00	×	100 Hours	=	800
Cost of cap promotion					$15,800

The Atlanta Braves should run the promotion if management expects it to produce additional revenues exceeding $15,800.

Estimated versus Actual Cost

The accumulated cost of the promotion—$15,800—is an *estimate*. Management cannot know *actual* costs and revenues until after running the promotion. While actual information is more accurate, it is not relevant for deciding whether to run the promotion because the decision must be made before the actual cost is known. Managers must accept a degree of inaccuracy in exchange for the relevance of timely information. Many business decisions are based on estimated rather than actual costs.

Managers use cost estimates to set prices, bid on contracts, evaluate proposals, distribute resources, plan production, and set goals. Certain circumstances, however, require actual cost data. For example, published financial reports and managerial performance evaluations use actual cost data. Managers frequently accumulate both estimated and actual cost data for the same cost object. For example, companies use cost estimates to establish goals and use actual costs to evaluate management performance in meeting those goals. The following discussion provides a number of business examples that use estimated data, actual data, or a combination of both.

Assignment of Costs to Objects in a Retail Business

Exhibit 12.1 displays the January income statement for In Style, Inc. (ISI), a retail clothing store. ISI subdivides its operations into women's, men's, and children's departments. To encourage the departmental managers to maximize sales, ISI began

paying the manager of each department a bonus based on a percentage of department sales revenue.

Although the bonus incentive increased sales revenue, it also provoked negative consequences. The departmental managers began to argue over floor space; each manager wanted more space to display merchandise. The managers reduced prices; they increased sales commissions. In the drive to maximize sales, the managers ignored the need to control costs. To improve the situation, the store manager decided to base future bonuses on each department's contribution to profitability rather than its sales revenue.

Identifying Direct and Indirect Costs

The new bonus strategy requires determining the cost of operating each department. Each department is a separate *cost object.* Assigning costs to the departments (cost objects) requires **cost tracing** and **cost allocation.** *Direct costs* can be easily traced to a cost object. **Indirect costs** cannot be easily traced to a cost object. Whether or not a cost is easily traceable requires *cost/benefit analysis.*

Some of ISI's costs can be easily traced to the cost objects (specific departments). The cost of goods sold is an example of an easily traced cost. Price tags on merchandise can be coded so cash register scanners capture the departmental code for each sale. The cost of goods sold is not only easily traceable but also very useful information. Companies need cost of goods sold information for financial reporting (income statement and balance sheet) and for management decisions (determining inventory reorder points, pricing strategies, and cost control). Because the cost of tracing *cost of goods sold* is small relative to the benefits obtained, cost of goods sold is a *direct cost.*

In contrast, the cost of supplies (shopping bags, sales slips, pens, staples, price tags) used by each department is much more difficult to trace. How could the number of staples used to seal shopping bags be traced to any particular department? The sales staff could count the number of staples used, but doing so would be silly for the benefits obtained. Although tracing the cost of supplies to each department may be possible, it is not worth the effort of doing so. The cost of supplies is therefore an *indirect cost.* Indirect costs are also called **overhead costs.**

Direct and indirect costs can be described as follows:

EXHIBIT 12.1
Income Statement

IN STYLE, INC.
Income Statement
For the Month Ended January 31

Sales	$360,000
Cost of goods sold	(216,000)
Gross margin	144,000
Sales commissions	(18,000)
Dept. managers' salaries	(12,000)
Store manager's salary	(9,360)
Depreciation	(16,000)
Rental fee for store	(18,400)
Utilities	(2,300)
Advertising	(7,200)
Supplies	(900)
Net income	$ 59,840

> **Direct costs** can be traced to cost objects in a *cost-effective* manner.
> **Indirect costs** cannot be traced to objects in a *cost-effective* manner.

By analyzing the accounting records, ISI's accountant classified the costs from the income statement in Exhibit 12.1 as direct or indirect, as shown in Exhibit 12.2. The next paragraph explains the classifications.

All figures represent January costs. Items 1 though 4 are direct costs, traceable to the cost objects in a cost-effective manner. Cost of goods sold is traced to departments at the point of sale using cash register scanners. Sales commissions are based on a percentage of departmental sales and are therefore easy to trace to the departments. Departmental managers' salaries are also easily traceable to the departments. Equipment, furniture, and fixtures are tagged with department codes that permit tracing depreciation charges directly to specific departments. Items 5 through 8 are incurred on behalf of the company as a whole and are therefore not directly traceable to a specific department.

EXHIBIT 12.2

Income Statement Classification of Costs

Cost Item	Direct Costs			Indirect Costs
	Women's	Men's	Children's	
1. Cost of goods sold—$216,000	$120,000	$58,000	$38,000	
2. Sales commissions—$18,000	9,500	5,500	3,000	
3. Dept. managers' salaries—$12,000	5,000	4,200	2,800	
4. Depreciation—$16,000	7,000	5,000	4,000	
5. Store manager's salary				$ 9,360
6. Rental fee for store				18,400
7. Utilities				2,300
8. Advertising				7,200
9. Supplies				900
Totals	$141,500	$72,700	$47,800	$38,160

Although Item 9 could be traced to specific departments, the cost of doing so would exceed the benefits. The cost of supplies is therefore also classified as indirect.

Cost Classifications—Independent and Context Sensitive

Whether a cost is direct or indirect is independent of whether it is fixed or variable. In the ISI example, both cost of goods sold and the cost of supplies vary relative to sales volume (both are variable costs), but cost of goods sold is direct and the cost of supplies is indirect. Furthermore, the cost of rent and the cost of depreciation are both fixed relative to sales volume, but the cost of rent is indirect and the cost of depreciation is direct. In fact, the very same cost can be classified as direct or indirect, depending on the cost object. The store manager's salary is not directly traceable to a specific department, but it is traceable to a particular store. As these examples demonstrate, cost classification depends on the context in which the costs occur.

ALLOCATING INDIRECT COSTS TO OBJECTS

LO 12-2

Allocate indirect costs to cost objects.

Common costs support multiple cost objects but cannot be directly traced to any specific object. In the case of In Style, Inc., the cost of renting the store (common cost) supports the women's, men's, and children's departments (cost objects). The departmental managers may shirk responsibility for the rental cost by claiming that others higher up the chain of command are responsible. Responsibility can be motivated at the departmental level by assigning (*allocating*) a portion of the total rental cost to each department.

To accomplish appropriate motivation, authority must accompany responsibility. In other words, the departmental managers should be held responsible for a portion of rental cost only if they are able to exercise some degree of control over that cost. For example, if managers are assigned a certain amount of the rental cost for each square foot of space they use, they should have the authority to establish the size of the space used by their departments. **Controllable costs** are costs that can be influenced by a manager's decisions and actions. The controllability concept is discussed in more detail in a later chapter.

Cost **allocation** involves dividing a total cost into parts and assigning the parts to designated cost objects. How should ISI allocate the $38,160 of indirect costs to each of the three departments? First, identify a cost driver for each cost to be allocated. For example, there is a cause-and-effect relationship between store size and rent cost;

REALITY BYTES

How does Southwest Airlines know the cost of flying a passenger from Houston, Texas, to Los Angeles, California? The fact is that Southwest does not know the actual cost of flying particular passengers anywhere. There are many indirect costs associated with flying passengers. Some of these include the cost of planes, fuel, pilots, office buildings, and ground personnel. Indeed, besides insignificant food and beverage costs, there are few costs that could be traced directly to customers. Southwest and other airlines are forced to use allocation and averaging to determine the estimated cost of providing transportation services to customers. Estimated rather than actual cost is used for decision-making purposes.

Consider that in its 2011 annual report Southwest reported the average operating expenses of flying one passenger one mile (called a *passenger mile*) were 12.4¢. However, this number was based on 120.6 billion "available passenger miles." In 2011, Southwest operated at 80.9 percent of capacity, not 100 percent, so it was only able to charge passengers for 97.6 billion passenger miles. Thus, its average operating expenses were closer to 15.3¢ for each mile for which it was able to charge. Had it operated at a higher capacity, its average costs would have been lower.

the larger the building, the higher the rent cost. This relationship suggests that the more floor space a department occupies, the more rent cost that department should bear. To illustrate, assume ISI's store capacity is 23,000 square feet and the women's, men's, and children's departments occupy 12,000, 7,000, and 4,000 square feet, respectively. ISI can achieve a rational allocation of the rent cost using the following two-step process.[1]

Step 1. Compute the *allocation rate* by dividing the *total cost to be allocated* ($18,400 rental fee) by the *cost driver* (23,000 square feet of store space). *The cost driver is also called the* **allocation base.** This computation produces the **allocation rate,** as follows:

Total cost to be allocated	÷	Cost driver (allocation base)	=	Allocation rate
$18,400 rental fee	÷	23,000 square feet	=	$0.80 per square foot

Step 2. Multiply the *allocation rate* by the *weight of the cost driver* (weight of the base) to determine the allocation *per cost object,* as follows:

Cost Object	Allocation Rate	×	Number of Square Feet	=	Allocation per Cost Object
Women's department	$0.80	×	12,000	=	$ 9,600
Men's department	0.80	×	7,000	=	5,600
Children's department	0.80	×	4,000	=	3,200
Total			23,000		$18,400

It is also plausible to presume utilities cost is related to the amount of floor space a department occupies. Larger departments will consume more heating, lighting, air

---

[1]Other mathematical approaches achieve the same result. This text consistently uses the two-step method described here. Specifically, the text determines allocations by (1) computing a *rate* and (2) multiplying the *rate* by the *weight of the base* (cost driver).

conditioning, and so on than smaller departments. Floor space is a reasonable cost driver for utility cost. Based on square footage, ISI can allocate utility cost to each department as follows:

Step 1.   Compute the allocation rate by dividing the total cost to be allocated ($2,300 utility cost) by the cost driver (23,000 square feet of store space):

Total cost to be allocated ÷   Cost driver   =   Allocation rate

$2,300 utility cost   ÷ 23,000 square feet = $0.10 per square foot

Step 2.   Multiply the *allocation rate* by the *weight of the cost driver* to determine the allocation *per cost object:*

Cost Object	Allocation Rate	×	Number of Square Feet	=	Allocation per Cost Object
Women's department	$0.10	×	12,000	=	$1,200
Men's department	0.10	×	7,000	=	700
Children's department	0.10	×	4,000	=	400
Total			23,000		$2,300

☑ CHECK YOURSELF 12.1

HealthCare, Inc., wants to estimate the cost of operating the three departments (Dermatology, Gynecology, and Pediatrics) that serve patients in its Health Center. Each department performed the following number of patient treatments during the most recent year of operation: Dermatology, 2,600; Gynecology, 3,500; and Pediatrics, 6,200. The annual salary of the Health Center's program administrator is $172,200. How much of the salary cost should HealthCare allocate to the Pediatrics Department?

Answer

Step 1   Compute the *allocation rate.*

Total cost to be allocated ÷ Cost driver (patient treatments) =   Allocation rate

$172,200 salary cost   ÷   (2,600 + 3,500 + 6,200)   = $14 per patient treatment

Step 2   Multiply the *allocation rate* by the *weight of the cost driver* (weight of the base) to determine the allocation per *cost object.*

Cost Object	Allocation Rate	×	No. of Treatments	=	Allocation per Cost Object
Pediatrics department	$14	×	6,200	=	$86,800

Determining the Cost to Be Allocated Using Cost Pools

Allocating *individually* every single indirect cost a company incurs would be tedious and not particularly useful relative to the benefit obtained. Instead, companies frequently accumulate many individual costs into a single **cost pool.** The total of the pooled cost is then allocated to the cost objects. For example, a company may accumulate costs for gas, water, electricity, and telephone service into a single utilities cost pool. It would then allocate the total cost in the utilities cost pool to the cost objects rather than individually allocating each of the four types of utility costs.

How far should pooling costs go? Why not pool utility costs with indirect labor costs? If the forces driving the utility costs are different from the forces driving the labor costs, pooling the costs will likely reduce the reliability of any associated cost allocations. To promote accuracy, pooling should be limited to costs with common cost drivers.

Costs that have been pooled for one purpose may require disaggregation for a different purpose. Suppose all overhead costs are pooled for the purpose of determining the cost of making a product. Further, suppose that making the product requires two processes that are performed in different departments. A cutting department makes heavy use of machinery to cut raw materials into product parts. An assembly department uses human labor to assemble the parts into a finished product. Now suppose the objective changes from determining the cost of making the product to determining the cost of operating each department. Under these circumstances, it may be necessary to disaggregate the total overhead cost into smaller pools such as a utility cost pool, an indirect labor cost pool, and so on so that different drivers can be used to allocate these costs to the two departments.

SELECTING THE COST DRIVER

Companies can frequently identify more than one cost driver for a particular indirect cost. For example, ISI's cost of shopping bags provided to customers can be linked to both the number of sales transactions and the total amount of sales. More specifically, since the store normally uses at least one shopping bag each time a sales transaction occurs, the number of sales transactions drives the cost of shopping bags. Likewise, a $500 sales transaction is likely to require the company to provide more shopping bags to a customer than would a $100 sales transaction. Therefore, the total amount of sales also drives the use of shopping bags. Given this scenario, should ISI use the *number of sales transactions* or the *total amount of sales* as the driver of the cost of shopping bags? The answer is, ISI should use the driver with the strongest cause-and-effect relationship.

LO 12-3

Identify the most appropriate cost driver.

Cause and Effect versus Availability of Information

To illustrate, consider shopping bag usage for T-shirts sold in the children's department versus T-shirts sold in the men's department. Assume ISI studied T-shirt sales during the first week of June and found the following:

Department	Children's	Men's
Number of sales transactions	120	92
Amount of total sales	$1,440	$1,612

Given that every sales transaction uses a shopping bag, the children's department uses far more shopping bags than the men's department (120 versus 92) even though it has a lower amount of total sales ($1,440 versus $1,612). A reasonable explanation for this circumstance is that children's T-shirts sell for less than men's T-shirts. The number of sales transactions is the better cost driver because it has a stronger cause-and-effect relationship with shopping bag usage than does the amount of sales. Should ISI therefore use the number of sales transactions to allocate supply cost to the departments? Not necessarily.

The *availability of information* also influences cost driver selection. While the number of sales transactions is the more accurate cost driver, ISI could not use this allocation base unless it maintains records of the number of sales transactions per department. If the store tracks the amount of sales but not the number of transactions, it must use the amount of sales even if the number of transactions is the better cost driver. For ISI, total sales appears to be the best *available* cost driver for allocating supply cost.

Assuming that total sales for the women's, men's, and children's departments was $190,000, $110,000, and $60,000, respectively, ISI can allocate the supplies cost as follows:

Step 1. Compute the allocation rate by dividing the total cost to be allocated ($900 supplies cost) by the cost driver ($360,000 total sales):

Total cost to be allocated ÷ Cost driver = Allocation rate

$900 supplies cost ÷ $360,000 total sales = $0.0025 per sales dollar

Step 2. Multiply the allocation rate by the weight of the cost driver to determine the allocation per cost object:

Cost Object	Allocation Rate	×	Total Sales	=	Allocation per Cost Object
Women's department	$0.0025	×	$190,000	=	$475
Men's department	0.0025	×	110,000	=	275
Children's department	0.0025	×	60,000	=	150
Total			$360,000		$900

ISI believes the amount of sales is also the appropriate allocation base for advertising cost. The sales generated in each department were likely influenced by the general advertising campaign. ISI can allocate advertising cost as follows:

Step 1. Compute the allocation rate by dividing the total cost to be allocated ($7,200 advertising cost) by the cost driver ($360,000 total sales):

Total cost to be allocated ÷ Cost driver = Allocation rate

$7,200 advertising cost ÷ $360,000 total sales = $0.02 per sales dollar

Step 2. Multiply the allocation rate by the weight of the cost driver to determine the allocation per cost object:

Cost Object	Allocation Rate	×	Total Sales	=	Allocation per Cost Object
Women's department	$0.02	×	$190,000	=	$3,800
Men's department	0.02	×	110,000	=	2,200
Children's department	0.02	×	60,000	=	1,200
Total			$360,000		$7,200

There is no strong cause-and-effect relationship between the store manager's salary and the departments. ISI pays the store manager the same salary regardless of sales level, square footage of store space, number of labor hours, or any other identifiable variable. Because no plausible cost driver exists, ISI must allocate the store manager's salary arbitrarily. Here the manager's salary is simply divided equally among the departments as follows:

Step 1. Compute the allocation rate by dividing the total cost to be allocated ($9,360 manager's monthly salary) by the allocation base (number of departments):

Total cost to be allocated ÷ Cost driver = Allocation rate

$9,360 store manager's salary ÷ 3 departments = $3,120 per department

Step 2. Multiply the allocation rate by the weight of the cost driver to determine the allocation per cost object:

Cost Object	Allocation Rate	×	Number of Departments	=	Allocation per Cost Object
Women's department	$3,120	×	1	=	$3,120
Men's department	3,120	×	1	=	3,120
Children's department	3,120	×	1	=	3,120
Total			3		$9,360

As the allocation of the store manager's salary demonstrates, many allocations are arbitrary or based on a weak relationship between the allocated cost and the allocation base (cost driver). Managers must use care when making decisions using allocated costs.

Behavioral Implications

Using the indirect cost allocations just discussed, Exhibit 12.3 shows the profit each department generated in January. ISI paid the three departmental managers bonuses based on each department's contribution to profitability. The store manager noticed an immediate change in the behavior of the departmental managers. For example, the manager of the women's department offered to give up 1,000 square feet of floor space because she believed reducing the selection of available products would not reduce sales significantly. Customers would simply buy different brands. Although sales would not decline dramatically, rent and utility cost allocations to the women's department would decline, increasing the profitability of the department.

In contrast, the manager of the children's department wanted the extra space. He believed the children's department was losing sales because it did not have enough floor space to display a competitive variety of merchandise. Customers came to the store to shop at the women's department, but they did not come specifically for children's wear. With additional space, the children's department could carry items that would draw customers to the store specifically to buy children's clothing. He believed the extra space would increase sales enough to cover the additional rent and utility cost allocations.

EXHIBIT 12.3

Profit Analysis by Department

	Women's	Men's	Children's	Total
		Department		
Sales	$190,000	$110,000	$60,000	$360,000
Cost of goods sold	(120,000)	(58,000)	(38,000)	(216,000)
Sales commissions	(9,500)	(5,500)	(3,000)	(18,000)
Dept. managers' salary	(5,000)	(4,200)	(2,800)	(12,000)
Depreciation	(7,000)	(5,000)	(4,000)	(16,000)
Store manager's salary	(3,120)	(3,120)	(3,120)	(9,360)
Rental fee for store	(9,600)	(5,600)	(3,200)	(18,400)
Utilities	(1,200)	(700)	(400)	(2,300)
Advertising	(3,800)	(2,200)	(1,200)	(7,200)
Supplies	(475)	(275)	(150)	(900)
Departmental profit	$ 30,305	$ 25,405	$ 4,130	$ 59,840

Answers to The Curious Accountant

When we compare the cost that a hospital charges for an aspirin to the price we pay for an aspirin, we are probably not considering the full cost that we incur to purchase aspirin. If someone were to ask you what you pay for an aspirin, you would probably take the price of a bottle, say $2, and divide it by the number of pills in the bottle, say 100. This would suggest their cost is $0.02 each. Now, consider what it costs to buy an aspirin when all costs are considered. First, there is your time to drive to the store; what do you get paid per hour? Then, there is the cost of operating your automobile. You get the idea; in reality, the cost of an aspirin, from a business perspective, is much more than just the cost of the pill itself.

The exhibit below shows the income statement of Hospital Corporation of America (HCA) for three recent years. HCA claims to be ". . . one of the leading health care services companies in the United States." In 2011, it operated 271 facilities in 20 states and England. As you can see, while it generated over $32.5 billion in revenue, it also incurred a lot of expenses. Look at its first two expense categories. Although it incurred $5.2 billion in supplies expenses, it incurred almost two and a half times this amount in compensation expense. In other words, it costs a lot more to have someone deliver the aspirin to your bed than the aspirin itself costs.

In 2011, HCA earned $2.5 billion from its $32.5 billion in revenues. This is a return on sales percentage of 7.6 percent ($2,465 ÷ $32,506). Therefore, on a $7 aspirin, HCA would earn 53 cents of profit, which is still not a bad profit for selling one aspirin. As a comparison, in 2011, Walgreens' return on sales was 3.8 percent.

HCA, INC.
Consolidated Income Statements
For the Years Ended December 31, 2011, 2010, and 2009
(Dollars in millions)

	2011	2010	2009
Revenues before the provision for doubtful accounts	$32,506	$30,683	$30,052
Provision for doubtful accounts	2,824	2,648	3,276
Revenues	29,682	28,035	26,776
Salaries and benefits	13,440	12,484	11,958
Supplies	5,179	4,961	4,868
Other operating expenses	5,470	5,004	4,724
Electronic health record incentive income	(210)		
Equity in earnings of affiliates	(258)	(282)	(246)
Depreciation and amortization	1,465	1,421	1,425
Interest expense	2,037	2,097	1,987
Losses (gains) on sales of facilities	(142)	(4)	15
Gain on acquisition of controlling interest in equity investment	(1,522)		
Impairments of long-lived assets		123	43
Losses on retirement of debt	481		
Termination of management agreement	181		
Total expenses	26,121	25,804	24,774
Income before income taxes	3,561	2,231	2,002
Provision for income taxes	719	658	627
Net income	2,842	1,573	1,375
Net income attributable to noncontrolling interests	377	366	321
Net income attributable to HCA Holdings, Inc.	$ 2,465	$ 1,207	$ 1,054

The store manager was pleased with the emphasis on profitability that resulted from tracing and assigning costs to specific departments.

Cost Drivers for Variable Overhead Costs

A *causal relationship* exists between variable overhead product costs (indirect materials, indirect labor, inspection costs, utilities, etc.) and the volume of production. For example, the cost of indirect materials such as glue, staples, screws, nails, and varnish will increase or decrease in proportion to the number of desks a furniture manufacturing company makes. *Volume measures are good cost drivers* for allocating variable overhead costs.

Volume can be expressed by such measures as the number of units produced, the number of labor hours worked, or the amount of *direct* materials used in production. Given the variety of possible volume measures, how does management identify the most appropriate cost driver (allocation base) for assigning particular overhead costs? Consider the case of Filmier Furniture Company.

Using Units as the Cost Driver

During the most recent year, Filmier Furniture Company produced 4,000 chairs and 1,000 desks. It incurred $60,000 of *indirect materials* cost during the period. How much of this cost should Filmier allocate to chairs versus desks? Using number of units as the cost driver produces the following allocation:

Step 1. Compute the allocation rate.

Total cost to be allocated ÷ Cost driver = Allocation rate

$60,000 indirect materials cost ÷ 5,000 units = $12 per unit

Step 2. Multiply the allocation rate by the weight of the cost driver to determine the allocation per cost object.

Product	Allocation Rate	×	Number of Units Produced	=	Allocated Cost
Desks	$12	×	1,000	=	$12,000
Chairs	12	×	4,000	=	48,000
Total			5,000	=	$60,000

Using Direct Labor Hours as the Cost Driver

Using the number of units as the cost driver assigns an *equal amount* ($12) of indirect materials cost to each piece of furniture. However, if Filmier uses more indirect materials to make a desk than to make a chair, assigning the same amount of indirect materials cost to each is inaccurate. Assume Filmier incurs the following direct costs to make chairs and desks:

	Desks	Chairs	Total
Direct labor hours	3,500 hrs.	2,500 hrs.	6,000 hrs.
Direct materials cost	$1,000,000	$500,000	$1,500,000

Both direct labor hours and direct materials cost are volume measures that indicate Filmier uses more indirect materials to make a desk than a chair. It makes sense that the amount of direct labor used is related to the amount of indirect materials used. Because production workers use materials to make furniture, it is plausible to assume that the more hours they work, the more materials they use. Using this reasoning, Filmier could assign the indirect materials cost to the chairs and desks as follows:

Step 1. Compute the allocation rate.

Total cost to be allocated   ÷ Cost driver = Allocation rate

$60,000 indirect materials cost ÷ 6,000 hours = $10 per hour

Step 2. Multiply the allocation rate by the weight of the cost driver.

Product	Allocation Rate	×	Number of Labor Hours	=	Allocated Cost
Desks	$10.00	×	3,500	=	$35,000
Chairs	10.00	×	2,500	=	25,000
Total			6,000	=	$60,000

Basing the allocation on labor hours rather than number of units assigns a significantly larger portion of the indirect materials cost to desks ($35,000 versus $12,000). Is this allocation more accurate? Suppose the desks, but not the chairs, require elaborate, labor-intensive carvings. A significant portion of the labor is then not related to consuming indirect materials (glue, staples, screws, nails, and varnish). It would therefore be inappropriate to allocate the indirect materials cost based on direct labor hours.

Using Direct Material Dollars as the Cost Driver

If labor hours is an inappropriate allocation base, Filmier can consider direct materials usage, measured in material dollars, as the allocation base. It is likely that the more lumber (direct material) Filmier uses, the more glue, nails, and so forth (indirect materials) it uses. It is reasonable to presume direct materials usage drives indirect materials usage. Using direct materials dollars as the cost driver for indirect materials produces the following allocation:

Step 1. Compute the allocation rate.

Total cost to be allocated ÷   Cost driver   = Allocation rate

$$\frac{\$60,000 \text{ indirect}}{\text{materials cost}} \div \frac{\$1,500,000 \text{ direct}}{\text{material dollars}} = \frac{\$0.04 \text{ per direct}}{\text{material dollar}}$$

Step 2. Multiply the allocation rate by the weight of the cost driver.

Product	Allocation Rate	×	Number of Direct Material Dollars	=	Allocated Cost
Desks	$0.04	×	$1,000,000	=	$40,000
Chairs	0.04	×	500,000	=	20,000
Total			$1,500,000	=	$60,000

Selecting the Best Cost Driver

Which of the three volume-based cost drivers (units, labor hours, or direct material dollars) results in the most accurate allocation of the overhead cost? Management must use judgment to decide. In this case, direct material dollars appears to have the most convincing relationship to indirect materials usage. If the cost Filmier was allocating were fringe benefits, however, direct labor hours would be a more appropriate cost driver. If the cost Filmier was allocating were machine maintenance cost, a different volume-based cost driver, machine hours, would be an appropriate base. The most accurate allocations of indirect costs may actually require using multiple cost drivers.

☑ CHECK YOURSELF 12.2

Boston Boat Company builds custom sailboats for customers. During the current accounting period, the company built five different-sized boats that ranged in cost from $35,000 to $185,000. The company's manufacturing overhead cost for the period was $118,000. Would you recommend using the number of units (boats) or direct labor hours as the base for allocating the overhead cost to the five boats? Why?

Answer Using the number of units as the allocation base would assign the same amount of overhead cost to each boat. Since larger boats require more overhead cost (supplies, utilities, equipment, etc.) than smaller boats, there is no logical link between the number of boats and the amount of overhead cost required to build a particular boat. In contrast, there is a logical link between direct labor hours used and overhead cost incurred. The more labor used, the more supplies, utilities, equipment, and so on used. Since larger boats require more direct labor than smaller boats, using direct labor hours as the allocation base would allocate more overhead cost to larger boats and less overhead cost to smaller boats, producing a logical overhead allocation. Therefore, Boston should use direct labor hours as the allocation base.

Cost Drivers for Fixed Overhead Costs

Fixed costs present a different cost allocation problem. By definition, the volume of production does not drive fixed costs. Suppose Lednicky Bottling Company rents its manufacturing facility for $28,000 per year. The rental cost is fixed regardless of how much product Lednicky bottles. However, Lednicky may still use a volume-based cost driver as the allocation base. The object of allocating fixed costs to products is to distribute a *rational share* of the overhead cost to each product. Selecting an allocation base that spreads total overhead cost equally over total production often produces a rational distribution. For example, assume Lednicky produced 2,000,000 bottles of apple juice during the current accounting period. If it sold 1,800,000 bottles of the juice during this period, how much of the $28,000 rental cost should Lednicky allocate to ending inventory and to cost of goods sold? A rational allocation follows:

Step 1. Compute the allocation rate.

Total cost to be allocated ÷ Allocation base (cost driver) = Allocation rate

$28,000 rental cost ÷ 2,000,000 units = $0.014 per bottle of juice

Because the base (number of units) used to allocate the cost does not drive the cost, it is sometimes called an *allocation base* instead of a *cost driver*. However, many managers use the term cost driver in conjunction with fixed cost even though that usage is technically inaccurate. The terms allocation base and cost driver are frequently used interchangeably.

Step 2. Multiply the allocation rate by the weight of the cost driver.

Financial Statement Item	Allocation Rate	×	Number of Bottles	=	Allocated Cost
Inventory	$0.014	×	200,000	=	$ 2,800
Cost of goods sold	0.014	×	1,800,000	=	25,200

Using number of units as the allocation base assigns equal amounts of the rental cost to each unit of product. Equal allocation is appropriate so long as the units are homogeneous. If the units are not identical, however, Lednicky may need to choose a different allocation base to rationally distribute the rental cost. For example, if some of the bottles are significantly larger than others, Lednicky may find using some physical measure, like liters of direct material used, to be a more appropriate allocation base. Whether an indirect cost is fixed or variable, selecting the most appropriate allocation base requires sound reasoning and judgment.

Allocating Fixed Costs When the Volume of Production Varies

Under certain circumstances products may be made before or after the costs associated with making them have been incurred. Suppose, for example, premiums for an annual insurance policy are paid in March. The insurance cost benefits the products made in the months before and after March as well as those produced in March. Allocation can be used to spread the insurance cost over products made during the entire accounting period rather than charging the total cost only to products made in March.

Monthly fluctuations in production volume complicate fixed cost allocations. To illustrate, assume Grave Manufacturing pays its production supervisor a monthly salary of $3,000. Furthermore, assume Grave makes 800 units of product in January and 1,875 in February. How much salary cost should Grave assign to the products made in January and February, respectively? The allocation seems simple. Just divide the $3,000 monthly salary cost by the number of units of product made each month as follows:

January $3,000 ÷ 800 units = $3.75 cost per unit

February $3,000 ÷ 1,875 units = $1.60 cost per unit

If Grave Manufacturing based a cost-plus pricing decision on these results, it would price products made in January significantly higher than products made in February. It is likely such price fluctuations would puzzle and drive away customers. Grave needs an allocation base that will spread the annual salary cost evenly over annual production. A timing problem exists, however, because Grave must allocate the salary cost before the end of the year. In order to price its products, Grave needs to know the allocated amount before the actual cost information is available. Grave can manage the timing problem by using estimated rather than actual costs.

Grave Manufacturing can *estimate* the annual cost of the supervisor's salary (indirect labor) as $36,000 ($3,000 × 12 months). The *actual* cost of indirect labor may differ because the supervisor might receive a pay raise or be replaced with a person who earns less. Based on current information, however, $36,000 is a reasonable estimate of the annual indirect labor cost. Grave must also estimate total annual production volume. Suppose Grave produced 18,000 units last year and expects no significant change in the current year. It can allocate indirect labor cost for January and February as follows:

Step 1.   Compute the allocation rate.

Total cost to be allocated ÷ Allocation base = Allocation rate
(cost driver)

$36,000   ÷   18,000 units   = $2.00 per unit

Step 2.   Multiply the rate by the weight of the base (number of units per month) to determine how much of the salary cost to allocate to each month's production.

Month	Allocation Rate	×	Number of Units Produced	=	Allocation per Month
January	$2.00	×	800	=	$1,600
February	2.00	×	1,875	=	3,750

Grave Manufacturing will add these indirect cost allocations to other product costs to determine the total estimated product cost to use in cost-plus pricing or other managerial decisions.

Because the overhead allocation rate is determined *before* actual cost and volume data are available, it is called the **predetermined overhead rate.** Companies use predetermined overhead rates for product costing estimates and pricing decisions during a year, but they must use actual costs in published year-end financial statements. If necessary, companies adjust their accounting records at year-end when they have used estimated data on an interim basis.

THE HUMAN FACTOR: A COMPREHENSIVE EXAMPLE

Cost allocations significantly affect individuals. They may influence managers' performance evaluations and compensation. They may dictate the amount of resources various departments, divisions, and other organizational subunits receive. Control over resources usually offers managers prestige and influence over organization operations. The following scenario illustrates the emotional impact and perceptions of fairness of cost allocation decisions.

LO 12-4

Recognize the effects of cost allocation on employee motivation.

Using Cost Allocations in a Budgeting Decision

Sharon Southport, dean of the School of Business at a major state university, is in dire need of a budgeting plan. Because of cuts in state funding, the money available to the School of Business for copying costs next year will be reduced substantially. Dean Southport supervises four departments: management, marketing, finance, and accounting. The dean knows the individual department chairpersons will be unhappy and frustrated with the deep cuts they face.

Using Cost Drivers to Make Allocations

To address the allocation of copying resources, Dean Southport decided to meet with the department chairs. She explained that the total budgeted for copying costs will be $36,000. Based on past usage, department allocations would be as follows: $12,000 for management, $10,000 for accounting, $8,000 for finance, and $6,000 for marketing.

Dr. Bill Thompson, the management department chair, immediately protested that his department could not operate on a $12,000 budget for copy costs. Management has more faculty members than any other department. Dr. Thompson argued that copy costs are directly related to the number of faculty members, so copy funds should be allocated based on the number of faculty members. Dr. Thompson suggested that number of faculty members rather than past usage should be used as the allocation base.

Since the School of Business has 72 faculty members (29 in management, 16 in accounting, 12 in finance, and 15 in marketing), the allocation should be as follows:

Step 1.   Compute the allocation rate.

Total cost to be allocated ÷ Cost driver =   Allocation rate

$36,000   ÷   72   = $500 per faculty member

Step 2.   Multiply the rate by the weight of the driver (the number of faculty per department) to determine the allocation per object (department).

Department	Allocation Rate	×	Number of Faculty	=	Allocation per Department	Allocation Based on Past Usage
Management	$500	×	29		$14,500	$12,000
Accounting	500	×	16		8,000	10,000
Finance	500	×	12		6,000	8,000
Marketing	500	×	15		7,500	6,000
Total					$36,000	$36,000

Seeing these figures, Dr. Bob Smethers, chair of the accounting department, questioned the accuracy of using the number of faculty members as the cost driver. Dr. Smethers suggested the number of *students* rather than the number of *faculty members* drives the cost of copying. He argued that most copying results from duplicating syllabi, exams, and handouts. The accounting department teaches mass sections of introductory accounting that have extremely high student/teacher ratios. Because his department teaches more students, it spends more on copying costs even though it has fewer faculty members. Dr. Smethers recomputed the copy cost allocation as follows:

Step 1. Compute the allocation rate based on number of students. University records indicate that the School of Business taught 1,200 students during the most recent academic year. The allocation rate (copy cost per student) follows.

Total cost to be allocated ÷ Cost driver = Allocation rate

$36,000   ÷   1,200   = $30 per student

Step 2. Multiply the rate by the weight of the driver (number of students taught by each department) to determine the allocation per object (department).

Department	Allocation Rate	×	Number of Students	=	Allocation per Department	Allocation Based on Past Usage
Management	$30	×	330		$ 9,900	$12,000
Accounting	30	×	360		10,800	10,000
Finance	30	×	290		8,700	8,000
Marketing	30	×	220		6,600	6,000
Total					$36,000	$36,000

Choosing the Best Cost Driver

Dr. Thompson objected vigorously to using the number of students as the cost driver. He continued to argue that the size of the faculty is a more appropriate allocation base. The chair of the finance department sided with Dr. Smethers, the chair of the marketing department kept quiet, and the dean had to settle the dispute.

Dean Southport recognized that the views of the chairpersons were influenced by self-interest. The allocation base affects the amount of resources available to each department. Furthermore, the dean recognized that the size of the faculty does drive some of the copying costs. For example, the cost of copying manuscripts that faculty submit for publication relates to faculty size. The more articles faculty submit, the higher the copying cost. Nevertheless, the dean decided the number of students has the most significant impact on copying costs. She also wanted to encourage faculty members to minimize the impact of funding cuts on student services. Dean Southport therefore decided to allocate copying costs based on the number of students taught by each department. Dr. Thompson stormed angrily out of the meeting. The dean developed a budget by assigning the available funds to each department using the number of students as the allocation base.

Controlling Emotions

Dr. Thompson's behavior may relieve his frustration but it doesn't indicate clear thinking. Dean Southport recognized that Dr. Thompson's contention that copy costs were related to faculty size had some merit. Had Dr. Thompson offered a compromise rather than an emotional outburst, he might have increased his department's share of the funds. Perhaps a portion of the allocation could have been based on the number of faculty members with the balance allocated based on the number of students. Had Dr. Thompson controlled his anger, the others might have agreed to compromise. Technical expertise in computing numbers is of little use without the interpersonal skills to persuade others. Accountants may provide numerical measurements, but they should never forget the impact of their reports on the people in the organization.

A Look Back

Managers need to know the costs of products, processes, departments, activities, and so on. The target for which accountants attempt to determine cost is a *cost object*. Knowing the cost of specific objects enables management to control costs, evaluate performance, and price products. *Direct costs* can be cost-effectively traced to a cost object. *Indirect costs* cannot be easily traced to designated cost objects.

The same cost can be direct or indirect, depending on the cost object to which it is traced. For example, the salary of a Burger King restaurant manager can be directly traced to a particular store but cannot be traced to particular food items made and sold in the store. Classifying a cost as direct or indirect is independent of whether the cost behaves as fixed or variable; it is also independent of whether the cost is relevant to a given decision. A direct cost could be either fixed or variable or either relevant or irrelevant, depending on the context and the designated cost object.

Indirect costs are assigned to cost objects using *cost allocation*. Allocation divides an indirect cost into parts and distributes the parts among the relevant cost objects. Companies frequently allocate costs to cost objects in proportion to the *cost drivers* that cause the cost to be incurred. The first step in allocating an indirect cost is to determine the allocation rate by dividing the total cost to be allocated by the chosen cost driver. The next step is to multiply the allocation rate by the amount of the cost driver for a particular object. The result is the amount of indirect cost to assign to the cost object.

A particular indirect cost may be related to more than one driver. The best cost driver is the one that most accurately reflects the amount of the resource used by the cost object. Objects that consume the most resources should be allocated a proportionately greater share of the costs. If no suitable cost driver exists, companies may use arbitrary allocations such as dividing a total cost equally among cost objects.

Cost allocations have behavioral implications. Using inappropriate cost drivers can distort allocations and lead managers to make choices that are detrimental to the company's profitability.

A Look Forward

The next chapter introduces the concept of *cost relevance*. Applying the concepts you have learned to real-world business problems can be challenging. Frequently, so much data is available that it is difficult to distinguish important from useless information. The next chapter will help you learn to identify information that is relevant in a variety of short-term decision-making scenarios including special offers, outsourcing, segment elimination, and asset replacement.

 Video lectures and accompanying self-assessment quizzes are available for all learning objectives through McGraw-Hill *Connect*® *Accounting*.

SELF-STUDY REVIEW PROBLEM

New budget constraints have pressured Body Perfect Gym to control costs. The owner of the gym, Mr. Ripple, has notified division managers that their job performance evaluations will be highly influenced by their ability to minimize costs. The gym has three divisions: weight lifting, aerobics, and spinning. The owner has formulated a report showing how much it cost to operate each of the three divisions last year. In preparing the report, Mr. Ripple identified several indirect costs that must be allocated among the divisions. These indirect costs are $4,200 of laundry expense, $48,000 of supplies, $350,000 of office rent, $50,000 of janitorial services, and $120,000 for administrative salaries. To provide a reasonably accurate cost allocation, Mr. Ripple has identified several potential cost drivers. These drivers and their association with each division follow.

Cost Driver	Weight Lifting	Aerobics	Spinning	Total
Number of participants	26	16	14	56
Number of instructors	10	8	6	24
Square feet of gym space	12,000	6,000	7,000	25,000
Number of staff	2	2	1	5

Required

a. Identify the appropriate cost objects.
b. Identify the most appropriate cost driver for each indirect cost, and compute the allocation rate for assigning each indirect cost to the cost objects.
c. Determine the amount of supplies expense that should be allocated to each of the three divisions.
d. The spinning manager wants to use the number of staff rather than the number of instructors as the allocation base for the supplies expense. Explain why the spinning manager would take this position.
e. Identify two cost drivers other than your choice for Requirement *b* that could be used to allocate the cost of the administrative salaries to the three divisions.

Solution to Requirement *a*

The objective is to determine the cost of operating each division. Therefore, the cost objects are the three divisions (weight lifting, aerobics, and spinning).

Solution to Requirement *b*

The costs, appropriate cost drivers, and allocation rates for assigning the costs to the departments follow:

Cost	Base	Computation	Allocation Rate
Laundry expense	Number of participants	$ 4,200 ÷ 56	$75 per participant
Supplies	Number of instructors	48,000 ÷ 24	$2,000 per instructor
Office rent	Square feet	350,000 ÷ 25,000	$14 per square foot
Janitorial service	Square feet	50,000 ÷ 25,000	$2 per square foot
Administrative salaries	Number of divisions	120,000 ÷ 3	$40,000 per division

There are other logical cost drivers. For example, the cost of supplies could be allocated based on the number of staff. It is also logical to use a combination of cost drivers. For example, the allocation for the cost of supplies could be based on the combined number of instructors and staff. For this problem, we assumed that Mr. Ripple chose the number of instructors as the base for allocating supplies expense.

Solution to Requirement *c*

Department	Cost to Be Allocated	Allocation Rate	×	Weight of Base	=	Amount Allocated
Weight lifting	Supplies	$2,000	×	10	=	$20,000
Aerobics	Supplies	2,000	×	8	=	16,000
Spinning	Supplies	2,000	×	6	=	12,000
Total						$48,000

Solution to Requirement d

If the number of staff were used as the allocation base, the allocation rate for supplies would be as follows:

$$\$48,000 \div 5 \text{ staff} = \$9,600 \text{ per staff member}$$

Using this rate, the total cost of supplies would be allocated among the three divisions as follows:

Department	Cost to Be Allocated	Allocation Rate	×	Weight of Base	=	Amount Allocated
Weight lifting	Supplies	$9,600	×	2	=	$19,200
Aerobics	Supplies	9,600	×	2	=	19,200
Spinning	Supplies	9,600	×	1	=	9,600
Total						$48,000

By using the number of staff as the allocation base instead of the number of instructors, the amount of overhead cost allocated to the spinning division falls from $12,000 to $9,600. Since managers are evaluated based on minimizing costs, it is clearly in the spinning manager's self-interest to use the number of staff as the allocation base.

Solution to Requirement e

Among other possibilities, bases for allocating the administrative salaries include the number of participants, the number of lessons, or the number of instructors.

KEY TERMS

Allocation 440	Controllable costs 440	Cost objects 436	Indirect cost 439
Allocation base 441	Cost accumulation 438	Cost pool 442	Overhead costs 439
Allocation rate 441	Cost allocation 439	Cost tracing 439	Predetermined overhead
Common costs 440	Cost driver 438	Direct cost 439	rate 451

QUESTIONS

1. What is a cost object? Identify four different cost objects in which an accountant would be interested.

2. Why is cost accumulation imprecise?

3. If the cost object is a manufactured product, what are the three major cost categories to accumulate?

4. What is a direct cost? What criteria are used to determine whether a cost is a direct cost?

5. Why are the terms *direct cost* and *indirect cost* independent of the terms *fixed cost* and *variable cost*? Give an example to illustrate.

6. Give an example of why the statement, "All direct costs are avoidable," is incorrect.

7. What are the important factors in determining the appropriate cost driver to use in allocating a cost?

8. How is an allocation rate determined? How is an allocation made?

9. In a manufacturing environment, which costs are direct and which are indirect in product costing?

10. Why are some manufacturing costs not directly traceable to products?

11. What is the objective of allocating indirect manufacturing overhead costs to the product?

12. On January 31, the managers of Integra Inc. seek to determine the cost of producing their product during January for product pricing and control purposes. The company can easily determine the

costs of direct materials and direct labor used in January production, but many fixed indirect costs are not affected by the level of production activity and have not yet been incurred. The managers can reasonably estimate the overhead costs for the year based on the fixed indirect costs incurred in past periods. Assume the managers decide to allocate an equal amount of these estimated costs to the products produced each month. Explain why this practice may not provide a reasonable estimate of product costs in January.

13. Respond to the following statement: "The allocation base chosen is unimportant. What is important in product costing is that overhead costs be assigned

to production in a specific period by an allocation process."

14. Larry Kwang insists that the costs of his school's fund-raising project should be determined after the project is complete. He argues that only after the project is complete can its costs be determined accurately and that it is a waste of time to try to estimate future costs. Georgia Sundum counters that waiting until the project is complete will not provide timely information for planning expenditures. How would you arbitrate this discussion? Explain the trade-offs between accuracy and timeliness.

15. Define the term *cost pool*. How are cost pools important in allocating costs?

MULTIPLE-CHOICE QUESTIONS

Multiple-choice questions are provided on the text website at www.mhhe.com/edmondssurvey4e.

EXERCISES

 connect All applicable Exercises are available with McGraw-Hill
|ACCOUNTING *Connect® Accounting.*

Exercise 12-1 *Direct versus indirect costs*

LO 12-1

Tapper Construction Company is composed of two divisions: (1) Home Construction and (2) Commercial Construction. The Home Construction Division is in the process of building 12 houses and the Commercial Construction Division is working on three projects. Cost items of the company follow:

Depreciation on home office building
Salary of corporate office manager
Wages of workers assigned to a specific construction project
Supplies used by the Commercial Construction Division
Labor on a particular house
Salary of the supervisor of commercial construction projects
Supplies, such as glue and nails, used by the Home Construction Division
Cost of building permits
Materials used in commercial construction projects
Depreciation on home building equipment (small tools such as hammers or saws)
Company president's salary
Depreciation on crane used in commercial construction

Required

a. Identify each cost as being a direct or indirect cost assuming the cost objects are the individual products (houses or projects).
b. Identify each cost as being a direct or indirect cost, assuming the cost objects are the two divisions.
c. Identify each cost as being a direct or indirect cost assuming the cost object is Tapper Construction Company as a whole.

Exercise 12-2 *Allocating costs between divisions*

LO 12-2

Kaplan Services Company (KSC) has 60 employees, 36 of whom are assigned to Division A and 24 to Division B. KSC incurred $330,000 of fringe benefits cost during 2014.

Required

Determine the amount of the fringe benefits cost to be allocated to Division A and to Division B.

Exercise 12-3 *Allocating overhead cost to accomplish smoothing*

LO 12-2

Kenneth Corporation expects to incur indirect overhead costs of $72,000 per month and direct manufacturing costs of $18 per unit. The expected production activity for the first four months of 2013 is as follows.

	January	February	March	April
Estimated production in units	5,000	6,500	2,500	4,000

Required

a. Calculate a predetermined overhead rate based on the number of units of product expected to be made during the first four months of the year.

b. Allocate overhead costs to each month using the overhead rate computed in Requirement *a*.

c. Calculate the total cost per unit for each month using the overhead allocated in Requirement *b*.

LO 12-2

Exercise 12-4   *Pooling overhead cost*

Eaton Manufacturing Company produced 1,600 units of inventory in January 2014. It expects to produce an additional 10,400 units during the remaining 11 months of the year. In other words, total production for 2014 is estimated to be 12,000 units. Direct materials and direct labor costs are $64 and $52 per unit, respectively. Eaton Company expects to incur the following manufacturing overhead costs during the 2014 accounting period.

Production supplies	$ 10,000
Supervisor salary	160,000
Depreciation on equipment	65,000
Utilities	20,000
Rental fee on manufacturing facilities	45,000

Required

a. Combine the individual overhead costs into a cost pool and calculate a predetermined overhead rate assuming the cost driver is number of units.

b. Determine the cost of the 1,600 units of product made in January.

c. Is the cost computed in Requirement *a* actual or estimated? Could Eaton improve accuracy by waiting until December to determine the cost of products? Identify two reasons that a manager would want to know the cost of products in January. Discuss the relationship between accuracy and relevance as it pertains to this problem.

LO 12-2, 12-3

Exercise 12-5   *Cost Pools*

Moineau Department Stores, Inc., has three departments: women's, men's, and children's. The following are the indirect costs related to its operations:

Vacation pay

Sewer bill

Staples

Natural gas bill

Pens

Ink cartridges

Payroll taxes

Paper rolls for cash registers

Medical insurance

Salaries of secretaries

Water bill

Required

a. Organize the costs in the following three pools: indirect materials, indirect labor, and indirect utilities, assuming that each department is a cost object.

b. Identify an appropriate cost driver for each pool.

c. Explain why accountants use cost pools.

LO 12-3

Exercise 12-6   *Allocating overhead cost among products*

Chandler Hats Corporation manufactures three different models of hats: Vogue, Beauty, and Glamour. Chandler expects to incur $360,000 of overhead costs during the next fiscal year. Other budget information follows.

	Vogue	Beauty	Glamour	Total
Direct labor hours	2,000	4,000	6,000	12,000
Machine hours	1,200	1,400	1,400	4,000

Required

a. Use direct labor hours as the cost driver to compute the allocation rate and the budgeted overhead cost for each product.

b. Use machine hours as the cost driver to compute the allocation rate and the budgeted overhead cost for each product.

c. Describe a set of circumstances where it would be more appropriate to use direct labor hours as the allocation base.

d. Describe a set of circumstances where it would be more appropriate to use machine hours as the allocation base.

Exercise 12-7 *Allocating overhead costs among products*

LO 12-3

Cain Company makes three products in its factory: plastic cups, plastic tablecloths, and plastic bottles. The expected overhead costs for the next fiscal year include the following.

Factory manager's salary	$175,000
Factory utility cost	64,000
Factory supplies	11,000
Total overhead costs	$250,000

Cain uses machine hours as the cost driver to allocate overhead costs. Budgeted machine hours for the products are as follows:

Cups	200 Hours
Tablecloths	600
Bottles	800
Total machine hours	1,600

Required

a. Allocate the budgeted overhead costs to the products.

b. Provide a possible explanation as to why Cain chose machine hours, instead of labor hours, as the allocation base.

Exercise 12-8 *Allocating costs among products*

LO 12-3

Longman Construction Company expects to build three new homes during a specific accounting period. The estimated direct materials and labor costs are as follows.

Expected Costs	Home 1	Home 2	Home 3
Direct labor	$30,000	$45,000	$85,000
Direct materials	45,000	65,000	90,000

Assume Longman needs to allocate two major overhead costs ($60,000 of employee fringe benefits and $20,000 of indirect materials costs) among the three jobs.

Required

Choose an appropriate cost driver for each of the overhead costs and determine the total cost of each house. Round your figures to 3 decimal points.

LO 12-3

Exercise 12-9   *Allocating to smooth cost over varying levels of production*

Production workers for Kennedy Manufacturing Company provided 300 hours of labor in January and 600 hours in February. Kennedy expects to use 5,000 hours of labor during the year. The rental fee for the manufacturing facility is $7,500 per month.

Required

Explain why allocation is needed. Based on this information, how much of the rental cost should be allocated to the products made in January and to those made in February?

LO 12-3

Exercise 12-10   *Allocating to solve a timing problem*

Production workers for Soloman Manufacturing Company provided 3,000 hours of labor in January and 2,000 hours in February. The company, whose operation is labor intensive, expects to use 40,000 hours of labor during the year. Soloman paid a $96,000 annual premium on July 1 of the prior year for an insurance policy that covers the manufacturing facility for the following 12 months.

Required

Explain why allocation is needed. Based on this information, how much of the insurance cost should be allocated to the products made in January and to those made in February?

LO 12-3

Exercise 12-11   *Allocating to solve a timing problem*

Lubbock Air is a large airline company that pays a customer relations representative $6,000 per month. The representative, who processed 1,000 customer complaints in January and 1,300 complaints in February, is expected to process 32,000 customer complaints during the year.

Required

a. Determine the total cost of processing customer complaints in January and in February.
b. Explain why allocating the cost of the customer relations representative would or would not be relevant to decision making.

LO 12-3

Exercise 12-12   *How the allocation of fixed cost affects a pricing decision*

Oxmoor Manufacturing Co. expects to make 40,000 chairs during the current accounting period. The company made 4,000 chairs in January. Materials and labor costs for January were $20,000 and $30,000, respectively. Oxmoor produced 3,200 chairs in February. Material and labor costs for February were $16,000 and $24,000, respectively. The company paid the $360,000 annual rental fee on its manufacturing facility on January 1.

Required

Assuming that Oxmoor desires to sell its chairs for cost plus 40 percent of cost, what price should be charged for the chairs produced in January and February?

LO 12-4

Exercise 12-13   *Human factor*

Talbot Clinics provides medical care in three departments: internal medicine (IM), pediatrics (PD), and obstetrics gynecology (OB). The estimated costs to run each department follow:

	IM	PD	OB
Physicians	$600,000	$400,000	$500,000
Nurses	80,000	120,000	160,000

Talbot expects to incur $450,000 of indirect (overhead) costs in the next fiscal year.

Required

a. Name four allocation bases that could be used to assign the overhead cost to each department.

b. Assume the manager of each department is permitted to recommend how the overhead cost should be allocated to the departments. Which of the allocation bases named in Requirement *a* is the manager of OB most likely to recommend? Explain why. What argument may the manager of OB use to justify his choice of the allocation base?

c. Which of the allocation bases would result in the fairest allocation of the overhead cost from the perspective of the company president?

d. Explain how classifying overhead costs into separate pools could improve the fairness of the allocation of the overhead costs.

PROBLEMS

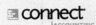 **All applicable Problems are available with McGraw-Hill Connect® Accounting.**

Problem 12-14   *Cost accumulation and allocation*

LO 12-1, 12-2, 12-3

Mogoul Manufacturing Company makes two different products, M and N. The company's two departments are named after the products; for example, Product M is made in Department M. Mogoul's accountant has identified the following annual costs associated with these two products.

CHECK FIGURE
c. $536.55

Financial data	
Salary of vice president of production division	$200,000
Salary of supervisor Department M	80,000
Salary of supervisor Department N	60,000
Direct materials cost Department M	300,000
Direct materials cost Department N	420,000
Direct labor cost Department M	240,000
Direct labor cost Department N	680,000
Direct utilities cost Department M	120,000
Direct utilities cost Department N	24,000
General factorywide utilities	36,000
Production supplies	36,000
Fringe benefits	138,000
Depreciation	720,000
Nonfinancial data	
Machine hours Department M	5,000
Machine hours Department N	1,000

Required

a. Identify the costs that are (1) direct costs of Department M, (2) direct costs of Department N, and (3) indirect costs.

b. Select the appropriate cost drivers for the indirect costs and allocate these costs to Departments M and N.

c. Determine the total estimated cost of the products made in Departments M and N. Assume that Mogoul produced 2,000 units of Product M and 4,000 units of Product N during the year. If Mogoul prices its products at cost plus 40 percent of cost, what price per unit must it charge for Product M and for Product N?

Problem 12-15   *Selecting an appropriate cost driver (What is the base?)*

LO 12-1, 12-2, 12-3

The Federer School of Vocational Technology has organized the school training programs into three departments. Each department provides training in a different area as follows:

nursing assistant, dental hygiene, and office technology. The school's owner, Joyce Federer, wants to know how much it costs to operate each of the three departments. To accumulate the total cost for each department, the accountant has identified several indirect costs that must be allocated to each. These costs are $15,000 of phone expense, $24,000 of office supplies, $720,000 of office rent, $144,000 of janitorial services, and $150,000 of salary paid to the dean of students. To provide a reasonably accurate allocation of costs, the accountant has identified several possible cost drivers. These drivers and their association with each department follow.

Cost Driver	Department 1	Department 2	Department 3
Number of telephones	20	30	50
Number of faculty members	20	16	24
Square footage of office space	14,000	8,000	14,000
Number of secretaries	2	2	2

Required

a. Identify the appropriate cost objects.

b. Identify the appropriate cost driver for each indirect cost and compute the allocation rate for assigning each indirect cost to the cost objects.

c. Determine the amount of telephone expense that should be allocated to each of the three departments.

d. Determine the amount of supplies expense that should be allocated to Department 3.

e. Determine the amount of office rent that should be allocated to Department 2.

f. Determine the amount of janitorial services cost that should be allocated to Department 1.

g. Identify two cost drivers not listed here that could be used to allocate the cost of the dean's salary to the three departments.

LO 12-1, 12-2, 12-3

CHECK FIGURE
b. To NY: $1,080

Problem 12-16   *Cost allocation in a service industry*

Pascal Airlines is a small airline that occasionally carries overload shipments for the overnight delivery company Never-Fail, Inc. Never-Fail is a multimillion-dollar company started by Wes Never immediately after he failed to finish his first accounting course. The company's motto is "We Never-Fail to Deliver Your Package on Time." When Never-Fail has more freight than it can deliver, it pays Pascal to carry the excess. Pascal contracts with independent pilots to fly its planes on a per-trip basis. Pascal recently purchased an airplane that cost the company $6,000,000. The plane has an estimated useful life of 20,000,000 miles and a zero salvage value. During the first week in January, Pascal flew two trips. The first was a round-trip flight from Chicago to San Francisco, for which Pascal paid $350 for the pilot and $500 for fuel. The second flight was a round-trip from Chicago to New York. For this trip, it paid $300 for the pilot and $300 for fuel. The round-trip between Chicago and San Francisco is approximately 4,400 miles and the round-trip between Chicago and New York is 1,600 miles.

Required

a. Identify the direct and indirect costs that Pascal incurs for each trip.

b. Determine the total cost of each trip.

c. In addition to depreciation, identify three other indirect costs that may need to be allocated to determine the cost of each trip.

LO 12-1, 12-2, 12-3

CHECK FIGURE
d. Feb.: $3,600

Problem 12-17   *Cost allocation in a manufacturing company*

Neal Manufacturing Company makes tents that it sells directly to camping enthusiasts through a mail-order marketing program. The company pays a quality control expert $60,000 per year to inspect completed tents before they are shipped to customers. Assume that the company completed 1,600 tents in January and 1,200 tents in February. For the entire year, the company expects to produce 20,000 tents.

Required

a. Explain how changes in the cost driver (number of tents inspected) affect the total amount of fixed inspection cost.

b. Explain how changes in the cost driver (number of tents inspected) affect the amount of fixed inspection cost per unit.

c. If the cost objective is to determine the cost per tent, is the expert's salary a direct or an indirect cost?

d. How much of the expert's salary should be allocated to tents produced in January and February?

Problem 12-18 *Allocation to accomplish smoothing*

LO 12-1, 12-2, 12-3

Maureen Corporation estimated its overhead costs would be $30,000 per month except for January when it pays the $90,000 annual insurance premium on the manufacturing facility. Accordingly, the January overhead costs were expected to be $120,000 ($90,000 + $30,000). The company expected to use 7,000 direct labor hours per month except during July, August, and September when the company expected 9,000 hours of direct labor each month to build inventories for high demand that normally occurs during the Christmas season. The company's actual direct labor hours were the same as the estimated hours. The company made 3,500 units of product in each month except July, August, and September, in which it produced 4,500 units each month. Direct labor costs were $30 per unit, and direct materials costs were $25 per unit.

CHECK FIGURES
a. $5
c. March: $65

Required

a. Calculate a predetermined overhead rate based on direct labor hours.

b. Determine the total allocated overhead cost for January, March, and August.

c. Determine the cost per unit of product for January, March, and August.

d. Determine the selling price for the product, assuming that the company desires to earn a gross margin of $20 per unit.

Problem 12-19 *Allocating indirect costs between products*

LO 12-2, 12-3

Janet Garcia is considering expanding her business. She plans to hire a salesperson to cover trade shows. Because of compensation, travel expenses, and booth rental, fixed costs for a trade show are expected to be $6,000. The booth will be open 30 hours during the trade show. Ms. Garcia also plans to add a new product line, ProOffice, which will cost $120 per package. She will continue to sell the existing product, EZRecords, which costs $90 per package. Ms. Garcia believes that the salesperson will spend approximately 20 hours selling EZRecords and 10 hours marketing ProOffice.

CHECK FIGURES
a. Cost/unit for EZRecords: $140
b. Cost/unit for ProOffice: $140

Required

a. Determine the estimated total cost and cost per unit of each product, assuming that the salesperson is able to sell 80 units of EZRecords and 50 units of ProOffice.

b. Determine the estimated total cost and cost per unit of each product, assuming that the salesperson is able to sell 200 units of EZRecords and 100 units of ProOffice.

c. Explain why the cost per unit figures calculated in Requirement *a* are different from the amounts calculated in Requirement *b*. Also explain how the differences in estimated cost per unit will affect pricing decisions.

Problem 12-20 *Fairness and cost pool allocations*

LO 12-3, 12-4

Jocey Manufacturing Company uses two departments to make its products. Department I is a cutting department that is machine intensive and uses very few employees. Machines cut and form parts and then place the finished parts on a conveyor belt that carries them to Department II, where they are assembled into finished goods. The assembly department is labor intensive and requires many workers to assemble parts into finished goods. The company's manufacturing facility incurs two significant overhead costs: employee fringe benefits and utility costs. The annual costs of fringe benefits are $360,000 and utility costs are $240,000. The typical consumption patterns for the two departments are as follows.

	Department I	Department II	Total
Machine hours used	20,000	4,000	24,000
Direct labor hours used	2,000	14,000	16,000

The supervisor of each department receives a bonus based on how well the department controls costs. The company's current policy requires using a single allocation base (machine hours or labor hours) to allocate the total overhead cost of $540,000.

Required

a. Assume that you are the supervisor of Department I. Choose the allocation base that would minimize your department's share of the total overhead cost. Calculate the amount of overhead that would be allocated to both departments using the base that you selected.

b. Assume that you are the supervisor of Department II. Choose the allocation base that would minimize your department's share of the total overhead cost. Calculate the amount of overhead that would be allocated to both departments using the base that you selected.

c. Assume that you are the plant manager and have the authority to change the company's overhead allocation policy. Formulate an overhead allocation policy that would be fair to the supervisors of both Department I and Department II. Compute the overhead allocations for each department using your policy.

d. Explain why it is necessary to disaggregate the overhead cost pool in order to accomplish fairness.

ANALYZE, THINK, COMMUNICATE

ATC 12-1   Business Applications Case   *Allocating fixed costs at HealthSouth Corporation*

HealthSouth Corporation claims to be ". . . the nation's largest owner and operator of inpatient rehabilitation hospitals in terms of revenues, number of hospitals, and patients treated and discharged." As of December 31, 2011, the company derived 92 percent of its revenues from inpatient services. During 2011 it treated and discharged 118,354 patients, and the average length of a patient's stay was 13.5 days. If one patient occupying one bed for one day represents a "patient-day," then HealthSouth produced 1,597,779 patient-days of output during 2011 (118,354 × 13.5 = 1,597,779). During this period, HealthSouth incurred depreciation costs of $52,500,000. For the purpose of this problem, assume that all of this depreciation related to the property, plant, and equipment of inpatient hospitals.

Required

a. Indicate whether the depreciation cost is a:

   (1) Product (i.e., patient) cost or a general, selling, and administrative cost.

   (2) Fixed or variable cost relative to the volume of production.

   (3) Direct or indirect cost if the cost object is the cost of patient services provided in 2011.

b. Assume that HealthSouth incurred depreciation of $4,375,000 during each month of the 2011 fiscal year, but that it produced 140,000 patient-days of service during February and 120,000 patient-days of service during March. Based on monthly costs and service levels, what was the average amount of depreciation cost per patient-day of service provided during each of these two months, assuming each patient-day of service was charged the same amount of depreciation?

c. If HealthSouth expected to produce 1,650,000 patient-days of service during 2011 and estimated its annual depreciation costs to be $53,000,000, what would have been its predetermined overhead charge per patient-day of service for depreciation? Explain the advantage of using this amount to determine the cost of providing one patient-day of service in February and March versus the amounts you computed in Requirement b.

d. If HealthSouth's management had estimated the profit per patient-day of service based on its budgeted production of 1,650,000 units, would you expect its actual profit per patient-day of service to be higher or lower than expected? Explain.

ATC 12-2   Group Assignment   *Selection of the cost driver*

Vulcan College School of Business is divided into three departments: accounting, marketing, and management. Relevant information for each of the departments follows.

Cost Driver	Accounting	Marketing	Management
Number of students	1,400	800	400
Number of classes per semester	64	36	28
Number of professors	20	24	10

Vulcan is a private school that expects each department to generate a profit. It rewards departments for profitability by assigning 20 percent of each department's profits back to that department. Departments have free rein as to how to use these funds. Some departments have used them to supply professors with computer technology. Others have expanded their travel budgets. The practice has been highly successful in motivating the faculty to control costs. The revenues and direct costs for the year 2014 follow:

	Accounting	Marketing	Management
Revenue	$29,600,000	$16,600,000	$8,300,000
Direct costs	24,600,000	13,800,000	6,600,000

Vulcan allocates to the School of Business $4,492,800 of indirect overhead costs such as administrative salaries and the costs of operating the registrar's office and the bookstore.

Required

a. Divide the class into groups and organize the groups into three sections. Assign each section a department. For example, groups in Sections 1, 2, and 3 should represent the Accounting Department, the Marketing Department, and the Management Department, respectively. Assume that the dean of the school is planning to assign an equal amount of the college overhead to each department. Have the students in each group prepare a response to the dean's plan. Each group should select a spokesperson who is prepared to answer the following questions.

   (1) Is your group in favor of or opposed to the allocation plan suggested by the dean?

   (2) Does the plan suggested by the dean provide a fair allocation? Why?

   The instructor should lead a discussion designed to assess the appropriateness of the dean's proposed allocation plan.

b. Have each group select the cost driver (allocation base) that best serves the self-interest of the department it represents.

c. Consensus on Requirement *c* should be achieved before completing Requirement *d*. Each group should determine the amount of the indirect cost to be allocated to each department using the cost driver that best serves the self-interest of the department it represents. Have a spokesperson from each section go to the board and show the resulting income statement for each department.

d. Discuss the development of a cost driver(s) that would promote fairness rather than self-interest in allocating the indirect costs.

ATC 12-3   Research Assignment   *Using real-world data from Coca-Cola Bottling Co. Consolidated*

Use the 2011 Form 10-K (year ended on January 1, 2012) for Coca-Cola Bottling Co. Consolidated to complete the requirements below. Be aware that Coca-Cola Bottling Co. Consolidated

(COKE) is a separate company from The Coca-Cola Company (KO), so do not confuse them. To obtain the Form 10-K, you can use the EDGAR system (see Appendix A at the back of this text for instructions), or it can be found under the "Investor Relations" link on the company's corporate website at www.cokeconsolidated.com. The company's Form 10-K can be found under "SEC Filings." Be sure to read carefully the following sections of the document:

> Under "Item 1. Business," read the subsection titled "Seasonality" on page 9.
>
> Under "Item 2. Properties," read pages 18 and 19.
>
> In the footnotes section of the report, under "Note 1—Summary of Significant Accounting Policies," read the following subsections:
>
> "Marketing Programs and Sales Incentives" on page 66; "Cost of Sales" on page 68; "Selling, Delivery and Administrative Expenses" on page 68; and "Shipping and Handling Costs" on page 69.

Required

a. Does COKE consider *shipping and handling costs* and *advertising costs* to be direct or indirect costs in relation to the manufacturing of its products? Explain.

b. Assume that when COKE ships orders of finished goods from manufacturing locations to sales distribution centers each shipment includes several different products such as Coca-Cola, Sprite, Dr Pepper, and Seagrams Ginger Ale. If COKE wanted to allocate the shipping costs among the various products, what would be an appropriate cost driver? Explain the rationale for your choice.

c. Based on COKE's discussion of the seasonality of its business, should the depreciation of production equipment recorded in a given month be based on the volume of drinks produced that month, or should the depreciation for each month be 1/12th of the estimated annual depreciation COKE expects to incur? Explain your answer.

d. As Item 2. *Properties* indicates, COKE appears to have significant excess capacity at its plants. Approximately what percentage of available production capacity was *not* being used by COKE in 2011? What are some possible reasons COKE might want to have this much excess capacity? Explain.

ATC 12-4   Writing Assignment   *Selection of the appropriate cost driver*

Bullions Enterprises, Inc. (BEI), makes gold, silver, and bronze medals used to recognize outstanding athletic performance in regional and national sporting events. The per-unit direct costs of producing the medals follow.

	Gold	Silver	Bronze
Direct materials	$300	$130	$ 35
Labor	120	120	120

During 2012, BEI made 1,200 units of each type of medal for a total of 3,600 (1,200 × 3) medals. All medals are created through the same production process, and they are packaged and shipped in identical containers. Indirect overhead costs amounted to $324,000. BEI currently uses the number of units as the cost driver for the allocation of overhead cost. As a result, BEI allocated $90 ($324,000 ÷ 3,600 units) of overhead cost to each medal produced.

Required

The president of the company has questioned the wisdom of assigning the same amount of overhead to each type of medal. He believes that overhead should be assigned on the basis of the cost to produce the medals. In other words, more overhead should be charged to expensive gold medals, less to silver, and even less to bronze. Assume that you are BEI's chief financial officer. Write a memo responding to the president's suggestion.

ATC 12-5   Ethical Dilemma   *Allocation to achieve fairness*

The American Acupuncture Association offers continuing professional education courses for its members at its annual meeting. Instructors are paid a fee for each student attending their courses but are charged a fee for overhead costs that is deducted from their compensation.

Overhead costs include fees paid to rent instructional equipment such as overhead projectors, provide supplies to participants, and offer refreshments during coffee breaks. The number of courses offered is used as the allocation base for determining the overhead charge. For example, if overhead costs amount to $5,000 and 25 courses are offered, each course is allocated an overhead charge of $200 ($5,000 ÷ 25 courses). Heidi McCarl, who taught one of the courses, received the following statement with her check in payment for her instructional services.

Instructional fees (20 students × $50 per student)	$1,000
Less: Overhead charge	(200)
Less: Charge for sign language assistant	(240)
Amount due instructor	$ 560

Although Ms. McCarl was well aware that one of her students was deaf and required a sign language assistant, she was surprised to find that she was required to absorb the cost of this service.

Required

a. Given that the Americans with Disabilities Act stipulates that the deaf student cannot be charged for the cost of providing sign language, who should be required to pay the cost of sign language services?

b. Explain how allocation can be used to promote fairness in distributing service costs to the disabled. Describe two ways to treat the $240 cost of providing sign language services that improve fairness.

CHAPTER 13

Relevant Information for Special Decisions

LEARNING OBJECTIVES

After you have mastered the material in this chapter, you will be able to:

LO 13-1   Identify the characteristics of relevant information.

LO 13-2   Make appropriate special order decisions.

LO 13-3   Make appropriate outsourcing decisions.

LO 13-4   Make appropriate segment elimination decisions.

LO 13-5   Make appropriate asset replacement decisions.

 Video lectures and accompanying self-assessment quizzes are available for all learning objectives through McGraw-Hill Connect® Accounting.

CHAPTER OPENING

Mary Daniels paid $25,000 to purchase a car that was used in her rental business. After one year, the car had a book value of $21,000. Ms. Daniels needs cash and is considering selling the car. After advertising the vehicle for sale, the best offer she received was $19,000. Ms. Daniels really needed the money, but ultimately decided not to sell because she did not want to incur a $2,000 loss ($21,000 market value − $19,000 book value). Did Ms. Daniels make the right decision?

Whether Ms. Daniels will be better off selling the car or keeping it is unknown. However, it is certain that she based her decision on irrelevant data. Ms. Daniels incurred a loss when the market value of the car dropped. She cannot avoid a loss that already exists. Past mistakes should not affect current decisions. The current value of the car is $19,000. Ms. Daniels's decision is whether to take the money or keep the car. The book value of the car is not relevant. This chapter explains how to isolate and focus on the variables that are relevant in the decision-making process.

The Curious Accountant

The authors compared the prices of six of the top selling, nongeneric, heart-disease drugs at two large online pharmacies, one in the United States and one in Canada. The analysis showed the Canadian prices for these six popular prescription drugs, such as Lipitor and Zocor, were only 37 percent of prices charged in the United States.

Major pharmaceutical companies have earnings before tax that average around 25 percent of sales, indicating that their costs average around 75 percent of the prices they charge. In other words, it costs approximately $75 to generate $100 of revenue. Given that drugs are sold in Canada for 37 percent of the U.S. sales price, a drug that is sold in the United States for $100 would be sold in Canada for only $37.

How can drugs be sold in Canada for less ($37) than cost ($75)? (Answer on page 474.)

470   Chapter 13

RELEVANT INFORMATION

How can you avoid irrelevant information when making decisions? Two primary characteristics distinguish relevant from useless information. Specifically, **relevant information** (1) differs among the alternatives and (2) is future oriented.

The first characteristic recognizes that relevant information differs for one or more of the alternatives being considered. Suppose the car Ms. Daniels is considering selling is due for a state-required safety inspection. Further assume that the inspection must be completed before the car can be sold or driven. Since the inspection fee must be paid regardless of whether Ms. Daniels keeps or sells the car, it does not differ among the alternatives and therefore is not relevant to her decision. In contrast, assume the car is due for an oil change that can be delayed until after the car is sold. Since Ms. Daniels can avoid the cost of the oil change if she sells the car but must pay for the oil change if she keeps the car, the cost of the oil change differs between the alternatives and is relevant to her decision.

The second characteristic of relevant information is that it impacts the future. "Don't cry over spilt milk." "It's water over the dam." These aphorisms remind people they cannot change the past. With regard to business decisions, the principle means you cannot avoid a cost that has already been incurred. In the Daniels example, the historical cost ($25,000) of the car is not relevant to a decision regarding whether to sell the car today. The current market value of $19,000 is relevant to the decision regarding whether to sell the car today.

It is interesting to note that the two characteristics are merely different views of the same concept because historical information does not differ between the alternatives. In other words, we could say that historical costs are not relevant because they do not differ between alternatives associated with current decisions.

Sunk Cost

Historical costs are frequently called *sunk costs.* Since **sunk costs** have been incurred in past transactions, they cannot be changed and are not relevant for making current decisions. The $25,000 original cost of the car in the Daniels example is a sunk cost.

Why even bother to collect historical information if it is not relevant? Historical information may be useful in predicting the future. A company that earned $5 million last year is more likely to earn $5 million this year than a company that earned $5,000 last year. The predictive capacity is relevant because it provides insight into the future.

Opportunity Costs

An **opportunity cost** is the sacrifice that is incurred in order to obtain an alternative opportunity. For example, in the above case, Ms. Daniels must give up the opportunity to obtain $19,000 in order to keep the car. So, the opportunity cost of owning the car is $19,000. Since this cost differs between the alternatives of owning the car versus selling it and since it affects the present or future, it is relevant to the decision regarding whether to keep or sell the car.

The best offer that Ms. Daniels received for the car was $19,000. Suppose Ms. Daniels also received a less favorable offer of $18,000. Does this mean that the opportunity cost of keeping the car is $37,000 ($18,000 + $19,000)? No. Opportunity costs are not cumulative. Ms. Daniels really has only one opportunity. If she accepts the $19,000 offer, she must reject the $18,000 offer or vice versa. Accountants normally measure opportunity cost as the highest value of the available alternatives. In this case, the opportunity cost of keeping the car is $19,000.

☑ **CHECK YOURSELF 13.1**

Aqua, Inc., makes statues for use in fountains. On January 1, 2014, the company paid $13,500 for a mold to make a particular type of statue. The mold had an expected useful life of four years and a salvage value of $1,500. On January 1, 2016, the mold had a market value of $3,000 and a salvage value of $1,200. The expected useful life did not change. What is the relevant cost of using the mold during 2016?

Answer   The relevant cost of using the mold in 2016 is the opportunity cost [(Market value − Salvage value) ÷ Remaining useful life], in this case, ($3,000 − $1,200) ÷ 2 = $900. The book value of the asset and associated depreciation is based on a sunk cost that cannot be avoided because it has already been incurred and therefore is not relevant to current decisions. In contrast, Aqua could avoid the opportunity cost (market value) by selling the mold.

Relevance Is an Independent Concept

The concept of relevance is independent from the concept of cost behavior. In a given circumstance, **relevant costs** could be either fixed or variable. Consider the following illustration. Executives of Better Bakery Products are debating whether to add a new product, either cakes or pies, to the company's line. Projected costs for the two options follow.

Cost of Cakes		Cost of Pies	
Materials (per unit)	$ 1.50	Materials (per unit)	$ 2.00
Direct labor (per unit)	1.00	Direct labor (per unit)	1.00
Supervisor's salary*	25,000.00	Supervisor's salary*	25,000.00
Franchise fee†	50,000.00	Advertising‡	40,000.00

*It will be necessary to hire a new production supervisor at a cost of $25,000 per year.

†Cakes will be distributed under a nationally advertised label. Better Bakery pays an annual franchise fee for the right to use the product label. Because of the established brand name, Better Bakery will not be required to advertise the product.

‡Better Bakery will market the pies under its own name and will advertise the product in the local market in which the product sells.

Which costs are relevant? Fifty cents per unit of the materials can be avoided by choosing cakes instead of pies. A portion of the materials cost is therefore relevant. Labor costs will be one dollar per unit whether Better Bakery makes cakes or pies. Labor cost is therefore not relevant. Although both materials and direct labor are variable costs, one is relevant but the other is not.

Since Better Bakery must hire a supervisor under either alternative, the supervisor's salary is not relevant. The franchise fee can be avoided if Better Bakery makes pies and advertising costs can be avoided if it makes cakes. All three of these costs are fixed, but only two are relevant. Finally, all the costs (whether fixed or variable) could be avoided if Better Bakery rejects both products. Whether a cost is fixed or variable has no bearing on its relevance.

Relevance Is Context Sensitive

A particular cost that is relevant in one context may be irrelevant in another. Consider a store that carries men's, women's, and children's clothing. The store manager's salary could not be avoided by eliminating the children's department, but it could be avoided if the entire store were closed. The salary is not relevant to deciding whether to eliminate the children's department but is relevant with respect to deciding to close the store. In one context, the salary is not relevant. In the other context, it is relevant.

Relationship between Relevance and Accuracy

Information need not be exact to be relevant. You may decide to delay purchasing a laptop computer you want if you know its price is going to drop even if you don't know exactly how much the price decrease will be. You know part of the cost can be avoided by waiting; you are just not sure of the amount.

The most useful information is both relevant and precise. Totally inaccurate information is useless. Likewise, irrelevant information is useless regardless of its accuracy.

Quantitative versus Qualitative Characteristics of Decision Making

Relevant information can have both **quantitative** and **qualitative characteristics.** The previous examples focused on quantitative data. Now consider qualitative issues. Suppose you are deciding which of two laptop computers to purchase. Computer A costs $300 more than Computer B. Both computers satisfy your technical requirements; however, Computer A has a more attractive appearance. From a quantitative standpoint, you would select Computer B because you could avoid $300 of cost. However, if the laptop will be used in circumstances where clients need to be impressed, appearance—a qualitative characteristic—may be more important than minimizing cost. You might purchase Computer A even though quantitative factors favor Computer B. Both qualitative and quantitative data are relevant to decision making.

As with quantitative data, qualitative features must *differ* between the alternatives to be relevant. If the two computers were identical in appearance, attractiveness would not be relevant to making the decision.

Differential Revenue and Avoidable Cost

Since relevant revenue *differs* among the alternatives, it is sometimes called **differential revenue.** To illustrate, assume Pecks Department Stores sells men's, women's, and children's clothing and is considering eliminating the children's line. The revenue generated by the children's department is differential (relevant) revenue because Pecks's total revenue would be different if the children's department were eliminated.

Why would Pecks consider eliminating the children's department and thereby lose the differential (relevant) revenue? Pecks may be able to save more by eliminating the cost of operating the department than it loses in differential revenue. Some but not all of the costs associated with operating the children's department can be saved. For example, if Pecks Department Stores eliminates the children's department, the company can eliminate the cost of the department manager's salary but cannot get rid of the salary of the company president. The costs that stay the same are not relevant. The costs that can be *avoided* by closing the department are relevant. Indeed, relevant costs are frequently called *avoidable costs.*

Avoidable costs are the costs managers can eliminate by making specific choices. In the Pecks example, the cost of the department manager's salary is an avoidable (relevant) cost. The cost of the president's salary is not avoidable and is not relevant to the elimination decision.

Relationship of Cost Avoidance to a Cost Hierarchy

Classifying costs into one of four hierarchical levels helps identify avoidable costs.[1]

1. *Unit-level costs.* Costs incurred each time a company generates one unit of product are **unit-level costs.**[2] Examples include the cost of direct materials, direct labor, inspections, packaging, shipping, and handling. Incremental (additional) unit-level costs increase *with each additional unit of product generated. Unit-level costs can be avoided by eliminating the production of a single unit of product.*

---

[1] R. Cooper and R. S. Kaplan, *The Design of Cost Management Systems* (Englewood Cliffs, NJ: Prentice-Hall, 1991). Our classifications are broader than those typically presented. They encompass service and merchandising companies as well as manufacturing businesses.

[2] Recall that we use the term *product* in a generic sense to represent producing goods or services.

2. *Batch-level costs.* Many products are generated in batches rather than individual units. For example, a heating and air conditioning technician may service a batch of air conditioners in an apartment complex. Some of the job costs apply only to individual units, and other costs relate to the entire batch. For instance, the labor to service each air conditioner is a unit-level cost, but the cost of driving to the site is a **batch-level cost.**

    Classifying costs as unit- versus batch-level frequently depends on the context rather than the type of cost. For example, shipping and handling costs to send 200 computers to a university are batch-level costs. In contrast, the shipping and handling cost to deliver a single computer to each of a number of individual customers is a unit-level cost. Eliminating a batch of work avoids both batch-level and unit-level costs. Similarly, adding a batch of work increases batch-level and unit-level costs. Increasing the number of units in a particular batch increases unit-level but not batch-level costs. Decreasing the number of units in a batch reduces unit-level costs but not batch-level costs.

3. *Product-level costs.* Costs incurred to support specific products or services are called **product-level costs.** Product-level costs include quality inspection costs, engineering design costs, the costs of obtaining and defending patents, the costs of regulatory compliance, and inventory holding costs such as interest, insurance, maintenance, and storage. *Product-level costs can be avoided by discontinuing a product line.* For example, suppose the Snapper Company makes the engines used in its lawn mowers. Buying engines from an outside supplier instead of making them would allow Snapper to avoid the product-level costs such as legal fees for patents, manufacturing supervisory costs of producing the engines, and the maintenance and inventory costs of holding engine parts.

4. *Facility-level costs.* **Facility-level costs** are incurred to support the entire company. They are not related to any specific product, batch, or unit of product. Because these costs maintain the facility as a whole, they are frequently called *facility-sustaining costs.* Facility-level costs include building rent or depreciation, personnel administration and training, property and real estate taxes, insurance, maintenance, administrative salaries, general selling costs, landscaping, utilities, and security. Total facility-level costs cannot be avoided unless the entire company is dissolved. However, eliminating a business segment (such as a division, department, or office) may enable a company to avoid some facility-level costs. For example, if a bank eliminates one of its branches, it can avoid the costs of renting, maintaining, and insuring that particular branch building. In general, *segment-level* facility costs can be avoided when a segment is eliminated. In contrast, *corporate-level* facility costs cannot be avoided unless the corporation is eliminated.

Precise distinctions between the various categories are often difficult to draw. One company may incur sales staff salaries as a facility-level cost while another company may pay sales commissions traceable to product lines or even specific units of a product line. Cost classifications cannot be memorized. Classifying specific cost items into the appropriate categories requires thoughtful judgment.

RELEVANT INFORMATION AND SPECIAL DECISIONS

Five types of special decisions are frequently encountered in business practice: (1) special order, (2) outsourcing, (3) segment elimination, (4) asset replacement, and (5) scarce resource allocation. The following sections discuss using relevant information in making the first four types of special decisions.

LO 13-2

Make appropriate special order decisions.

474   Chapter 13

EXHIBIT 13.1

EXHIBIT 13.1

Budgeted Cost for Expected Production of 2,000 Printers

Unit-level costs		
Materials costs (2,000 units × $90)	$180,000	
Labor costs (2,000 units × $82.50)	165,000	
Overhead (2,000 units × $7.50)	15,000	
Total unit-level costs (2,000 × $180)		$360,000
Batch-level costs		
Assembly setup (10 batches × $1,700)	17,000	
Materials handling (10 batches × $500)	5,000	
Total batch-level costs (10 batches × $2,200)		22,000
Product-level costs		
Engineering design	14,000	
Production manager salary	63,300	
Total product-level costs		77,300
Facility-level costs		
Segment-level costs:		
Division manager's salary	85,000	
Administrative costs	12,700	
Allocated—corporate-level costs:		
Company president's salary	43,200	
Building rental	27,300	
General expenses	31,000	
Total facility-level costs		199,200
Total expected cost		$658,500

Cost per unit: $658,500 ÷ 2,000 = $329.25

Special Order Decisions

Occasionally, a company receives an offer to sell its goods at a price significantly below its normal selling price. The company must make a **special order decision** to accept or reject the offer.

Quantitative Analysis

Assume Premier Office Products manufactures printers. Premier expects to make and sell 2,000 printers in 10 batches of 200 units per batch during the coming year. Expected production costs are summarized in Exhibit 13.1.

Adding its normal markup to the total cost per unit, Premier set the selling price at $360 per printer.

Suppose Premier receives a *special order* from a new customer for 200 printers. If Premier accepts the order, its expected sales would increase from 2,000 units to 2,200 units. But the special order customer is willing to pay only $250 per printer. This price is well below not only Premier's normal selling price of $360 but also the company's expected per-unit cost of $329.25. Should Premier accept or reject the special order? At first glance, it seems Premier should reject the special order because the customer's offer is

Answers to The Curious Accountant

There are several factors that enable drug companies to reduce their prices to certain customers. One significant factor is the issue of relevant cost. Pharmaceutical manufacturers have a substantial amount of fixed cost, such as research and development. For example, in 2011 Pfizer Inc. had research and development expenses that were 13.5 percent of sales, while its cost of goods sold expense was 22.4 percent of sales. With respect to a special order decision, the research and development costs would not change and therefore would not be relevant. In contrast, the unit-level cost of goods sold would increase and therefore would be relevant. Clearly, relevant costs are significantly less than the total cost. If Canadian prices are based on relevant costs, that is, if drug companies view Canadian sales as a special order opportunity, the lower prices may provide a contribution to profitability even though they are significantly less than the prices charged in the United States.

It is interesting to compare the costs and profit percentages of a generic pharmaceutical manufacturer, such as Watson Pharmaceutical, Inc., to a company such as Pfizer that produces "patent drugs." In 2011, while Pfizer's cost of goods sold was 22.4 percent of sales, Watson's was 55.9 percent; however, Pfizer spent 13.5 percent of sales on research and development, while Watson spent only 6.4 percent. Finally, Pfizer's profit was 14.8 percent of sales while Watson's profit was only 5.7 percent. Clearly, patents do add value to a company, though a profit margin of 5.7 percent is not considered to be bad.

below the expected cost per unit. Analyzing relevant costs and revenue leads, however, to a different conclusion.

The quantitative analysis follows in three steps.

Step 1. **Determine the amount of the relevant (differential) revenue Premier will earn by accepting the special order.** Premier's alternatives are (1) to accept or (2) to reject the special order. If Premier accepts the special order, additional revenue will be $50,000 ($250 × 200 units). If Premier rejects the special order, additional revenue will be zero. Since the amount of revenue differs between the alternatives, the $50,000 is relevant.

Step 2. **Determine the amount of the relevant (differential) cost Premier will incur by accepting the special order.** Examine the costs in Exhibit 13.1. If Premier accepts the special order, it will incur additional unit-level costs (materials, labor, and overhead). It will also incur the cost of one additional 200-unit batch. The unit- and batch-level costs are relevant because Premier could avoid them by rejecting the special order. The other costs in Exhibit 13.1 are not relevant because Premier will incur them whether it accepts or rejects the special order.

Step 3. **Accept the special order if the relevant revenue exceeds the relevant (avoidable) cost. Reject the order if relevant cost exceeds relevant revenue.** Exhibit 13.2 summarizes the relevant figures. Since the relevant revenue exceeds the relevant cost, Premier should accept the special order because profitability will increase by $11,800.

EXHIBIT 13.2

Relevant Information for Special Order of 200 Printers

Differential revenue ($250 × 200 units)	$50,000
Avoidable unit-level costs ($180 × 200 units)	(36,000)
Avoidable batch-level costs ($2,200 × 1 batch)	(2,200)
Contribution to income	$11,800

Opportunity Costs

Premier can consider the special order because it has enough excess productive capacity to make the additional units. Suppose Premier has the opportunity to lease its excess capacity (currently unused building and equipment) for $15,000. If Premier uses the excess capacity to make the additional printers, it must forgo the opportunity to lease the excess capacity to a third party. Sacrificing the potential leasing income represents an opportunity cost of accepting the special order. Adding this opportunity cost to the other relevant costs increases the cost of accepting the special order to $53,200 ($38,200 unit-level and batch-level costs + $15,000 opportunity cost). The avoidable costs would then exceed the differential revenue, resulting in a projected loss of $3,200 ($50,000 differential revenue − $53,200 avoidable costs). Under these circumstances Premier would be better off rejecting the special order and leasing the excess capacity.

Relevance and the Decision Context

Assume Premier does not have the opportunity to lease its excess capacity. Recall the original analysis indicated the company could earn an $11,800 contribution to profit by accepting a special order to sell 200 printers at $250 per unit (see Exhibit 13.2). Because Premier can earn a contribution to profit by selling printers for $250 each, can the company reduce its normal selling price (price charged to existing customers) to $250? The answer is no, as illustrated in Exhibit 13.3.

EXHIBIT 13.3

Projections Based on 2,200 Printers at a Sales Price of $250 per Unit

Revenue ($250 × 2,200 units)		$ 550,000
Unit-level supplies and inspection ($180 × 2,200 units)	$396,000	
Batch-level costs ($2,200 × 11 batches)	24,200	
Product-level costs	77,300	
Facility-level costs	199,200	
Total cost		(696,700)
Projected loss		$(146,700)

If a company is to be profitable, it must ultimately generate revenue in excess of total costs. Although the facility-level and product-level costs are not relevant to the special order decision, they are relevant to the operation of the business as a whole.

Qualitative Characteristics

Should a company ever reject a special order if the relevant revenues exceed the relevant costs? Qualitative characteristics may be even more important than quantitative ones. If Premier's regular customers learn the company sold printers to another buyer at $250 per unit, they may demand reduced prices on future purchases. Exhibit 13.3 shows Premier cannot reduce the price for all customers. Special order customers should therefore come from outside Premier's normal sales territory. In addition, special order customers should be advised that the special price does not apply to repeat business. Cutting off a special order customer who has been permitted to establish a continuing relationship is likely to lead to ill-feelings and harsh words. A business's reputation can depend on how management handles such relationships. Finally, at full capacity, Premier should reject any special orders at reduced prices because filling those orders reduces its ability to satisfy customers who pay full price.

LO 13-3

Make appropriate outsourcing decisions.

Outsourcing Decisions

Companies can sometimes purchase products they need for less than it would cost to make them. This circumstance explains why automobile manufacturers purchase rather than make many of the parts in their cars or why a caterer might buy gourmet desserts

REALITY BYTES

Sometimes companies make special pricing decisions that appear to violate the rule of rejecting an offer when its relevant cost exceeds its relevant revenue. Consider companies that use the services of Groupon or LivingSocial.

In these special pricing decisions, retail customers are offered a reduced price on goods or services if they make the purchase through Groupon or LivingSocial. For example, a restaurant may offer to sell a customer $20 worth of food for only $10. This appears to be a deal where the restaurant is selling its food for 50 percent off, but actually it is probably selling the food for 75 percent off. The restaurant will only receive around $5 of the $10 the customer pays to Groupon. Groupon keeps the remaining $5 for itself. Thus, the restaurant is selling $20 of food for $5.

At Darden Concepts Inc., the company that owns several restaurant chains including Red Lobster and Olive Garden, the cost of goods sold averages 75 percent of revenue. In other words, if a customer buys $20 worth of food, approximately $15 of those dollars are costs of providing the food to the customer. Not all of these costs are unit-level costs, but many of them are. Therefore, when a restaurant sells a customer $20 worth of food for only $5, as in the Groupon example above, it appears to be selling the goods for much less than their relevant cost. Why would the restaurant do this?

Obviously, the restaurant is hoping that it will attract new customers with its special pricing offer and that these new customers will become repeat customers who pay full price for future meals. In this situation, the true relevant revenue is not the $5 received for the first meal, but includes the revenue from future meals the customer buys. Of course there is no guarantee the customer will ever return, but as with most business decisions, managers must make decisions with less than perfect information.

from a specialty company. Buying goods and services from other companies rather than producing them internally is commonly called **outsourcing.**

Quantitative Analysis

Assume Premier Office Products is considering whether to outsource production of the printers it currently makes. A supplier has offered to sell an unlimited supply of printers to Premier for $240 each. The estimated cost of making the printers is $329.25 per unit (see Exhibit 13.1). The data suggest that Premier could save money by outsourcing. Analyzing relevant costs proves this presumption wrong.

A two-step quantitative analysis for the outsourcing decision follows:

Step 1. **Determine the production costs Premier can avoid if it outsources printer production.** A review of Exhibit 13.1 discloses the costs Premier could avoid by outsourcing. If Premier purchases the printers, it can avoid the unit-level costs (materials, labor, overhead), and the batch-level costs (assembly setup and materials handling). It can also avoid the product-level costs (engineering design costs and production manager salary). Deciding to outsource will not, however, affect the facility-level costs. Because Premier will incur them whether or not it outsources printer production, the facility-level costs are not relevant to the outsourcing decision. Exhibit 13.4 shows the avoidable (relevant) costs of outsourcing.

Step 2. **Compare the avoidable (relevant) production costs with the cost of buying the product and select the lower-cost option.** Because the relevant production cost is less than the purchase price of the printers ($229.65 per unit versus $240.00), the quantitative analysis suggests that Premier should continue to make the printers. Profitability would decline by $20,700 [$459,300 − ($240 × 2,000)] if printer production were outsourced.

Opportunity Costs

Suppose Premier's accountant determines that the space Premier currently uses to manufacture printers could be leased to a third party for $40,000 per year. By using the space to manufacture printers, Premier is *forgoing the opportunity* to earn $40,000. Because this *opportunity cost* can be avoided by purchasing the printers, it is relevant to the outsourcing decision. After adding the opportunity cost to the other relevant costs, the total relevant cost increases to $499,300 ($459,300 + $40,000) and the relevant cost per unit becomes $249.65 ($499,300 ÷ 2,000). Since Premier can purchase printers for $240, it should outsource printer production. It would be better off buying the printers and leasing the manufacturing space.

EXHIBIT 13.4

Relevant Cost for Expected Production for Outsourcing 2,000 Printers

Unit-level costs ($180 × 2,000 units)	$360,000
Batch-level costs ($2,200 × 10 batches)	22,000
Product-level costs	77,300
Total relevant cost	$459,300

Cost per unit: $459,300 ÷ 2,000 = $229.65

Evaluating the Effect of Growth on the Level of Production

The decision to outsource would change if expected production increased from 2,000 to 3,000 units. Because some of the avoidable costs are fixed relative to the level of production, cost per unit decreases as volume increases. For example, the product-level costs (engineering design, production manager's salary, and opportunity cost) are fixed relative to the level of production. Exhibit 13.5 shows the relevant cost per unit if Premier expects to produce 3,000 printers.

EXHIBIT 13.5

Relevant Cost for Expected Production for Outsourcing 3,000 Printers

Unit-level costs ($180 × 3,000 units)	$540,000
Batch-level costs ($2,200 × 15 batches)	33,000
Product-level costs	77,300
Opportunity cost	40,000
Total relevant cost	$690,300

Cost per unit: $690,300 ÷ 3,000 units = $230.10

478   Chapter 13

FOCUS ON INTERNATIONAL ISSUES

ARE YOU SURE YOUR GERMAN CAR WAS MADE IN GERMANY?

In recent years, there has been much discussion about American companies outsourcing work to workers in other countries. However, some activities that are seldom outsourced by American companies are routinely outsourced by companies in other countries. In fact, sometimes the "foreign country" who provides the outsourcing is the United States.

   Consider an example from the automotive industry. While American automobile companies may use parts that were manufactured in another country, the final assembly of cars they sell in the United States is usually performed in their own plants in the United States or Canada. Japanese auto companies also tend to perform the final assembly of their cars in their own plants, which may be located in another country. In contrast, European car makers are more willing to outsource the final assembly, as well as engineering and parts production, to independent companies. For example, most, if not all BMW X3s are not assembled at a BMW plant, but by the employees of Magna Steyr in Graz, Austria. This company, by the way, is a subsidiary of Magna International, which is a Canadian company. Likewise, for most of its existence, the Porsche Boxster was not built by Porsche but by Valmet Automotive of Finland. However, in recent years Porsche has decided to reduce its level of outsourcing. Its agreement with Valmet ended on January 31, 2012.

Source: Companies' annual reports.

At 3,000 units of production, the relevant cost of making printers is less than the cost of outsourcing ($230.10 versus $240.00). If management believes the company is likely to experience growth in the near future, it should reject the outsourcing option. Managers must consider potential growth when making outsourcing decisions.

Qualitative Features

A company that uses **vertical integration** controls the full range of activities from acquiring raw materials to distributing goods and services. Outsourcing reduces the level of vertical integration, passing some of a company's control over its products to outside suppliers. The reliability of the supplier is critical to an outsourcing decision. An unscrupulous supplier may lure an unsuspecting manufacturer into an outsourcing decision using **low-ball pricing.** Once the manufacturer is dependent on the supplier, the supplier raises prices. If a price sounds too good to be true, it probably is too good to be true. Other potential problems include product quality and delivery commitments. If the printers do not work properly or are not delivered on time, Premier's customers will be dissatisfied with Premier, not the supplier. Outsourcing requires that Premier depend on the supplier to deliver quality products at designated prices according to a specified schedule. Any supplier failures will become Premier's failures.

   To protect themselves from unscrupulous or incompetent suppliers, many companies establish a select list of reliable **certified suppliers.** These companies seek to become the preferred customers of the suppliers by offering incentives such as guaranteed volume purchases with prompt payments. These incentives motivate the suppliers to ship high-quality products on a timely basis. The purchasing companies recognize that prices ultimately depend on the suppliers' ability to control costs, so the buyers and suppliers work together to minimize costs. For example, buyers may share confidential information about their production plans with suppliers if such information would enable the suppliers to more effectively control costs.

   Companies must approach outsourcing decisions cautiously even when relationships with reliable suppliers are ensured. Outsourcing has both internal and external effects. It usually displaces employees. If the supplier experiences difficulties, reestablishing internal production capacity is expensive once a trained workforce has been released. Loyalty and trust are difficult to build but easy to destroy. In fact, companies must consider not only the employees who will be discharged but also the morale of those who remain. Cost reductions achieved through outsourcing are of little benefit if they are acquired at the expense of low morale and reduced productivity.

In spite of the potential pitfalls outsourcing entails, the vast majority of U.S. businesses engage in some form of it. Such widespread acceptance suggests that most companies believe the benefits achieved through outsourcing exceed the potential shortcomings.

 CHECK YOURSELF 13.2

Addison Manufacturing Company pays a production supervisor a salary of $48,000 per year. The supervisor manages the production of sprinkler heads that are used in water irrigation systems. Should the production supervisor's salary be considered a relevant cost to a special order decision? Should the production supervisor's salary be considered a relevant cost to an outsourcing decision?

Answer   The production supervisor's salary is not a relevant cost to a special order decision because Addison would pay the salary regardless of whether it accepts or rejects a special order. Since the cost does not differ for the alternatives, it is not relevant. In contrast, the supervisor's salary would be relevant to an outsourcing decision. Addison could dismiss the supervisor if it purchased the sprinkler heads instead of making them. Since the salary could be avoided by purchasing heads instead of making them, the salary is relevant to an outsourcing decision.

Segment Elimination Decisions

Businesses frequently organize their operations into subcomponents called **segments.** Segment data are used to make comparisons among different products, departments, or divisions. For example, in addition to the companywide income statement provided for external users, JCPenney may prepare separate income statements for each retail store for internal users. Executives can then evaluate managerial performance by comparing profitability measures among stores. *Segment reports* can be prepared for products, services, departments, branches, centers, offices, or divisions. These reports normally show segment revenues and costs. The primary objective of segment analysis is to determine whether relevant revenues exceed relevant costs.

LO 13-4

 Make appropriate segment elimination decisions.

Quantitative Analysis

Assume Premier Office Products makes copy equipment and computers as well as printers. Each product line is made in a separate division of the company. Division (segment) operating results for the most recent year are shown in Exhibit 13.6. Initial review of the results suggests the copier division should be eliminated because it is operating at a loss. However, analyzing the relevant revenues and expenses leads to a different conclusion.

A three-step quantitative analysis for the segment elimination decision follows:

Step 1. **Determine the amount of relevant (differential) revenue that pertains to eliminating the copier division.** The alternatives are (1) to eliminate or (2) to continue to operate the copier division. If Premier eliminates the copier line, it will lose the $550,000 of revenue the copier division currently produces. If the division continues to operate, Premier will earn the revenue. Since the revenue differs between the alternatives, it is relevant.

Step 2. **Determine the amount of cost Premier can avoid if it eliminates the copier division.** If it eliminates copiers, Premier can avoid the unit-level, batch-level,

EXHIBIT 13.6

Projected Revenues and Costs by Segment

	Copiers	Computers	Printers	Total
Projected revenue	$550,000	$850,000	$720,000	$2,120,000
Projected costs				
Unit-level costs				
Materials costs	(120,000)	(178,000)	(180,000)	(478,000)
Labor costs	(160,000)	(202,000)	(165,000)	(527,000)
Overhead	(30,800)	(20,000)	(15,000)	(65,800)
Batch-level costs				
Assembly setup	(15,000)	(26,000)	(17,000)	(58,000)
Materials handling	(6,000)	(8,000)	(5,000)	(19,000)
Product-level costs				
Engineering design	(10,000)	(12,000)	(14,000)	(36,000)
Production manager salary	(52,000)	(55,800)	(63,300)	(171,100)
Facility-level costs				
Segment level				
Division manager salary	(82,000)	(92,000)	(85,000)	(259,000)
Administrative costs	(12,200)	(13,200)	(12,700)	(38,100)
Allocated—corporate-level				
Company president salary	(34,000)	(46,000)	(43,200)	(123,200)
Building rental	(19,250)	(29,750)	(27,300)	(76,300)
General facility expenses	(31,000)	(31,000)	(31,000)	(93,000)
Projected income (loss)	$(22,250)	$136,250	$ 61,500	$ 175,500

product-level, and segment-level facility-sustaining costs. The relevant revenue and the avoidable costs are shown in Exhibit 13.7.

Premier will incur the corporate-level facility-sustaining costs whether it eliminates the copier segment or continues to operate it. Since these costs do not differ between the alternatives, they are not relevant to the elimination decision.

Step 3. **If the relevant revenue is less than the avoidable cost, eliminate the segment (division). If not, continue to operate it.** Because operating the segment is contributing $62,000 per year to company profitability (see Exhibit 13.7), Premier should not eliminate the copier division. Exhibit 13.8 shows Premier's estimated revenues and costs if the computer and printer divisions were operated without the copier division. Projected company profit declines by $62,000 ($175,500 − $113,500) without the copier segment, confirming that eliminating it would be detrimental to Premier's profitability.

Qualitative Considerations in Decisions to Eliminate Segments

As with other special decisions, management should consider qualitative factors when determining whether to eliminate segments. Employee lives will be disrupted; some employees may be reassigned elsewhere in the company, but others will be discharged. As with outsourcing decisions, reestablishing internal production capacity is difficult once a trained workforce has been released. Furthermore, employees in other segments, suppliers, customers, and investors may believe that the elimination of a segment implies the company as a whole is experiencing financial difficulty. These individuals may lose confidence in the company and seek business contacts with other companies they perceive to be more stable.

EXHIBIT 13.7

Relevant Revenue and Cost Data for Copier Segment

Projected revenue	$550,000
Projected costs	
Unit-level costs	
Materials costs	(120,000)
Labor costs	(160,000)
Overhead	(30,800)
Batch-level costs	
Assembly setup	(15,000)
Materials handling	(6,000)
Product-level costs	
Engineering design	(10,000)
Production manager salary	(52,000)
Facility-level costs	
Segment level	
Division manager salary	(82,000)
Administrative costs	(12,200)
Projected income (loss)	$ 62,000

EXHIBIT 13.8

Projected Revenues and Costs without Copier Division

	Computers	Printers	Total
Projected revenue	$850,000	$720,000	$1,570,000
Projected costs			
Unit-level costs			
Materials costs	(178,000)	(180,000)	(358,000)
Labor costs	(202,000)	(165,000)	(367,000)
Overhead	(20,000)	(15,000)	(35,000)
Batch-level costs			
Assembly setup	(26,000)	(17,000)	(43,000)
Materials handling	(8,000)	(5,000)	(13,000)
Product-level costs			
Engineering design	(12,000)	(14,000)	(26,000)
Production manager salary	(55,800)	(63,300)	(119,100)
Facility-level costs			
Segment level			
Division manager salary	(92,000)	(85,000)	(177,000)
Administrative costs	(13,200)	(12,700)	(25,900)
Allocated—corporate-level*			
Company president salary	(63,000)	(60,200)	(123,200)
Building rental	(39,375)	(36,925)	(76,300)
General facility expenses	(46,500)	(46,500)	(93,000)
Projected income (loss)	$ 94,125	$ 19,375	$ 113,500

*The corporate-level facility costs that were previously *allocated* to the copier division have been reassigned on the basis of one-half to the computer division and one-half to the printer division.

Management must also consider the fact that sales of different product lines are frequently interdependent. Some customers prefer one-stop shopping; they want to buy all their office equipment from one supplier. If Premier no longer sells copiers, customers may stop buying its computers and printers. Eliminating one segment may reduce sales of other segments.

What will happen to the space Premier used to make the copiers? Suppose Premier decides to make telephone systems in the space it previously used for copiers. The contribution to profit of the telephone business would be an *opportunity cost* of operating the copier segment. As demonstrated in previous examples, adding the opportunity cost to the avoidable costs of operating the copier segment could change the decision.

As with outsourcing, volume changes can affect elimination decisions. Because many costs of operating a segment are fixed, the cost per unit decreases as production increases. Growth can transform a segment that is currently producing real losses into a segment that produces real profits. Managers must consider growth potential when making elimination decisions.

☑ CHECK YOURSELF 13.3

Capital Corporation is considering eliminating one of its operating segments. Capital employed a real estate broker to determine the marketability of the building that houses the segment. The broker obtained three bids for the building: $250,000, $262,000, and $264,000. The book value of the building is $275,000. Based on this information alone, what is the relevant cost of the building?

Answer   The book value of the building is a sunk cost that is not relevant. There are three bids for the building, but only one is relevant because Capital could sell the building only once. The relevant cost of the building is the highest opportunity cost, which in this case is $264,000.

482   Chapter 13

Summary of Relationships between Avoidable Costs and the Hierarchy of Business Activity

A relationship exists between the cost hierarchy and the different types of special decisions just discussed. A special order involves making additional units of an existing product. Deciding to accept a special order affects unit-level and possibly batch-level costs. In contrast, outsourcing a product stops the production of that product. Outsourcing can avoid many product-level as well as unit- and batch-level costs. Finally, if a company eliminates an entire business segment, it can avoid some of the facility-level costs. The more complex the decision level, the more opportunities there are to avoid costs. Moving to a higher category does not mean, however, that all costs at the higher level of activity are avoidable. For example, all product-level costs may not be avoidable if a company chooses to outsource a product. The company may still incur inventory holding costs or advertising costs whether it makes or buys the product. Understanding the relationship between decision type and level of cost hierarchy helps when identifying avoidable costs. The relationships are summarized in Exhibit 13.9. For each type of decision, look for avoidable costs in the categories marked with an X. Remember also that sunk costs cannot be avoided.

EXHIBIT 13.9

Relationship between Decision Type and Level of Cost Hierarchy

Decision Type	Unit level	Batch level	Product level	Facility level
Special order	X	X		
Outsourcing	X	X	X	
Elimination	X	X	X	X

Equipment Replacement Decisions

Equipment may become technologically obsolete long before it fails physically. Managers should base **equipment replacement decisions** on profitability analysis rather than physical deterioration. Assume Premier Office Products is considering replacing an existing machine with a new one. The following table summarizes pertinent information about the two machines:

Old Machine		New Machine	
Original cost	$90,000	Cost of the new machine	$29,000
Accumulated depreciation	(33,000)	Salvage value (in 5 years)	4,000
Book value	$57,000	Operating expenses	
		($4,500 × 5 years)	22,500
Market value (now)	$14,000		
Salvage value (in 5 years)	2,000		
Annual depreciation expense	11,000		
Operating expenses			
($9,000 × 5 years)	45,000		

Quantitative Analysis

First determine what relevant costs Premier will incur if it keeps the *old machine*.

1. The *original cost* ($90,000), *current book value* ($57,000), *accumulated depreciation* ($33,000), and *annual depreciation expense* ($11,000) are different measures of a cost that was incurred in a prior period. They represent irrelevant sunk costs.

2. The $14,000 market value represents the current sacrifice Premier must make if it keeps using the existing machine. In other words, if Premier does not keep the machine, it can sell it for $14,000. In economic terms, *forgoing the opportunity* to sell the machine costs as much as buying it. The *opportunity cost* is therefore relevant to the replacement decision.

3. The salvage value of the old machine reduces the opportunity cost. Premier can sell the old machine now for $14,000 or use it for five more years and then sell it for $2,000. The opportunity cost of using the old machine for five more years is therefore $12,000 ($14,000 − $2,000).

4. Because the $45,000 ($9,000 × 5) of operating expenses will be incurred if the old machine is used but can be avoided if it is replaced, the operating expenses are relevant costs.

Next, determine what relevant costs will be incurred if Premier purchases and uses the *new machine*.

1. The cost of the new machine represents a future economic sacrifice Premier must incur if it buys the new machine. It is a relevant cost.

2. The salvage value reduces the cost of purchasing the new machine. Part ($4,000) of the $29,000 cost of the new machine will be recovered at the end of five years. The relevant cost of purchasing the new machine is $25,000 ($29,000 − $4,000).

3. The $22,500 ($4,500 × 5) of operating expenses will be incurred if the new machine is purchased; it can be avoided if the new machine is not purchased. The operating expenses are relevant costs.

The relevant costs for the two machines are summarized here:

Old Machine		New Machine	
Opportunity cost	$14,000	Cost of the new machine	$29,000
Salvage value	(2,000)	Salvage value	(4,000)
Operating expenses	45,000	Operating expenses	22,500
Total	$57,000	Total	$47,500

The analysis suggests that Premier should acquire the new machine because buying it produces the lower relevant cost. The $57,000 cost of using the old machine can be *avoided* by incurring the $47,500 cost of acquiring and using the new machine. Over the five-year period, Premier would save $9,500 ($57,000 − $47,500) by purchasing the new machine. One caution: This analysis ignores income tax effects and the time value of money, which are explained later. The discussion in this chapter focuses on identifying and using relevant costs in decision making.

A Look Back

Decision making requires managers to choose from alternative courses of action. Successful decision making depends on a manager's ability to identify *relevant information*. Information that is relevant for decision making differs among the alternatives and is future oriented. Relevant revenues are sometimes called *differential revenues* because they differ among the alternatives. Relevant costs are sometimes called *avoidable costs* because they can be eliminated or avoided by choosing a specific course of action.

Costs that do not differ among the alternatives are not avoidable and therefore not relevant. *Sunk costs* are not relevant in decision making because they have been incurred in past transactions and therefore cannot be avoided. *Opportunity costs* are relevant because they represent potential benefits that may or may not be realized, depending on the decision maker's choice. In other words, future benefits that differ among the alternatives are relevant. Opportunity costs are not recorded in the financial accounting records.

Cost behavior (fixed or variable) is independent from the concept of relevance. Furthermore, a cost that is relevant in one decision context may be irrelevant in another context. Decision making depends on qualitative as well as quantitative information. *Quantitative information refers to information that can be measured using numbers. Qualitative information* is nonquantitative information such as personal preferences or opportunities.

Classifying costs into one of four hierarchical levels facilitates identifying relevant costs. *Unit-level costs* such as materials and labor are incurred each time a single unit of product is made. These costs can be avoided by eliminating the production of a single unit of product. *Batch-level costs* are associated with producing a group of products. Examples include setup costs and inspection costs related to a batch (group) of work rather than a single unit. Eliminating a batch would avoid both batch-level costs and unit-level costs. *Product-level costs* are incurred to support specific products or services (design and regulatory compliance costs). Product-level costs can be avoided by discontinuing a product line. *Facility-level costs,* like the president's salary, are incurred on behalf of the whole company or a segment of the company. In segment elimination decisions, the facility-level costs related to a particular segment being considered for elimination are relevant and avoidable. Those applying to the company as a whole are not avoidable.

Four types of special decisions that are frequently encountered in business are (1) *special orders,* (2) *outsourcing,* (3) *elimination decisions,* and (4) *asset replacement.* The relevant costs in a special order decision are the unit-level and batch-level costs that will be incurred if the special order is accepted. If the differential revenues from the special order exceed the relevant costs, the order should be accepted. Outsourcing decisions determine whether goods and services should be purchased from other companies. The relevant costs are the unit-level, batch-level, and product-level costs that could be avoided if the company outsources the product or service. If these costs are more than the cost to buy and the qualitative characteristics are satisfactory, the company should outsource. Segment-related unit-level, batch-level, product-level, and facility-level costs that can be avoided when a segment is eliminated are relevant. If the segment's avoidable costs exceed its differential revenues, it should be eliminated, assuming favorable qualitative factors. Asset replacement decisions compare the relevant costs of existing equipment with the relevant costs of new equipment to determine whether replacing the old equipment would be profitable.

>> A Look Forward

The next chapter introduces key concepts associated with planning and cost control. It shows you how to develop a master budget including the preparation of four operating budgets: (1) a sales budget, (2) an inventory purchases budget, (3) a selling and administrative expense budget and (4) a cash budget. The chapter explains how data from the operating budgets are used to prepare pro forma (budgeted) financial statements. In addition to the quantitative aspects, the chapter discusses the effect of the budgeting process on human behavior.

Video lectures and accompanying self-assessment quizzes are available for all learning objectives through McGraw-Hill *Connect® Accounting.*

SELF-STUDY REVIEW PROBLEM

Flying High, Inc. (FHI), is a division of The Master Toy Company. FHI makes remote-controlled airplanes. During 2014, FHI incurred the following costs in the process of making 5,000 planes:

Unit-level materials costs (5,000 units × $80)	$ 400,000
Unit-level labor costs (5,000 units × $90)	450,000
Unit-level overhead costs (5,000 × $70)	350,000
Depreciation cost on manufacturing equipment*	50,000
Other manufacturing overhead†	140,000
Inventory holding costs	240,000
Allocated portion of The Master Toy Company's facility-level costs	600,000
Total costs	$2,230,000

*The manufacturing equipment, which originally cost $250,000, has a book value of $200,000, a remaining useful life of four years, and a zero salvage value. If the equipment is not used in the production process, it can be leased for $30,000 per year.

†Includes supervisors' salaries and rent for the manufacturing building.

Required

a. FHI uses a cost-plus pricing strategy. FHI sets its price at product cost plus $100. Determine the price that FHI should charge for its remote-controlled airplanes.

b. Assume that a potential customer that operates a chain of high-end toy stores has approached FHI. A buyer for this chain has offered to purchase 1,000 planes from FHI at a price of $275 each. Ignoring qualitative considerations, should FHI accept or reject the order?

c. FHI has the opportunity to purchase the planes from Arland Manufacturing Company for $325 each. Arland maintains adequate inventories so that it can supply its customers with planes on demand. Should FHI accept the opportunity to outsource the making of its planes?

d. When completing this requirement, use the sales price computed in Requirement *a*. Use the contribution margin format to prepare an income statement based on historical cost data. Prepare a second income statement that reflects the relevant cost data that Master Toy should consider in a segment elimination decision. Based on a comparison of these two statements, indicate whether Master Toy should eliminate the FHI division.

e. FHI is considering replacing the equipment it currently uses to manufacture its planes. It could purchase replacement equipment for $480,000 that has an expected useful life of four years and a salvage value of $40,000. The new equipment would increase productivity substantially, reducing unit-level labor costs by 20 percent. Assume that FHI would maintain its production and sales at 5,000 planes per year. Prepare a schedule that shows the relevant costs of operating the old equipment versus the costs of operating the new equipment. Should FHI replace the equipment?

Solution to Requirement *a*

Product Cost for Remote-Controlled Airplanes	
Unit-level materials costs (5,000 units × $80)	$ 400,000
Unit-level labor costs (5,000 units × $90)	450,000
Unit-level overhead costs (5,000 units × $70)	350,000
Depreciation cost on manufacturing equipment	50,000
Other manufacturing overhead	140,000
Total product cost	$1,390,000

The cost per unit is $278 ($1,390,000 ÷ 5,000 units). The sales price per unit is $378 ($278 + $100). Depreciation expense is included because cost-plus pricing is usually based on historical cost rather than relevant cost. To be profitable in the long run, a company must ultimately recover the amount it paid for the equipment (the historical cost of the equipment).

Solution to Requirement b

The incremental (relevant) cost of making 1,000 additional airplanes follows. The depreciation expense is not relevant because it represents a sunk cost. The other manufacturing overhead costs are not relevant because they will be incurred regardless of whether FHI makes the additional planes.

Per-Unit Relevant Product Cost for Airplanes	
Unit-level materials costs	$ 80
Unit-level labor costs	90
Unit-level overhead costs	70
Total relevant product cost	$240

Since the relevant (incremental) cost of making the planes is less than the incremental revenue, FHI should accept the special order. Accepting the order will increase profits by $35,000 [($275 Incremental revenue − $240 Incremental cost) × 1,000 Units].

Solution to Requirement c

Distinguish this decision from the special order opportunity discussed in Requirement b. That special order (Requirement b) decision hinged on the cost of making additional units with the existing production process. In contrast, a make-or-buy decision compares current production with the possibility of making zero units (closing down the entire manufacturing process). If the manufacturing process were shut down, FHI could avoid the unit-level costs, the cost of the lost opportunity to lease the equipment, the other manufacturing overhead costs, and the inventory holding costs. Since the planes can be purchased on demand, there is no need to maintain any inventory. The allocated portion of the facility-level costs is not relevant because it would be incurred regardless of whether FHI manufactured the planes. The relevant cost of making the planes follows.

Relevant Manufacturing Cost for Airplanes	
Unit-level materials costs (5,000 units × $80)	$ 400,000
Unit-level labor costs (5,000 units × $90)	450,000
Unit-level overhead costs (5,000 units × $70)	350,000
Opportunity cost of leasing the equipment	30,000
Other manufacturing overhead costs	140,000
Inventory holding cost	240,000
Total product cost	$1,610,000

The relevant cost per unit is $322 ($1,610,000 ÷ 5,000 units). Since the relevant cost of making the planes ($322) is less than the cost of purchasing them ($325), FHI should continue to make the planes.

Solution to Requirement d

Income Statements		
	Historical Cost Data	Relevant Cost Data
Revenue (5,000 units × $378)	$1,890,000	$1,890,000
Less variable costs:		
Unit-level materials costs (5,000 units × $80)	(400,000)	(400,000)
Unit-level labor costs (5,000 units × $90)	(450,000)	(450,000)
Unit-level overhead costs (5,000 units × $70)	(350,000)	(350,000)
Contribution margin	690,000	690,000
Depreciation cost on manufacturing equipment	(50,000)	
Opportunity cost of leasing manufacturing equipment		(30,000)
Other manufacturing overhead costs	(140,000)	(140,000)
Inventory holding costs	(240,000)	(240,000)
Allocated facility-level administrative costs	(600,000)	
Net loss	$ (340,000)	
Contribution to Master Toy's profitability		$ 280,000

Master Toy should not eliminate the segment (FHI). Although it appears to be incurring a loss, the allocated facility-level administrative costs are not relevant because Master Toy would incur these costs regardless of whether it eliminated FHI. Also, the depreciation cost on the manufacturing equipment is not relevant because it is a sunk cost. However, since the company could lease the equipment if the segment were eliminated, the $30,000 potential rental fee represents a relevant opportunity cost. The relevant revenue and cost data show that FHI is contributing $280,000 to the profitability of The Master Toy Company.

Solution to Requirement *e*

The relevant costs of using the old equipment versus the new equipment are the costs that differ for the two alternatives. In this case, relevant costs include the purchase price of the new equipment, the opportunity cost of the old equipment, and the labor costs. These items are summarized in the following table. The data show the total cost over the four-year useful life of the replacement equipment.

Relevant Cost Comparison		
	Old Equipment	New Equipment
Opportunity to lease the old equipment ($30,000 × 4 years)	$ 120,000	
Cost of new equipment ($480,000 − $40,000)		$ 440,000
Unit-level labor costs (5,000 units × $90 × 4 years)	1,800,000	
Unit-level labor costs (5,000 units × $90 × 4 years × .80)		1,440,000
Total relevant costs	$1,920,000	$1,880,000

Since the relevant cost of operating the new equipment is less than the cost of operating the old equipment, FHI should replace the equipment.

KEY TERMS

Avoidable costs 472	Facility-level costs 473	Qualitative	Segment 479
Batch-level costs 473	Low-ball pricing 478	characteristics 472	Special order
Certified suppliers 478	Opportunity cost 470	Quantitative	decisions 474
Differential revenue 472	Outsourcing 477	characteristics 472	Sunk costs 470
Equipment replacement	Product-level	Relevant costs 471	Unit-level costs 472
decisions 482	costs 473	Relevant information 470	Vertical integration 478

QUESTIONS

1. Identify the primary qualities of revenues and costs that are relevant for decision making.

2. Are variable costs always relevant? Explain.

3. Identify the four hierarchical levels used to classify costs. When can each of these levels of costs be avoided?

4. Describe the relationship between relevance and accuracy.

5. "It all comes down to the bottom line. The numbers never lie." Do you agree with this conclusion? Explain your position.

6. Carmon Company invested $300,000 in the equity securities of Mann Corporation. The current market value of Carmon's investment in Mann is $250,000. Carmon currently needs funds for operating purposes. Although interest rates are high, Carmon's president has decided to borrow the needed funds instead of selling the investment in Mann. He explains that his company cannot afford to take a $50,000 loss on the Mann stock. Evaluate the president's decision based on this information.

7. What is an opportunity cost? How does it differ from a sunk cost?

8. A local bank advertises that it offers a free noninterest-bearing checking account if the depositor maintains a $500 minimum balance in the account. Is the checking account truly free?

9. A manager is faced with deciding whether to replace machine A or machine B. The original cost of machine A was $20,000 and that of

machine B was $30,000. Because the two cost figures differ, they are relevant to the manager's decision. Do you agree? Explain your position.

10. Are all fixed costs unavoidable?

11. Identify two qualitative considerations that could be associated with special order decisions.

12. Which of the following would not be relevant to a make-or-buy decision?

    (a) Allocated portion of depreciation expense on existing facilities.

(b) Variable cost of labor used to produce products currently purchased from suppliers.

(c) Warehousing costs for inventory of completed products (inventory levels will be constant regardless of whether products are purchased or produced).

(d) Cost of materials used to produce the items currently purchased from suppliers.

(e) Property taxes on the factory building.

13. What two factors should be considered in deciding how to allocate shelf space in a retail establishment?

14. What level(s) of costs is(are) relevant in special order decisions?

15. Why would a company consider outsourcing products or services?

16. Chris Sutter, the production manager of Satellite Computers, insists that the floppy drives used in the company's upper-end computers be outsourced since they can be purchased from a supplier at a lower cost per unit than

the company is presently incurring to produce the drives. Jane Meyers, his assistant, insists that if sales growth continues at the current levels, the company will be able to produce the drives in the near future at a lower cost because of the company's predominately fixed cost structure. Does Ms. Meyers have a legitimate argument? Explain.

17. Identify some qualitative factors that should be considered in addition to quantitative costs in

deciding whether to outsource.

18. The managers of Wilcox, Inc., are suggesting that the company president eliminate one of the company's segments that is operating at a loss. Why may this be a hasty decision?

19. Why would a supervisor choose to continue using a more costly old machine instead of replacing it with a less costly new machine?

MULTIPLE-CHOICE QUESTIONS

Multiple-choice questions are provided on the text website at www.mhhe.com/edmondssurvey4e.

EXERCISES

 All applicable Exercises are available with McGraw-Hill Connect® Accounting.

LO 13-1

Exercise 13-1   *Distinction between relevance and cost behavior*

Tiffani Franks is trying to decide which of two different kinds of candy to sell in her retail candy store. One type is a name-brand candy that will practically sell itself. The other candy is cheaper to purchase but does not carry an identifiable brand name. Ms. Franks believes that she will have to incur significant advertising costs to sell this candy. Several cost items for the two types of candy are as follows:

Brandless Candy		Name-Brand Candy	
Cost per box	$ 5.00	Cost per box	$ 8.00
Sales commissions per box	1.00	Sales commissions per box	1.00
Rent of display space	1,500.00	Rent of display space	1,500.00
Advertising	3,000.00	Advertising	2,000.00

Required

Identify each cost as being relevant or irrelevant to Ms. Franks's decision and indicate whether it is fixed or variable relative to the number of boxes sold.

LO 13-1

Exercise 13-2   *Distinction between relevance and cost behavior*

Castro Company makes and sells a single product. Castro incurred the following costs in its most recent fiscal year.

Cost Items Appearing on the Income Statement	
Materials cost ($9 per unit)	Sales commissions (1.50% of sales)
Company president's salary	Salaries of administrative personnel
Depreciation on manufacturing equipment	Shipping and handling ($0.50 per unit)
Customer billing costs (1% of sales)	Depreciation on office furniture
Rental cost of manufacturing facility	Manufacturing supplies ($0.25 per unit)
Advertising costs ($200,000 per year)	Production supervisor's salary
Labor cost ($8 per unit)	

Castro could purchase the products that it currently makes. If it purchased the items, the company would continue to sell them using its own logo, advertising program, and sales staff.

Required

Identify each cost as relevant or irrelevant to the outsourcing decision and indicate whether the cost is fixed or variable relative to the number of products manufactured and sold.

Exercise 13-3   *Distinction between avoidable costs and cost behavior*   LO 13-1

Lallone Company makes fine jewelry that it sells to department stores throughout the United States. Lallone is trying to decide which of two bracelets to manufacture. Cost data pertaining to the two choices follow.

	Bracelet A	Bracelet B
Cost of materials per unit	$ 16	$ 30
Cost of labor per unit	32	32
Advertising cost per year	7,500	5,000
Annual depreciation on existing equip.	5,000	4,000

Required

a. Identify the fixed costs and determine the amount of fixed cost for each product.
b. Identify the variable costs and determine the amount of variable cost per unit for each product.
c. Identify the avoidable costs and determine the amount of avoidable cost for each product.

Exercise 13-4   *Cost hierarchy*   LO 13-1

Costs can be classified into one of four categories, including unit-level, batch-level, product-level, or facility-level costs.

Required

Classify each of the items listed below into one of the four categories listed above. The first item has been categorized as an example.

Cost Description	Cost Classification
Salary of company president	Facility-level cost
Research and development cost	
Factory lawn care cost	
Cost of patent	
Startup cost to change color of a product	
Cost of resetting sewing machines to change shirt size	
Real estate tax for the factory	
Direct labor	

LO 13-1

Exercise 13-5   *Opportunity costs*

Justin Brimer owns his own taxi, for which he bought a $20,000 permit to operate two years ago. Mr. Brimer earns $60,000 a year operating as an independent but has the opportunity to sell the taxi and permit for $73,000 and take a position as dispatcher for Carter Taxi Co. The dispatcher position pays $55,000 a year for a 40-hour week. Driving his own taxi, Mr. Brimer works approximately 55 hours per week. If he sells his business, he will invest the $73,000 and can earn a 10 percent return.

Required

a. Determine the opportunity cost of owning and operating the independent business.

b. Based solely on financial considerations, should Mr. Brimer sell the taxi and accept the position as dispatcher?

c. Discuss the qualitative as well as quantitative factors that Mr. Brimer should consider.

LO 13-2

Exercise 13-6   *Special order decision*

Packer Concrete Company pours concrete slabs for single-family dwellings. Wolff Construction Company, which operates outside Packer's normal sales territory, asks Packer to pour 40 slabs for Wolff's new development of homes. Packer has the capacity to build 300 slabs and is presently working on 250 of them. Wolff is willing to pay only $2,750 per slab. Packer estimates the cost of a typical job to include unit-level materials, $1,200; unit-level labor, $600; and an allocated portion of facility-level overhead, $1,000.

Required

Should Packer accept or reject the special order to pour 40 slabs for $2,750 each? Support your answer with appropriate computations.

LO 13-2

Exercise 13-7   *Special order decision*

Miko Company manufactures a personal computer designed for use in schools and markets it under its own label. Miko has the capacity to produce 40,000 units a year but is currently producing and selling only 32,000 units a year. The computer's normal selling price is $600 per unit with no volume discounts. The unit-level costs of the computer's production are $200 for direct materials, $180 for direct labor, and $50 for indirect unit-level manufacturing costs. The total product- and facility-level costs incurred by Miko during the year are expected to be $1,600,000 and $400,000, respectively. Assume that Miko receives a special order to produce and sell 6,000 computers at $450 each.

Required

Should Miko accept or reject the special order? Support your answer with appropriate computations.

LO 13-2

Exercise 13-8   *Identifying qualitative factors for a special order decision*

Required

Describe the qualitative factors that Miko should consider before accepting the special order described in Exercise 13-7.

LO 13-2

Exercise 13-9   *Using the contribution margin approach for a special order decision*

Elsea Company, which produces and sells a small digital clock, bases its pricing strategy on a 25 percent markup on total cost. Based on annual production costs for 25,000 units of product, computations for the sales price per clock follow.

Unit-level costs	$190,000
Fixed costs	50,000
Total cost (a)	240,000
Markup (a × 0.25)	60,000
Total sales (b)	$300,000
Sales price per unit (b ÷ 25,000)	$ 12

Required

a. Elsea has excess capacity and receives a special order for 8,000 clocks for $10 each. Calculate the contribution margin per unit. Based on this, should Elsea accept the special order?

b. Support your answer by preparing a contribution margin income statement for the special order.

Exercise 13-10   *Outsourcing decision*   LO 13-3

Jordan Bicycle Manufacturing Company currently produces the handlebars used in manufacturing its bicycles, which are high-quality racing bikes with limited sales. Jordan produces and sells only 10,000 bikes each year. Due to the low volume of activity, Jordan is unable to obtain the economies of scale that larger producers achieve. For example, Jordan could buy the handlebars for $29 each; they cost $31 each to make. The following is a detailed breakdown of current production costs.

Item	Unit Cost	Total
Unit-level costs		
Materials	$15	$150,000
Labor	10	100,000
Overhead	2	20,000
Allocated facility-level costs	4	40,000
Total	$31	$310,000

After seeing these figures, Jordan's president remarked that it would be foolish for the company to continue to produce the handlebars at $31 each when it can buy them for $29 each.

Required

Do you agree with the president's conclusion? Support your answer with appropriate computations.

Exercise 13-11   *Establishing price for an outsourcing decision*   LO 13-3

Rimes Company makes and sells lawn mowers for which it currently makes the engines. It has an opportunity to purchase the engines from a reliable manufacturer. The annual costs of making the engines are shown here.

Cost of materials (20,000 Units × $24)	$ 480,000
Labor (20,000 Units × $26)	520,000
Depreciation on manufacturing equipment*	42,000
Salary of supervisor of engine production	85,000
Rental cost of equipment used to make engines	23,000
Allocated portion of corporate-level facility-sustaining costs	80,000
Total cost to make 20,000 engines	$1,230,000

*The equipment has a book value of $90,000 but its market value is zero.

Required

a. Determine the maximum price per unit that Rimes would be willing to pay for the engines.

b. Would the price computed in Requirement *a* change if production increased to 24,000 units? Support your answer with appropriate computations.

Exercise 13-12   *Outsourcing decision with qualitative factors*   LO 13-3

Daisuke Corporation, which makes and sells 85,000 radios annually, currently purchases the radio speakers it uses for $5 each. Each radio uses one speaker. The company has idle capacity and is considering the possibility of making the speakers that it needs. Daisuke estimates that the cost of materials and labor needed to make speakers would be a total of $4.50 for each speaker. In addition, supervisory salaries, rent, and other manufacturing costs would be $89,000. Allocated facility-level costs would be $50,000.

Required

a. Determine the change in net income Daisuke would experience if it decides to make the speakers.

b. Discuss the qualitative factors that Daisuke should consider.

LO 13-3

Exercise 13-13 *Outsourcing decision affected by opportunity costs*

Freeman Electronics currently produces the shipping containers it uses to deliver the electronics products it sells. The monthly cost of producing 10,000 containers follows.

Unit-level materials	$ 6,000
Unit-level labor	6,600
Unit-level overhead	4,200
Product-level costs*	10,800
Allocated facility-level costs	26,400

*One-third of these costs can be avoided by purchasing the containers.

Baxi Container Company has offered to sell comparable containers to Freeman for $2.50 each.

Required

a. Should Freeman continue to make the containers? Support your answer with appropriate computations.

b. Freeman could lease the space it currently uses in the manufacturing process. If leasing would produce $8,000 per month, would your answer to Requirement *a* be different? Explain.

LO 13-4

Exercise 13-14 *Segment elimination decision*

Patterson Company operates three segments. Income statements for the segments imply that profitability could be improved if Segment A were eliminated.

PATTERSON COMPANY			
Income Statements for the Year 2014			
Segment	A	B	C
Sales	$165,000	$240,000	$250,000
Cost of goods sold	(121,000)	(92,000)	(95,000)
Sales commissions	(15,000)	(22,000)	(22,000)
Contribution margin	29,000	126,000	133,000
General fixed oper. exp. (allocation of president's salary)	(44,000)	(52,000)	(44,000)
Advertising expense (specific to individual divisions)	(3,000)	(10,000)	0
Net income	$ (18,000)	$ 64,000	$ 89,000

Required

a. Explain the effect on profitability if Segment A is eliminated.

b. Prepare comparative income statements for the company as a whole under two alternatives: (1) the retention of Segment A and (2) the elimination of Segment A.

LO 13-4

Exercise 13-15 *Segment elimination decision*

Mason Transport Company divides its operations into four divisions. A recent income statement for its West Division follows.

MASON TRANSPORT COMPANY	
West Division	
Income Statement for the Year 2015	
Revenue	$250,000
Salaries for drivers	(175,000)
Fuel expenses	(25,000)
Insurance	(35,000)
Division-level facility-sustaining costs	(20,000)
Companywide facility-sustaining costs	(65,000)
Net loss	$ (70,000)

Required

a. Should West Division be eliminated? Support your answer by explaining how the division's elimination would affect the net income of the company as a whole. By how much would companywide income increase or decrease?

b. Assume that West Division is able to increase its revenue to $270,000 by raising its prices. Would this change the decision you made in Requirement *a*? Determine the amount of the increase or decrease that would occur in companywide net income if the segment were eliminated if revenue were $270,000.

c. What is the minimum amount of revenue required to justify continuing the operation of West Division?

Exercise 13-16   *Identifying avoidable cost of a segment*   LO 13-4

Ramos Corporation is considering the elimination of one of its segments. The segment incurs the following fixed costs. If the segment is eliminated, the building it uses will be sold.

Advertising expense	$ 70,000
Supervisory salaries	150,000
Allocation of companywide facility-level costs	65,000
Original cost of building	110,000
Book value of building	50,000
Market value of building	80,000
Maintenance costs on equipment	56,000
Real estate taxes on building	6,000

Required

Based on this information, determine the amount of avoidable cost associated with the segment.

Exercise 13-17   *Opportunity cost*   LO 13-5

Brewton Freight Company owns a truck that cost $35,000. Currently, the truck's book value is $20,000, and its expected remaining useful life is four years. Brewton has the opportunity to purchase for $26,000 a replacement truck that is extremely fuel efficient. Fuel cost for the old truck is expected to be $5,000 per year more than fuel cost for the new truck. The old truck is paid for but, in spite of being in good condition, can be sold for only $12,000.

Required

Should Brewton replace the old truck with the new fuel-efficient model, or should it continue to use the old truck until it wears out? Explain.

Exercise 13-18   *Asset replacement decision*   LO 13-5

A machine purchased three years ago for $360,000 has a current book value using straight-line depreciation of $200,000; its operating expenses are $30,000 per year. A replacement machine would cost $240,000, have a useful life of nine years, and would require $13,000 per year in operating expenses. It has an expected salvage value of $65,000 after nine years. The current disposal value of the old machine is $85,000; if it is kept nine more years, its residual value would be $10,000.

Required

Based on this information, should the old machine be replaced? Support your answer.

LO 13-5

Exercise 13-19 *Asset replacement decision*

Adam Company is considering the replacement of some of its manufacturing equipment. Information regarding the existing equipment and the potential replacement equipment follows.

Existing Equipment		Replacement Equipment	
Cost	$150,000	Cost	$125,000
Operating expenses*	120,000	Operating expenses*	80,000
Salvage value	20,000	Salvage value	20,000
Market value	60,000	Useful life	8 years
Book value	45,000		
Remaining useful life	8 years		

*The amounts shown for operating expenses are the cumulative total of all such expected expenses to be incurred over the useful life of the equipment.

Required

Based on this information, recommend whether to replace the equipment. Support your recommendation with appropriate computations.

LO 13-5

Exercise 13-20 *Asset replacement decision*

Bach Company paid $120,000 to purchase a machine on January 1, 2012. During 2014, a technological breakthrough resulted in the development of a new machine that costs $150,000. The old machine costs $50,000 per year to operate, but the new machine could be operated for only $18,000 per year. The new machine, which will be available for delivery on January 1, 2015, has an expected useful life of four years. The old machine is more durable and is expected to have a remaining useful life of four years. The current market value of the old machine is $40,000. The expected salvage value of both machines is zero.

Required

Based on this information, recommend whether to replace the machine. Support your recommendation with appropriate computations.

LO 13-5

Exercise 13-21 *Annual versus cumulative data for replacement decision*

Because of rapidly advancing technology, Southern Publications Corporation is considering replacing its existing typesetting machine with leased equipment. The old machine, purchased two years ago, has an expected useful life of six years and is in good condition. Apparently, it will continue to perform as expected for the remaining four years of its expected useful life. A four-year lease for equipment with comparable productivity can be obtained for $20,000 per year. The following data apply to the old machine:

Original cost	$240,000
Accumulated depreciation	80,000
Current market value	95,000
Estimated salvage value	5,000

Required

a. Determine the annual opportunity cost of using the old machine. Based on your computations, recommend whether to replace it.

b. Determine the total cost of the lease over the four-year contract. Based on your computations, recommend whether to replace the old machine.

PROBLEMS

 All applicable Problems are available with McGraw-Hill *Connect® Accounting.*

Problem 13-22 *Context-sensitive relevance*   LO 13-1

Required

Respond to each requirement independently.

a. Describe two decision-making contexts, one in which unit-level materials costs are avoidable, and the other in which they are unavoidable.

b. Describe two decision-making contexts, one in which batch-level setup costs are avoidable, and the other in which they are unavoidable.

c. Describe two decision-making contexts, one in which advertising costs are avoidable, and the other in which they are unavoidable.

d. Describe two decision-making contexts, one in which rent paid for a building is avoidable, and the other in which it is unavoidable.

e. Describe two decision-making contexts, one in which depreciation on manufacturing equipment is avoidable, and the other in which it is unavoidable.

Problem 13-23 *Context-sensitive relevance*   LO 13-1

Bennett Construction Company is a building contractor specializing in small commercial buildings. The company has the opportunity to accept one of two jobs; it cannot accept both because they must be performed at the same time and Bennett does not have the necessary labor force for both jobs. Indeed, it will be necessary to hire a new supervisor if either job is accepted. Furthermore, additional insurance will be required if either job is accepted. The revenue and costs associated with each job follow.

CHECK FIGURES
a. Contribution to profit for Job A: $324,000
b. Contribution to profit for Job B: $76,130

Cost Category	Job A	Job B
Contract price	$900,000	$800,000
Unit-level materials	250,000	220,000
Unit-level labor	260,000	310,000
Unit-level overhead	40,000	30,000
Supervisor's salary	116,670	116,670
Rental equipment costs	26,000	29,000
Depreciation on tools (zero market value)	19,900	19,900
Allocated portion of companywide facility-sustaining costs	10,400	8,600
Insurance cost for job	18,200	18,200

Required

a. Assume that Bennett has decided to accept one of the two jobs. Identify the information relevant to selecting one job versus the other. Recommend which job to accept and support your answer with appropriate computations.

b. Assume that Job A is no longer available. Bennett's choice is to accept or reject Job B alone. Identify the information relevant to this decision. Recommend whether to accept or reject Job B. Support your answer with appropriate computations.

Problem 13-24 *Effect of order quantity on special order decision*   LO 13-2

Levy Quilting Company makes blankets that it markets through a variety of department stores. It makes the blankets in batches of 1,000 units. Levy made 20,000 blankets during the prior accounting period. The cost of producing the blankets is summarized as follows.

CHECK FIGURE
a. Relevant cost per unit: $49

Materials cost ($20 per unit × 20,000)	$ 400,000
Labor cost ($18 per unit × 20,000)	360,000
Manufacturing supplies ($3 × 20,000)	60,000
Batch-level costs (20 batches at $4,000 per batch)	80,000
Product-level costs	160,000
Facility-level costs	290,000
Total costs	$1,350,000

Cost per unit = $1,350,000 ÷ 20,000 = $67.50

Required

a. Rios Motels has offered to buy a batch of 500 blankets for $47 each. Levy's normal selling price is $90 per unit. Based on the preceding quantitative data, should Levy accept the special order? Support your answer with appropriate computations.

b. Would your answer to Requirement *a* change if Rios offered to buy a batch of 1,000 blankets for $56 per unit? Support your answer with appropriate computations.

c. Describe the qualitative factors that Levy Quilting Company should consider before accepting a special order to sell blankets to Rios Motels.

LO 13-3

Problem 13-25 *Effects of the level of production on an outsourcing decision*

Koch Chemical Company makes a variety of cosmetic products, one of which is a skin cream designed to reduce the signs of aging. Koch produces a relatively small amount (15,000 units) of the cream and is considering the purchase of the product from an outside supplier for $7.20 each. If Koch purchases from the outside supplier, it would continue to sell and distribute the cream under its own brand name. Koch's accountant constructed the following profitability analysis.

CHECK FIGURE
a. Total relevant cost: $120,000

Revenue (15,000 units × $16)	$240,000
Unit-level materials costs (15,000 units × $2.00)	(30,000)
Unit-level labor costs (15,000 units × $1.50)	(22,500)
Unit-level overhead costs (15,000 × $0.50)	(7,500)
Unit-level selling expenses (15,000 × $0.80)	(12,000)
Contribution margin	168,000
Skin cream production supervisor's salary	(60,000)
Allocated portion of facility-level costs	(30,000)
Product-level advertising cost	(40,000)
Contribution to companywide income	$ 38,000

Required

a. Identify the cost items relevant to the make-or-outsource decision.

b. Should Koch continue to make the product or buy it from the supplier? Support your answer by determining the change in net income if Koch buys the cream instead of making it.

c. Suppose that Koch is able to increase sales by 10,000 units (sales will increase to 25,000 units). At this level of production, should Koch make or buy the cream? Support your answer by explaining how the increase in production affects the cost per unit.

d. Discuss the qualitative factors that Koch should consider before deciding to outsource the skin cream. How can Koch minimize the risk of establishing a relationship with an unreliable supplier?

LO 13-3, 13-5

Problem 13-26 *Outsourcing decision affected by equipment replacement*

Cruger Bike Company (CBC) makes the frames used to build its bicycles. During 2014, CBC made 20,000 frames; the costs incurred follow.

Unit-level materials costs (20,000 units × $30)	$ 600,000
Unit-level labor costs (20,000 units × $40)	800,000
Unit-level overhead costs (20,000 × $10)	200,000
Depreciation on manufacturing equipment	120,000
Bike frame production supervisor's salary	70,000
Inventory holding costs	290,000
Allocated portion of facility-level costs	500,000
Total costs	$2,580,000

CHECK FIGURES
a. Avoidable cost per unit: $98.60
b. Avoidable cost per unit with new equipment: $26.50

CBC has an opportunity to purchase frames for $85 each.

Additional Information

1. The manufacturing equipment, which originally cost $550,000, has a book value of $450,000, a remaining useful life of four years, and a zero salvage value. If the equipment is not used to produce bicycle frames, it can be leased for $70,000 per year.
2. CBC has the opportunity to purchase for $910,000 new manufacturing equipment that will have an expected useful life of four years and a salvage value of $70,000. This equipment will increase productivity substantially, reducing unit-level labor costs by 60 percent. Assume that CBC will continue to produce and sell 20,000 frames per year in the future.
3. If CBC outsources the frames, the company can eliminate 80 percent of the inventory holding costs.

Required

a. Determine the avoidable cost per unit of making the bike frames, assuming that CBC is considering the alternatives of making the product using the existing equipment or outsourcing the product to the independent contractor. Based on the quantitative data, should CBC outsource the bike frames? Support your answer with appropriate computations.
b. Assuming that CBC is considering whether to replace the old equipment with the new equipment, determine the avoidable cost per unit to produce the bike frames using the new equipment and the avoidable cost per unit to produce the bike frames using the old equipment. Calculate the impact on profitability if the bike frames were made using the old equipment versus the new equipment.
c. Assuming that CBC is considering whether to either purchase the new equipment or outsource the bike frame, calculate the impact on profitability between the two alternatives.
d. Discuss the qualitative factors that CBC should consider before making a decision to outsource the bike frame. How can CBC minimize the risk of establishing a relationship with an unreliable supplier?

Problem 13-27   *Eliminating a segment*

LO 13-4

Niklos Boot Co. sells men's, women's, and children's boots. For each type of boot sold, it operates a separate department that has its own manager. The manager of the men's department has a sales staff of nine employees, the manager of the women's department has six employees, and the manager of the children's department has three employees. All departments are housed in a single store. In recent years, the children's department has operated at a net loss and is expected to continue to do so. Last year's income statements follow.

CHECK FIGURE
a. Contribution to profit: $8,000

	Men's Department	Women's Department	Children's Department
Sales	$500,000	$600,000	$120,000
Cost of goods sold	(210,000)	(250,000)	(70,000)
Gross margin	290,000	350,000	50,000
Department manager's salary	(52,000)	(60,000)	(24,000)
Sales commissions	(86,000)	(98,000)	(18,000)
Rent on store lease	(21,000)	(21,000)	(21,000)
Store utilities	(4,000)	(4,000)	(4,000)
Net income (loss)	$127,000	$167,000	$ (17,000)

Required

a. Determine whether to eliminate the children's department.

b. Confirm the conclusion you reached in Requirement *a* by preparing income statements for the company as a whole with and without the children's department.

c. Eliminating the children's department would increase space available to display men's and women's boots. Suppose management estimates that a wider selection of adult boots would increase the store's net earnings by $20,000. Would this information affect the decision that you made in Requirement *a*? Explain your answer.

LO 13-4

CHECK FIGURE

a. Contribution to profit: $(18,000)

Problem 13-28 *Effect of activity level and opportunity cost on segment elimination decision*

Borris Manufacturing Co. produces and sells specialized equipment used in the petroleum industry. The company is organized into three separate operating branches: Division A, which manufactures and sells heavy equipment; Division B, which manufactures and sells hand tools; and Division C, which makes and sells electric motors. Each division is housed in a separate manufacturing facility. Company headquarters is located in a separate building. In recent years, Division B has been operating at a net loss and is expected to continue to do so. Income statements for the three divisions for 2013 follow.

	Division A	Division B	Division C
Sales	$2,000,000	$ 600,000	$2,500,000
Less: Cost of goods sold			
Unit-level manufacturing costs	(1,200,000)	(400,000)	(1,500,000)
Rent on manufacturing facility	(270,000)	(150,000)	(200,000)
Gross margin	530,000	50,000	800,000
Less: Operating expenses			
Unit-level selling and admin. expenses	(125,000)	(28,000)	(156,000)
Division-level fixed selling and			
admin. expenses	(160,000)	(40,000)	(200,000)
Headquarters facility-level costs	(100,000)	(100,000)	(100,000)
Net income (loss)	$ 145,000	$(118,000)	$ 344,000

Required

a. Based on the preceding information, recommend whether to eliminate Division B. Support your answer by preparing companywide income statements before and after eliminating Division B.

b. During 2013, Division B produced and sold 20,000 units of hand tools. Would your recommendation in response to Requirement *a* change if sales and production increase to 30,000 units in 2014? Support your answer by comparing differential revenue and avoidable cost for Division B, assuming that it sells 30,000 units.

c. Suppose that Borris could sublease Division B's manufacturing facility for $320,000. Would you operate the division at a production and sales volume of 30,000 units, or would you close it? Support your answer with appropriate computations.

LO 13-2, 13-3, 13-4

CHECK FIGURE

a. CM: $5,000

Problem 13-29 *Comprehensive problem including special order, outsourcing, and segment elimination decisions*

Lang Corporation makes and sells state-of-the-art electronics products. One of its segments produces The Math Machine, an inexpensive calculator. The company's chief accountant recently prepared the following income statement showing annual revenues and expenses associated with the segment's operating activities. The relevant range for the production and sale of the calculators is between 30,000 and 60,000 units per year.

Revenue (40,000 units × $9.00)	$360,000
Unit-level variable costs	
Materials cost (40,000 × $2.25)	(90,000)
Labor cost (40,000 × $1.00)	(40,000)
Manufacturing overhead (40,000 × $1.00)	(40,000)
Shipping and handling (40,000 × $0.25)	(10,000)
Sales commissions (40,000 × $1.00)	(40,000)
Contribution margin	140,000
Fixed expenses	
Advertising costs	(20,000)
Salary of production supervisor	(60,000)
Allocated companywide facility-level expenses	(80,000)
Net loss	$ (20,000)

Required (Consider each of the requirements independently.)

a. A large discount store has approached the owner of Lang about buying 5,000 calculators. It would replace The Math Machine's label with its own logo to avoid affecting Lang's existing customers. Because the offer was made directly to the owner, no sales commissions on the transaction would be involved, but the discount store is willing to pay only $5.50 per calculator. Based on quantitative factors alone, should Lang accept the special order? Support your answer with appropriate computations. Specifically, by what amount would the special order increase or decrease profitability?

b. Lang has an opportunity to buy the 40,000 calculators it currently makes from a reliable competing manufacturer for $5.60 each. The product meets Lang's quality standards. Lang could continue to use its own logo, advertising program, and sales force to distribute the products. Should Lang buy the calculators or continue to make them? Support your answer with appropriate computations. Specifically, how much more or less would it cost to buy the calculators than to make them? Would your answer change if the volume of sales were increased to 60,000 units?

c. Because the calculator division is currently operating at a loss, should it be eliminated from the company's operations? Support your answer with appropriate computations. Specifically, by what amount would the segment's elimination increase or decrease profitability?

ANALYZE, THINK, COMMUNICATE

ATC 13-1 Business Application Case *Analyzing inventory reductions at Supervalu*

On January 12, 2010, Supervalu, Inc., announced it was planning to reduce the number of different items it carries in its inventory by as much as 25 percent. Supervalu is one of the largest grocery store companies in the United States. As of February 25, 2012, it operated more than 2,400 stores under 12 different brand names, including Albertsons, Farm Fresh, Jewel-Osco, and Save-A-Lot. The company also has a wholesale segment that distributes goods to other retailers.

Most of the planned reduction in inventory items was going to be accomplished by reducing the number of different package sizes rather than by reducing entire product brands. The new approach was intended to allow the company to get better prices from its vendors and to put more emphasis on its own store brands.

Required

a. Identify some cost savings Supervalu might realize by reducing the number of items it carries in inventory. Be as specific as possible, and use your imagination.

b. Consider the additional information presented below, which is hypothetical. All dollar amounts are in thousands; unit amounts are not. Assume that Supervalu decides to eliminate one product line, Corn Clusters, for one of its segments that currently produces three products. As a result, the following are expected to occur:

(1) The number of units sold for the segment is expected to drop by only 125,000 because of the elimination of Corn Clusters, since many customers are expected to purchase an Oat Flakes or Fiber Squares product instead. The shift of sales from Corn Clusters to Oat Flakes and Fiber Squares is expected to be evenly split. In other words, the sales of Oat Flakes and Fiber Squares will each increase by 50,000 units.

(2) Rent is paid for the entire production facility, and the space used by Corn Clusters cannot be sublet.

(3) Utilities costs are expected to be reduced by $40,000.

(4) All of the supervisors for Corn Clusters will be terminated. No new supervisors will be hired for Oat Flakes or Fiber Squares.

(5) Half of the equipment being used to produce Corn Clusters is also used to produce the other two products, and its depreciation cost must be absorbed by them. The remaining equipment has a book value of $340,000 but can be sold for only $60,000.

(6) Facility-level costs will continue to be allocated between the product lines based on the number of units produced.

Product-Line Earnings Statements
(Dollar amounts are in thousands)

Annual Costs of Operating Each Product Line	Oat Flakes	Fiber Squares	Corn Clusters	Total
Sales in units	450,000	450,000	225,000	1,125,000
Sales in dollars	$900,000	$900,000	$450,000	$2,250,000
Unit-level costs:				
Cost of production	85,500	85,500	46,200	217,200
Sales commissions	11,700	11,700	6,000	29,400
Shipping and handling	20,250	18,000	9,000	47,250
Miscellaneous	6,750	4,500	2,250	13,500
Total unit-level costs	68,400	66,000	36,000	170,400
Product-level costs:				
Supervisors' salaries	9,600	7,200	2,400	19,200
Facility-level costs:				
Rent	100,000	100,000	50,000	250,000
Utilities	112,500	112,500	56,250	281,250
Depreciation on equipment	400,000	400,000	200,000	1,000,000
Allocated companywide expenses	22,500	22,500	11,250	56,250
Total facility-level costs	312,000	312,000	156,000	780,000
Total product cost	385,200	381,600	193,200	960,000
Profit on products	$ 94,800	$ 98,400	$ 46,800	$ 240,000

Prepare revised product-line earnings statements based on the elimination of Corn Clusters. (*Hint:* It will be necessary to calculate some per-unit data to accomplish this).

ATC 13-2   Group Assignment   *Relevance and cost behavior*

Maccoa Soft, a division of Zayer Software Company, produces and distributes an automated payroll software system. A contribution margin format income statement for Maccoa Soft for the past year follows.

Revenue (12,000 units × $1,200)	$14,400,000
Unit-level variable costs	
Product materials cost (12,000 × $60)	(720,000)
Installation labor cost (12,000 × $200)	(2,400,000)
Manufacturing overhead (12,000 × $2)	(24,000)
Shipping and handling (12,000 × $25)	(300,000)
Sales commissions (12,000 × $300)	(3,600,000)
Nonmanufacturing miscellaneous costs (12,000 × $5)	(60,000)
Contribution margin (12,000 × $608)	7,296,000
Fixed costs	
Research and development	(2,700,000)
Legal fees to ensure product protection	(780,000)
Advertising costs	(1,200,000)
Rental cost of manufacturing facility	(600,000)
Depreciation on production equipment (zero market value)	(300,000)
Other manufacturing costs (salaries, utilities, etc.)	(744,000)
Division-level facility sustaining costs	(1,730,000)
Allocated companywide facility-level costs	(1,650,000)
Net loss	$ (2,408,000)

a. Divide the class into groups and then organize the groups into three sections. Assign Task 1 to the first section, Task 2 to the second section, and Task 3 to the third section. Each task should be considered independently of the others.

Group Tasks

(1) Assume that Maccoa has excess capacity. The sales staff has identified a large franchise company with 200 outlets that is interested in Maccoa's software system but is willing to pay only $800 for each system. Ignoring qualitative considerations, should Maccoa accept the special order?

(2) Maccoa has the opportunity to purchase a comparable payroll system from a competing vendor for $600 per system. Ignoring qualitative considerations, should Maccoa outsource producing the software? Maccoa would continue to sell and install the software if the manufacturing activities were outsourced.

(3) Given that Maccoa is generating a loss, should Zayer eliminate it? Would your answer change if Maccoa could increase sales by 1,000 units?

b. Have a representative from each section explain its respective conclusions. Discuss the following:

(1) Representatives from Section 1 should respond to the following: The analysis related to the special order (Task 1) suggests that all variable costs are always relevant. Is this conclusion valid? Explain your answer.

(2) Representatives from Section 2 should respond to the following: With respect to the outsourcing decision, identify a relevant fixed cost and a nonrelevant fixed cost. Discuss the criteria for determining whether a cost is or is not relevant.

(3) Representatives from Section 3 should respond to the following: Why did the segment elimination decision change when the volume of production and sales increased?

ATC 13-3   Research Assignment   *Challenging times at the USPS*

In recent years, the United States Postal Service (USPS) has experienced declining revenues, largely due to the increase in digital communications such as e-mail. These declining revenues have led the USPS to experience financial losses. On February 16, 2012, the USPS issued a report titled *Plan to Profitability: 5 Year Business Plan,* which outlined the problems facing the USPS and the actions needed to address them.

To obtain a copy of the report, type "USPS Plan to Profitability" into an Internet search engine or search for "USPS Release 12-029." This should take you to a link where you can view and download the 28-page PDF document. You may want to review the entire document, but at a minimum you need to read the following pages: 3–5, 8–10, 12–14, and 26. (This is not as much as it seems as the print is large and there are lots of graphics.) Note: the report uses the acronym RHB, but does not define it. RHB stands for Retiree Health Benefits and represents money that Congress appropriated to help the USPS.

Required

a. Based on the information on page 4, summarize the basic factors contributing to the USPS's financial difficulties.

b. Based on the information on pages 8 and 9, in 2011 what percentage of the USPS mail *volume* resulted from delivery of first-class mail, and what percent of the USPS "*profit*" was derived from first-class mail?

c. What percentage of the USPS costs is due to compensation costs? From the USPS's point of view, are these costs more fixed or variable in nature, relative to the volume of mail delivered?

d. Page 26 of the report discusses "sensitivity analysis." Based on these data, if USPS's volume of activity were to increase by 1 percent, by how many dollars would revenues and profits be expected to increase? If USPS's *price* were to increase by 1 percent, by how many dollars would revenues and profits be expected to increase? With respect to the increase in *price*, how can the USPS expect that the dollar amount of increase in profit would be higher than the increase in revenue? (See the footnote.)

e. Based on the information on pages 12 through 14, summarize the proposals the USPS made to return to profitability. What percent of the proposals can be implemented without the approval of Congress? Do most of the proposals for cost reductions relate to reducing fixed costs or variable costs? Explain.

ATC 13-4   Writing Assignment   *Relevant versus full cost*

State law permits the State Department of Revenue to collect taxes for municipal governments that operate within the state's jurisdiction and allows private companies to collect taxes for municipalities. To promote fairness and to ensure the financial well-being of the state, the law dictates that the Department of Revenue must charge municipalities a fee for collection services that is above the cost of providing such services but does not define the term *cost*. Until recently, Department of Revenue officials have included a proportionate share of all departmental costs such as depreciation on buildings and equipment, supervisory salaries, and other facility-level overhead costs when determining the cost of providing collection services, a measurement approach known as *full costing*. The full costing approach has led to a pricing structure that places the Department of Revenue at a competitive disadvantage relative to private collection companies. Indeed, highly efficient private companies have been able to consistently underbid the Revenue Department for municipal customers. As a result, it has lost 30 percent of its municipal collection business over the last two years. The inability to be price competitive led the revenue commissioner to hire a consulting firm to evaluate the current practice of determining the cost to provide collection services.

The consulting firm concluded that the cost to provide collection services should be limited to the relevant costs associated with providing those services, defined as the difference between the costs that would be incurred if the services were provided and the costs that would be incurred if the services were not provided. According to this definition, the costs of depreciation, supervisory salaries, and other facility-level overhead costs are not included because they are the same regardless of whether the Department of Revenue provides collection services to municipalities. The Revenue Department adopted the relevant cost approach and immediately reduced the price it charges municipalities to collect their taxes and rapidly recovered the collection business it had lost. Indeed, several of the private collection companies were forced into bankruptcy. The private companies joined together and filed suit against the Revenue Department, charging that the new definition of cost violates the intent of the law.

Required

a. Assume that you are an accountant hired as a consultant for the private companies. Write a brief memo explaining why it is inappropriate to limit the definition of the costs of providing collection services to relevant costs.

b. Assume that you are an accountant hired as a consultant for the Department of Revenue. Write a brief memo explaining why it is appropriate to limit the definition of the costs of providing collection services to relevant costs.

c. Speculate on how the matter will be resolved.

ATC 13-5   Ethical Dilemma   *Asset replacement clouded by self-interest*

John Dillworth is in charge of buying property used as building sites for branch offices of the National Bank of Commerce. Mr. Dillworth recently paid $110,000 for a site located in a growing section of the city. Shortly after purchasing this lot, Mr. Dillworth had the opportunity to purchase a more desirable lot at a significantly lower price. The traffic count at the new site is virtually twice that of the old site, but the price of the lot is only $80,000. It was immediately apparent that he had overpaid for the previous purchase. The current market value of the purchased property is only $75,000. Mr. Dillworth believes that it would be in the bank's best interest to buy the new lot, but he does not want to report a loss to his boss, Kelly Fullerton. He knows that Ms. Fullerton will severely reprimand him, even though she has made her share of mistakes. In fact, he is aware of a significant bad loan that Ms. Fullerton recently approved. When confronted with the bad debt by the senior vice president in charge of commercial lending, Ms. Fullerton blamed the decision on one of her former subordinates, Ira Sacks. Ms. Fullerton implied that Mr. Sacks had been dismissed for reckless lending decisions when, in fact, he had been an excellent loan officer with an uncanny ability to assess the creditworthiness of his customers. Indeed, Mr. Sacks had voluntarily resigned to accept a better position.

Required

a. Determine the amount of the loss that would be recognized on the sale of the existing branch site.

b. Identify the type of cost represented by the $110,000 original purchase price of the land. Also identify the type of cost represented by its current market value of $75,000. Indicate which cost is relevant to a decision as to whether the original site should be replaced with the new site.

c. Is Mr. Dillworth's conclusion that the old site should be replaced supported by quantitative analysis? If not, what facts do justify his conclusion?

d. Assuming that Mr. Dillworth is a certified management accountant (CMA), do you believe the failure to replace the land violates any of the standards of ethical professional practice in Exhibit 10.17 in Chapter 10? If so, which standards would be violated?

CHAPTER 14

Planning for Profit and Cost Control

LEARNING OBJECTIVES

After you have mastered the material in this chapter, you will be able to:

LO 14-1   Describe the budgeting process and the benefits it provides.

LO 14-2   Prepare a sales budget and related schedule of cash receipts.

LO 14-3   Prepare an inventory purchases budget and related schedule of cash payments.

LO 14-4   Prepare a selling and administrative expense budget and related schedule of cash payments.

LO 14-5   Prepare a cash budget.

LO 14-6   Prepare a pro forma income statement, balance sheet, and statement of cash flows.

 Video lectures and accompanying self-assessment quizzes are available for all learning objectives through McGraw-Hill Connect® Accounting.

CHAPTER OPENING

Planning is crucial to operating a profitable business. Expressing business plans in financial terms is commonly called **budgeting.** The budgeting process involves coordinating the financial plans of all areas of the business. For example, the production department cannot prepare a manufacturing plan until it knows how many units of product to produce. The number of units to produce depends on the marketing department's sales projection. The marketing department cannot project sales volume until it knows what products the company will sell. Product information comes from the research and development department. The point should be clear: A company's master budget results from combining numerous specific plans prepared by different departments.

Master budget preparation is normally supervised by a committee. The budget committee is responsible for settling disputes among various departments over budget matters. The committee also monitors reports on how various segments are progressing toward achieving their budget goals. The budgeting committee is not an accounting committee. It is a high-level committee that normally includes the company president, vice presidents of marketing, purchasing, production, and finance, and the controller.

The Curious Accountant

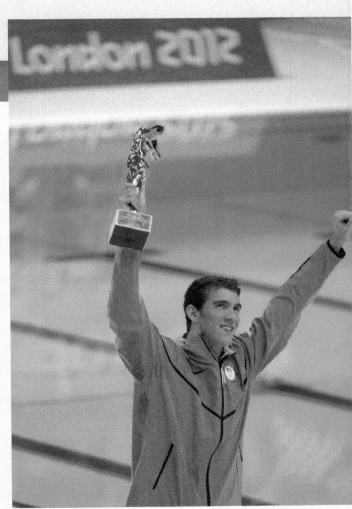

People in television commercials often say they shop at a particular store because, "my family is on a budget." The truth is, most families do not have a formal budget. What these people mean is that they need to be sure their spending does not exceed their available cash.

When a family expects to spend more money in a given year than it will earn, it must plan on borrowing funds needed to make up the difference. However, even if a family's income for a year will exceed its spending, it may still need to borrow money because the timing of its cash inflows may not match the timing of its cash outflows. Whether a budget is being prepared for a family or a business, those preparing the budget must understand the specific issues facing that entity if potential financial problems are to be anticipated. There is no such thing as a "one size fits all" budget.

The United States Olympic Committee (USOC), like all large organizations, devotes considerable effort to budget planning.

Think about the Olympic Games and how the USOC generates revenues and incurs expenditures. Can you identify any unusual circumstances facing the USOC that complicate its budgeting efforts? (Answer on page 519.)

THE PLANNING PROCESS

LO 14-1

Describe the budgeting process and the benefits it provides.

Planning normally addresses short, intermediate, and long-range time horizons. Short-term plans are more specific than long-term plans. Consider, for example, your decision to attend college. Long-term planning requires considering general questions such as:

- Do I want to go to college?
- How do I expect to benefit from the experience?
- Do I want a broad knowledge base, or am I seeking to learn specific job skills?
- In what field do I want to concentrate my studies?

Many students go to college before answering these questions. They discover the disadvantages of poor planning the hard way. While their friends are graduating, they are starting over in a new major.

Intermediate-range planning usually covers three to five years. In this stage, you consider which college to attend, how to support yourself while in school, and whether to live on or off campus.

Short-term planning focuses on the coming year. In this phase, you plan specific courses to take, decide which instructors to choose, schedule part-time work, and join a study group. Short-term plans are specific and detailed. Their preparation may seem tedious, but careful planning generally leads to efficient resource use and high levels of productivity.

Three Levels of Planning for Business Activity

Businesses describe the three levels of planning as *strategic planning, capital budgeting,* and *operations budgeting.* **Strategic planning** involves making long-term decisions such as defining the scope of the business, determining which products to develop or discontinue, and identifying the most profitable market niche. Upper-level management is responsible for these decisions. Strategic plans are descriptive rather than quantitative. Objectives such as "to have the largest share of the market" or "to be the best-quality producer" result from strategic planning. Although strategic planning is an integral component of managing a business, an in-depth discussion of it is beyond the scope of this text.

Capital budgeting focuses on intermediate range planning. It involves such decisions as whether to buy or lease equipment, whether to stimulate sales, or whether to increase the company's asset base. Capital budgeting is discussed in detail in a later chapter.

Operations budgeting concentrates on short-term plans. A key component of operations budgeting is the *master budget,* which describes short-term objectives in specific amounts of sales targets, production goals, and financing plans. The master budget describes how management intends to achieve its objectives and directs the company's short-term activities.

The master budget normally covers one year. It is frequently divided into quarterly projections and often subdivides quarterly data by month. Effective managers cannot wait until year-end to know whether operations conform to budget targets. Monthly data provide feedback to permit making necessary corrections promptly.

Many companies use **perpetual,** or **continuous, budgeting** covering a 12-month reporting period. As the current month draws to a close, an additional month is added at the end of the budget period, resulting in a continuous 12-month budget. A perpetual budget offers the advantage of keeping management constantly focused on thinking ahead to the next 12 months. The more traditional annual approach to budgeting invites a frenzied stop-and-go mentality, with managers preparing the budget in a year-end rush that is soon forgotten. Changing conditions may not be discussed until the next year-end budget is due. A perpetual budget overcomes these disadvantages.

Advantages of Budgeting

Budgeting is costly and time-consuming. The sacrifices, however, are more than offset by the benefits. Budgeting promotes planning and coordination; it enhances performance measurement and corrective action.

Planning

Almost everyone makes plans. Each morning, most people think about what they will do during the day. Thinking ahead is planning. Most business managers think ahead about how they will direct operations. Unfortunately, planning is frequently as informal as making a few mental notes. Informal planning cannot be effectively communicated. The business manager might know what her objectives are, but neither her superiors nor her subordinates know. Because it serves as a communication tool, budgeting can solve these problems. The budget formalizes and documents managerial plans, clearly communicating objectives to both superiors and subordinates.

Coordination

Sometimes a choice benefits one department at the expense of another. For example, a purchasing agent may order large quantities of raw materials to obtain discounts from suppliers. But excessive quantities of materials pose a storage problem for the inventory supervisor who must manage warehouse costs. The budgeting process forces coordination among departments to promote decisions in the best interests of the company as a whole.

Performance Measurement

Budgets are specific, quantitative representations of management's objectives. Comparing actual results to budget expectations provides a way to evaluate performance. For example, if a company budgets sales of $10 million, it can judge the performance of the sales department against that level. If actual sales exceed $10 million, the company should reward the sales department; if actual sales fall below $10 million, the company should seek an explanation for the shortfall from the sales manager.

Corrective Action

Budgeting provides advance notice of potential shortages, bottlenecks, or other weaknesses in operating plans. For example, a cash budget alerts management to when the company can expect cash shortages during the coming year. The company can make borrowing arrangements well before it needs the money. Without knowing ahead of time, management might be unable to secure necessary financing on short notice, or it may have to pay excessively high interest rates to obtain funds. Budgeting advises managers of potential problems in time for them to carefully devise effective solutions.

Budgeting and Human Behavior

Effective budgeting requires genuine sensitivity on the part of upper management to the effect on employees of budget expectations. People are often uncomfortable with budgets. Budgets are constraining. They limit individual freedom in favor of an established plan. Many people find evaluation based on budget expectations stressful. Most students experience a similar fear about testing. Like examinations, budgets represent standards by which performance is evaluated. Employees worry about whether their performance will meet expectations.

The attitudes of high-level managers significantly impact budget effectiveness. Subordinates are keenly aware of management's expectations. If upper-level managers degrade, make fun of, or ignore the budget, subordinates will follow suit. If management uses budgets to humiliate, embarrass, or punish subordinates, employees will resent the treatment and the budgeting process. Upper-level managers must demonstrate that they view the budget as a sincere effort to express realistic goals employees are expected to meet. An honest, open, respectful atmosphere is essential to budgeting success.

Participative budgeting has frequently proved successful in creating a healthy atmosphere. This technique invites participation in the budget process by personnel at all levels of the organization, not just upper-level managers. Information flows from the bottom up as well as from the top down during budget preparation. Because they are directly responsible for meeting budget goals, subordinates can offer more realistic targets. Including them in budget preparation fosters development of a team effort. Participation fosters more cooperation and motivation, and less fear. With participative budgeting, subordinates cannot complain that the budget is management's plan. The budget is instead a self-imposed constraint. Employees can hold no one responsible but themselves if they fail to accomplish the budget objectives they established.

Upper management participates in the process to ensure that employee-generated objectives are consistent with company objectives. Furthermore, if subordinates were granted complete freedom to establish budget standards, they might be tempted to adopt lax standards to ensure they will meet them. Both managers and subordinates must cooperate if the participatory process is to produce an effective budget. If developed carefully, budgets can motivate employees to achieve superior performance. Normal human fears must be overcome, and management must create an honest budget atmosphere.

The Master Budget

The **master budget** is a group of detailed budgets and schedules representing the company's operating and financial plans for a future accounting period. The master budget usually includes (1) *operating budgets,* (2) *capital budgets,* and (3) *pro forma financial statements.* The budgeting process normally begins with preparing the **operating budgets,** which focus on detailed operating activities. This chapter illustrates operating budgets and pro forma statements for Hampton Hams, a retail sales company that uses (1) a sales budget, (2) an inventory purchases budget, (3) a selling and administrative (S&A) expense budget, and (4) a cash budget. As previously stated, capital budgets are discussed in a later chapter.

The sales budget includes a schedule of cash receipts from customers. The inventory purchases and S&A expense budgets include schedules of cash payments for inventory and expenses. Preparing the master budget begins with the sales forecast. Based on the sales forecast, the detailed budgets for inventory purchases and operating expenses are developed. The schedules of cash receipts and cash payments provide the foundation for preparing the cash budget.

The operating budgets are used to prepare *pro forma statements.* **Pro forma financial statements** are based on projected (budgeted) rather than historical information. Hampton Hams prepares a pro forma income statement, balance sheet, and statement of cash flows.

Exhibit 14.1 shows how information flows in a master budget.

EXHIBIT 14.1

Information Flows in the Master Budget

HAMPTON HAMS BUDGETING ILLUSTRATION

Hampton Hams (HH), a major corporation, sells cured hams nationwide through retail outlets in shopping malls. By focusing on a single product and standardized operations, the company controls costs stringently. As a result, it offers high-quality hams at competitive prices.

Hampton Hams has experienced phenomenal growth during the past five years. It opened two new stores in Indianapolis, Indiana, last month and plans to open a third new store in October. Hampton Hams finances new stores by borrowing on a line of credit arranged with National Bank. National's loan officer has requested monthly budgets for each of the first three months of the new store's operations. The accounting department is preparing the new store's master budget for October, November, and December. The first step is developing a sales budget.

Sales Budget

Preparing the master budget begins with the sales forecast. The accuracy of the sales forecast is critical because all the other budgets are derived from the sales budget. Normally, the marketing department coordinates the development of the sales forecast. Sales estimates frequently flow from the bottom up to the higher management levels. Sales personnel prepare sales projections for their products and territories and pass them up the line where they are combined with the estimates of other sales personnel to develop regional and national estimates. Using various information sources, upper-level sales managers adjust the estimates generated by sales personnel. Adjustment information comes from industry periodicals and trade journals, economic analysis, marketing surveys, historical sales figures, and changes in competition. Companies assimilate these data using sophisticated computer programs, statistical techniques, and quantitative methods, or, simply, professional judgment. Regardless of the technique, the senior vice president of sales ultimately develops a sales forecast for which she is held responsible.

To develop the sales forecast for HH's new store, the sales manager studied the sales history of existing stores operating in similar locations. He then adjusted for start-up conditions. October is an opportune time to open a new store because customers will learn the store's location before the holiday season. The sales manager expects significant

LO 14-2

Prepare a sales budget and related schedule of cash receipts.

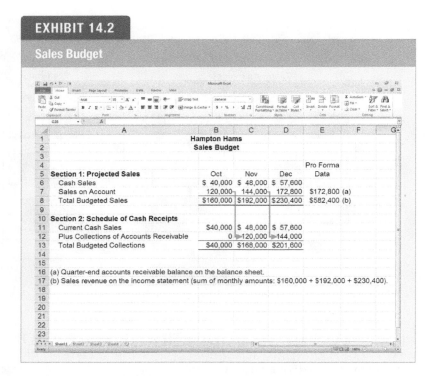

EXHIBIT 14.2

Sales Budget

	A	B	C	D	E	F
1			**Hampton Hams**			
2			**Sales Budget**			
3						
4					Pro Forma	
5	**Section 1: Projected Sales**	Oct	Nov	Dec	Data	
6	Cash Sales	$ 40,000	$ 48,000	$ 57,600		
7	Sales on Account	120,000	144,000	172,800	$172,800 (a)	
8	Total Budgeted Sales	$160,000	$192,000	$230,400	$582,400 (b)	
9						
10	**Section 2: Schedule of Cash Receipts**					
11	Current Cash Sales	$40,000	$ 48,000	$ 57,600		
12	Plus Collections of Accounts Receivable	0	120,000	144,000		
13	Total Budgeted Collections	$40,000	$168,000	$201,600		
14						
15						
16	(a) Quarter-end accounts receivable balance on the balance sheet.					
17	(b) Sales revenue on the income statement (sum of monthly amounts: $160,000 + $192,000 + $230,400).					

growth in November and December as customers choose the company's hams as the centerpiece for many Thanksgiving and winter holiday dinner tables.

The new store's sales are expected to be $160,000 in October ($40,000 in cash and $120,000 on account). Sales are expected to increase 20 percent per month during November and December. Based on these estimates, the sales manager prepared the sales budget in Exhibit 14.2.

Projected Sales

The sales budget has two sections. Section 1 shows the projected sales for each month. The November sales forecast reflects a 20 percent increase over October sales. For example, November *cash sales* are calculated as $48,000 [$40,000 + ($40,000 × 0.20)], and December *cash sales* are calculated as $57,600 [$48,000 + ($48,000 × 0.20)]. *Sales on account* are similarly computed.

Schedule of Cash Receipts

Section 2 is a schedule of the cash receipts for the projected sales. This schedule is used later to prepare the cash budget. The accountant has assumed in this schedule that Hampton Hams will collect accounts receivable from credit sales *in full* in the month following the sale. In practice, collections may be spread over several months, and some receivables may become bad debts that are never collected. Regardless of additional complexities, the objective is to estimate the amount and timing of expected cash receipts.

In the HH case, *total cash receipts* are determined by adding the current month's *cash sales* to the cash collected from the previous month's *credit sales* (accounts receivable balance). Cash receipts for each month are determined as follows:

- October receipts are projected to be $40,000. Because the store opens in October, no accounts receivable from September exist to be collected in October. Cash receipts for October equal the amount of October's cash sales.

- November receipts are projected to be $168,000 ($48,000 November cash sales + $120,000 cash collected from October sales on account).

- December receipts are projected to be $201,600 ($57,600 December cash sales + $144,000 cash collected from November sales on account).

FOCUS ON INTERNATIONAL ISSUES

CASH FLOW PLANNING IN BORDEAUX

The year 2010 was considered a great year for wine in the Bordeaux region of France, and the winemakers could look forward to selling their wines for high prices, but there was one catch: These wines would not be released to consumers until late in 2013. The winemakers had incurred most of their costs in 2010 when the vines were being tended and the grapes were being processed into wine. In many industries, this would mean the companies would have to finance their inventory for almost four years—not an insignificant cost. The company must finance the inventory by either borrowing the money, which results in out-of-pocket interest expense, or using its own funds. The second option generates an opportunity cost resulting from the interest revenue that could have been earned if these funds were not being used to finance the inventory.

To address this potential cash flow problem, many of the winemakers in Bordeaux offer some of their wines for sale as "futures." That means the wines are purchased and paid for while they are still aging in barrels in France. Selling wine as futures reduces the time inventory must be financed from four years to only one to two years. Of course there are other types of costs in such deals. For one, the wines must be offered at lower prices than they are expected to sell for upon release. The winemakers have obviously decided this cost is less than the cost of financing inventory through borrowed money, or they would not do it.

Recently, one major Bordeaux winery announced a contrarian approach. Chateau Latour said that beginning with the 2012 vintage, not only would it no longer sell futures, but it would no longer sell its wines until it thinks they have aged sufficiently to be at their prime drinking age, which might be 12 years after the vintage. Obviously the winery believes this will allow it to sell its wine at a higher price, but it will need large sums of cash to finance many years of production while it waits. Clearly, this will complicate Chateau Latour's cash-flow planning.

Companies in other industries use similar techniques to speed up cash flow, such as factoring of accounts receivable. A major reason entities prepare cash budgets is to be sure they will have enough cash on hand to pay bills as they come due. If the budget indicates a temporary cash-flow deficit, action must be taken to avoid the problem, and new budgets must be prepared based on these options. Budgeting is not a static process.

Source: Wine Spectator, June 30, 2012.

Pro Forma Financial Statement Data

The Pro Forma Data column in the sales budget displays two figures HH will report on the quarter-end (December 31) budgeted financial statements. Since HH expects to collect December credit sales in January, the *accounts receivable balance* will be $172,800 on the December 31 pro forma balance sheet (shown later in Exhibit 14.7).

The $582,400 of *sales revenue* in the Pro Forma Data column will be reported on the budgeted income statement for the quarter (shown later in Exhibit 14.6). The sales revenue represents the sum of October, November, and December sales ($160,000 + $192,000 + $230,400 = $582,400).

Inventory Purchases Budget

The inventory purchases budget shows the amount of inventory HH must purchase each month to satisfy the demand projected in the sales budget. The *total inventory needed* each month equals the amount of inventory HH plans to sell that month plus the amount of inventory HH wants on hand at month-end. To the extent that total inventory needed exceeds the inventory on hand at the beginning of the month, HH will need to purchase additional inventory. The amount of inventory to purchase is computed as follows:

LO 14-3

Prepare an inventory purchases budget and related schedule of cash payments.

Cost of budgeted sales	XXX
Plus: Desired ending inventory	XXX
Total inventory needed	XXX
Less: Beginning inventory	(XXX)
Required purchases	XXX

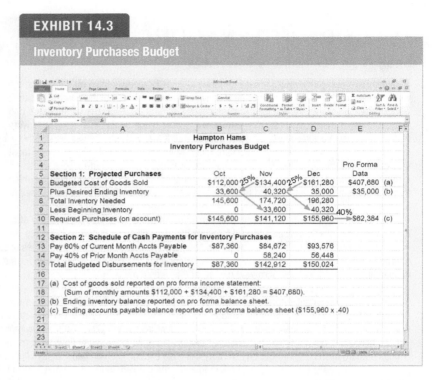

EXHIBIT 14.3

Inventory Purchases Budget

It is HH's policy to maintain an ending inventory equal to 25 percent of the next month's *projected cost of goods sold.* HH's cost of goods sold normally equals 70 percent of *sales.* Using this information and the sales budget, the accounting department prepared the inventory purchases budget shown in Exhibit 14.3.

Section 1 of the inventory purchases budget shows required purchases for each month. HH determined *budgeted cost of goods sold* for October by multiplying October *budgeted sales* by 70 percent ($160,000 × 0.70 = $112,000). Budgeted cost of goods sold for November and December were similarly computed. The October *desired ending inventory* was computed by multiplying November *budgeted cost of goods sold* by 25 percent ($134,400 × 0.25 = $33,600). Desired ending inventory for November is $40,320 ($161,280 × .25). Desired ending inventory for December is based on January projected cost of goods sold (not shown in the exhibit). HH expects ham sales to decline after the winter holidays. Because January projected cost of goods sold is only $140,000, the December desired ending inventory falls to $35,000 ($140,000 × .25).

Schedule of Cash Payments for Inventory Purchases

Section 2 is the schedule of cash payments for inventory purchases. HH makes all inventory purchases on account. The supplier requires that HH pay for 60 percent of inventory purchases in the month goods are purchased. HH pays the remaining 40 percent the month after purchase.

Cash payments are projected as follows (amounts are rounded to the nearest whole dollar):

- October cash payments for inventory are $87,360. Because the new store opens in October, no accounts payable balance from September remains to be paid in October. Cash payments for October equal 60 percent of October inventory purchases.

- November cash payments for inventory are $142,912 (40 percent of October purchases + 60 percent of November purchases).

- December cash payments for inventory are $150,024 (40 percent of November purchases + 60 percent of December purchases).

Pro Forma Financial Statement Data

The Pro Forma Data column in the inventory purchases budget displays three figures HH will report on the quarter-end budgeted financial statements. The $407,680 *cost of goods sold* reported on the pro forma income statement (shown later in Exhibit 14.6) is the sum of the monthly cost of goods sold amounts ($112,000 + $134,400 + $161,280 = $407,680).

The $35,000 *ending inventory* as of December 31 is reported on the pro forma balance sheet (shown later in Exhibit 14.7). December 31 is the last day of both the month of December and the three-month quarter represented by October, November, and December.

The $62,384 of *accounts payable* reported on the pro forma balance sheet (shown later in Exhibit 14.7) represents the 40 percent of December inventory purchases HH will pay for in January ($155,960 × .40).

☑ CHECK YOURSELF 14.1

Main Street Sales Company purchased $80,000 of inventory during June. Purchases are expected to increase by 2 percent per month in each of the next three months. Main Street makes all purchases on account. It normally pays cash to settle 70 percent of its accounts payable during the month of purchase and settles the remaining 30 percent in the month following purchase. Based on this information, determine the accounts payable balance Main Street would report on its July 31 balance sheet.

Answer Purchases for the month of July are expected to be $81,600 ($80,000 × 1.02). Main Street will pay 70 percent of the resulting accounts payable in cash during July. The remaining 30 percent represents the expected balance in accounts payable as of July 31. Therefore, the balance would be $24,480 ($81,600 × 0.3).

Selling and Administrative Expense Budget

Section 1 of Exhibit 14.4 shows the selling and administrative (S&A) expense budget for Hampton Hams's new store. Most of the projected expenses are self-explanatory; depreciation and interest, however, merit comment. The depreciation expense is based on projections in the *capital expenditures budget*. Although not presented in this chapter, the capital budget calls for the cash purchase of $130,000 of store fixtures. The fixtures were purchased on October 1. The supplier allows a 30-day inspection period. As a result, payment for the fixtures was made at the end of October. The fixtures are expected to have a useful life of 10 years and a $10,000 salvage value. Using the straight-line method, HH estimates annual depreciation expense at $12,000 ([$130,000 − $10,000] ÷ 10). Monthly depreciation expense is $1,000 ($12,000 annual charge ÷ 12 months).

Interest expense is missing from the S&A expense budget. HH cannot estimate interest expense until it completes its borrowing projections. Expected borrowing (financing activities) and related interest expense are shown in the cash budget.

LO 14-4

Prepare a selling and administrative expense budget and related schedule of cash payments.

Schedule of Cash Payments for Selling and Administrative Expenses

Section 2 of the S&A expense budget shows the schedule of cash payments. There are several differences between the S&A expenses recognized on the pro forma income statement and the cash payments for S&A expenses. First, Hampton Hams pays sales commissions and utilities expense the month following their incurrence. Since the store opens in October there are no payments due from September. Cash payments for sales commissions and utilities in October are zero. In November, HH will pay the October expenses for these items and in December it will pay the November sales commissions and utilities expenses. Depreciation expense does not affect the cash payments schedule. The cash outflow for the store fixtures occurs when the assets are purchased, not when they are depreciated. The cost of the investment in store fixtures is in the cash budget, not in the cash outflow for S&A expenses.

514   Chapter 14

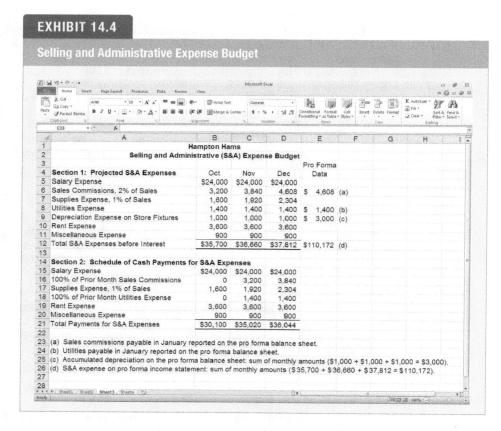

EXHIBIT 14.4

Selling and Administrative Expense Budget

	A	B	C	D	E	F
1			Hampton Hams			
2		Selling and Administrative (S&A) Expense Budget				
3					Pro Forma	
4	**Section 1: Projected S&A Expenses**	Oct	Nov	Dec	Data	
5	Salary Expense	$24,000	$24,000	$24,000		
6	Sales Commissions, 2% of Sales	3,200	3,840	4,608	$ 4,608 (a)	
7	Supplies Expense, 1% of Sales	1,600	1,920	2,304		
8	Utilities Expense	1,400	1,400	1,400	$ 1,400 (b)	
9	Depreciation Expense on Store Fixtures	1,000	1,000	1,000	$ 3,000 (c)	
10	Rent Expense	3,600	3,600	3,600		
11	Miscellaneous Expense	900	900	900		
12	Total S&A Expenses before Interest	$35,700	$36,660	$37,812	$110,172 (d)	
13						
14	**Section 2: Schedule of Cash Payments for S&A Expenses**					
15	Salary Expense	$24,000	$24,000	$24,000		
16	100% of Prior Month Sales Commissions	0	3,200	3,840		
17	Supplies Expense, 1% of Sales	1,600	1,920	2,304		
18	100% of Prior Month Utilities Expense	0	1,400	1,400		
19	Rent Expense	3,600	3,600	3,600		
20	Miscellaneous Expense	900	900	900		
21	Total Payments for S&A Expenses	$30,100	$35,020	$36,044		
22						
23	(a) Sales commissions payable in January reported on the pro forma balance sheet.					
24	(b) Utilities payable in January reported on the pro forma balance sheet.					
25	(c) Accumulated depreciation on the pro forma balance sheet: sum of monthly amounts ($1,000 + $1,000 + $1,000 = $3,000).					
26	(d) S&A expense on pro forma income statement: sum of monthly amounts ($35,700 + $36,660 + $37,812 = $110,172).					
27						
28						

Pro Forma Financial Statement Data

The Pro Forma Data column of the S&A expense budget displays four figures HH will report on the quarter-end budgeted financial statements. The first and second figures are the sales commissions payable ($4,608) and utilities payable ($1,400) (shown later

REALITY BYTES

THE ULTIMATE CASH PLANNING

Most companies have to spend money to buy inventory before they can collect money from selling those goods. For example, if you are manufacturing television sets, you need to purchase the parts needed to make the TVs and pay workers to assemble the TVs before you can sell them to retailers—who generally take 30 to 60 days to pay you for the TVs they purchase. Some companies are in the enviable position of being able to collect cash from their customers before having to pay cash to their own suppliers for the goods they sell. For example, Dell Computer, Inc., takes only 12 days to sell its inventory and 38 days to collect accounts receivable from those sales, for a total operating cycle of 50 days. However, it waits 87 days to pay its suppliers for its inventory purchases. Thus, Dell collects cash from its customers 37 days before it has to pay its suppliers.

Costco Wholesale Corporation also does a good job with cash management, but more from quick collection of its receivables than from slow payment to its suppliers, which is Dell's strategy. On average, Costco sells its inventory in 29 days and collects the receivables from those sales in 4 days, for a total operating cycle of 33 days. It takes 29 days to pay its suppliers for the inventory that it sells. So, although not as efficient as Dell, Costco still manages to get its cash from customers at about the same time it needs the cash to pay its suppliers, thus reducing its reliance on financing from sources such as bank loans.

Source: Companies' annual reports.

on the pro forma balance sheet in Exhibit 14.7). Because December sales commissions and utilities expense are not paid until January, these amounts represent liabilities as of December 31. The third figure in the column ($3,000) is the amount of accumulated depreciation on the pro forma balance sheet (shown later in Exhibit 14.7). Since depreciation accumulates, the $3,000 balance is the sum of the monthly depreciation amounts ($1,000 + $1,000 + $1,000 = $3,000). The final figure in the Pro Forma Data column ($110,172) is the total S&A expenses reported on the pro forma income statement (shown later in Exhibit 14.6). The total S&A expense is the sum of the monthly amounts ($35,700 + $36,660 + $37,812 = $110,172).

Cash Budget

Little is more important to business success than effective cash management. If a company experiences cash shortages, it will be unable to pay its debts and may be forced into bankruptcy. If excess cash accumulates, a business loses the opportunity to earn investment income or reduce interest costs by repaying debt. Preparing a **cash budget** alerts management to anticipated cash shortages or excess cash balances. Management can plan financing activities, making advance arrangements to cover anticipated shortages by borrowing and planning to repay past borrowings and making appropriate investments when excess cash is expected.

LO 14-5

Prepare a cash budget.

The cash budget is divided into three major sections: (1) a cash receipts section, (2) a cash payments section, and (3) a financing section. Much of the data needed to prepare the cash budget are included in the cash receipts and payments schedules previously discussed; however, further refinements to project financing needs and interest costs are sometimes necessary. The completed cash budget is shown in Exhibit 14.5.

EXHIBIT 14.5

Cash Budget

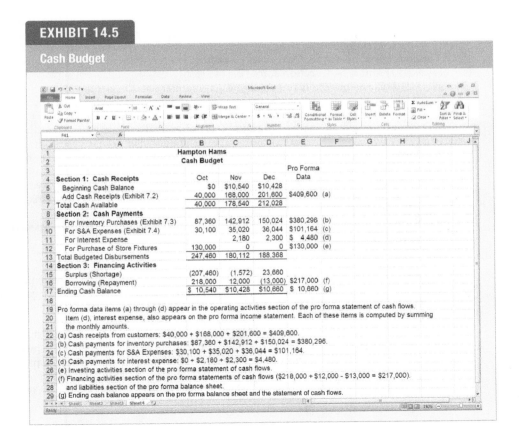

516   Chapter 14

REALITY BYTES
BUDGETING IN GOVERNMENTAL ENTITIES

This chapter has presented several reasons organizations should prepare budgets, but for governmental entities, budgets are not simply good planning tools—law requires them. If a manager at a commercial enterprise does not accomplish the budget objectives established for his or her part of the business, the manager may receive a poor performance evaluation. At worst, they may be fired. If managers of governmental agencies spend more than their budgets allow, they may have broken the law. In some cases, the manager could be required to personally repay the amount by which the budget was exceeded. Since governmental budgets are enacted by the relevant elected bodies, to violate the budget is to break the law.

Because budgets are so important for governments and are not to be exceeded, government accounting practices require that budgeted amounts be formally entered into the bookkeeping system. As you learned in your first accounting course, companies do not make formal accounting entries when they order goods; they only make an entry when the goods are received. Governmental accounting systems are different. Each time goods or services are ordered by a government, an "encumbrance" is recorded against the budgeted amount so that agencies do not commit to spending more money than their budgets allow.

Cash Receipts Section

The total cash available (Exhibit 14.5, row 7) is determined by adding the beginning cash balance to the cash receipts from customers. There is no beginning cash balance in October because the new store is opening that month. The November beginning cash balance is the October ending cash balance. The December beginning cash balance is the November ending cash balance. Cash receipts from customers comes from the *schedule of cash receipts* in the sales budget (Exhibit 14.2, section 2, row 13).

Cash Payments Section

Cash payments include expected cash outflows for inventory purchases, S&A expenses, interest expense, and investments. The cash payments for inventory purchases comes from the *schedule of cash payments for inventory purchases* (Exhibit 14.3, section 2, row 15). The cash payments for S&A expenses come from the *schedule of cash payments for S&A expenses* (Exhibit 14.4, section 2, row 21).

HH borrows or repays principal and pays interest on the last day of each month. The cash payments for interest are determined by multiplying the loan balance for the month by the monthly interest rate. Since there is no outstanding debt during October, there is no interest payment at the end of October. HH expects an outstanding debt of $218,000 during the month of November. The bank charges interest at the rate of 12 percent per year, or 1 percent per month. The November interest expense and cash payment for interest is $2,180 ($218,000 × .01). The outstanding loan balance during December is $230,000. The December interest expense and cash payment for interest is $2,300 ($230,000 × .01). Determining the amount to borrow or repay at the end of each month is discussed in more detail in the next section of the text.

Finally, the cash payment for the store fixtures comes from the *capital expenditures budget* (not shown in this chapter).

Financing Section

HH has a line of credit under which it can borrow or repay principal in increments of $1,000 at the end of each month as needed. HH desires to maintain an ending cash balance of at least $10,000 each month. With the $207,460 projected cash shortage in row 15 of the cash budget ($40,000 cash balance in row 7 less $247,460 budgeted cash payments in row 13), HH must borrow $218,000 on October 31 to maintain an ending cash balance of at least $10,000. This $218,000 balance is outstanding during November. On November 30, HH must borrow an additional $12,000 to cover the November projected cash shortage of $1,572 plus the $10,000 desired ending cash balance. HH projects a surplus of $23,660 for the month of December. This surplus will allow HH to repay $13,000 of debt and still maintain the desired $10,000 cash balance.

Pro Forma Financial Statement Data

Figures in the Pro Forma Data column of the cash budget (Exhibit 14.5) are alphabetically referenced. The cash receipts from customers, item (a), and the cash payment items (b), (c), and (d) are reported in the operating activities section of the pro forma statement of cash flows (shown later in Exhibit 14.8). The interest expense, item (d), is also reported on the pro forma income statement (shown later in Exhibit 14.6). The figures are determined by summing the monthly amounts. The $130,000 purchase of store fixtures, item (e), is reported in the investing activities section of the pro forma statement of cash flows. The $217,000 net borrowings, item (f), is reported in the financing activities section of the pro forma statement of cash flows (shown later in Exhibit 14.8) and also as a liability on the pro forma balance sheet (shown later in Exhibit 14.7). The $10,660 ending cash balance, item (g), is reported as the ending balance on the pro forma statement of cash flows and as an asset on the pro forma balance sheet.

 CHECK YOURSELF 14.2

Astor Company expects to incur the following operating expenses during September: Salary Expense, $25,000; Utility Expense, $1,200; Depreciation Expense, $5,400; and Selling Expense, $14,000. In general, it pays operating expenses in cash in the month in which it incurs them. Based on this information alone, determine the total amount of cash outflow Astor would report in the Operating Activities section of the pro forma statement of cash flows.

Answer Depreciation is not included in cash outflows because companies do not pay cash when they recognize depreciation expense. The total cash outflow is $40,200 ($25,000 + $1,200 + $14,000).

PRO FORMA FINANCIAL STATEMENTS

The information contained in the operating budgets is used to prepare pro forma financial statements. This section of the chapter shows how the pro forma income statement, balance sheet, and statement of cash flows are prepared using data from Hampton Hams's operating budgets.

LO 14-6

 Prepare a pro forma income statement, balance sheet, and statement of cash flows.

Pro Forma Income Statement

Exhibit 14.6 shows the budgeted income statement for Hampton Hams's new store. The figures for this statement come from Exhibits 14.2, 14.3, 14.4, and 14.5. The budgeted income statement provides an advance estimate of the new store's expected profitability. If expected profitability is unsatisfactory, management could decide to abandon the

EXHIBIT 14.6

HAMPTON HAMS
Pro Forma Income Statement
For the Quarter Ending December 31

		Data Source
Sales revenue	$582,400	Exhibit 14.2
Cost of goods sold	(407,680)	Exhibit 14.3
Gross margin	174,720	
Selling and administrative expenses	(110,172)	Exhibit 14.4
Operating income	64,548	
Interest expense	(4,480)	Exhibit 14.5
Net income	$ 60,068	

project or modify planned activity. Perhaps HH could lease less costly store space, pay employees a lower rate, or reduce the number of employees hired. The pricing strategy could also be examined for possible changes.

Budgets are usually prepared using spreadsheets or computerized mathematical models that allow managers to easily undertake "what-if" analysis. What if the growth rate differs from expectations? What if interest rates increase or decrease? Exhibits 14.2 through 14.5 in this chapter were prepared using Microsoft Excel. When variables such as growth rate, collection assumptions, or interest rates are changed, the spreadsheet software instantly recalculates the budgets. Although managers remain responsible for data analysis and decision making, computer technology offers powerful tools to assist in those tasks.

Pro Forma Balance Sheet

Most of the figures on the pro forma balance sheet in Exhibit 14.7 already have been explained. The new store has no contributed capital because its operations will be financed through debt and retained earnings. The amount of retained earnings equals the amount of net income because no earnings from prior periods exist and no distributions are planned.

EXHIBIT 14.7

HAMPTON HAMS
Pro Forma Balance Sheet
As of the Quarter Ending December 31

			Data Source
Assets			
Cash		$ 10,660	Exhibit 14.5
Accounts receivable		172,800	Exhibit 14.2
Inventory		35,000	Exhibit 14.3
Store fixtures	$130,000		Exhibit 14.4 Discussion
Accumulated depreciation	(3,000)		Exhibit 14.4 Discussion
Book value of store fixtures		127,000	
Total assets		$345,460	
Liabilities			
Accounts payable		$ 62,384	Exhibit 14.3
Sales commissions payable		4,608	Exhibit 14.4
Utilities payable		1,400	Exhibit 14.4
Line of credit borrowings		217,000	Exhibit 14.5
Equity			
Retained earnings		60,068	
Total liabilities and equity		$345,460	

Pro Forma Statement of Cash Flows

Exhibit 14.8 shows the pro forma statement of cash flows for Hampton Hams. All information for this statement comes from the cash budget in Exhibit 14.5.

 CHECK YOURSELF 14.3

How do pro forma financial statements differ from the financial statements presented in a company's annual report to stockholders?

Answer Pro forma financial statements are based on estimates and projections about business events that a company expects to occur in the future. The financial statements presented in a company's annual report to stockholders are based on historical events that occurred prior to the preparation of the statements.

Answers to The Curious Accountant

Budget preparation at the USOC is complicated by the fact that the timing of its revenues does not match the timing of its expenditures. The USOC spends a lot of money helping to train athletes for the United States Olympic team. Training takes place year-round, every year, for many athletes. The USOC's training facilities in Colorado must also be maintained continuously.

Conversely, much of the USOC's revenues are earned in big batches, received every two years. This money comes from fees the USOC receives for the rights to broadcast the Olympic games on television in the United States. Most companies have a one-year budget cycle during which they attempt to anticipate the coming year's revenues and expenses. This model would not work well for the USOC. For example, in 2010, a year of summer Olympics, the USOC reported revenues of $250.6 million and a surplus of $59.0 million. In 2011, a year with no Olympic games, the USOC reported revenues of $140.7 million and a deficit of $44.4 million.

Every business, like every family, faces its own set of circumstances. Those individuals responsible for preparing an entity's budget must have a thorough understanding of the environment in which the entity operates. This is the reason the budget process must be participatory if it is to be successful. No one person, or small group, can anticipate all the issues that a large organization will face in the coming budget period; input from employees at all levels is necessary.

Source: Form 990s filed by the USOC with the IRS.

EXHIBIT 14.8

HAMPTON HAMS
Pro Forma Statement of Cash Flows
For the Quarter Ending December 31

Cash flow from operating activities		
Cash receipts from customers	$409,600	
Cash payments for inventory	(380,296)	
Cash payments for S&A expenses	(101,164)	
Cash payments for interest expense	(4,480)	
Net cash flow for operating activities		$ (76,340)
Cash flow from investing activities		
Cash outflow to purchase fixtures		(130,000)
Cash flow from financing activities		
Inflow from borrowing on line of credit		217,000
Net change in cash		10,660
Plus beginning cash balance		0
Ending cash balance		$ 10,660

A Look Back

The planning of financial matters is called *budgeting.* The degree of detail in a company's budget depends on the budget period. Generally, the shorter the time period, the more specific the plans. *Strategic planning* involves long-term plans, such as the overall objectives of the business. Examples of strategic planning include which products to manufacture and sell and which market niches to pursue. Strategic plans are stated in broad, descriptive terms. Capital budgeting deals with intermediate investment planning. *Operations budgeting* focuses on short-term plans and is used to create the master budget.

A budgeting committee is responsible for consolidating numerous departmental budgets into a master budget for the whole company. The *master budget* has detailed objectives stated in specific amounts; it describes how management intends to achieve its objectives. The master budget usually covers one year. Budgeting supports planning, coordination, performance measurement, and corrective action.

Employees may be uncomfortable with budgets, which can be constraining. Budgets set standards by which performance is evaluated. To establish an effective budget system, management should recognize the effect on human behavior of budgeting. Upper-level management must set a positive atmosphere by taking budgets seriously and avoiding using them to humiliate subordinates. One way to create the proper atmosphere is to encourage subordinates' participation in the budgeting process; *participative budgeting* can lead to goals that are more realistic in terms of what can be accomplished and can help to establish a team effort in trying to reach those goals.

The primary components of the master budget are the *operating budgets,* the *capital budgets,* and the *pro forma financial statements.* The budgeting process begins with preparing the operating budgets, which consist of detailed schedules and budgets prepared by various company departments. The first operating budget to be prepared is the sales budget. The detailed operating budgets for inventory purchases and S&A expenses are based on the projected sales from the sales budget. The information in the schedules of cash receipts (prepared in conjunction with the sales budget) and cash payments (prepared in conjunction with the inventory purchases and S&A expense budgets) is used in preparing the cash budget. The cash budget subtracts cash payments from cash receipts; the resulting cash surplus or shortage determines the company's financing activities.

The capital budget describes the company's long-term plans regarding investments in facilities, equipment, new products, or other lines of business. The information from the capital budget is used as input to several of the operating budgets.

The pro forma financial statements are prepared from information in the operating budgets. The operating budgets for sales, inventory purchases, and S&A expenses contain information that is used to prepare the income statement and balance sheet. The cash budget includes the amount of interest expense reported on the income statement, the ending cash balance, the capital acquisitions reported on the balance sheet, and most of the information included in the statement of cash flows.

>> A Look Forward

Once a company has completed its budget, it has defined its plans. Then the plans must be followed. The next chapter investigates the techniques used to evaluate performance. You will learn to compare actual results to budgets, calculate variances, and identify the parties who are normally accountable for deviations from expectations. Finally, you will learn about the human impact management must consider in taking corrective action when employees fail to accomplish budget goals.

Video lectures and accompanying self-assessment quizzes are available for all learning objectives through McGraw-Hill *Connect® Accounting.*

SELF-STUDY REVIEW PROBLEM

The Getaway Gift Company operates a chain of small gift shops that are located in prime vacation towns. Getaway is considering opening a new store on January 1, 2015. Getaway's president recently attended a business seminar that explained how formal budgets could be useful in judging the new store's likelihood of succeeding. Assume you are the company's accountant. The president has asked you to explain the budgeting process and to provide sample reports that show the new store's operating expectations for the first three months (January, February, and March). Respond to the following specific requirements:

Required

a. List the operating budgets and schedules included in a master budget.

b. Explain the difference between pro forma financial statements and the financial statements presented in a company's annual reports to shareholders.

c. Prepare a sample sales budget and a schedule of expected cash receipts using the following assumptions. Getaway estimates January sales will be $400,000, of which $100,000 will be cash and $300,000 will be credit. The ratio of cash sales to sales on account is expected to remain constant over the three-month period. The company expects sales to increase 10 percent per month. The company expects to collect 100 percent of the accounts receivable generated by credit sales in the month following the sale. Use this information to determine the amount of accounts receivable that Getaway would report on the March 31 pro forma balance sheet and the amount of sales it would report on the first quarter pro forma income statement.

d. Prepare a sample inventory purchases budget using the following assumptions. Cost of goods sold is 60 percent of sales. The company desires to maintain a minimum ending inventory equal to 25 percent of the following month's cost of goods sold. Getaway makes all inventory purchases on account. The company pays 70 percent of accounts payable in the month of purchase. It pays the remaining 30 percent in the following month. Prepare a schedule of expected cash payments for inventory purchases. Use this information to determine the amount of cost of goods sold Getaway would report on the first quarter pro forma income statement and the amounts of ending inventory and accounts payable it would report on the March 31 pro forma balance sheet.

Solution to Requirement *a*

A master budget would include (1) a sales budget and schedule of cash receipts, (2) an inventory purchases budget and schedule of cash payments for inventory, (3) a general, selling, and administrative expenses budget and a schedule of cash payments related to these expenses, and (4) a cash budget.

Solution to Requirement *b*

Pro forma statements result from the operating budgets listed in the response to Requirement *a*. Pro forma statements describe the results of expected future events. In contrast, the financial statements presented in a company's annual report reflect the results of events that have actually occurred in the past.

Solution to Requirement *c*

General Information				
				Pro Forma Statement Data
Sales growth rate 10%				
Sales Budget	January	February	March	
Sales				
Cash sales	$100,000	$110,000	$121,000	
Sales on account	300,000	330,000	363,000	$ 363,000*
Total sales	$400,000	$440,000	$484,000	$1,324,000†
Schedule of Cash Receipts				
Current cash sales	$100,000	$110,000	$121,000	
Plus 100% of previous month's credit sales	0	300,000	330,000	
Total budgeted collections	$100,000	$410,000	$451,000	

*Ending accounts receivable balance reported on March 31 pro forma balance sheet.

†Sales revenue reported on first quarter pro forma income statement (sum of monthly sales).

522   Chapter 14

Solution to Requirement *d*

General Information

Cost of goods sold percentage 60%
Desired ending inventory percentage of CGS 25%

                                                                    Pro Forma
                                                                  Statement Data

Inventory Purchases Budget	January	February	March	
Budgeted cost of goods sold	$240,000	$264,000	$290,400	$794,400*
Plus: Desired ending inventory	66,000	72,600	79,860	79,860†
Inventory needed	306,000	336,600	370,260	
Less: Beginning inventory	0	(66,000)	(72,600)	
Required purchases	$306,000	$270,600	$297,660	89,298‡
Schedule of Cash Payments for Inventory Purchases				
70% of current purchases	$214,200	$189,420	$208,362	
30% of prior month's purchases	0	91,800	81,180	
Total budgeted payments for inventory	$214,200	$281,220	$289,542	

*Cost of goods sold reported on first quarter pro forma income statement (sum of monthly amounts).
†Ending inventory balance ($484,000 × 1.10 × .60 × .25) reported on March 31 pro forma balance sheet.
‡Ending accounts payable balance reported on pro forma balance sheet ($297,660 × 0.3).

KEY TERMS

Budgeting 504
Capital
  budgeting 506
Cash budget 515

Master budget 508
Operating budgets 508
Operations
  budgeting 506

Participative
  budgeting 508
Perpetual (continuous)
  budgeting 506

Pro forma financial
  statements 508
Strategic planning 506

QUESTIONS

1. Budgets are useful only for small companies that can estimate sales with accuracy. Do you agree with this statement?

2. Why does preparing the master budget require a committee?

3. What are the three levels of planning? Explain each briefly.

4. What is the primary factor that distinguishes the three different levels of planning from each other?

5. What is the advantage of using a perpetual budget instead of the traditional annual budget?

6. What are the advantages of budgeting?

7. How may budgets be used as a measure of performance?

8. Ken Shilov, manager of the marketing department, tells you that "budgeting simply does not work." He says that he made budgets for his employees and when he reprimanded them for failing to accomplish budget goals, he got unfounded excuses. Suggest how Mr. Shilov could encourage employee cooperation.

9. What is a master budget?

10. What is the normal starting point in developing the master budget?

11. How does the level of inventory affect the production budget? Why is it important to manage the level of inventory?

12. What are the components of the cash budget? Describe each.

13. The primary reason for preparing a cash budget is to determine the amount of cash to include on the budgeted balance sheet. Do you agree or disagree with this statement? Explain.

14. What information does the pro forma income statement provide? How does its preparation depend on the operating budgets?

15. How does the pro forma statement of cash flows differ from the cash budget?

MULTIPLE-CHOICE QUESTIONS

Multiple-choice questions are provided on the text website at www.mhhe.com/edmondssurvey4e.

EXERCISES

 All applicable Exercises are available with McGraw-Hill
Connect® Accounting.

Exercise 14-1   *Budget responsibility*

LO 14-1

Stacey Weller, the accountant, is a perfectionist. No one can do the job as well as she can. Indeed, she has found budget information provided by the various departments to be worthless. She must change everything they give her. She has to admit that her estimates have not always been accurate, but she shudders to think of what would happen if she used the information supplied by the marketing and operating departments. No one seems to care about accuracy. Indeed, some of the marketing staff have even become insulting. When Ms. Weller confronted one of the salesmen with the fact that he was behind in meeting his budgeted sales forecast, he responded by saying, "They're your numbers. Why don't you go out and make the sales? It's a heck of a lot easier to sit there in your office and make up numbers than it is to get out and get the real work done." Ms. Weller reported the incident, but, of course, nothing was done about it.

Required

Write a short report suggesting how the budgeting process could be improved.

Exercise 14-2   *Preparing a sales budget*

LO 14-1

Sycamore Company, which expects to start operations on January 1, 2014, will sell digital cameras in shopping malls. Sycamore has budgeted sales as indicated in the following table. The company expects a 10 percent increase in sales per month for February and March. The ratio of cash sales to sales on account will remain stable from January through March.

Sales	January	February	March
Cash sales	$ 60,000	?	?
Sales on account	140,000	?	?
Total budgeted sales	$200,000	?	?

Required

a. Complete the sales budget by filling in the missing amounts.
b. Determine the amount of sales revenue Sycamore will report on its first quarter pro forma income statement.

Exercise 14-3   *Preparing a schedule of cash receipts*

LO 14-2

The budget director of Natalia's Florist has prepared the following sales budget. The company had $100,000 in accounts receivable on July 1. Natalia's Florist normally collects 100 percent of accounts receivable in the month following the month of sale.

	July	August	September
Sales Budget			
Cash sales	$ 80,000	$ 85,000	$ 90,000
Sales on account	90,000	108,000	129,600
Total budgeted sales	$170,000	$193,000	$219,000
Schedule of Cash Receipts			
Current cash sales	?	?	?
Plus: Collections from accounts receivable	?	?	?
Total budgeted collections	$180,000	$175,000	$198,000

Required

a. Complete the schedule of cash receipts by filling in the missing amounts.
b. Determine the amount of accounts receivable the company will report on its third quarter pro forma balance sheet.

LO 14-2

Exercise 14-4   *Preparing sales budgets with different assumptions*

Norton Corporation, which has three divisions, is preparing its sales budget. Each division expects a different growth rate because economic conditions vary in different regions of the country. The growth expectations per quarter are 4 percent for East Division, 2 percent for West Division, and 5 percent for South Division.

Division	First Quarter	Second Quarter	Third Quarter	Fourth Quarter
East Division	$150,000	?	?	?
West Division	250,000	?	?	?
South Division	200,000	?	?	?

Required

a. Complete the sales budget by filling in the missing amounts. (Round figures to the nearest dollar.)

b. Determine the amount of sales revenue that the company will report on its quarterly pro forma income statements.

LO 14-2

Exercise 14-5   *Determining cash receipts from accounts receivable*

Laura's Dress Delivery operates a mail-order business that sells clothes designed for frequent travelers. It had sales of $800,000 in December. Because Laura's Dress Delivery is in the mail-order business, all sales are made on account. The company expects a 30 percent drop in sales for January. The balance in the Accounts Receivable account on December 31 was $120,000 and is budgeted to be $82,000 as of January 31. Laura's Dress Delivery normally collects accounts receivable in the month following the month of sale.

Required

a. Determine the amount of cash Laura's Dress Delivery expects to collect from accounts receivable during January.

b. Is it reasonable to assume that sales will decline in January for this type of business? Why or why not?

LO 14-2

Exercise 14-6   *Using judgment in making a sales forecast*

Williams Company operates a candy store located in a large shopping mall.

Required

Write a brief memo describing the sales pattern that you would expect Williams to experience during the year. In which months will sales likely be high? In which months will sales likely be low? Explain why.

LO 14-3

Exercise 14-7   *Preparing an inventory purchases budget*

Spencer Company sells lamps and other lighting fixtures. The purchasing department manager prepared the following inventory purchases budget. Spencer's policy is to maintain an ending inventory balance equal to 10 percent of the following month's cost of goods sold. April's budgeted cost of goods sold is $80,000.

	January	February	March
Budgeted cost of goods sold	$60,000	$64,000	$70,000
Plus: Desired ending inventory	6,400	?	?
Inventory needed	66,400	?	?
Less: Beginning inventory	6,000	?	?
Required purchases (on account)	$60,400	?	?

Required

a. Complete the inventory purchases budget by filling in the missing amounts.
b. Determine the amount of cost of goods sold the company will report on its first quarter pro forma income statement.
c. Determine the amount of ending inventory the company will report on its pro forma balance sheet at the end of the first quarter.

Exercise 14-8   *Preparing a schedule of cash payments for inventory purchases*   LO 14-3

Vivian Books buys books and magazines directly from publishers and distributes them to grocery stores. The wholesaler expects to purchase the following inventory.

	April	May	June
Required purchases (on account)	$140,000	$160,000	$190,000

Vivian Books's accountant prepared the following schedule of cash payments for inventory purchases. Vivian Books's suppliers require that 90 percent of purchases on account be paid in the month of purchase; the remaining 10 percent are paid in the month following the month of purchase.

Schedule of Cash Payments for Inventory Purchases			
	April	May	June
Payment for current accounts payable	$126,000	?	?
Payment for previous accounts payable	8,000	?	?
Total budgeted payments for inventory	$134,000	?	?

Required

a. Complete the schedule of cash payments for inventory purchases by filling in the missing amounts.
b. Determine the amount of accounts payable the company will report on its pro forma balance sheet at the end of the second quarter.

Exercise 14-9   *Determining the amount of expected inventory purchases and cash payments*   LO 14-3

Widden Company, which sells electric razors, had $400,000 of cost of goods sold during the month of June. The company projects a 5 percent increase in cost of goods sold during July. The inventory balance as of June 30 is $30,000, and the desired ending inventory balance for July is $32,000. Widden pays cash to settle 70 percent of its purchases on account during the month of purchase and pays the remaining 30 percent in the month following the purchase. The accounts payable balance as of June 30 was $36,000.

Required

a. Determine the amount of purchases budgeted for July.
b. Determine the amount of cash payments budgeted for inventory purchases in July.

Exercise 14-10   *Preparing inventory purchases budgets with different assumptions*   LO 14-3

Executive officers of Weston Company are wrestling with their budget for the next year. The following are two different sales estimates provided by two difference sources.

Source of Estimate	First Quarter	Second Quarter	Third Quarter	Fourth Quarter
Sales manager	$450,000	$360,000	$320,000	$540,000
Marketing consultant	600,000	480,000	420,000	700,000

Weston's past experience indicates that cost of goods sold is about 60 percent of sales revenue. The company tries to maintain 10 percent of the next quarter's expected cost of goods sold as the current quarter's ending inventory. This year's ending inventory is $30,000. Next year's ending inventory is budgeted to be $36,000.

Required

a. Prepare an inventory purchases budget using the sales manager's estimate.

b. Prepare an inventory purchases budget using the marketing consultant's estimate.

LO 14-4

Exercise 14-11   *Preparing a schedule of cash payments for selling and administrative expenses*

The budget director for Yardley Cleaning Services prepared the following list of expected selling and administrative expenses. All expenses requiring cash payments are paid for in the month incurred except salary expense and insurance. Salary is paid in the month following the month in which it is incurred. The insurance premium for six months is paid on October 1. October is the first month of operations; accordingly, there are no beginning account balances.

	October	November	December
Budgeted S&A Expenses			
Equipment lease expense	$ 7,500	$ 7,500	$ 7,500
Salary expense	8,200	8,700	9,000
Cleaning supplies	2,800	2,730	3,066
Insurance expense	1,200	1,200	1,200
Depreciation on computer	1,800	1,800	1,800
Rent	1,700	1,700	1,700
Miscellaneous expenses	700	700	700
Total operating expenses	$23,900	$24,330	$24,966
Schedule of Cash Payments for S&A Expenses			
Equipment lease expense	?	?	?
Prior month's salary expense, 100%	?	?	?
Cleaning supplies	?	?	?
Insurance premium	?	?	?
Depreciation on computer	?	?	?
Rent	?	?	?
Miscellaneous expenses	?	?	?
Total disbursements for operating expenses	$19,900	$20,830	$21,666

Required

a. Complete the schedule of cash payments for S&A expenses by filling in the missing amounts.

b. Determine the amount of salaries payable the company will report on its pro forma balance sheet at the end of the fourth quarter.

c. Determine the amount of prepaid insurance the company will report on its pro forma balance sheet at the end of the fourth quarter.

LO 14-4

Exercise 14-12   *Determining the amount of cash payments and pro forma statement data for selling and administrative expenses*

January budgeted selling and administrative expenses for the retail shoe store that Nadege Weib plans to open on January 1, 2014, are as follows: sales commissions, $40,000; rent, $24,000; utilities, $8,000; depreciation, $4,000; and miscellaneous, $2,000. Utilities are paid in the month after incurrence. Other expenses are expected to be paid in cash in the month in which they are incurred.

Required

a. Determine the amount of budgeted cash payments for January selling and administrative expenses.

b. Determine the amount of utilities payable the store will report on the January 31st pro forma balance sheet.

c. Determine the amount of depreciation expense the store will report on the income statement for the year 2014, assuming that monthly depreciation remains the same for the entire year.

Exercise 14-13 *Preparing a cash budget*

LO 14-5

The accountant for Erica's Dress Shop prepared the following cash budget. Erica's desires to maintain a cash cushion of $20,000 at the end of each month. Funds are assumed to be borrowed and repaid on the last day of each month. Interest is charged at the rate of 1 percent per month.

Cash Budget	July	August	September
Section 1: Cash receipts			
Beginning cash balance	$ 50,000	$?	$?
Add cash receipts	180,000	200,000	240,600
Total cash available (a)	230,000	?	?
Section 2: Cash payments			
For inventory purchases	165,500	140,230	174,152
For S&A expenses	54,500	60,560	61,432
For interest expense	0	?	?
Total budgeted disbursements (b)	220,000	?	?
Section 3: Financing activities			
Surplus (shortage)	10,000	?	?
Borrowing (repayments) (c)	10,000	?	?
Ending cash balance (a − b + c)	$ 20,000	$ 20,000	$ 20,000

Required

a. Complete the cash budget by filling in the missing amounts. Round all computations to the nearest whole dollar.

b. Determine the amount of net cash flows from operating activities Erica's will report on the third quarter pro forma statement of cash flows.

c. Determine the amount of net cash flows from financing activities Erica's will report on the third quarter pro forma statement of cash flows.

Exercise 14-14 *Determining amount to borrow and pro forma statement balances*

LO 14-5

Abebe Helton owns a small restaurant in New York City. Ms. Helton provided her accountant with the following summary information regarding expectations for the month of June. The balance in accounts receivable as of May 31 is $80,000. Budgeted cash and credit sales for June are $200,000 and $500,000, respectively. Credit sales are made through Visa and MasterCard and are collected rapidly. Eighty percent of credit sales is collected in the month of sale, and the remainder is collected in the following month. Ms. Helton's suppliers do not extend credit. Consequently, she pays suppliers on the last day of the month. Cash payments for June are expected to be $660,000. Ms. Helton has a line of credit that enables the restaurant to borrow funds on demand; however, they must be borrowed on the last day of the month. Interest is paid in cash also on the last day of the month. Ms. Helton desires to maintain a $30,000 cash balance before the interest payment. Her annual interest rate is 9 percent.

Required

a. Compute the amount of funds Ms. Helton needs to borrow for June.

b. Determine the amount of interest expense the restaurant will report on the June pro forma income statement.

c. What amount will the restaurant report as interest expense on the July pro forma income statement?

528   Chapter 14

LO 14-6

Exercise 14-15 *Preparing pro forma income statements with different assumptions*

Daniel Singh, the controller of Meier Corporation, is trying to prepare a sales budget for the coming year. The income statements for the last four quarters follow.

	First Quarter	Second Quarter	Third Quarter	Fourth Quarter	Total
Sales revenue	$180,000	$200,000	$210,000	$260,000	$850,000
Cost of goods sold	108,000	120,000	126,000	156,000	510,000
Gross profit	72,000	80,000	84,000	104,000	340,000
Selling & admin. expenses	17,000	20,000	21,000	26,000	84,000
Net income	$ 55,000	$ 60,000	$ 63,000	$ 78,000	$256,000

Historically, cost of goods sold is about 60 percent of sales revenue. Selling and administrative expenses are about 10 percent of sales revenue.

Joe Meier, the chief executive officer, told Mr. Singh that he expected sales next year to be 8 percent for each respective quarter above last year's level. However, Ashley Odom, the vice president of sales, told Mr. Singh that she believed sales growth would be only 5 percent.

Required

a. Prepare a pro forma income statement including quarterly budgets for the coming year using Mr. Meier's estimate.

b. Prepare a pro forma income statement including quarterly budgets for the coming year using Ms. Odom's estimate.

c. Explain why two executive officers in the same company could have different estimates of future growth.

PROBLEMS

 All applicable Problems are available with McGraw-Hill *Connect® Accounting.*

LO 14-1

CHECK FIGURES
a. NI: $315,000
c. NI: $345,000

Problem 14-16   *Behavioral impact of budgeting*

Butler Corporation has three divisions, each operating as a responsibility center. To provide an incentive for divisional executive officers, the company gives divisional management a bonus equal to 15 percent of the excess of actual net income over budgeted net income. The following is French Division's current year's performance.

	Current Year
Sales revenue	$2,000,000
Cost of goods sold	1,250,000
Gross profit	750,000
Selling & admin. expenses	450,000
Net income	$ 300,000

The president has just received next year's budget proposal from the vice president in charge of French Division. The proposal budgets a 5 percent increase in sales revenue with an extensive explanation about stiff market competition. The president is puzzled. French has enjoyed revenue growth of around 10 percent for each of the past five years. The president had consistently approved the division's budget proposals based on 5 percent growth in the past. This time, the president wants to show that he is not a fool. "I will impose a 15 percent revenue increase to teach them a lesson!" the president says to himself smugly.

Assume that cost of goods sold and selling and administrative expenses remain stable in proportion to sales.

Required

a. Prepare the budgeted income statement based on French Division's proposal of a 5 percent increase.

b. If growth is actually 10 percent as usual, how much bonus would French Division's executive officers receive if the president had approved the division's proposal?

c. Prepare the budgeted income statement based on the 15 percent increase the president imposed.

d. If the actual results turn out to be a 10 percent increase as usual, how much bonus would French Division's executive officers receive since the president imposed a 15 percent increase?

e. Propose a better budgeting procedure for Butler Corporation.

Problem 14-17 *Preparing a sales budget and schedule of cash receipts*

LO 14-2

CHECK FIGURES
c. Feb: $224,400
March: $259,620

Sutton Pointers Corporation expects to begin operations on January 1, 2015; it will operate as a specialty sales company that sells laser pointers over the Internet. Sutton expects sales in January 2015 to total $240,000 and to increase 5 percent per month in February and March. All sales are on account. Sutton expects to collect 70 percent of accounts receivable in the month of sale, 20 percent in the month following the sale, and 10 percent in the second month following the sale.

Required

a. Prepare a sales budget for the first quarter of 2015.

b. Determine the amount of sales revenue Sutton will report on the first 2015 quarterly pro forma income statement.

c. Prepare a cash receipts schedule for the first quarter of 2015.

d. Determine the amount of accounts receivable as of March 31, 2015.

Problem 14-18 *Preparing an inventory purchases budget and schedule of cash payments*

LO 14-3

CHECK FIGURES
a. May: $67,200
c. June: $64,680

Peabody, Inc., sells fireworks. The company's marketing director developed the following cost of goods sold budget for April, May, June, and July.

	April	May	June	July
Budgeted cost of goods sold	$75,000	$68,000	$60,000	$90,000

Peabody had a beginning inventory balance of $3,600 on April 1 and a beginning balance in accounts payable of $14,800. The company desires to maintain an ending inventory balance equal to 10 percent of the next period's cost of goods sold. Peabody makes all purchases on account. The company pays 60 percent of accounts payable in the month of purchase and the remaining 40 percent in the month following purchase.

Required

a. Prepare an inventory purchases budget for April, May, and June.

b. Determine the amount of ending inventory Peabody will report on the end-of-quarter pro forma balance sheet.

c. Prepare a schedule of cash payments for inventory for April, May, and June.

d. Determine the balance in accounts payable Peabody will report on the end-of-quarter pro forma balance sheet.

Problem 14-19 *Preparing a schedule of cash payments for selling and administrative expenses*

LO 14-4

CHECK FIGURE
a. Sept: $34,810

Ruddy is a retail company specializing in men's hats. Its budget director prepared the list of expected operating expenses that follows. All items are paid when incurred except sales commissions and utilities, which are paid in the month following their incurrence. July is the first month of operations, so there are no beginning account balances.

	July	August	September
Salary expense	$24,000	$24,000	$24,000
Sales commissions (4 percent of sales)	2,000	2,000	2,000
Supplies expense	360	390	420
Utilities	1,100	1,100	1,100
Depreciation on store equipment	3,000	3,000	3,000
Rent	6,600	6,600	6,600
Miscellaneous	690	690	690
Total S&A expenses before interest	$37,750	$37,780	$37,810

Required

a. Prepare a schedule of cash payments for selling and administrative expenses.
b. Determine the amount of utilities payable as of September 30.
c. Determine the amount of sales commissions payable as of September 30.

LO 14-5

CHECK FIGURE
Feb. cash surplus before financing
activities: $7,010

Problem 14-20   *Preparing a cash budget*

Newman Medical Clinic has budgeted the following cash flows.

	January	February	March
Cash receipts	$120,000	$116,000	$136,000
Cash payments			
For inventory purchases	110,000	82,000	95,000
For S&A expenses	31,000	32,000	27,000

Newman Medical had a cash balance of $8,000 on January 1. The company desires to maintain a cash cushion of $5,000. Funds are assumed to be borrowed, in increments of $1,000, and repaid on the last day of each month; the interest rate is 1 percent per month. Repayments may be made in any amount available. Newman pays its vendors on the last day of the month also. The company had a monthly $40,000 beginning balance in its line of credit liability account from this year's quarterly results.

Required

Prepare a cash budget. (Round all computations to the nearest whole dollar.)

LO 14-6

CHECK FIGURE
a. 13.59%

Problem 14-21   *Preparing pro forma income statements with different assumptions*

Top executive officers of Preston Company, a merchandising firm, are preparing the next year's budget. The controller has provided everyone with the current year's projected income statement.

	Current Year
Sales revenue	$3,200,000
Cost of goods sold	2,240,000
Gross profit	960,000
Selling & admin. expenses	380,000
Net income	$ 580,000

Cost of goods sold is usually 70 percent of sales revenue, and selling and administrative expenses are usually 10 percent of sales plus a fixed cost of $60,000. The president has announced that the company's goal is to increase net income by 15 percent.

Required

The following items are independent of each other.

a. What percentage increase in sales would enable the company to reach its goal? Support your answer with a pro forma income statement.

b. The market may become stagnant next year, and the company does not expect an increase in sales revenue. The production manager believes that an improved production procedure can cut cost of goods sold by 2 percent. What else can the company do to reach its goal? Prepare a pro forma income statement illustrating your proposal.

c. The company decides to escalate its advertising campaign to boost consumer recognition, which will increase selling and administrative expenses to $460,000. With the increased advertising, the company expects sales revenue to increase by 15 percent. Assume that cost of goods sold remains a constant proportion of sales. Can the company reach its goal?

Problem 14-22 *Preparing budgets with multiple products*

LO 14-2, 14-3, 14-4, 14-6

Mulligan Fruits Corporation wholesales peaches and oranges. Kimberly Priest is working with the company's accountant to prepare next year's budget. Ms. Priest estimates that sales will increase 5 percent for peaches and 10 percent for oranges. The current year's sales revenue data follow.

CHECK FIGURES
c. 1st QTR purchases for peaches: $103,320
2nd QTR purchases for oranges: $304,920

	First Quarter	Second Quarter	Third Quarter	Fourth Quarter	Total
Peaches	$160,000	$200,000	$320,000	$280,000	$ 960,000
Oranges	400,000	450,000	570,000	380,000	1,800,000
Total	$560,000	$650,000	$890,000	$660,000	$2,760,000

Based on the company's past experience, cost of goods sold is usually 60 percent of sales revenue. Company policy is to keep 10 percent of the next period's estimated cost of goods sold as the current period's ending inventory. (*Hint:* Use the cost of goods sold for the first quarter to determine the beginning inventory for the first quarter.)

Required

a. Prepare the company's sales budget for the next year for each quarter by individual product.

b. If the selling and administrative expenses are estimated to be $700,000, prepare the company's budgeted annual income statement.

c. Ms. Priest estimates next year's ending inventory will be $20,000 for peaches and $40,000 for oranges. Prepare the company's inventory purchases budgets for the next year, showing quarterly figures by product.

Problem 14-23 *Preparing a master budget for retail company with no beginning account balances*

LO 14-2, 14-3, 14-4, 14-5, 14-6

Haas Company is a retail company that specializes in selling outdoor camping equipment. The company is considering opening a new store on October 1, 2015. The company president formed a planning committee to prepare a master budget for the first three months of operation. As budget coordinator, you have been assigned the following tasks.

CHECK FIGURES
c. Dec. purchases: $169,464
g. Nov. surplus before financing activities: $60,973

Required

Round all computations to two decimal points.

a. October sales are estimated to be $250,000, of which 40 percent will be cash and 60 percent will be credit. The company expects sales to increase at the rate of 8 percent per month. Prepare a sales budget.

b. The company expects to collect 100 percent of the accounts receivable generated by credit sales in the month following the sale. Prepare a schedule of cash receipts.

c. The cost of goods sold is 60 percent of sales. The company desires to maintain a minimum ending inventory equal to 10 percent of the next month's cost of goods sold. However, ending inventory of December is expected to be $12,000. Assume that all purchases are made on account. Prepare an inventory purchases budget.

d. The company pays 70 percent of accounts payable in the month of purchase and the remaining 30 percent in the following month. Prepare a cash payments budget for inventory purchases.

e. Budgeted selling and administrative expenses per month follow.

Salary expense (fixed)	$18,000
Sales commissions	5 percent of Sales
Supplies expense	2 percent of Sales
Utilities (fixed)	$1,400
Depreciation on store fixtures (fixed)*	$4,000
Rent (fixed)	$4,800
Miscellaneous (fixed)	$1,200

*The capital expenditures budget indicates that Haas will spend $164,000 on October 1 for store fixtures, which are expected to have a $20,000 salvage value and a three-year (36-month) useful life.

Use this information to prepare a selling and administrative expenses budget.

f. Utilities and sales commissions are paid the month after they are incurred; all other expenses are paid in the month in which they are incurred. Prepare a cash payments budget for selling and administrative expenses.

g. Haas borrows funds, in increments of $1,000, and repays them on the last day of the month. Repayments may be made in any amount available. The company also pays its vendors on the last day of the month. It pays interest of 1 percent per month in cash on the last day of the month. To be prudent, the company desires to maintain a $12,000 cash cushion. Prepare a cash budget.

h. Prepare a pro forma income statement for the quarter.

i. Prepare a pro forma balance sheet at the end of the quarter.

j. Prepare a pro forma statement of cash flows for the quarter.

ANALYZE, THINK, COMMUNICATE

ATC 14-1   Business Applications Case   *Preparing and using pro forma statements*

Mary Helu and Randy Adams recently graduated from the same university. After graduation they decided not to seek jobs at established organizations but, rather, to start their own small business hoping they could have more flexibility in their personal lives for a few years. Mary's family has operated Mexican restaurants and taco-trucks for the past two generations, and Mary noticed there were no taco-truck services in the town where their university was located. To reduce the amount they would need for an initial investment, they decided to start a business operating a taco-cart rather than a taco-truck, from which they would cook and serve traditional Mexican-styled street food.

They bought a used taco-cart for $18,000. This cost, along with the cost for supplies to get started, a business license, and street vendor license brought their initial expenditures to $22,000. Five-thousand dollars came from personal savings they had accumulated by working part time during college, and they borrowed $17,000 from Mary's parents. They agreed to pay interest on the outstanding loan balance each month based on an annual rate of 5 percent. They will repay the principal over the next few years as cash becomes available. They were able to rent space in a parking lot near the campus they had attended, believing that the students would welcome their food as an alternative to the typical fast food that was currently available.

After two months in business, September and October, they had average monthly revenues of $25,000 and out-of-pocket costs of $22,000 for rent, ingredients, paper supplies, and so on, but not interest. Randy thinks they should repay some of the money they borrowed, but Mary thinks they should prepare a set of forecasted financial statements for their first year in business before deciding whether or not to repay any principal on the loan. She remembers a bit about budgeting from a survey of accounting course she took and thinks the results from their first two months in business can be extended over the next 10 months to prepare the budget they need. They estimate the cart will last at least four years, after which they expect to sell it for $6,000 and move on to something else in their lives. Mary agrees to prepare a forecasted (pro forma) income statement, balance sheet, and statement of cash flows for their first year in business, which includes the two months already passed.

Required

a. Prepare the annual pro forma financial statements that you would expect Mary to prepare based on her comments about her expectations for the business. Assume no principal will be repaid on the loan.

b. Review the statements you prepared for the first requirement and prepare a list of reasons why actual results for Randy and Mary's business probably will not match their budgeted statements.

ATC 14-2   Group Assignment   *Master budget and pro forma statements*

The following trial balance was drawn from the records of Havel Company as of October 1, 2014.

Cash	$ 16,000	
Accounts receivable	60,000	
Inventory	40,000	
Store equipment	200,000	
Accumulated depreciation		$ 76,800
Accounts payable		72,000
Line of credit loan		100,000
Common stock		50,000
Retained earnings		17,200
Totals	$316,000	$316,000

Required

a. Divide the class into groups, each with four or five students. Organize the groups into three sections. Assign Task 1 to the first section, Task 2 to the second section, and Task 3 to the third section.

Group Tasks

(1) Based on the following information, prepare a sales budget and a schedule of cash receipts for October, November, and December. Sales for October are expected to be $180,000, consisting of $40,000 in cash and $140,000 on credit. The company expects sales to increase at the rate of 10 percent per month. All accounts receivable are collected in the month following the sale.

(2) Based on the following information, prepare a purchases budget and a schedule of cash payments for inventory purchases for October, November, and December. The inventory balance as of October 1 was $40,000. Cost of goods sold for October is expected to be $72,000. Cost of goods sold is expected to increase by 10 percent per month. The company expects to maintain a minimum ending inventory equal to 20 percent of the current month cost of goods sold. Seventy-five percent of accounts payable is paid in the month that the purchase occurs; the remaining 25 percent is paid in the following month.

(3) Based on the following selling and administrative expenses budgeted for October, prepare a selling and administrative expenses budget for October, November, and December.

Sales commissions (10% increase per month)	$ 7,200
Supplies expense (10% increase per month)	1,800
Utilities (fixed)	2,200
Depreciation on store equipment (fixed)	1,600
Salary expense (fixed)	34,000
Rent (fixed)	6,000
Miscellaneous (fixed)	1,000

Cash payments for sales commissions and utilities are made in the month following the one in which the expense is incurred. Supplies and other operating expenses are paid in cash in the month in which they are incurred.

b. Select a representative from each section. Have the representatives supply the missing information in the following pro forma income statement and balance sheet for the fourth quarter of 2014. The statements are prepared as of December 31, 2014.

Income Statement		
Sales revenue	$	?
Cost of goods sold		?
Gross margin		357,480
Operating expenses		?
Operating income		193,290
Interest expense		(2,530)
Net income		$190,760

Balance Sheet		
Assets		
Cash		$ 9,760
Accounts receivable		?
Inventory		?
Store equipment	$200,000	
Accumulated depreciation store equipment	?	
Book value of equipment		118,400
Total assets		$314,984
Liabilities		
Accounts payable		?
Utilities payable		?
Sales commissions payable		?
Line of credit		23,936
Equity		
Common stock		50,000
Retained earnings		?
Total liabilities and equity		$314,984

c. Indicate whether Havel will need to borrow money during October.

ATC 14-3   Research Assignment   *Analyzing budget data for the United States government*

The annual budget of the United States is very complex, but this case requires that you analyze only a small portion of the historical tables that are presented as a part of each year's budget. The fiscal year of the federal government ends on September 30. Obtain the budget documents needed at http://www.gpo.gov/fdsys/search/home.action and follow these steps:

- Under the "Featured Collections" heading (top right side of screen), click on "Budget of the U.S. Government."
- Click on the "Fiscal Year 2012" link.
- Scroll down and select "Historical Tables."
- There are two options that can be used to download each historical data table. One is an XLS (Excel) file format. This option will make completing this assignment easier.
- You will need to use Table 1.1, Table 1.2, and Table 4.2 to complete the requirements below.

Required

a. Table 1.2 shows the budget as a percentage of gross domestic product (GDP). Using the data in the third column, "Surplus of Deficit," determine how many years since 1960 the budget has shown a surplus and how many times it has shown a deficit. Ignore the "TQ" data between 1976 and 1977. This was a year that the government changed the ending date of its fiscal year.

b. Based on the data in Table 1.2, identify the three years with the highest deficits as a percentage of GDP. What were the deficit percentages for these years? Which year had the largest surplus and by what percentage?

c. Using your findings for Requirement *b* regarding the year with the highest deficit as a percentage of GDP, go to Table 1.1 and calculate the deficit for that year as a **percentage of revenues.** What percent of each dollar spent by the federal government in that year was paid for with tax revenues and what percent was paid for with borrowed funds?

d. The president of the United States from 1993 through 2000 was Bill Clinton, a Democrat. The president from 2001 through 2009 was George Bush, a Republican. These men had significant input into the federal budget for the fiscal years 1994–2001 and 2002–2009, respectively. Table 4.2 shows what percentage of the total federal budget was directed toward each department within the government. Compare the data on Table 4.2 for 1994–2001, the Clinton years, to the data for 2002–2009, the Bush years. Identify the five departments that appear to have changed the most from the Clinton years to the Bush years. Ignore "Allowances" and "Undistributed offsetting receipts." Note, to approach this assignment more accurately, you should compute the average percentage for each department for the eight years each president served, and compare the two averages.

ATC 14-4   Writing Assignment   *Continuous budgeting*

The Curious Accountant in this chapter discussed some of the budgeting issues facing the United States Olympic Committee (USOC). First, to get a basic understanding of the sources of revenues and expenses of the USOC, review its Form 990, which shows its revenues and expenditures as reported to the IRS, by accessing the following link: http://www.teamusa.org/About-the-USOC/Organization/Financial.aspx. You only need to review the information on the first page of the Form 990, but reviewing pages 9 and 10 of the form will provide additional insight as to the USOC's revenues and expenses.

Required

Assume the OSOC had not previously used continuous budgeting but was considering implementing a continuous budgeting system. Also assume you had been asked to identify some of the challenges the USOC would face in implementing this system. Write a memorandum explaining the challenges you identify.

ATC 14-5   Ethical Dilemma   *Bad budget system or unethical behavior?*

Clarence Cleaver is the budget director for the Harris County School District. Mr. Cleaver recently sent an urgent e-mail message to Sally Simmons, principal of West Harris County High. The message severely reprimanded Ms. Simmons for failing to spend the funds allocated to her to purchase computer equipment. Ms. Simmons responded that her school already has a sufficient supply of computers; indeed, the computer lab is never filled to capacity and usually is less than half filled. Ms. Simmons suggested that she would rather use the funds for teacher training. She argued that the reason the existing computers are not fully utilized is that the teachers lack sufficient computer literacy necessary to make assignments for their students.

Mr. Cleaver responded that it is not Ms. Simmons's job to decide how the money is to be spent; that is the school board's job. It is the principal's job to spend the money as the board directed. He informed Ms. Simmons that if the money is not spent by the fiscal closing date, the school board would likely reduce next year's budget allotment. To avoid a potential budget cut, Mr. Cleaver reallocated Ms. Simmons's computer funds to Jules Carrington, principal of East Harris County High. Mr. Carrington knows how to buy computers regardless of whether they are needed. Mr. Cleaver's final words were, "Don't blame me if parents of West High students complain that East High has more equipment. If anybody comes to me, I'm telling them that you turned down the money."

Required

a. Do Mr. Cleaver's actions violate the standards of ethical professional practice shown in Exhibit 10.17 of Chapter 10?

b. Explain how participative budgeting could improve the allocation of resources for the Harris County School District.

CHAPTER 15

Performance Evaluation

LEARNING OBJECTIVES

After you have mastered the material in this chapter, you will be able to:

LO 15-1   Describe the concept of decentralization.

LO 15-2   Distinguish between flexible and static budgets.

LO 15-3   Classify variances as being favorable or unfavorable.

LO 15-4   Compute and interpret sales and variable cost volume variances.

LO 15-5   Compute and interpret flexible budget variances.

LO 15-6   Evaluate investment opportunities using return on investment.

LO 15-7   Evaluate investment opportunities using residual income.

 Video lectures and accompanying self-assessment quizzes are available for all learning objectives through McGraw-Hill Connect® Accounting.

CHAPTER OPENING

Walter Keller, a production manager, complained to the accountant, Kelly Oberson, that the budget system failed to control his department's labor cost. Ms. Oberson responded, "People, not budgets, control costs." Budgeting is one of many tools management uses to control business operations. Managers are responsible for using control tools effectively. **Responsibility accounting** focuses on evaluating the performance of individual managers. For example, expenses controlled by a production department manager are presented in one report and expenses controlled by a marketing department manager are presented in a different report. This chapter discusses the development and use of a responsibility accounting system.

The Curious Accountant

Art in a Cup is a coffee shop located in an arts district of a major metropolitan area. Its owner, Melanie Tonkin, managed a coffee shop owned by a national chain while attending college. Even though there were more than 10,000 Starbucks coffee shops in the United States in 2012 and McDonald's had more than 14,000 restaurants selling coffee, Melanie opened her shop believing that patrons of an arts district would favor doing business with an independent coffee shop if the quality was high and the atmosphere eclectic.

In order to prepare a budget for her store, among other things, Melanie calculated the cost of making an average cup of coffee. She estimated the cost of coffee beans to be 18 cents per cup. This estimate was based on paying $8.00 per pound for the beans and getting 45 cups per pound. However, after six months in business, she had spent $7,450 on coffee beans and had sold 36,000 cups of coffee. This resulted in an actual cost per cup of 20.7 cents.

What are two general reasons that may explain why the materials cost for coffee beans was higher than Melanie estimated? (Answer on page 545.)

DECENTRALIZATION CONCEPT

Describe the concept of decentralization.

Effective responsibility accounting requires clear lines of authority and responsibility. Divisions of authority and responsibility normally occur as a natural consequence of managing business operations. In a small business, one person can control everything: marketing, production, management, accounting. In contrast, large companies are so complex that authority and control must be divided among many people.

Consider the hiring of employees. A small business usually operates in a limited geographic area. The owner works directly with employees. She knows the job requirements, local wage rates, and the available labor pool. She is in a position to make informed hiring decisions. In contrast, a major corporation may employ thousands of employees throughout the world. The employees may speak different languages and have different social customs. Their jobs may require many different skills and pay a vast array of wage rates. The president of the corporation cannot make informed hiring decisions for the entire company. Instead, he delegates *authority* to a professional personnel manager and holds that manager *responsible* for hiring practices.

Decision-making authority is similarly delegated to individuals responsible for managing specific organization functions such as production, marketing, and accounting. Delegating authority and responsibility is referred to as **decentralization.**

Responsibility Centers

Decentralized businesses are usually subdivided into distinct reporting units called responsibility centers. A **responsibility center** is an organizational unit that controls identifiable revenue or expense items. The unit may be a division, a department, a subdepartment, or even a single machine. For example, a transportation company may identify a semitrailer truck as a responsibility center. The company holds the truck driver responsible for the revenues and expenses associated with operating the truck. Responsibility centers may be divided into three categories: cost, profit, and investment.

A **cost center** is an organizational unit that incurs expenses but does not generate revenue. Cost centers normally fall on the lower levels of an organization chart. The manager of a cost center is judged on his ability to keep costs within budget parameters.

A **profit center** differs from a cost center in that it not only incurs costs but also generates revenue. The manager of a profit center is judged on his ability to produce revenue in excess of expenses.

Investment center managers are responsible for revenues, expenses, and the investment of capital. Investment centers normally appear at the upper levels of an organization chart. Managers of investment centers are accountable for assets and liabilities as well as earnings.

Controllability Concept

The **controllability concept** is crucial to an effective responsibility accounting system. Managers should only be evaluated based on revenues or costs they control. Holding individuals responsible for things they cannot control is demotivating. Isolating control, however, may be difficult, as illustrated in the following case.

Dorothy Pasework, a buyer for a large department store chain, was criticized when stores could not resell the merchandise she bought at the expected price. Ms. Pasework countered that the sales staff caused the sluggish sales by not displaying the merchandise properly. The sales staff charged that the merchandise had too little sales potential to justify setting up more enticing displays. The division of influence between the buyer and the sales staff clouds the assignment of responsibility.

Because the exercise of control may be clouded, managers are usually held responsible for items over which they have *predominant* rather than *absolute* control. At times responsibility accounting may be imperfect. Management must strive to ensure that praise or criticism is administered as fairly as possible.

PREPARING FLEXIBLE BUDGETS

A **flexible budget** is an extension of the *master budget* discussed previously. The master budget is based solely on the planned volume of activity. The master budget is frequently called a **static budget** because it remains unchanged even if the actual volume of activity differs from the planned volume. Flexible budgets differ from static budgets in that they show expected revenues and costs at a *variety* of volume levels.

To illustrate the differences between static and flexible budgets, consider Melrose Manufacturing Company, a producer of small, high-quality trophies used in award ceremonies. Melrose plans to make and sell 18,000 trophies during 2014. Management's best estimates of the expected sales price and per-unit costs for the trophies are called *standard* prices and costs. The standard price and costs for the 18,000 trophies follow.

Per-unit sales price and variable costs	
Expected sales price	$ 80.00
Standard materials cost	12.00
Standard labor cost	16.80
Standard overhead cost	5.60
Standard general, selling, and administrative cost	15.00
Total fixed costs	$291,600

The static budget is highlighted with red shading in Exhibit 15.1. Sales revenue is determined by multiplying the expected sales price per unit times the planned volume of activity ($80 × 18,000 = $1,440,000). Similarly, the variable costs are calculated by multiplying the standard cost per unit times the planned volume of activity. For example, the manufacturing materials cost is $216,000 ($12 × 18,000). The same computational procedures apply to the other variable costs. The variable costs are subtracted from the sales revenue to produce a contribution margin of $550,800. The fixed costs are subtracted from the contribution margin to produce a budgeted net income of $259,200.

EXHIBIT 15.1

Static and Flexible Budgets in Excel Spreadsheet

	Per Unit Standards	Static Budget		Flexible Budgets				
Number of Units		18,000		16,000	17,000	18,000	19,000	20,000
Sales Revenue	$80.00	$1,440,000		$1,280,000	$1,360,000	$1,440,000	$1,520,000	$1,600,000
Variable Manuf. Costs								
Materials	$12.00	216,000		192,000	204,000	216,000	228,000	240,000
Labor	16.80	302,400		268,800	285,600	302,400	319,200	336,000
Overhead	5.60	100,800		89,600	95,200	100,800	106,400	112,000
Variable G,S, &A	15.00	270,000		240,000	255,000	270,000	285,000	300,000
Contribution Margin		550,800		489,600	520,200	550,800	581,400	612,000
Fixed Costs		291,600		291,600	291,600	291,600	291,600	291,600
Net Income		$ 259,200		$ 198,000	$ 228,600	$ 259,200	$ 289,800	$ 320,400

What happens if the number of units sold is different from the planned volume? In other words, *what* happens to net income *if* Melrose sells more or less than 18,000 units? Managers frequently use flexible budgets to examine such *what if* scenarios. Flexible budget income statements for Melrose at sales volumes of 16,000, 17,000, 18,000, 19,000, and 20,000 are shown in Exhibit 15.1.

The flexible budgets are prepared with the same per-unit standard amounts and fixed cost data used to produce the static budget. The only difference is the expected number of units sold. For example, the sales revenue at 16,000 units is $1,280,000 ($80 × 16,000), at 17,000 units it is $1,360,000 ($80 × 17,000), and so on. The variable materials cost at 16,000 units is $192,000 ($12 × 16,000), at 17,000 units it is $204,000 ($12 × 17,000), and so on. The other variable costs are computed in the same manner. Note that the fixed costs are the same at all levels of activity because, by definition, they are not affected by changes in volume.

Other flexible budgets are possible. Indeed, a flexible budget can be prepared for any number of units sold. You have probably noticed that Exhibit 15.1 was prepared using an Excel spreadsheet. Excel offers the opportunity to prepare an unlimited number of flexible budgets with minimal effort. For example, formulas can be created with cell references so that new budgets can be created simply by changing the number of units entered in a single cell.

Managers use flexible budgets for both planning and performance evaluation. For example, managers may assess whether the company's cash position is adequate by assuming different levels of volume. They may judge if the number of employees, amounts of materials, and equipment and storage facilities are appropriate for a variety of different potential levels of volume. In addition to helping plan, flexible budgets are critical to implementing an effective performance evaluation system.

 CHECK YOURSELF 15.1

The static (master) budget of Parcel, Inc., called for a production and sales volume of 25,000 units. At that volume, total budgeted fixed costs were $150,000 and total budgeted variable costs were $200,000. Prepare a flexible budget for an expected volume of 26,000 units.

Answer   Budgeted fixed costs would remain unchanged at $150,000 because changes in the volume of activity do not affect budgeted fixed costs. Budgeted variable costs would increase to $208,000, computed as follows: Calculate the budgeted variable cost per unit ($200,000 ÷ 25,000 units = $8) and then multiply that variable cost per unit by the expected volume ($8 × 26,000 units = $208,000).

DETERMINING VARIANCES FOR PERFORMANCE EVALUATION

 LO 15-3

Classify variances as being favorable or unfavorable.

One means of evaluating managerial performance is to compare *standard* amounts with *actual* results. The differences between the standard and actual amounts are called **variances;** variances can be either *favorable* or *unfavorable*. When actual sales revenue is greater than expected (planned) revenue, a company has a favorable sales variance because higher sales increase net income. When actual sales are less than expected, an unfavorable sales variance exists. When actual costs are *less* than standard costs, cost variances are favorable because lower costs increase net income. Unfavorable cost variances exist when actual costs are *more* than standard costs. These relationships are summarized below.

- When actual sales exceed expected sales, variances are favorable.
- When actual sales are less than expected sales, variances are unfavorable.
- When actual costs exceed standard costs, variances are unfavorable.
- When actual costs are less than standard costs, variances are favorable.

SALES AND VARIABLE COST VOLUME VARIANCES

The amount of a **sales volume variance** is the difference between the static budget (which is based on planned volume) and a flexible budget based on actual volume. Likewise, the **variable cost volume variances** are determined by calculating the differences between the static and flexible budget amounts. These variances measure management effectiveness in attaining the planned volume of activity. To illustrate, assume Melrose Manufacturing Company actually makes and sells 19,000 trophies during 2014. The planned volume of activity was 18,000 trophies. Exhibit 15.2 shows Melrose's static budget, flexible budget, and volume variances.

LO 15-4

 Compute and interpret sales and variable cost volume variances.

EXHIBIT 15.2

Melrose Manufacturing Company's Volume Variances

	Static Budget	Flexible Budget	Volume Variances	
Number of units	18,000	19,000	1,000	Favorable
Sales revenue	$1,440,000	$1,520,000	$80,000	Favorable
Variable manufacturing costs				
Materials	216,000	228,000	12,000	Unfavorable
Labor	302,400	319,200	16,800	Unfavorable
Overhead	100,800	106,400	5,600	Unfavorable
Variable SG&A	270,000	285,000	15,000	Unfavorable
Contribution margin	550,800	581,400	30,600	Favorable
Fixed costs	291,600	291,600	0	
Net income	$ 259,200	$ 289,800	$30,600	Favorable

Interpreting the Sales and Variable Cost Volume Variances

Because the static and flexible budgets are based on the same standard sales price and per-unit variable costs, the variances are solely attributable to the difference between the planned and actual volume of activity. Marketing managers are usually responsible for the volume variances. Because the sales volume drives production levels, production managers have little control over volume. Exceptions occur; for example, if poor production quality control leads to inferior goods that are difficult to sell, the production manager is responsible. The production manager is responsible for production delays that affect product availability, which may restrict sales volume. Under normal circumstances, however, the marketing campaign determines the volume of sales. Upper-level marketing managers develop the promotional program and create the sales plan; they are in the best position to explain why sales goals are or are not met. When marketing managers refer to **making the numbers,** they usually mean reaching the sales volume in the static (master) budget.

In the case of Melrose Manufacturing Company, the marketing manager not only achieved but also exceeded by 1,000 units the planned volume of sales. Exhibit 15.2 shows the activity variances resulting from the extra volume. At the standard price, the additional volume produces a favorable revenue variance of $80,000 (1,000 units × $80 per unit). The increase in volume also produces unfavorable variable cost variances. The net effect of producing and selling the additional 1,000 units is an increase of $30,600 in the contribution margin, a positive result. These preliminary results suggest that the marketing manager is to be commended. The analysis, however, is incomplete. For example, examining market share could reveal whether the manager won customers from competitors or whether the manager simply reaped the benefit of an unexpected industrywide increase in demand. The increase in sales volume could have been attained by reducing the sales price; the success of that strategy will be analyzed further in a later section of this chapter.

Since the variable costs in the flexible budget are higher than the variable costs in the static budget, the variable cost volume variances are *unfavorable.* The unfavorable classification may be misleading because it focuses solely on the cost component of the income statement. While costs are higher than expected, so too may be revenue. Indeed, as shown in Exhibit 15.2, the total of the unfavorable variable cost variances is more than offset by the favorable revenue variance, resulting in a higher contribution margin. Frequently, the assessment of variances requires a holistic perspective.

Fixed Cost Considerations

The fixed costs are the same in both the static and flexible budgets. By definition, the budgeted amount of fixed costs remains unchanged regardless of the volume of activity. However, this does not mean that there will be no fixed cost variances. Companies may certainly pay more or less than expected for a fixed cost. For example, a supervisor may receive an unplanned raise, causing actual salary costs to be more than the costs shown in the static budget. The difference between the *budgeted* fixed costs and the *actual* fixed costs is called a **spending variance.** At this point, it is important to note that the reason the fixed cost variances shown in Exhibit 15.2 are zero is because we are comparing two budgets (static versus flexible). Because total fixed cost is not affected by the level of activity, there will be no fixed cost variances associated with static versus flexible budgets.

While total fixed cost does not change in response to changes in the volume of activity, fixed cost per unit does change. Changes in the fixed cost per unit have important implications for decision making. For example, consider the impact on cost-plus pricing decisions. Because actual volume is unknown until the end of the year, selling prices must be based on planned volume. At the *planned volume* of activity of 18,000 units, Melrose's fixed cost per unit is expected to be $16.20 ($291,600 ÷ 18,000 units).

Based on the *actual volume* of 19,000 units, the fixed cost per unit is actually $15.35 per trophy ($291,600 ÷ 19,000 units). Because Melrose's prices were established using the $16.20 budgeted cost at planned volume rather than the $15.35 budgeted cost at actual volume, the trophies were overpriced, giving competitors a price advantage. Although Melrose sold more trophies than expected, sales volume might have been even greater if the trophies had been competitively priced.

Underpricing (not encountered by Melrose in this example) can also be detrimental. If planned volume is overstated, the estimated fixed cost per unit will be understated and prices will be set too low. When the higher amount of actual costs is subtracted from revenues, actual profits will be lower than expected. To monitor the effects of volume on fixed cost per unit, companies frequently calculate a **fixed cost volume variance.**

The fixed cost volume variance is *unfavorable* if actual volume is less than planned because cost per unit is higher than expected. Conversely, if actual volume is greater than planned, cost per unit is less than expected, resulting in a *favorable* variance. Both favorable and unfavorable variances can have negative consequences. Managers should strive for the greatest possible degree of accuracy.

FLEXIBLE BUDGET VARIANCES

LO 15-5

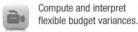

Compute and interpret flexible budget variances.

For performance evaluation, management compares actual results to a flexible budget based on the *actual* volume of activity. Because the actual results and the flexible budget reflect the same volume of activity, any variances in revenues and variable costs result from differences between standard and actual per-unit amounts. To illustrate computing and analyzing flexible budget variances, we assume that Melrose's *actual* per-unit amounts during 2014 were those shown in the following table. The 2014 per-unit *standard* amounts are repeated here for your convenience.

	Standard	Actual
Sales price	$80.00	$78.00
Variable materials cost	12.00	11.78
Variable labor cost	16.80	17.25
Variable manufacturing overhead cost	5.60	5.75
Variable G, S, & A	15.00	14.90

Actual and budgeted fixed costs are shown in Exhibit 15.3.

Exhibit 15.3 shows Melrose's 2014 flexible budget, actual results, and flexible budget variances. The flexible budget is the same one compared to the static budget in Exhibit 15.2.

EXHIBIT 15.3

Flexible Budget Variances for Melrose Manufacturing Company

	Flexible Budget	Actual Results	Flexible Budget Variances	
Number of units	19,000	19,000	0	
Sales revenue	$1,520,000	$1,482,000	$38,000	Unfavorable
Variable manufacturing costs				
Materials	228,000	223,820	4,180	Favorable
Labor	319,200	327,750	8,550	Unfavorable
Overhead	106,400	109,250	2,850	Unfavorable
Variable SG&A	285,000	283,100	1,900	Favorable
Contribution margin	581,400	538,080	43,320	Unfavorable
Fixed costs	291,600	295,000	3,400	Unfavorable
Net income	$ 289,800	$ 243,080	$46,720	Unfavorable

Recall the flexible budget amounts come from multiplying the standard per-unit amounts by the actual volume of production. For example, the sales revenue in the flexible budget comes from multiplying the standard sales price by the actual volume ($80 × 19,000). The variable costs are similarly computed. The *actual results* are calculated by multiplying the actual per-unit sales price and cost figures from the preceding table by the actual volume of activity. For example, the sales revenue in the Actual Results column comes from multiplying the actual sales price by the actual volume ($78 × 19,000 = $1,482,000). The actual cost figures are similarly computed. The differences between the flexible budget figures and the actual results are the **flexible budget variances.**

Calculating the Sales Price Variance

Because both the flexible budget and actual results are based on the actual volume of activity, the flexible budget variance is attributable to sales price, not sales volume. In this case, the actual sales price of $78 per unit is less than the standard price of $80 per unit. Because Melrose sold its product for less than the standard sales price, the **sales price variance** is *unfavorable.* Even though the price variance is unfavorable, however, sales volume was 1,000 units more than expected. It is possible the marketing manager generated the additional volume by reducing the sales price. Whether the combination of lower sales price and higher sales volume is favorable or unfavorable depends on the amount of the unfavorable sales price variance versus the amount of the favorable sales volume variance. The *total* sales variance (price and volume) follows:

Actual sales (19,000 units × $78 per unit)	$1,482,000	
Expected sales (18,000 units × $80 per unit)	1,440,000	
Total sales variance	$ 42,000	Favorable

Alternatively,

Activity variance (sales volume)	$ 80,000	Favorable
Sales price variance	(38,000)	Unfavorable
Total sales variance	$ 42,000	Favorable

This analysis indicates that reducing the sales price had a favorable impact on the *total* amount of sales revenue. Use caution when interpreting variances as good or bad; in this instance, the favorable sales variance must be compared with the related cost variances to determine whether the price reduction strategy actually increased or decreased profitability. All unfavorable variances are not bad; all favorable variances are not good. Variances should not be considered the final answer, but instead be seen as a signal to investigate.

☑ CHECK YOURSELF 15.2

Scott Company's master budget called for a planned sales volume of 30,000 units. Budgeted direct materials cost was $4 per unit. Scott actually produced and sold 32,000 units with an actual materials cost of $3.90 per unit. Determine the volume variance for materials cost and identify the organizational unit most likely responsible for this variance. Determine the flexible budget variance for materials cost and identify the organizational unit most likely responsible for this variance.

Answer

Planned Volume	30,000	Actual Volume	32,000	Actual Volume	32,000
×	×	×	×	×	×
Standard Cost	$4.00	Standard Cost	$4.00	Actual Cost	$3.90
	$120,000		$128,000		$124,800

	Volume Variance for Materials Cost	Flexible Budget Variance for Materials Cost
	$8,000 Unfavorable	$3,200 Favorable

The materials volume variance is unfavorable because the materials cost ($128,000) is higher than was expected ($120,000). However, this could actually be positive because higher volume was probably caused by increasing sales. Further analysis would be necessary to determine whether the overall effect on the company's profitability was positive or negative. The marketing department is most likely to be responsible for the volume variance.

The flexible budget materials cost variance is favorable because the cost of materials was less than expected at the actual volume of activity. Either the production department (used less than the expected amount of materials) or the purchasing department (obtained materials at a favorable price) is most likely to be responsible for this variance.

The Human Element Associated with Flexible Budget Variances

The flexible budget cost variances offer insight into management efficiency. For example, Melrose Manufacturing Company's favorable materials variance could mean purchasing agents were shrewd in negotiating price concessions, discounts, or delivery terms and therefore reduced the price the company paid for materials. Similarly, production

Answers to The Curious Accountant

As this chapter demonstrates, there are two primary reasons a company spends more or less to produce a product than it estimated. First, the company may have paid more or less than estimated to purchase the inputs needed to produce the product. Second, the company may have used a greater or lesser quantity of these inputs than expected. In the case of Art in a Cup, it may have had to pay more for coffee beans than the owner estimated. Coffee prices, like most agricultural commodities, can be very volatile due to factors such as weather. Or, it may have used more coffee beans per cup than expected. For example, if brewed coffee sits around too long before being served, it has to be thrown out. This waste was not anticipated when computing the cost to make only one cup of coffee. Of course, the higher than expected cost could have been a combination of price and quantity factors.

Art in a Cup needs to determine if the difference between its expected costs and actual costs was because the estimates were faulty or because the production process was inefficient. If the estimates were to blame, the owner needs to revise them so she can charge the proper price to her customers. If the production process is inefficient, she needs to correct it if she is to earn an acceptable level of profit.

employees may have used materials efficiently, using less than expected. The unfavorable labor variance could mean managers failed to control employee wages or motivate employees to work hard. As with sales variances, cost variances require careful analysis. A favorable variance may, in fact, mask unfavorable conditions. For example, the favorable materials variance might have been caused by paying low prices for inferior goods. Using substandard materials could have required additional labor in the production process, which would explain the unfavorable labor variance. Again, we caution that variances, whether favorable or unfavorable, alert management to investigate further.

Need for Standards

As the previous discussion suggests, standards are the building blocks for preparing the static and flexible budgets. Standard costs help managers plan and also establish benchmarks against which actual performance can be judged. Highlighting differences between standard (expected) and actual performance focuses management attention on the areas of greatest need. Because management talent is a valuable and expensive resource, businesses cannot afford to have managers spend large amounts of time on operations that are functioning normally. Instead, managers should concentrate on areas not performing as expected. In other words, management should attend to the exceptions; this management philosophy is known as **management by exception.**

Standard setting fosters using the management by exception principle. By reviewing performance reports that show differences between actual and standard costs, management can focus its attention on the items that show significant variances. Areas with only minor variances need little or no review.

MANAGERIAL PERFORMANCE MEASUREMENT

As previously discussed, managers are assigned responsibility for certain cost, profit, or investment centers. They are then evaluated based on how their centers perform relative to specific goals and objectives. The measurement techniques (variance analysis and contribution margin format income reporting) used for cost and profit centers have been discussed in this and previous chapters. The remainder of this chapter discusses performance measures for investment centers.

RETURN ON INVESTMENT

LO 15-6

Evaluate investment opportunities using return on investment.

Society confers wealth, prestige, and power upon those who have control of assets. Unsurprisingly, managers are motivated to increase the amount of assets employed by the investment centers they control. When companies have additional assets available to invest, how do upper-level managers decide which centers should get them? The additional assets are frequently allotted to the managers who demonstrate the greatest potential for increasing the company's wealth. Companies often assess managerial performance by comparing the return on investment ratios of various investment centers. The **return on investment (ROI)** is the ratio of wealth generated (operating income) to the amount invested (operating assets) to generate the wealth. ROI is commonly expressed with the following equation.

$$ROI = \frac{\text{Operating income}}{\text{Operating assets}}$$

To illustrate using ROI for comparative evaluations, assume Panther Holding Company's corporate (first level) chief financial officer (CFO) determined the ROIs for the company's three divisions (second level investment centers). The CFO used the following accounting data from the records of each division:

	Lumber Manufacturing Division	Home Building Division	Furniture Manufacturing Division
Operating income	$ 60,000	$ 46,080	$ 81,940
Operating assets	300,000	256,000	482,000

The ROI for each division is:

Lumber manufacturing: $\dfrac{\text{Operating income}}{\text{Operating assets}} = \$60{,}000 \div \$300{,}000 = 20\%$

Home building: $\dfrac{\text{Operating income}}{\text{Operating assets}} = \$46{,}080 \div \$256{,}000 = 18\%$

Furniture manufacturing: $\dfrac{\text{Operating income}}{\text{Operating assets}} = \$81{,}940 \div \$482{,}000 = 17\%$

All other things being equal, higher ROIs indicate better performance. In this case, the Lumber Manufacturing Division manager is the best performer. Assume Panther obtains additional funding for expanding the company's operations. Which investment center is most likely to receive the additional funds?

If the manager of the Lumber Manufacturing Division convinces the upper-level management team that his division would continue to outperform the other two divisions, the Lumber Manufacturing Division would most likely get the additional funding. The manager of the lumber division would then invest the funds in additional operating assets, which would in turn increase the division's operating income. As the division prospers, Panther would reward the manager for exceptional performance. Rewarding the manager of the lumber division would likely motivate the other managers to improve their divisional ROIs. Internal competition would improve the performance of the company as a whole.

Qualitative Considerations

Why do companies compute ROI using operating income and operating assets instead of using net income and total assets? Suppose Panther's corporate headquarters closes a furniture manufacturing plant because an economic downturn temporarily reduces the demand for furniture. It would be inappropriate to include these nonoperating plant assets in the denominator of the ROI computation. Similarly, if Panther sells the furniture plant and realizes a large gain on the sale, including the gain in the numerator of the ROI formula would distort the result. Since the manager of the Furniture Manufacturing Division does not control closing the plant or selling it, it is unreasonable to include the effects of these decisions in computing the ROI. These items would, however, be included in computing net income and total assets. Most companies use operating income and operating assets to compute ROI because those variables measure performance more accurately.

 CHECK YOURSELF 15.3

Green View is a lawn services company whose operations are divided into two districts. The District 1 manager controls $12,600,000 of operating assets. District 1 produced $1,512,000 of operating income during the year. The District 2 manager controls $14,200,000 of operating assets. District 2 reported $1,988,000 of operating income for the same period. Use return on investment to determine which manager is performing better.

Answer

District 1

$$ROI = \text{Operating income} \div \text{Operating assets} = \$1,512,000 \div \$12,600,000 = 12\%$$

District 2

$$ROI = \text{Operating income} \div \text{Operating assets} = \$1,988,000 \div \$14,200,000 = 14\%$$

Because the higher ROI indicates the better performance, the District 2 manager is the superior performer. This conclusion is based solely on quantitative results. In real-world practice, companies also consider qualitative factors.

Factors Affecting Return on Investment

Management can gain insight into performance by dividing the ROI formula into two separate ratios as follows:

$$ROI = \frac{\text{Operating income}}{\text{Sales}} \times \frac{\text{Sales}}{\text{Operating assets}}$$

The first ratio on the right side of the equation is called the margin. The **margin** is a measure of management's ability to control operating expenses relative to the level of sales. In general, high margins indicate superior performance. Management can increase the margin by reducing the level of operating expenses necessary to generate sales. Decreasing operating expenses increases profitability.

The second ratio in the expanded ROI formula is called turnover. **Turnover** is a measure of the amount of operating assets employed to support the achieved level of sales. Operating assets are scarce resources. To maximize profitability, they must be used wisely. Just as excessive expenses decrease profitability, excessive investments in operating assets also limit profitability.

Both the short and expanded versions of the ROI formula produce the same end result. To illustrate, we will use the ROI for the Lumber Manufacturing Division of

Panther Holding Company. Recall that the division employed $300,000 of operating assets to produce $60,000 of operating income, resulting in the following ROI:

$$\text{ROI} = \frac{\text{Operating income}}{\text{Operating assets}} = \frac{\$60,000}{\$300,000} = 20\%$$

Further analysis of the accounting records indicates the Lumber Manufacturing Division had sales of $600,000. The following computation demonstrates that the expanded ROI formula produces the same result as the short formula:

$$\text{ROI} = \text{Margin} \times \text{Turnover}$$

$$= \frac{\text{Operating income}}{\text{Sales}} \times \frac{\text{Sales}}{\text{Operating assets}}$$

$$= \frac{\$60,000}{\$600,000} \times \frac{\$600,000}{\$300,000}$$

$$= .10 \times 2$$

$$= 20\%$$

Dividing the ROI formula into a margin and a turnover computation encourages managers to examine the benefits of controlling assets as well as expenses.

Because ROI blends many aspects of managerial performance into a single ratio that enables comparisons between companies, comparisons between investment centers within companies, and comparisons between different investment opportunities within an investment center, ROI has gained widespread acceptance as a performance measure.

 CHECK YOURSELF 15.4

What three actions can a manager take to improve ROI?

Answer

1. Increase sales
2. Reduce expenses
3. Reduce the investment base

RESIDUAL INCOME

LO 15-7

 Evaluate investment opportunities using residual income.

Suppose Panther Holding Company evaluates the manager of the Lumber Manufacturing Division (LMD) based on his ability to maximize ROI. The corporation's overall ROI is approximately 18 percent. LMD, however, has consistently outperformed the other investment centers. Its ROI is currently 20 percent. Now suppose the manager has an opportunity to invest additional funds in a project likely to earn a 19 percent ROI. Would the manager accept the investment opportunity?

These circumstances place the manager in an awkward position. The corporation would benefit from the project because the expected ROI of 19 percent is higher than the corporate average ROI of 18 percent. Personally, however, the manager would suffer from accepting the project because it would reduce the division ROI to less than the current 20 percent. The manager is forced to choose between his personal best interests and the best interests of the corporation. When faced with decisions such as these, many managers choose to benefit themselves at the expense of their corporations, a condition described as **suboptimization.**

To avoid *suboptimization,* many businesses base managerial evaluation on **residual income.** This approach measures a manager's ability to maximize earnings above some

FOCUS ON INTERNATIONAL ISSUES

DO MANAGERS IN DIFFERENT COMPANIES STRESS THE SAME PERFORMANCE MEASURES?

About the only ratio companies are required to disclose in their annual reports to stockholders is the earnings per share ratio. Nevertheless, many companies choose to show their performance as measured by other ratios, as well as providing nonratio data not required by GAAP. The types of ratio data companies choose to include in their annual reports provide a sense of what performance measure they consider most important.

A review of several publicly traded companies from the United Kingdom, Japan, and the United States will show that the most common ratios presented are variations of the return on sales percentage and the return on investment percentage, although they may be called by different names. The country in which the company is located does not seem to determine which ratio it will emphasize.

One nonratio performance measure that is popular with companies in all three countries is free cash flow, and it is usually reported in total pounds, yen, or dollars. Be sure to exercise caution before comparing one company's free cash flow, return on sales, or return on investment to those of other companies. There are no official rules governing how these data are calculated, and different companies make different interpretations about how to compute these measurements.

targeted level. The targeted level of earnings is based on a minimum desired ROI. Residual income is calculated as follows:

$$\text{Residual income} = \text{Operating income} - (\text{Operating assets} \times \text{Desired ROI})$$

To illustrate, recall that LMD currently earns $60,000 of operating income with the $300,000 of operating assets it controls. ROI is 20 percent ($60,000 ÷ $300,000). Assume Panther's desired ROI is 18 percent. LMD's residual income is therefore:

$$\text{Residual income} = \text{Operating income} - (\text{Operating assets} \times \text{Desired ROI})$$
$$= \$60,000 - (\$300,000 \times .18)$$
$$= \$60,000 - \$54,000$$
$$= \$6,000$$

Now assume that Panther Holding Company has $50,000 of additional funds available to invest. Because LMD consistently performs at a high level, Panther's corporate management team offers the funds to the LMD manager. The manager believes he could invest the additional $50,000 at a 19 percent rate of return.

If the LMD manager's evaluation is based solely on ROI, he is likely to reject the additional funding because investing the funds at 19 percent would lower his overall ROI. If the LMD manager's evaluation is based on residual income, however, he is likely to accept the funds because an additional investment at 19 percent would increase his residual income as follows:

$$\text{Operating income} = \$50,000 \times .19$$
$$= \$9,500$$
$$\text{Residual income} = \text{Operating income} - (\text{Operating assets} \times \text{Desired ROI})$$
$$= \$9,500 - (\$50,000 \times .18)$$
$$= \$9,500 - \$9,000$$
$$= \$500$$

550   Chapter 15

REALITY BYTES

Thinking about investments usually conjures up images of buildings and equipment, but investments typically include a much broader range of expenditures. For example, if Walmart plans to open a new store, it has to make an investment in inventory to stock the store that is as permanent as the building. But investment expenditures can be for items much less tangible than inventory. Consider the making of a movie.

While it is true that making a movie can require expenditures for items such as cameras and sets, the single highest cost can often be for actors' salaries. Although movie fans may focus on how much a movie grosses at the box office, from a business perspective it is the movie's ROI that matters.

From an ROI perspective, the question is, "Which actor generates the highest (or lowest) dollars of return for each dollar he or she is paid?" To this end, for the past several years Forbes has calculated the "Best Actors for the Buck" and "Worst Actors for the Buck" lists. Calculating the ROI for an actor in a movie, rather than for the entire investment in the movie, can be tricky and requires several estimates. For example, should the credit for the spectacular success of the Harry Potter movies go to the main actor, Daniel Radcliffe; the special effects; or the author, J. K. Rowling? Despite these challenges, Forbes reviews the financial performance of the 40 highest paid actors who have starred in at least three movies in the past five years and creates its best and worst lists.

And the winner is . . . ? In 2012, the actor with the highest return per dollar paid was Natalie Portman, who starred in the *Black Swan* and *No Strings Attached*. According to Forbes, she returned $42.70 for each $1.00 of salary she was paid. *And the loser is . . . ?* Eddie Murphy, who returned $2.30 for each dollar he was paid.

Source: Forbes.com.

Accepting the new project would add $500 to LMD's residual income. If the manager of LMD is evaluated based on his ability to maximize residual income, he would benefit by investing in any project that returns an ROI in excess of the desired 18 percent. The reduction in LMD's overall ROI does not enter into the decision. The residual income approach solves the problem of suboptimization.

The primary disadvantage of the residual income approach is that it measures performance in absolute dollars. As a result, a manager's residual income may be larger simply because her investment base is larger rather than because her performance is superior.

To illustrate, return to the example where Panther Holding Company has $50,000 of additional funds to invest. Assume the manager of the Lumber Manufacturing Division (LMD) and the manager of the Furniture Manufacturing Division (FMD) each have investment opportunities expected to earn a 19 percent return. Recall that Panther's desired ROI is 18 percent. If corporate headquarters allots $40,000 of the funds to the manager of LMD and $10,000 to the manager of FMD, the increase in residual income earned by each division is as follows:

LMD's Residual income = ($40,000 × .19) − ($40,000 × .18) = $400

FMD's Residual income = ($10,000 × .19) − ($10,000 × .18) = $100

Does LMD's higher residual income mean LMD's manager is outperforming FMD's manager? No. It means LMD's manager received more operating assets than FMD's manager received.

Calculating Multiple ROIs and/or RIs for the Same Company

You may be asked to calculate different ROI and RI measures for the same company. For example, ROI and/or RI may be calculated for the company as a whole, for segments of the company, for specific investment opportunities, and for individual managers. An example is shown in Check Yourself 15.5.

Responsibility Accounting and the Balanced Scorecard

Throughout the text, we have discussed many financial measures companies use to evaluate managerial performance. Examples include standard cost systems to evaluate cost center managers; the contribution margin income statement to evaluate profit center managers; and ROI or residual income to evaluate the performance of investment center managers. Many companies may have goals and objectives such as "satisfaction guaranteed" or "we try harder" that are more suitably evaluated using nonfinancial measures. To assess how well they accomplish the full range of their missions, many companies use a *balanced scorecard.*

 CHECK YOURSELF 15.5

Tambor Incorporated (TI) earned operating income of $4,730,400 on operating assets of $26,280,000 during 2014. The Western Division earned $748,000 on operating assets of $3,400,000. TI has offered the Western Division $1,100,000 of additional operating assets. The manager of the Western Division believes he could use the additional assets to generate operating income amounting to $220,000. TI has a desired return on investment (ROI) of 17 percent. Determine the ROI and RI for TI, the Western Division, and the additional investment opportunity.

Answer

Return on investment (ROI) = Operating income ÷ Operating assets
ROI for TI = $4,730,400 ÷ $26,280,000 = 18%
ROI for Western Division = $748,000 ÷ $3,400,000 = 22%
ROI for investment opportunity = $220,000 ÷ $1,100,000 = 20%

Residual income (RI) = Operating income − (Operating assets × Desired ROI)
RI for TI = $4,730,400 − ($26,280,000 × .17) = $262,800
RI for Western Division = $748,000 − ($3,400,000 × .17) = $170,000
RI for investment opportunity = $220,000 − ($1,100,000 × .17) = $33,000

A **balanced scorecard** includes financial and nonfinancial performance measures. Standard costs, income measures, ROI, and residual income are common financial measures used in a balanced scorecard. Nonfinancial measures include defect rates, cycle time, on-time deliveries, number of new products or innovations, safety measures, and customer satisfaction surveys. Many companies compose their scorecards to highlight leading versus lagging measures. For example, customer satisfaction survey data are a leading indicator of sales growth, which is a lagging measure. The balanced scorecard is a holistic approach to evaluating managerial performance. It is gaining widespread acceptance among world-class companies.

A Look Back

The practice of delegating authority and responsibility is referred to as *decentralization.* Clear lines of authority and responsibility are essential in establishing a responsibility accounting system. In a responsibility accounting system, segment managers are held accountable for profits based on the amount of control they have over the profits in their segment.

Responsibility reports are used to compare actual results with budgets. The reports should be simple with variances highlighted to promote the *management by exception* doctrine. Individual managers should be held responsible only for those revenues or costs they control. Each manager should receive only summary information about the performance of the responsibility centers under her supervision.

552   Chapter 15

A *responsibility center* is the point in an organization where control over revenue or expense is located. *Cost centers* are segments that incur costs but do not generate revenues. *Profit centers* incur costs and also generate revenues, producing a measurable profit. *Investment centers* incur costs, generate revenues, and use identifiable capital investments.

One of the primary purposes of responsibility accounting is to evaluate managerial performance. Comparing actual results with standards and budgets and calculating *return on investment* are used for this purpose. Because return on investment uses revenues, expenses, and investment, problems with measuring these parameters must be considered. The return on investment can be analyzed in terms of the margin earned on sales as well as the turnover (asset utilization) during the period. The *residual income approach* is sometimes used to avoid *suboptimization,* which occurs when managers choose to reject investment projects that would benefit their company's ROI but would reduce their investment center's ROI. The residual income approach evaluates managers based on their ability to generate earnings above some targeted level of earnings.

 # A Look Forward

The next chapter expands on the concepts in this chapter. You will see how managers select investment opportunities that will affect their future ROIs. You will learn to apply present value techniques to compute the net present value and the internal rate of return for potential investment opportunities. You will also learn to use less sophisticated analytical techniques such as payback and the unadjusted rate of return.

 Video lectures and accompanying self-assessment quizzes are available for all learning objectives through McGraw-Hill *Connect®* *Accounting.*

SELF-STUDY REVIEW PROBLEM 1

Bugout Pesticides Inc. established the following standard price and costs for a termite control product that it sells to exterminators.

Variable price and cost data (per unit)	Standard	Actual
Sales price	$52.00	$49.00
Materials cost	10.00	10.66
Labor cost	12.00	11.90
Overhead cost	7.00	7.05
General, selling, and administrative (G, S, & A) cost	8.00	7.92
Expected fixed costs (in total)		
Manufacturing	$150,000	$140,000
General, selling, and administrative	60,000	64,000

The 2014 master budget was established at an expected volume of 25,000 units. Actual production and sales volume for the year was 26,000 units.

Required

a. Prepare the pro forma income statement for Bugout's 2014 master budget.

b. Prepare a flexible budget income statement at the actual volume.

c. Determine the sales activity (volume) variances and indicate whether they are favorable or unfavorable. Comment on how Bugout would use the variances to evaluate performance.

d. Determine the flexible budget variances and indicate whether they are favorable or unfavorable.

e. Identify the two variances Bugout is most likely to analyze further. Explain why you chose these two variances. Who is normally responsible for the variances you chose to investigate?

Solution to Requirements *a*, *b*, and *c*

Number of units		25,000	26,000	
	Per Unit Standards	Master Budget	Flexible Budget	Volume Variances
Sales revenue	$52	$1,300,000	$1,352,000	$52,000 F
Variable manufacturing costs				
Materials	10	(250,000)	(260,000)	10,000 U
Labor	12	(300,000)	(312,000)	12,000 U
Overhead	7	(175,000)	(182,000)	7,000 U
Variable G, S, & A	8	(200,000)	(208,000)	8,000 U
Contribution margin		375,000	390,000	15,000 F
Fixed costs				
Manufacturing		(150,000)	(150,000)	0
G, S, & A		(60,000)	(60,000)	0
Net income		$ 165,000	$ 180,000	$15,000 F

The sales activity variances are useful in determining how changes in sales volume affect revenues and costs. Because the flexible budget is based on standard prices and costs, the variances do not provide insight into differences between standard prices and costs versus actual prices and costs.

Solution to Requirement *d*

Number of units		26,000	26,000	
	Actual Unit Price/Cost	Flexible Budget*	Actual Results	Flexible Budget Variances
Sales revenue	$49.00	$1,352,000	$1,274,000	$78,000 U
Variable manufacturing costs				
Materials	10.66	(260,000)	(277,160)	17,160 U
Labor	11.90	(312,000)	(309,400)	2,600 F
Overhead	7.05	(182,000)	(183,300)	1,300 U
Variable G, S, & A	7.92	(208,000)	(205,920)	2,080 F
Contribution margin		390,000	298,220	91,780 U
Fixed costs				
Manufacturing		(150,000)	(140,000)	10,000 F
G, S, & A		(60,000)	(64,000)	4,000 U
Net income		$ 180,000	$ 94,220	$85,780 U

*The price and cost data for the flexible budget come from the previous table.

Solution to Requirement *e*

The management by exception doctrine focuses attention on the sales price variance and the materials variance. The two variances are material in size and are generally under the control of management. Upper-level marketing managers are responsible for the sales price variance. These managers are normally responsible for establishing the sales price. In this case, the actual sales price is less than the planned sales price, resulting in an unfavorable flexible budget variance. Mid-level production supervisors and purchasing agents are normally responsible for the materials cost variance. This variance could have been caused by waste or by paying more for materials than the standard price.

SELF-STUDY REVIEW PROBLEM 2

The following financial statements apply to Hola Division, one of three investment centers operated by Costa Corporation. Costa Corporation has a desired rate of return of 15 percent. Costa Corporation Headquarters has $80,000 of additional operating assets to assign to the investment centers.

HOLA DIVISION
Income Statement
For the Year Ended December 31, 2014

Sales revenue	$ 78,695
Cost of goods sold	(50,810)
Gross margin	27,885
Operating expenses	
Selling expenses	(1,200)
Depreciation expense	(1,125)
Operating income	25,560
Nonoperating expense	
Loss on sale of land	(3,200)
Net income	$ 22,360

HOLA DIVISION
Balance Sheet
As of December 31, 2014

Assets	
Cash	$ 8,089
Accounts receivable	22,870
Merchandise inventory	33,460
Equipment less acc. dep.	77,581
Nonoperating assets	8,250
Total assets	$150,250
Liabilities	
Accounts payable	$ 5,000
Notes payable	58,000
Stockholders' equity	
Common stock	55,000
Retained earnings	32,250
Total liab. and stk. equity	$150,250

Required

a. Should Costa use operating income or net income to determine the rate of return (ROI) for the Hola investment center? Explain.

b. Should Costa use operating assets or total assets to determine the ROI for the Hola investment center? Explain.

c. Calculate the ROI for Hola.

d. The manager of the Hola division has an opportunity to invest the funds at an ROI of 17 percent. The other two divisions have investment opportunities that yield only 16 percent. The manager of Hola rejects the additional funding. Why would the manager of Hola reject the funds under these circumstances?

e. Calculate the residual income from the investment opportunity available to Hola and explain how residual income could be used to encourage the manager to accept the additional funds.

Solution to Requirement *a*

Costa should use operating income because net income frequently includes items over which management has no control, such as the loss on sale of land.

Solution to Requirement *b*

Costa should use operating assets because total assets frequently includes items over which management has no control, such as assets not currently in use.

Solution to Requirement *c*

$$\text{ROI} = \text{Operating income}/\text{Operating assets} = \$25{,}560/\$142{,}000 = 18\%$$

Solution to Requirement *d*

Since the rate of return on the investment opportunity (17 percent) is below Hola's current ROI (18 percent), accepting the opportunity would decrease Hola's average ROI, which would have a negative effect on the manager's performance evaluation. While it is to the advantage of the company as a whole for Hola to accept the investment opportunity, it will reflect negatively on the manager to do so. This phenomenon is called *suboptimization*.

Solution to Requirement *e*

Operating income from the investment opportunity is $13,600 ($80,000 × .17)

$$\text{Residual income} = \text{Operating income} - (\text{Operating assets} \times \text{Desired ROI})$$

$$\text{Residual income} = \$13{,}600 - (\$80{,}000 \times .15)$$

$$\text{Residual income} = \$13{,}600 - \$12{,}000$$

$$\text{Residual income} = \$1{,}600$$

Because the investment opportunity would increase Hola's residual income, the acceptance of the opportunity would improve the manager's performance evaluation, thereby motivating the manager to accept it.

KEY TERMS

Balanced scorecard 551	Flexible budget variance 543	Residual income 548	Spending variance 542
Controllability concept 538	Investment center 538	Responsibility	Static budget 539
Cost center 538	Making the numbers 541	accounting 536	Suboptimization 548
Decentralization 538	Management by	Responsibility center 538	Turnover 547
Fixed cost volume	exception 545	Return on investment 546	Variable cost volume
variance 542	Margin 547	Sales price variance 543	variance 541
Flexible budget 539	Profit center 538	Sales volume variance 541	Variances 540

QUESTIONS

1. Pam Kelly says she has no faith in budgets. Her company, Kelly Manufacturing Corporation, spent thousands of dollars to install a sophisticated budget system. One year later the company's expenses are still out of control. She believes budgets simply do not work. How would you respond to Ms. Kelly's beliefs?

2. What is a responsibility center?

3. What are the three types of responsibility centers? Explain how each differs from the others.

4. What is the difference between a static budget and a flexible budget? When is each used?

5. When the operating costs for Bill Smith's production department were released, he was sure that he would be getting a raise. His costs were $20,000 less than the planned cost in the master budget. His supervisor informed him that the results look good but that a more in-depth analysis is necessary before raises can be assigned. What other considerations could Mr. Smith's

supervisor be interested in before she rates his performance?

6. When are sales and cost variances favorable and unfavorable?

7. Joan Mason, the marketing manager for a large manufacturing company, believes her unfavorable sales volume variance is the responsibility of the

556   Chapter 15

production department. What production circumstances that she does not control could have been responsible for her poor performance?

8. When would variable cost volume variances be expected to be unfavorable? How should unfavorable variable cost volume variances be interpreted?

9. What factors could lead to an increase in sales revenues that would not merit congratulations to the marketing manager?

10. With respect to fixed costs, what are the consequences of the actual volume of activity exceeding the planned volume?

11. How are flexible budget variances determined? What causes these variances?

12. Minnie Divers, the manager of the marketing department for one of the industry's leading retail businesses, has been notified by the accounting department that her department experienced an unfavorable sales volume variance in the preceding period but a favorable sales price variance.

Based on these contradictory results, how would you interpret her overall performance as suggested by her variances?

13. How do variance reports promote the management by exception doctrine?

14. Carmen Douglas claims that her company's performance evaluation system is unfair. Her company uses return on investment (ROI) to evaluate performance. Ms. Douglas says that even though her ROI is lower than another manager's, her performance is far superior. Is it

possible that Ms. Douglas is correct? Explain your position.

15. What two factors affect the computation of return on investment?

16. What three ways can a manager increase the return on investment?

17. How can a residual income approach to performance evaluation reduce the likelihood of suboptimization?

18. Is it true that the manager with the highest residual income is always the best performer?

MULTIPLE-CHOICE QUESTIONS

Multiple-choice questions are provided on the text website at www.mhhe.com/edmondssurvey4e.

EXERCISES

≡ connect | ACCOUNTING   **All applicable Exercises are available with McGraw-Hill Connect® Accounting.**

LO 15-1

Exercise 15-1   *Evaluating a profit center*

Ericka Riku, the president of Besant Toys Corporation, is trying to determine this year's pay raises for the store managers. Besant Toys has seven stores in the southwestern United States. Corporate headquarters purchases all toys from different manufacturers globally and distributes them to individual stores. Additionally, headquarters makes decisions regarding location and size of stores. These practices allow Besant Toys to receive volume discounts from vendors and to implement coherent marketing strategies. Within a set of general guidelines, store managers have the flexibility to adjust product prices and hire local employees. Ms. Riku is considering three possible performance measures for evaluating the individual stores: cost of goods sold, return on sales (net income divided by sales), and return on investment.

Required

a. Using the concept of controllability, advise Ms. Riku about the best performance measure.
b. Explain how a balanced scorecard can be used to help Ms. Riku.

LO 15-2

Exercise 15-2   *Preparing master and flexible budgets*

Allard Manufacturing Company established the following standard price and cost data.

Sales price	$10.00 per unit
Variable manufacturing cost	$6 per unit
Fixed manufacturing cost	$3,000 total
Fixed selling and administrative cost	$1,000 total

Allard planned to produce and sell 2,000 units. Actual production and sales amounted to 2,200 units.

Required

a. Prepare the pro forma income statement in contribution format that would appear in a master budget.

b. Prepare the pro forma income statement in contribution format that would appear in a flexible budget.

Exercise 15-3 *Using a flexible budget to accommodate market uncertainty*

LO 15-2

According to its original plan, Bailey Consulting Services Company plans to charge its customers for service at $160 per hour in 2014. The company president expects consulting services provided to customers to reach 45,000 hours at that rate. The marketing manager, however, argues that actual results may range from 40,000 hours to 50,000 hours because of market uncertainty. Bailey's standard variable cost is $60 per hour, and its standard fixed cost is $1,800,000.

Required

Develop flexible budgets based on the assumptions of service levels at 40,000 hours, 45,000 hours, and 50,000 hours.

Exercise 15-4 *Classifying variances as favorable or unfavorable*

LO 15-3

Required

Indicate whether each of the following variances is favorable or unfavorable. The first one has been done as an example.

Item to Classify	Standard	Actual	Type of Variance
Sales volume	40,000 units	42,000 units	Favorable
Sales price	$3.60 per unit	$3.63 per unit	
Materials cost	$2.90 per pound	$3.00 per pound	
Materials usage	91,000 pounds	90,000 pounds	
Labor cost	$10.00 per hour	$9.60 per hour	
Labor usage	61,000 hours	61,800 hours	
Fixed cost spending	$400,000	$390,000	
Fixed cost per unit (volume)	$3.20 per unit	$3.16 per unit	

Exercise 15-5 *Determining amount and type (favorable vs. unfavorable) of variance*

LO 15-3

Required

Compute variances for the following items and indicate whether each variance is favorable (F) or unfavorable (U).

Item	Budget	Actual	Variance	F or U
Sales price	$800	$780		
Sales revenue	$720,000	$780,000		
Cost of goods sold	$385,000	$360,000		
Material purchases at 5,000 pounds	$275,000	$280,000		
Materials usage	$180,000	$178,000		
Production volume	950 units	900 units		
Wages at 4,000 hours	$60,000	$58,700		
Labor usage at $16 per hour	$96,000	$97,000		
Research and development expense	$22,000	$25,000		
Selling and administrative expenses	$49,000	$40,000		

LO 15-3

Exercise 15-6   *Income statement for internal use*

Titov Company has provided the following 2014 data.

Budget	
Sales	$800,000
Variable product costs	326,000
Variable selling expense	80,000
Other variable expenses	6,000
Fixed product costs	21,000
Fixed selling expense	40,000
Other fixed expenses	3,200
Interest expense	1,300
Variances	
Sales	6,400 U
Variable product costs	5,200 F
Variable selling expense	2,500 U
Other variable expenses	1,200 U
Fixed product costs	220 F
Fixed selling expense	390 F
Other fixed expenses	150 U
Interest expense	100 F

Required

a. Prepare in good form a budgeted and actual income statement for internal use. Separate operating income from net income in the statements.

b. Calculate variances and identify them as favorable (F) or unfavorable (U) by comparing the budgeted and actual amounts determined in Requirement *a*.

LO 15-3, 15-4

Exercise 15-7   *Determining sales and variable cost volume variances*

Required

Use the information provided in Exercise 15-2.

a. Determine the sales and variable cost volume variances.

b. Classify the variances as favorable (F) or unfavorable (U).

c. Comment on the usefulness of the variances with respect to performance evaluation and identify the member of the management team most likely to be responsible for these variances.

d. Determine the amount of fixed cost that will appear in the flexible budget.

e. Determine the fixed cost per unit based on planned activity and the fixed cost per unit based on actual activity. Assuming Allard uses information in the master budget to price the company's product, comment on how the fixed cost volume variance could affect the company's profitability.

LO 15-3, 15-5

Exercise 15-8   *Determining flexible budget variances*

Use the standard price and cost data provided in Exercise 15-2. Assume that the actual sales price is $9.80 per unit and that the actual variable cost is $5.75 per unit. The actual fixed manufacturing cost is $2,500, and the actual selling and administrative costs are $1,025.

Required

a. Determine the flexible budget variances.

b. Classify the variances as favorable (F) or unfavorable (U).

c. Provide another name for the fixed cost flexible budget variances.

d. Comment on the usefulness of the variances with respect to performance evaluation and identify the member(s) of the management team who is (are) most likely to be responsible for these variances.

Exercise 15-9 *Responsibility for the fixed cost volume variance*

LO 15-5

Daisy Company expected to sell 400,000 of its pagers during 2014. It set the standard sales price for the pager at $30 each. During June, it became obvious that the company would be unable to attain the expected volume of sales. Daisy's chief competitor, Cruz Corporation, had lowered prices and was pulling market share from Daisy. To be competitive, Daisy matched Cruz's price, lowering its sales price to $28 per pager. Cruz responded by lowering its price even further to $24 per pager. In an emergency meeting of key personnel, Daisy's accountant, Miriana Hope, stated, "Our cost structure simply won't support a sales price in the $24 range." The production manager, Borris Cooper, said, "I don't understand why I'm here. The only unfavorable variance on my report is a fixed manufacturing overhead cost volume variance and that one is not my fault. We shouldn't be making the product if the marketing department isn't selling it."

Required

a. Describe a scenario in which the production manager is responsible for the fixed cost volume variance.

b. Describe a scenario in which the marketing manager is responsible for the fixed cost volume variance.

c. Explain how a decline in sales volume would affect Daisy's ability to lower its sales price.

Exercise 15-10 *Evaluating a cost center including flexible budgeting concepts*

LO 15-3, 15-4, 15-5

Koch Medical Equipment Company makes a blood pressure measuring kit. Albert Kaiser is the production manager. The production department's static budget and actual results for 2015 follow.

	Static Budget	Actual Results
Production in units	60,000 kits	64,000 kits
Direct materials	$ 420,000	$ 524,000
Direct labor	360,000	371,200
Variable manufacturing overhead	96,000	108,000
Total variable costs	876,000	1,003,200
Fixed manufacturing overhead	420,000	410,000
Total manufacturing cost	$1,296,000	$1,413,200

Required

a. Convert the static budget into a flexible budget with a production volume of 64,000 kits.

b. Use the flexible budget to evaluate Mr. Kaiser's performance.

c. Explain why Mr. Kaiser's performance evaluation does not include sales revenue and net income.

Exercise 15-11 *Evaluating a decision to increase sales volume by lowering sales price*

LO 15-3, 15-4, 15-5

Austen Educational Services had budgeted its training service charge at $100 per hour. The company planned to provide 30,000 hours of training services during 2015. By lowering the service charge to $95 per hour, the company was able to increase the actual number of hours to 31,500.

Required

a. Determine the sales volume variance, and indicate whether it is favorable (F) or unfavorable (U).

b. Determine the flexible budget variance, and indicate whether it is favorable (F) or unfavorable (U).

c. Did lowering the price of training services increase revenue? Explain.

Exercise 15-12 *Return on investment*

LO 15-6

An investment center of Aguilar Corporation shows an operating income of $8,000 on total operating assets of $120,000.

Required

Compute the return on investment. Round the computation to two decimal points.

LO 15-6

Exercise 15-13 *Return on investment*

Albany Company calculated its return on investment as 10 percent. Sales are now $300,000, and the amount of total operating assets is $480,000.

Required

a. If expenses are reduced by $30,000 and sales remain unchanged, what return on investment will result?
b. If both sales and expenses cannot be changed, what change in the amount of operating assets is required to achieve the same result?

LO 15-7

Exercise 15-14 *Residual income*

Applin Corporation has a desired rate of return of 8 percent. Troy Anderson is in charge of one of Applin's three investment centers. His center controlled operating assets of $5,000,000 that were used to earn $480,000 of operating income.

Required

Compute Mr. Anderson's residual income.

LO 15-7

Exercise 15-15 *Residual income*

Alder Cough Drops operates two divisions. The following information pertains to each division for 2013.

	Division A	Division B
Sales	$360,000	$150,000
Operating income	$ 26,000	$ 16,000
Average operating assets	$125,000	$100,000
Company's desired rate of return	16%	16%

Required

a. Compute each division's residual income.
b. Which division increased the company's profitability more?

LO 15-6, 15-7

Exercise 15-16 *Return on investment and residual income*

Required

Supply the missing information in the following table for Blair Company.

Sales	$484,000
ROI	?
Operating assets	?
Operating income	?
Turnover	2.2
Residual income	?
Operating profit margin	0.08
Desired rate of return	10%

LO 15-6, 15-7

Exercise 15-17 *Comparing return on investment with residual income*

The Bishop Division of Kingley Corporation has a current ROI of 12 percent. The company target ROI is 8 percent. The Bishop Division has an opportunity to invest $6,000,000 at 10 percent but is reluctant to do so because its ROI will fall to 11.25 percent. The present investment base for the division is $10,000,000.

Required

Demonstrate how Kingley can motivate the Bishop Division to make the investment by using the residual income method.

PROBLEMS

 All applicable Problems are available with McGraw-Hill Connect® Accounting.

Problem 15-18 *Different types of responsibility centers*

Southern National Bank is a large municipal bank with several branch offices. The bank's computer department handles all data processing for bank operations. In addition, the bank sells the computer department's expertise in systems development and excess machine time to several small business firms, serving them as a service bureau.

The bank currently treats the computer department as a cost center. The manager of the computer department prepares a cost budget annually for senior bank officials to approve. Monthly operating reports compare actual and budgeted expenses. Revenues from the department's service bureau activities are treated as other income by the bank and are not reflected on the computer department's operating reports. The costs of servicing these clients are included in the computer department reports, however.

The manager of the computer department has proposed that bank management convert the computer department to a profit or investment center.

Required

a. Describe the characteristics that differentiate a cost center, a profit center, and an investment center from each other.

b. Would the manager of the computer department be likely to conduct the operations of the department differently if the department were classified as a profit center or an investment center rather than as a cost center? Explain.

Problem 15-19 *Flexible budget planning*

Curtis Salter, the president of Kasimer Computer Services, needs your help. He wonders about the potential effects on the firm's net income if he changes the service rate that the firm charges its customers. The following basic data pertain to fiscal year 2015.

CHECK FIGURES
a. NI = $155,000
c. NI = $162,500

Standard rate and variable costs	
Service rate per hour	$75.00
Labor cost	40.00
Overhead cost	7.20
Selling, general, and administrative cost	4.30
Expected fixed costs	
Facility maintenance	$400,000
Selling, general, and administrative	150,000

Required

a. Prepare the pro forma income statement that would appear in the master budget if the firm expects to provide 30,000 hours of services in 2015.

b. A marketing consultant suggests to Mr. Salter that the service rate may affect the number of service hours that the firm can achieve. According to the consultant's analysis, if Kasimer charges customers $70 per hour, the firm can achieve 38,000 hours of services. Prepare a flexible budget using the consultant's assumption.

c. The same consultant also suggests that if the firm raises its rate to $80 per hour, the number of service hours will decline to 25,000. Prepare a flexible budget using the new assumption.

d. Evaluate the three possible outcomes you determined in Requirements *a*, *b*, and *c* and recommend a pricing strategy.

Problem 15-20 *Determining sales and variable cost volume variances*

Lloyd Publications established the following standard price and costs for a hardcover picture book that the company produces.

Standard price and variable costs	
Sales price	$45.00
Materials cost	9.00
Labor cost	4.50
Overhead cost	6.30
Selling, general, and administrative costs	7.20
Planned fixed costs	
Manufacturing overhead	$135,000
Selling, general, and administrative	54,000

Lloyd planned to make and sell 30,000 copies of the book.

Required

a. Prepare the pro forma income statement that would appear in the master budget.

b. Prepare flexible budget income statements, assuming production volumes of 29,000 and 31,000 units.

c. Determine the sales and variable cost volume variances, assuming volume is actually 31,000 units.

d. Indicate whether the variances are favorable (F) or unfavorable (U).

e. Comment on how Lloyd could use the variances to evaluate performance.

LO 15-5

Problem 15-21   *Determining and interpreting flexible budget variances*

Use the standard price and cost data supplied in Problem 15-20. Assume that Lloyd actually produced and sold 32,000 books. The actual sales price and costs incurred follow.

Actual price and variable costs	
Sales price	$43.50
Materials cost	9.20
Labor cost	4.40
Overhead cost	6.35
Selling, general, and administrative costs	7.00
Actual fixed costs	
Manufacturing overhead	$125,000
Selling, general, and administrative	58,000

Required

a. Determine the flexible budget variances. Provide another name for the fixed cost flexible budget variances.

b. Indicate whether each variance is favorable (F) or unfavorable (U).

c. Identify the management position responsible for each variance. Explain what could have caused the variance.

LO 15-6

Problem 15-22   *Return on investment*

Helton Corporation's balance sheet indicates that the company has $500,000 invested in operating assets. During 2014, Helton earned operating income of $50,000 on $1,000,000 of sales.

Required

a. Compute Helton's profit margin for 2014.

b. Compute Helton's turnover for 2014.

c. Compute Helton's return on investment for 2014.

d. Recompute Helton's ROI under each of the following independent assumptions.

(1) Sales increase from $1,000,000 to $1,200,000, thereby resulting in an increase in operating income from $50,000 to $56,000.

(2) Sales remain constant, but Helton reduces expenses, resulting in an increase in operating income from $50,000 to $52,000.

(3) Helton is able to reduce its invested capital from $500,000 to $400,000 without affecting operating income.

Problem 15-23 *Comparing return on investment and residual income*

LO 15-6, 15-7

Cole Corporation operates three investment centers. The following financial statements apply to the investment center named Morrison Division.

CHECK FIGURE
c. 23.05%

MORRISON DIVISION Income Statement For the Year Ended December 31, 2014	
Sales revenue	$135,000
Cost of goods sold	78,500
Gross margin	56,500
Operating expenses	
Selling expenses	(5,000)
Depreciation expense	(8,000)
Operating income	43,500
Nonoperating item	
Loss on sale of land	(15,000)
Net income	$ 28,500

MORRISON DIVISION Balance Sheet As of December 31, 2014	
Assets	
Cash	$ 18,580
Accounts receivable	42,266
Merchandise inventory	37,578
Equipment less accum. dep.	90,258
Nonoperating assets	9,000
Total assets	$197,682
Liabilities	
Accounts payable	$ 9,637
Notes payable	72,000
Stockholders' equity	
Common stock	80,000
Retained earnings	36,045
Total liab. and stk. equity	$197,682

Required

a. Which should be used to determine the rate of return (ROI) for the Morrison investment center, operating income or net income? Explain your answer.

b. Which should be used to determine the ROI for the Morrison investment center, operating assets or total assets? Explain your answer.

c. Calculate the ROI for Morrison. Round the computation to two decimal points.

d. Cole has a desired ROI of 10 percent. Headquarters has $96,000 of funds to assign to its investment centers. The manager of the Morrison Division has an opportunity to invest the funds at an ROI of 12 percent. The other two divisions have investment opportunities that yield only 11 percent. Even so, the manager of Morrison rejects the additional funding.

Explain why the manager of Morrison would reject the funds under these circumstances. Round the computation to two decimal points.

e. Explain how residual income could be used to encourage the manager to accept the additional funds. Round the computation to whole dollars.

Problem 15-24   *Comparing return on investment and residual income*

The manager of the Cranston Division of Wynn Manufacturing Corporation is currently producing a 20 percent return on invested capital. Wynn's desired rate of return is 16 percent. The Cranston Division has $6,000,000 of capital invested in operating assets and access to additional funds as needed. The manager is considering a new investment in operating assets that will require a $1,500,000 capital commitment and promises an 18 percent return.

Required

a. Would it be advantageous for Wynn Manufacturing Corporation if the Cranston Division makes the investment under consideration?

b. What effect would the proposed investment have on the Cranston Division's return on investment? Show computations.

c. What effect would the proposed investment have on the Cranston Division's residual income? Show computations.

d. Would return on investment or residual income be the better performance measure for the Cranston Division's manager? Explain.

ANALYZE, THINK, COMMUNICATE

ATC 15-1   Business Applications Case   *Static versus flexible budget variances*

Anthony Bennett is the manufacturing production supervisor for Green Bottle Works (GBW), a company that manufactures stainless-steel water bottles. Trying to explain why he did not get the year-end bonus that he had expected, he told his wife, "This is the dumbest place I ever worked. Last year the company set up this budget assuming it would sell 250,000 units. Well, it sold only 240,000. The company lost money and gave me a bonus for not using as much materials and labor as was called for in the budget. This year, the company has the same 250,000 units goal and it sells 260,000. The company's making all kinds of money. You'd think I'd get this big fat bonus. Instead, management tells me I used more materials and labor than was budgeted. They said the company would have made a lot more money if I'd stayed within my budget. I guess I gotta wait for another bad year before I get a bonus. Like I said, this is the dumbest place I ever worked."

GBW's master budget and the actual results for the most recent year of operating activity follow.

	Master Budget	Actual Results	Variances	F or U
Number of units	250,000	260,000	10,000	
Sales revenue	$3,750,000	$3,950,000	$200,000	F
Variable manufacturing costs				
Materials	(600,000)	(622,200)	22,200	U
Labor	(312,500)	(321,000)	8,500	U
Overhead	(337,500)	(354,700)	17,200	U
Variable selling, general,				
and admin. costs	(475,000)	(501,300)	26,300	U
Contribution margin	2,025,000	2,150,800	125,800	F
Fixed costs				
Manufacturing overhead	(1,275,000)	(1,273,100)	1,900	F
Selling, general, and admin. costs	(470,000)	(479,300)	9,300	U
Net income	$ 280,000	$ 398,400	$118,400	F

Required

a. Did GBW increase unit sales by cutting prices or by using some other strategy?

b. Is Mr. Bennett correct in his conclusion that something is wrong with the company's performance evaluation process? If so, what do you suggest be done to improve the system?

c. Prepare a flexible budget and recompute the budget variances.

d. Explain what might have caused the fixed costs to be different from the amount budgeted.

e. Assume that the company's materials price variance was favorable and its materials usage variance was unfavorable. Explain why Mr. Bennett may not be responsible for these variances. Now, explain why he may have been responsible for the materials usage variance.

f. Assume the labor price variance is unfavorable. Was the labor usage variance favorable or unfavorable?

g. Is the fixed cost volume variance favorable or unfavorable? Explain the effect of this variance on the cost of each unit produced.

ATC 15-2   Group Assignment   *Return on investment versus residual income*

Bellco, a division of Becker International Corporation, is operated under the direction of Antoin Sedatt. Bellco is an independent investment center with approximately $72,000,000 of assets that generate approximately $8,640,000 in annual net income. Becker International has additional investment capital of $12,000,000 that is available for the division managers to invest. Mr. Sedatt is aware of an investment opportunity that will provide an 11 percent annual net return. Becker International's desired rate of return is 10 percent.

Required

Divide the class into groups of four or five students and then organize the groups into two sections. Assign Task 1 to the first section and Task 2 to the second section.

Group Tasks

1. Assume that Mr. Sedatt's performance is evaluated based on his ability to maximize return on investment (ROI). Compute ROI using the following two assumptions: Bellco retains its current asset size and Bellco accepts and invests the additional $12,000,000 of assets. Determine whether Mr. Sedatt should accept the opportunity to invest additional funds. Select a spokesperson to present the decision made by the group.

2. Assume that Mr. Sedatt's performance is evaluated based on his ability to maximize residual income. Compute residual income using the following two assumptions: Bellco retains its current asset base and Bellco accepts and invests the additional $12,000,000 of assets. Determine whether Mr. Sedatt should accept the opportunity to invest additional funds. Select a spokesperson to present the decision made by the group.

3. Have a spokesperson from one of the groups in the first section report the two ROIs and the group's recommendation for Mr. Sedatt. Have the groups in this section reach consensus on the ROI and the recommendation.

4. Have a spokesperson from the second section report the two amounts of residual income and disclose the group's recommendation for Mr. Sedatt. Have this section reach consensus on amounts of residual income.

5. Which technique (ROI or residual income) is more likely to result in suboptimization?

ATC 15-3   Research Assignment   *Using real-world data from Target Corporation*

Obtain the income statements for Target Corporation for the fiscal years ending in 2008, 2009, 2010, 2011, and 2012. Target's fiscal year ends near the end of January or the beginning of February. The 2010–2012 statements are included in Target's 2012 annual report and Form 10-K, dated March 15, 2012. The 2008 and 2009 statements are in its 2009 annual report and Form 10-K, dated March 13, 2009.

To obtain the Form 10-Ks, you can use the EDGAR system (see Appendix A at the back of this text for instructions), or they can be found under the "Investors Relations" link on the company's corporate website, www.target.com. The company's annual reports are also available on its website. Note that this problem ignores Target's revenues and expenses related to its credit card operations.

566   Chapter 15

Required

a. Compute the percentage change for each of the following categories of revenues and expenses for 2008 to 2009, 2009 to 2010, and 2010 to 2011:

> Sales (not total revenues)
> Cost of sales
> Selling, general, and administrative expenses
> Depreciation and amortization

Using an Excel spreadsheet will make this task much easier. After you have obtained these averages (you should have three averages for each of the six revenue and expense items), calculate an average of the changes for each item. The answer for the "Depreciation and amortization" item is shown as an example:

	Percentage Change
2008–2009	10.1%
2009–2010	10.8
2010–2011	3.0
Average of the changes	8.0%

b. Prepare a budgeted income statement for 2012 (the fiscal year ending January 28, 2012), and compare the budgeted data to the actual results for 2012. To calculate budgeted amounts, multiply (1 + Average percentage change) in each revenue and expense item from Requirement *b* by the dollar amount of the corresponding revenue or expense item from 2011. This will represent the budgeted amount for that item for 2012. Don't forget to use decimal data and not percentage data. Subtract the actual 2012 results from the budgeted results. Finally, divide the actual versus budgeted difference by the budgeted amount to determine a percentage variance from the budget. The answer for the "Depreciation and amortization" item is shown as an example (dollar amounts are in millions):

	(1) 2011 Actual	(2) Average 3-year Change	(3) [1 + (1 × 2)] 2012 Budget	(4) 2012 Actual	(5) (3 − 4) Variance	(5 ÷ 3) Percentage Variance from Budget
Depreciation and amortization	$2,084	.080	$2,251	$2,131	$120	.053 [5.3%]

ATC 15-4   Business Applications Case   *Analyzing segments at Coca-Cola*

The following excerpt is from Coca-Cola Company's 2011 annual report filed with the SEC.

> *Management evaluates the performance of our operating segments separately to individually monitor the different factors affecting financial performance. Our Company manages income taxes and certain treasury-related items, such as interest income and expense, on a global basis within the Corporate operating segment. We evaluate segment performance based on income or loss before income taxes.*

Below are selected segment data for Coca-Cola Company for the 2011 and 2010 fiscal years. Dollar amounts are in millions.

	Eurasia & Africa	Europe	Latin America	North America	Pacific
2011 Fiscal Year					
Net operating revenues	$2,689	$4,777	$4,403	$20,559	$5,454
Income before taxes	1,089	3,134	2,832	2,325	2,154
Identifiable operating assets	1,245	3,204	2,446	33,422	2,085
2010 Fiscal Year					
Net operating revenues	$2,426	$4,424	$3,880	$11,140	$4,941
Income before taxes	1,000	3,020	2,426	1,523	2,049
Identifiable operating assets	1,278	2,724	2,298	32,793	1,827

Required

a. Compute the ROI for each of Coke's geographical segments for each fiscal year. Which segment appears to have the best performance during 2011 based their ROIs? Which segment showed the most improvement from 2010 to 2011?

b. Assuming Coke's management expects a minimum return of 30 percent, calculate the residual income for each segment for each fiscal year. Which segment appears to have the best performance based on residual income? Which segment showed the most improvement from 2010 to 2011?

c. Explain why the segment with the highest ROI in 2011 was not the segment with the highest residual income.

d. Assume the management of Coke is considering a major expansion effort for the next five years. On which geographic segment would you recommend Coke focus its expansion efforts? Explain the rationale for your answer.

ATC 15-5   Ethics Dilemma   *Fudging the standards*

Eric Dawson is a department manager at Lemhi, Inc., a manufacturing company. His department is responsible for assembling various products. Lemhi uses a standard costing system to help manage operations and evaluate its managers. In addition to his salary, Mr. Dawson has the potential to earn a bonus based on how well his department performs, and he, in turn, evaluates the workers in his department based on how well they perform their duties, based on the standard costing system.

Lemhi, Inc., has just received a contract to manufacture a new toy, called LogicBlock, for the Toys for the Imagination Company, and Mr. Dawson's department will be responsible for its assembly. The product designers and engineers at Lemhi believe it should take the workers in Mr. Dawson's department 23 minutes to assemble each toy. However, Mr. Dawson told his workers the standard time allowed to assemble each unit of LogicBlock is 21 minutes.

Required

a. Explain what Mr. Dawson is hoping to achieve by telling workers the time expected to assemble a toy is 21 minutes versus 23 minutes.

b. What do you think the short-term and long-term implications of his strategy are likely to be? Explain.

CHAPTER 16

Planning for Capital Investments

LEARNING OBJECTIVES

After you have mastered the material in this chapter, you will be able to:

LO 16-1   Explain the time value of money concept.

LO 16-2   Determine and interpret the net present value of an investment opportunity.

LO 16-3   Determine and interpret the internal rate of return of an investment opportunity.

LO 16-4   Evaluate investment opportunities using the payback method and the unadjusted rate of return.

 Video lectures and accompanying self-assessment quizzes are available for all learning objectives through McGraw-Hill Connect® Accounting.

CHAPTER OPENING

The president of EZ Rentals (EZ) is considering expanding the company's rental service business to include LCD projectors that can be used with notebook computers. A marketing study forecasts that renting projectors could generate revenue of $200,000 per year. The possibility of increasing revenue is alluring, but EZ's president has a number of unanswered questions. How much do the projectors cost? What is their expected useful life? Will they have a salvage value? Does EZ have the money to buy them? Does EZ have the technical expertise to support the product? How much will training cost? How long will customer demand last? What if EZ buys the projectors and they become technologically obsolete? How quickly will EZ be able to recover the investment? Are there more profitable ways to invest EZ's funds?

Spending large sums of money that will have long-term effects on company profits makes most managers anxious. What if a cell phone manufacturer spends millions of dollars to build a factory in the United States and its competitors locate their manufacturing facilities in countries that provide cheap labor? The manufacturer's cell phones will be overpriced, but it cannot move overseas because it cannot find a buyer for the factory. What if a pharmaceutical company spends millions of dollars to develop a drug which then fails to receive FDA approval? What if a communications company installs underground cable but satellite transmission steals its market? What if a company buys computer equipment that rapidly becomes technologically obsolete? Although these possibilities may be remote, they can be expensive when they do occur. For example, Wachovia Bank's 1997 annual report discloses a $70 million write-off of computer equipment. This chapter discusses some of the analytical techniques companies use to evaluate major investment opportunities.

The Curious Accountant

The March 25, 2011, drawing for the Mega Millions multistate lottery produced one winning ticket. The ticket, which was purchased in New York, had an advertised value of $312 million. This amount, however, was based on the assumption that the winner would take his or her prize as 26 equal annual payments of $12 million. If the winnings were taken in this manner, the first payment would be made immediately, and the others would be paid annually over the next 25 years. The winner also had the option of taking an immediate, lump-sum payment of $203 million.

Assume that you work as a personal financial planner and that one of your clients held the winning lottery ticket. If you think you could invest your client's winnings and earn an annual return of 7 percent, would you advise your client to take the lump-sum payment or the annual payments? Why? (The answer is on page 583.)

CAPITAL INVESTMENT DECISIONS

Purchases of long-term operational assets are **capital investments.** Capital investments differ from stock and bond investments in an important respect. Investments in stocks and bonds can be sold in organized markets such as the New York Stock Exchange. In contrast, investments in capital assets normally can be recovered only by using those assets. Once a company purchases a capital asset, it is committed to that investment for an extended period of time. If the market turns sour, the company is stuck with the consequences. It may also be unable to seize new opportunities because its capital is committed. Business profitability ultimately hinges, to a large extent, on the quality of a few key capital investment decisions.

A capital investment decision is essentially a decision to exchange current cash outflows for the expectation of receiving future cash inflows. For EZ Rentals, purchasing LCD projectors, cash outflows today, provides the opportunity to collect $200,000 per year in rental revenue, cash inflows in the future. Assuming the projectors have useful lives of four years and no salvage value, how much should EZ be willing to pay for the future cash inflows? If you were EZ's president, would you spend $700,000 today to receive $200,000 each year for the next four years? You would give up $700,000 today for the opportunity to receive $800,000 (4 × $200,000) in the future. What if you collect less than $200,000 per year? If revenue is only $160,000 per year, you would lose $60,000 [$700,000 − (4 × $160,000)]. Is $700,000 too much to pay for the opportunity to receive $200,000 per year for four years? If $700,000 is too much, would you spend $600,000? If not, how about $500,000? There is no one right answer to these questions. However, understanding the *time value of money* concept can help you develop a rational response.

Time Value of Money

The **time value of money** concept recognizes that *the present value of a dollar received in the future is less than a dollar.* For example, you may be willing to pay only $0.90 today for a promise to receive $1.00 one year from today. The further into the future the receipt is expected to occur, the smaller is its present value. In other words, one dollar to be received two years from today is worth less than one dollar to be received one year from today. Likewise, one dollar to be received three years from today is less valuable than one dollar to be received two years from today, and so on.

The present value of cash inflows decreases as the time until expected receipt increases for several reasons. First, you could deposit today's dollar in a savings account to earn *interest* that increases its total value. If you wait for your money, you lose the opportunity to earn interest. Second, the expectation of receiving a future dollar carries an element of *risk*. Changed conditions may result in the failure to collect. Finally, *inflation* diminishes the buying power of the dollar. In other words, the longer you must wait to receive a dollar, the less you will be able to buy with it.

When a company invests in capital assets, it sacrifices present dollars in exchange for the opportunity to receive future dollars. Since trading current dollars for future dollars is risky, companies expect compensation before they invest in capital assets. The compensation a company expects is called *return on investment (ROI).* As discussed previously, ROI is expressed as a percentage of the investment. For example, the ROI for a $1,000 investment that earns annual income of $100 is 10 percent ($100 ÷ $1,000 = 10%).

Determining the Minimum Rate of Return

To establish the minimum expected *return on investment* before accepting an investment opportunity, most companies consider their cost of capital. To attract capital, companies must provide benefits to their creditors and owners. Creditors expect interest payments; owners expect dividends and increased stock value. Companies that earn lower returns than their cost of capital eventually go bankrupt; they cannot continually pay out more than they collect. *The **cost of capital** represents the **minimum rate of return** on investments.* Calculating the cost of capital is a complex exercise which is beyond the scope of this text. It is addressed in finance courses. We discuss how management accountants *use* the cost of capital to evaluate investment opportunities. Companies describe the cost of capital in a variety of ways: the *minimum rate of return*, the *desired rate of return*, the *required rate of return*, the *hurdle rate*, the *cutoff rate*, or the *discount rate*. These terms are used interchangeably throughout this chapter.

 CHECK YOURSELF 16.1

Study the following cash inflow streams expected from two different potential investments.

	Year 1	Year 2	Year 3	Total
Alternative 1	$2,000	$3,000	$4,000	$9,000
Alternative 2	4,000	3,000	2,000	9,000

Based on visual observation alone, which alternative has the higher present value? Why?

Answer   Alternative 2 has the higher present value. The size of the discount increases as the length of the time period increases. In other words, a dollar received in year 3 has a lower present value than a dollar received in year 1. Since most of the expected cash inflows from Alternative 2 are received earlier than those from Alternative 1, Alternative 2 has a higher present value even though the total expected cash inflows are the same.

Converting Future Cash Inflows to Their Equivalent Present Values

Given a desired rate of return and the amount of a future cash flow, present value can be determined using algebra. To illustrate, refer to the $200,000 EZ expects to earn the first year it leases LCD projectors.[1] Assuming EZ desires a 12 percent rate of return, what amount of cash would EZ be willing to invest today (present value outflow) to obtain a $200,000 cash inflow at the end of the year (future value)? The answer follows:[2]

$$\text{Investment} + (0.12 \times \text{Investment}) = \text{Future cash inflow}$$

$$1.12 \text{ Investment} = \$200,000$$

$$\text{Investment} = \$200,000 \div 1.12$$

$$\text{Investment} = \$178,571$$

If EZ invests $178,571 cash on January 1 and earns a 12 percent return on the investment, EZ will have $200,000 on December 31. An investor who is able to earn a 12 percent return on investment is indifferent between having $178,571 now or receiving

---

[1] The following computations assume the $200,000 cash inflow is received on the last day of each year. In actual practice, the timing of cash inflows is less precise and present value computations are recognized to be approximate, not exact.

[2] All computations in this chapter are rounded to the nearest whole dollar.

$200,000 one year from now. The two options are equal, as shown in the following mathematical proof:

$$\text{Investment} + (0.12 \times \text{Investment}) = \$200,000$$

$$\$178,571 + (0.12 \times \$178,571) = \$200,000$$

$$\$178,571 + \$21,429 = \$200,000$$

$$\$200,000 = \$200,000$$

Present Value Table for Single-Amount Cash Inflows

The algebra illustrated above is used to convert a one-time future receipt of cash to its present value. One-time receipts of cash are frequently called **single-payment,** or **lump-sum,** cash flows. Because EZ desires a 12 percent rate of return, the present value of the first cash inflow is $178,571. We can also determine the present value of a $200,000 single amount (lump sum) at the end of the second, third, and fourth years. Instead of using cumbersome algebraic computations to convert these future values to their present value equivalents, financial analysts frequently use a table of conversion factors to convert future values to their present value equivalents. The table of conversion factors used to convert future values into present values is commonly called a **present value table.**[3] A typical present value table presents columns with different return rates and rows with different periods of time, like Table 1 in the Appendix located at the end of this chapter.

To illustrate using the present value table, locate the conversion factor in Table 1 at the intersection of the 12% column and the one-period row. The conversion factor is 0.892857. Multiplying this factor by the $200,000 expected cash inflow yields $178,571 ($200,000 × 0.892857). This is the same value determined algebraically in the previous section of this chapter. The conversion factors in the present value tables simplify converting future values to present values.

The conversion factors for the second, third, and fourth periods are 0.797194, 0.711780, and 0.635518, respectively. These factors are in the 12% column at rows 2, 3, and 4, respectively. Locate these factors in Table 1 of the Appendix. Multiplying the conversion factors by the future cash inflow for each period produces their present value equivalents, shown in Exhibit 16.1. Exhibit 16.1 indicates that investing $607,470 today at a 12 percent rate of return is equivalent to receiving $200,000 per year for four years. Because EZ Rentals desires to earn (at least) a 12 percent rate of return, the company should be willing to pay up to $607,470 to purchase the LCD projectors.

Present Value Table for Annuities

The algebra described previously for converting equal lump-sum cash inflows to present value equivalents can be further simplified by adding the present value table factors

EXHIBIT 16.1

Present Value of a $200,000 Cash Inflow to Be Received for Four Years

PV	=	FV	×	Present Value Table Factor	=	Present Value Equivalent
Period 1 PV	=	$200,000	×	0.892857	=	$178,571
Period 2 PV	=	200,000	×	0.797194	=	159,439
Period 3 PV	=	200,000	×	0.711780	=	142,356
Period 4 PV	=	200,000	×	0.635518	=	127,104
Total						$607,470

[3]The present value table is based on the formula $[1 \div (1 + r)^n]$ where r equals the rate of return and n equals the number of periods.

together before multiplying them by the cash inflows. The total of the present value table factors in Exhibit 16.1 is 3.037349 (0.892857 + 0.797194 + 0.711780 + 0.635518). Multiplying this **accumulated conversion factor** by the expected annual cash inflow results in the same present value equivalent of $607,470 ($200,000 × 3.037349). As with lump-sum conversion factors, accumulated conversion factors can be calculated and organized in a table with *columns* for different rates of return and *rows* for different periods of time. Table 2 in the Appendix is a present value table of accumulated conversion factors. Locate the conversion factor at the intersection of the 12% column and the fourth time-period row. The factor at this intersection is 3.037349, confirming that the accumulated conversion factors represent the sum of the single-payment conversion factors.

The conversion factors in Appendix Table 2 apply to annuities. An **annuity** is a series of cash flows that meets three criteria: (1) equal payment amounts; (2) equal time intervals between payments; and (3) a constant rate of return. For EZ Rentals, the expected cash inflows from renting LCD projectors are all for equivalent amounts ($200,000); the expected intervals between cash inflows are equal lengths of time (one year); and the rate of return for each inflow is constant at 12 percent. The series of expected cash inflows from renting the projectors is therefore an annuity. The present value of an annuity table can be used only if all of these conditions are satisfied.

The present value of an annuity table (Appendix Table 2) simplifies converting future cash inflows to their present value equivalents. EZ Rentals can convert the cash inflows as shown in Exhibit 16.1, using four conversion factors, multiplying each con-version factor by the annual cash inflow (four multiplications), and adding the resulting products. In contrast, EZ can recognize that the series of payments is an annuity, which requires multiplying a single conversion factor from Appendix Table 2 by the amount of the annuity payment. Regardless of the conversion method, the result is the same (a present value of $607,470). Recall that EZ can also make the conversion using algebra. The table values are derived from algebraic formulas. The present value tables reduce the computations needed to convert future values to present values.

Software Programs that Calculate Present Values

Software programs offer an even more efficient means of converting future values into present value equivalents. These programs are frequently built into handheld financial calculators and computer spreadsheet programs. As an example, we demonstrate the procedures used in a Microsoft Excel spreadsheet.

An Excel spreadsheet offers a variety of financial functions, one of which converts a future value annuity into its present value equivalent. This present value function uses the syntax *PV(rate,nper,pmt)* in which *rate* is the desired rate of return, *nper* is the num-ber of periods, and *pmt* is the amount of the payment (periodic cash inflow). To convert a future value annuity into its present value equivalent, provide the function with the appropriate amounts for the rate, number of periods, and amount of the annuity (cash inflows) into a spreadsheet cell. Press the Enter key and the present value equivalent appears in the spreadsheet cell.

The power of the spreadsheet to perform computations instantly is extremely use-ful for answering what-if questions. Exhibit 16.2 demonstrates this power by providing spreadsheet conversions for three different scenarios. The first scenario demonstrates the annuity assumptions for EZ Rentals, providing the present value equivalent ($607,470) of a four-year cash inflow of $200,000 per year at a 12 percent rate of inter-est. The present value is a *negative* number. This format indicates that an initial $607,470 *cash outflow* is required to obtain the four-year series of cash inflows. The present value equivalent in Scenario 2 shows the present value if the annuity assumptions reflect a 14 percent, rather than 12 percent, desired rate of return. The present value equivalent in Scenario 3 shows the present value if the annuity assumptions under Scenario 1 are changed to reflect annual cash inflows of $300,000, rather than $200,000. A wide range of scenarios could be readily considered by changing any or all of the variables in the spreadsheet function. In each case, the computer does the calculations, giving the manager more time to analyze the data rather than compute it.

Although software is widely used in business practice, the diversity of interfaces used by different calculators and spreadsheet programs makes it unsuitable for textbook

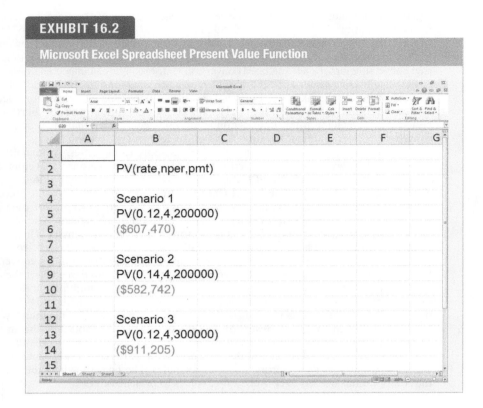

EXHIBIT 16.2

Microsoft Excel Spreadsheet Present Value Function

presentations. This text uses the present value tables in the Appendix in the text illustrations and the end-of-chapter exercises and problems. If you use software to solve these problems, your answers will be the same. All of these tools—formulas, conversion tables, and software—are based on the same mathematical principles and will produce the same results.

Ordinary Annuity Assumption

All of the conversion methods described above assume the cash inflows occur at the *end* of each accounting period. This distribution pattern is called an **ordinary annuity.**[4] In practice, cash inflows are likely to be received throughout the period, not just at the end. For example, EZ Rentals is likely to collect cash revenue from renting projectors each month rather than in a single lump-sum receipt at the end of each of the four years. Companies frequently use the ordinary annuity assumption in practice because it simplifies time value of money computations. Because capital investment decisions are necessarily based on uncertain projections about future cash inflows, the lives of investment opportunities, and the appropriate rates of return, achieving pinpoint accuracy is impossible. Sacrificing precision for simplicity by using the ordinary annuity assumption is a reasonable trade-off in the decision-making process.

Reinvestment Assumption

The present value computations in the previous sections show that investing $607,470 today at a 12 percent rate of return is equivalent to receiving four individual $200,000 payments at the end of four successive years. Exhibit 16.3 illustrates that a cash inflow

---

[4]When equal cash inflows occur at the *beginning* of each accounting period, the distribution is called an *annuity due*. Although some business transactions are structured as annuities due, they are less common than ordinary annuities. This text focuses on the ordinary annuity assumption.

EXHIBIT 16.3

Cash Flow Classifications for EZ's Investment in Projectors

Time Period	(a) Investment Balance During the Year	(b) Annual Cash Inflow	(c) Return on Investment (a × 0.12)	(d) Recovered Investment (b − c)	(e) Year-End Investment Balance (a − d)
1	$607,470	$200,000	$ 72,896	$127,104	$480,366
2	480,366	200,000	57,644	142,356	338,010
3	338,010	200,000	40,561	159,439	178,571
4	178,571	200,000	21,429	178,571	0
Totals		$800,000	$192,530	$607,470	

of $200,000 per year is equivalent to earning a 12 percent rate of return on a $607,470 investment.[5]

It is customary to assume that the desired rate of return includes the effects of *compounding*.[6] Saying an investment is "earning the desired rate of return," assumes the cash inflows generated by the investment are reinvested at the desired rate of return. In this case, we are assuming that EZ will reinvest the $200,000 annual cash inflows in other investments that will earn a 12 percent return.

TECHNIQUES FOR ANALYZING CAPITAL INVESTMENT PROPOSALS

Managers can choose from among numerous analytical techniques to help them make capital investment decisions. Each technique has advantages and disadvantages. A manager may apply more than one technique to a particular proposal to take advantage of more information. Since most companies have computer capabilities that include a variety of standard capital budgeting programs, applying different techniques to the same proposal normally requires little extra effort. Limiting analysis to only one tool could produce biased results. Obtaining more than one perspective offers substantial benefit.

Net Present Value

By using the present value conversion techniques described earlier, EZ Rentals' management determined it would be willing to invest $607,470 today (present value) to obtain a four-year, $200,000 future value annuity cash inflow. The $607,470 investment is *not* the cost of the LCD projectors; it is the amount EZ is willing to pay for them. The projectors may cost EZ Rentals more or less than their present value. To determine whether EZ should invest in the projectors, management must compare the present value of the future cash inflows ($607,470) to the cost of the projectors (the current cash outflow required to purchase them). Subtracting the cost of the investment from the present value of the future cash inflows determines the **net present value** of the investment opportunity. A positive net present value indicates the investment will yield a rate of return higher than 12 percent. A negative net present value means the return is less than 12 percent.

LO 16-2

Determine and interpret the net present value of an investment opportunity.

[5]Exhibit 16.3 is analogous to an amortization table for a long-term note with equal payments of principal and interest.

[6]*Compounding* refers to reinvesting investment proceeds so the total amount of invested capital increases, resulting in even higher returns. For example, assume $100 is invested at a 10 percent compounded annual rate of return. At the end of the first year, the investment yields a $10 return ($100 × 0.10). The $10 return plus any recovered investment is reinvested so that the total amount of invested capital at the beginning of the second year is $110. The return for the second year is $11 ($110 × 0.10). All funds are reinvested so that the return for the third year is $12.10 [($110 + $11) × 0.10].

To illustrate, assume EZ can purchase the projectors for $582,742. Assuming the desired rate of return is 12 percent, EZ should buy them. The net present value of the investment opportunity is computed as follows.

Present value of future cash inflows	$607,470
Cost of investment (required cash outflow)	(582,742)
Net present value	$ 24,728

The positive net present value suggests the investment will earn a rate of return in excess of 12 percent (if cash flows are indeed $200,000 each year). Because the projected rate of return is higher than the desired rate of return, this analysis suggests EZ should accept the investment opportunity. Based on the above analysis, we are able to establish the following decision rule:

Net present value decision rule: If the net present value is equal to or greater than zero, accept the investment opportunity.

☑ CHECK YOURSELF 16.2

To increase productivity, Wald Corporation is considering the purchase of a new machine that costs $50,000. Wald expects using the machine to increase annual net cash inflows by $12,500 for each of the next five years. Wald desires a minimum annual rate of return of 10 percent on the investment. Determine the net present value of the investment opportunity and recommend whether Wald should acquire the machine.

Answer

Present value of future cash flows = Future cash flow × Table 2 factor ($n = 5, r = 10\%$)

Present value of future cash flows = $12,500 × 3.790787 = $47,385

Net present value = PV of future cash flows − Cost of machine

Net present value = $47,385 − $50,000 = ($2,615)

The negative net present value indicates the investment will yield a rate of return below the desired rate of return. Wald should not acquire the new machine.

Internal Rate of Return

LO 16-3

Determine and interpret the internal rate of return of an investment opportunity.

The net present value method indicates EZ's investment in the projectors will provide a return in excess of the desired rate, but it does not provide the actual rate of return to expect from the investment. If EZ's management team wants to know the rate of return to expect from investing in the projectors, it must use the *internal rate of return method*. The **internal rate of return** is the rate at which the present value of cash inflows equals the cash outflows. It is the rate that will produce a zero net present value. For EZ Rentals, the internal rate of return can be determined as follows. First, compute the *present value table factor* for a $200,000 annuity that would yield a $582,742 present value cash outflow (cost of investment).

Present value table factor × $200,000 = $582,742

Present value table factor = $582,742 ÷ $200,000

Present value table factor = 2.91371

Second, since the expected annual cash inflows represent a four-year annuity, scan Table 2 in the Appendix at period $n = 4$. Try to locate the table factor 2.91371. The rate listed at the top of the column in which the factor is located is the internal rate of return. Turn to Appendix Table 2 and determine the internal rate of return for EZ Rentals before you read further. The above factor is in the 14 percent column. The difference in the table value (2.913712) and the value computed here (2.91371) is not significant. If EZ invests $582,742 in the projectors and they produce a $200,000 annual cash flow for four years, EZ will earn a 14 percent rate of return on the investment.

The *internal rate of return* may be compared with a *desired rate of return* to determine whether to accept or reject a particular investment project. Assuming EZ desires to earn a minimum rate of return of 12 percent, the preceding analysis suggests it should accept the investment opportunity because the internal rate of return (14 percent) is higher than the desired rate of return (12 percent). An internal rate of return below the desired rate suggests management should reject a particular proposal. The desired rate of return is sometimes called the *cutoff rate* or the *hurdle rate*. To be accepted, an investment proposal must provide an internal rate of return higher than the hurdle rate, cutoff rate, or desired rate of return. These terms are merely alternatives for the *cost of capital*. Ultimately, to be accepted, an investment must provide an internal rate of return higher than a company's cost of capital. Based on the above analysis, we are able to establish the following decision rule:

> **Internal rate of return decision rule:** If the internal rate of return is equal to or greater than the desired rate of return, accept the investment opportunity.

TECHNIQUES FOR MEASURING INVESTMENT CASH FLOWS

The EZ Rentals example represents a simple capital investment analysis. The investment option involved only one cash outflow and a single annuity inflow. Investment opportunities often involve a greater variety of cash outflows and inflows. The following section of this chapter discusses different types of cash flows encountered in business practice.

Cash Inflows

Cash inflows generated from capital investments come from *four basic sources*. As in the case of EZ Rentals, the most common source of cash inflows is incremental revenue. **Incremental revenue** refers to the *additional* cash inflows from operating activities generated by using additional capital assets. For example, a taxi company expects revenues from taxi fares to increase if it purchases additional taxicabs. Similarly, investing in new apartments should increase rent revenue; opening a new store should result in additional sales revenue.

A second type of cash inflow results from *cost savings*. Decreases in cash outflows have the same beneficial effect as increases in cash inflows. Either way, a firm's cash position improves. For example, purchasing an automated computer system may enable a company to reduce cash outflows for salaries. Similarly, relocating a manufacturing facility closer to its raw materials source can reduce cash outflows for transportation costs.

An investment's *salvage value* provides a third source of cash inflows. Even when one company has finished using an asset, the asset may still be useful to another company. Many assets are sold after a company no longer wishes to use them. The salvage value represents a one-time cash inflow obtained when a company terminates an investment.

Companies can also experience a cash inflow through a *reduction in the amount of* **working capital** needed to support an investment. A certain level of working capital is required to support most business investments. For example, a new retail store outlet requires cash, receivables, and inventory to operate. When an investment is terminated, the decrease in the working capital commitment associated with the investment normally results in a cash inflow.

Cash Outflows

Cash outflows fall into *three primary categories.* One category consists of outflows for the *initial investment.* Managers must be alert to all the cash outflows connected with purchasing a capital asset. The purchase price, transportation costs, installation costs, and training costs are examples of typical cash outflows related to an initial investment.

A second category of cash outflows may result from *increases in operating expenses.* If a company increases output capacity by investing in additional equipment, it may experience higher utility bills, labor costs, and maintenance expenses when it places the equipment into service. These expenditures increase cash outflows.

Third, *increases in working capital* commitments result in cash outflows. Frequently, investments in new assets must be supported by a certain level of working capital. For example, investing in a copy machine requires spending cash to maintain a supply of paper and toner. Managers should treat an increased working capital commitment as a cash outflow in the period the commitment occurs.

Exhibit 16.4 lists the cash inflows and outflows discussed above. The list is not exhaustive but does summarize the most common cash flows businesses experience.

EXHIBIT 16.4

Typical Cash Flows Associated with Capital Investments

Inflows	Outflows
1. Incremental revenue	1. Initial investment
2. Cost savings	2. Incremental expenses
3. Salvage values	3. Working capital commitments
4. Recovery of working capital	

TECHNIQUES FOR COMPARING ALTERNATIVE CAPITAL INVESTMENT OPPORTUNITIES

The management of Torres Transfer Company is considering two investment opportunities. One alternative, involving the purchase of new equipment for $80,000, would enable Torres to modernize its maintenance facility. The equipment has an expected useful life of five years and a $4,000 salvage value. It would replace existing equipment that had originally cost $45,000. The existing equipment has a current book value of $15,000 and a trade-in value of $5,000. The old equipment is technologically obsolete but can operate for an additional five years. On the day Torres purchases the new equipment, it would also pay the equipment manufacturer $3,000 for training costs to teach employees to operate the new equipment. The modernization has two primary advantages. One, it will improve management of the small parts inventory. The company's accountant believes that by the end of the first year, the carrying value of the small parts inventory could be reduced by $12,000. Second, the modernization is expected to increase efficiency, resulting in a $21,500 reduction in annual operating expenses.

The other investment alternative available to Torres is purchasing a truck. Adding another truck would enable Torres to expand its delivery area and increase revenue. The truck costs $115,000. It has a useful life of five years and a $30,000 salvage value. Operating the truck will require the company to increase its inventory of supplies, its petty cash account, and its accounts receivable and payable balances. These changes would add $5,000 to the company's working capital base immediately upon buying the truck. The working capital cash outflow is expected to be recovered at the end of the truck's useful life. The truck is expected to produce $69,000 per year in additional revenues. The driver's salary and other operating expenses are expected to be $32,000 per year. A major overhaul costing $20,000 is expected to be required at the end of the third year of operation. Assuming Torres desires to earn a rate of return of 14 percent, which of the two investment alternatives should it choose?

Net Present Value

Begin the analysis by calculating the net present value of the two investment alternatives. Exhibit 16.5 shows the computations. Study this exhibit. Each alternative is analyzed using three steps. Step 1 requires identifying all cash inflows; some may be annuities, and

EXHIBIT 16.5

Net Present Value Analysis

	Amount	×	Conversion Factor	=	Present Value
Alternative 1: Modernize Maintenance Facility					
Step 1: Cash inflows					
1. Cost savings	$21,500	×	3.433081*	=	$ 73,811
2. Salvage value	4,000	×	0.519369†	=	2,077
3. Working capital recovery	12,000	×	0.877193‡	=	10,526
Total					$ 86,414
Step 2: Cash outflows					
1. Cost of equipment					
($80,000 cost—$5,000 trade-in)	$75,000	×	1.000000§	=	$ 75,000
2. Training costs	3,000	×	1.000000§	=	3,000
Total					$ 78,000
Step 3: Net present value					
Total present value of cash inflows					$ 86,414
Total present value of cash outflows					(78,000)
Net present value					$ 8,414
Alternative 2: Purchase Delivery Truck					
Step 1: Cash inflows					
1. Incremental revenue	$69,000	×	3.433081*	=	$236,883
2. Salvage value	30,000	×	0.519369†	=	15,581
3. Working capital recovery	5,000	×	0.519369†	=	2,597
Total					$255,061
Step 2: Cash outflows					
1. Cost of truck	$115,000	×	1.000000§	=	$115,000
2. Working capital increase	5,000	×	1.000000§	=	5,000
3. Increased operating expense	32,000	×	3.433081§§	=	109,859
4. Major overhaul	20,000	×	0.674972§§	=	13,499
Total					$243,358
Step 3: Net present value					
Total present value of cash inflows					$255,061
Total present value of cash outflows					(243,358)
Net present value					$ 11,703

*Present value of annuity table 2, $n = 5$, $r = 14\%$.
†Present value of single payment table 1, $n = 5$, $r = 14\%$.
‡Present value of single payment table 1, $n = 1$, $r = 14\%$.
§Present value at beginning of period 1.
§§Present value of single payment table 1, $n = 3$, $r = 14\%$.

others may be lump-sum receipts. In the case of Alternative 1, the cost saving is an annuity, and the inflow from the salvage value is a lump-sum receipt. Once the cash inflows have been identified, the appropriate conversion factors are identified and the cash inflows are converted to their equivalent present values. Step 2 follows the same process to determine the present value of the cash outflows. Step 3 subtracts the present value of the outflows from the present value of the inflows to determine the net present value. The same three-step approach is used to determine the net present value of Alternative 2.

With respect to Alternative 1, the original cost and the book value of the existing equipment are ignored. As indicated in a previous chapter, these measures represent *sunk costs;* they are not relevant to the decision. The concept of relevance applies to long-term capital investment decisions just as it applies to the short-term special decisions. To be relevant to a capital investment decision, costs or revenues must involve different present and future cash flows for each alternative. Since the historical cost of the old equipment does not differ between the alternatives, it is not relevant.

Since the *net present value* of each investment alternative is *positive,* either investment will generate a return in excess of 14 percent. Which investment is the more favorable? The data could mislead a careless manager. Alternative 2 might seem the better choice because it has a greater present value than Alternative 1 ($11,703 vs. $8,414). Net present value, however, is expressed in *absolute dollars.* The net present value of a more costly capital investment can be greater than the net present value of a smaller investment even though the smaller investment earns a higher rate of return.

To compare different size investment alternatives, management can compute a **present value index** by dividing the present value of cash inflows by the present value of cash outflows. *The higher the ratio, the higher the rate of return per dollar invested in the proposed project.* The present value indexes for the two alternatives Torres Transfer Company is considering are as follows.

$$\text{Present value index for Alternative 1} = \frac{\text{Present value of cash inflows}}{\text{Present value of cash outflows}} = \frac{\$86,414}{\$78,000} = 1.108$$

$$\text{Present value index for Alternative 2} = \frac{\text{Present value of cash inflows}}{\text{Present value of cash outflows}} = \frac{\$255,061}{\$243,358} = 1.048$$

Management can use the present value indexes to rank the investment alternatives. In this case, Alternative 1 yields a higher return than Alternative 2.

Internal Rate of Return

Management can also rank investment alternatives using the internal rate of return for each investment. Generally, *the higher the internal rate of return, the more profitable the investment.* We previously demonstrated how to calculate the internal rate of return for an investment that generates a simple cash inflow annuity. The computations are significantly more complex for investments with uneven cash flows. Recall that the internal rate of return is the rate that produces a zero net present value. Manually computing the rate that produces a zero net present value is a tedious trial-and-error process. You must first estimate the rate of return for a particular investment, then calculate the net present value. If the calculation produces a negative net present value, you try a lower estimated rate of return and recalculate. If this calculation produces a positive net present value, the actual internal rate of return lies between the first and second estimates. Make a third estimate and once again recalculate the net present value, and so on. Eventually you will determine the rate of return that produces a net present value of zero.

Many calculators and spreadsheet programs are designed to make these computations. We illustrate the process with a Microsoft Excel spreadsheet. Excel uses the syntax *IRR (values, guess)* in which *values* refers to cells that specify the cash flows for which you want to calculate the internal rate of return and *guess* is a number you estimate is close to the actual internal rate of return (IRR). The IRRs for the two investment alternatives available to Torres Transfer Company are shown in Exhibit 16.6. Study this exhibit. Excel requires netting cash outflows against cash inflows for each period in which both outflows and inflows are expected. For your convenience, we have labeled the net cash flows in the spreadsheet. Labeling is not necessary to execute the IRR function. The entire function, including values and guess, can be entered into a single cell of the spreadsheet. Persons familiar with spreadsheet programs learn to significantly simplify the input required.

The IRR results in Exhibit 16.6 confirm the ranking determined using the present value index. Alternative 1 (modernize maintenance facility), with an internal rate of return of 18.69 percent, ranks above Alternative 2 (purchase a truck) with an internal rate of return of 17.61 percent, even though Alternative 2 has a higher net present value (see Exhibit 16.5). Alternative 2, however, still may be the better investment option, depending on the amount available to invest. Suppose Torres has $120,000 of available funds to invest. Because Alternative 1 requires an initial investment of only $78,000, $42,000 ($120,000 − $78,000) of capital will not be invested. If Torres has no other

REALITY BYTES

Developing proficiency with present value mathematics is usually the most difficult aspect of capital budgeting for students taking their first managerial accounting course. In real-world companies, the most difficult aspect of capital budgeting is forecasting cash flows for several years into the future. Consider the following capital budgeting project.

In 1965, representatives from the Georgia Power Company visited Ms. Taylor's fifth grade class to tell her students about the Edwin I. Hatch Nuclear Plant that was going to be built nearby. One of the authors of this text was a student in that class.

In 1966, construction began on the first unit of the plant, and the plant started producing electricity in 1975. The next year, 10 years after hearing the presentation in his fifth grade class, the author worked on construction of the second unit of the plant during the summer before his senior year of college. This second unit began operations in 1978.

In its 2011 annual report, the Southern Company, which is now the major owner of the plant, stated that the Hatch plant is expected to operate until 2038, and that decommissioning of the plant will continue until 2063. The cost to construct both units of the plant was $934 million. The estimated cost to dismantle and decommission the plant is over $600 million.

It seems safe to assume that the students in Ms. Taylor's fifth grade class were not among the first to hear about the power company's plans for the Hatch plant. Thus, we can reasonably conclude that the life of this capital project will be over 100 years, from around 1960 until 2063.

Try to imagine that you were assigned the task of predicting the cost inflows and outflows for a project that was expected to last 100 years. Clearly, mastering present value mathematics would not be your biggest worry.

EXHIBIT 16.6

Microsoft Excel Spreadsheet Internal Rate of Return Function

2	Internal Rate of Return for Alternative 1
3	IRR (Values, Guess)
4	IRR (B6:B11, 10%) = 18.6932%
5	
6	-78000 *($80,000 Cost of Equipment - $5,000 Trade-In + $3,000 Training Cost)*
7	33500 *($21,500 Cost Savings + $12,000 Working Capital Recovery)*
8	21500 *(Cost Savings)*
9	21500 *(Cost Savings)*
10	21500 *(Cost Savings)*
11	25500 *($21,500 Cost Savings + $4,000 Salvage Value)*
12	
13	
14	Internal Rate of Return for Alternative 2
15	IRR (Values, Guess)
16	IRR (B18:B23, 10%) = 17.6083%
17	
18	-120000 *($115,000 Cost of Truck + $5,000 Working Capital Increase)*
19	37000 *($69,000 Revenue - $32,000 Operating Expense)*
20	37000 *($69,000 Revenue - $32,000 Operating Expense)*
21	17000 *($69,000 Revenue - $32,000 Operating Expense - $20,000 Overhaul)*
22	37000 *($69,000 Revenue - $32,000 Operating Expense)*
23	72000 *($69,000 Revenue - $32,000 Operating Expense +$30,000 Salvage + $5,000 Working Capital Recovery)*

investment opportunities for this $42,000, the company would be better off investing the entire $120,000 in Alternative 2 ($115,000 cost of truck + $5,000 working capital increase). Earning 17.61 percent on a $120,000 investment is better than earning 18.69 percent on a $78,000 investment with no return on the remaining $42,000. Management accounting requires exercising judgment when making decisions.

Relevance and the Time Value of Money

Suppose you have the opportunity to invest in one of two capital projects. Both projects require an immediate cash outflow of $6,000 and will produce future cash inflows of $8,000. The only difference between the two projects is the timing of the inflows. The receipt schedule for both projects follows.

Year	Project 1	Project 2
1	$3,500	$2,000
2	3,000	2,000
3	1,000	2,000
4	500	2,000
Total	$8,000	$8,000

Because both projects cost the same and produce the same total cash inflows, they may appear to be equal. Whether you select Project 1 or Project 2, you pay $6,000 and receive $8,000. Because of the time value of money, however, Project 1 is preferable to Project 2. To see why, determine the net present value of both projects, assuming a 10 percent desired rate of return.

Computation of Net Present Value for Project 1 and Project 2

Net Present Value for Project 1

Period	Cash Inflow	×	Conversion Factor Table 1, $r = 10\%$	=	Present Value
1	$3,500	×	0.909091	=	$3,182
2	3,000	×	0.826446	=	2,479
3	1,000	×	0.751315	=	751
4	500	×	0.683013	=	342
Present value of future cash inflows					6,754
Present value of cash outflow					(6,000)
Net present value Project 1					$ 754

Net Present Value for Project 2

	Cash Inflow Annuity	×	Conversion Factor Table 2, $r = 10\%$, $n = 4$	
Present value of cash inflow	$2,000	×	3.169865	$6,340
Present value of cash outflow				(6,000)
Net present value Project 2				$ 340

The net present value of Project 1 ($754) exceeds the net present value of Project 2 ($340). The timing as well as the amount of cash flows has a significant impact on capital investment returns. Recall that to be relevant, costs or revenues must differ between alternatives. Differences in the timing of cash flow payments or receipts are also relevant for decision-making purposes.

Answers to The Curious Accountant

One way to answer your client's question is to determine which option has the highest net present value. The present value of the lump-sum payment option is simple; it is the $203 million the lottery is prepared to pay the winner now. The present value of the annuity option must be calculated, and it consists of two parts. The first of the 26 payments of $12 million will be paid immediately, so it is worth $12 million today. The remaining 25 payments will occur at one-year intervals, so their present value is computed as:

$$\$12,000,000 \times 11.6536^* = \$139,843,200$$

Adding $12,000,000 to $139,843,200 yields a present value of $151,843,200, which is a lot less than $203 million. This suggests your client should take the lump-sum payment. Of course, the risk of the lottery not making its annual payments is very low. There is a greater risk that a financial planner may not find investments to earn a 7 percent annual return, so the winner would have to consider his or her tolerance for risk before making a final decision.

In the case of this particular lottery example, the winning ticket was purchased by seven co-workers. They chose the lump-sum payment.

*This factor is not included in the tables at the end of the chapter, so it is provided here for the purposes of this illustration.

Tax Considerations

The previous examples have ignored the effect of income taxes on capital investment decisions. Taxes affect the amount of cash flows generated by investments. To illustrate, assume Wu Company purchases an asset that costs $240,000. The asset has a four-year useful life, no salvage value, and is depreciated on a straight-line basis. The asset generates cash revenue of $90,000 per year. Assume Wu's income tax rate is 40 percent. What is the net present value of the asset, assuming Wu's management desires to earn a 10 percent rate of return after taxes? The first step in answering this question is to calculate the annual cash flow generated by the asset, as shown in Exhibit 16.7.

Because recognizing depreciation expense does not require a cash payment (cash is paid when assets are purchased, not when depreciation is recognized), depreciation expense must be added back to after-tax income to determine the annual cash

EXHIBIT 16.7

Determining Cash Flow from Investment

	Period 1	Period 2	Period 3	Period 4
Cash revenue	$90,000	$90,000	$90,000	$90,000
Depreciation expense (noncash)	(60,000)	(60,000)	(60,000)	(60,000)
Income before taxes	30,000	30,000	30,000	30,000
Income tax at 40%	(12,000)	(12,000)	(12,000)	(12,000)
Income after tax	18,000	18,000	18,000	18,000
Depreciation add back	60,000	60,000	60,000	60,000
Annual cash inflow	$78,000	$78,000	$78,000	$78,000

584 Chapter 16

inflow. Once the cash flow is determined, the net present value is computed as shown here.

Cash flow annuity	×	Conversion factor Table 2, $r = 10\%$, $n = 4$	=	Present value cash inflows	−	Present value cash outflows	=	Net present value
$78,000	×	3.169865	=	$247,249	−	$240,000	=	$7,249

The depreciation sheltered some of the income from taxation. Income taxes apply to income after deducting depreciation expense. Without depreciation expense, income taxes each year would have been $36,000 ($90,000 × 0.40) instead of $12,000 ($30,000 × 0.40). The $24,000 difference ($36,000 − $12,000) is known as a *depreciation tax shield*. The amount of the depreciation tax shield can also be computed by multiplying the depreciation expense by the tax rate ($60,000 × 0.40 = $24,000).

Because of the time value of money, companies benefit by maximizing the depreciation tax shield early in the life of an asset. For this reason, most companies calculate depreciation expense for tax purposes using the *modified accelerated cost recovery system (MACRS)* permitted by tax law rather than using straight-line depreciation. MACRS recognizes depreciation on an accelerated basis, assigning larger amounts of depreciation in the early years of an asset's useful life. The higher depreciation charges result in lower amounts of taxable income and lower income taxes. In the later years of an asset's useful life, the reverse is true, and lower depreciation charges result in higher taxes. Accelerated depreciation does not allow companies to avoid paying taxes but to delay them. The longer companies can delay paying taxes, the more cash they have available to invest.

TECHNIQUES THAT IGNORE THE TIME VALUE OF MONEY

LO 16-4

Evaluate investment opportunities using the payback method and the unadjusted rate of return.

Several techniques for evaluating capital investment proposals ignore the time value of money. Although these techniques are less accurate, they are quick and simple. When investments are small or the returns are expected within a short time, these techniques are likely to result in the same decisions that more sophisticated techniques produce.

Payback Method

The **payback method** is simple to apply and easy to understand. It shows how long it will take to recover the initial cash outflow (the cost) of an investment. The formula for computing the payback period, measured in years, is as follows.

Payback period = Net cost of investment ÷ Annual net cash inflow

To illustrate, assume Winston Cleaners can purchase a new ironing machine that will press shirts in half the time of the one currently used. The new machine costs $100,000 and will reduce labor cost by $40,000 per year over a four-year useful life. The payback period is computed as follows.

Payback period = $100,000 ÷ $40,000 = 2.5 years

Interpreting Payback

Generally, investments with shorter payback periods are considered better. Because the payback method measures only investment recovery, not profitability, however, this conclusion can be invalid when considering investment alternatives. To illustrate, assume Winston Cleaners also has the opportunity to purchase a different machine that costs $100,000 and provides an annual labor savings of $40,000. However, the second machine will last for five instead of four years. The payback period is still 2.5 years ($100,000 ÷ $40,000), but the second machine is a better investment because it improves profitability by providing an additional year of cost savings. The payback analysis does not measure this difference between the alternatives.

Unequal Cash Flows

The preceding illustration assumed Winston's labor cost reduction saved the same amount of cash each year for the life of the new machine. The payback method requires adjustment when cash flow benefits are unequal. Suppose a company purchases a machine for $6,000. The machine will be used sporadically and is expected to provide incremental revenue over the next five years as follows.

2014	2015	2016	2017	2018
$3,000	$1,000	$2,000	$1,000	$500

Based on this cash inflow pattern, what is the payback period? There are two acceptable solutions. One accumulates the incremental revenue until the sum equals the amount of the original investment.

Year	Annual Amount	Cumulative Total
2014	$3,000	$3,000
2015	1,000	4,000
2016	2,000	6,000

This approach indicates the payback period is three years.

A second solution uses an averaging concept. The average annual cash inflow is determined. This figure is then used in the denominator of the payback equation. Using the preceding data, the payback period is computed as follows.

1. Compute the average annual cash inflow.

$$2014 \ + \ 2015 \ + \ 2016 \ + \ 2017 \ + 2018 = \ \text{Total} \ \div \ 5 = \text{Average}$$

$$\$3,000 + \$1,000 + \$2,000 + \$1,000 + \$500 = \$7,500 \div 5 = \ \$1,500$$

2. Compute the payback period.

$$\frac{\text{Net cost of investment}} \div \frac{\text{Average annual net cash inflow}} = 6,000 \div 1,500 = 4 \text{ years}$$

The average method is useful when a company purchases a number of similar assets with differing cash return patterns.

Unadjusted Rate of Return

The **unadjusted rate of return** method is another common evaluation technique. Investment cash flows are not adjusted to reflect the time value of money. The unadjusted rate of return is sometimes called the *simple rate of return*. It is computed as follows.

$$\frac{\text{Unadjusted}}{\text{rate of return}} = \frac{\text{Average incremental increase in annual net income}}{\text{Net cost of original investment}}$$

To illustrate computing the unadjusted rate of return, assume The Dining Table, Inc., is considering establishing a new restaurant that will require a $2,000,000 original investment. Management anticipates operating the restaurant for 10 years before significant renovations will be required. The restaurant is expected to provide an average after-tax return of $280,000 per year. The unadjusted rate of return is computed as follows.

$$\text{Unadjusted rate of return} = \$280,000 \div \$2,000,000 = 14\% \text{ per year}$$

The accuracy of the unadjusted rate of return suffers from the failure to recognize the recovery of invested capital. With respect to a depreciable asset, the capital investment is normally recovered through revenue over the life of the asset. To illustrate, assume we purchase a $1,000 asset with a two-year life and a zero salvage value. For simplicity, ignore income taxes. Assume the asset produces $600 of cash revenue per year. The income statement for the first year of operation appears as follows.

Revenue	$600
Depreciation expense	(500)
Net income	$100

What is the amount of invested capital during the first year? First, a $1,000 cash outflow was used to purchase the asset (the original investment). Next, we collected $600 of cash revenue of which $100 was a *return on investment* (net income) and $500 was a **recovery of investment.** As a result, $1,000 was invested in the asset at the beginning of the year and $500 was invested at the end of the year. Similarly, we will recover an additional $500 of capital during the second year of operation, leaving zero invested capital at the end of the second year. Given that the cash inflows from revenue are collected somewhat evenly over the life of the investment, the amount of invested capital will range from a beginning balance of $1,000 to an ending balance of zero. On average, we will have $500 invested in the asset (the midpoint between $1,000 and zero). The average investment can be determined by dividing the total original investment by 2 ($1,000 ÷ 2 = $500). The unadjusted rate of return based on average invested capital can be calculated as follows.

$$\text{Unadjusted rate of return (Based on average investment)} = \frac{\text{Average incremental increase in annual net income}}{\text{Net cost of original investment} \div 2}$$

$$= \frac{\$100}{\$1,000 \div 2} = 20\%$$

To avoid distortions caused by the failure to recognize the recovery of invested capital, the unadjusted rate of return should be based on the *average investment* when working with investments in depreciable assets.

✓ CHECK YOURSELF 16.3

EZ Rentals can purchase a van that costs $24,000. The van has an expected useful life of three years and no salvage value. EZ expects rental revenue from the van to be $12,000 per year. Determine the payback period and the unadjusted rate of return.

Answer

Payback = Cost of the investment ÷ Annual cash inflow

Payback = $24,000 ÷ $12,000 = 2 years

Unadjusted rate of return = Net income ÷ Average cost of the investment

Revenue	$12,000	
Depreciation expense	(8,000)	[$24,000 ÷ 3 years]
Net income	$ 4,000	

Unadjusted rate of return = $4,000 ÷ ($24,000 ÷ 2) = 33.33%

REAL-WORLD REPORTING PRACTICES

In a study, researchers found that companies in the forest products industry use discounted cash flow techniques more frequently when the capital project being considered is a long-term timber investment. The use of techniques that ignore the time value of money increased when other shorter-term capital investment projects were being considered. Exhibit 16.8 shows the researchers' findings.

EXHIBIT 16.8

Forestry Industry Investments

Long-term investments in timber

Net present value **38%** · **9%** Unadjusted rate of return · Internal **38%** rate of return · **15%** Payback period

Investments in other assets

Net present **22%** value · **13%** Unadjusted rate of return · Internal **33%** rate of return · **32%** Payback period

Data Source: J. Bailes, J. Nielsen, and S. Lawton, "How Forest Product Companies Analyze Capital Budgets," *Management Accounting,* October 1998, pp. 24–30.

POSTAUDITS

The analytical techniques for evaluating capital investment proposals depend highly on estimates of future cash flows. Although predictions cannot be perfectly accurate, gross miscalculations can threaten the existence of an organization. For example, optimistic projections of future cash inflows that do not materialize will lead to investments that do not return the cost of capital. Managers must take their projections seriously. A postaudit policy can encourage managers to carefully consider their capital investment decisions. A **postaudit** is conducted at the completion of a capital investment project, using the same analytical technique that was used to justify the original investment. For example, if an internal rate of return was used to justify approving an investment project, the internal rate of return should be computed in the postaudit. In the postaudit computation, *actual* rather than estimated cash flows are used. Postaudits determine whether the expected results were achieved.

Postaudits should focus on continuous improvement rather than punishment. Managers who are chastised for failing to achieve expected results might become overly cautious when asked to provide estimates for future projects. Being too conservative can create problems as serious as those caused by being too optimistic. Managers can err two ways with respect to capital investment decisions. First, a manager might accept a project that should have been rejected. This mistake usually stems from excessively optimistic future cash flow projections. Second, a manager might reject a project that should have been accepted. These missed opportunities are usually the result of underestimating future cash flows. A too cautious manager can become unable to locate enough projects to fully invest the firm's funds.

Idle cash earns no return. If projects continue to outperform expectations, managers are probably estimating future cash flows too conservatively. If projects consistently fail to live up to expectations, managers are probably being too optimistic in their projections of future cash flows. Either way, the company suffers. The goal of a postaudit is

588   Chapter 16

to provide feedback that will help managers improve the accuracy of future cash flow projections, maximizing the quality of the firm's capital investments.

 A Look Back

Capital expenditures have a significant, long-term effect on profitability. They usually involve major cash outflows that are recovered through future cash inflows. The most common cash inflows include incremental revenue, operating cost savings, salvage value, and working capital releases. The most common outflows are the initial investment, increases in operating expenses, and working capital commitments.

Several techniques for analyzing the cash flows associated with capital investments are available. The techniques can be divided into two categories: (1) techniques that use time value of money concepts and (2) techniques that ignore the time value of money. Generally, techniques that ignore the time value of money are less accurate but simpler and easier to understand. These techniques include the *payback method* and the *unadjusted rate of return method*.

The techniques that use time value of money concepts are the *net present value method* and the *internal rate of return method*. These methods offer significant improvements in accuracy but are more difficult to understand. They may involve tedious computations and require using experienced judgment. Computer software and programmed calculators that ease the tedious computational burden are readily available to most managers. Furthermore, the superiority of the techniques justifies learning how to use them. These methods should be used when investment expenditures are larger or when cash flows extend over a prolonged time period.

APPENDIX

TABLE 1		Present Value of $1								
n	4%	5%	6%	7%	8%	9%	10%	12%	14%	16%	20%
1	0.961538	0.952381	0.943396	0.934579	0.925926	0.917431	0.909091	0.892857	0.877193	0.862069	0.833333
2	0.924556	0.907029	0.889996	0.873439	0.857339	0.841680	0.826446	0.797194	0.769468	0.743163	0.694444
3	0.888996	0.863838	0.839619	0.816298	0.793832	0.772183	0.751315	0.711780	0.674972	0.640658	0.578704
4	0.854804	0.822702	0.792094	0.762895	0.735030	0.708425	0.683013	0.635518	0.592080	0.552291	0.482253
5	0.821927	0.783526	0.747258	0.712986	0.680583	0.649931	0.620921	0.567427	0.519369	0.476113	0.401878
6	0.790315	0.746215	0.704961	0.666342	0.630170	0.596267	0.564474	0.506631	0.455587	0.410442	0.334898
7	0.759918	0.710681	0.665057	0.622750	0.583490	0.547034	0.513158	0.452349	0.399637	0.353830	0.279082
8	0.730690	0.676839	0.627412	0.582009	0.540269	0.501866	0.466507	0.403883	0.350559	0.305025	0.232568
9	0.702587	0.644609	0.591898	0.543934	0.500249	0.460428	0.424098	0.360610	0.307508	0.262953	0.193807
10	0.675564	0.613913	0.558395	0.508349	0.463193	0.422411	0.385543	0.321973	0.269744	0.226684	0.161506
11	0.649581	0.584679	0.526788	0.475093	0.428883	0.387533	0.350494	0.287476	0.236617	0.195417	0.134588
12	0.624597	0.556837	0.496969	0.444012	0.397114	0.355535	0.318631	0.256675	0.207559	0.168463	0.112157
13	0.600574	0.530321	0.468839	0.414964	0.367698	0.326179	0.289664	0.229174	0.182069	0.145227	0.093464
14	0.577475	0.505068	0.442301	0.387817	0.340461	0.299246	0.263331	0.204620	0.159710	0.125195	0.077887
15	0.555265	0.481017	0.417265	0.362446	0.315242	0.274538	0.239392	0.182696	0.140096	0.107927	0.064905
16	0.533908	0.458112	0.393646	0.338735	0.291890	0.251870	0.217629	0.163122	0.122892	0.093041	0.054088
17	0.513373	0.436297	0.371364	0.316574	0.270269	0.231073	0.197845	0.145644	0.107800	0.080207	0.045073
18	0.493628	0.415521	0.350344	0.295864	0.250249	0.211994	0.179859	0.130040	0.094561	0.069144	0.037561
19	0.474642	0.395734	0.330513	0.276508	0.231712	0.194490	0.163508	0.116107	0.082948	0.059607	0.031301
20	0.456387	0.376889	0.311805	0.258419	0.214548	0.178431	0.148644	0.103667	0.072762	0.051385	0.026084

TABLE 2		Present Value of an Annuity of $1									
n	4%	5%	6%	7%	8%	9%	10%	12%	14%	16%	20%
1	0.961538	0.952381	0.943396	0.934579	0.925926	0.917431	0.909091	0.892857	0.877193	0.862069	0.833333
2	1.886095	1.859410	1.833393	1.808018	1.783265	1.759111	1.735537	1.690051	1.646661	1.605232	1.527778
3	2.775091	2.723248	2.673012	2.624316	2.577097	2.531295	2.486852	2.401831	2.321632	2.245890	2.106481
4	3.629895	3.545951	3.465106	3.387211	3.312127	3.239720	3.169865	3.037349	2.913712	2.798181	2.588735
5	4.451822	4.329477	4.212364	4.100197	3.992710	3.889651	3.790787	3.604776	3.433081	3.274294	2.990612
6	5.242137	5.075692	4.917324	4.766540	4.622880	4.485919	4.355261	4.111407	3.888668	3.684736	3.325510
7	6.002055	5.786373	5.582381	5.389289	5.206370	5.032953	4.868419	4.563757	4.288305	4.038565	3.604592
8	6.732745	6.463213	6.209794	5.971299	5.746639	5.534819	5.334926	4.967640	4.638864	4.343591	3.837160
9	7.435332	7.107822	6.801692	6.515232	6.246888	5.995247	5.759024	5.328250	4.946372	4.606544	4.030967
10	8.110896	7.721735	7.360087	7.023582	6.710081	6.417658	6.144567	5.650223	5.216116	4.833227	4.192472
11	8.760477	8.306414	7.886875	7.498674	7.138964	6.805191	6.495061	5.937699	5.452733	5.028644	4.327060
12	9.385074	8.863252	8.383844	7.942686	7.536078	7.160725	6.813692	6.194374	5.660292	5.197107	4.439217
13	9.985648	9.393573	8.852683	8.357651	7.903776	7.486904	7.103356	6.423548	5.842362	5.342334	4.532681
14	10.563123	9.898641	9.294984	8.745468	8.244237	7.786150	7.366687	6.628168	6.002072	5.467529	4.610567
15	11.118387	10.379658	9.712249	9.107914	8.559479	8.060688	7.606080	6.810864	6.142168	5.575456	4.675473
16	11.652296	10.837770	10.105895	9.446649	8.851369	8.312558	7.823709	6.973986	6.265060	5.668497	4.729561
17	12.165669	11.274066	10.477260	9.763223	9.121638	8.543631	8.021553	7.119630	6.372859	5.748704	4.774634
18	12.659297	11.689587	10.827603	10.059087	9.371887	8.755625	8.201412	7.249670	6.467420	5.817848	4.812195
19	13.133939	12.085321	11.158116	10.335595	9.603599	8.905115	8.364920	7.365777	6.550369	5.877455	4.843496
20	13.590326	12.462210	11.469921	10.594014	9.818147	9.128546	8.513564	7.469444	6.623131	5.928841	4.869580

 Video lectures and accompanying self-assessment quizzes are available for all learning objectives through McGraw-Hill *Connect® Accounting*.

SELF-STUDY REVIEW PROBLEM

The CFO of Advo Corporation is considering two investment opportunities. The expected future cash inflows for each opportunity follow:

	Year 1	Year 2	Year 3	Year 4
Project 1	$144,000	$147,000	$160,000	$178,000
Project 2	204,000	199,000	114,000	112,000

Both investments require an initial payment of $400,000. Advo's desired rate of return is 16 percent.

Required

a. Compute the net present value of each project. Which project should Advo adopt based on the net present value approach?

b. Use the incremental revenue summation method to compute the payback period for each project. Which project should Advo adopt based on the payback approach?

Solution to Requirement *a*

Project 1				
	Cash Inflows	Table Factor*		Present Value
Year 1	$144,000	× 0.862069	=	$124,138
Year 2	147,000	× 0.743163	=	109,245
Year 3	160,000	× 0.640658	=	102,505
Year 4	178,000	× 0.552291	=	98,308
PV of cash inflows				434,196
Cost of investment				(400,000)
Net present value				$ 34,196

*Table 1, *n* = 1 through 4, *r* = 16%

Project 2				
	Cash Inflows	Table Factor*		Present Value
Year 1	$204,000	× 0.862069	=	$175,862
Year 2	199,000	× 0.743163	=	147,889
Year 3	114,000	× 0.640658	=	73,035
Year 4	112,000	× 0.552291	=	61,857
PV of cash inflows				458,643
Cost of investment				(400,000)
Net present value				$ 58,643

*Table 1, *n* = 1 through 4, *r* = 16%

Advo should adopt Project 2 since it has a greater net present value.

Solution to Requirement *b*

Cash Inflows	Project 1	Project 2
Year 1	$144,000	$204,000
Year 2	147,000	199,000
Total	$291,000	$403,000

By the end of the second year, Project 2's cash inflows have more than paid for the cost of the investment. In contrast, Project 1 still falls short of investment recovery by $109,000 ($400,000 − $291,000). Advo should adopt Project 2 since it has a shorter payback period.

KEY TERMS

Accumulated conversion factor 573	Incremental revenue 577	Payback method 584	Single-payment (lump-sum) 572
Annuity 573	Internal rate of return 576	Postaudit 587	Time value of money 570
Capital investments 570	Minimum rate of return 571	Present value index 580	Unadjusted rate of return 585
Cost of capital 571	Net present value 575	Present value table 572	Working capital 577
	Ordinary annuity 574	Recovery of investment 586	

QUESTIONS

1. What is a capital investment? How does it differ from an investment in stocks or bonds?

2. What are three reasons that cash is worth more today than cash to be received in the future?

3. "A dollar today is worth more than a dollar in the future." "The present value of a future dollar is worth less than one dollar." Are these two statements synonymous? Explain.

Planning for Capital Investments 591

4. Define the term *return on investment*. How is the return normally expressed? Give an example of a capital investment return.

5. How does a company establish its minimum acceptable rate of return on investments?

6. If you wanted to have $500,000 one year from today and desired to earn a 10 percent return, what amount would you need to invest today? Which amount has more value, the amount today or the $500,000 a year from today?

7. Why are present value tables frequently used to convert future values to present values?

8. Define the term *annuity*. What is one example of an annuity receipt?

9. How can present value "what-if" analysis be enhanced by using software programs?

10. Receiving $100,000 per year for five years is equivalent to investing what amount today at 14 percent? Provide a mathematical formula to solve this problem, assuming use of a present value annuity table to convert the future cash flows to their present value equivalents. Provide the expression for the Excel spreadsheet function that would perform the present value conversion.

11. Maria Espinosa borrowed $15,000 from the bank and agreed to repay the loan at 8 percent annual interest over four years, making payments of $4,529 per year. Because part of the bank's payment from Ms. Espinosa is a recovery of the original investment, what assumption must the bank make to earn its desired 8 percent compounded annual return?

12. Two investment opportunities have positive net present values. Investment A's net present value amounts to $40,000 while B's is only $30,000. Does this mean that A is the better investment opportunity? Explain.

13. What criteria determine whether a project is acceptable under the net present value method?

14. Does the net present value method provide a measure of the rate of return on capital investments?

15. Which is the best capital investment evaluation technique for ranking investment opportunities?

16. Paul Henderson is a manager for Spark Company. He tells you that his company always maximizes profitability by accepting the investment opportunity with the highest internal rate of return. Explain to Mr. Henderson how his company may improve profitability by sometimes selecting investment opportunities with lower internal rates of return.

17. What is the relationship between desired rate of return and internal rate of return?

18. What typical cash inflow and outflow items are associated with capital investments?

19. "I always go for the investment with the shortest payback period." Is this a sound strategy? Why or why not?

20. "The payback method cannot be used if the cash inflows occur in unequal patterns." Do you agree or disagree? Explain.

21. What are the advantages and disadvantages associated with the unadjusted rate of return method for evaluating capital investments?

22. How do capital investments affect profitability?

23. What is a postaudit? How is it useful in capital budgeting?

MULTIPLE-CHOICE QUESTIONS

Multiple-choice questions are provided on the text website at www.mhhe.com/edmondssurvey4e.

EXERCISES

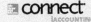 **All applicable Exercises are available with McGraw-Hill** *Connect® Accounting.*

Exercise 16-1 *Identifying cash inflows and outflows*   LO 16-1

Required

Indicate which of the following items will result in cash inflows and which will result in cash outflows. The first one is shown as an example.

Item	Type of Cash Flow
a. Initial investment	Outflow
b. Salvage values	
c. Recovery of working capital	
d. Incremental expenses	
e. Working capital commitments	
f. Cost savings	
g. Incremental revenue	

LO 16-1

Exercise 16-2   *Determining the present value of a lump-sum future cash receipt*

Adam Wilton turned 20 years old today. His grandfather had established a trust fund that will pay him $80,000 on his next birthday. However, Adam needs money today to start his college education, and his father is willing to help. Mr. Wilton has agreed to give Adam the present value of the $80,000 future cash inflow, assuming a 6 percent rate of return.

Required

Round your figures to the nearest whole dollar.

a. Use a present value table to determine the amount of cash that Adam Wilton's father should give him.
b. Use an algebraic formula to prove that the present value of the trust fund (the amount of cash computed in Requirement *a*) is equal to its $80,000 future value.

LO 16-1

Exercise 16-3   *Determining the present value of a lump-sum future cash receipt*

Brooks Long expects to receive a $600,000 cash benefit when she retires five years from today. Ms. Long's employer has offered an early retirement incentive by agreeing to pay her $360,000 today if she agrees to retire immediately. Ms. Long desires to earn a rate of return of 8 percent.

Required

Round your figures to the nearest whole dollar.

a. Assuming that the retirement benefit is the only consideration in making the retirement decision, should Ms. Long accept her employer's offer?
b. Identify the factors that cause the present value of the retirement benefit to be less than $600,000.

LO 16-1

Exercise 16-4   *Determining the present value of an annuity*

The dean of the School of Fine Arts is trying to decide whether to purchase a copy machine to place in the lobby of the building. The machine would add to student convenience, but the dean feels compelled to earn an 8 percent return on the investment of funds. Estimates of cash inflows from copy machines that have been placed in other university buildings indicate that the copy machine would probably produce incremental cash inflows of approximately $20,000 per year. The machine is expected to have a three-year useful life with a zero salvage value.

Required

Round your figures to two decimal points.

a. Use Present Value Table 1 in the Appendix to determine the maximum amount of cash the dean should be willing to pay for a copy machine.
b. Use Present Value Table 2 in the Appendix to determine the maximum amount of cash the dean should be willing to pay for a copy machine.
c. Explain the consistency or lack of consistency in the answers to Requirements *a* and *b*.

LO 16-2

Exercise 16-5   *Determining net present value*

Callaghan Company is considering investing in two new vans that are expected to generate combined cash inflows of $28,000 per year. The vans' combined purchase price is $91,000. The expected life and salvage value of each are four years and $21,000, respectively. Callaghan has an average cost of capital of 7 percent.

Required

Round your figures to two decimal points.

a. Calculate the net present value of the investment opportunity.
b. Indicate whether the investment opportunity is expected to earn a return that is above or below the cost of capital and whether it should be accepted.

LO 16-2

Exercise 16-6   *Determining net present value*

Brett Dunlop is seeking part-time employment while he attends school. He is considering purchasing technical equipment that will enable him to start a small training services company that will offer tutorial services over the Internet. Brett expects demand for the service to grow rapidly in the first two years of operation as customers learn about the availability of the Internet assistance. Thereafter, he expects demand to stabilize. The following table presents the expected cash flows.

Year of Operation	Cash Inflow	Cash Outflow
2015	$16,000	$10,000
2016	20,000	12,000
2017	21,000	12,600
2018	21,000	12,600

In addition to these cash flows, Mr. Dunlop expects to pay $21,000 for the equipment. He also expects to pay $3,600 for a major overhaul and updating of the equipment at the end of the second year of operation. The equipment is expected to have a $1,500 salvage value and a four-year useful life. Mr. Dunlop desires to earn a rate of return of 8 percent.

Required

Round your computations to two decimal points.

a. Calculate the net present value of the investment opportunity.
b. Indicate whether the investment opportunity is expected to earn a return that is above or below the desired rate of return and whether it should be accepted.

Exercise 16-7 *Using the present value index*   LO 16-2

Drinkwater Company has a choice of two investment alternatives. The present value of cash inflows and outflows for the first alternative is $100,000 and $80,000, respectively. The present value of cash inflows and outflows for the second alternative is $240,000 and $210,000, respectively.

Required

Round your computation to two decimal points.

a. Calculate the net present value of each investment opportunity.
b. Calculate the present value index for each investment opportunity.
c. Indicate which investment will produce the higher rate of return.

Exercise 16-8 *Determining the cash flow annuity with income tax considerations*   LO 16-2

To open a new store, Linton Tire Company plans to invest $360,000 in equipment expected to have a four-year useful life and no salvage value. Linton expects the new store to generate annual cash revenues of $400,000 and to incur annual cash operating expenses of $210,000. Linton's average income tax rate is 30 percent. The company uses straight-line depreciation.

Required

Determine the expected annual net cash inflow from operations for each of the first four years after Linton opens the new store.

Exercise 16-9 *Determining the internal rate of return*   LO 16-3

Merton Manufacturing Company has an opportunity to purchase some technologically advanced equipment that will reduce the company's cash outflow for operating expenses by $1,280,000 per year. The cost of the equipment is $7,865,045.76. Merton expects it to have a 10-year useful life and a zero salvage value. The company has established an investment opportunity hurdle rate of 9 percent and uses the straight-line method for depreciation.

Required

Round your computations to two decimal points.

a. Calculate the internal rate of return of the investment opportunity.
b. Indicate whether the investment opportunity should be accepted.

Exercise 16-10 *Using the internal rate of return to compare investment opportunities*   LO 16-3

Hosier and Wogan (H&W) is a partnership that owns a small company. It is considering two alternative investment opportunities. The first investment opportunity will have a five-year useful life, will cost $9,840.48, and will generate expected cash inflows of $2,400 per year. The second investment is expected to have a useful life of three years, will cost $6,442.74, and will generate expected cash inflows of $2,500 per year. Assume that H&W has the funds available to accept only one of the opportunities.

Required

a. Calculate the internal rate of return of each investment opportunity.

b. Based on the internal rates of return, which opportunity should H&W select?

c. Discuss other factors that H&W should consider in the investment decision.

LO 16-2, 16-3

Exercise 16-11   *Evaluating discounted cash flow techniques*

Lucy Bennett is angry with Austin Lyte. He is behind schedule developing supporting material for tomorrow's capital budget committee meeting. When she approached him about his apparent lackadaisical attitude in general and his tardiness in particular, he responded, "I don't see why we do this stuff in the first place. It's all a bunch of estimates. Who knows what future cash flows will really be? I certainly don't. I've been doing this job for five years, and no one has ever checked to see if I even came close at these guesses. I've been waiting for marketing to provide the estimated cash inflows on the projects being considered tomorrow. But, if you want my report now, I'll have it in a couple of hours. I can make up the marketing data as well as they can."

Required

Does Mr. Lyte have a point? Is there something wrong with the company's capital budgeting system? Write a brief response explaining how to improve the investment evaluation system.

LO 16-4

Exercise 16-12   *Determining the payback period*

Bailey Airline Company is considering expanding its territory. The company has the opportunity to purchase one of two different used airplanes. The first airplane is expected to cost $9,000,000; it will enable the company to increase its annual cash inflow by $3,000,000 per year. The plane is expected to have a useful life of five years and no salvage value. The second plane costs $18,000,000; it will enable the company to increase annual cash flow by $4,500,000 per year. This plane has an eight-year useful life and a zero salvage value.

Required

a. Determine the payback period for each investment alternative and identify the alternative Bailey should accept if the decision is based on the payback approach.

b. Discuss the shortcomings of using the payback method to evaluate investment opportunities.

LO 16-4

Exercise 16-13   *Determining the payback period with uneven cash flows*

Barker Company has an opportunity to purchase a forklift to use in its heavy equipment rental business. The forklift would be leased on an annual basis during its first two years of operation. Thereafter, it would be leased to the general public on demand. Barker would sell it at the end of the fifth year of its useful life. The expected cash inflows and outflows follow.

Year	Nature of Item	Cash Inflow	Cash Outflow
2015	Purchase price		$72,000
2015	Revenue	$30,000	
2016	Revenue	30,000	
2017	Revenue	21,000	
2017	Major overhaul		9,000
2018	Revenue	18,000	
2019	Revenue	14,400	
2019	Salvage value	9,600	

Required

a. Determine the payback period using the accumulated cash flows approach.

b. Determine the payback period using the average cash flows approach. Round your computation to one decimal point.

Exercise 16-14 *Determining the unadjusted rate of return*   LO 16-4

Scarlett Painting Company is considering whether to purchase a new spray paint machine that costs $8,000. The machine is expected to save labor, increasing net income by $800 per year. The effective life of the machine is 15 years according to the manufacturer's estimate.

Required

a. Determine the unadjusted rate of return based on the average cost of the investment.
b. What is the predominant shortcoming of using the unadjusted rate of return to evaluate investment opportunities?

Exercise 16-15 *Computing the payback period and unadjusted rate of return for the*   LO 16-5
same investment opportunity

Norman Rentals can purchase a van that costs $45,000; it has an expected useful life of three years and no salvage value. Norman uses straight-line depreciation. Expected revenue is $25,000 per year. Assume that depreciation is the only expense associated with this investment.

Required

a. Determine the payback period.
b. Determine the unadjusted rate of return based on the average cost of the investment. Compute the percentage rate to one decimal point.

PROBLEMS

 All applicable Problems are available with McGraw-Hill
Connect® Accounting.

Problem 16-16 *Using present value techniques to evaluate alternative investment*   LO 16-2
opportunities

Speedy Delivery is a small company that transports business packages between New York and Chicago. It operates a fleet of small vans that moves packages to and from a central depot within each city and uses a common carrier to deliver the packages between the depots in the two cities. Speedy Delivery recently acquired approximately $6 million of cash capital from its owners, and its president, Mason Faith, is trying to identify the most profitable way to invest these funds.

Zach Singh, the company's operations manager, believes that the money should be used to expand the fleet of city vans at a cost of $720,000. He argues that more vans would enable the company to expand its services into new markets, thereby increasing the revenue base. More specifically, he expects cash inflows to increase by $260,000 per year. The additional vans are expected to have an average useful life of four years and a combined salvage value of $80,000. Operating the vans will require additional working capital of $40,000, which will be recovered at the end of the fourth year.

In contrast, Joshua Vines, the company's chief accountant, believes that the funds should be used to purchase large trucks to deliver the packages between the depots in the two cities. The conversion process would produce continuing improvement in operating savings and reduce cash outflows as follows:

CHECK FIGURES
a. NPV of the trucks investment: $147,280.99
b. NPV index of the trucks investment: 1.18

Year 1	Year 2	Year 3	Year 4
$140,000	$300,000	$360,000	$400,000

The large trucks are expected to cost $800,000 and to have a four-year useful life and a $65,000 salvage value. In addition to the purchase price of the trucks, up-front training costs are expected to amount to $16,000. Speedy Delivery's management has established a 10 percent desired rate of return.

Required

Round your computations to two decimal points.

a. Determine the net present value of the two investment alternatives.
b. Calculate the present value index for each alternative.
c. Indicate which investment alternative you would recommend. Explain your choice.

Problem 16-17 *Applying the net present value approach with and without tax considerations*

Troy Batkin, the chief executive officer of Batkin Corporation, has assembled his top advisers to evaluate an investment opportunity. The advisers expect the company to pay $400,000 cash at the beginning of the investment and the cash inflow for each of the following four years to be the following.

Year 1	Year 2	Year 3	Year 4
$84,000	$96,000	$120,000	$180,000

Mr. Batkin agrees with his advisers that the company should use the discount rate (required rate of return) of 7 percent to compute net present value to evaluate the viability of the proposed project.

Required

Round your computation to the nearest whole dollar.

a. Compute the net present value of the proposed project. Should Mr. Batkin approve the project?
b. Ruchin Oruh, one of the advisers, is wary of the cash flow forecast and she points out that the advisers failed to consider that the depreciation on equipment used in this project will be tax deductible. The depreciation is expected to be $80,000 per year for the four-year period. The company's income tax rate is 30 percent per year. Use this information to revise the company's expected cash flow from this project.
c. Compute the net present value of the project based on the revised cash flow forecast. Should Mr. Batkin approve the project?

Problem 16-18 *Postaudit evaluation*

Kerri Bates is reviewing his company's investment in a cement plant. The company paid $15,000,000 five years ago to acquire the plant. Now top management is considering an opportunity to sell it. The president wants to know whether the plant has met original expectations before he decides its fate. The company's discount rate for present value computations is 8 percent. Expected and actual cash flows follow.

	Year 1	Year 2	Year 3	Year 4	Year 5
Expected	$3,300,000	$4,920,000	$4,560,000	$4,980,000	$4,200,000
Actual	2,700,000	3,060,000	4,920,000	3,900,000	3,600,000

Required

Round your computations to the nearest whole dollar.

a. Compute the net present value of the expected cash flows as of the beginning of the investment.
b. Compute the net present value of the actual cash flows as of the beginning of the investment.
c. What do you conclude from this postaudit?

CHECK FIGURES
a. NPV of A: $8,664.00
b. Rate of return of B: 12%

Problem 16-19 *Using net present value and internal rate of return to evaluate investment opportunities*

Pedro Spier, the president of Spier Enterprises, is considering two investment opportunities. Because of limited resources, he will be able to invest in only one of them. Project A is to purchase a machine that will enable factory automation; the machine is expected to have a useful life of four years and no salvage value. Project B supports a training program that will improve the skills of employees operating the current equipment. Initial cash expenditures for Project A are $200,000 and for Project B are $80,000. The annual expected cash inflows are $63,000 for Project A and $26,400 for Project B. Both investments are expected to provide cash flow benefits for the next four years. Spier Enterprises' cost of capital is 8 percent.

Required

a. Compute the net present value of each project. Which project should be adopted based on the net present value approach? Round your computations to two decimal points.

b. Compute the approximate internal rate of return of each project. Which one should be adopted based on the internal rate of return approach? Round your rates to six decimal points.

c. Compare the net present value approach with the internal rate of return approach. Which method is better in the given circumstances? Why?

Problem 16-20 *Using the payback period and unadjusted rate of return to evaluate alternative investment opportunities*

LO 16-4

CHECK FIGURE
a. Payback period of the yogurt investment: 1.69 years
Unadjusted rate of return of the cappuccino investment: 52.99%

Austen Ren owns a small retail ice cream parlor. He is considering expanding the business and has identified two attractive alternatives. One involves purchasing a machine that would enable Mr. Ren to offer frozen yogurt to customers. The machine would cost $8,100 and has an expected useful life of three years with no salvage value. Additional annual cash revenues and cash operating expenses associated with selling yogurt are expected to be $6,200 and $900, respectively.

Alternatively, Mr. Ren could purchase for $10,080 the equipment necessary to serve cappuccino. That equipment has an expected useful life of four years and no salvage value. Additional annual cash revenues and cash operating expenses associated with selling cappuccino are expected to be $8,500 and $2,430, respectively.

Income before taxes earned by the ice cream parlor is taxed at an effective rate of 20 percent.

Required

Round your figures, including percentage rates, to two decimal points.

a. Determine the payback period and unadjusted rate of return (use average investment) for each alternative.

b. Indicate which investment alternative you would recommend. Explain your choice.

Problem 16-21 *Using net present value and payback period to evaluate investment opportunities*

LO 16-2, 16-4

CHECK FIGURES
a. NPV of #1: $37,724.66
b. Payback period of #2: less than two years.

Roger Rosich saved $300,000 during the 30 years that he worked for a major corporation. Now he has retired at the age of 60 and has begun to draw a comfortable pension check every month. He wants to ensure the financial security of his retirement by investing his savings wisely and is currently considering two investment opportunities. Both investments require an initial payment of $200,000. The following table presents the estimated cash inflows for the two alternatives.

	Year 1	Year 2	Year 3	Year 4
Opportunity #1	$ 55,000	$ 59,000	$79,000	$100,000
Opportunity #2	102,000	108,000	20,000	20,000

Mr. Rosich decides to use his past average return on mutual fund investments as the discount rate; it is 8 percent.

Required

Round your computation to two decimal points.

a. Compute the net present value of each opportunity. Which should Mr. Rosich adopt based on the net present value approach?

b. Compute the payback period for each project. Which should Mr. Rosich adopt based on the payback approach?

c. Compare the net present value approach with the payback approach. Which method is better in the given circumstances?

LO 16-2, 16-4

Problem 16-22 *Effects of straight-line versus accelerated depreciation on an investment decision*

Cole Electronics is considering investing in manufacturing equipment expected to cost $200,000. The equipment has an estimated useful life of four years and a salvage value of $20,000. It is expected to produce incremental cash revenues of $100,000 per year. Cole has an effective income tax rate of 30 percent and a desired rate of return of 10 percent.

Required

Round your financial figures to the nearest dollar and all other figures to two decimal points.

a. Determine the net present value and the present value index of the investment, assuming that Cole uses straight-line depreciation for financial and income tax reporting.

b. Determine the net present value and the present value index of the investment, assuming that Cole uses double-declining-balance depreciation for financial and income tax reporting.

c. Why do the net present values computed in Requirements *a* and *b* differ?

d. Determine the payback period and unadjusted rate of return (use average investment), assuming that Cole uses straight-line depreciation.

e. Determine the payback period and unadjusted rate of return (use average investment), assuming that Cole uses double-declining-balance depreciation. (*Note:* Use average annual cash flow when computing the payback period and average annual income when determining the unadjusted rate of return.)

f. Why are there no differences in the payback periods or unadjusted rates of return computed in Requirements *d* and *e*?

LO 16-3, 16-4

Problem 16-23 *Comparing internal rate of return with unadjusted rate of return*

Desny Auto Repair, Inc., is evaluating a project to purchase equipment that will not only expand the company's capacity but also improve the quality of its repair services. The board of directors requires all capital investments to meet or exceed the minimum requirement of a 10 percent rate of return. However, the board has not clearly defined the rate of return. The president and controller are pondering two different rates of return: unadjusted rate of return and internal rate of return. The equipment, which costs $100,000, has a life expectancy of five years. The increased net profit per year will be approximately $7,000, and the increased cash inflow per year will be approximately $27,700.

Required

Round rates to six decimal points.

a. If it uses the unadjusted rate of return (use average investment) to evaluate this project, should the company invest in the equipment?

b. If it uses the internal rate of return to evaluate this project, should the company invest in the equipment?

c. Which method is better for this capital investment decision?

ANALYZE, THINK, COMMUNICATE

ATC 16-1 Business Application Case *Pension planning in state governments*

In recent years, there has been a lot of media coverage about the funding status of pension plans for state employees. In many states, the amount of money invested in employee pension plans is far less than the amount estimated to be needed to pay them the retirement benefits they have been promised. Basically, pension plans work by investing enough money while employees are working so that the money invested, plus the investment income it earns over the years, will be sufficient to pay the workers their retirement incomes once they have retired.

There are many complicated assumptions, estimates, and calculations needed to determine how much money a state should invest in its pension fund each year. One of the most important assumptions is the rate of return the plan's investments will earn in the future. As you have seen in this chapter, the higher the rate of return used to calculate the present value of future cash flows, the lower the present value will be. To determine a pension plan's funded status, actuaries (1) estimate the future cash payments expected to be made to employees, (2) calculate the present value of those cash flows using an assumed rate of return (this present value is the gross liability of the fund), and (3) subtract the amount of money that has been invested from the gross liability calculated in step 2 (this amount is the funded status of the pension plan). Essentially, this is the same as calculating the net present value of an investment. If the plan has less money in its investments than the present value of its estimated future cash flows, it has a net liability and is considered to be underfunded by that amount.

Many states' pension plans have assumed they will earn 8 percent or more on their investments, even though many experts think a more appropriate assumption would be 6.5 percent. As an example, the state of Virginia used an assumed rate of return of 7.5 percent in 2009 but reduced the rate to 7.0 percent in 2011. In 2011, Virginia paid out approximately $3.3 billion in benefits to retirees.

Required

a. Assume Virginia's annual payments will continue to be $3.3 billion, and that retirees will receive benefits for 20 years on average. Using an assumed rate of return of 8 percent, calculate the liability of the state's pension plan. The liability is the present value of the future cash payments. (Be aware that the real-world calculation for a state's pension plan liability involves many more assumptions than just these two.)

b. Assume the annual payments will continue to be $3.3 billion, and that retirees will receive benefits for 20 years on average. Using an assumed rate of return of 6 percent, calculate the liability of the state's pension plan.

c. Reviewing your answers from Requirements *a* and *b*, provide an explanation as to why states may wish to assume a higher rate of return on their pension plan's investments than actuaries might recommend.

ATC 16-2   Group Assignment   *Net present value*

Espada Real Estate Investment Company (EREIC) purchases new apartment complexes, establishes a stable group of residents, and then sells the complexes to apartment management companies. The average holding time is three years. EREIC is currently investigating two alternatives.

1. EREIC can purchase Harding Properties for $4,500,000. The complex is expected to produce net cash inflows of $360,000, $502,500, and $865,000 for the first, second, and third years of operation, respectively. The market value of the complex at the end of the third year is expected to be $5,175,000.
2. EREIC can purchase Summit Apartments for $3,450,000. The complex is expected to produce net cash inflows of $290,000, $435,000, and $600,000 for the first, second, and third years of operation, respectively. The market value of the complex at the end of the third year is expected to be $4,050,000.

EREIC has a desired rate of return of 12 percent.

Required

a. Divide the class into groups of four or five students per group and then divide the groups into two sections. Assign Task 1 to the first section and Task 2 to the second section.

Group Tasks

   (1) Calculate the net present value and the present value index for Harding Properties.

   (2) Calculate the net present value and the present value index for Summit Apartments.

b. Have a spokesperson from one group in the first section report the amounts calculated by the group. Make sure that all groups in the section have the same result. Repeat the process for the second section. Have the class as a whole select the investment opportunity that EREIC should accept given that the objective is to produce the higher rate of return.

c. Assume that EREIC has $4,500,000 to invest and that any funds not invested in real estate properties must be invested in a certificate of deposit earning a 5 percent return. Would this information alter the decision made in Requirement *b*?

d. This requirement is independent of Requirement *c*. Assume there is a 10 percent chance that the Harding project will be annexed by the city of Hoover, which has an outstanding school district. The annexation would likely increase net cash flows by $37,500 per year and would increase the market value at the end of year 3 by $300,000. Would this information change the decision reached in Requirement *b*?

ATC 16-3   Research Assignment   *Capital expenditures at CarMax, Inc.*

Obtain CarMax, Inc.'s Form 10-K for the fiscal year ending on February 29, 2012. To obtain the Form 10-K, you can use the EDGAR system (see Appendix A at the back of this text for instructions), or it can be found under the "Investor Relations" link on the company's website at www.carmax.com. Read the following sections of the 10-K: "Used Car Superstores as of February 29, 2012" on page 14, "Expansion" on page 15, "Fiscal 2013 Planned Superstore Openings" on page 32, and the Consolidated Statements of Cash Flows on page 41.

Required

a. How many superstores did CarMax plan to open during its 2013 fiscal year? By what percentage would these new stores increase the size of CarMax's superstore operations? How much did CarMax estimate these expansions will cost?

b. How much cash did CarMax spend on capital expenditures during its 2010, 2011, and 2012 fiscal years? Do you think the amount spent on "capital expenditures" represents the full costs that CarMax incurred to open new stores? Explain your answer.

c. Where did CarMax get the cash used to make these investments?

ATC 16-4   Writing Assignment   *Limitations of capital investment techniques*

Webb Publishing Company is evaluating two investment opportunities. One is to purchase an Internet company with the capacity to open new marketing channels through which Webb can sell its books. This opportunity offers a high potential for growth but involves significant risk. Indeed, losses are projected for the first three years of operation. The second opportunity is to purchase a printing company that would enable Webb to better control costs by printing its own books. The potential savings are clearly predictable but would make a significant change in the company's long-term profitability.

Required

Write a response discussing the usefulness of capital investment techniques (net present value, internal rate of return, payback, and unadjusted rate of return) in making a choice between these two alternative investment opportunities. Your response should discuss the strengths and weaknesses of capital budgeting techniques in general. Furthermore, it should include a comparison between techniques based on the time value of money versus those that are not.

ATC 16-5   Ethical Dilemma   *Postaudit*

Gaines Company recently initiated a postaudit program. To motivate employees to take the program seriously, Gaines established a bonus program. Managers receive a bonus equal to 10 percent of the amount by which actual net present value exceeds the projected net present value. Victor Holt, manager of the North Western Division, had an investment proposal on his desk when the new system was implemented. The investment opportunity required a $250,000 initial cash outflow and was expected to return cash inflows of $90,000 per year for the next five years. Gaines' desired rate of return is 10 percent. Mr. Holt immediately reduced the estimated cash inflows to $70,000 per year and recommended accepting the project.

Required

a. Assume that actual cash inflows turn out to be $91,000 per year. Determine the amount of Mr. Holt's bonus if the original computation of net present value were based on $90,000 versus $70,000.

b. Is Mr. Holt's behavior in violation of any of the standards of ethical professional practice in Exhibit 10.17 of Chapter 10?

c. Speculate about the long-term effect the bonus plan is likely to have on the company.

d. Recommend how to compensate managers in a way that discourages gamesmanship.

APPENDIX A

Accessing the EDGAR Database through the Internet

Successful business managers need many different skills, including communication, interpersonal, computer, and analytical. Most business students become very aware of the data analysis skills used in accounting, but they may not be as aware of the importance of "data-finding" skills. There are many sources of accounting and financial data. The more sources you are able to use, the better.

One very important source of accounting information is the EDGAR database. Others are probably available at your school through the library or business school network. Your accounting instructor will be able to identify these for you and make suggestions regarding their use. By making the effort to learn to use electronic databases, you will enhance your abilities as a future manager and your marketability as a business graduate.

These instructions assume that you know how to access and use an Internet browser. Follow the instructions to retrieve data from the Securities and Exchange Commission's EDGAR database. Be aware that the SEC may have changed its interface since this appendix was written. Accordingly, be prepared for slight differences between the following instructions and what appears on your computer screen. Take comfort in the fact that changes are normally designed to simplify user access. If you encounter a conflict between the following instructions and the instructions provided in the SEC interface, remember that the SEC interface is more current and should take precedence over the following instructions.

Most companies provide links to their SEC filings from their corporate website. These links are often simpler to use and provide more choices regarding file formats than SEC's EDGAR site. On company websites, links to their SEC filings are usually found under one of the following links: "Investor Relations," "Company Info," or "About Us."

1. Connect to the EDGAR database through the following address: **http://www.sec.gov/.**

2. After the SEC homepage appears, click on **Investors,** then **Filings and Forms,** then click on **Search for Company Filings.**

3. On the screen that appears, click on **Company or Fund Name. . . .**

4. On the screen that appears, enter the name of the company whose file you wish to retrieve in the "Company Name" window and click the **Search** button.

5. The following screen will present a list of companies that have the same, or similar, names to the one you entered. Identify the company you want and click on the CIK number beside it.

6. Enter the SEC form number that you want to retrieve in the window titled **Filling Type** that appears in the upper left portion of the screen. For example, if you want Form 10-K, which will usually be the case, enter **10-K** and click on the **Search** button.

7. A list of the forms you requested will be presented, along with the date they were filed. Click on the **Document** button next to the file you wish to retrieve.

8. You will be presented with a list of documents from which to select; usually you will want to choose the file **form10k.htm.**

9. Once the 10-K has been retrieved, you can search it online or save it on your computer.

10. Often the 10-K will have a table of contents that can help locate the part of the report you need. The financial statements are seldom located at the beginning of the Form 10-K. They are usually in either Section 8 or Section 15.

APPENDIX B

The Double-Entry Accounting System

INTRODUCTION

*To prepare financial statements, a company must have a system that captures the vast numbers of business transactions in which it engages each year. The most widely used system, **double-entry accounting,** is so effective it has been in use for hundreds of years! This Appendix explains the rules for recording transactions using double-entry accounting.*

DEBIT/CREDIT TERMINOLOGY

An account form known as a **T-account** is a good starting point for learning double-entry recording procedures. A T-account looks like the letter "T" drawn on a piece of paper. The account title is written across the top of the horizontal bar of the T. The left side of the vertical bar is the **debit** side, and the right side is the **credit** side. An account has been *debited* when an amount is written on the left side and *credited* when an amount is written on the right side. For any given account, the difference between the total debit and credit amounts is the **account balance.**

The rules for using debits and credits to record transactions in T-accounts are as follows.

			Claims			
Assets		=	**Liabilities**	+	**Equity**	
Debit	Credit		Debit	Credit	Debit	Credit
+	−		−	+	−	+

Notice that a debit can represent an increase or a decrease. Likewise, a credit can represent an increase or a decrease. Whether a debit or credit is an increase or a decrease depends on the type of account (asset, liability, or stockholders' equity) in question. The rules of debits and credits are summarized as follows.

1. Debits increase asset accounts; credits decrease asset accounts.
2. Debits decrease liability and stockholders' equity accounts; credits increase liability and stockholders' equity accounts.

We now demonstrate the use of debits and credits in the double-entry accounting system.

The General Journal

Businesses find it impractical to record every individual transaction directly into accounts. Imagine the number of cash transactions a grocery store has each day. To simplify recordkeeping, businesses rely on **source documents** such as cash register tapes as the basis for entering transaction data into the accounting system. Other source documents include invoices, time cards, check stubs, and deposit tickets.

Accountants further simplify recordkeeping by initially recording data from source documents into **journals.** Journals provide a chronological record of business transactions. *Transactions are recorded in journals before they are entered into ledger accounts.* Journals are therefore **books of original entry.** Companies may use different **special journals** to record specific types of recurring transactions. For example, a company may use one special journal to record sales on account, another to record purchases on account, a third to record cash receipts, and a fourth to record cash payments. Transactions that do not fall into any of these categories are recorded in the **general journal.** Although special journals can be useful, companies can keep records without them by recording all transactions in the general journal. For simplicity, this appendix illustrates a general journal only.

At a minimum, the general journal shows the dates, the account titles, and the amounts of each transaction. The date is recorded in the first column, followed by the title of the account to be debited. The title of the account to be credited is indented and written on the line directly below the account to be debited. The dollar amount of the transaction is recorded in the Debit and Credit columns. For example, providing services for $1,000 cash on August 1 would be recorded in general journal format as follows:

Date	Account Title	Debit	Credit
Aug. 1	Cash	1,000	
	Service Revenue		1,000

THE GENERAL LEDGER

The collection of all the accounts used by a particular business is called the **general ledger.** In a manual system, the ledger could be a book with pages for each account where entries are recorded by hand. In more sophisticated systems, the general ledger is maintained in electronic form. Data is entered into electronic ledgers using computer keyboards or scanners. Companies typically assign each ledger account a name and a number. A list of all ledger accounts and their account numbers is called the **chart of accounts.** As previously stated, accounting data are first recorded in journals. The data are then transferred to the ledger accounts through a process called **posting.** The posting process for the August 1, $1,000 revenue transaction is shown below.

Date	Account Title	Debit	Credit
Aug. 1	Cash	1,000	
	Service Revenue		1,000

Case		Service Revenue	
Aug. 1	1,000	Aug. 1	1,000

ILLUSTRATION OF RECORDING PROCEDURES

We use the following transactions data to illustrate the process of recording transactions into a general journal and then posting them into a general ledger. The transactions data

EXHIBIT A.1

Event No.	Account Title	Debit	Credit
1	Cash	28,000	
	Common Stock		28,000
2	Supplies	1,100	
	Accounts Payable		1,100
3	Prepaid Rent	12,000	
	Cash		12,000
4	Accounts Receivable	23,000	
	Consulting Revenue		23,000
5	General Operating Expenses	16,000	
	Accounts Payable		16,000
6	Cash	20,000	
	Accounts Receivable		20,000
7	Accounts Payable	13,000	
	Cash		13,000
8	Dividends	1,000	
	Cash		1,000
9	Rent Expense	900	
	Supplies		900
10	Rent Expense	3,000	
	Prepaid Rent		3,000
11	Salaries Expense	1,200	
	Salaries Payable		1,200

applies to the Mestro Financial Services Company. The journal entries are shown in Exhibit A.1. The general ledger after posting is shown in Exhibit A.2.

1. Acquired $28,000 cash by issuing common stock on January 1, 2014.
2. Purchased $1,100 of supplies on account.
3. Paid $12,000 cash in advance for a one-year lease on office space.
4. Earned $23,000 of consulting revenue on account.
5. Incurred $16,000 of general operating expenses on account.
6. Collected $20,000 cash from receivables.
7. Paid $13,000 cash on accounts payable.
8. Paid a $1,000 cash dividend to stockholders.

Information for Adjusting Entries

9. There was $200 of supplies on hand at the end of the accounting period.
10. The one-year lease on the office space was effective beginning on October 1, 2014.
11. There was $1,200 of accrued salaries at the end of 2014.

EXHIBIT A.2

MESTRO FINANCIAL SERVICES COMPANY
T-Accounts, 2014

Assets	=	Liabilities	+	Equity

Cash

1.	28,000	3.	12,000
6.	20,000	7.	13,000
		8.	1,000
Bal.	22,000		

Accounts Receivable

4.	23,000	6.	20,000
Bal.	3,000		

Supplies

2.	1,100	9.	900
Bal.	200		

Prepaid Rent

3.	12,000	10.	3,000
Bal.	9,000		

Accounts Payable

7.	13,000	2.	1,100
		5.	16,000
		Bal.	4,100

Salaries Payable

		11.	1,200
		Bal.	1,200

Common Stock

		1.	28,000
		Bal.	28,000

Dividends

8.	1,000	

Consulting Revenue

		4.	23,000

General Operating Expenses

5.	16,000	

Salaries Expense

11.	1,200	

Supplies Expense

9.	900	

Rent Expense

10.	3,000	

Trial Balance

To test accuracy, accountants regularly prepare an internal accounting schedule called a **trial balance.** A trial balance lists every ledger account and its balance. Debit balances are listed in one column and credit balances are listed in an adjacent column. The columns are totaled and the totals are compared. Exhibit A.3 displays the trial balance for Mestro Financial Services Company after the adjusting entries have been posted to the ledger.

If the debit total does not equal the credit total, the accountant knows to search for an error. Even if the totals are equal, however, there may be errors in the accounting records. For example, equal trial balance totals would not disclose errors like the following: failure to record transactions; misclassifications, such as debiting the wrong account; or incorrectly recording the amount of a transaction, such as recording a $200 transaction as $2,000. Equal debits and credits in a trial balance provide evidence rather than proof of accuracy.

Financial Statements

Supplemented with details from the Cash and Common Stock ledger accounts, the trial balance (Exhibit A.3) provides the information to prepare the financial statements shown in Exhibit A.4.

EXHIBIT A.3

MESTRO FINANCIAL SERVICES COMPANY
Trial Balance
December 31, 2014

Account Titles	Debit	Credit
Cash	$22,000	
Accounts receivable	3,000	
Supplies	200	
Prepaid rent	9,000	
Accounts payable		$ 4,100
Salaries payable		1,200
Common stock		28,000
Dividends	1,000	
Consulting revenue		23,000
General operating expenses	16,000	
Salaries expense	1,200	
Supplies expense	900	
Rent expense	3,000	
Totals	$56,300	$56,300

EXHIBIT A.4

MESTRO FINANCIAL SERVICES COMPANY
Financial Statements
For 2014

Income Statement
For the Year Ended December 31, 2014

Consulting revenue		$23,000
Expenses		
General operating expenses	$16,000	
Salaries expense	1,200	
Supplies expense	900	
Rent expense	3,000	
Total expenses		(21,100)
Net income		$ 1,900

Statement of Changes in Stockholders' Equity
For the Year Ended December 31, 2014

Beginning common stock	$ 0	
Plus: Common stock issued	28,000	
Ending common stock		$28,000
Beginning retained earnings	0	
Plus: Net income	1,900	
Less: Dividends	(1,000)	
Ending retained earnings		900
Total stockholders' equity		$28,900

continued

Balance Sheet		
As of December 31, 2014		
Assets		
Cash	$22,000	
Accounts receivable	3,000	
Supplies	200	
Prepaid rent	9,000	
Total assets		$34,200
Liabilities		
Accounts payable	$ 4,100	
Salaries payable	1,200	
Total liabilities		$ 5,300
Stockholders' equity		
Common stock	28,000	
Retained earnings	900	
Total stockholders' equity		28,900
Total liabilities and stockholders' equity		$34,200

Statement of Cash Flows		
For the Year Ended December 31, 2014		
Cash flows from operating activities		
Inflow from customers	$20,000	
Outflow for expenses	(25,000)	
Net cash flow for operating activities		$ (5,000)
Cash flows from investing activities		0
Cash flows from financing activities		
Inflow from issue of common stock	28,000	
Outflow for dividends	(1,000)	
Net cash flow from financing activities		27,000
Net change in cash		22,000
Plus: Beginning cash balance		0
Ending cash balance		$22,000

KEY TERMS

Account balance 602	Debit 602	General ledger 603	Special journals 603
Books of original entry 603	Double-entry	Journals 603	T-account 602
Chart of accounts 603	accounting 602	Posting 603	Trial balance 605
Credit 602	General journal 603	Source documents 602	

EXERCISES

Appendix 1-1   *Debit/credit terminology*

Required

For each of the following independent events, identify the account that would be debited and the account that would be credited. The accounts for the first event are identified as an example.

Event	Account Debited	Account Credited
a	Cash	Common Stock

a. Received cash by issuing common stock.
b. Received cash for services to be performed in the future.
c. Provided services on account.
d. Paid accounts payable.
e. Paid cash in advance for one year's rent.
f. Paid cash for operating expenses.
g. Paid salaries payable.
h. Purchased supplies on account.
i. Paid cash dividends to the stockholders.
j. Recognized revenue for services completed; previously collected the cash in Event *b*.
k. Received cash in payment of accounts receivable.
l. Paid salaries expense.
m. Recognized expense for prepaid rent that had been used up by the end of the accounting period.

Appendix 1-2   *Recording transactions in general journal and T-accounts*

The following events apply to Pearson Service Co. for 2014, its first year of operation.

1. Received cash of $50,000 from the issue of common stock.
2. Performed $90,000 worth of services on account.
3. Paid $64,000 cash for salaries expense.
4. Purchased supplies for $12,000 on account.
5. Collected $78,000 of accounts receivable.
6. Paid $8,500 of the accounts payable.
7. Paid a $5,000 dividend to the stockholders.
8. Had $1,500 of supplies on hand at the end of the period.

Required

a. Record these events in general journal form.
b. Post the entries to T-accounts and determine the ending balance in each account.
c. Determine the amount of total assets at the end of 2014.
d. Determine the amount of net income for 2014.

Appendix 1-3   *Recording events in the general journal, posting to T-accounts, and preparing a trial balance*

The following events apply to Complete Business Service in 2014, its first year of operations.

1. Received $30,000 cash from the issue of common stock.
2. Earned $25,000 of service revenue on account.
3. Incurred $10,000 of operating expenses on account.
4. Received $20,000 cash for performing services.
5. Paid $8,000 cash to purchase land.
6. Collected $22,000 of cash from accounts receivable.
7. Received a $6,000 cash advance for services to be provided in the future.
8. Purchased $900 of supplies on account.
9. Made a $7,500 payment on accounts payable.
10. Paid a $5,000 cash dividend to the stockholders.
11. Recognized $500 of supplies expense.
12. Recognized $5,000 of revenue for services provided to the customer in Event 7.

Required

a. Record the events in the general journal.
b. Post the events to T-accounts and determine the ending account balances.
c. Test the equality of the debit and credit balances of the T-accounts by preparing a trial balance.

Appendix 1-4 *One complete accounting cycle*

The following events apply to Paradise Vacations's first year of operations.

1. Acquired $20,000 cash from the issue of common stock on January 1, 2014.
2. Purchased $800 of supplies on account.
3. Paid $4,200 cash in advance for a one-year lease on office space.
4. Earned $28,000 of revenue on account.
5. Incurred $12,500 of other operating expenses on account.
6. Collected $24,000 cash from accounts receivable.
7. Paid $9,000 cash on accounts payable.
8. Paid a $3,000 cash dividend to the stockholders.

Information for Adjusting Entries

9. There was $150 of supplies on hand at the end of the accounting period.
10. The lease on the office space covered a one-year period beginning November 1.
11. There was $3,600 of accrued salaries at the end of the period.

Required

a. Record these transactions in general journal form.
b. Post the transaction data from the journal to ledger T-accounts.
c. Prepare a trial balance.
d. Prepare an income statement, statement of changes in stockholders' equity, a balance sheet, and a statement of cash flows.

GLOSSARY

absolute amounts Dollar totals reported in accounts on financial reports that can be misleading because they make no reference to the relative size of the company being analyzed. *p. 327*

accelerated depreciation methods Depreciation methods that recognize depreciation expense more rapidly in the early stages of an asset's life than in the later stages of its life. *p. 214*

account balance Difference between total debits and total credits in an account. *p. 602*

account receivable Expected future cash receipt arising from permitting a customer to *buy now and pay later;* typically a relatively small balance due within a short time period. *pp. 51, 162*

accounting Service-based profession that provides reliable and relevant financial information useful in making decisions. *p. 3*

accounting equation Expression of the relationship between the assets and the claims on those assets. *p. 12*

accounting event Economic occurrence that causes changes in an enterprise's assets, liabilities, or equity. *p. 13*

accounting period Span of time covered by the financial statements, normally one year, but may be a quarter, a month or some other time span. *p. 23*

accounts Records used for classifying and summarizing transaction data; subclassifications of financial statement elements. *p. 11*

accounts receivable turnover Financial ratio that measures how fast accounts receivable are turned into cash; computed by dividing sales by accounts receivable. *p. 333*

accrual Recognition of events before exchanging cash. *p. 49*

accrual accounting Accounting system that recognizes expenses or revenues when they occur regardless of when cash is exchanged. *p. 49*

accrued expenses Expenses that are recognized before cash is paid. An example is accrued salaries expense. *p. 52*

accrued interest Interest revenue or expense that is recognized before cash has been exchanged. *p. 173*

accumulated conversion factors Factors used to convert a series of future cash inflows into their present value equivalent and that are applicable to cash inflows of equal amounts spread over equal interval time periods and that can be determined by computing the sum of the individual single factors used for each period. *p. 573*

accumulated depreciation Contra asset account that indicates the sum of all depreciation expense recognized for an asset since the date of acquisition. *p. 212*

acid-test ratio (quick ratio) Measure of immediate debt-paying ability; calculated by dividing very liquid assets (cash, receivables, and marketable securities) by current liabilities. *p. 332*

activities The actions taken by an organization to accomplish its mission. *p. 381*

activity base Factor that causes changes in variable cost; is usually some measure of volume when used to define cost behavior. *p. 411*

activity-based management (ABM) Management of the activities of an organization to add the greatest value by developing products that satisfy the needs of that organization's customers. *p. 381*

adjusting entry Entry that updates account balances prior to preparing financial statements. *pp. 52, 174*

adverse opinion Opinion issued by a certified public accountant that means one or more departures from GAAP in a company's financial statements are so very material the auditors believe the financial statements do not fairly represent the company's status; contrast with *unqualified opinion. p. 147*

aging of accounts receivable Classifying each account receivable by the number of days it has been outstanding. The aging schedule is used to develop an estimate of the amount of the allowance for doubtful accounts. *p. 171*

AICPA (American Institute of Certified Public Accountants) National association that serves the educational and professional interests of members of the public accounting profession; membership is voluntary. *p. 143*

allocation Process of dividing a total cost into parts and apportioning the parts among the relevant cost objects. *p. 440*

allocation base Cost driver used as the basis for the allocation process. *p. 441*

allocation rate Factor used to allocate or assign costs to a cost object; determined by taking the total cost to be allocated and dividing it by the appropriate cost driver. *p. 441*

allowance for doubtful accounts Contra asset account that contains an amount equal to the accounts receivable that are expected to be uncollectible. *p. 164*

allowance method of accounting for uncollectible accounts Method of accounting for bad debts in which bad debts are estimated and expensed in the same period in which the corresponding sales are recognized. The receivables are reported in the financial statements at net realizable value (the amount expected to be collected in cash). *p. 164*

amortization Method of systematically allocating the costs of intangible assets to expense over their useful lives; also term for converting the discount on a note or a bond to interest expense over a designated period. *pp. 208, 254*

amortizing See *amortization.*

annual report Document in which an organization provides information to stockholders, usually on an annual basis. *p. 28*

annuity Series of equal payments made over a specified number of periods. *p. 573*

appropriated retained earnings Retained earnings restricted by the board of directors for a specific purpose (e.g., to repay debt or for future expansion); although a part of total retained earnings, not available for distribution as dividends. *p. 307*

articles of incorporation Items on an application filed with a state agency for the formation of a corporation; contains such information as the corporation's name, its purpose, its location, its expected life, provisions for its capital stock, and a list of the members of its board of directors. *p. 294*

articulation Characteristic of financial statements that means they are interrelated. For example, the amount of net income reported on the income statement is added to beginning retained earnings as a component in calculating the ending retained earnings balance reported on the statement of changes in stockholders' equity. *p. 21*

asset exchange transaction A transaction that decreases one asset while increasing another asset so that total assets do not change; for example, the purchase of land with cash. *pp. 14, 51*

asset source transaction Transaction that increases an asset and a claim on assets; three types of asset source transactions are acquisitions from owners (equity), borrowings from creditors (liabilities), or earnings from operations (revenues). *pp. 13, 50*

asset turnover ratio   The amount of net income divided by average total assets. *p. 328*

asset use transaction   Transaction that decreases an asset and a claim on assets; the three types are distributions (transfers to owners), liability payments (to creditors), or expenses (used to operate the business). *pp. 15, 51*

assets   Economic resources used by a business to produce revenue. *p. 11*

audits   Detailed examination of some aspect of a company's accounting records or operating procedures in order to report the results to interested parties. *p. 145*

authority manual   A document that outlines the chain of command for authority and responsibility. The authority manual provides guidelines for specific positions such as personnel officer as well as general authority such as all vice presidents are authorized to spend up to a designated limit. *p. 133*

authorized stock   Number of shares that the corporation is approved by the state to issue. *p. 299*

average cost   The total cost of making products divided by the total number of products made. *p. 366*

average number of days to collect receivables   Length of the average collection period for accounts receivable; computed by dividing 365 by the accounts receivable turnover ratio. *p. 334*

average number of days to sell inventory   Financial ratio that measures the average number of days that inventory stays in stock before being sold. *p. 334*

avoidable costs   Future costs that can be avoided by taking a specified course of action. To be avoidable in a decision-making context, costs must differ among the alternatives. For example, if the cost of material used to make two different products is the same for both products, that cost could not be avoided by choosing to produce one product over the other. Therefore, the material's cost would not be an avoidable cost. *p. 472*

balanced score card   A management evaluation tool that includes financial and nonfinancial measures. *p. 551*

balance sheet   Statement that lists the assets of a business and the corresponding claims (liabilities and equity) on those assets. *p. 23*

bank reconciliation   Schedule that identifies and explains differences between the cash balance reported by the bank and the cash balance in the firm's accounting records. *p. 137*

bank statement   Statement issued by a bank (usually monthly) that denotes all activity in the bank account for that period. *p. 137*

bank statement credit memo   Memorandum that describes an increase in the account balance. *p. 137*

bank statement debit memo   Memorandum that describes a decrease in the account balance. *p. 137*

basket purchase   Acquisition of several assets in a single transaction with no specific cost attributed to each asset. *p. 209*

batch-level costs   The costs associated with producing a batch of products. For example, the cost of setting up machinery to produce 1,000 products is a batch-level cost. The classification of batch-level costs is context sensitive. Postage for one product would be classified as a unit-level cost. In contrast, postage for a large number of products delivered in a single shipment would be classified as a batch-level cost. *p. 473*

benchmarking   Identifying the best practices used by world-class competitors. *p. 381*

best practices   Practices used by world-class companies. *p. 381*

board of directors   Group of individuals elected by the stockholders of a corporation to oversee its operations. *p. 296*

bond certificates   Debt securities used to obtain long-term financing in which a company borrows funds from a number of lenders, called *bondholders*; usually issued in denominations of $1,000. *p. 257*

bond discount   Difference between the selling price and the face amount of a bond sold for less than the face amount. *p. 262*

bond premium   Difference between the selling price and the face amount of a bond that is sold for more than the face amount. *p. 266*

bondholder   The party buying a bond (the lender or creditor). *p. 257*

book of original entry   A journal in which transactions are first recorded. *p. 603*

book value   Historical (original) cost of an asset minus the accumulated depreciation; alternatively, undepreciated amount to date. *p. 212*

book value per share   Value of stock determined by dividing the total stockholders' equity by the number of shares of stock. *pp. 299, 340*

break-even point   Point where total revenue equals total cost; can be expressed in units or sales dollars. *p. 412*

budgeting   Form of planning that formalizes a company's goals and objectives in financial terms. *p. 504*

capital budgeting   Financial planning activities that cover the intermediate range of time such as whether to buy or lease equipment, whether to purchase a particular investment, or whether to increase operating expenses to stimulate sales. *p. 506*

capital expenditures   (on an existing asset) Substantial amounts of funds spent to improve an asset's quality or to extend its life. *p. 220*

capital investments   Expenditures for the purchase of operational assets that involve a long-term commitment of funds that can be critically important to the company's ultimate success; normally recovered through the use of the assets. *p. 570*

carrying value   Face amount of a bond liability less any unamortized bond discount or plus any unamortized bond premium. *p. 263*

cash   Coins, currency, checks, balances in checking and certain savings accounts, money orders, bank drafts, certificates of deposit, and other items that are payable on demand. *p. 135*

cash budget   A budget that focuses on cash receipts and payments that are expected to occur in the future. *p. 515*

cash discount   Discount offered on merchandise sold to encourage prompt payment; offered by sellers of merchandise and represent sales discounts to the seller when they are used and purchase discounts to the purchaser of the merchandise. *p. 100*

certified check   Check guaranteed by a bank to be drawn on an account having funds sufficient to pay the check. *p. 139*

certified public accountant (CPA)   Accountant who, by meeting certain educational and experiential requirements, is licensed by the state government to provide audit services to the public. *p. 145*

certified suppliers   Suppliers who have gained the confidence of the buyer by providing quality goods and services at desirable prices and usually in accordance with strict delivery specifications; frequently provide the buyer with preferred customer status in exchange for guaranteed purchase quantities and prompt payment schedules. *p. 478*

chart of accounts   List of all ledger accounts and their corresponding account numbers. *p. 603*

checks   Prenumbered forms, sometimes multicopy, with the name of the business issuing them preprinted on the face, indicating to whom they are paid, the amount of the payment, and the transaction date. *p. 137*

claims   Owners' and creditors' interests in a business's assets. *p. 12*

claims exchange transaction   Transaction that decreases one claim and increases another so that total claims do not change. For example, the accrual of interest expense is a claims exchange transaction; liabilities increase, and the recognition of the expense causes retained earnings to decrease. *p. 53*

classified balance sheet   Balance sheet that distinguishes between current and noncurrent items. *p. 268*

closely held corporation   Corporation whose stock is exchanged between a limited number of individuals. *p. 294*

closing   See *closing the books.*

closing the books   Process of transferring balances from temporary accounts (Revenue, Expense, and Dividends) to the permanent account (Retained Earnings). *p. 25*

Code of Professional Conduct   A set of guidelines established by the American Institute of Certified Public Accountants (AICPA) to promote high ethical conduct among its membership. *p. 143*

collateral   Assets pledged as security for a loan. *pp. 173, 267*

common costs   Costs that are incurred to support more than one cost object but cannot be traced to any specific object. *p. 440*

common size financial statements   Financial statements in which amounts are converted to percentages to allow a better comparison of period-to-period and company-to-company financial data since all information is placed on a common basis. *p. 109*

common stock   Basic class of corporate stock that carries no preferences as to claims on assets or dividends; certificates that evidence ownership in a company. *pp. 12, 300*

confidentiality   Code of ethics requirement that prohibits CPAs from voluntarily disclosing information they acquire as a result of accountant-client relationships. *p. 147*

conservatism   A principle that guides accountants in uncertain circumstances to select the alternative that produces the lowest amount of net income. *p. 58*

consistency   The generally accepted accounting principle that a company should, in most circumstances, continually use the same accounting method(s) so that its financial statements are comparable across time. *p. 183*

contingent liability   A potential obligation, the amount of which depends on the outcome of future events. *p. 250*

continuity   Concept that describes the fact that a corporation's life may extend well beyond the time at which any particular shareholder decides to retire or to sell his or her stock. *p. 296*

continuous improvement   Total quality management (TQM) feature that refers to an ongoing process through which employees learn to eliminate waste, reduce response time, minimize defects, and simplify the design and delivery of products and services to customers. *p. 381*

contra asset account   Account subtracted from another account with which it is associated; has the effect of reducing the asset account with which it is associated. *pp. 166, 212*

contribution margin   Difference between a company's sales revenue and total variable cost; represents the amount available to cover fixed cost and thereafter to provide a profit. *p. 408*

contribution margin per unit   The contribution margin per unit is equal to the sales price per unit minus the variable cost per unit. *p. 413*

controllability concept   Evaluating managerial performance based only on revenue and costs under the manager's direct control. *p. 538*

controllable costs   Costs that can be influenced by a particular manager's decisions and actions. *p. 440*

copyright   Legal protection of writings, musical compositions, and other intellectual property for the exclusive use of the creator or persons assigned the right by the creator. *p. 223*

corporation   Legal entity separate from its owners; formed when a group of individuals with a common purpose join together in an organization according to state laws. *p. 294*

cost   Measure of resources used to acquire an asset or to produce revenue. *p. 59*

cost accumulation   Process of determining the cost of a particular object by accumulating many individual costs into a single total cost. *p. 438*

cost allocation   Process of dividing a total cost into parts and assigning the parts to relevant objects. *pp. 372, 439*

cost behavior   How a cost reacts (goes up, down, or remains the same) relative to changes in some measure of activity (e.g., the behavior pattern of the cost of raw materials is to increase as the number of units of product made increases). *p. 404*

cost center   Type of responsibility center which incurs costs but does not generate revenue. *p. 538*

cost driver   Any factor, usually some measure of activity, that causes cost to be incurred, sometimes referred to as *activity base* or *allocation base*. Examples are labor hours, machine hours, or some other measure of activity whose change causes corresponding changes in the cost object. *p. 438*

cost method of accounting for treasury stock   Method of accounting for treasury stock in which the purchase of treasury stock is recorded at its cost to the firm but does not consider the original issue price or par value. *p. 304*

cost objects   Objects for which managers need to know the cost; can be products, processes, departments, services, activities, and so on. *p. 436*

cost of capital   Return paid to investors and creditors for the use of their assets (capital); usually represents a company's minimum rate of return. *p. 571*

cost of goods available for sale   Total costs paid to obtain goods and to make them ready for sale, including the cost of beginning inventory plus purchases and transportation-in costs, less purchase returns and allowances and purchase discounts. *p. 95*

cost of goods sold   Total cost incurred for the goods sold during a specific accounting period. *p. 95*

cost-plus pricing   Pricing strategy that sets the price at cost plus a markup equal to a percentage of the cost. *p. 365*

cost pool   A collection of costs organized around a common cost driver. The cost pool as opposed to individual costs is allocated to cost objects using the common cost driver thereby promoting efficiency in the allocation process. *p. 442*

cost tracing   Relating specific costs to the objects that cause their incurrence. *p. 439*

credit   Entry that increases liability and equity accounts or decreases asset accounts. *p. 602*

creditors   Individuals or institutions that have loaned goods or services to a business. *p. 4*

cumulative dividends   Preferred dividends that accumulate from year to year until paid. *p. 301*

current (short-term) assets   Assets that will be converted to cash or consumed within one year or an operating cycle, whichever is longer. *pp. 206, 267*

current (short-term) liability   Obligation due within one year or an operating cycle, whichever is longer. *p. 267*

current ratio   Measure of liquidity (short-term debt-paying ability); calculated by dividing current assets by current liabilities. *p. 332*

date of record   Date that establishes who will receive the dividend payment: shareholders who actually own the stock on the record date will be paid the dividend even if the stock is sold before the dividend is paid. *p. 305*

debit   Entry that increases asset accounts or decreases liability and equity accounts. *p. 602*

debt to assets ratio   Financial ratio that measures a company's level of risk. *p. 335*

debt to equity ratio   Financial ratio that compares creditor financing to owner financing, expressed as the dollar amount of liabilities for each dollar of stockholder's equity. *p. 335*

decentralization   Practice of delegating authority and responsibility for the operation of business segments. *p. 538*

declaration date Date on which the board of directors actually declares a dividend. *p. 305*

deferral Recognition of revenue or expense in a period after the cash is exchanged. *p. 49*

depletion Method of systematically allocating the costs of natural resources to expense as the resources are removed from the land. *p. 208*

deposits in transit Deposits recorded in a depositor's books but not received and recorded by the bank. *p. 138*

deposit ticket Bank form that accompanies checks and cash deposited into a bank account; normally specifies the account number, name of the account, and a record of the checks and cash being deposited. *p. 137*

depreciable cost Original cost minus salvage value (of a long-term depreciable asset). *p. 210*

depreciation Decline in value of long-term tangible assets such as buildings, furniture, or equipment. It is systematically recognized by accountants as depreciation expense over the useful lives of the affected assets. *p. 208*

depreciation expense Portion of the original cost of a long-term tangible asset systematically allocated to an expense account in a given period. *p. 210*

differential revenues Future-oriented revenues that differ among the alternatives under consideration. *p. 472*

direct cost Cost that is easily traceable to a cost object and for which the sacrifice to trace is small in relation to the information benefits attained. *p. 439*

direct labor Wages paid to production workers whose efforts can be easily and conveniently traced to products. *p. 369*

direct raw materials Costs of raw materials used to make products that can be easily and conveniently traced to those products. *p. 369*

disclaimer of opinion Report on financial statements issued when the auditor is unable to obtain enough information to determine if the statements conform to GAAP; is neither positive nor negative. *p. 147*

discount on bonds payable Contra liability account used to record the amount of discount on a bond issue. *p. 262*

dividend Transfer of wealth from a business to its owners. *p. 16*

dividends in arrears Cumulative dividends on preferred stock that have not been paid; must be paid prior to paying dividends to common stockholders. *p. 301*

dividend yield Ratio for comparing stock dividends paid in relation to the market price; calculated as dividends per share divided by market price per share. *p. 341*

double-declining-balance depreciation Depreciation method that recognizes larger amounts of depreciation in the early stages of an asset's life and progressively smaller amounts as the asset ages. *p. 214*

double-entry accounting (bookkeeping) Method of keeping records that provides a system of checks and balances by recording transactions in a dual format. *pp. 13, 602*

double taxation Policy to tax corporate profits distributed to owners twice, once when the income is reported on the corporation's income tax return and again when the dividends are reported on the individual's return. *p. 295*

downstream costs Costs, such as delivery costs and sales commissions, incurred after the manufacturing process is complete. *p. 375*

earnings The difference between revenues and expenses. Same as net income or profit. *p. 4*

earnings per share Measure of the value of a share of common stock in terms of company earnings; calculated as net income available to common stockholders divided by the average number of outstanding common shares. *p. 340*

effective interest rate Yield rate of bonds, equal to the market rate of interest on the day the bonds are sold. *p. 262*

effective interest rate method Method of amortizing bond discounts and premiums that bases interest computations on the carrying value of liability. As the liability increases or decreases, the amount of interest expense also increases or decreases. *p. 270*

elements Primary components of financial statements including assets, liabilities, equity, contributions, revenue, expenses, distributions, and net income. *p. 10*

entity See *reporting entities.*

entrenched management Management that may have become ineffective but because of political implications may be difficult to remove. *p. 297*

equation method Cost-volume-profit analysis technique that uses the algebraic relationship among sales, variable costs, fixed costs, and desired net income before taxes to solve for required sales volume. *p. 412*

equipment replacement decisions Decisions regarding whether existing equipment should be replaced with newer equipment based on identification and comparison of the avoidable costs of the old and new equipment to determine which equipment is more profitable to operate. *p. 482*

equity Portion of assets remaining after the creditors' claims have been satisfied (i.e., Assets Liabilities Equity); also called *residual interest* or *net assets. p. 10*

estimated useful life Time for which an asset is expected to be used by a business. *p. 210*

ex-dividend Stock traded after the date of record but before the payment date; does not receive the benefit of the upcoming dividend. *p. 306*

expenses Economic sacrifices (decreases in assets or increase in liabilities) that are incurred in the process of generating revenue. *pp. 15, 54*

face value Amount of the bond to be paid back (to the bondholders) at maturity. *p. 257*

facility-level costs Costs incurred on behalf of the whole company or a segment of the company; not related to any specific product, batch, or unit of production or service and unavoidable unless the entire company or segment is eliminated. *p. 473*

favorable variance Variance that occurs when actual costs are less than standard costs or when actual sales are higher than standard sales. *p. 542*

fidelity bond Insurance policy that a company buys to insure itself against loss due to employee dishonesty. *p. 133*

financial accounting Field of accounting designed to meet the information needs of external users of business information (creditors, investors, governmental agencies, financial analysts, etc.); its objective is to classify and record business events and transactions to facilitate the production of external financial reports (income statement, balance sheet, statement of cash flows, and statement of changes in equity). *pp. 6, 362*

Financial Accounting Standards Board (FASB) Privately funded organization with the primary authority for the establishment of accounting standards in the United States. *pp. 8, 365*

financial resources Money or credit supplied to a business by investors (owners) and creditors. *p. 4*

financial statement audit Detailed examination of a company's accounting records and the documents that support the information reported in the financial statements; includes testing the reliability of the underlying accounting system used to produce the financial reports. *p. 146*

financial statements Primary means of communicating the financial information of an organization to the external users. The four general-purpose financial statements are the income statement, statement of changes in equity, balance sheet, and statement of cash flows. *p. 10*

financing activities Cash inflows and outflows from transactions with investors and creditors (except interest). These cash flows include cash receipts from the issue of stock, borrowing activities, and cash disbursements associated with dividends. *p. 24*

finished goods inventory Asset account used to accumulate the product costs (direct materials, direct labor, and overhead) associated with completed products that have not yet been sold. *pp. 178, 374*

first-in, first-out (FIFO) cost flow method Inventory cost flow method that treats the first items purchased as the first items sold for the purpose of computing cost of goods sold. *p. 178*

fixed cost Cost that in total remains constant when activity volume changes; varies per unit inversely with changes in the volume of activity. *p. 402*

fixed cost volume variance The difference between the budgeted fixed cost and the applied fixed cost. *p. 542*

fixed interest rate Interest rate (charge for the use of money) that does not change over the life of the loan. *p. 253*

flexible budgets Budgets that show expected revenues and costs at a variety of different activity levels. *p. 539*

flexible budget variances Differences between budgets based on standard amounts at the actual level of activity and actual results; caused by differences in standard and actual unit cost since the volume of activity is the same. *p. 543*

FOB (free on board) destination Term that designates the seller as the responsible party for freight costs (transportation-in costs). *p. 101*

FOB (free on board) shipping point Term that designates the buyer as the responsible party for freight costs (transportation-in costs). *p. 101*

franchise Exclusive right to sell products or perform services in certain geographic areas. *p. 223*

full disclosure The accounting principle that financial statements should include all information relevant to an entity's operations and financial condition. Full disclosure frequently requires adding footnotes to the financial statements. *p. 183*

gains Increases in assets or decreases in liabilities that result from peripheral or incidental transactions. *p. 105*

general authority Policies and procedures that apply across different levels of a company's management, such as everyone flies coach class. *p. 133*

general journal Journal in which all types of accounting transactions can be entered but which is commonly used to record adjusting and closing entries and unusual types of transactions. *p. 603*

general ledger Complete set of accounts used in accounting systems. *pp. 16, 603*

generally accepted accounting principles (GAAP) Rules and regulations that accountants agree to follow when preparing financial reports for public distribution. *pp. 8, 365*

general uncertainties Uncertainties inherent in operating a business, such as competition and damage from storms. Unlike contingent liabilities, these uncertainties arise from future rather than past events. *p. 250*

going concern assumption Accounting presumption that a company will continue to operate indefinitely, benefiting from its assets and paying its obligations in full; justifies reporting assets and liabilities in the financial statements. *p. 19*

goodwill Added value of a successful business that is attributable to factors—reputation, location, and superior products—that enable the business to earn above-average profits; stated differently, the excess paid for an existing business over the appraised value of the net assets. *p. 224*

gross margin (gross profit) Difference between sales revenue and cost of goods sold; the amount a company makes from selling goods before subtracting operating expenses. *p. 96*

gross profit See *gross margin.*

historical cost concept Actual price paid for an asset when it was purchased. *pp. 16, 209*

horizontal analysis Analysis technique that compares amounts of the same item over several time periods. *p. 327*

horizontal statements model Arrangement of a set of financial statements horizontally across a sheet of paper. *p. 26*

income Added value created in transforming resources into more desirable states. *p. 4*

income statement Statement that measures the difference between the asset increases and the asset decreases associated with running a business. This definition is expanded in subsequent chapters as additional relationships among the elements of the financial statements are introduced. *p. 21*

incremental revenue Additional cash inflows from operations generated by using an additional capital asset. *p. 577*

independent auditor Licensed certified public accountant engaged to audit a company's financial statements; not an employee of the audited company. *p. 146*

indirect cost Cost that cannot be easily traced to a cost object and for which the economic sacrifice to trace is not worth the informational benefits. *pp. 371, 439*

information overload Situation in which presentation of too much information confuses the user of the information. *p. 326*

installment notes Obligations that require regular payments of principal and interest over the life of the loan. *p. 254*

intangible assets Assets that may be represented by pieces of paper or contracts that appear tangible; however, the true value of an intangible asset lies in the rights and privileges extended to its owners. *p. 208*

interest Fee paid for the use of borrowed funds; also refers to revenue from debt securities. *pp. 4, 173*

internal controls A company's policies and procedures designed to reduce the opportunity for fraud and to provide reasonable assurance that its objectives will be accomplished. *p. 132*

internal rate of return Rate that will produce a present value of an investment's future cash inflows that equals cash outflows required to acquire the investment; alternatively, the rate that produces in a net present value of zero. *p. 576*

International Accounting Standards Board (IASB) Private, independent body that establishes International Financial Reporting Standards (IFRS). The IASB's authority is established by various governmental institutions that require or permit companies in their jurisdiction to use IFRS. To date, more than 100 countries require or permit companies to prepare their financial statements using IFRS. One notable exception is the United States of America. *p. 9*

International Financial Reporting Standards (IFRS) Pronouncement established by the International Accounting Standards Board (IASB) that provides guidance for the preparation of financial statements. *p. 9*

inventory cost flow methods Methods used to allocate the cost of goods available for sale between cost of goods sold and inventory. *p. 180*

inventory holding costs Costs associated with acquiring and retaining inventory including cost of storage space; lost, stolen, or damaged merchandise; insurance; personnel and management costs; and interest. *p. 376*

inventory turnover Ratio of cost of goods sold to inventory that indicates how many times a year the average inventory is sold (turned over). *p. 334*

investing activities One of the three categories of cash inflows and outflows shown on the statement of cash flows; includes cash received and spent by the business on operating assets and investments in the debt and equity of other companies. *p. 24*

investment center   Type of responsibility center for which revenue, expense and capital investments can be measured. *p. 538*

investors   Company or individual who gives assets or services in exchange for security certificates representing ownership interests. *p. 4*

issued stock   Stock sold to the public. *p. 299*

issuer   Individual or business that issues a note payable, bonds payable, or stock (the party receiving cash). See also *maker*. *pp. 248, 257*

journals   Books of original entry in which accounting data are entered chronologically before posting to the ledger accounts. *p. 603*

just in time (JIT)   Inventory flow system that minimizes the amount of inventory on hand by making inventory available for customer consumption on demand, therefore eliminating the need to store inventory. The system reduces explicit holding costs including financing, warehouse storage, supervision, theft, damage, and obsolescence. It also eliminates hidden opportunity costs such as lost revenue due to the lack of availability of inventory. *p. 376*

labor resources   Both intellectual and physical efforts of individuals used in the process of providing goods and services to customers. *p. 5*

last-in, first-out (LIFO) cost flow method   Inventory cost flow method that treats the last items purchased as the first items sold for the purpose of computing cost of goods sold. *p. 178*

legal capital   Amount of assets that should be maintained as protection for creditors; the number of shares multiplied by the par value. *p. 299*

liabilities   Obligations of a business to relinquish assets, provide services, or accept other obligations. *p. 12*

limited liability   Concept that investors in a corporation may not be held personally liable for the actions of the corporation (the creditors cannot lay claim to the owners' personal assets as payment for the corporation's debts). *p. 296*

limited liability companies (LLC)   Organizations offering many of the best features of corporations and partnerships and with many legal benefits of corporations (e.g., limited liability and centralized management) but permitted by the Internal Revenue Service to be taxed as a partnership, thereby avoiding double taxation of profits. *p. 295*

line of credit   Preapproved credit arrangement with a lending institution in which a business can borrow money by simply writing a check up to the approved limit. *p. 257*

liquidation   Process of dividing up the assets and returning them to the resource providers. Creditors normally receive first priority in business liquidations; in other words, assets are distributed to creditors first. After creditor claims have been satisfied, the remaining assets are distributed to the investors (owners) of the business. *p. 19*

liquidity   Ability to convert assets to cash quickly and meet short-term obligations. *pp. 23, 175*

liquidity ratios   Measures of short-term debt-paying ability. *p. 331*

long-term liabilities   Liabilities with maturity dates beyond one year or the company's operating cycle, whichever is longer; noncurrent liabilities. *p. 253*

long-term operational assets   Assets used by a business to generate revenue; condition of being used distinguishes them from assets that are sold (inventory) and that are held (investments). *p. 206*

losses   Decreases in assets or increases in liabilities that result from peripheral or incidental transactions. *p. 105*

low-ball pricing   Pricing a product below competitors' price to lure customers away and then raising the price once customers depend on the supplier for the product. *p. 478*

maker   The party issuing a note (the borrower). *p. 173*

making the numbers   Expression that indicates marketing managers attained the planned master budget sales volume. *p. 541*

management by exception   The philosophy of focusing management attention and resources only on those operations where performance deviates significantly from expectations. *p. 545*

managerial accounting   Branch of accounting that provides information useful to internal decision makers and managers in operating an organization. *pp. 6, 362*

manufacturing business   Companies that make the goods they sell to customers. *p. 27*

manufacturing overhead   Production costs that cannot be traced directly to products. *p. 371*

margin   Component in the determination of the return on investment. Computed by dividing operating income by sales. *p. 547*

margin of safety   Difference between break-even sales and budgeted sales expressed in units, dollars, or as a percentage; the amount by which actual sales can fall below budgeted sales before a loss is incurred. *p. 416*

market   Group of people or entities organized to buy and sell resources. *p. 4*

market rate of interest   Interest rate currently available on a wide range of alternative investments with similar levels of risk. *p. 266*

market value   The price at which securities sell in the secondary market; also called fair value. *p. 299*

master budget   Composition of the numerous separate but interdependent departmental budgets that cover a wide range of operating and financial factors such as sales, production, manufacturing expenses, and administrative expenses. *p. 508*

matching concept   Process of matching expenses with the revenues they produce; three ways to match expenses with revenues include matching expenses directly to revenues, matching expenses to the period in which they are incurred, and matching expenses systematically with revenues. *pp. 21, 57, 174*

material   The point at which knowledge of information would influence a user's decision; can be measured in absolute, percentage, quantitative, or qualitative terms. The concept allows nonmaterial matters to be handled in any convenient way, such as charging a pencil sharpener to expense rather than recording periodic depreciation over its useful life. *p. 146*

materiality   Concept that recognizes practical limits in financial reporting by allowing flexible handling of matters not considered material; information is considered material if the decisions of a reasonable person would be influenced by its omission or misstatement; can be measured in absolute, percentage, quantitative, or qualitative terms. *p. 327*

maturity date   The date a liability is due to be settled (the date the borrower is expected to repay a debt). *p. 173*

merchandise inventory   Supply of finished goods held for resale to customers. *p. 92*

merchandising businesses   Companies that buy and resell merchandise inventory. *pp. 27, 92*

minimum rate of return   Minimum amount of profitability required to persuade a company to accept an investment opportunity; also known as *desired rate of return, required rate of return, hurdle rate, cutoff rate,* and *discount rate. p. 571*

mixed costs (semivariable costs)   Costs composed of a mixture of fixed and variable components. *p. 410*

multistep income statement   Income statement format that matches particular revenue items with related expense items and distinguishes between recurring operating activities and nonoperating items such as gains and losses. *p. 106*

natural resources   Mineral deposits, oil and gas reserves, and reserves of timber, mines, and quarries are examples; sometimes called *wasting assets* because their value wastes away as the resources are removed. *p. 208*

net income   Increase in net assets resulting from operating the business. *p. 21*

616   Glossary

net loss Decrease in net assets resulting from operating the business. *p. 21*

net margin Profitability measurement that indicates the percentage of each sales dollar resulting in profit; calculated as net income divided by net sales. *p. 337*

net present value Evaluation technique that uses a desired rate of return to discount future cash flows back to their present value equivalents and then subtracts the cost of the investment from the present value equivalents to determine the net present value. A zero or positive net present value (present value of cash inflows equals or exceeds the present value of cash outflows) implies that the investment opportunity provides an acceptable rate of return. *p. 575*

net realizable value Face amount of receivables less an allowance for accounts whose collection is doubtful (amount actually expected to be collected). *p. 164*

net sales Sales less returns from customers and allowances or cash discounts given to customers. *p. 109*

non-sufficient-funds (NSF) check Customer's check deposited but returned by the bank on which it was drawn because the customer did not have enough funds in its account to pay the check. *p. 139*

nonvalue-added activities Tasks undertaken that do not contribute to a product's ability to satisfy customer needs. *p. 381*

note payable A liability that results from executing a legal document called a *promissory note* which describes the interest rate, maturity date, collateral, and so on. *p. 248*

notes receivable Notes that evidence rights to receive cash in the future from the maker of a *promissory note;* usually specify the maturity date, interest rate, and other credit terms. *p. 163*

not-for-profit entities Organizations (also called *nonprofit* or *nonbusiness entities*) established primarily for motives other than making a profit, such as providing goods and services for the social good. Examples include state-supported universities and colleges, hospitals, public libraries, and public charities. *p. 6*

operating activities Cash inflows and outflows associated with operating the business. These cash flows normally result from revenue and expense transactions including interest. *p. 24*

operating budgets Budgets prepared by different departments within a company that will become a part of the company's master budget; typically include a sales budget, an inventory purchases budget, a selling and administrative budget, and a cash budget. *p. 508*

operating cycle Time required to turn cash into inventory, inventory into receivables, and receivables back to cash. *p. 267*

operating income (or loss) Income statement subtotal representing the difference between operating revenues and operating expenses, but before recognizing gains and losses from peripheral activities which are added to or subtracted from operating income to determine net income or loss. *p. 106*

operating leverage Operating condition in which a percentage change in revenue produces a proportionately larger percentage change in net income; measured by dividing the contribution margin by net income. The higher the proportion of fixed cost to total costs, the greater the operating leverage. *p. 404*

operations budgeting Short-range planning activities such as the development and implementation of the master budget. *p. 506*

opportunity An element of the fraud triangle that recognizes weaknesses in internal controls that enable the occurrence of fraudulent or unethical behavior. *p. 144*

opportunity cost Cost of lost opportunities such as the failure to make sales due to an insufficient supply of inventory or the wage a working student forgoes to attend class. *pp. 366, 470*

ordinary annuity Annuity whose cash inflows occur at the end of each accounting period. *p. 574*

outsourcing The practice of buying goods and services from another company rather than producing them internally. *p. 477*

outstanding checks Checks deducted from the depositor's cash account balance but not yet presented to the bank for payment. *p. 139*

outstanding stock Stock owned by outside parties; normally the amount of stock issued less the amount of treasury stock. *p. 299*

overhead Costs associated with producing products that cannot be cost effectively traced to products including indirect costs such as indirect materials, indirect labor, utilities, rent, and depreciation. *p. 336*

overhead costs Indirect costs of doing business that cannot be directly traced to a product, department, or process, such as depreciation. *p. 439*

paid-in capital in excess of par (or stated) value Any amount received above the par or stated value of stock when stock is issued. *p. 302*

participative budgeting Budget technique that allows subordinates to participate with upper-level managers in setting budget objectives, thereby encouraging cooperation and support in the attainment of the company's goals. *p. 508*

partnership agreement Legal document that defines the responsibilities of each partner and describes the division of income and losses. *p. 294*

partnerships Business entities owned by at least two people who share talents, capital, and the risks of the business. *p. 294*

par value Arbitrary value assigned to stock by the board of directors. *p. 299*

patent Legal right granted by the U.S. Patent Office ensuring a company or an individual the exclusive right to a product or process. *p. 222*

payback method Technique that evaluates investment opportunities by determining the length of time necessary to recover the initial net investment through incremental revenue or cost savings; the shorter the period, the better the investment opportunity. *p. 584*

payee The party collecting cash. *p. 173*

payment date Date on which a dividend is actually paid. *p. 306*

percentage analysis Analysis of relationships between two different items to draw conclusions or make decisions. *p. 328*

percent of receivables method Estimating the amount of the allowance for doubtful accounts as a percentage of the outstanding receivables balance. The percentage is typically based on a combination of factors such as historical experience, economic conditions, and the company's credit policies. *p. 170*

percent of revenue method Estimating the amount of uncollectible accounts expense as a percentage of the revenue earned on account during the accounting period. The percentage is typically based on a combination of factors such as historical experience, economic conditions, and the company's credit policies. *p. 169*

period costs General, selling, and administrative costs that are expensed in the period in which the economic sacrifice is made. *pp. 57, 95, 371*

periodic inventory system Method of accounting for changes in the Inventory account only at the end of the accounting period. *p. 112*

permanent accounts Accounts that contain information transferred from one accounting period to the next. *p. 25*

perpetual (continuous) budgeting Continuous budgeting activity normally covering a 12-month time span by replacing the current month's budget at the end of each month with a new budget; keeps management constantly involved in the budget process so that changing conditions are incorporated on a timely bases. *p. 506*

perpetual inventory system Method of accounting for inventories that increases the Inventory account each time merchandise is purchased and decreases it each time merchandise is sold. *p. 96*

physical flow of goods Physical movement of goods through the business; normally a FIFO flow so that the first goods purchased are the first goods delivered to customers, thereby reducing the likelihood of obsolete inventory. *p. 178*

physical resources Natural resources that businesses transform to create more valuable resources. *p. 5*

plant assets to long-term liabilities Financial ratio that suggests how well a company manages its long-term debt. *p. 337*

postaudit Repeat calculation using the techniques originally employed to analyze an investment project; accomplished with the use of actual data available at the completion of the investment project so that the actual results can be compared with expected results based on estimated data at the beginning of the project. Its purpose is to provide feedback as to whether the expected results were actually accomplished in improving the accuracy of future analysis. *p. 587*

posting Process of copying information from journals to ledgers. *p. 603*

predetermined overhead rate Allocation rate calculated before actual costs or activity are known; determined by dividing the estimated overhead costs for the coming period by some measure of estimated total production activity for the period, such as the number of labor-hours or machine-hours. The base should relate rationally to overhead use. The rate is used throughout the accounting period to allocate overhead costs to work in process inventory based on actual production activity. *p. 451*

preferred stock Stock that receives some form of preferential treatment (usually as to dividends) over common stock; normally has no voting rights. *p. 300*

premium on bonds payable Difference between the selling price and the face amount of a bond that is sold for more than the face amount. *p. 266*

prepaid items Deferred expenses. An example is prepaid insurance. *p. 59*

present value index Present value of cash inflows divided by the present value of cash outflows. Higher index numbers indicate higher rates of return. *p. 580*

present value table Table that consists of a list of factors to use in converting future values into their present value equivalents; composed of columns that represent different return rates and rows that depict different periods of time. *p. 572*

pressure An element of the fraud triangle that recognizes conditions that motivate fraudulent or unethical behavior. *p. 145*

price-earnings (P/E) ratio Measurement used to compare the values of different stocks in terms of earnings; calculated as market price per share divided by earnings per share. *p. 340*

principal Amount of cash actually borrowed. *p. 173*

procedures manual Manual that sets forth the accounting procedures to be followed. *p. 133*

product costing Classification and accumulation of individual inputs (materials, labor, and overhead) for determining the cost of making a good or providing a service. *p. 365*

product costs All costs related to obtaining or manufacturing a product intended for sale to customers; are accumulated in inventory accounts and expensed as cost of goods sold at the point of sale. For a manufacturing company, product costs include direct materials, direct labor, and manufacturing overhead. *pp. 95, 365*

product-level costs Costs incurred to support different kinds of products or services; can be avoided by the elimination of a product line or a type of service. *p. 473*

profit Value added by transforming resources into products or services desired by customers. *p. 4*

profit center Type of responsibility center for which both revenues and costs can be indentified. *p. 538*

profitability ratios Measurements of a firm's ability to generate earnings. *p. 337*

pro forma financial statements Budgeted financial statements prepared from the information in the master budget. *p. 508*

promissory note A legal document representing a credit agreement between a lender and a borrower. The note specifies technical details such as the maker, payee, interest rate, maturity date, payment terms, and any collateral. *p. 172*

property, plant, and equipment Category of assets, sometimes called *plant assets*, used to produce products or to carry on the administrative and selling functions of a business; includes machinery and equipment, buildings, and land. *p. 208*

purchase discount Reduction in the gross price of merchandise extended under the condition that the purchaser pay cash for the merchandise within a stated time (usually within 10 days of the date of the sale). *p. 100*

purchase returns and allowances A reduction in the cost of purchases resulting from dissatisfaction with merchandise purchased. *p. 99*

qualified opinion Opinion issued by a certified public accountant that means the company's financial statements are, for the most part, in compliance with GAAP, but there is some circumstance (explained in the auditor's report) about which the auditor has reservations; contrast with *unqualified opinion*. *p. 147*

qualitative characteristics Nonquantifiable features such as company reputation, welfare of employees, and customer satisfaction that can be affected by certain decisions. *p. 472*

quantitative characteristics Numbers in decision making subject to mathematical manipulation, such as the dollar amounts of revenues and expenses. *p. 472*

quick ratio See *acid-test ratio*. *p. 332*

ratio analysis See *percentage analysis*. *p. 330*

rationalization An element of the fraud triangle that recognizes a human tendency to justify fraudulent or unethical behavior. *p. 145*

raw materials Physical commodities (e.g., wood, metal, paint) used in the manufacturing process. *p. 369*

raw materials inventory Asset account used to accumulate the costs of materials (such as lumber, metals, paints, chemicals) that will be used to make a company's products. *p. 374*

realization A term that usually refers to actually collecting cash. *p. 49*

recognition Reporting an accounting event in the financial statements. *p. 49*

recovery of investment Recovery of the funds used to acquire the original investment. *p. 586*

reengineering Business practices designed by companies to make production and delivery systems more competitive in world markets by eliminating or minimizing waste, errors, and costs. *p. 381*

reinstate Recording an account receivable previously written off back into the accounting records, generally when cash is collected long after the original due date. *p. 168*

relative fair market value method Method of assigning value to individual assets acquired in a basket purchase in which each asset is assigned a percentage of the total price paid for all assets. The percentage assigned equals the market value of a particular asset divided by the total of the market values of all assets acquired in the basket purchase. *p. 209*

relevant costs Future-oriented costs that differ between business alternatives; also known as *avoidable costs*. *p. 471*

relevant information Decision-making information about costs, costs savings, or revenues that have these features: (1) future-oriented information and (2) the information differs between the alternatives; decision-specific (information that is relevant in one decision may not be relevant in another decision). *p. 470*

relevant range Range of activity over which the definitions of fixed and variable costs are valid. *p. 411*

reporting entities Particular businesses or other organizations for which financial statements are prepared. *p. 9*

residual income Approach that evaluates managers on their ability to maximize the dollar value of earnings above some targeted level of earnings. *p. 548*

responsibility accounting Performance measure that evaluates managers based on how well they maximize the dollar value of earning above some target level of earnings. *p. 536*

responsibility center Point in an organization where the control over revenue or expense items is located. *p. 538*

restrictive covenants Special provisions specified in the loan contract that are designed to prohibit management from taking certain actions that place creditors at risk. *p. 267*

retail companies Companies that sell goods to consumers. *p. 92*

retained earnings Portion of stockholders' equity that includes all earnings retained in the business since inception (revenues minus expenses and distributions for all accounting periods). *p. 12*

return on assets Profitability measure based on earnings a company generates relative to its asset base; calculated as net income divided by average total assets. *p. 338*

return on equity Measure of the profitability of a firm based on earnings generated in relation to stockholders' equity; calculated as net income divided by stockholders' equity. *p. 339*

return on investment Measure of profitability based on the asset base of the firm. It is calculated as net income divided by average total assets. ROI is a product of net margin and asset turnover. *pp. 338, 546*

return on sales Percent of net income generated by each $1 of sales; computed by dividing net income by net sales. *p. 337*

revenue The economic benefit (increase in assets or decrease in liabilities) gained by providing goods or services to customers. *p. 64*

revenue expenditures Costs incurred for repair or maintenance of long-term operational assets; recorded as expenses and subtracted from revenue in the accounting period in which incurred. *p. 219*

salaries payable Amounts of future cash payments owed to employees for services that have already been performed. *p. 52*

sales discount Cash discount extended by the seller of goods to encourage prompt payment. When the buyer of the goods takes advantage of the discount to pay less than the original selling price, the difference between the selling price and the cash collected is the sales discount. *p. 107*

sales price variance Difference between actual sales and expected sales based on the standard sales price per unit times the actual level of activity. *p. 543*

sales return and allowances A reduction in sales revenue resulting from dissatisfaction with merchandise sold. *p. 109*

sales volume variance Difference between sales based on a static budget (standard sales price times standard level of activity) and sales based on a flexible budget (standard sales price times actual level of activity). *p. 541*

salvage value Expected selling price of an asset at the end of its useful life. *p. 210*

schedule of cost of goods manufactured and sold Internal accounting report that summarizes the manufacturing product costs for the period; its result, cost of goods sold, is reported as a single line item on the company's income statement. *p. 374*

schedule of cost of goods sold Schedule that reflects the computation of the amount of the cost of goods sold under the periodic inventory system; an internal report not shown in the formal financial statements. *p. 112*

Securities Act of 1933 and Securities Exchange Act of 1934 Acts passed after the stock market crash of 1929 designed to regulate the issuance of stock and govern the stock exchanges; created the Securities and Exchange Commission (SEC), which has the authority to establish accounting policies for companies registered on the stock exchanges. *p. 295*

Securities and Exchange Commission (SEC) Government agency responsible for overseeing the accounting rules to be followed by companies required to be registered with it. *p. 365*

segment Component part of an organization that is designated as a reporting entity. *p. 479*

selling and administrative costs Costs that cannot be directly traced to products that are recognized as expenses in the period in which they are incurred. Examples include advertising expense and rent expense. *p. 95*

selling, general, and administrative costs (SG&A) All costs not associated with obtaining or manufacturing a product; sometimes called *period costs* because they are normally expensed in the period in which the economic sacrifice is incurred. *p. 371*

separation of duties Internal control feature of, whenever possible, assigning the functions of authorization, recording, and custody to different individuals. *p. 132*

service business Organizations such as accounting and legal firms, dry cleaners, and insurance companies that provide services to consumers. *p. 27*

service charges Fees charged by a bank for services performed or a penalty for the depositor's failing to maintain a specified minimum cash balance throughout the period. *p. 139*

shrinkage A term that reflects decreases in inventory for reasons other than sales to customers. *p. 104*

signature card Bank form that records the bank account number and the signatures of the people authorized to write checks on an account. *p. 136*

single-payment (lump-sum) A one-time receipt of cash which can be converted to its present value using a conversion factor. *p. 572*

single-step income statement Single comparison between total revenues and total expenses. *p. 106*

sole proprietorships Businesses (usually small) owned by one person. *p. 294*

solvency Ability of a business to pay liabilities in the long run. *p. 335*

solvency ratios Measures of a firm's long-term debt-paying ability. *p. 335*

source documents Documents such as a cash register tape, invoice, time card, or check stub that provide accounting information to be recorded in the accounting journals and ledgers. *p. 602*

special journals Journals designed to improve the efficiency of recording specific types of repetitive transactions. *p. 603*

special order decisions Decisions of whether to accept orders from nonregular customers who want to buy goods or services significantly below the normal selling price. If the order's relevant revenues exceed its avoidable costs, the order should be accepted. Qualitative features such as the order's effect on the existing customer base if accepted must also be considered. *p. 474*

specific authorizations Policies and procedures that apply to designated levels of management, such as the policy that the right to approve overtime pay may apply only to the plant manager. *p. 133*

specific identification Inventory method that allocates costs between cost of goods sold and ending inventory using the cost of the specific goods sold or retained in the business. *p. 178*

spending variance The difference between the actual fixed overhead costs and the budgeted fixed overhead costs. *p. 542*

stakeholders Parties interested in the operations of a business, including owners, lenders, employees, suppliers, customers, and government agencies. *p. 5*

stated interest rate Rate of interest specified in the bond contract that will be paid at specified intervals over the life of the bond. *p. 258*

stated value Arbitrary value assigned to stock by the board of directors. *p. 299*

statement of cash flows Statement that explains how a business obtained and used cash during an accounting period. *p. 24*

statement of changes in stockholders' equity Statement that summarizes the transactions occurring during the accounting period that affected the owners' equity. *p. 23*

static budgets Budgets such as the master budget based solely on the level of planned activity; remain constant even when volume of activity changes. *p. 539*

stewardship A duty to protect and use the assets of a business for the benefit of the owners. *p. 18*

stock certificate Evidence of ownership interest issued when an investor contributes assets to a corporation; describes the rights and privileges that accompany ownership. *p. 294*

stock dividend Proportionate distribution of additional shares of the declaring corporation's stock. *p. 306*

stockholders Owners of a corporation. *pp. 12, 296*

stockholders' equity Stockholders' equity represents the portion of the assets that is owned by the stockholders. *p. 12*

stock split Proportionate increase in the number of outstanding shares; designed to reduce the market value of the stock and its par value. *p. 307*

straight-line amortization Method of amortization in which equal amounts of the account being reduced (e.g., Bond Discount, Bond Premium, Patent) are transferred to the appropriate expense account over the relevant time period. *p. 263*

straight-line depreciation Method of computing depreciation that allocates the cost of an asset to expense in equal amounts over its life. The formula for calculating straight line depreciation is [(Cost − Salvage)/Useful Life]. *p. 211*

strategic planning Planning activities associated with long-range decisions such as defining the scope of the business, determining which products to develop, deciding whether to discontinue a business segment, and determining which market niche would be most profitable. *p. 506*

suboptimization Situation in which managers act in their own self-interests even though the organization as a whole suffers. *p. 548*

sunk costs Costs that have been incurred in past transactions and therefore are not relevant for decision making. *p. 470*

T-account Simplified account form, named for its shape, with the account title placed at the top of a horizontal bar, debit entries listed on the left side of the vertical bar, and credit entries shown on the right side. *p. 602*

tangible assets Assets that can be touched, such as equipment, machinery, natural resources, and land. *p. 208*

temporary accounts Accounts used to collect information for a single accounting period (usually revenue, expense, and distribution accounts). *p. 25*

times interest earned ratio Ratio that computes how many times a company would be able to pay its interest by using the amount of earnings available to make interest payments; amount of earnings is net income before interest and income taxes. *pp. 335–336*

time value of money Recognition that the present value of a promise to receive a dollar some time in the future is worth less than a dollar because of interest, risk, and inflation factors. For example, a person may be willing to pay $0.90 today for the right to receive $1.00 one year from today. *p. 570*

total quality management (TQM) Management philosophy that includes: (1) a continuous systematic problem-solving philosophy that engages personnel at all levels of the organization to eliminate waste, defects, and nonvalue-added activities; and (2) the effort to manage quality costs in a manner that leads to the highest level of customer satisfaction. *p. 381*

trademark Name or symbol that identifies a company or an individual product. *p. 222*

transaction Particular event that involves the transfer of something of value between two entities. *p. 13*

transferability Concept referring to the practice of dividing the ownership of corporations into small units that are represented by shares of stock, which permits the easy exchange of ownership interests. *p. 296*

transportation-in (freight-in) Cost of freight on goods purchased under terms FOB shipping point that is usually added to the cost of inventory and is a product cost. *p. 101*

transportation-out (freight-out) Freight cost for goods delivered to customers under terms FOB destination; a period cost expensed when it is incurred. *p. 101*

treasury stock Stock first issued to the public and then bought back by the corporation. *p. 299*

trend analysis Study of the performance of a business over a period of time. *p. 327*

trial balance List of ledger accounts and their balances that provides a check on the mathematical accuracy of the recording process. *p. 605*

true cash balance Actual balance of cash owned by a company at the close of business on the date of the bank statement. *p. 137*

turnover Component in the determination of the return on investment. Computed by dividing sales by operating assets. *p. 547*

2/10, n/30 Expression meaning the seller will allow the purchaser a 2 percent discount off the gross invoice price if the purchaser pays cash for the merchandise within 10 days from the date of purchase. *p. 100*

unadjusted bank balance Ending cash balance reported by the bank as of the date of the bank statement. *p. 137*

unadjusted book balance Balance of the Cash account as of the date of the reconciliation before making any adjustments. *p. 137*

unadjusted rate of return Measure of profitability computed by dividing the average incremental increase in annual net income by the average cost of the original investment (original cost ÷ 2). *p. 585*

uncollectible accounts expense Expense associated with uncollectible accounts receivable; the amount recognized may be estimated using the percent of revenue or the percent of receivables method, or actual losses may be recorded using the direct write-off method. *p. 165*

unearned revenue Revenue for which cash has been collected but the service has not yet been performed. *p. 60*

unfavorable variance Variance that occurs when actual costs exceed standard costs or when actual sales are less than standard sales. *p. 542*

unit-level costs Costs incurred each time a company makes a single product or performs a single service and that can be avoided by eliminating a unit of product or service. Likewise, unit-level costs increase with each additional product produced or service provided. *p. 472*

units-of-production depreciation Depreciation method based on a measure of production rather than a measure of time; for example, an automobile may be depreciated based on the expected miles to be driven rather than on a specific number of years. *p. 217*

unqualified opinion Opinion issued by a certified public accountant that means the company's financial statements are, in all material respects, in compliance with GAAP; the auditor has no reservations. Contrast with qualified opinion. *p. 147*

upstream costs Costs incurred before the manufacturing process begins, for example, research and development costs. *p. 375*

users Individuals or organizations that use financial information for decision making. Also called *stakeholders*. *p. 5*

value-added activity Any unit of work that contributes to a product's ability to satisfy customer needs. *p. 381*

value-added principle The benefits attained (value added) from the process should exceed the cost of the process. *p. 365*

value chain Linked sequence of activities that create value for the customer. *p. 381*

variable cost Cost that in total changes in direct proportion to changes in volume of activity; remains constant per unit when volume of activity changes. *p. 402*

variable cost volume variance The difference between a variable cost calculated at the planned volume of activity and the same variable cost calculated at the actual volume of activity. *p. 541*

variable interest rate Interest rate that fluctuates (may change) from period to period over the life of the loan. *p. 253*

variances Differences between standard and actual amounts. *p. 540*

vertical analysis Analysis technique that compares items on financial statements to significant totals. *p. 329*

vertical integration Attainment of control over the entire spectrum of business activity from production to sales; as an example a grocery store that owns farms. *p. 478*

vertical statements model Arrangement of a full set of financial statements on a single page with account titles arranged from the top to the bottom of the page. *p. 66*

warranties Promises to correct deficiencies or dissatisfactions in quality, quantity, or performance of products or services sold. *p. 251*

weighted-average cost flow method Inventory cost flow method in which the cost allocated between inventory and cost of goods sold is based on the average cost per unit, which is determined by dividing total costs of goods available for sale during the accounting period by total units available for sale during the period. If the average is recomputed each time a purchase is made, the result is called a *moving average. p. 178*

wholesale companies Companies that sell goods to other businesses. *p. 92*

withdrawals Distributions to the owners of proprietorships and partnerships. *p. 297*

work in process inventory Asset account used to accumulate the product costs (direct materials, direct labor, and overhead) associated with incomplete products that have been started but are not yet completed. *p. 374*

working capital Current assets minus current liabilities. *pp. 331, 577*

working capital ratio Another term for the current ratio; calculated by dividing current assets by current liabilities. *p. 332*

PHOTO CREDITS

Page 2 © AP Photo/Mark Lennihan; 4 © David Buffington/Getty Image; 8 © Lars Niki; 9 © Denny Henry/epa/Corbis; 20 © The McGraw-Hill Companies, Inc./John Flournoy, photographer; 28 (left) © Digital Vision/PunchStock; 28 (center) © The McGraw-Hill Companies, Inc./Andrew Resek, photographer; 28 (right) © Monty Rakusen/Getty Images; 29 © AP Photo/US Navy - Justin E. Stumberg; 50 © AP Photo/Charlie Neibergall; 58 © Getty Images/Stockbyte; 70 © AP Photo/Ted S. Warren; 93 © AP Photo/Damian Dovarganes; 104 © Digital Vision/Getty Images; 131 © Mario Tama/Getty Images; 136 © Royalty-Free/Corbis; 163 © Alessandro Abbonizio/AFP/Getty Images; 184 (top) © Martial Colomb/Getty Images; 184 (bottom) © Stan Honda/Getty Images; 207 © Stephen Reynolds; 223 © Pixtal/AGE Fotostock; 224 © PRNewsFoto/Jackson Hewitt Tax Service Inc.; 247 © Stephen Reynolds; 253 © The McGraw-Hill Companies, Inc./Christopher Kerrigan, photographer; 258 © The McGraw-Hill Companies, Inc.; 269 © Royalty-Free/Corbis; 293 © Royalty-Free/Corbis; 300 © Brand X Pictures; 306 © AP Photo/Bebeto Matthews; 325 (top) © Brent Lewin/Bloomberg via Getty Images; 325 (bottom) © Justin Sullivan/Getty Images; 326 © Susan Van Etten/PhotoEdit; 338 © Niall Carson/PA Wire UAN: 15879677; 363 © AP Photo/Mark Lennihan; 365 © AP Photo/Susan Walsh; 377 Courtesy of Ford Motor Company; 378 © Adam Roundtree/Bloomberg via Getty Images; 379 © Purestock/SuperStock/RF; 403 © AP Photo/Denis Poroy; 405 © Kyodo via AP Images; 415 © AP Photo/Keith Srakocic; 437 © Stockbyte/PunchStock; 438 © Lynn Seldon; 441 Courtesy of Southwest Airlines; 449 © John A. Rizzo/Getty Images; 469 © Scott Olson/Getty Images; 473 © Ryan Pyle/Corbis; 476 © AP Photo/Groupon.com; 478 © AP Photo/Markus Leodolter; 505 © Christophe Simon/AFP/Getty Images; 507 © Alistair Berg/Digital Vision/Getty Images; 511 © F. Schussler/PhotoLink/Getty Images; 514 © AP Photo/Harry Cabluck; 516 © AP Photo/J. Scott Applewhite; 537 © Greg Kuchik/Getty Images; 541 © Thomas Barwick/Getty Images; 549 © Stockbyte/PunchStock; 550 © Jordan Strauss/Invision/AP Images; 569 © AP Photo/Paul Sakuma; 570 © C. Zachariasen/PhotoAlto; 577 © Image 100/Corbis; 581 © Creatas/PunchStock.

INDEX

McGraw Hill Education connect®

Edmonds/Edmonds/Olds/McNair/Tsay: *Survey of Accounting, 4e,* offers a seamless content and technology solution to improve student engagement and comprehension, automation of assignments and grading, and easy reporting to ensure that learning objectives are being met.

Connect® Accounting provides a wide array of tools and content to improve instructor productivity and student performance. In fact, the aggregated results of 34 Connect adoptions showed an 11% improvement in pass rates, a 16% improvement in retention, two times as many students receiving an A, and a 77% reduction in instructor grading time.

Connect Performance Metrics

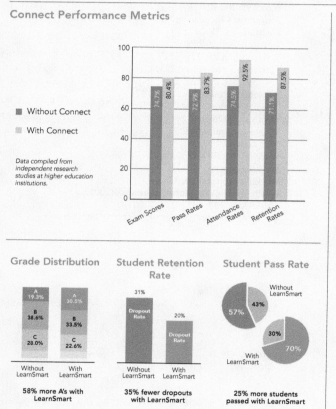

■ Without Connect
▨ With Connect

Data compiled from independent research studies at higher education institutions.

Exam Scores: 74.7% / 80.4%
Pass Rates: 72.9% / 83.7%
Attendance Rates: 74.5% / 92.5%
Retention Rates: 71.1% / 87.5%

Grade Distribution

A 19.3% / A 30.5%
B 38.6% / B 33.5%
C 28.0% / C 22.6%

Without LearnSmart / With LearnSmart

58% more A's with LearnSmart

Student Retention Rate

Dropout Rate 31% / Dropout Rate 20%

Without LearnSmart / With LearnSmart

35% fewer dropouts with LearnSmart

Student Pass Rate

Without LearnSmart 57% / 43%
With LearnSmart 30% / 70%

25% more students passed with LearnSmart

Average Grade Distribution

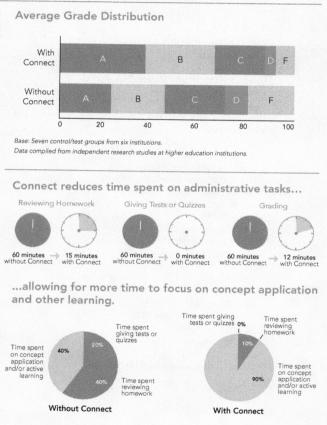

With Connect: A B C D F
Without Connect: A B C D F

0   20   40   60   80   100

Base: Seven control/test groups from six institutions.
Data compiled from independent research studies at higher education institutions.

Connect reduces time spent on administrative tasks...

Reviewing Homework
60 minutes without Connect → 15 minutes with Connect

Giving Tests or Quizzes
60 minutes without Connect → 0 minutes with Connect

Grading
60 minutes without Connect → 12 minutes with Connect

...allowing for more time to focus on concept application and other learning.

Without Connect
Time spent on concept application and/or active learning 40%
Time spent giving tests or quizzes 20%
Time spent reviewing homework 40%

With Connect
Time spent giving tests or quizzes 0%
Time spent reviewing homework 10%
Time spent on concept application and/or active learning 90%

CONNECT FEATURES

Lecture Videos

Edmonds' Connect Accounting Lecture Videos, new to this edition, teach each chapter's core learning objectives and concepts through an engaging, hands-on presentation, bringing the text content to life. The videos have been developed by the author team and have the touch and feel of a live lecture, as opposed to a canned presentation. Paired with self-assessment questions, students can learn at their own pace. Harnessing the full power of technology to truly engage and appeal to all learning styles, the lecture videos are ideal in all class formats—online, face-to-face, flipped, and hybrid.

Intelligent Response Technology

Intelligent Response Technology (IRT) is a redesigned student interface for our end-of-chapter assessment content. In addition to a streamlined interface, IRT provides improved answer acceptance to reduce students' frustration with formatting issues (such as rounding), and, for select questions, provides an expanded table that guides students through the process of solving the problem. Many questions have been redesigned to more fully test students' mastery of the content.

eBook

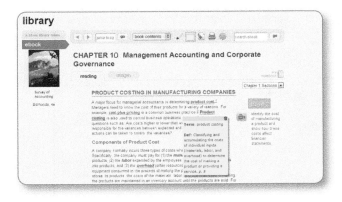

Connect Plus includes a media-rich eBook that allows you to share your notes with your students. Your students can insert and review their own notes, highlight the text, search for specific information, and interact with media resources. Using an eBook with Connect Plus gives your students a complete digital solution that allows them to access their materials from any computer.

Tegrity

Make your classes available anytime, anywhere. With simple, one-click recording, students can search for a word or phrase and be taken to the exact place in your lecture that they need to review.

EASY TO USE

Learning Management System Integration

McGraw-Hill Campus is a one-stop teaching and learning experience available to use with any learning management system. McGraw-Hill Campus provides single sign-on to faculty and students for all McGraw-Hill material and technology from within the school website. McGraw-Hill Campus also allows instructors instant access to all supplements and teaching materials for all McGraw-Hill products.

Blackboard users also benefit from McGraw-Hill's industry-leading integration, providing single sign-on to access all Connect assignments and automatic feeding of assignment results to the Blackboard grade book.

POWERFUL REPORTING

Connect generates comprehensive reports and graphs that provide instructors with an instant view of the performance of individual students, a specific section, or multiple sections. Since all content is mapped to learning objectives, Connect reporting is ideal for accreditation or other administrative documentation.